W9-BQZ-196

HISTORY OF DOGMA

HISTORY OF DOGMA

BY

Dr. ADOLPH HARNACK

ORDINARY PROF. OF CHURCH HISTORY IN THE UNIVERSITY, AND FELLOW OF
THE ROYAL ACADEMY OF SCIENCE, BERLIN

*TRANSLATED FROM THE THIRD GERMAN
EDITION*

BY

NEIL BUCHANAN

VOLUME VI
and
VOLUME VII

DOVER PUBLICATIONS, INC.
NEW YORK

Published in the United Kingdom by Constable
and Company Limited, 10 Orange Street, London
W. C. 2.

This new Dover edition, first published in 1961,
is an unabridged republication of the English translation of the third German edition that appeared
circa 1900. This Dover edition is an unaltered republication except that minor typographical errors
in Volume VII have been corrected.

The original English edition appeared as seven
separate volumes, whereas this Dover edition is
published complete in four separate volumes.

Manufactured in the United States of America

Dover Publications, Inc.
180 Varick Street
New York 14, N.Y.

HISTORY OF DOGMA

BY

DR. ADOLPH HARNACK

Volume VI

TRANSLATOR'S NOTE.

As at several places in this volume Latin quotations are largely introduced, so as to form portions of the text, these have in many cases been simply reproduced in English. Where the meaning is less obvious, and the reader might desire to be made acquainted with the original, the Latin has been inserted within brackets.

CONTENTS.

PART II.

DEVELOPMENT OF ECCLESIASTICAL DOGMA.

BOOK II., *Continued.*

Expansion and Remodelling of Dogma into a Doctrine of Sin,
Grace, and Means of Grace on the basis of the Church.

[1] The two chapters which make up this volume answer to Chapters VII. and VIII. of Part II., Book II., in the Original German Edition.

CHAPTER I.

HISTORY OF DOGMA IN THE PERIOD OF CLUGNY, ANSELM, AND BERNARD, TILL THE CLOSE OF THE TWELFTH CENTURY.

A TENACIOUSLY maintained tradition relates that in the closing years of the tenth century the Christians of the West looked forward with fear and trembling to the destruction of the world in the year 1000, and that a kind of reformation, expressing itself in the keenest activity in all branches of religion, was the consequence of this expectation. This representation has long since been proved a legend ;[1] but there lies at the basis of it, as is the case with so many legends, an accurate historic observation. From the end of the tenth century [2] we really discern the beginnings of a powerful rise of religious and ecclesiastical life. This revival grew in strength, suffering from no reaction of any consequence, till the beginning of the thirteenth century. During this period it released, and took command of all the forces of mediæval manhood. All institutions of the past, and all the new elements of culture that had been added were subjected to its influence, and even the most hostile powers were ultimately

---

[1] The eschatological ideas were always strong and vigorous in the Middle Ages, but for a time they certainly asserted themselves with special intensity ; see Wadstein, Die Eschat. Ideengruppe (Antichrist, world-Sabbath, world-end and world-judgment) in den Hauptmomenten ihrer christlich-mittelalterlichen Gesammtentwickelung, 1896. But Wadstein again thinks that the year 1000 was contemplated with special suspense (p. 16 f.).

[2] On the tenth century, see Reuter, l.c. I., p. 67 ff.

made to yield it service and support. In the thirteenth century
the supremacy of the Church and the system of the mediæval
view of the world appear in perfected form.[1]

*This perfecting is the conclusion, not only of Mediæval Church
history, but also of that historical development of Christianity, the
beginnings of which lie as far back as the history of the primitive
Church.* Certainly, if Christianity is regarded only as *doctrine*,
the Middle Ages appear almost as a supplement to the history
of the ancient Church ; but if it is regarded as *life*, our judgment
must be that it was only in the Western Church of the Middle
Ages that the Christianity of the early Church came to its completion.   In ancient times the Church was confronted with restrictions in the motives, standards, and ideas of ancient life.
These restrictions it was never able to break through, and so it
continued to be with the Church of the Eastern Empire :
Monachism stood *alongside* the Church ; the Church of the
world was the old world itself with Christian manners. It was
otherwise in the West.   Here the Church was able to apply
much more effectively its peculiar standards of monastic asceticism and domination of this world by the world beyond,[2] because
it had not to subdue an ancient civilisation, but met with its
restrictions simply in the most elementary forces of human life,
in the desire to live, hunger, love and cupidity.   It was thus
able to propagate here through all circles, from the highest to
the lowest, a view of the world which would inevitably have
driven all into the cloisters, had not these elementary forces
been stronger than even the fear of hell.

It is not the task of the History of Dogma to show how the
mediæval view of the world was fully constructed and applied
from the end of the tenth (for here the beginnings lie) till the
thirteenth century.   *Substantially* not much that is new would
be discovered, for it is still the old well-known body of thought ;
what is new is merely the application of the material to all
provinces of life, the comprehensive control in the hands of the
Pope, and the gradual progressive development in its prior

[1] See v. Eicken, Gesch. und System der mittelalterlichen Weltanschauung, 1887.

[2] From this there resulted a new kind of dominion over the world, which certainly
became very like the old, for there is only *one* way of exercising dominion.

stages of religious individualism. But before we describe the changes, partly really, and partly apparently slight, which dogma underwent down to the time of the Mendicant Orders, it is necessary to indicate in a few lines the conditions under which these changes came about. We must direct our attention to the fresh rise of *piety*, to the development of *ecclesiastical law*, and to the beginnings of mediæval *science*.

1. *The Fresh Rise of Piety.*

The Monastery of Clugny, founded in the tenth century, became the centre of the great reform which the Church in the West passed through in the eleventh century.[1] Instituted by monks, it was at first supported against the secularised mona-chism, priesthood (Episcopate),[2] and papacy by pious and prudent princes and bishops, above all, by the Emperor, the representative of God on earth, until the great Hildebrand laid hold of it, and, as Cardinal and successor of Peter, set it in

[1] The following partly corresponds with my Lecture on Monachism (3rd ed. 1886, p. 43 ff.).   Two sources appear in the tenth century from which the religious awakening proceeded, the Monastery of Clugny, and the Saxon dynasty.   We cannot attach too much importance to the influence of Matilda (cf. in general the Essay by Lamprecht, Das deutsche Geistesleben unter den Ottonen in the deutsche Zeitschrift f. Geschichtswissensch. Vol. VII., part 1, p. i. ff.).   It extended to Henry II., and even, indeed, to the third Henry; v. Nitzsch, Gesch. des deutschen Volkes I., p. 318 f.   For the history of the world the ecclesiastical sympathies of the dynasty, and the spirit of ascetic piety that emanated from the saintly devotee in the Quedlinburg Convent were of as great importance as the reformed monachism of Clugny.   The history of mediæval Germanic piety may be said to have begun with Matilda.   Charlemagne is still in many respects a Christian of the type of Constantius and Theodosius.

[2] From Hauck (K.-Gesch. Deutschlands III., p. 342 ff.) and the work of Sackur, Die Cluniacenser in ihrer Kirchl. und allgemeingesch. Wirksamkeit bis zur Mitte des 11. Jahrh. (2 vols., 1892-1894) we learn that the reform of Clugny had for centuries to contend with the same difficulties against the secularised Church and the secularised, but also more independent monachism (see also Hauck, " Zur Erklärung von Ekkeh. Cas. s. Galli " c. 87 in the Festschrift f. Luthardt, p. 107 ff.) as had the old monachism formerly on its introduction about 400 into Gaul and Spain (and as had the Minorites at a later time).   It is instructive to notice the attitude of the laity in connection with these three great reforms of the Church.   Towards the first they were substantially indifferent, in the second they took a share from the outset (against the secularised clergy), the third (the Minorite) was simply carried out by them.

opposition to the princes, the secularised clergy, and the Emperor. What the West obtained in it was a monastic reform of the Church, that rested on the idea of a view of the world that made everything alike, and that consequently favoured the universal supremacy of Rome over the Church. What were the aims of this new movement which took hold of the entire Church in the second half of the eleventh century? In the first instance, and chiefly, the restoration *in the monasteries themselves* of the " old " discipline, of the true abnegation of the world, and piety ; but then, also, first, *the monastic training of the whole secular clergy ;* second, *the supremacy of the monastically trained clergy over the lay world, over princes and nations ;* third, *the reduction of national churches, with their pride and secularity, in favour of the uniform supremacy of Rome.*[1]

---

[1] Sackur (II., p. 464 f.) characterises this French monastic reform thus : " The movement of Clugny did not start with announcing a programme : it was the product of a view of the world. It had no other aim than to oppose the coarse materialism of those days by reviving those institutions that admitted of an existence in sympathy with evangelical injunctions, even in the midst of a barbarised society. It was a formation of autonomous associations, such as usually arise in disorganised States under a weak central government, and serve to supplement by self-help the great social unions of, *e.g.*, State and Church. From this there resulted the design of influencing from these institutions those around, and winning them for religion. The restored monasteries increased in number, the task became always greater ; but it became in no way different. The winning of souls was, and continued to be, the real end. Connections became extended ; we have seen how ready the princes were to support the efforts of the monks. Very soon every family of mark had its family monastery. . . . Monachism found its way to the courts . . . by means of a conspicuous social activity monachism gained hold of the masses. . . . Not a few bishops, especially in the South, were carried away by the current, friends of the movement came to occupy the Episcopal Sees. What followed was a spiritual transformation (but no transformation of any consequence of a literary and scientific kind. See what Sackur has stated, II., p. 327 ff.), giving pain to those who had previously built their house out of the ruins of the Carlovingian order of society, giving annoyance especially to a part of the Episcopate. . . . With this the opposition also was given. The ascetic *Romanic* movement issuing from the South mastered in the end the French North, captured the new Capetian dynasty, and here found itself confronted with an Episcopate which defended itself, in some cases, with desperation, against the assaults of a monachism that set out from the idea of a view of the world that made all things alike, from the thought of the universal Romanism, and that had no understanding for the independent pride of national churches. . . . The strict organisation of the German Imperial Church, its close union with the monarchy, the morality of the clergy (of a higher character as compared with the West-Frankian Church), still kept back the movement (at first) from the borders of Germany. It

The attempt to control the life of the whole clergy by monastic rules had already begun in the Carlovingian period; but in part it had failed, in part the Chapters had only become thoroughly secularised. Now, however, it was undertaken anew and with greater efficiency. In the Cluniacensian reform Western monachism raised for the first time the decided claim to apply, and find recognition for, itself as the Christian order of life for all Christians of full age—the priests. This Western monachism could not withdraw from the task of serving the Church and urging itself upon it, *i.e.*, upon the clergy of the day, as Christianity. The Christian freedom which it strove for was for it, with all wavering, not only a freedom from the world, but *the freedom of Christendom for unrestricted preparation for the life beyond, and for the service of God in this world.* But no man can serve two masters.

Herewith there was given also its relation to the laity, with the position of the latter. If the mature confessors of Christianity must be trained according to monastic rules, then the immature —and these are the laity—must leave an entirely free course to the former, and must at least pay respect to their majesty, that it may be possible to stand approved in the coming judgment. If Clugny and its great Popes required the strict observance of celibacy, the estrangement of the priests from secular life, and especially the extirpation of all " simony," then this last demand of itself involved, under the then existing distribution of power and property, the subjection of the laity, inclusive of the civil power, to the Church. But what was the Church's dominion over the world to mean, side by side with the renunciation of the world exacted of all priests? How does that power over the earth harmonise with exclusive concern for the soul's salvation in the world beyond? How can the same man who exclaims to his brother who thinks of leaving him all the patrimonial property, "What an unjust division,—for thee, heaven, and for me, the earth," and who then himself enters a monastery—how

was only the process of ecclesiastical and civil dissolution, which began under Henry IV., that opened the breaches through which the monastic Romanic spirit could penetrate into the organism of the German State."—On Clugny and Rome, see Sackur II., p. 441 ff.

can this same man bring himself to contend from within the monastery for dominion over the world? Now in a certain sense this dominion is *something substitutionary*, so long as and because the *true, universal* Christianising has not been carried out. As long as all are not genuine Christians, the obstinate world and the half-developed Christendom must be governed and educated, for otherwise the gospel would be captured by the powers hostile to it, and would not be in the position to fulfil its mission. But the dominion is certainly not merely something substitutionary. *Christianity is asceticism and the City of God.* All earthly relations must be moulded by the transcendent and universal idea of God's kingdom, and all national political forms of life must be brought under control in accordance therewith. But the kingdom of God has its existence on this side of things in the Church. The States, therefore, must become subject to the divine ends of the Church; they must merge themselves in the kingdom of righteousness and of the victorious Christ, which is a truly heavenly kingdom, because it has its source in heaven, and is ruled by Christ's representative. Thus out of the programme of renunciation of the world and out of the supra-mundane world that was to permeate this world, out of the Augustinian idea of the city of God and out of the idea of the *one* Roman world-empire, an idea that had never disappeared, but that had reached its glorification in the papal supremacy, there developed itself the claim to world-dominion, though the ruin of many an individual monk might be involved in making it. With sullied consciences and broken courage many monks, whose only desire was to seek after God, yielded to the plans of the great monastic Popes, and became subservient to their aims. And those whom they summoned from the retirement of the cloisters were just those who wished to think least of the world. They knew very well that it was only the monk who fled from the world, and would be rid of it, that could give help in subduing the world. Abandonment of the world in the service of the world-ruling Church, dominion over the world in the service of renunciation of the world,—this was the problem, and the ideal of the Middle Ages! What an innocent simplicity, what a wealth of illusions, was involved in

believing that this ideal could be realised, and in working for
it ! What a childlike reverence for the Church was necessary
for developing that paradoxical " flight from the world," which
at one and the same moment could join the fight and pray,
utter cursing and blessing, exercise dominion and do penance !
What a spirit of romance filled those souls, which at a single
view could see in nature and all sensuous life an enchantment of
the devil, and could behold in it at the same time, as illumined
by the Church, the reflection of the world beyond ! What kind
of men were they, who abandoned the world and gladsome life,
and then took back from the hand of the Church the good
things of earth, love-making, combat and victory, speculating
and money-making, feasting, and the joys of sense ! Of course,
with a slight turn of the kaleidoscope, all these things were in
ruins ; there must be fasting and repentance ; but again a
slight turn, and everything was back again which the world
could afford—but glorified with the light of the Church and of
the world beyond.

At the close of this period (about 1200) the Church was
victorious. If ever ideals were carried out in the world and
gained dominion over souls it happened then. " It was as if the
world had cast aside its old garment and clothed itself in the
white robe of the Church." [1] Negation of the world and rule of
the world by the Church appeared to men identical. That age
bore in its culture " the pained look of world-renunciation on the
one hand, and the look of strong character suggesting world-
conquest on the other." [2] But in the period we are reviewing the
development, which had to cancel itself when it seemed to have
come near its completion, was still in process. Much was still
to be done in the way of excavating secularised Christendom

[1] The Cluniacensian monk, Rudolph Glaber, Hist. lib. III., 4.
[2] v. Eicken, l.c., p. 155 f. If the early Church had had this latter characteristic
expressed in its piety, it would inevitably have developed into Islam, or rather would
have been crushed by the Roman world-empire. *But the Mediæval Church from its
origin* (period of the migration of the nations) *had absorbed into itself the Roman
world-empire as an idea and as a force*, and stood face to face with uncivilised nations ;
hence its aggressive character, which, moreover, it only developed after Charlemagne
had shown it how the *vicarius Christi* on earth must rule. Nicolas I. learned from
Charles I., the Gregorian popes from Otto I., Henry II., and Henry III., how the
rector ecclesiæ must administer his office.

from its rough surroundings.   And the masses were really
changed in temper and set on fire—set on fire to contend against
the secularised clergy and against simonistic princes in the whole
of Europe.   A new enthusiasm of a religious kind stirred the
nations of the West, especially the Romanic.   The ardour of the
Crusades was the direct fruit of the monastic papal reform movement of the eleventh century.   In them most vividly the religious
revival which had passed over the West revealed itself in its
specific character.   The supremacy of the Church must be given
effect to on earth.   It was the ideas of the world-ruling monk of
Clugny that guided the Crusaders on their path.   The Holy
Land and Jerusalem were parts of heaven on earth.   They must
be conquered.   The dreadful and affecting scenes at the taking
of the sacred city illustrate the spirit of mediæval piety.

Christianity is ascetism and the City of God—but the Church,
which really fired souls for these ideas, lit also thereby the flame
of *religious individualism ;* it awakened the power which was
ultimately strong enough to burst through the strict bonds of
system and sever the chain.   But it was long before things
went so far as this.   The Cluniacensian reform, if I see aright,
produced as yet no religious individualism at all, in the sense of
manifold expressions of piety.   The enthusiastic religious spirit
of the eleventh century was quite of the same kind in individual
cases.   Among the numerous founders of orders during this
period, there still prevailed the greatest uniformity: spiritual need,
flight from the world, contemplation—all of them are expressed
in similar forms and by the same means.[1]   An appeal must not
be made to the Sectaries, already numerous in this century ;
they stood in scarcely any connection with the *ecclesiastical*
revival, and had as yet no influence upon it.[2]

---

[1] See Neander, K.-Gesch. V., 1, pp. 449-564.

[2] Their doctrines were imported from the East—from Bulgaria ; that old remnants of
sects survived in the West itself (Priscillians) is not impossible.   But spontaneous
developments also must be recognised, such as have arisen in all ages of the Church's
history, from reading Scripture and the Fathers, and from old reminiscences.   In the
twelfth century, heresy became an organised power, frightfully dangerous to the
Church, in some regions—indeed, superior to it ; see Reuter I., p. 153 f., and Döllinger's
work, Beiträge zur Sectengesch. des Mittelalters, 2 Thl., München 1890, in which
the Paulicians, Bogomili, Apostolic Brethren and Catharists are described.

Through the Crusades this became changed. The primitive Christian intuitions were restored. The sacred places stirred the imagination, and led it to the Christ of the Gospels. Piety was quickened by the most vivid view of the suffering and dying Redeemer ; He must be followed through all the stages of His path of sorrow! Negative asceticism thus obtained a positive form, and a new and more certain aim. The notes of the Christ-Mysticism, which Augustine had struck only singly and with uncertainty,[1] became a ravishing melody. Beside the sacramental Christ the image of the historical took its place [2]— majesty in humility, innocence in penal suffering, life in death. That dialectic of piety without dialectic, that combined spectacle of suffering and of glory, that living picture of the true *communicatio idiomatum* (communication of attributes) developed itself, before which mankind stood worshipping, adoring with equal reverence the sublimity and the abasement. The sensuous and the spiritual, the earthly and the heavenly, shame and honour, renunciation and fulness of life were no longer tumultuously intermingled : they were united in serene majesty in the " Ecce homo." And so this piety broke forth into the solemn hymn : " Salve caput cruentatum " (" O Lamb of God once wounded "). We cannot measure the effects which this newly-tempered piety produced, nor can we calculate the manifold types it assumed, and the multitude of images it drew within its range. We need only recall the picture—new, and certainly only derived from the cross—of the mother and child, the God in the cradle, omnipotence in weakness. Where this piety appears without dogmatic formulæ, without fancifulness, without subtlety, or studied calculation, it is the simple expression, now brought back again, of the Christian religion itself; for in reverence for the suffering Christ, and in the power which proceeds from His image, all the forces of religion are embraced. But even where it does not appear in its purity, where there is intermingled with it the trivial—down even to the heart-of-Jesus-worship [3]—the

[1] See Vol. V., p. 124 f.

[2] Bernh., Sermo LXII. 7, in cant. cantic : " quid enim tam efficax ad curanda conscientiæ vulnera nec non ad purgandam mentis aciem quam Christi vulnerum sedula meditatio ? "

[3] This certainly is also very old, and that, too, in bad forms ; it is not otherwise

over-refined and studied, it can still be salutary and worthy of
honour, more salutary and worthy of honour, at least, than the
strivings of a purely negative asceticism governed by no living
conception. Even, indeed, where it manifestly degenerates into
paganism, there will still remain some remnant of that liberating
message, that the divine is to be found in humility and in
patient suffering, and that the innocent suffers that the guilty
may have peace.

In the period under review, this newly attuned piety, born of
the Crusades, and nurtured on Augustine as now understood, was
still in process of growth. But we have already alluded to the man
who stood at the beginning, though he was himself no initiator,
Saint Bernard.[1] Bernard is the religious genius of the twelfth
century, and therefore also the leading spirit of the age. Above
all, in him the Augustinian contemplation was revived. Too
much is not asserted when it is said that he was *Augustinus
redivivus,* that he moulded himself entirely on the pattern of the
great African,[2] and that from him what lay at the foundation of
his pious contemplations was derived.   So far as Bernard furnishes a system of contemplation, and describes the development
of love,[3] on to its fourth and highest stage, at which man, rising
above self-love, is wholly absorbed in the love of God, and
experiences that momentary ecstasy in which he becomes one
with God—so far Bernard has simply experienced anew what
Augustine experienced before him. Even his language indeed
is to a very large extent dependent on the language of the
Confessions.[4] But Bernard has also learned his relation to

with the limb-worship of Mary.   In the Vitt. Fratrum of Gérard de Frachet (about
1260), published in the Monum. Ord. Fratr. Prædic. Hist. I. (Louvain, 1896) the
following is related of a brother : "Consueverat venerari beatam virginem, cor ejus,
quo in Christum credidit et ipsum amavit, uterum, quo eum portavit, ubera, quibus
eum lactavit, manus ejus tornatiles, quibus ei servivit, et pectus ejus, in quo recubuit,
virtutum omnium apothecam specialiter venerans, ad singula faciens frequenter
singulas venias cum totidem Ave Maria, adaptando illi virtutes, quibus meruit fieri
mater dei," etc.

[1] See the Monograph by Neander, new edit. (edited by Deutsch, 1889) ; Hüffer,
Der hl. Bernard von Clairvaux, vol. I., 1886.

[2] This is true to a much greater extent than Neander has shown.

[3] Caritas and humilitas are the fundamental conceptions in Bernard's Ethics.

[4] v. the Treatise De diligendo deo.

Jesus Christ from the great leader.   Like the latter[1] he writes : " Dry is all food of the soul if it is not sprinkled with the oil of Christ.   When thou writest, promise me nothing, unless I read Jesus in it.   When thou conversest with me on religious themes, promise me nothing if I hear not Jesus' voice. Jesus—honey to the taste, melody to the ear, gladness to the soul." [2]   But here Bernard has taken a step beyond Augustine. " Reverence for what is beneath us " dawned upon him, as it had never dawned upon any Christian of the older world (not even upon Augustine) ; for these earlier Christians, while revering asceticism as the means of escape from the body, still, as men of the ancient world, were unable to see in suffering and shame, in the cross and death, the form of the divine.   The study of the Song of Songs (under the direction of Ambrose), and the spirit enkindled by the Crusades, led him before the image of the crucified Saviour as the bridegoom of the soul.   In this picture he became absorbed.   From the features of the suffering Christ there shone forth upon him truth and love.   In a literal sense He hangs on His lips and gazes on His limbs : " My beloved, saith the Spouse, is white and ruddy : in this we see both the white light of truth and the ruddy glow of love " (in hoc nobis et candet veritas et rubet caritas), says Gilbert in the spirit of Bernard.[3]   The basis for this Christ-contemplation—the wounds of Christ as the clearest token of His love—was laid by Ambrose and Augustine (Christ, mediator as man), and the image of the soul's bridegroom goes back to Origen and Valentinus (cf. also Ignatius) ; but Bernard was the first to give to the pious spirit its historic Christian intuitions ; he united the Neoplatonic self-discipline for rising to God with contemplation of the suffer-

---

[1] v. the numerous passages in the Confessions.

[2] Jesus mel in ore, in aure melos, in corde jubilus.   In cantic. cantic. XV. 6.

[3] How the cross of Christ is for Bernard the sum and substance of all reflection and all wisdom, see Sermo XLIII. ; on loftiness in abasement see XXVIII. and XLII. ; de osculo pedis, manus et oris domini III. ; de triplici profectu animæ, qui fit per osculum pedis, manus et oris domini IV. ; de spiritu, qui est deus, et quomodo misericordia et judicium dicantur pedes domini VI. ; de uberibus sponsi, i.e., Christi IX. ; de duplice humilitate, una vid. quam parit veritas et altera quam inflammat caritas XLII., etc. etc.

ing and dying Redeemer, and released the subjectivity of the
Christ-Mysticism and the Christ-Lyricism.[1]

But in spite of all quickening of the imagination, and in spite
of his most ardent devotion to the *person* of Christ, even
Bernard was obliged to pay the heavy tribute that is exacted of

[1] See the Poems of Bernard and the 86 Sermons on the Song of Songs, which
determined the character of the piety of the following generations. These sermons
became the source of the Catholic Christ-mysticism. Ritschl, however, (Lesefrüchte
aus dem hl. Bernhard, Stud. u. Krit. 1879, pp. 317-335) has noted (see Neander, l.c.
p. 116), that in these sermons true evangelical thoughts also find expression. " The
cause of that I was constrained to see in this, that the preacher did not handle his
doctrinal material in the historical order which dogmatic theology adheres to among both
Catholics and Evangelicals—an order according to which the doctrines treated first
are dealt with without regard to those that follow. We can see rather, without
difficulty, that the preacher uses the points of doctrine as they present themselves in
the *practical* circle of vision." Ritschl points to the following passages (see also Wolff,
Die Entw. d. einen christl, K. 1889, p. 165 ff.) : Sermo LXIX. 3 (the gravity of
original sin : the degree of injury is determined by regeneration) ; Sermo LXXII. 8
(significance of death : among the redeemed "propter quos omnia fiunt," it must be
regarded as an expression, not of God's wrath, but of His mercy, as the act of redemption from the conflict between the law in the members and the sanctified will) ;
Sermo XXII. 7-11 (righteousness by faith ; it is not equivalent to power given for
good works, but "unde vera justitia nisi de Christi misericordia? . . . soli justi qui
de ejus misericordia veniam peccatorum consecuti sunt . . . *quia non modo justus
sed et beatus, cui non imputabit deus peccatum*") ; Sermo XX. 2 ; XI. 3 ; VI. 3
(redemptive work of Christ : the work of love ["non in omni mundi fabrica tantum
fatigationis auctor assumpsit"], of which the modus is the exinanitio of God, its fruit
nostri de illo repletio, and which is divine, because Christ here kept in view the way
of acting which is God's way, who makes His sun to rise on the evil and the good.
The communicatio idiomatum is not understood here in the Greek sense, but is
exhibited in the motives of Christ ; VI. 3 : "dum in carne et per carnem facit opera,
non carnis sed dei . . . manifeste ipsum se esse judicat, per quem eadem et ante
fiebant, quando fiebant. In carne, inquam, et per carnem potenter et patienter operatus
mira, locutus salubria, passus indigna evidentur ostendit, quia ipse sit, qui potenter
sed invisibiliter sæcula condidisset, sapienter regeret, benigne protegeret. Denique
dum evangelizat ingratis, signa præbet infidelibus, pro suis crucifixoribus orat, nonne
liquido ipsum se esse declarat, qui cum patre suo quotidie oriri facit solem super bonos
et malos, pluit super justos et injustos?") : Sermo XXI. 6, 7 ; LXXXV. 5 (the
restored image of God in man) ; Sermo LXVIII. 4 ; LXXI. 11 (the founding of the
Church as the aim of redemption) ; LXXVIII. 3 (Church and predestination) ; Sermo
VIII. 2, XII. 11, XLVI. 4, LI. 5 (conception and marks of the historic Church,
where the rigidly juristic view is quite absent : in XII. 11, it is said that no individual
may declare himself the bride of Christ ; the members of the Church only share in the
honour which belongs to the Church as bride). Cf. also Ritschl, Gesch. des Pietismus
I., p. 46 ff., and Rechtfert. u. Versöhn, I.[2] p. 109 ff., where it is shown how for
Bernard the thought of grace controls everything.

every mystic,—the mood of *abandonment* after the blessed feeling of union, and the exchange of the historic Christ for the
dissolving picture of the ideal. With him the latter is specially
remarkable. It might have been expected that for one who
became so absorbed in the picture of the suffering Christ, it
would have been impossible to repeat the direction given by
Origen and Augustine, that we must rise from the word of
scripture, and from the Incarnate Word, to the " Spirit." And
yet this final and most questionable direction of mysticism,
which nullifies historical Christianity and leads on to pantheism,
was most distinctly repeated by Bernard. No doubt what he
has written in ep. 106, on the uselessness of the study of Scripture, as compared with practical devotion to Christ,[1] may still be
interpreted in the light of the thought, that Christianity must be
experienced, not known. But there is no ambiguity in the expositions in the twentieth sermon on the Song of Songs. Here
the love to Christ that is stirred by what Christ did or offered in
the flesh is described as still to some extent fleshly. It is no
doubt a valuable circumstance that Bernard does not regard the
distress and anguish awakened by the picture of the man Jesus
as the highest thing, that he rather sees in it a portion of the
fleshly love. But he then goes on to say, that in true spiritual
love we must rise altogether from the picture of the historic
Christ to the Christ κατὰ πνεῦμα (after the spirit), and for this
he appeals to John VI. and 2 Cor. V. 16. All the mysticism of
after times retained this feature. It learned from Bernard the
Christ-contemplation ;[2] but, at the same time, it adopted the pan-

---

[1] " Why dost thou seek in the Word for the Word that already stands before thine
eyes as Incarnate? He that hath ears to hear, let him hear Him crying in the
temple, If any man thirst, let him come unto me and drink. . . . O, if thou only
once tastedst of the rich marrow of the grain with which the heavenly Jerusalem is
satisfied, how willingly wouldst thou leave the Jewish scribes to gnaw at their bread-
crusts. . . . Experto crede, aliquid amplius invenies in silvis, quam in libris. Ligna
et lapides docebunt, quod a magistris audire non possis."

[2] Bernard was reverenced as an apostle and prophet " among all nations of Gaul
and Germany." The lament of Odo of Morimond (see Hüffer, l.c. p. 21 ff.) is
very touching, and proves at the same time the incomparable influence of his personality. Since Augustine, no such man had been given to the Church. " Vivit
Bernardus et nardus ejus dedit odorem suum etiam in morte." " His life is hid
with Christ in God," with this the disciple comforted himself at the grave.

theistic tendency of the Neoplatonists and Augustine.[1]   In the
second half of the twelfth century the new piety was already a
powerful force in the Church.[2]   The subjectivity of pious feeling
was unfettered in the monasteries.[3]   But as the same man who,

"Verba ejus spiritus et vita erant." The recollection of the days when Bernard
wandered as a preacher of the cross through the districts of Germany long survived ;
for the Germans had never heard such a preacher.   See the Historia miraculorum in
itinere Germanico patratorum in Migne CLXXXV. ; Hüffer, p. 70 ff. (who certainly
is remarkably credulous).   The correspondence of Bernard stands alone in the
twelfth century as regards importance and extent.   Almost 500 letters by himself
are extant.

[1] The "excedere et cum Christo esse" (S. LXXXV.) was understood even by
Bernard as meaning, that the soul loses itself, and in the embraces of the bridegroom
ceases to be a proper ego.   But where the soul is merged in the Godhead, the
Godhead becomes resolved into the All-One.

[2] Follow Christ became the watchword ; it broke through the restrictions which
dogmatic had drawn, and turned to the Lord Himself.   For all relations of life, the
suffering, humble, and patient Saviour was presented as an example.   What a
quickening was the result !   But from this point it was possible that a familiarity of
feeling should develop itself, which conflicts with reverence for the Redeemer, and
because the value of Christ was seen, in a one-sided way, in His example, other sides
necessarily suffered neglect.   With Bernard that was not yet the case ; but already
in him it is astonishing how the Greek dogmatic scheme of Christology had to give
place in praxi to a scheme quite different.   After he has shown in the 16th sermon
that the rapid spread of Christianity was due simply to the preaching of the person of
Jesus, that the image of Jesus had assuaged wrath, humbled pride, healed the wounds
of envy, checked luxury, quenched lust, bridled avarice, and, in short, had driven out
all the lower passions of men, he continues : Siquidem cum nomino Jesum,
hominem mihi propono mitem et humilem corde, benignum, sobrium, castum,
misericordem et omni denique honestate et sanctitate conspicuum eundemque ipsum
deum omnipotentem, *qui suo me et exemplo sanet et roboret adjutorio.*   Hæc omnia
simul mihi sonant, cum insonuerit Jesus.   *Sumo itaque mihi exempla de homine et
auxilium de potente.*"   Thus did one write, while in theory rejecting Adoptianism !
This Bernardine Christology, of which the roots lie in Augustine, requires no two-
nature doctrine ; it excludes it.   It is fully represented by the formula that Jesus is
the sinless man, approved by suffering, to whom the divine grace by which He lives
has lent such power that His image takes shape in other men, *i.e.,* incites to counter
love and imparts humility.   *Caritas* and *humilitas* were practical Christianity, till
St. Francis gave as much vividness of form to the latter in his demand for poverty as
was to be exhibited by love in imitation of Christ in His course of suffering.   All the
ascetic treatises of the period speak of humility ; see Petrus Comestor, Hist. evang.
c. 133 : "est debita humilitas subdere se majori propter deum, abundans (humilitas)
subdere se pari, superabundans subdere se minori."   Note the distinction also, so
important subsequently in the doctrine of the merit of Christ, between debita,
abundans, and superabundans.

[3] It counterbalanced the legal righteousness and "meritoriousness" that lay close
at hand from other sides.   Ritschl remarks very correctly (Rechtf. und Versöhn.

in the seclusion of his monastery, spoke a new language of adoration, preached flight from the world, and called to the Pope that he sat in Peter's chair to serve and not to rule—as this man at the same time continued fettered by all the hierarchical prejudices of his age, and himself guided the policy of the world-ruling Church, even the pious in the Church in the twelfth century had not yet felt the contrast between Church and Christianity. The attachment of monachism to the Church was still of a naïve kind ; the contradiction between the actual form of the world-ruling Church and the gospel which it preached was felt, indeed, but always suppressed again.[1] That great mendicant monk had not yet come on the scene whose appearing was to work the crisis in the fluctuating struggle between renunciation of the world and lordship over it. But already the Church was beset all around by the wrathful curses of the "heretics," who saw in the Church's powerful exercise of her dominion and in the alienation of her gifts of grace the features of the ancient Babylon.

I.[2], p. 117) : "It is an erroneous view that the Latin Catholicism of the Middle Ages was summed up in the cultivation of legal righteousness and meritoriousness." It has as its correlate the mysticism that sacrifices the personal ego, to which at one time a theologico-acosmistic, at another time a christologico-lyrical character is given. But the simple trust in God, who reveals His grace in Christ, with the confession : "Sufficit mihi ad omnem justitiam solum habere propitium, cui soli peccavi" (Bernh. serm. in cant. xxiii. 15), was certainly not wanting in individual cases. Here and there, but above all in view of death, it triumphed, both over the calculations of legal righteousness and over the vagueness of mysticism. Flacius and Chemnitz were right in seeking and collecting testimonies for the evangelical doctrine of justification from the Middle Ages, and as Augustine in his day could justly assert that his doctrine of grace had its tradition in the *prayers* of the Church, so Chemnitz also was entitled to affirm that the cardinal evangelical doctrine could produce evidence for itself from earlier times, "Non in declamatoriis rhetoricationibus nec in otiosis disputationibus, sed in seriis exercitiis pænitentiæ et fidei, quando conscientia in tentationibus cum sua indignitate vel coram ipso judicio dei vel in agone mortis luctatur. Hoc enim solo modo rectissime intelligi potest doctrina de justificatione, sicut in scriptura traditur."

[1] The "eternal gospel" of Joachim of Fiore belongs to the close of our period, and for a time remained latent ; see Reuter, l.c. II., p. 198 ff.

2. *The Development of Ecclesiastical Law.*[1]

Let us notice at least in a few words the increased activity in ecclesiastical law in the period under review, which was not without its influence on the mode of conceiving of dogma, and on the history of dogma.

First, it is a fact of importance that from the middle of the second half of the ninth century, Church law was framed more and more on a *Pseudoisidorian* basis. *Second*, the preponderating attention given to law in general, and the growing subjection of all ecclesiastical questions to *legal conceptions* are characteristics of the period. As to the first point, it is well known that the Popes always continued to take more to do with the administration of the dioceses,[2] that the old metropolitan constitution lost its importance, and that the old constitutional state of things in general—during the first half of our period—fell into decay and ceased to exist. The Episcopal power, it is true, strengthened itself in many places by assuming a civil character, and on the other hand, the Emperors, from Otto I. to Henry III. after having reformed the enfeebled papacy, brought it for a time into dependence on the imperial crown. But as they also deprived all laymen, who were not princes, of all share in the direction of ecclesiastical affairs, and as they suppressed the independence of the local ecclesiastical bodies (the congregations), in the interests of imperialism and of "piety," only the Emperor (who called himself rector ecclesiæ and vicarius Christi), the Pope, and the bishops remained as independent powers. It was about the property of the bishops, and on the question as to who was the true ruler of the divine state and the vicar of Christ, that the great battle was really waged between the empire and the reformed papacy. In this struggle the latter, acting on the

1 For the earliest period see Maassen, Gesch. der Quellen und Litt. des Kanonischen Rechts I. vol. (till Pseudoisidore) 1870. For the later period see v. Schulte, Gesch. der Quellen und Lit. des Kanonischen Rechts von Gratian bis auf Gregor IX., 1875. See the introductions to von Friedberg's edition of the corp. jur. can.

2 Nicholas I., Leo IX., Alexander II., Alexander III. represent the stages prior to Innocent III. But Gregory VII. was the soul of the great movement in the eleventh century.

impulse given by Gregory VII., developed itself into the *autocratic* power in the Church, and accordingly after having freed itself in Rome from the last remnants of older constitutional conditions, framed its legislation by means of numerous decretals. At the "œcumenical" Lateran Synods of 1123 and 1139, the papacy left no doubt as to this new position which it meant to assert.[1] The Popes after-

[1] The numbering of the Œcumenical Councils, which has now become a sententia communis among the curialist theologians, has been established on the authority of Bellarmin (see Döllinger and Reusch, Die Selbstbiographie des Cardinals Bellarmin, 1887, p. 226 ff. That previous to him Antonius Augustinus [ob. 1586] counted them in the same way, has been pointed out by Buschball : " Die Professiones fidei der Päpste," separately printed from the Röm. Quartalschr. 10 Bd., 1896, p. 62). In the sixteenth century there still prevailed the greatest diversity in the enumeration : indeed the majority did not regard those Councils in which the Greek Church did not take part as œcumenical at all. There was likewise conflict of opinion as to whether the Councils of Bâsle, Florence (and Constance), were to be reckoned in. Antonius Augustinus and Bellarmin (in the Roman edition of the Concilia generalia of 1608 f.), included the Lateran Councils of 1123 and 1139 (and left out the Council of Bâsle). " The question, it is true, was of subordinate importance for Bellarmin, in as much as he places on the same level with the decrees of the General Councils those of the ' Particular ' Councils held under the presidency of the Pope, or sanctioned by him ; but having in view those who held, not that the Pope, but that the General Council was infallible, it was certainly necessary for him to discuss the question as to what Councils are to be regarded as general." But in thus determining the question, he naturally allowed himself to be influenced by his strong curialistic standpoint, that is, he set aside the Council of Constance and Bâsle, and placed among the Œcumenical Councils that of Florence, the fourth and fifth Lateran Councils, the first of Lyons, and that of Vienna, on the ground that these favoured the papacy. He thus arrived at the number of eighteen *approved* General Councils (eight from the first ten centuries, the Lateran Councils of 1123, 1139, 1179, 1215, those of Lyons in 1245 and 1274, that of Vienna in 1311, that of Florence, the fifth Lateran Council, and that of Trent). But here also, as everywhere in Catholic dogmatics, there are "half" authorities, and half genuine coin, in spite of the Holy Ghost who guides into all truth. That is to say, several Councils are " partly ratified, partly rejected," those of Constance and Bâsle being among them, and the Council of Pisa in 1409 the question about "neither manifestly ratified nor manifestly rejected." Since the year 1870, the question about the number of the Councils has completely lost all real interest for Catholics. But reactionary Protestantism has every reason to feel interested in it. Buschball (l.c. pp. 60, 74, 79), holds that *in the Middle Ages* a distinction in principle was not made between the view taken of the Councils of the first thousand years and that taken of those that were later. But he adduces no proof that prior to the Council of Constance the later Councils were placed quite on a level with the earlier, and even by what he adduces for the time subsequent uncertainty is suggested. How could the Mediæval Councils be regarded even before the Council of Trent as quite of equal standing with those of the first ten centuries, when, up to the time of this Council, the general

wards, till the time of Innocent III., defended and strengthened their autocratic position in the Church amid severe but
victorious struggles.   No doubt, they had to hear many an
anxious word from their most faithful sons ; but the rise of the
papacy to despotic power in the Church, and thereby to dominion
over the world, was promoted by the piety and by all the ideal
forces of the period.   Not in opposition to the spirit of the times
—how would that have been possible ?—but in union with it, the
papacy ascended the throne of the world's history in the eleventh
and twelfth centuries.   Its opponents, so far as they possessed
religion, were its secret allies, or contended with doubtful
consciences, or, at least, were unable to show that the benefits
for which they fought (national churchism, etc.) were the highest
and the holiest.   Under such circumstances the papal decretals
obtained an ever-increasing authority.[1]   They took their place

opinion was certainly to the effect that *dogma* was contained in fundamental and final
form in the twelve articles, and in the interpretation relating to them which they had
received from the older Councils !   The process of equalising was probably begun by
the Councils of Florence and Bâsle, with their high degree of self-consciousness.
That Councils at all could be pointed to in the long period between the ninth and the
fifteenth centuries, was necessarily of more importance than the taking account of
what was decided at these Councils, of how they were constituted, and of the authority
that guided them.   We may very well venture to say therefore : in the fifteenth century
the equalising had begun with some hesitation, the Council of Trent favoured it by
its weight, and it then became established.

1 On the development of the primacy in the eleventh and twelfth centuries, see
Döllinger, Janus, p. 107 ff. (Schwane, Dogmengesch. des Mittelalters, p. 530 ff.).
How much stronger was the Gregorian party in the eleventh century than the
Pseudoisidorian in the ninth, and how much more revolutionary and aware of his aim
was Gregory VII. than Nicolas I.!   " He was the first who, with full, clear consciousness, was determined to introduce a new condition of things into the Church by
new means.   He regarded himself not merely as the reformer of the Church, but as
the divinely chosen founder of an order of things such as had never before existed."
His chief means were Synods held by the Pope (this was begun by Leo IX.) and new
ecclesiastical law-books.   The nephew of Pope Alexander II., Anselm of Lucca,
became the founder of the new Gregorian Church law, this being effected by him
partly by making apt use of that of Pseudoisidore, and partly by a new set of fictions
(*e.g.*, that the episcopacy everywhere originated from Peter) and forgeries.   He was
followed by Deusdedit, Bonizo, and Cardinal Gregorius.   Deusdedit formulated the
new principle, that contradictions in the traditional Church law must always be
harmonised by letting, not the older, but the *greater* authority, that is, the dictum of
the Pope cancel the opposite view.   In this way the autocracy of the Popes was
established.   On the series of new fictions and falsifications of the old tradition, see

beside the old canons,[1] nay even beside the decrees of the Œcumenical Councils. Yet, strictly speaking, the measure of their authority remained still quite uncertain, and prior to Innocent III. *dogmatic* questions were not treated in them, or treated only very seldom, while the Popes in general, in the period of 150 years from the Synod of Sutri till 1198, had their hands fully occupied with establishing the Roman autocratic and monastic Church order. [2]

In developing itself as the supreme court of *jurisdiction*, the papacy could never have obtained in the *Church*, which assuredly is fellowship in *faith* and *worship*, monarchical rule as regards *faith* and *morals*, had not the amalgamation of *dogma* and *law* become perfect in this period. It was not the Popes who brought about this fusion; they merely turned to account a mode of view which prevailed everywhere, and from which scarcely an individual dissented. In what has been represented from the beginning of Book II. of our Second Part, it has been shown that the *legal* view of religion was an old inheritance of the Latin Church; religion is lex dei, lex Christi. In principle, it is true, this view had been radically corrected by Augustinianism; but Augustine himself allowed the legal schemes to remain in many important particulars. Then there followed the mission of the Western Church among the foreign nations, pagan and Arian. With these it came into contact, not merely as an institution

Janus, p. 112 ff. Specially important is the way in which history was induced to furnish testimony in proof of the infallibility of the papal decretals, and in which even Augustine was pronounced an authority for this new doctrine (p. 119 ff.). A sentence of his was so manipulated that it came to mean that the papal letters stood on a level with canonical Scripture. Since then the defenders of the infallibility of the Pope, to which Gregory VII. already made a distinct claim, and, indeed, treated it as concessum (p. 124 ff.), have always appealed to Augustine. Indeed, Gregory VII., following an earlier precedent, claimed for the Popes a complete *personal* holiness— for they have all that Peter had—and the Pope's holiness, in addition to his infallibility, was so boldly taught by the Gregorians (imputation of the merit of Peter) that anything stronger in the way of claim became impossible.

[1] Alexander II. wrote to King Philip of France, requesting him to rank the papal decrees along with the canons; see Jaffé, Regesta, 2 Edit., Nr. 4525.

[2] The Lateran Synods of 1123, 1139, 1179, contain nothing whatever of a dogmatic character (excepting the twenty-seventh canon of the Council of 1179, which urges the extermination of the Cathari, but says nothing of their doctrine) ; see Mansi XXI., XXII., Hefele V.[2], pp. 378 ff., 438 ff., 710 ff.

for religious worship, but as the *Roman Christian system of civilisation and law.* Not simply as a system of faith did it wish and venture to assert itself; it could assert itself at all, rather, only by placing its entire equipment, and all its principles, some of which had an extremely profane origin, under the protection of the *divine* law. Thus the Germanic and Romanic nations came to regard all *legal ordinances* of the Church as *ordinances of faith,* and *vice versâ.* Boniface and Charlemagne then set themselves to secure that the two would harmonise. The "must" became identical in the three sentences: "He who will be saved *must* believe as follows"; "the Christian *must* pay tithes"; "adultery *must* be atoned for by this particular penalty." How busily the framing, or the codification, of Church law was carried on from the time when Dionysius Exiguus made his collection till the time of Pseudoisidore, is shown by the numerous collections which were everywhere produced—even in Rome still—by the rich synodical life of the provincial Churches, and which were meant to guard the independence, the rights, and the distinctive life of the Church in the new world of Germanic manners. Everywhere (prior to the ninth century) dogma fell quite into the background; but just on that account the feeling became habitual, of regarding all deliverances of the Church as *legal ordinances.* The Cluniacensian-Gregorian reform of the eleventh century put an end to numerous traditional ordinances pertaining to constitution and law, and replaced them with new ones, in which the independence of the Church in relation to the State, and of Roman universalism in relation to the national Churches, found ever stronger expression. As the result of this, there developed itself in the eleventh century an imposing legislation, which was gathered up and completed in Gratian's collection—though this collection was in so far out of date and behind the facts, as in it the legislation was not yet determined throughout by the thought of the concentration of ecclesiastical power in the hands of the Pope.[1] But besides their adoption of the Gregorian doctrines, this collection, and some older ones that preceded it, show quite a new turn of things, for they are the product of a *study of law.* Here also Gregory VII. was

[1] See v. Schulte, Lehrbuch des Kathol. und evang. Kirchenrechts 4 Aufl., p. 20.

epoch-making. He was the great jurist in the papal chair, *and from his time onward, the treatment of all functions of the Church in accordance with juristic science began to be the main problem.* The study of law, carried on chiefly in Bologna,[1] exercised an immeasurable influence on the intellectual vision of the Church throughout its whole extent; the study of law, indeed, moulded thought in general. Hellenism also at that time exerted an incalculable influence in the way of fostering this study. The Romo-Grecian legislation came into the West, and although, at the first, it began by modifying what was still a "barbarian" form of secular legal life there, and by building up a sovereign State with its laws and officials, it yet gradually exercised also a furthering influence on the construction of the strict monarchical Church system; for what is legal for the Emperor is allowable for the Pope; or rather—he is in truth the Emperor. It cannot be doubted that here also Rome knew how to gather grapes of thorns and figs of thistles. The new rights of its adversary, the Emperor, it applied to itself.

What had formerly developed itself under the force of circumstances—the Church as a legal institution—was now strengthened and built up by thought.[2] Juristic thought laid its arrest on everything. And yet even here need controlled the situation. For when the impulse to reflect is once awakened, what else can those at first become, who still live in a world of abstractions and are blind to nature and history, but jurists and dialecticians? Thus there settled down upon the whole Church, even upon its faith, the spirit of jurisprudence, now grown conscious of itself. Everything was laid hold of by it. It was a strong force in what is styled "Scholasticism"; it governed the most powerful Popes (Alexander III. as Magister Rolandus), and it began to bring

[1] See Denifle, Die Univ. des Mittelalters I. 1885. Kaufmann, Gesch. der deutschen Univers. I., p. 157 ff.

[2] See v. Schulte, Gesch. der Quellen, etc., I., p. 92 ff.; II., p. 512 f. As Gregory VII. held still more strongly than any of his predecessors that the Church is the *kingdom* founded upon Peter, and that everything is to be traced back to the *power* given to it, the *legal organism* was placed in the foreground ; see Kahl, Die Verschiedenheit Kathol. und Evang. Anschauung über das Verhältniss von Staat und Kirche (1886), p. 7 f. : "The character of the Catholic Church as a legal organism is already involved in the doctrine of its founding, and in the conception of it." The fullest and most reliable historic proofs in Hinschius, Kath. Kirchenrecht.

within its sweep the form in which the traditional dogmas were presented. Certainly this was an easy matter for it ; for in their practical conclusions these dogmas had already been made to serve quite as legal means in a legal process. What still remained was to submit to juristic exposition even the central tenets of faith themselves, and so to justify and defend them " scientifically." Here too, indeed, the material was not entirely in a raw state ; to some extent, rather, the foundation stones had received a juristic shaping from the Latin fathers of dogma themselves (cf. Tertullian) ; but there was still an immense task presenting itself, to the full accomplishment of which an approach even had never been made ; it was to re-think the whole dogmatic tradition in the spirit of jurisprudence, to represent everything under the categories of judge (God), accused, advocate, legal measures, satisfactions, penalties, indulgences, to make out of dogmas as many distinctions as obtain in secular legal order between universally valid, relatively valid, probable, consuetudinary law, positive law, etc., and to convert dogmatics into a chamber of justice, out of which there was afterwards to develop the merchant's hall and the den of thieves.

But in the period we are considering, the Church was certainly the basis and sum of the highest ideals of the mediæval man, and the enormous contradiction on which one proceeded—had proceeded indeed, from the time of Augustine—of regarding the Church as at once the society of the faithful (societas fidelium), and as the hierarchically organised assemblage (coetus), of recognising the secular power in its divine right and yet suppressing its authority, was by many scarcely felt.[1] Only at the end of the epoch did the inner antagonism become apparent ; but the hierarchy had then already become the Church. just at that time, therefore, the claim of the hierarchy, and specially of the papacy, was proclaimed as dogma, and the struggle of the

[1] In the valuable inquiry of Mirbt, Die Stellung Augustin's in der Publicistik des gregorianischen Kirchenstreits (1888)—cf. the same author's work " Die Publicistik im Zeitalter Gregor's VII.," 1894—the significance of Augustine for the struggles in Church politics in the eleventh century has for the first time been methodically and thoroughly described. It amounted *directly* to less than one would have expected, and it is noteworthy that the Antigregorians can show a larger heritage of Augustinian thoughts than their opponents (see Theol. Lit. Ztg., 1889, Col. 599).

civil powers against the despotism of the Pope was declared to be as really rebellion against Christ as was the assertion of the sects that the true Church is the opposite of the hierarchy. This will have to be dealt with in the following chapter.

3. *The Revival of Science.*[1]

Theologians and philosophers have vied with one another in endeavouring to find a specific definition of Scholasticism, and to differentiate what this term is meant to denote, from the theology and philosophy of the old (Greek) Church on the one hand, and from modern science on the other. These efforts have led to no accepted result ; nor could they lead to any such, for Scholasticism is simply nothing but *scientific thought.* That this thought was governed by prejudices,[2] and that from these it in some respects did not free itself at all, and in some respects freed itself only slowly, is shared by the science of the Middle Ages with the science of every age. Neither dependence on authorities, nor the preponderance of the deductive method, was specially characteristic of Scholasticism ; for science in fetters has existed in every period—our descendants will find that present-day science is in many respects not controlled merely by pure experience—and the dialectico-deductive method is the means that must be used by all science that has the courage to emphasise strongly the conviction of the unity of all that is. But it is not even correct to say that within mediæval science that method prevailed alone, or chiefly. The realism that was represented by Albert and Thomas, acting upon impulses re-

---

[1] See the histories of philosophy by Ueberweg, Erdmann and Stöckl; Prantl, Gesch. der Logik Bd. II.-IV. ; Bach, l.c., I. and II. ; Reuter, Gesch. der Aufkl. I. and II. : Löwe, Der Kampf zwischen dem Nominalismus und Realismus, 1876 ; Nitzsch, Art. Scholastische Theologie in der R.-E., XIII.[2], p. 650 ff., where in p. 674 ff., the literature is noted. Dilthey, Einl. in die Geisteswissensch. I. Denifle, l.c. ; Kaufmann, l.c., p. 1 ff. ; Denifle in the Archiv f. Litt.-u. Kirchengesch. des Mittelalters, I. and II. ; v. Eicken, l.c., p. 589 ff.

[2] The fundamental prejudice, which, however, Scholasticism shared with the theology of antiquity, and unfortunately also of modern times, was that theology is cognition of the world, or that it has to verify and complete cognition of the world. If it is said to-day that it has to supplement it, seeing that it steps in where knowledge fails, modesty has extorted the expression, but the same thing is still meant.

ceived from Augustine, made excellent use of experience, and
Scotism and Nominalism in particular are partly based on the
empiric method, though as compared with the deductive, Duns
may have found fault with this method as confused. What is
of importance here is only this, that the observation of the
external world was extremely imperfect, that, in a word, natural
science, and the science of history did not exist, the reason being
that men knew how to observe spirit, but not how to observe
things of sense.[1] But least of all must Scholasticism be reproached with treating "artificial," "fabricated" problems. On
its premises they were not artificial, and if they were boldly
wrought out, it was only a proof of scientific energy.

The Scholasticism of the Middle Ages, then, was simply
science, and it is merely perpetuating an unwarranted mistrust
when it is thought that this part of the general history of science
may be designated by a special name.[2] As if science in general
had not its stages, as if the mediæval stage was distinguished
from the rest by its unparalleled and culpable obscurity! On

[1] Yet even this does not apply to the whole of Scholasticism. Especially in its
later period, it pointed also to the book of nature.

[2] Kaufmann remarks correctly, p. 5 : " There still attaches to the term Scholasticism something of the hatred and contempt which the Humanists poured upon it."
This hostile spirit is, no doubt, intelligible, inasmuch as Scholasticism still threatens
our present-day science. Yet in more recent years a complete change of judgment
has appeared, which comes to the help of the Pope in his renewed recommendations
of St. Thomas. Indeed, in the effort to be just, the once disparaged Scholasticism
is beginning to be extravagantly belauded, as is shown by the pronouncement of a
very celebrated jurist. With this praise the circumstance may also have some connection, that the Schoolmen are now being read again, and readers find to their
surprise that they are not so irrational as had been believed. The strongest contribution to the glorification of Thomas has been furnished by Otto Willmann in the
second volume of his " Gesch. des Idealismus " (1896). Here Idealism and Thomism
(of the strictest type) are simply placed on a level. Nominalism is the corrupt tree,
which can bear no good fruit, and is to be regarded, moreover, merely as an episode,
as a nubicula ; for since its rising, the sun of the Thomist Realism has been always in
the heavens, and has given warmth to every century. The real enemy of Thomas
and of Idealism is Kantianism, which has slowly prepared itself, that, on its assuming
its perfect form, it may forthwith be assailed and overthrown by the true Idealism.
Protestantism is viewed as the continuation of monistic Mysticism (!), because it (v.
the strict determinism) does not take account of the causæ secundæ. So Thomism
alone, sans phrase, is the saviour of the holy things of humanity ! Augustinianism at
the same time still finds recognition here, but yet it is still no completed system ; it
only represents the way to the right one.

the contrary, it may rather be said that Scholasticism furnishes a unique and luminous example of the fact that thought finds its way even under the most adverse conditions, and that even the gravest prejudices that weigh it down are not heavy enough to quench its life. The science of the Middle Ages gives practical proof of eagerness in thinking, and exhibits an energy in subjecting all that is real and valuable to thought, to which we can find, perhaps, no parallel in any other age.[1]

Hence it is useless to direct one's ingenuity to answering the question as to what *kind* of science presents itself in Scholasticism ; we have simply rather to inquire into the *conditions* under which scientific thought was placed at that time. Not equally useless, but vaguely treated, is the academic question, much discussed and marked by confusion and wearisomeness, with regard to the relation of Scholasticism to Mysticism.[2] If by Scholasticism there is understood (though this is arbitrary) " the hand-maid of hierarchism," or, with sudden change of front, the " construction of systems without concern for the needs of the inner life," or the " rationalistic craving for proof," and if Mysticism is then placed alongside as the free pectoral theology, then the most beautiful contrasts can be drawn—Hagar and Sarah, Martha and Mary. But with little trouble Scholasticism and Mysticism can, on the other hand, be resolved into each other, and a daring dialectic performance can be carried on with these terms, which does honour to the acuteness of the author, but which has only the disadvantage that one is as wise after, as before, the definitions have been given. The thing to be dealt with here is simple. Scholasticism is science, applied to religion, and—at least, till the time when it underwent self-disintegration —science setting out from the axiom, that all things are to be understood from *theology*, that all things therefore must be

---

[1] We may say, indeed, with the poet about that age : " Everything now aims at fathoming man from within and from without ; truth, where hast thou an escape from the wild chase ? "

[2] On Mysticism, see the works which Karl Müller has cited in his krit. Uebersicht (Zeitschr. f. K.-Gesch. VII., p. 102 ff.). Above all the numerous works of Denifle and Preger (Gesch. der deutschen Mystik I., II.) have to be consulted ; as also Greith, Die deutsche Mystik im Predigerorden, 1861. For the earlier Mysticism, cf. the monographs on Anselm, Bernard, and the Victorinians.

traced back to *theology*.   This axiom regularly presupposes
that the thinker feels himself to be in entire dependence on
God, that he seeks to *know* this dependence ever more deeply,
and that he uses every means for the strengthening of his own
religious life ; for only in the measure in which he finds, and
knows himself to be, under and in God, is he made capable
of understanding all else, since, of course, to *understand* things
means nothing else than to know their relation to the One and
All, or to the Author (*i.e.*, in both cases, to God).   From this it
follows at once *that personal piety is the presupposition of science.*
But in so far as personal piety at that time was always thought
of as *contemplation* of the relation of the ego to God accompanied by asceticism,[1] *Mysticism is the presupposition of Scholasticism ;* in other words, mediæval science bases itself on piety,
and on piety, too, which is itself *contemplation*, which lives therefore in an *intellectual* element.   From this it follows, *that this
piety itself prompts to thought ;* for the strong impulse to become
acquainted with the relation of one's own ego to God necessarily
leads to the determination of the relation of the creation, of
which one knows himself to be a part, to God.   Now, where this
knowledge is so pursued that insight into the relation of the
world to God is sought for solely or chiefly with the view of
understanding the position of one's own soul to God, and of
inwardly growing through such understanding, we speak of
Mystic theology.[2]   But where this reflex aim of the process of
knowledge does not present itself so distinctly, where, rather,
the knowledge of the world in its relation to God acquires a
more independent objective interest,[3] the term *Scholastic theology*

---

[1] Piety is, above all, not the hidden temper of feeling and will, from which spring
love to one's neighbour, humility and patience, but it is growing *cognition*, begotten
of steadfast reflection on the relation of the soul to God.

[2] How largely dependent on Scholasticism the later Mystic theology in particular
was ; or, more correctly, how identical the two were, has been shown especially by
the works of Denifle (against Preger in the histor. polit. Blättern, 1875, p. 679 ff.,
and on Master Eckhart in the Archiv f. Litt.-u. K.-Gesch. des Mittelalters II. Bd.).

[3] It is only a question of difference of degree ; very correctly Karl Müller says
(Zeitschr. f. K.-Gesch. VII., p. 118): " The character of mediæval piety always
expresses itself, more or less, even in the theoretic discussions of Scholasticism,
because among the representatives of the latter the entire half of the way of salvation
is dominated throughout by the interests and points of view of Mysticism, this circum-

is employed.   From this it appears that we have not before us two magnitudes that run parallel, or that, forsooth, collide with each other, but that Mystic theology and Scholastic theology are one and the same phenomenon, which only present themselves in manifold gradations, according as the subjective or objective interest prevails.[1]   The former interest was so little lacking even to the most distinguished Schoolmen that their whole theology can be unhesitatingly described as *also* Mystic theology—for Thomas, Mysticism is the starting-point and practical application of Scholasticism—and, on the other hand, there are theologians who are described as Mystics, but who, in the strength of their desire to know the *world*, and to understand in a systematic way the Church doctrine, are not a whit behind the so-called Schoolmen.   But in saying this the further position is already stated, that a specific difference between the scientific *means* had likewise no existence.   Here also it is simply a question of shade (nuance).   The view of the God in whom, and from whom, all things must be understood, was given by the Church tradition.   But in this view also subjective piety was

stance having a connection with their monastic training and education.   As soon as these men come to deal in their theoretical discussions with the appropriation of salvation, they bring along with them the presuppositions of their practical Mysticism."

[1] Even in Nitzsch's determination of the relationship (l.c., pp. 651 ff., 655) I cannot find a clearing up, while in Thomasius-Seeberg the distinct vision of the matter is completely obscured by a mass of details.   Nitzsch first accentuates strongly the formalistic character of Scholasticism, then, with a view to understanding Mystic theology, points to its origin, the Pseudo-Dionysian doctrine, and now concludes : "It is obvious that this theology of the soul, of feeling, and of *direct* intuition is fundamentally distinct from the Scholastico-dialectic theology."   But the assertion that the Scholastic theology is formalistic is scarcely cum grano salis correct, as will appear more clearly below.   How can one call a mode of thought formalistic which takes the greatest interest in relating everything to a living unity ?   And if the means employed cannot secure the proposed end (as *we* think), have we therefore a right to reproach these scholars with a merely formalistic interest in things ?   But, further, the Pseudo-Dionysian theology is as much the presupposition of Scholasticism as of Mysticism, and that which Nitzsch calls "theology of the soul, of feeling, and of direct intuition" plays in both the same part, as alpha and omega, while the Mystic theology certainly keeps manifestly to its point of departure throughout the whole alphabet, the Scholastic, on the other hand, apparently forsakes it, but in the end (doctrine of the way of salvation) always returns to it, thereby showing that it has never really lost sight of it.

trained.   The formal shaping elements were likewise everywhere
the same.   Inasmuch as the scientific means were derived entirely from the same three sources, the authoritative dogma, inner
experience, and the traditional philosophy, any differences that
would be more than varieties cannot be made out (a greater or
less passing into the background of logical formalism, a preference for inner observation over authoritative tradition [1]).

Yet it is said that great inner antagonisms entered into
mediæval science.   Anselm and his opponents are pointed to,
Bernard and Abelard, the German theologians of the fourteenth
century and the Churchmen who pronounced them heretics, and
from the contrasted positions in these cases the formula is
framed, that here Mysticism is in conflict with Scholasticism.
Differences certainly there are here ; but that stock controversial
term throws a very uncertain light on them.   Above all, the
phenomena here gathered together can by no means be united
in *one* group.   But before we deal with them, it will be well to
answer the main question stated above, under what conditions
the scientific thought of the Middle Ages was placed, or, let us
say, how it developed itself, and what were the concrete factors
which determined it (in the way of advancing or retarding), and
thereby gave it its peculiar stamp.   From this inquiry the proper
light will naturally be thrown upon these " antagonisms " which
are erroneously represented when they are described as a struggle
of two opposing principles.

The Middle Ages received from the ancient Church not only
the substantially completed dogma, but also—as a living force—
the philosophy, or say, the theology which had been employed
in the shaping of dogma, and together with this also a treasury
of classical literature, which had little or no connection with the
philosophy and the dogma, but which answered to an element in
the antique view of life in Italy and Byzantium that had never
quite disappeared.   These three things constituted the legacy of
the old world to the new.   But they already contained in them
all the contrasts that came to view in the inner life of the Middle
Ages, when consciousness of that inheritance had been awakened.

[1] Scholasticism shares with Mysticism the "finis," and Mysticism uses essentially
the same means as Scholasticism.

These " antagonisms " were as actively at work in the Greek
Church from the days of Origen and Jerome as they afterwards
were in the Mediæval Church.   In this sense all scientific
developments of the West in the Middle Ages were simply a
continuation of what the Greek Church had already partly
passed through, and was partly still continuing to pass through
in feeble movements.   The difference consisted only in this, that
in the West everything gradually developed itself to a higher
degree of energy ; that the Church, as the visible commonwealth
of God on earth, impressed its stamp on all secular life, taking
even science into closer connection with itself, giving it a higher
flight, and at the same time requiring it by its authority to
adopt juristic thought ; and finally in this, that from Greek
science Augustinianism was absent.

We have remarked above that along with the substantially
completed dogma the Middle Ages received from antiquity the
related philosophy or theology.   But this very circumstance
introduced strain : for while this theology was certainly " related,"
yet as certainly also did it contain, as a living force, elements
that were hostile to dogma, whether we think of Neoplatonism
or Aristotelianism.   It is well known that in the Greek Church,
from the fifth and sixth centuries, both schools worked upon
dogma, and that " heresies " to the right and left were the result
(pantheism and tritheism, spiritualistic Mysticism and rationalistic
Criticism), and that then, from the Justinian age, the Scholasticism
evolved itself which found the via media between the Areopagite
and John Philoponus.[1]

In the theological science of John of Damascus there presents
itself the reconciliation of dogma with Neoplatonism and
Aristotelianism.[2]   Here the former plays the principal part in
the principles, the latter in the working out ; for with the help
of dialectic distinction one can remove all difficulties and contradictions that emerge.   But the *independent* force of the Neoplatonic and Aristotelian philosophies was not broken by the harmonising.   The books in which they were contained continued to be
read, and thus in Byzantium the strain did not cease.   Mystic

[1] v. Vol. IV. p. 232 f. of this work.
[2] Vol. IV. p. 264 f. ; see also p. 331 ff.

theology was further cultivated, Aristotle was studied, and
although the acts of aggression always grew feebler, both of them
threatened the Church with its dogma, the Church that was
meanwhile growing more powerless in the embraces of the State.
There were the further circumstances that memories of the
theologically unconcerned age of antiquity had never died out,
that a certain worldly culture, indifferent to religion, and often
indeed degenerating into barbarism, still survived, which was
strong enough to hinder the Eastern Church from ever making
even an approach to the carrying out of its ideals and aims in
secular life and *secular* culture.   From the days of the Alexandrian Theophilus monks and pious laymen might lament over
the godlessness of the ancient literature and wish it in hell, but
no one was able either to banish it, or to purify it, and bring it
entirely into the service of ecclesiastical science.

If we pass now to the Carlovingian period, *i.e.*, to the first
epoch of scientific advance in the West, we find exactly the same
elements side by side, only with one important addition
(Augustinianism).   There is an eager endeavour to become
acquainted with the traditional dogma and to think it out, and,
as the Adoptian controversy shows, there is at the same time a
surrender to entire dependence on the Greeks.   In the writings of
Boethius and Isidore there is possessed a source, rich enough for
that period, from which the dialectic science of method may be
learned.   As the work of John Scotus shows, the Neoplatonic
Mysticism had already become known to the West from the
writings of Dionysius and Maximus ; besides this, however, it
was represented in a *theistic* setting, and with incomparable
attractiveness, by Augustine.   Finally, the ancient literature
(poets and historians) was sought out, and through contact with
Italy there arose the seductive pictures of a blithesome life that
had never altogether vanished.

But the forces which the West had at its command at that
time were still too weak to admit of working independently with
the capital that had been inherited.   To become familiar with
Augustine and Gregory I., to understand the christological speculations of the Greeks, and to master the simplest rules of logic and
method—that was the real task of the period.   What was

attempted beyond this, Scotus excepted, was a feeble renaissance : indeed the union of the antique with the theological at
the court of Charles the Great has something childish.   This
union therefore was soon dissolved again.   Not for the first
time under Louis the Pious, but as early as the last years of
Charles I. himself, the ascetic thought of the ancient Church
asserted its influence even in science.   And so it continued to
be afterwards ; we can observe indeed, on till the thirteenth
century, a steady increase of aversion to the antique, while, no
doubt, some bold spirits sought more than before to learn from
it.   In theory secular studies were discarded.   Ancient literature
was regarded as a source of temptations.   All science which did
not place itself under theology, *i.e.*, which did not refer everything to the knowledge of God, was held to be pernicious, nay,
to be a seduction of the devil.   But as what is characteristic, in
all fields, of the mediæval view of the world consists in this, that
it aims at uniting the ununitable, and requires that negation of
the world shall be attained in the form of dominion over it, so
we observe here also that what is rejected is again adopted.
Ancient literature and philosophy were certainly employed as a
formal means of culture, and with a view also to the refutation
of pagans, Jews, and heretics, and to a fathoming of the divine
mysteries.   It was to some extent the same persons who rejected them in the end, who on their slow, toilsome journey to
the summit made use of them.   And where they were different
persons, yet there was at bottom between the two an elective
affinity ; for *all* thinkers who came to be influential, though
some of them may appear to us "illuminists" (Aufklärer) and
others traditionalists, were dominated by the same fundamental thought of tracing back all things to God and understanding them from Him.   And when in the end the Church
released Aristotle and allowed full use to be made of him, that
was not done by way of yielding to outward constraint, but
because the Church theology was now strong enough to master
this master, and because he could furnish it with the most effectual
help against the dangers of a bold idealism which threatened
dogma.   Though the schools, the universities, might not be
ecclesiastical institutions in the strict sense of the term, science

was *ecclesiastical, theological.* There was no lay science. The thought of such science was for that age equivalent to paganism and nihilism.

From the Carlovingian period a chain of scientific tradition and schools of learning extends into the eleventh century ;[1] but a *continuous* increase of scientific activity cannot be ascertained, and even the greatest masters (Gerbert of Rheims) did not produce effects that were epoch-making. Not till the middle of the century was the advancement begun that was followed by no further declension, and the thread formed that was not again to break. The inner rise of the Church was unquestionably the determining cause of this upward movement of science, although we are surprised at meeting quite at the beginning with a trained skill in dialectic for which we had not been prepared, and which must have gone on developing in the dark ages (sæculum obscurum) in spite of their darkness. But how could the inner revival of the Church have continued without results for science ? The Church conceived itself at that time as *spiritual* power, as the power of the supersensuous life over the sensuous ; the subject of science was the supersensuous ; science, therefore, was challenged by this revival ! But even the science which revels in the transcendental, and which readily attaches itself to revelations, cannot deny its character as *science.* Even where it is, and wishes to be, the handmaid of revelation, it will always embrace an element by which it offends the faith which desires rest ; it will exhibit a freshness and joy which to devoutness appears as insolence ; nay, even when it knows itself to be one with the Church in its starting-point and aims, it will never be able to deny a negative tendency, for it will always be justified in finding that the principles of the Church suffer deterioration in the concrete expressions of life, and are disfigured by superstition.

In the dazzling light in which Reuter, the marvellous master of that literature, has presented the conflicts between young mediæval science and the men of the Church (Berengar and Lanfranc, Anselm and his opponents, Abelard and Bernard),

[1] Berengar was a disciple of Fulbert of Chartres (ob. 1028) ; the latter had studied under Gerbert.

the persons engaged appear like spectral caricatures. Because this scholar tries to find "negative illuminism" everywhere in the movements, things are deprived of their proportion, and the common ground on which the combatants stand almost entirely disappears. With wonder and astonishment we see one Herostratus after another cross the stage, surrounded by troops of like-minded disciples ; the "primacy of infallible reason" is set up by them, after they have destroyed authority; the antitheses become as abrupt as cliffs, and frightful chasms open up. But the biographer of these heroes, so far as he does not charge them with hypocrisy, must himself regularly acknowledge in some stray turn of thought, that they stood in closest connection with their age and with their opponents, that their enormously magnified performances were of a much more modest kind, and that the great illuminists were obedient sons of the Church. In opposition to this representation we follow out the hints given above, in order to elucidate and understand these struggles.

In the higher rise of science three things were involved : the *penetrating more deeply into the Neoplatonic-Augustinian principles of all theology, the dialectic art of analysis*, and, united with both, *a certain knowledge of the ancient classics and of the Church Fathers.* As regards those principles, it was the spirit of the *so-called Platonic Realism* that prevailed. By means of it, as it had been derived from Augustine and from dogma itself, and from a hundred little sources also, dogma—but the world, too, as well—came to be understood, and all things came to be known from and in God. Till the beginning of the twelfth century this Platonic Realism, with its spiritualistic sublimating tendency and its allegorical method, reigned pretty much unbroken. It reigned all the more securely, the less a conception of it had as yet been consciously formed (as a theory of knowledge).[1] It

---

[1] Till far on in the twelfth century the scholars were not first philosophers and then theologians ; they possessed as yet no philosophic system at all ; their philosophy rather was quite essentially dialectic art ; see Deutsch, Abælard, p. 96 : "The relation of philosophy to theology in the initial period of Scholasticism was essentially different from what it was at its maturity. In the earlier period a proper philosophic system, a view of the world developed on different sides, had as yet no existence. Only logic was known with some completeness . . . but, as a distinct discipline,

was peculiar to it that it set out from faith, and then made itself master of dogma in the way in which dogma had formerly arisen ("credo ut intelligam"—this position of Augustine was not merely reasserted by Anselm, but was willingly assented to by all Church thinkers of the period). But it was, further, peculiar to it *that it took a flight beyond dogma.* This had occurred in Greek Mysticism as well as with Augustine, and it repeated itself, without the danger being observed, from the eleventh century (and just, too, among the "most pious" philosophers). Here lay the first antagonism. As one got to understand dogma by the help of the same means by which it had arisen, that idea of the immanence of God, of all things existing in God, asserted itself, before which the historical, and dogma itself, threatened to vanish, *i.e.,* were viewed as the final stage needing sublimation. So Origen thought, so also had Augustine felt, and had expressed it at the outskirts of his speculation,[1] so was it taught by the Greek Mystics.[2] From this point, as by a circuit, a complete rehabilitation of reason could take place. After getting its dismissal at the beginning—revelation decides and authority—reason was now the means for removing out of the way whatever hindered the thought of the absoluteness, the *immutability* and immanence of God. It neutralised miracle, in order to give expression to the strict uniformity of the operation

metaphysic did not yet exist for the philosophers of that period. What they had of it consisted in single propositions, partly Platonic, partly Aristotelian. . . . Only when the Aristotelian writings became known in the second half of the twelfth century did the West learn to know a real philosophic system."

[1] See Vol. V., p. 125 ff.

[2] Hence even in the question about the universals, which was already dealt with at that time on the basis of passages from Porphyry and Boethius, the treatment was almost entirely realistic : general notions exist in and of themselves, or they exist in things as their real essence (though very different turns of thought were possible here in matters of detail ; see Prantl, Gesch. der Logik, II., p. 118 ff.). Certainly there were already to be found also in this period representatives of Nominalism, according to which general notions are intellectus, or, say, only voces ; indeed, it probably always existed side by side with Realism ; but theology still treated it with indifference. When the Nominalist Roscellin, the teacher of Abelard, applied the Nominalist view to the doctrine of the Trinity, he was resisted by Anselm (v. Deutsch, p. 100 f.). The latter had no doubt that those who held the universales substantiæ to be mere voces, must err from the Christian faith, and were heretics. But how did it stand with those who logically applied the substantiality of general notions ?

of the All-One ; it neutralised even the history of salvation, and history in general, or transformed it into the circulating course of the operative Being that is, was, and shall be ; it neutralised, finally, the creature. The " illuminist " of the eleventh and twelfth centuries would still have to be found who did not play his " illuminist " part under the influence of this mysticism, who did not likewise take the " credo ut intelligam " as his starting-point. Though, like Berengar, he might compare the literally understood Jewish law with the laws of the Romans, Athenians, and Spartans in order to give the palm to the latter, though like Abelard, he might unite into one the history of salvation and general history in the " philosophy of religion on a historic basis "—this was still done on the understanding that there was to be absolute validity obtained for all that the Church offered of material content, by means of sublimating (allegory) ; it was done in the name of the conception of God and of the theology which prevailed also among the opponents, so far as they thought at all, and these latter started back before conclusions which Justin, Origen, and the great group of Greek and Latin Fathers had long before drawn.[1] So it was not that principle stood opposed to principle, but the amount of application was disputed [2]—unless we should have to regard as the real principle

[1] The inquiry would be interesting and important that would lead us to determine whether, and through what channels, the older Pre-Jeromic Church literature influenced Scholasticism ; *e.g.*, are the agreements of Abelard with Justin and Origen accidental, or only indirect, or direct ? That the Shepherd of Hermas and the Didache continued to have influence admits of proof. Contradictions within tradition, between the older and the later, and again between tradition (the sacred canons) and Scripture had already been discovered in the Gregorian period, and up to a certain point had been admitted (see Mirbt, Augustine, p. 3 f.) ; but Abelard was the first to emphasise the importance of these contradictions, while on the other hand, certainly, he began to have an inkling of what his contemporaries were far from thinking of, namely, that errors promote the progress of truth.

[2] It surely does not require to be specially noted, that no teacher of importance in this period drew all the conclusions of Platonic Realism (as little as Augustine did). They lay only on the horizon of their view, and were touched on in passages here and there. Till Abelard taught him better, William of Champeaux, it is true, seems to have asserted the full immanence of the generic notion, conceived of substantially, in every individual, a view which must necessarily have led to the doctrine of the *one* latent substance, and of the negating of all that is individual as mere semblance or mere contingency. This doctrine certainly lay on the outskirts of the view then taken

of mediæval ecclesiastical theology, lack of thought, or blind surrender. But that was not what the Church Fathers taught, nor was
it what the Church itself wished when it again conceived of itself
as spiritual power in the eleventh century. How slight really is
the distinction between Berengar and Anselm as theologians !
It often entirely disappears ; for how far were those represented
as wild destroyers from drawing the conclusions *in their totality*,
and from repeating, say, the thoughts of Erigena ! They were
not innovators, but restorers ; not a trace is to be found in them
of negative illuminism.

In the Greek Church Aristotelianism had made its appearance when dogma and speculation could no longer be reconciled,
and it rendered the Church invaluable service as the Horos
which kept the Sophia of the Mystics from plunging into the
abyss of the primeval Father. But along with these services
it had at the same time brought at first unpleasant gifts in addition. While it checked unrestrained idealism, and at the same
time set to work to make paradoxical and burdensome formulæ
tolerable by means of distinctions, it also subjected to revision
formulæ that collapsed as soon as their basis of Platonic Realism
was taken from them. This Aristotelianism, which was so
necessary, but of which there had been such bad experiences,
as it appeared in John Philoponus and other Greeks, not to
speak of the old Antiochian School, was known also to those in
the West, through Boethius, and from other sources (in a poor
enough form, no doubt, more directly as logical method), and
long before had concluded (in the case of Boethius himself, *e.g.*), an
irregular marriage with the Neoplatonic doctrine of principles.
To the spirit of the West, which had more of understanding
than of reason, and, as juristic also, constantly strove after distinctions, this Aristotelianism was congenial. From it there
developed " dialectic," at first, too, as scientific art. And as this
scientific art always encourages insolence and pride where it is
held to be the sum of all wisdom, so was it at the beginning of
the Middle Ages. The schooled " dialecticians " of the eleventh

of the world, and made its appearance in Mysticism as the expression of pious contemplation, afterwards even as a theoretic conviction. On Abelard's having the credit
of discarding it see below.

century looked proudly down on the obscurantists who did not understand art, while these again became concerned about the traditional Church doctrine, although the operations of the youthful science only seldom touched the kernel of things, unless it was that one here and there ventured too far with his art in regard to dogmas that stood in the centre of vision (doctrines of the Trinity, of the two natures, of the Eucharist), and, anticipating the later Nominalism, or recalling unpleasant facts in the history of tradition, served up a questionable attempt at solving the trinitarian problem (tritheistic, Sabellian), or approached too near the old Adoptianism, or threw doubt on the current opinion about the external miracle in the Eucharist. In this way the first conflicts arose, which were lacking in real sharpness, however, because the dialectic itself stood in league with Platonic Realism, and at bottom did not know very often what it really wanted. At the same time it must not be denied, that wherever the understanding is brought in, it will assert its own rights and will overleap the limits of a purely formal activity. But it is shown, e.g., by the science of Anselm, how peacefully, under certain conditions, dogma, Platonic Realism, and dialectic harmonised.

Yet in the twelfth century that came to be otherwise. In Abelard [1] both the critical tendency of Platonic Realism (cf. his

---

[1] See the excellent monograph of Deutsch upon him (1883), the best book we possess on the history of the theological science of that period, distinguished preeminently by calmness and caution of judgment, as compared with the overstrained biographies to the right and left. In the introduction, p. 11 f., it is denied on good grounds that there was a widely prevailing negative illuminism in this period. What widely prevailed was not negative but ecclesiastical, and what was negative (frivolity of course there has been in every age; "the frivolity and avarice of the jeunesse dorée that vaunted itself in the apostolic chair up to the middle of the eleventh century": Sackur) or expressly heretical had no widespread influence (to what extent at the time of the establishment of Clugny practical and theoretical atheism, frivolous criticism of the Bible, etc., prevailed among the West-Frankian lay circles is shown by Sackur). That to Abelard there belongs a unique position in his time, Deutsch has grounds for asserting, but he is far from characterising him simply as an illuminist. If it were necessary to describe him as such, then it would be peculiar to Catholic religion to be purely acquiescent faith—but at that time at least it certainly had not yet made that claim; then Justin, Origen, and Augustine would be "creedless free-thinkers"; then Abelard himself would be a double-tongued hypocrite, for his wish was to be a Church theologian, believing in revelation, and yet at the same time one who could give account of his faith and was capable of showing it to be plain truth. That while this was his aim he became entangled in contradictions, that in under-

view of history) and the critical tendency of dialectic grew
stronger, *without his abandoning, however, in the fundamental
theses, his relation of dependence on the Church doctrine.* Abelard
was the boldest theologian of his time, because he understood
how to derive the critical side from *all* elements of tradition, and
was really persuaded of the defectiveness just of what was held
valid. His opponents of his day thought that the dangers of
his science arose quite essentially from his *dialectic,* and, accordingly, discredited this above everything else. In point of fact,
boldness in submitting particulars to the treatment of the
understanding was an outstanding feature in Abelard; the
understanding, too, when once released, asserted its own rights,
frequently overleapt the boundaries theoretically recognised,
scorned authority, and proclaimed, with the support of a certain
knowledge of ancient history, the eternal right of reasonable
thought as the highest court of appeal. But that the most
dangerous theses of the restless scholar sprang from Platonic
(Augustinian) Realism, *i.e.,* from the fundamental view that was
adhered to by one's self, was not observed. *In principle Abelard
certainly moderated this view by means of his critico-dialectic
reflections.* He was no more a representative of thorough-going
Realism. He was rather the first to introduce into epistemology
a kind of conceptualism,[1] to break through the strict doctrine of
immanence, and, by beginning to restore independence to the
creature, to begin also to emancipate the conception of God
itself from pantheism. For Abelard, the dialectic art ceases to
be mere art; it begins to become a material principle, and to
correct the traditional (Neoplatonic-Augustinian) doctrines of
the first and last things. *The paradox in Abelard's position
consists in this, that on the one hand in contemplating history he*

taking to commend religion to the understanding he frequently had more regard to
the judge than to the client, was certainly not peculiar to him as a theologian! For
ascertaining the theology of Abelard the sentences of his disciple, Magister Roland
Alexander III. (see the edition by Gietl, 1891, and Denifle in Archiv, Vol. I., pp.
434 ff. 603 ff.) may be consulted.

[1] How his theory of knowledge is to be understood is a disputed point among
scholars (v. Deutsch, p. 104 ff.). It is certain that he held a sceptical attitude
towards Platonic Realism, that he rejected it indeed, without however passing over
to Nominalism.

drew certain conclusions from the Mystic doctrine of God (cf. Justin, Origen, but also Augustine himself) *more confidently than his contemporaries, while, on the other hand, he allowed sober thought to have a material influence on the view taken of ground principles.* His opponents saw in him only the negative theologian. *This negative theologian really laid the foundation for the classical structure of mediæval conservative theology.*[1]   For

---

[1] This seems paradoxical, and certainly other things come more prominently to view in Abelard at first : his genuine, unquenchable scientific ardour, his sense for the natural (sound human understanding), his ambitious striving, not devoid of vanity, his dialectic acuteness, his critical spirit, finally, the conviction animating him that the ratio has its own field of play, and that there are many questions on which it first, and it alone, must be heard (on his learning, which has often been over-rated, see Deutsch, p. 53 ff.). But on the other hand the following factors in his mode of teaching are to be noted, which obtained quite a *positive* importance for the time that followed (while we pass over what is an understood matter, viz., that even by him all knowledge was ultimately traced up to the revelation of God) : (1) The man charged with "rationalism" has no great confidence in the capabilities of the human power of knowledge, and openly expressed this, in opposition to the self-assurance of the dialecticians and mystics ; he did not possess it, but pointed to revelation, because he (2) did not regard thought and being as identical, but took up a critico-sceptical attitude towards the reigning Realism, such as was just required for the defence of the Church doctrine—as was taught by the time that followed. With this there is connected (3) that, while keeping very much on Augustine's lines in the conception of God, he avoided those conclusions from his conception which led at one time to the assumption of a rigid, unchangeable divine working (a rigid order of nature), at another time to an unlimited arbitrariness on God's part. This he effected by bringing in again (with Origen, partly *against* Augustine) very strongly though not at every point, the thought of the *ethically* determined character of the divine action, and of the limitation of the divine power by the notion of purpose (and so by what actually happens). With this he also drew a sharp distinction between God and the creature, and asserted the independence of the latter, corrected thereby the questionable Mystic conception of God, and prepared the way for the conception of God held by the great Schoolmen. His opponents, on the other hand, such as Hugo (and afterwards also the Lombard) adhered to that conception of God which afterwards proved more convenient in defending any kind of Church doctrine ; but there is no question that Abelard was really the *more positive.* If he has nevertheless been classed with Spinoza, that only proves that there has been ignorance of the notion of God which elsewhere prevailed in his time among Church theologians, and that just that side in Abelard's notion of God has been emphasised which was *not* peculiar to him, for he sought to unite the standpoints of immanence and transcendence, while his opponents assailed him from the standpoint of the "Spinozist" notion of God. (4) As with the doctrine of God so is it with all the other doctrines of the faith : here Abelard always set out from Augustine (see Deutsch's account), keeps essentially to his formulations, but, with more courage and confidence than the great master, fettered by his Neoplatonism, strives to free theology and the objects of faith from the embraces of a

the Church dogma could not be held by the thinking mind under the entire domination of the Mystic Neoplatonic theology. Although it was by this theology that it had been chiefly elaborated, yet the *Church* had always reserved to itself the *supra-mundane* God and the independence of the creature, and had formed a set of dogmas which Platonism could only sublimate, but could not justify as the *final* expression of the matter itself. The Church needed, therefore, the

Mysticism which is ultimately philosophy of nature. The *ethical* interest, the assurance that what answers to the moral law is also the holy and good before and for God, dominates Abelard (hence also his special interest in moral philosophy), and so far as this interest corrected the Mystical scheme of Christian doctrine in the thirteenth century, Abelard must be thought of as the pioneer. But if in this sense it may be said that Abelard laid the foundation for the great structures of Scholasticism in the thirteenth century—not only because he was the teacher of the Lombard, nor only because he was the acutest thinker of the period, *but because he was the first to attempt that amalgamation of the immanence and transcendence doctrines*, and taught that lower estimation of the principles of knowledge, which became the presuppositions of *ecclesiastical* systems—yet it cannot be denied that the following age did not attach itself directly to him. What he found independently the following age learned from Aristotle, who became more and more known to it from the second half of the twelfth century; it learned it only indirectly, or not at all, from Abelard. But that cannot diminish his fame. He was the first to show how all Church doctrines can and must be so treated that the *principles of morality* (the moral law) shall have as much justice done to them in the system as the *fundamental thoughts of theological speculation on nature.* That he did not solve this problem no one will make the ground of a reproach, for it is insoluble. But that it must be set down as the task of all ecclesiastical science—so long as this science at all declares that its ideal is that of knowing the world—is quite obvious. The contemporaries of Abelard were not willing to learn enough from him, and that, as a rule, determines the amount of influence that belongs to a teacher. They felt repelled (1) by the still novel form of the science in general; (2) by many propositions of Abelard, which were afterwards found to be tolerable—indeed to be the only correct ones; (3) by many individual negative, or critical judgments, both in regard to history and the validity of opinion prevailing at the time, and in regard to particular ecclesiastical doctrines, of which his defensive presentation was felt to be questionable (Sabellianism in the doctrine of the Trinity, yet see Augustine; strong inner variance in the Christology, which thus approached Nestorianism, yet see likewise Augustine). (4) It must not be denied that Abelard himself injured the influence of his doctrines by many contradictions and by the immaturity of his systematising. But how much could have been learned from him; compare only his admirable discussions of love, reconciliation, and the Church! The Church had no genius between Augustine and Luther; but among the men of second rank, Abelard deserves to be named. Karl Müller (Abhandl. f. Weizsäcker 1892, pp. 308 f., 319 f.) has strongly emphasised the importance of Abelard for the ways of stating problems and for the positive views of the following period.

help of dialectics (of sober intelligence, and of juristic acuteness
directed to the given formulæ) and of a lowering of the lofty
flight of speculation, and this help Aristotelianism alone could
afford it, *i.e.*, the Aristotelianism, which was then understood as
such, and which was then exercising its influence, as the view
of things according to which it is held—not that the phenomenal
and creaturely are the form transitorily expressing the divine—
but that the supernatural God, as Creator in the proper sense of
the word, has created the creature and endowed it with independence. It needed the help of Aristotelianism to defend a
set of dogmas in the form in which they were already established.[1] But still more was the "Aristotelianism" to do for
it. Reason will never ultimately make a compact with
authority, but the understanding will. Whoever has entered
into the spirit of the All-One and embraces the doctrine of
immanence, will feel himself to be as "God," and will therefore
reject all authority, of whatever kind it be. Whoever, on the
other hand, feels his independence, side by side with other forms
of independence, will become certain of his dependence also.
He will no longer take part in the dialectic performance of
exchanging his estimate of himself as the perfect nothing (as an
individual) for an estimate of himself as the perfect being (as
spirit); but while within certain limits, and perhaps with great

---

[1] Very correctly v. Eicken l.c. p. 602 : " The importance which Plato and Aristotle
acquired in mediæval philosophy was really in the inverse relation to the position
which the two had taken up in the history of the development of Greek philosophy.
The Platonic philosophy had placed the substance of things in the general ideas, and
had deduced from this assumption the transcendence of the latter, and especially of
the highest idea, that is, the idea of God.   But the extreme Realism of the Middle
Ages adopted the Platonic doctrine of ideas, not to derive from it the transcendence
of the supreme idea, but to derive rather the harmonious co-existence of all things in
the supreme idea, and just with this aim before it it arrived at that doctrine of God
which bore a pantheistic character, as compared with the strict transcendence of the
Church doctrine.   On the other hand the Aristotelian philosophy had asserted the
reality of the general ideas in the individuals, with the view of refuting Plato's transcendent doctrine of ideas.   The Aristotelian Realism, however, attached itself to the
Aristotelian doctrine, in order that, by guarding the substantial character of the
individuals, it might prove their extra-divine subsistence, and accordingly also the
divine transcendence that harmonised with the Church doctrine.   This view, which
quite inverted the historical and logical relation of the Platonic and Aristotelian
philosophies, was maintained till the close of the Middle Ages."

tenacity, he will embrace a rational mode of view, he will, in
that which lies beyond these limits, be ready to recognise
authorities.

Yet for the great inaugurator of Mediæval Scholasticism (for
Anselm everything is still naïve)—for Abelard, the elements
were still vaguely intermingled. He set down already as force
all that, in the time following, the period when Scholasticism
flourished, was conceived of as mutually limiting potencies, or
that then became differentiated as distinct tendencies. His
contemporaries had as yet no presentiment, that an element in
him which they specially censured would yet become the means
of saving the Church doctrine. Orthodoxy and the Platonic
Realism were still in closest union. The French Mystics declared the efforts of the "dialecticians" heretical ; Aristotle was
hated. When the great disciple of Abelard, Petrus Lombardus,
published his Sentences, and in them fittingly placed the learning of his master at the service of the Church theology—as yet
the Middle Ages had not possessed a compendium for the study
of theology[1]—much would not have been required for even this
book to be set aside on suspicion. No doubt, this work, because, from the patristic tradition being uncertain, it still
frequently adds opinion to opinion, bears the stamp of a freedom
which was afterwards lost. But the mere fact that it became
the authoritative compendium of the thirteenth century is a
proof that on the part of the Church free inquiry, dialectic investigation, and Aristotelian philosophy were now tolerated, not
because inward freedom had increased, but because the faculty
had grown for making friends with these forces, and because
there began to be observed what the Aristotelian method and
mode of thought could do for dogma. In the second half of
the twelfth century the turn round of things was already preparing itself. The "pious" theologians (the Mystics), so far as
they gave themselves up to the work of expounding and establishing dogma, were forced to see that by means of thorough-

[1] Only since Abelard's times were there somewhat more comprehensive statements
of Christian doctrine, which, besides, were still in many respects different. He himself and Hugo of St. Victor took the lead in producing them ; see Abelard's "Introductio" ; faith, love, the sacraments as subjects of dogmatic.

going Realism contemplation might be enriched, but the objective doctrine could not be defended. The coalition of naïve faith on authority with a Mysticism that, in its ultimate ground, was not without danger, came to an end. Church faith, Mysticism, and Aristotelian science formed a close alliance. On the other hand, the dialecticians, in the degree in which they passed from the Aristotelian formalism to Aristotle's doctrine of principles (perhaps the increasing knowledge of this philosophy contributed most to this), lost that audacity which had once given so much offence, and which, certainly, had often been only a sign of playing with empty forms. No doubt in connection with this many a fresh piece of knowledge came to be lost.[1] One who has much to carry gets more anxious, and moves more slowly, than one who marches under an easy burden. To this there came to be added, that from decade to decade the authority of the Church grew stronger. Though there was a growth also of opposition, which forced to anxious reflection (Mohammedans, Jews, heretics, knowledge of the ancient classics),[2] at the end of the twelfth century the Church outshone all else with its lustre. Its *rights* in respect of life and doctrine became the worthiest subject of investigation and exposition. Into this task blended the other, of referring all things to God and construing the knowledge of the world as theology. *The theology of the ecclesiastical facts pressed itself on the theology of speculation.* Under what other auspices could this great structure be erected than under those of that *Aristotelian Realism*, which was at bottom a *dialectic* between the Platonic Realism and Nominalism, and which was represented as capable of uniting immanence and transcendence, history and miracle, the immutability of God and mutability, Idealism and Realism, reason and authority? Thus it was only

---

[1] In the writings of the earlier Schoolmen, *i.e.*, of Abelard chiefly, there are not a few thoughts that were *directly* fitted either to enrich or to modify dogma. But at that time the Church accepted nothing from the Schoolmen, and when it was prepared to have the doctrine interpreted to it by them, these men had no longer the freedom and boldness to say anything new to the Church.

[2] What importance for Abelard the discussion with the Jew and the philosopher had may be learned from the "Dialogue" (v. Deutsch, p. 433 ff., against Reuter I., pp. 198-221.)

in the thirteenth century that there made its appearance the
theology adequate to the Church and its dogma, and no longer
viewed with suspicion,[1] after a new wave of piety (the Mendicant
Orders) had imparted to it the highest measure of power of
which the Catholic religion is at all capable. The fear of the
Lord was also the beginning of this new wisdom. In form and
contents, in its systematic method, and in the exhaustive fulness
of its material, it is related to the theology of the twelfth century
as, we might say, Origen was related to Clement of Alexandria.
This is more than a comparison, for the course of events really
repeated itself. Clement, the inaugurator, the *bolder* spirit, the
less "enlightened," who does not yet know that the full
authority of the Catholic Church is against him ; Origen, the
man of system, more comprehensive, but at the same time more
closely tied to the Church and its doctrine. The same relation
obtained between the theologians of the twelfth and thirteenth
centuries. (Compare, *e.g.*, the "aggregating" character of the
Sentences of Robert Pulleyn [Deutsch, p. 6 f.] with the Stro-
mateis of Clement, and the great "Sums" of the thirteenth
century with Origen's De principiis.) In the following chapter
we shall take up the thread here again. If we direct no further
attention here to the Lombard, and especially to Hugo, the
somewhat earlier, and, *in respect of matter*, the most influential
theologian of the twelfth century ("a second Augustine"), the
fact may serve as an excuse that the importance which the two
obtained for the *history of dogma* appeared only at the great
Lateran Council, and in the theologians of the thirteenth
century. On Hugo's Sentences see Denifle in the Archiv f.
L.-u. K.-Gesch. des Mittelalters III., p. 634 ff.

---

[1] The diminishing distrust of theology in contra-distinction to the former period is
also to be explained from the circumstance that the general average of culture among
the higher clergy became higher. The theologians of the thirteenth century were no
longer confronted with so much unreason as the "dialecticians" of the eleventh
century had to contend with in the wide development of the Church.

4. *Elaboration of Dogma.*

The theological conflicts of the eleventh and twelfth centuries, as they were fought out between the dialecticians and their opponents, do not belong to the history of dogma. This science has to confine itself to showing what position dogma asserted in connection with the revival and the crises of theology, what enrichments it received, and how far the Scholastic activity (or the theological systematising) already influenced it. As to the first of these questions, the statement may be quite brief: dogma, as it was fixed by the Councils, as it had been described by Augustine and Gregory I.,[1] was the presupposition of all theological thought, and was held inviolate. Isolated exceptions were without any importance. The dialectic experiments on dogma were always based on the traditional view of it. As regards the third question, an influence on dogma of Scholastic activity and systematic theology can already be pointed to in the twelfth century ; but the influence was still so much in its beginnings that it is better to treat it first in connection with the thirteenth century.[2] And so there remains only the question as to the "enrichments." Strictly speaking, this question also would have to be answered in the negative,[3] were it not that in the Berengarian controversy a movement presents itself, in which a dogma that had still always been the subject of dispute, attained a relatively complete form, and had not Anselm set up a doctrine of satisfaction, which, indeed, was a product of purely private work, and found few adherents, too, in the period that followed, but which brought before the Church a dogmatic problem that was hitherto unsolved, nay,

---

[1] So far as there was at all a single authoritative book here, it was Augustine's Enchiridion. But it is characteristic that Abelard, in his systematic work, already added the Sacraments to faith and love.

[2] The doctrine of the sacraments is chiefly thought of here.

[3] Almost everything that Bach has set forth in the second volume of his work on the history of dogma in the Middle Ages, including the "history of Adoptianism in the twelfth century" and the "systematic polemic against the dialecticians" (p. 390 ff. ; Gerhoch against the German Adoptians, p. 475 ff.), belongs simply to the history of theology, and has no significance for the history of dogma.

had scarcely ever been touched as yet, but which was not again to pass out of view. In what follows, therefore, we have to treat of these two movements.

A. *The Berengarian Controversy.*

Besides its dogmatic, this controversy[1] has a philosophic[2] interest, and an interest also in connection with Church politics.[3] The last of these interests may be left quite out of view here; the second is closely connected with the first. From the place which the dogma of the Eucharist held in the theory and practice of the Church, the criticism of it was a criticism of the reigning Church doctrine as a whole. When the youthful science, represented and led by Berengar of Tours, began at this point, charged the accepted view with error, and applied the scientific doctrine of method to the dogma of the Eucharist, expression was given to the thought, that there may not be a resting satisfied with mere Church tradition, with what is held as valid *to-day*. But this thought was not expressed in the name of a negative "illuminism,"[4] but, on the contrary rather, that the *true* tradition of the Church might be delivered from the embraces of a bad routine, that the spirit of the doctrine

[1] Besides Lessing's well-known work and Vischer, De sacra cœna adv. Lanfrancum lib. posterior, 1834; also the Acts of the Roman Council (Mansi XIX., p. 761 ff.), see Sudendorf, Berengarius, 1850; Schnitzer, Berengar v. Tours, sein Leben u. s. Lehre, 1890; Bach I., pp. 364-451; Reuter I., p. 91 ff., Dieckhoff, Die Abendmahlslehre im Reform.-Zeitalter I., p. 44 ff.

[2] Here, for the first time, the categories "subjectum," "quod in subjecto," "de subjecto," the distinction of "esse" from "secundum quod esse," in short, the dialectic manipulations of the notion of substance (according to Porphyry, Boethius, etc.) were applied to a dogma in the West.

[3] The outward political side of the controversy has been thoroughly treated by Schwane (Studien zur Gesch. des 2. Abendmahlsstreits, 1887, see Loofs, Gött. Gel.-Anz., 1888, No. 15), who follows Sudendorf. On the antagonism to Berengar, see the accounts of Schnitzer, l.c. p. 246 ff.

[4] Reuter's judgment is, I., p. 97 : "Thus the second controversy on the Eucharist became what the first was not, a struggle as to the supreme criteria of religious truth, a conflict of the tendency of negative 'illuminism,' directly with the authoritative ecclesiasticism of the time, indirectly with the Christianity of positive revelation." This is to me utterly unintelligible. Even the most deeply convinced Romish theologian will hesitate to endorse this opinion.

might be protected against a coarse and superstitious realism, that the λογικὴ λατρεία (reasonable service) might be maintained against a barbarian craving for mysteries, and that the mystery of faith might not be profaned. But combined with this interest, which was by no means merely pretended, there was the pleasure in thinking, and the daring reliance on dialectics as on "reason" in general. As theologians, Berengar and his followers were Augustinians, but, at the same time, Berengar had an enjoyment in criticism as such, and a confidence in "science," that were not Augustinian.

Berengar, Director of the Cathedral School in Tours, from about 1040 Archdeacon in Angers (ob. 1088), had instituted studies on the doctrine of the Eucharist, searched through the Church Fathers, occupied himself with the first Eucharist controversy, and rejected [1] the doctrine of Paschasius, long before a controversy developed itself. In the doctrine as it prevailed at the time he saw apostacy from the Church Fathers and unreason; for he saw in it only the view, that after the consecration bread and wine have disappeared, and in place of them there exist the real flesh and blood of Christ in so sensibly palpable a form that they are present as pieces (portions) of His bloody body. He was right; so the widely prevailing superstition taught; [2] yet

---

[1] See on this Reuter I., p. 95, "Paschasius ineptus ille monachus Corbeiensis." Berengar is correct in seeing contradictions in Paschasius. The book of Ratramnus was then regarded as a work of John Scotus, and was condemned as such at Vercelli in 1050.

[2] The confession of faith which was forced upon him in 1059 (composed by Cardinal Humbert), also contained the coarse view. Even Bach I., p. 366, n. 4, declares the confession "at least objectionable." In Lanfranc de corp. et sang. dom. 2 (Migne CL.) the words occur : "panem et vinum quæ in altari ponuntur post consecrationem non solum sacramentum sed etiam verum corpus et sanguinem J. Christi esse et sensualiter, non solum in sacramento sed et in veritate, manibus sacerdotum tractari et frangi et fidelium dentibus atteri." The most characteristic thing is that those who were quite logical declared even the word "sacrament" to be unsatisfactory : " The Eucharist is the mystery (sacramentum) in which there is no mystery, but all takes place vere et sensualiter." That is the fundamental thought of Berengar's opponents. That this was a falling away from tradition stands beyond doubt. But the traditional theologians, as is well known, are most fanatical, when to the old beaten track which they call tradition, or to their fancies, which, from their lack of understanding, they surround with the halo of the venerable, there is opposed the truth *that has the protection of the true tradition.*

Paschasius had certainly taken also a more spiritual view of the change, and among the authoritative churchmen of that period such a "conversion" was not taught by all the more prominent.[1] By means of a letter to Lanfranc, Berengar himself opened the controversy.[2] We have his doctrine fully stated for us for the first time in his work de sacra cœna. adv. Lanfrancum (ab. 1073; anything earlier is almost entirely lost). His leading idea was to introduce reason into the Church doctrine, or, more correctly, to bring to light by means of reason the reason that lies in the divine doctrines of the Church. Dialectics, the science which had always differentiated, is nowhere more in its proper place than where there is a question about two objects, which, in one respect, are one, and in another respect are different. Thus the two-nature doctrine is very peculiarly its province; and so also is the doctrine of the Eucharist, with its earthly elements and its heavenly gift.[3] Berengar showed that the doctrine of the bodily transmutation was absurd (" ineptia "), and went directly in the face of the old traditions, as well as of reason, which we must make use of as reasonable beings created in the image of God.[4] He accordingly adopted the standpoint of Scotus (Ratramnus), as he understood it. He taught that the words are to be understood *tropically ;* but he held this interpretation

---

[1] The controversy is also so uninspiring, because, as usual, the opponents exaggerated. Berengar proceeded as if he had only the view against him that parts of the bloody body of Christ are chewed by the teeth, while his adversaries asserted that according to him the elements were empty symbols. He had at any rate more right on his side in his description; yet not only Fulbert (Bach I., p. 365), but some also who were later, did not think of a *spatial* extension of the body of Christ in the converted elements.

[2] See Mansi T. XIX., p. 768.

[3] Of course the chief arguments of Berengar are derived from Scripture and tradition. To them he attaches decisive weight. The distinction that already prejudges everything, between the sensible, the visible, and the sacrament, the invisible—Berengar had made it the basis of his doctrine and the starting-point of his dialectic, as long as he could think—originates with Augustine. With the dialectic there mingle the beginnings of a more independent, a critical view of history. Yet Berengar meddles with no decree of any Council. Only, the decrees connected with his subject are ridiculed by him.

[4] See Vischer, p. 600: " maximi plane cordis est, per omnia ad dialecticam confugere, quia confugere ad eam ad rationem est confugere, quo qui non confugit, cum secundum rationem sit factus ad imaginem dei, suum honorem reliquit nec potest renovari de die in diem ad imaginem dei."

with much greater firmness than his predecessor, and gave it
an exclusiveness of which his predecessor had not thought;
Christ is spoken of under many symbols, hence the bread is also
a symbol;[1] Scripture teaches that, till His return, Christ
remains in heaven;[2] a piece of bread is not capable of taking
into itself the body born of the Virgin, and yet it is a question
about the *whole* Christ;[3] a destruction of the subject (the
elements) involves the destruction of all essential attributes of
the elements, for concretely (in concreto) these cannot be distinguished from the subject itself (Nominalist tendency).[4] Yet
the tropical view, as he did not stand by it, was not equivalent
for Berengar to the symbolical. This latter view rather he
explicitly rejected, in so far as he followed the old tradition, and
recognised two things in the Eucharist, sign and sacrament.
The elements become sacrament through consecration, and this
implies that they now include something objectively holy. A
" conversio " takes place ; but for Berengar this expression has
certainly an unusual sense.[5] It is meant to suggest that the

---

[1] Berengar compares the description of Christ as a lion, lamb, corner-stone.

[2] P. 199 : "constabit, eum qui opinetur, Christi corpus cœlo devocatum adesse
sensualiter in altari, ipsum se dejicere, quod vecordium est, dum confirmat se manu
frangere, dente atterere Christi corpus, quod tamen ipsum negare non possit impossibile esse et incorruptibile."

[3] The last point was for Berengar of the greatest weight. He always regards his
opponents as assuming that there are " portiunculæ " of the body of Christ on the
altar, and objects to this, (1) that it is a question of the *whole* body (see pp. 148, 199
f.); (2) that the body of Christ is not something " corruptible," which can be touched,
broken, and bitten. Then, again, the bread is not capable of affording room for such
a body, and then the "sensualiter" is above all objected to. The incorruptibility
and uniqueness of the body of Christ are the presuppositions of his dialectic. A body
so constituted cannot become sensible, and it cannot be at the same time in a thousand
places. The expedient also of supposing a creating-anew of the body of Christ is
effectively refuted by him ; this would involve us in the thought of two bodies.

[4] Here Berengar emphasised the correct logical reflection, "quod in subjecto erat
superesse quacunque ratione non potest corrupto subjecto " (p. 93), *i.e* , when the
substance is destroyed, the essential attributes (taste, colour, form) cannot remain
behind ; or p. 59 : "non potest res ulla aliquid esse, si desinat ipsum esse." Even
Protestant historians will take no account of such reasons.

[5] It must be assumed that it rests on accommodation ; for although there answers
to the sacrament a res sacramenti, which is created by the consecration, yet it is
certainly not a question of transmutation. Nor did the old tradition furnish this
term. In substance Berengar is a correct Augustinian ; hence it is unnecessary to
quote further passages. The proper expression for what Berengar means would be a

elements remain what they are, but *at the same time* become the
body of Christ.   They become *in a certain respect* something
different, *i.e.*, there is now added to the visible a second element,
which is real, but *invisible*.   The consecrated elements remain
in one respect what they are, but in another respect they become
the sacraments, *i.e.*, as the visible, temporal, and mutable subjects,
they become the guarantees (pignora, figuræ, signa) of the
reception of the *whole* heavenly Christ by the believer.   While
the mouth therefore receives the " sacrament," the truly genuine
Christian receives by discernment (" in cognitione "), and into
his heart that which the sacramental elements represent, namely,
Christ as food, the power of the heavenly Christ.   Hence the
enjoyment and the effect of the Eucharist are spiritual : the
inner man (so it depends on faith, in addition to the consecration) receives the true body of Christ, and appropriates the death
of the crucified Christ through believing remembrance.[1]

Augustine would have had nothing to object to this doctrine
of the Eucharist, even though some dialectic arguments and
devices in it had surprised him.   But the men of the period were
shocked, both at the result, and partly also at the course of
thought that led to this result.   At Rome and Vercelli (1050),
in Berengar's absence, the doctrine was condemned, on the
ground of the letter to Lanfranc.   Nine years later, after it had
become artificially mixed up in France with ecclesiastico-
political questions, but had thereby become for the time more
tolerable for Rome, and after its author had suffered much from
slander and imprisonment, Berengar was compelled to subscribe
at Rome, under Nicolas II., a formula of faith, which made it
clear that his worst fears with regard to the tyranny of superstition in the Church were not exaggerated.[2]   Having returned to
France, he kept in retirement at first ; but subsequently he

---

divine " auctio " in the elements, and so also he has expressed himself, p. 98.   On
the other hand, it is said, p. 125 : " per consecrationem altaris fiunt panis et vinum
sacramenta religionis, non ut desinat esse quæ fuerant, sed ut sint quæ erant et in
aliud commutentur."

[1] "Christi corpus totum constat accipi ab interiore homine, fidelium corde, non
ore" (p. 148).   At the same time also a memorial feast : " spiritualis comestio, quæ
fit in mente."

[2] v. above p. 47, note 2.

could have no rest.   He came to the front again with his
doctrine, for which he had influential supporters in Rome itself,
and a new, heated literary controversy was the result.   During
its course the most important writings on both sides were
produced.   Gregory VII. treated the controversy in a dilatory
way, and with much indulgence towards Berengar, who was
personally known to him: in all ages Rome has been clever
enough not to be hasty in making heretics, and a Pope who, in
ruling the world, must so often wink at things, knows also how
to exercise patience and forbearance, especially when personal
sympathy is not wanting.[1]   But in the end Gregory was compelled, in order not to shake his own authority, to force Berengar,
at the Synod of 1079, to recognise the transmutation doctrine.[2]
For a second time Berengar outwardly submitted; the Pope was
satisfied with the form; but with this the cause which the
broken scholar represented became lost.

The transmutation theory of Paschasius—the term transubstantiation was apparently first used casually by Hildebert of
Tours (beginning of twelfth century) in his 93rd Sermon
(Migne CLXXI., p. 776), and therefore already existed [3]—was
further developed by the opponents of Berengar.[4]   First, the
mystery was conceived of still more sensuously, at least by some
(manducatio infidelium);[5]   secondly, there was a beginning,

[1] On the interesting relation of Berengar to the Curia and Gregory VII., see
Reuter I., p. 116 ff., 120 ff.

[2] The formula (in Lanfranc, c. 2) was milder than that of 1059, but yet sufficiently
plain : "Ego Berengarius corde credo et ore confiteor panem et vinum quæ *ponuntur
in altari* per mysterium sacræ orationis et verba nostri redemptoris *substantialiter*
converta in veram et propriam et vivicatricem carnem et sanguinem J. Christi et
post consecrationem esse verum corpus Christi, quod natum est de virgine . . . et
quod sedet ad dexteram patris . . . *non tantum per signum et virtutem sacramenti
sed in proprietate naturæ et veritate substantiæ.*"

[3] In his two treatises (of date 1157) against the followers of Soterichos, in whose
opinion the mass was not offered to the Son, but only to the Father and Spirit, Nicolas
of Methone used the expression μεταστοιχείωσις, see Hefele V.[2], p. 568.   These
treatises were published by Dimitracopulos in the year 1865 (see Reusch, Theol. Lit.-
Blatt, 1866, No. 11).

[4] Yet everything acquired settled form only in the thirteenth century : the questions
resulting from the new doctrine are innumerable.

[5] Lanfranc, l.c. c. 20 : even sinners and the unworthy receive the true body of
Christ.   Only in this respect did Lanfranc develop the doctrine beyond Paschasius.

though with caution, to apply to dogma the " science " that was discredited in the opponent. The crude conceptions (which embraced the *total* conversion) were put aside, and an attempt was made to unite the older deliverances of tradition with the new transmutation doctrine, as also to adapt the Augustinian terminology, by means of dialectic distinctions, to the still coarsely realistic view of the object.[1] The struggle of Berengar, therefore, did not continue altogether without fruit; but the fruit consisted essentially in this, that science was left quite free,

[1] There was an aiming above all at recognising the *whole* Christ as present in the host, at reconciling the Augustinian, as well as the older rich and manifold conception of the Eucharist as a whole, with the transmutation doctrine, at rationalising the relation of element to verum corpus Christi by dialectic distinctions of accident and substance, at reconciling the presence of Christ in heaven with the sacramental presence, and at not forgetting, too, in these speculations the Church as corpus Christi. Note here as specially important the treatise de corp. et sang. Christi veritate in eucharistia, by Guitmund of Aversa (Migne CXLIX.), who certainly learned from Berengar. For the theories of other opponents of Berengar (Lanfranc, Adelmann of Brixen, Hugo of Langres, Durandus of Troanne, Alger of Lüttich, Abelard [he taught differently from Berengar, see Deutsch, l.c. pp. 401 f., 405 ff.], Walter of St. Victor, Honorius of Autun, etc.), see in Bach I., p. 382 ff. On the German theologians who occupied themselves with the doctrine of the Eucharist, see ibid., p. 399 ff. (the Reichersberg theologians, Gerhoch, Rupert of Deutz ; in the last named there is a peculiar, spiritualistic consubstantiation doctrine). Guitmund attributed the whole Christ to every particle, and thereby led on to the new view, first expressed by Anselm, that the whole Christ is contained in *one* form (ep. IV., 107) ; " in acceptione sanguinis totum Christum deum et hominem et in acceptione corporis similiter totum accipimus." In this the dogmatic basis was laid for withholding the cup, which afterwards became the rule. There is interest connected with the timid attempts that were made to teach also a " certain " incorruptibility of the *accidents* of the converted *substances* (these terms are now used even by the orthodox). Yet appearance witnessed against this assumption, and there was not yet resolution enough to adopt the doctrine that even here the empirical misleads. That Lutheran theologians take sides with Berengar's opponents (Thomasius-Seeberg, p. 48 : " really religious position as opposed to the rationalising misinterpretation of this man," cf. Reuter), although their final argument was the omnipotence of God, belongs to the peculiarities of the Romantic theology of the nineteenth century. Thomasius (p. 49) is specially delighted with the timid anticipations of the doctrine of the ubiquity of the substance of the body of the heavenly Christ in Alger (de sacram. corp. et sang. domini I., 11-16), whereby the difficulties which attach to the idea of the creatio of the Eucharistic body are to be set aside (Bach. I., p. 389 ff.) : " Christ can be corporeally present wherever he wills." For the rest (see Lanfranc), there was as yet no more declared than that with the body exalted to the right hand of God the Eucharistic body is identical, and yet not identical. How necessary here, therefore, was the so much despised dialectic of Berengar !

because it was gradually seen that in face of the gravity of the problems the simplicity of faith was powerless.   At the Fourth Lateran Council (1215) the mediæval doctrine of the Supper was solemnly framed as dogma in the famous confession of faith, which, previous to the Tridentine confession, was the most influential symbol (after the Niceno-Constantinopolitan ; see Mansi XXII., p. 982; Hefele V.², p. 878 ff.; and the Corpus juris canonici, where the topic finds a place under X. 1 : de summa trinitate [I. 1]).   What is important here is (1) that the doctrine of the Eucharist is immediately attached to the confession of the Trinity and Incarnation. *In this way it is represented even in the symbol as having a most intimate relation to these doctrines, as, indeed, forming with them a unity ; i.e.*, the state of things was now created that was disastrous even for the history of the Reformation : the real presence obtained the same value as the Trinity and the two-nature doctrine, so that every one was regarded as an ecclesiastical anarchist who called it in question.   This valuation certainly corresponds with the development of the doctrine of the Eucharist, inasmuch as the Eucharist appears as the continuously present, earthly incorporation of the mysteries of the Trinity and Incarnation, but it robs the Gospel of its spiritual character.   (2) Transubstantiation was now expressly taught ; the words run : " moreover there is one universal Church of the faithful, outside of which no one whatever can be saved, in which Jesus Christ is at once priest and sacrifice, whose body and blood are truly (veraciter) contained in the sacrifice of the altar under the appearances of bread and wine, the bread being *transubstantiated* into the body, and the wine into the blood by divine power, so that for the effecting of the mystery of unity (ad perficiendum mysterium unitatis) we receive of His what He received of ours (here the conjunction with the Christology is manifest).   And this sacrament especially (hoc utique sacramentum) no one can administer but the priest who has been duly ordained according to the Church authority (secundum claves ecclesiæ) which Jesus Christ Himself gave to the Apostles and their successors."   The symbol then immediately continues : " But the sacrament of baptism, which is consecrated in water on invoking the undivided Trinity, avails for salvation both to

infants and adults, by whomsoever it is duly administered in the
forms of the Church (in forma ecclesiæ). And if after receiving
baptism any one shall have fallen into sin, he can *always* be
restored (reparari) through true penitence." Thus this line of
development also is completed, and at the same time the related
one (see Vol. V., p. 325), according to which every Christian
must make confession of his sins before the parish priest
(parochus). It is laid down in the twenty-first chapter : " Every
believer, of either sex, after arriving at the years of discretion,
must by himself (solus) faithfully confess all his sins, at least
once a year, to his own priest, and must study to carry out to
the best of his ability the repentance enjoined upon him, receiving reverently, at least at Easter, the sacrament of the Eucharist."
The novelty in the symbol — the direct attachment of the
Eucharist dogma to the Trinity and Christology—is the most
distinctive and boldest act of the Middle Ages. Compared with
this immense innovation, the addition of the " filioque " weighs
very lightly. But on the other hand, the symbol certainly shows
also very plainly how the old dogmatic tradition still dominated
everything, for it contains *nothing* of the specific Augustinian-
Western propositions about sin, original sin, grace, and justification. " Dogma," in the strict sense of the word, consists of the
Trinity, Christology, the doctrine of the Eucharist, the doctrine
of Baptism, and of the Sacrament of Penance. All else is at
the most dogma of the second order. This state of things also
was of the greatest weight for the history of the Reformation ; the
doctrines of the Trinity, of Christ and of the Sacraments (*i.e.*,
the doctrine of the three Sacraments, Baptism, Penance,
Eucharist) constitute Catholic Christianity—nothing else.

*B. Anselm's Doctrine of Satisfaction, and the Doctrines of
Atonement of the Theologians of the Twelfth Century.*[1]

Ever since the days when an attempt was made to punish,
without decimating the Church, the great apostasy occasioned
by the Decian persecution, the positions were held as valid, that

_____
[1] See Baur, Lehre von der Versöhnung; Hasse, Anselm, 1853; Ritschl, Rechtfertigung und Versöhnung 2 Aufl. I., p. 31 ff.

God's mercy is unlimited, even as regards the baptised, but that only a satisfactio, consisting of legitimate penance (pœnitentia legitima), can move the offended God to regard the sinner again with favour.   Since that time these ideas had obtained the widest circulation,[1] united themselves at a later period with Germanic ideas, and dominated the whole penitential system of the Church.[2]   Connected with this system stood the conception of " merits," *i.e.*, of such supererogatory acts as establish a claim to reward, when no guilt exists to be expiated.   Through this idea a *calculation* of the *value* of particular deeds was introduced, and of these calculations the whole ethical system was full. Whether an act was obligatory, or abundans, or superabundans, whether, under given circumstances, it was compensatory (satis-factory), or meritorious, had to be established in each particular case, so that each one might know how his account stood with heaven.   The Augustinian conception of prevenient grace freely bestowed (gratia gratis data præveniens), which had been generally accepted, wrought no change on this view, but only made it more complicated.

Yet neither by Gregory the Great, nor by any theologian of the Carlovingian period, was this view applied to the work of Christ.   Frequent reference, it is true, was already made to the " *copiousness of the value* of the mystery of the passion " (pretü copiositas mysterii passionis ; see the fourth chapter of the Synod of Chiersey) ; but a theory had not been framed, because there was no reflection at all on the nature, the specific worth, and the effect of the redemption contained in the suffering and death of Christ.   The Fathers, Augustine included, had handed down nothing certain on this.   The only view taken by the Greeks was that the reign of death was broken by the cross and resurrection of Christ, or that mankind were thereby bought off, or cunningly wrested, from the devil.   All that they said of the *sacrifice* in the suffering was quite vague.   Only Athanasius spoke with noteworthy clearness of the penal suffering which Christ took from us and laid upon Himself.   But, from the days

---

[1] See the confidence in the unlimited mercy of God on the part of the Carlovingian theologians, especially Alcuin (Hauck, K.-Deutschlands II., p. 136 f.).

[2] See Vol. V., p. 323 ff.

of Paul, all of them testified *that Christ died for us,* and delivered us from the power of the devil. That was felt and proclaimed as the great act of redemption. Ambrose and Augustine had then emphasised the position that Christ is Mediator as *man,* and had given many instructions about particular points ; but the question why that Man, who was at the same time God, was obliged to *suffer* and *die,* was dealt with by pointing to His *example,* or by reciting biblical texts about ransom, sacrifice, and such like, without the necessity of the death here coming clearly to view.[1]　But Augustine certainly had laid the foundation for a new and vigorous apprehension of the significance of Christ's work, by emphasising so strongly the gravity of sin, and by representing the relation between God and man under the scheme of sin and grace.

At this point Anselm came in. The importance of his *doctrine of satisfaction,* as developed in Book II. of his " Cur deus homo," [2] composed as a dialogue, lies in this, that he made use of all the factors of the Augustinian theology, so far as they came into consideration here, but that at the same time he was the first of all to frame a *theory,* both of the necessity of the appearing of the God-man, and of the necessity of His death. This he did by *making the principles of the practice of penance the fundamental scheme of religion in general.*[3]　The " necessity "

---

[1] The necessity resulted, no doubt, when the right of the devil over mankind was thought of. Beyond this, it may be said that we have in one respect an anticipation of the Anselmic representation in the sermon composed about 500 by a contemporary of Faustus of Reji : Why Christ redeemed mankind from the power of the devil, not through the use of His divine might, but by becoming man, fulfilling the law, suffering and dying. (Caspari, Briefe, Abhandlungen und Predigten, 1890, pp. 202 ff. 411 ff.). The whole view of redemption, it is true, is still given here under the scheme of redemption from the devil, but the mode of redemption is dominated by the thought that " deus est rationis atque justitiæ et auctor et exactor." Something similar is also to be found in some homilies of Faustus (see Caspari, l.c. p. 418 ff.).

[2] Edit. II., by Fritzsche, 1886.

[3] Cremer (die Wurzeln des Anselm'schen Satisfactionsbegriff, in den Stud. und Krit. 1880, p. 7 ff.) has endeavoured to show that the fundamental thesis of Anselm's satisfaction theory (I. 13: "necesse est, ut aut ablatus honor solvatur aut pœna sequatur." I. 15 : " necesse est, ut omne peccatum satisfactio aut pœna sequatur ") is of Germanic origin. The correspondence is no doubt easily proved, but the Roman law also knows of this alternative in the case of private offences, and there can be no doubt that the Church, in its ordinances of penance, had acted on

was understood by Anselm in the sense of the strictest *reasonableness*, *i.e.*, his aim is to show that even if we knew nothing of
Christ, and such an One had never existed, reason would have

the principle, "aut pœnitentia legitima (satisfactio congrua) aut mors acterna,"
long ere it learned to know Germanic law. In Tertullian, certainly, there still prevails
another idea, when (de pudic. 2) he says : "omne delictum aut venia dispungit aut
pœna"; but the fatal turn of thought is already anticipated, when he forthwith adds:
"*venia ex castigatione*, pœna ex damnatione."—Thus I had written in the first
edition ; since then, Cremer has again described his standpoint in the Stud. u. Krit.,
1893 (pp. 316-345). I must adhere to the position that it is not necessary for understanding Anselm to have recourse to the Germanic notion of satisfaction, since the
material in hand, of which we have to take account, is quite sufficiently given in the
prevailing practice and theory of penance. These go back in the West to the time of
Cyprian, or say of Tertullian (see Wirth, Der Verdienstbegriff bei Tertullian, 1892 ;
see also Tertullian's notion of "compensatio," cf. Apolog. 50 : "veniam dei com-
pensatione sanguinis expedire"), and developed themselves everywhere in the same
way. It may be enough to point to Sulpitius Severus (Dial. II. 10), who was
certainly not affected by Germanic influence : "fornicatio deputatur ad *pœnam*, nisi
satisfactione purgatur." That is surely clearly enough the Anselmic scheme. (See other
passages in Karl Müller, Abhandl. f. Weizsäcker, 1892, p. 290 f. : God is satisfied
with a lesser performance ; this appears sometimes as mutatio of, sometimes as compensatio for, the eternal penalty.) Nor is it advisable here, or in Tertullian,
to speak of "compensating penalty" ("Ersatzstrafe") as distinct from "compensation for injury" ("Schadenersatz"), for these notions cannot at all be
strictly kept apart everywhere. "The sacrifices that are well-pleasing to God are
a broken spirit, a broken and contrite heart." From this passage and similar
ones, from the consensus gentium also, which may very well be appealed to here, and
finally from the rule, well-known even to the Romans, as to every other nation, that
private injuries are cancelled by indemnifications which restore to the injured party
his honour, it is quite sufficiently explained, how in the gemitus, lamentationes,
humiliationes, etc., there should both be recognised mortificationes temporales, and
also something seen which changes the feeling of the angry God and makes Him
again gracious. That is *compensation* for injury as regards the honour of God
(because voluntary self-humiliation), for in the normal relationship one is not obliged
in such a way to testify his subjection (therefore it is also a "merit"—*i.e.*, something
which God gladly sees and prizes—when in this condition one nevertheless offers
those performances, and under certain circumstances a saint can also offer them for a
sinner). But it can also be described as *compensating penalty*, for the satisfaction, it
is true, and even the Anselmic is no exception, is in no sense endurance of deserved
penalty, but it is a performance, which to the performer is painful and arduous. In
Roman public *law* the pœna is certainly the satisfactio—that has not been disputed—
but, so far as I know, in the penitential discipline of the ancient Church the satisfactio
was *never* thought of purely in the forms of Roman law (against Cremer, p. 316), but
was always the *evasion* of penalty by acts which were at once (as castigatio) compensating penalties and (as surplus exercise of lowly submission to God) compensations
for injury. It may be that to the man of the ancient world the compensating *penalty*
was more distinctly present than the compensation for injury, although all public penal

to confess that men can only be saved if a God-man appears
and dies for them.[1] Jews and pagans must be constrained to
acknowledge this necessity. They, and unbelieving Christians,
must see that it is *unreason* to assert that God could also have
redeemed us by another person (whether man or angel), or that
He could have redeemed us by a mere determination of His
will;[2] they must *perceive* that the mercy of God does not suffer
wrong through the death on the cross, and that it is not unworthy of God that Christ should have stooped to abasement
and taken upon Himself the uttermost suffering. No doubt it
holds good that we first believe and then see.[3] But though the
attempt may fail—faith, of course, would remain unshaken—we

---

procedure has developed itself from compensating *performances*, and the consciousness of this has never disappeared (even " pœna " is originally " ransom "). But
when Cremer asserts : " The term and conception ' penance ' (Busse), in the penal
law and current language of the Romish Church, springs from the satisfactio of
German law," that is an error which prejudices all his further exposition (see also
Loofs, Dogmengesch.[3], p. 273 f.). At the same time it may be held by way of
reservation that the transfusion of the penance discipline of the Church with Germanic
ideas strengthened the theory, and gave a casuistic tinge and externality to the
practice (Weregild, instead of, and in addition to, cor humiliatum and lamentationes).
So also the peculiar expression Anselm gives to the notion " honour " of God is
perhaps due to Germanic influence, although one must look very closely to discover
a shade of difference on this point between Anselm's God and the injured and wrathful God of Tertullian. Why then (according to Tertullian) is God injured by sins?
Because the obedience is withheld which is due to His commands. When Cremer
asserts (p. 329) that in the ancient penance discipline, the satisfactio congrua
(" congrua "—that is, determined by the penance regulations ; the expression can be
pointed out already in the fourth century) was *as much* penalty as the mors aeterna, that
is certainly a wonderful statement. When, finally (p. 326), he throws on me the
burden of proving that the Roman law, in the case of private injuries, recognises the
alternative : " aut pœna aut satisfactio," I grant that I expressed myself too strongly,
and in a way not incapable of being misunderstood. The law, so far as it was *publicly*
administered and codified, may no longer recognise this principle ; but a jurist like
Tertullian shows that the scheme must have been a familiar one, and how can we
think of the settlement of private wrongs at all otherwise than by supposing that a satisfactio is rendered to the injured ?

[1] Augustine already propounded the question of the absolute necessity of redemption
by means of the incarnation and death of the Logos, but answered it *in the negative*.
He saw in this means not the only, though certainly the worthiest, way.

[2] I. 1.

[3] I. 2: " Sicut rectus ordo exigit, ut profunda christianæ fidei prius credamus,
quam ea præsumamus ratione discutere."

must advance to the knowledge of what we believe, and in this case a perfect reasonable knowledge is possible.

At the outset Anselm rejects three ideas, one as insufficient, the others as erroneous.   It is not sufficient to justify redemption through the death on the cross by emphasising the "conveniens," *i.e.*, the correspondence of the person and work of Christ with the person and fall of Adam; that is an æsthetic view, which is correct, but which proves nothing until the "necessarium" is established.[1]   It is erroneous to think that a man could have redeemed us; for we should then become the servants of him who should have delivered us from eternal death.   But in that way our original dignity would not be restored, in virtue of which we were like the angels and servants of *God* alone.[2]   It is erroneous, finally, to think that by redemption legal claims of the devil upon us had to be wiped out; for although by reason of our sins we have justly come under the devil's power, yet the devil does not rule justly, but rather unjustly.   He has obtained no claim upon us, and over against God he has absolutely no right.[3]   Before Anselm begins his process of proof, he further endeavours—the arrangement is extremely unskilful—to refute the objection that the suffering and death of a God-man, just because he is man, are without effect, because every man is bound to be obedient unto death. He rejects this view, which is only apparently supported by passages of Scripture that teach that the death of Christ was obligatory, because it was fulfilment of the divine will; a sinless man, rather—and the God-man was such—was only under obligation to observe justitia and veritas (righteousness and truth), but not to die, for death follows only upon sin.[4]   Having now cleared the path for himself, he goes on to put the question thus: Assuming that we knew nothing whatever of the God-

---

[1] I. 3, 4: ". . . Multa alia, quæ studiose considerata inenarrabilem quandam nostræ redemptionis hoc modo procuratæ pulchritudinem (see Augustine) ostendunt . . . sed si non est aliquid solidum super quod sedeant, non videntur infidelibus sufficere."

[2] I. 5.

[3] I. 6, 7.

[4] I. 8-10.   In the 2nd Book this decisive point is repeatedly treated very fully in c. 10, 11 and 16, 18.

man and His action, what must take place, if men, who are
created for blessedness in the world beyond, but who can attain
to this blessedness only as *sinless*, have all become sinners?
The most natural answer is (for it has already been said in I. 4,
that it would not become God not to carry out His plan): *sins
must be forgiven.* But how must that be done? What is forgiveness of sin? What range has it? In order to answer
this question, we must first ask, What is sin? With this
the development begins.[1]

Every rational creature owes to God entire subjection to His
will. That is the only honour which God demands. He who
pays it is righteous; he who pays it not, sins; sin, indeed, is
nothing else than the dishonouring of God by withholding from
Him His own.[2] This robbery God cannot tolerate; He must
defend His honour. He must therefore demand that man
restore it to Him, and, indeed, " for the insult inflicted, that he
restore more than he took away "; otherwise he continues " in
culpa " (under guilt).[3] Every sinner, therefore, must furnish a
satisfaction.[4] God cannot dispense with this; for that would

[1] In the course of it (I. 16-18) the Augustinian theologoumenon, that the men
destined to salvation take the place of the fallen angels, fills a large space. But it is
in no way connected with the doctrine of satisfaction. Anselm differs from Augustine
in this, that he thinks that the number of saved men is greater than that of the fallen
angels; from the beginning God had in view the numerus beatorum as consisting of
angels and men. Otherwise the creation of men would be simply a consequence of
the fall among the angels, and there would result the inconveniens that we men
should have to rejoice over this fall. This correction of the Augustinian doctrine does
all honour to Anselm's heart; but as the doctrine has its point in the equally great
number of the fallen angels and saved men, it is really cancelled by Anselm. Yet he
was himself not quite sure of his case. See I. 18, p. 37.

[2] I. 11 : " non est aliud peccare quam non reddere deo debitum . . . debitum est
subjectum esse voluntate deo . . . hæc est justitia sive rectitudo voluntatis, quæ
justos facit sive rectos corde, *i.e.*, voluntate, hic est solus et totus honor quem debemus
deo . . . hunc honorem debitum qui deo non reddit, aufert deo quod suum est et
deum exhonorat, et hoc est peccare."

[3] I. 11 : " non sufficit solummodo reddere quod ablatum est, sed pro contumelia
illata plus debet reddere, quam abstulit, sicut enim qui lædit salutem alterius, non
sufficit si salutem restituit, nisi pro illata doloris injuria recompenset aliquid, ita qui
honorem alicujus violat, non sufficit honorem reddere, si non secundum exhonora-
tionis factam molestiam aliquid, quod placeat illi quem exhonoravit, restituit.
Hoc quoque attendendum, quod cum aliquis quod injuste abstulit solvit, hoc debet
dare, quod ab illo non posset exigi, si alienum non rapuisset."

[4] I. 11 fin.

be equivalent to the impunity of sin, and would violate the
divine honour. But the impunity of sin would be equivalent to
God's ceasing to be the controller of sin (ordinator peccatorum) ;
He would let something disorderly pass in His kingdom
("aliquid inordinatum in suo regno dimittere.") Right and
wrong also would then become the same ; the latter, indeed,
would have the advantage, because, as unrepented of and un-
punished, it would be subject to no law. No doubt we men
are enjoined simply to forgive those who sin against us. But
that is said to us, that we may not encroach upon the prerogative of God : "for it belongs to no one but Him to take
vengeance." Nor may we appeal against this to the omnipotence and goodness of God, and say that all that God does is
good, even when He simply forgives sin therefore ; for God's
power and goodness are determined by His *will* ("it is not to
be so understood that if God wills something improper [incon-
veniens], it is right because He wills it ; for it does not follow
that if God wills to lie, it is right to lie ") ; hence, as God wills
to do nothing wrong or disorderly (inordinate), the absolving
without penalty of a sinner who does not restore to Him what
he has robbed Him of, is not within the scope of the freedom or
the goodness or the will of God.[1] The supreme righteousness,
therefore, which is nothing else than God Himself, requires
restitution or—this turn of thought appears first here—penalty.[2]
Even the latter, that is to say, as deprivation of salvation
(damnation), restores the divine honour, in as much as by it
"man unwillingly pays back of his own what he took away . . .
as man by sinning seized what is God's, so God by punishing
takes away what is man's."[3] Even by penalty the beauty and
order of the universe are maintained, which must never be
shaken (of the honour of God in itself it holds good that it
cannot be shaken ; "for to Himself He is the incorruptible and
in no way mutable honour. . . . No one can honour or dis-
honour God so far as He is in Himself.")[4] But it is "extremely

[1] I. 12.
[2] I. 13, see above, p. 56, note 3.
[3] I. 14 : "deum impossibile est honorem suum perdere : aut enim peccator sponte
solvit quod debet aut deus ab invito accipit."
[4] I. 15.

alien to God " that He should abandon His costliest work, the
rational creature (creatura rationabilis), to complete ruin.[1] But
as, on the other hand, He cannot associate sinful men with the
holy angels, satisfaction must come in ("hold this most firmly,
because without satisfaction, *i.e.*, without spontaneous payment of
the debt, God cannot allow sin to pass with impunity ").[2] The
objection that we are directed to pray to God for forgiveness,
which would surely be unmeaning if only satisfaction were of
any avail, is met by saying *that the prayer for forgiveness is
itself a part of the satisfaction*.[3] Now the satisfaction is subject
to the twofold rule, that it must be, first, restitution, and secondly,
smart-money (Schmerzensgeld).[4] But what can man give to
God which he was not already required to give Him in any
case, since entire surrender is included in obligatory obedience ?
" If I owe Him myself and all I can do—even when I sin not,
that I do not sin (so there is no thought here of supererogatory
deeds), I have nothing that I can render back (reddam) for
my sin." The objection : " if I consider reasons (rationes), I do
not see how I can be saved, but if I fall back upon my faith,
then in Christian faith which worketh by love I hope that my
salvation is possible," is repelled ; for here it is just a question
of reason.[5] Man can therefore do nothing. And how much he
would have to do ! " Thou hast not yet considered of what
gravity thy sin is." Even the smallest disobedience entails an
infinite guilt (even to gain the whole world one may not commit

---

[1] In II. 4, it is said indeed (cf. I. 4) : " Si nihil pretiosius agnoscitur deus feci-se
quam rationalem naturam ad gau lendum de se, valde alienum est ab eo, ut *ullam*
rationalem naturam penitus perire sinat." I. 25, p. 52.

[2] I. 19.

[3] I. 19 : The Interlocutor says : " Quid est, quod dicimus deo : dimitte nobis
debita nostra, et omnis gens orat deum quem credit, ut dimittat sibi peccata? Si
enim solvimus quod debemus, cur oramus ut dimittat ? Numquid deus injustus est,
ut iterum exigat quod solutum est ? Si autem non solvimus, cur frustra oramus, ut
faciat quod, quia non convenit, facere non potest ? " To this Anselm replies : " *Qui
non solvit, frustra dicit : dimitte ;* qui autem solvit, supplicat, *quoniam hoc ipsum
pertinet ad solutionem ut supplicet ;* nam deus nulli quicquam debet, sed omnis
creatura illi debet ; et ideo non expedit homini, *ut agat cum deo, quemadmodum par
cum pari.*" Unfortunately Anselm has forgotten this last thought in his exposition
elsewhere.

[4] See above, p. 60, note 3.

[5] I. 20.

the smallest sin) for the guilt is to be measured by the God who is despised.[1]   Man has therefore to furnish an infinitely great satisfaction, since it is already an established rule, that God's honour does not permit of man's receiving salvation, "*if he does not restore to God all he has taken from Him, so that as God has lost by him, He may also recover by him.*"[2]   The incapacity of human nature to furnish satisfaction can make no change on this law, which follows from the honour of God.[3]   So therefore there remains only one solution, if the "convenientia" (the befitting) requires redemption[4]—namely, the *God-man.*   There must be someone "who shall pay to God for the sin of man something greater than all that is, apart from God . . . it is necessary, therefore, that he who shall be able to give *of his own* to God something that shall surpass all that is under God, shall be greater than all that is not God . . . but there is nothing above all that is not God, save God. . . . No one, therefore, is able to make this satisfaction save *God.*"   Again, "nor must that satisfaction be made by anyone save *man,* otherwise man does not satisfy."   Conclusion : "If, therefore, as is certain (sicut constat), it is necessary that that heavenly State be made perfect from men, and this cannot be unless there is made the aforesaid satisfaction, which no one can make save God, and no one owes save man, it is necessary that *the God-man* shall make it."[5]

---

[1] See the exposition in I. 21.   Because every sin is committed contra voluntatem dei, it is greater than the value of the world—infinitely great.   Further (I. 22), because man in paradise preferred the devil to God, it is "contra honorem dei, ut homo reconcilietur illi cum calumnia hujus contumeliæ deo irrogatæ, nisi prius honoraverit deum vincendo diabolum, sicut inhonoravit illum victus a diabolo." But how can he do that?

[2] I. 23.

[3] I. 24.

[4] I. 4, and the strongest passage, I. 25 : "Si deo inconveniens est, hominem cum aliqua macula perducere ad hoc, ad quod illum sine omni macula fecit, ne aut boni incepti pænitere aut propositum implere non posse videatur : *multo magis propter eandem inconvenientiam impossibile est nullum hominem ad hoc provehi, ad quo factus est.*"   In II. 4, 5, it is said, indeed, that while God "nihil facit necessitate, quia nullo modo cogitur aut prohibetur facere aliquid," yet an inner self-willed necessity exists for God's carrying out His work : "necesse est, ut bonitas dei propter immutabilitatem suam perficiat de homine quod incepit, quamvis totum sit gratia bonum quod facit."

[5] II. 6.

This God-man must possess the two natures unchanged
(otherwise he would be either only God or only man), un-
mingled, too (otherwise he would be neither God nor man), but
also unseparated (otherwise no work having unity is effected);
therefore he must possess them "entire in one person" (integras
in una persona).[1] The God must have derived the human
nature from Adam and Eve, but from a virgin,[2] and he must as
man have surrendered this nature to death voluntarily. His
dying was really free, for he was sinless.[3] If the supposed
God-man now surrenders his life voluntarily to God, the satisfaction sought for is obtained. It must be his *life*; for only
this he is not under obligation to offer to God; all that he could
give of his own, it behoved him in some way or other to offer to
God. "Let us see if, perhaps, this giving of his life, or parting
with his soul, or surrender of himself to death, is for the honour
of God. For God will not require it from him as a debt, because, as there shall be no sin in him, he shall not owe it to
die . . . if man has had a sweet experience in sinning, is it not
fitting that he should have a hard experience in satisfying?
And if he has been so easily prevailed upon by the devil to dis-
honour God by sinning that nothing could be easier, is it not
just that, in satisfying for sin, he should overcome the devil to
the honour of God with a measure of difficulty that could not
be exceeded? Is it not becoming (dignum) that as he who by
sinning so denied himself to God that he could not deny himself

---

[1] II. 7.

[2] II. 8: The former, because the descendants of Adam must make satisfaction;
the latter, because of the four ways in which God can create man (from man and
woman [the rule], neither from man nor woman [Adam], from man alone [Eve], from
woman alone), the fourth had not yet occurred. But that it must be a virgin, if it
was to be a woman, "non opus est disputare." Here is a piece of Scholasticsm in
the strictest sense of the term, and this kind of proof is continued in the following
chapter, where it is shown that it had to be the second person of the Trinity who
became man, because otherwise the predicates in the Trinity would have been
destroyed, and for other equally cogent reasons ("duo nepotes essent in trinitate,
quia, si pater incarnatus esset, esset nepos parentum virginis per hominem assumptum,
et verbum cum nihil habeat de homine, nepos tamen esset virginis, quia filii ejus erit
filius" II. 9). Here, besides, there is a working everywhere with "mundius,"
"honestius," in short, with relative notions.

[3] The prolix demonstration here in II. 10, 11 and 16 ff. shows that Anselm did not
understand how to make this point quite "rational."

in a greater degree, should by satisfying so give himself to God
that he could not give himself in a greater degree ? . . . But
there is nothing harder or more difficult that a man can suffer
for the honour of God spontaneously and not of debt than death,
*and in no way can man give himself more fully to God than when
he surrenders himself to death for His honour.*" Hence the man
sought for must be one who does not die " of necessity," because
he is almighty, nor " of debt," because he is sinless, who therefore can die " of free choice because it will be necessary " (ex
libera voluntate quia necessarium erit.)[1] The worth of such a
life as a satisfaction is infinite. Because the smallest violation
of this life has an infinitely negative worth, the voluntary surrender of it has an infinitely positive worth. Because sins are
as hate-worthy as they are bad, so that life also is as love-worthy
as it is good. Hence the acceptance of the death (acceptio
mortis) of such a God-man is an infinite good for God (!), which
far surpasses the loss by sin.[2] But the giving of life (datio vitæ)

[1] II. 11. In II. 12, 13 further allied questions are discussed. The God-man was
not "miser," although he took the incommoda on himself; he was omniscient,
because otherwise he would not have been perfectly good (!).

[2] II. 14: "Si omne bonum tam bonum est, quam mala est ejus destructio (!),
plus est bonum incomparabiliter quam sint ea peccata mala, quæ sine æstimatione
superat ejus interremptio . . . tantum bonum tam amabile potest sufficere ad solven-
dum quod debetur pro peccatis totius mundi, *immo plus potest in infinitum* (II. 17
fin. : plus in infinitum. II. 20 : "pretium majus omni debito") . . . si ergo dare
vitam est *mortem accipere (!)*, sicut datio hujus vitæ prævalet omnibus hominum
peccatis, ita et *acceptio* mortis." The question is next discussed, whether the death
of Christ can be of advantage even to His enemies who crucified Him (II. 15 : the
question is answered affirmatively; for they acted in ignorance), then how Christ
could be sinless (II. 16), for although He was conceived "absque carnalis delecta-
tionis peccato"—the sexual appetite is, after Augustine, original sin—yet Mary was
not sinless. This question is discussed with much prolixity. Anselm was apparently
at a loss for a rational solution. In the end, though with uncertainty, he offers the
explanation, that in prospect of the future effect of the work of Christ, Mary was
purified from her sins before her birth, *i.e.*, God purified her. After this the question
of the voluntariness of the death of Christ is again discussed ; for if Mary was only
purified in view of His death, while He needed a purified mother, it was *necessary*
that He should die. This question again occupies a very large space, and is only
solved by a subtle dialectic, which in the end cannot do without the support of the
proposition, "ad hoc valuit in Christo diversitas naturarum . . . ut quod opus erat
fieri ad hominum restaurationem si humana non posset natura, faceret divina, et si
divinæ minime conveniret, exhiberet humana " (II. 17, p. 85).

can only have taken place " to the honour of God ; " for another
spirit and purpose cannot be discovered. To this there is to
be added, no doubt, the further design of setting us an example,
so that by no sufferings we might let ourselves be drawn aside
from the righteousness which is due to God.   Others, it is true,
have given us such an example ; but his is the most powerful,
for he suffered without being obliged to suffer.[1]   Once again it
is asked, by way of objection, whether he was not really obliged,
because the creature " owes all to God, what he is, and what he
knows, and what he can do."   As the answer, there suddenly
appears the doctrine of surplus merit.   When God leaves us free
to offer Him something smaller or greater, a reward is the result
if we give the greater, " because we give spontaneously what is
our own."   When this is applied to the God-man, the conclusion
follows that his dying was necessary, because he willed it,
but at the same time was not necessary, because God did not
demand it.   His death therefore is voluntary.[2]   Now at length
can the long-looked-for solution be given.[3]   It follows in a surprising form, and, above all, with strange brevity : the God-man
acts for himself, by no means as the representative of mankind.
But the Father must *recompense* him for that.[4]   But nothing,
again, can be given to the Son, since he has all.   Yet it would
be outrageous to assume that the whole action of the Son
should remain without effect.   Hence it is *necessary* that it
should be for the advantage of another, and if that is willed by
the Son, the Father cannot object, otherwise He would be
unjust.   " But to whom *more fittingly* (convenientius) shall he
impart the fruit and recompence of his death than to those for
whose salvation, as true reason (ratio veritatis) has taught us,
he made himself man, and to whom, as we have said, he gave in
dying the example of dying for righteousness' sake ?   *In vain
surely shall they be imitators of him, if they are not to be partakers*

---

[1] This thought is dropped into the course of the discussion, II. 18.

[2] II. 18.

[3] II. 19 : "intueamur nunc prout possumus, quanta inde ratione *sequatur humana
salvatio.*"   The Interlocutor : " ad hoc tendit cor meum."

[4] II. 19 : "eum autem qui tantum donum sponte dat deo, sine retributione debere
esse non judicabis . . . alioquin aut injustus (!) videretur esse si nollet, aut impotens
si non posset."

of his merit.   Or whom shall he more justly make heirs of that which is due to him, but which he does not need, and of the superabundance of his plenitude (exundatiæ suæ plenitudinis) than his own *parents* and *brethren*, whom he looks on, burdened in their poverty with so many and so great debts, and languishing in the depths of misery, *that what they owe for their sin may be remitted to them, and what, by reason of their sin, they lack, may be given to them ?* "[1]   God accordingly now rejects no one who comes to Him in the name of this God-man, on condition that he comes as it befits him, *i.e.,* that he so approaches Him, and so lives, as Holy Scripture directs.[2]   The divine mercy, therefore, has not been made void by the death on the cross— so it would seem when sin and the divine righteousness are contemplated—but it appears rather as inconceivably great, and at the same time as in perfect harmony with righteousness. God's word, indeed, to the sinner is : " Take mine only-begotten Son and give him for thyself," and the Son's word is : " Take me and redeem thyself."[3]   Only the wicked angels cannot be redeemed.   Not as if the "price of His death would not be availing through its magnitude for all sins of men and angels "; but the condition of the angels (they are not descended from *one* angel, and fell without a tempter) excludes redemption.[4]   Anselm concludes with the lofty consciousness that " by the solution of one question " he has shown to be reasonable " all that is contained in the New and Old Testaments."[5]

Because it really is what Anselm, in the last sentence, has asserted, namely, a (new) construction of the *whole* of dogma from the point of view of sin and redemption, and because in this construction the disjecta membra of the Augustinian Mediæval view of Christianity were for the first time knit together into a unity, this representation deserves a searching criticism.   Standing on the shoulders of Augustine, but eliminating the " patristic," *i.e.,* the Greek elements of his mode of thought, Anselm has, by his book, " Cur deus homo," placed

[1] II. 19, p. 93 sq.   [4] II. 21.
[2] II. 19.   [5] II. 22.
[3] II. 20.

himself, as distinctively a dogmatic theologian, side by side with the Fathers of Greek dogma (Irenæus, Athanasius, and Origen). With the outline which John of Damascus had furnished another outline is now associated, which certainly, and not to its advantage, is still dependent on the old, but yet is evidently dominated by another *principle*. Anselm's representation, however, also deserves special consideration because it has given the impulse to permanent treatment of the subject, and because it is still regarded in our own day—and by evangelical theologians, too—as essentially a model.

First of all, as against misunderstandings, it must be stated what Anselm's theory is *not*, and is *not* meant to be. It is (1) no doctrine of reconciliation in the sense of showing how the opposition of will between God and sinful humanity is removed; it is (2) no theory of penal suffering, for Christ does not suffer penalty; the point rather at which penalty is inflicted is never reached, for God declares Himself satisfied with Christ's spontaneous acceptio mortis; just for this reason it is (3) no theory of vicarious representation in the strict sense of the term, for Christ does not suffer penalty in our stead, but rather provides a benefit, the value of which is not measured by the greatness of sin and sin's penalty, but by the value of His life, and which God accepts, as it weighs more for Him than the loss which He has suffered through sin (between sin, therefore, and the value of the life of Christ there exists only an external relation; both are infinite, but the latter is more infinite; hence it more than satisfies God);[1] it is, finally (4), not a theory which guarantees to the *individual* that he *really* becomes saved; *it aims rather at only showing for all the possibility of their being saved;* whether they shall be saved depends " on the measure in which men come to partake of so great grace, and on the degree in which they live under it," *i.e.*, on how they fulfil the commandments of holy scripture (II. 19, p. 94).

From this consideration of what the Anselmic theory is *not* and does *not* offer, it already appears how inadequate it is. Above all, its unevangelical character shows itself in the 4th

---

[1] The theory of a vicarious penal suffering is to be found, along with the theory of ransom of men from the devil, in Athanasius, see Vol. III. p. 308 of this work.

point. The entire ancient world, indeed, and, as Anselm shows, the mediæval world as well, rested satisfied *with the doctrine of redemption, as demonstrating the possibility of the redemption of the individual from sin ;* but as this "possibility" can afford no comfort whatever to any distressed conscience, as it only satisfies the understanding, it is a worthless substitute for a real doctrine of redemption—Luther would say it is of the *devil.*   If it cannot be shown from the person of Christ that we really *are redeemed,* if the *certainty of salvation* (certitudo salutis) is not derived therefrom, nothing is gained ; all, rather, is lost, when we rest satisfied with such a doctrine, and append to it, as Anselm does, the conclusion, "If thou fulfillest the commands of Scripture, then the great provision of the God-man has an effect for thee." For Anselm, the question of personal certitude of salvation, the fundamental question of religion, is simply not yet raised at all. He is an old-world, a mediæval, in a word, a *Catholic* Christian, inasmuch as he is satisfied with having made out that in virtue of Christ's provision *some* certainly from the "mass of perdition" *can* be saved, and in fact shall be saved, because they live piously.   But a second point is to be noted here. With every effort to express it as strongly as possible, the gravity of sin (pondus peccati) is not treated with sufficient earnestness if the thought of penalty, and therefore also of vicarious penal suffering, is entirely eliminated.   In the idea that sin can be compensated for by something else than penalty there lies an underestimate of its gravity that is extremely objectionable.   A recognition of the deep proposition that the innocent suffers for the guilty, that the *penalty* lies upon him, that we might have peace, is not to be found in the Anselmic *theory.*   It does not appear even in the statement, prompted by warm feeling, II. 20: "Accept mine only-begotten and give Him for thyself." "Take Me and redeem thyself," for nothing is said of a penal suffering (just as little in the equally warm line of exposition II. 16, pp. 77 sq.).

But before entering upon the objections to the theory, let us indicate its excellences. These are not small: (1) It must be held as greatly to the credit of Anselm that he laid hold of the problem at all, and made it the centre for a survey of faith ; (2)

that he so apprehended it that redemption from *guilt* is the question
dealt with (the Greeks had always thought primarily of redemption from the consequences of sin, liability to death); (3) it is
to be specially noted that he conceived of guilt exclusively as
guilt before *God* (disobedience), and entirely set aside the
traditional doctrine (see even Augustine) that in redemption
(by means of the crucifixion of the God-man) the question is
about satisfying the devil;[1] (4) that he discarded a merely
æsthetic, or an externally historical, grounding of the death on
the Cross (Christ did not die because it was prophesied, nor
because the accomplishment of redemption had to correspond
in its particulars with the history of Adam and the fall); (5) it
is a point of much importance that Anselm made earnest efforts
to prove the *moral* necessity of this precise mode of redemption.[2]
That which he calls "reason" (ratio) is, at least in many lines
of proof, nothing but the strict moral imperative, and is
accordingly entirely admissible here, and he expressly refuses
to lay at the basis of his investigation the conception of an
unrestricted divine arbitrariness; with deeper insight and more
courage than Augustine, he rather assumes everywhere that
God's omnipotence is in inner subjection to His holy will.
What, in his judgment, makes it possible to reflect rightly on
God's arrangements is just our title to feel assured that the
supreme righteousness and the supreme mercy, which He is
Himself, can be understood by us as righteousness and mercy.
Finally (6), according to Anselm, Jesus Christ, in His historic
person and through His death, is for us the redemption. The
grace of God is nothing but the redeeming work of Christ, *i.e.*,
the thought of grace is now for the first time entirely dissociated
from that of nature and located in history, *i.e.*, is connected
solely with the person of Christ.

But contrasted with these excellences there are so many
defects that this theory is entirely untenable. To a great
extent these defects lie so much on the surface, and do such

[1] Whether indeed what Anselm offered as a substitute was in every respect better,
or was not rather worse, will appear below.

[2] A noteworthy passage already in Tertullian (de jejun. 3) : "homo per eandem
materiam causæ deo satisfacere debet, per quam offenderat."

violence, equally to reason and to morality (not to speak of the attack on the gospel), that if the present-day theology stood under normal conditions not a word would have to be lost upon them.   But as the current theology stands under the dominating influence of traditional faith and Romanticism, and discards all the criteria of gospel, morality, logic, and culture, when it sees the "*necessity of the possibility*" *of the traditional objects of its faith* in some way justified, some discussion will here be in its right place.   Besides what has been already noted above, the following things fall to be observed :

First, the theory contains a series of imperfections, or, say contradictions ; for (1) the *necessarium* is to be strictly carried through, yet at important points Anselm does not get beyond the *conveniens*, above all at the most important point, that it is just to men that the merit of Christ is imparted (II. 19, pp. 93 fin.).   Moreover, that God *accepts* the death of the God-man for the wrong done to Him is not based on strict necessity, for the sin of men, and the nature of the satisfaction of Christ, have nothing *inwardly* in common ;[1] (2) the satisfaction theory must be brought to a point in a way that is foreign to it, that it may be proved to have any effect at all.   That is to say, the theory itself, strictly taken, only goes so far as to show that God's injured honour is vindicated and men take an example from the death of Christ to adhere steadfastly to righteousness, even under the severest sufferings.   *But how can they take an example ?*   Will the example, then, have the *power* to incite to earnest imitation ?   Will they not rather go on sinning ? Yet the whole provision, according to Anselm, avails only for those who regulate their life according to Holy Scripture.   So the provision will be a failure !   Anselm certainly felt this, and therefore passed quite beyond his theory by asserting that God sees occasion for His rewarding the voluntary action of the God-man, and for His conferring this reward on men, *by reckoning to them as the kinsmen of Christ the merit of Christ, without which they shall be quite unable to become imitators of*

---

[1] The keen criticism which the present-day Catholics apply to Anselm's theory (see Schwane, pp. 296 ff.) rests, on the contrary, on the strong Scotist antipathy to unconditional necessity.

Christ. This turn of thought does all honour to Anselm's
piety ; but it destroys his doctrine of satisfaction ; for if Christ's
suffering establishes *merit*, it does not contain strict reparation ;
but if it contains satisfaction, it establishes no merit.   Nor does
Anselm speak here of a *surplus* merit, *but he suddenly regards
the whole work of Christ as merit ;* but then it is not satisfaction.
Further, when men suddenly come to be considered as kinsmen
of Jesus, the question arises as to why this standpoint—that
Christ is to be regarded as the head of elect humanity—was not
asserted at the beginning of the inquiry.   (3) The way in which
the conceptions of the *righteousness* and *honour* of God are
treated is full of contradictions.   On the one hand righteousness, it is maintained, finds expression in penalty as much as in
the positive attainment of salvation as an end ; on the other
hand righteousness *requires* that this end be reached.   In keeping with this is the way the conception of honour is dealt with ;
indeed, three conceptions are here presupposed.   First of all, it
must be held entirely impossible for God to receive personal
wrong ; His honour can suffer absolutely no injury (I., 15 : "By
nothing can the honour of God, so far as it is concerned, be
increased or diminished ; since for itself it is the same incorruptible and absolutely immutable honour ").   Then it is asserted that His honour, certainly, can be injured, but that it
can likewise be restored, either by penalty (damnation of the
human race) or by satisfaction.   Lastly, it is asserted that the
honour of God cannot tolerate the destruction of His world-
plan, which culminates in the salvation of the reasonable
creature, that, accordingly, God must forego penalty, bring
about the salvation of the creature, and therefore choose satisfaction.   (4) While in general the idea is always carried through,
that on account of His honour God cannot simply pardon men,
the turn of thought occurs in c. 19, p. 41, that God cannot do
so *on man's account*, because a man polluted by sin, even though
he were restored to paradise, would not be as he was before the
fall.   Yet this important turn of thought is not wrought out to
a further issue.   (5) It is asserted of God that He stands above
all change of human conditions, and supports all things by His
holy omnipotence ; hence the rule holds good (l.c.): "it is not

for man to transact with God as an equal with an equal." Yet this rule is contravened by the *whole* exposition, which proceeds on the principle (I. 23, p. 47) : " Man never should, and never can, receive from God what God has proposed to give him, unless he restores to God all that he took from Him, so that as God has lost by him, He shall also recover by him." This principle places God and man entirely on the same footing as injured and injurer. God is wronged as a man is wronged. But if it is said, that in point of fact, as moral beings, they would stand on the same footing, yet this correct observation must not alter the fundamental relationship, that God is the Lord and man His creature. (6) The assumption that Christ's death was voluntary, in the sense that He could also have declined death, cannot be carried through without contradiction, and yet, as Anselm knew very well, everything in his theory depends on this point. First of all, Anselm can only set aside by clumsy sophisms the Bible passages that assert that death was included in the *obedience* of Christ, and that He drank the cup in trembling fulfilment of the will of the *Father*. Secondly, when the subject itself is dealt with, it cannot be proved that the obedience of Christ did not extend to the suffering of death, for as it was—according to Anselm—the *man* Christ that suffered, death is also included in what He owed to God, since man, even apart from sin, owes himself entirely to God. The action, moreover, which Christ offered up when He died " to the honour of God " was not objective ; it was personal. But— again according to Anselm—man is under obligation to direct all personal action " to the honour of God."[1]

Second, the old ecclesiastical material with which Anselm works is not adapted to the new purposes for which he employs it. From the time of Athanasius, and even earlier, the doctrine of the two natures was so understood as to imply *that the God-Logos is the subject*, and that He takes human nature into the unity of His divine being. This idea alone suits the purpose which the Greeks had in view, namely, to explain the reality of the conquest of death, and the deification of our nature. From this as a starting-point, Athanasius developed in detail a multi-

[1] See Ritschl l.c. I., pp. 44 f.

tude of points of view, this among the rest, that by His dying—
which was possible to Him through the human nature—the
God-Logos bore the penalty, and expelled death from human
nature. But Anselm wished to trace back everything to satisfaction, and he adhered strictly to the correct theory of Ambrose
and Augustine, that it was the *man* Jesus who died, and that it
is He therefore who is our mediator. At the same time, however, the impossibility of reconciling this view with the doctrine
of the two natures now at last found definite expression in him ;
*for where the subject of the redeeming personality is regarded, not
as the God-Logos, but as, with Anselm, the man, there is a cancelling, not, indeed, of the Godhead of Christ, but certainly of the
two-nature doctrine. The term, " the Godhead of Christ," occurs
in Anselm, within the lines of the strict theory, only as a determination of the value of the human person in his action.*[1] Christ
appears as the *man*, whose life has an infinite value. That that
is something quite different from the second person of the
Godhead is obvious.[2] When Anselm now continues to use the
two-nature doctrine as a hallowed tradition, a quite Nestorian
diremption of the person is the result (see I. 9, 10), such as had
regularly occurred in the West from the time of Augustine,
when there was an attempt to work out one's own Christology as
a doctrine of redemption, and yet a refusal to relinquish that
doctrine of natures. But further, the two-nature doctrine still
appears welcome on this ground also, namely, that by means of
it every difficulty whatever which the theory of redemption
offers can be got quit of ; for as everything conceivable can be
distributed between the predicates, "human and divine natures,"
one finds himself herewith equal to any difficulty, and can
suppress every doubt, and excuse all indolence of thought.

[1] See Ritschl I., pp. 43 f.

[2] Hence also the feeling in relation to Christ is quite different among the Latins from
what it is among the Greeks. The latter look for the most part to the God in Christ,
the former to the man. Ritschl has (p. 47) pointed out the remarkable, though by
no means solitary, passage in Anselm's Meditations (12) : "Certe nescio, quia non
plene comprehendere valeo, unde hoc est, quod longe dulcior es in corde diligentis
te in eo quod caro es, quam in eo quod verbum : dulcior in eo, quod humilis, quam in
eo quod sublimis . . . Hæc omnia (the human) formant et adaugent magis ac magis
exsultationem, fiduciam et consolationem, amorem ac desiderium."

Anselm confessed that himself in a naïve way (c. 17, p. 85):
"What does not answer to the man in Christ must be transferred to the God, what does not suit the God must be applied
to the man." In this way the earnest Greek speculation, which
always stood for the unity of the God-man, was discarded; and
thus it continued to be in the West. Among those who to-day
interject in discussion the "Godhead" of Christ, how many
reflect that the term obliges them to *prove the divine-human
unity*, and that, if they imagine they may disregard this obligation, an Athanasius and the Fathers of dogma would despise
them as empty talkers or as heretics? These men knew full
well that the mere term, "the divinity of Christ," affirms simply
nothing, is heretical, indeed, because the *God-manhood* must be
proved. But to those in the West that no longer occurs; for
they neither can, nor will, prove it, by employing the means of
the Greeks; nay, they follow quite a different scheme in the
doctrine of redemption : Christ is the *man* whose action has an
infinite value. If, then, the term, "doctrine of two-natures,"
continues in use, then among those who really reflect on Christ
as Redeemer it is deprived of its meaning through the Western
conception of it. Hence it is only used still in the service of
"conservative interests," or to secure an authorised exemption
from all energetic reflection on Christ as Redeemer by means of
the convenient formula ; this He did as God, and that as man.

Third, besides what has been set forth up to this point, there
is still a series of the gravest objections to be urged against the
whole character of the Anselmic doctrine. Let us only briefly
indicate them : (1) In many passages, and these, too, the most
important, Anselm proceeds according to a logic by which
already everything can be proved. The gravest malpractices
of Scholasticism already betray themselves in him; the self-
restraint of the ancient thinkers, modest as was the expression
given to it by the Fathers, is wanting to him. (2) Everything
is conceived of quite abstractly, very much in the way in which
a clever child thinks and speaks of such things, This theory
manages to describe the work of redemption by Jesus Christ
without adducing *a single* saying of His (what is brought
forward does not serve to elucidate, but consists in the *explaining*

away of important passages of Scripture). Anselm holds it as
superfluous to accentuate any one personal feature in the picture
of Christ; the sinless man with the infinitely valuable life is
enough. The death of Christ is entirely severed from His life-
work on earth, and isolated. This God-man need not have
preached, and founded a kingdom, and gathered disciples;
he only required to die. (3) There is no reference to the
eternal election of the Christian community, or the reference
is only feeble (see I. 16, and in connection with Mary). As
the Kingdom of God is not spoken of, so neither is the Church,
and its eternal existence in the view of God. The category of
the inner moral necessity of the good and holy even for God is
consistently confounded with that of reason (ratio), by means
of which, it is represented, one can constrain even a heathen to
believe in the God-man, the result being that the mystery
of faith is profaned. (4) Sin is conceived of certainly as guilt
before God; but this guilt is not the want of trust (faith) in
Him, but is conceived of as a personal injury. How any one
pleases to deal with personal injuries is a matter for himself;
on the other hand, the guilt which is want of child-like fear and
love, and which destroys God's world, must be *wiped out*,
whether it be in wrath or in love. Anselm fails to see that.
(5) And this brings us to the worst thing in Anselm's theory:
the mythological conception of God as the mighty private
man, who is incensed at the injury done to His honour
and does not forego His wrath till He has received an at
least adequately great equivalent; the quite Gnostic antagonism
between justice and goodness, the Father being the just one,
and the Son the good; the frightful idea (as compared with
which the views of the Fathers and the Gnostics are far to be
preferred) *that mankind are delivered from the wrathful God;* [1]

---

[1] Very correct statement by Bigg, The Christian Platonists of Alex., p. 290: "It
was reserved for Anselm, centuries afterwards, to array the justice against the
goodness of God, and thus to complete the resemblance of Christianity to its ancient
deadly foe" (namely, Gnosticism). Only, Gnosticism distinguished between the just
God (the demiurge) and the good God as two hostile deities. But the old patristic
theory was that by His death Christ has redeemed men from the devil. If we isolate
the death from the life of Christ, this is in fact the best theory, for it brings no
discord into the deity. It was no doubt a step of progress on Anselm's part that he

the illusory performance between Father and Son, while the Son is one with the Father ; the illusory performance of the Son with Himself, *for according to Anselm the Son offers Himself to Himself* (II. 18 : "filius ad honorem suum seipsum sibi obtulit ") ;[1] the blasphemous idea that the Son's giving of life (datio vitæ) is for God, as acceptance of death (acceptio mortis), a *benefit ;* the dreadful thought that God is superior to man, as having the prerogative of not being able to forgive from love, a payment always being needed by Him (I. 12); the vitiated conception of our prayer to God for forgiveness, that it is a part of our satisfaction, but can never in itself have the effect of forgiveness (I. 19 : "qui non solvit, frustra dicit : dimitte "). If it is now added that, as has been shown above, there is proved by all this only the *possibility* of our being saved, that the thought of the penalty of sin is eliminated (and therefore the righteousness of God too laxly conceived of), that here no innocent one suffers *penalty* for the guilty, and that, in the effect upon us, only the feeble thought of example comes clearly to view, then we must say, that in spite of Anselm's good intentions, and in spite of some correct perceptions, no theory so bad had

---

wished to carry through the thought that God is at the same time holy and merciful. But this thought cannot be carried through by means of the death of Christ as isolated, and thought of as satisfaction, if this is held as satisfaction to God Himself. So it is always better to let the satisfaction be paid to the devil, because even on that assumption the idea of righteousness is satisfied—in a mythological way, no doubt (the right view would be, that justice must be done to evil, namely by penalty)—without Christ the merciful and God the wrathful being brought into conflict, while Christ is nevertheless regarded as Himself God. That the latter is an impracticable thought was clearly seen, moreover, by Augustine, after he had weighed its possibility. Bigg points to de trinit. XIII. 11 : "Sed quid est justificati in sanguine ipsius ? Quæ vis est sanguinis hujus, obsecro, ut in eo justificentur credentes ? Et quid est reconciliati per mortem filii ejus ? Itane vero, cum irasceretur nobis deus pater, vidit mortem filii sui pro nobis et placatus est nobis ?" This cannot be ; "for omnia simul et pater et filius et amborum spiritus pariter et concorditer operantur." He therefore rejects the Anselmic theory in anticipation. This theory can only be explained from the fact that the thought of God as the *Father* who is nigh to us had fallen into the background in the Middle Ages, and the old view of the Trinity as *unity* was no longer held. Here too, therefore, the ancient traditional dogma was discarded, the term Trinity retained.

[1] In Constantinople the Synods from the year 1156 f. decided, that the mass is offered also to the Son, as He is at the same time the offerer and the offered, and the Trinity admits of no diremption. See Hefele V.[2], p. 567.

ever before his day been given out as *ecclesiastical*. But perhaps no
one can frame a better, who isolates the death of Christ from His
life, and wishes to see in this death something else than the consummation of the "service" which He rendered throughout His *life*.[1]

In its complete form Anselm's theory exercised little influence.
The conception, which he only touched on, of the "*meritoriousness*" of the work of Christ, very rapidly came to the front, and
made his satisfaction theory—which, moreover, conflicted with
the Augustinian tradition—without effect. Added to this was
the fact that interest in the proof of *our* reconciliation to God
was not satisfied by Him. At this point Abelard intervened,
without giving, certainly, a connected and exact development of
the doctrine.[2] After rejecting still more decidedly than Anselm
the relation of the death on the Cross to the devil, he sets out
from the fundamental thought of the love of God, and at the
same time makes it clear to himself that sin has separated men
from God, that it is a question therefore of bringing them back
to God, and of again imparting to them trust in God. Further,
he keeps it before him that the fruit of redemption relates to
the chosen, with regard to whom God's disposition did not first
need to be changed. Accordingly, the incarnation and death
of the Son of God can be conceived of only as an act of love,
and even the righteousness of God must be so defined that it is
subordinated to love, or, say, is identical with it. It was not
required then that Christ should first assuage the wrath of God.
It is as easy for God to forgive sin as it was for Him to bring
into existence a sinless man, who united himself to Christ. But
in order really to win *us* for Himself, Christ has given us the highest
proof of love, which kindles our cold hearts and leads us back
to the trust and love of God. Further (the reflections do not

---

[1] That Anselm himself, however, has, in other writings, carried through other
thoughts with regard to redemption has been shown by Ritschl, l.c. I., pp. 46 f., 109.
He surrendered himself to the certainty of grace even without such calculations, on
the other hand emphasised more strongly the conception of merit.

[2] See Ritschl, l.c. I., pp. 48 ff. ; Schwane, pp. 304 ff. ; Deutsch, Abälard, pp.
336 ff. ; Seeberg in the "Mittheil. u. Nachricht. f. die ev. K. in Russland," 1888,
March-April. Also Reuter in his 1st, and especially Bach in his 2nd, vol., pp. 68 f.
77 f., 88 ff.

stand in a strict order) in this deed of Christ in dying on the
Cross God beholds us, that is, He forgives us our sins, in so far
as He reckons to us the merit of Christ, because Christ stands
before God as the head of humanity; He likewise lets the merit
of the perfect righteousness of Christ fall to our advantage; for
in the *obedience* of Christ God is satisfied.   Finally, Christ goes
on working continuously for us, for inasmuch as He prays for
us unceasingly to the Father, it is in keeping with the righteousness of God to reckon to us this merit.   But by Christ's "merit"
Abelard never understands "a sum of distinct actions; the
fulness of love to God dwelling in Christ is His merit."   "Thus
it is in will, not in works, which are common to the good and
evil, that all merit consists."[1]   There is therefore here nothing
objective and nothing magical.   Even the death on the Cross is
not estimated as an objective deed, but belongs entirely—as a
chief part—to the evidences of the love of Christ which He
exhibited from the beginning.   *Christ's merit is His service of
love;* but love calls forth responsive love, and he who loves
(because Christ has first loved him) has forgiveness of sins
granted him, nay, in the interchange of love which springs from
Christ there lies the forgiveness of sins itself.[2]

Abelard has furnished no strict proof for the necessity of the
death on the Cross; his propositions, moreover, are inadequate,
because he has not clearly perceived that *that love* is the highest,
is indeed alone effectual, which, by taking the *penalty* upon
itself, reveals at the same time the greatness of the absolution
and the greatness of the cancelled guilt.   He did not perceive that
the sinner cannot be otherwise delivered from guilt than by
experiencing and seeing the penalty of guilt.   But he had too
keen a sense of the love of his God, and of the oneness of God

---

[1] So a disciple of Abelard, who hit upon his meaning; see Seeberg, p. 7, and
Deutsch, p. 378 ff.

[2] I do not transcribe here the passages, for in their isolation they do not give a
true view.   There fall to be considered more particularly several passages from the
Exposit. ep. Rom. (especially on chap. III. 22 ff., V. 12 ff.), from the Sermons V.,
X., XII., theolog. christ. IV., and the Dialogue.   How much Abelard's whole
Christology and doctrine of redemption are dominated by the thought of love and
counter love, how entirely love is "merit," could not be ascertained from separate
quotations.

and Christ, to entertain the Gnostic thought that God needs a
sacrifice or an equivalent, or that for Him Christ's death is a
benefit.   And he knew himself so intimately united to Christ in
living fellowship that it was he who first introduced again into
the doctrine of redemption the apostolic thought of the perpetual
intercession of Christ for us, and on the other hand saw also in
the earthly life of Christ, not *one* proof of love—the death—but
a continuous stream of love, in which the " work " of Christ also,
namely His "merit," *i.e.*, the operation of His loving will, is
included.[1]

[1] Deutsch says very correctly, p. 382 : " Accordingly the ultimate and deepest
thought of Abelard is this, that reconciliation rests on personal fellowship with Christ.
It is He who, by perfectly fulfilling the will of God as man, realised the divine
destination of humanity, *in this sense* satisfied God, and thereby opened again to mankind
the closed gates of paradise.   He who belongs to Him has through Him the forgiveness of sins, and with Him access to God, but at the same time also the power of the
new life, in which he fulfils the commands of God from love ; and so far as this fulfilment is still imperfect the righteousness of God comes in to complete it."   On the
other hand Reuter (I., p. 243) has given this perverted view of Abelard's doctrine :
" For one who wrought reconciliation, there was substituted one who proclaimed
that God was already reconciled [but according to Abelard Christ is no "proclaimer,"
and God is not reconciled, if we are not] ; instead of a passion of the Son, who alone
opens again the way to the Father [but that is just Abelard's meaning], a martyrdom
with psychological efficacy was held up to view [the word "psychological" is here
meant to create an impression of the profane, but we have surely only the choice
between this and physico-chemical] ; instead of change of disposition on God's part,
change of disposition on man's was spoken of."   [Is God love or is He of alienated
mood ?   Is it not the *penalty for man* that as a sinner he *must* think of a God of
terror, and can anything greater take place in heaven or earth than when a man's
feelings are revolutionised, *i.e.*, when his fear of a God of terror is transformed into
trust and love?   If it were possible to bring home to the sinner the thought of the
loving God, in whom he can have confidence, while he feels himself guilty, then
certainly Christ would have died in vain ; but that is a contradictio in adjecto.]
Even Seeberg, in spite of all his efforts to be impartial, has made a rationalistic
caricature of Abelard's doctrine, and in keeping with this has much bepraised sayings
of Bernard, some of which are to be found also in Abelard, some of which Abelard
has happily set aside (the justa potestas diaboli).   That which we really miss in
Abelard—that Christ bore our penalty—is also wanting in Bernard, and the
" example " of Christ is much more incautiously emphasised by the latter than by the
former, who always thinks of the *power* of love that proceeds from Christ.   But
Bernard, it is alleged, stands much higher than Abelard, because he can give a more
lyrical expression to the impassioned love to Christ, while Abelard thinks only of the
doctrine and the example (!), and because, it is asserted, something "objective" is
to be found in him which is supposed to be wanting in Abelard.   Even according to
Seeberg, indeed, this "objective" is quite falsely defined by Bernard, but that is of

The polemic against Abelard directed itself also against his theory of redemption ; but it was contested essentially from the basis of the Augustinian theory of redemption (vanquishment of the claim of the devil), while there was no following of Anselm.[1] At the same time all were increasingly at one in this, that the point of view of merit must be applied, and that Christ must be contemplated as Redeemer in the light of His human quality. With this understanding also the Lombard drew up his connected account of the opinions of the Fathers in his doctrinal compendium. As in the case of Augustine, the "man" (homo) in Christ takes the prominent place, as the moral personality chosen and sustained by God, and the whole life of Christ is understood from this point of view.[2] At the same time, in order to understand the peculiar nature of redemption, all points of view were combined that were furnished by the past : obedience, redemption from the devil, death and penalty, but, above all, the *merit* of death, then also sacrifice. With Augustine, the strict necessity of this precise means (death on the Cross) is rejected; with him and the other Fathers, the buying off of the devil (including deception) is asserted. With Abelard, the death is viewed as a proof of love, which awakens counter love ; with him Christ is regarded as the representative of humanity before God ; with Augustine, the necessity for a reconciliation of God through the death of Christ is rejected (God loves even His enemies ; He has loved us beforehand from eternity, and we are reconciled, not with the wrathful, but with the loving God); finally, a penal value in the death of Christ is asserted, in the sense that by it the eternal penalty is remitted (see Athanasius), the temporal penalty in future (after death) falls away. On the other hand the Anselmic theory is not mentioned at all.[3] The Lombard shows there-

no consequence, if only there is "something" there. When will there be a getting rid in Protestantism of this "something," which at best only establishes the possibility of redemption ; and when will there be a distinguishing between a vicarious penal suffering and a satisfaction demanded by God?

[1] See Bach II., pp. 88-122. Besides Bernard, William of St. Thierry specially comes into view here.

[2] Sentent. lib. III., dist. 18, 19.

[3] Ritschl I., p. 56 f.

fore that the patristic tradition still continued to be the only
subject of doctrine, and that it was only with an effort that
what was new asserted itself against it. Yet the whole undertaking to give a combined and connected view was itself new
(on which account the Lombard was regarded with much
distrust as an Abelardian).[1]

Not till the thirteenth century did the new dogmatic impulses
of the eleventh and twelfth centuries take their place with equal
rights, materially, though not formally, alongside the mass of
traditional patristic tenets. By the latter, which were represented partly by a voluminous exegetical tradition, and partly

---

[1] This was not without ground ; for apart from the objective redemption which consists in deliverance from the fetters of the devil (yet even to this a subjective turn is
given, see Sentent. III. Dist. 19 A : "si ergo recte fidei intuitu in illum respicimus
qui pro nobis pependit in ligno, a vinculis diaboli solvimur, *i.e.*, *a peccatis*, et ita a
diabolo liberamur, ut nec post hanc vitam in nobis inveniat quod puniat. Morte
quippe sua, uno verissimo sacrificio, quidquid culparum erat, unde nos diabolus ad
luenda supplicia detinebat, Christus exstinxit, ut in hac vita tentando nobis non
prævaleat ") the Lombard knows only of a *subjective* redemption ; l.c. "quo modo a
peccatis per Christi mortem soluti sumus? Quia per ejus mortem, ut ait apostolus,
commendatur nobis caritas dei, *i.e.*, apparet eximia et commendabilis caritas dei erga
nos in hoc, quod filium suum tradidit in mortem pro nobis peccatoribus. Exhibita
autem tantæ erga nos dilectionis arrha, *et nos movemur accendimurque ad diligendum
deum*, qui pro nobis tanta fecit, *et per hoc justificamur, i.e., soluti a peccatis justi
efficimur. Mors ergo Christi nos justificat, dum per eam caritas excitatur in cordibus
nostris.*" Yet along with this the other turn of thought is found : "dicimur quoque et
aliter per mortem Christi justificati, *quia per fidem mortis ejus a peccatis mundamur.*"
But his thought is not further followed out ; on the contrary, it is said again Dist. 19
F : "reconciliati sumus deo, ut ait apostolus, per mortem christi. Quod non sic intelligendum est quasi nos sic reconciliaverit Christus, *ut inciperet amare quos oderat,*
sicut reconciliatur inimicus inimico, ut deinde sint amici qui ante se oderant, *sed jam
nos diligenti deo reconciliati sumus;* non enim ex quo ei reconciliati sumus per
sanguinem filii nos coepit diligere, sed ante mundum, priusquam nos aliquid essemus.
Quomodo ergo nos diligenti deo sumus reconciliati? *Propter peccatum cum eo habe-
bamus inimicitias, qui habebat erga nos caritatem,* etiam cum inimicitias exercebamus
adversus eum operando iniquitatem. Ita ergo inimici eramus deo, sicut justitiæ sunt
inimica peccata et ideo dimissis peccatis tales inimicitiæ finiuntur, et reconciliamur
justo quos ipse justificat. Christus ergo dicitur *mediator,* eo quod medius inter deum
et homines ipsos reconciliat deo." But here again another thought comes in, when
the Lombard immediately continues : "reconciliat autem dum *offendicula hominum
tollit ab oculis dei,* id est dum peccata delet quibus deus *offendebatur* et nos inimici
ejus eramus." The prevading thought of the awakening of counter love, which the
Lombard took over from Abelard, is already to be found in Augustine ; see *e.g.*, de
catech. rud. 4 : "Nulla est major ad amorem invitatio, quam *prævenire* amando, et
nimis durus est animus, qui dilectionem si nolebat impendere, nolit rependere."

by theological positions no longer understood in their original connection, the trivial spirit of mediæval theology was fostered, which mingled in a marvellous way with its energy and with its juristic acuteness.   The statement of the thesis in scholastic science was invariably lofty and great; "but by its love for details even heaven was dragged down."   From the scientific standpoint, and from the standpoint of "juristic thinking," we cannot find fault, certainly, with this spirit; for does not science require that the problems be thought out to their ultimate consequences?   The error lay simply in the premises, and in the idea that that thinking was thinking about religion.   But even that idea it was necessary then to entertain, for religion was of course contemplation !

CHAPTER II.

IF in this chapter we again direct our attention in the first
instance to the history of ecclesiastical *piety*, of ecclesiastical
law and of ecclesiastical *science*, it is less with the view of understanding the *changes* which dogma passed through in this
period, *than in order to show how the conditions under which it
stood served to make it ever more stable and to protect it from all
attack.* It must, above all, be shown how it was possible that
the enormous revolution of the sixteenth century—keeping out
of view the Anabaptist movements—stayed its course before
the old dogma. This can only be understood, however, when
we consider what *confirmations* dogma received from the thirteenth to the fifteenth century. These confirmations were a
consequence of the peculiar history of piety, of ecclesiastical
law and of science in this period. All of these sought, not for
an "unmoved mover" in the background—for dogma was
simply no longer a "mover"—but for an immovable *basis*.
Mysticism, the development of ecclesiastical law, Nominalist
theology—all of them could only develop themselves on the
basis of an authoritative dogma, or, say, could only protect
themselves on that basis against dangerous consequences.

It is only in the second place that there fall to be considered
how far the general conditions produced also certain *changes* in
dogma, then how far an *individual* piety developed itself, how
from this piety the need for individual certainty of salvation
arose, and how this need gathered itself into a mighty force.
Of itself the force was strong enough to demand, and to carry
out, a revision of the entire ecclesiastical tradition. But it will

appear in the last Book (see below) that it was impeded in its
unfolding by the still greater power of a fifteen century long
development.

1. *On the History of Piety.*

What was germinating in the twelfth century, the century of
the Crusades—namely, the piety of which Bernard was the
subject and delineator, which derives its power from *humility*
before God and from *love* to the sorely suffering Redeemer—
opened into blossom in the holy beggar of Assisi, and "its
fragrance filled the world."   In Francis mediæval piety attained
its clearest and most forcible expression.   In him it uttered
itself most simply, and therefore most powerfully and most
impressively, because its chord—"humility, love and obedience"
—was here struck with the greatest purity, while the quality of
tone which Francis lent to it was the most melting.[1]

Humility—that is entire *poverty*.   The reverence for that
which is beneath us, which Bernard and his followers proclaimed, admits of no other robe than that of perfect poverty
and humility.   Long ago no doubt, nay, on from the beginning,
Greek monks had striven after this ideal; but in their hands it
became a torch, which consumed, along with the body, the imagination also, the powers of perception, and the wealth of the
inner life.   It was to be the means of emancipation from the
body ; but often enough it made a wilderness of the spirit.
*Here, on the other hand, it is the imitation of the poor life of
Jesus,* and while it thus acquired a personal ideal, it also developed out of itself, in the inexhaustibly fresh imagination of

[1] Müller, Die Anfänge des Minoritenordens und der Bussbruderschaften, 1885.
Sabatier, Leben des h. Franz v. Assisi, German by M. L., 1895.   R. Mariano,
Francesco d' Assisi e alcuni dei suoi più recenti biografi. Napoli, 1896.   Mariano
brings a sharp, and in many respects well-deserved, criticism to bear on the work of
Sabatier, which is captivatingly written and instructive, but, after the style of Renan,
mingles confusedly past and present, religion and poetry.   Mariano has made a substantial contribution to the estimation of St. Francis, by correcting the partly rhetorical, partly material, exaggerations of Sabatier.   An excellent lecture, taking a survey
of all the principal points, has been published recently by Hegler " Franciskus von
Assisi und die Gründung des Franziskanerordens " (Zeitschr. f. Theol. u. K. 6 Bd.
p. 395 ff.

St. Francis, a wealth of intuitions from which all provinces
of the outer and inner life derived profit. A spirited investigator has shown us what effects were produced by St. Francis
in the field of art.[1]   But in all spheres of human life, even including that of strict science, the new impulse took effect—the
godly fear which gives honour to God alone, the living view of
Christ, which brought the personal into the foreground, the
holy simplicity which shed its light into the heart and over the
world.   In the sunny soul of the sacred singer of Assisi, the
troubadour of God ("joculator domini") and of poverty, the
world mirrored itself, not as merely the struggle for existence,
or the realm of the devil, but as the paradise of God with our
brothers and sisters, the sun, the moon and the stars, the wind
and the water, the flowers and the living creatures.   In poverty,
which is nothing else but sister of the humility by which the
soul becomes like the eye, which sees everything save only
itself, a new organ was obtained for contemplating God and the
world.   But poverty is not only imitation of the poor life of
Jesus, it is also, nay pre-eminently, imitation of the *apostolic*
life, the life without care, of "the pilgrim preacher and herald
of love."   The oldest rule of St. Francis presented this ideal
with the utmost clearness, and created the joyous, devout
Franciscan "family." [2]

With the spirit of which poverty and humility are the
evidence, *love* must unite itself.   Going forth in pairs, the new
Apostles must *serve* in lowly love ; there is no work for which
they must hold themselves too feeble ; " for the love of Jesus
Christ " they must " expose themselves to enemies, both visible
and invisible " ; acording to the Sermon on the Mount, they
must willingly suffer wrong ; above all, wherever they come, in
house and hall, they must render to men the loving service of
preaching repentance, must deliver the message : " fear ye and
honour, praise and bless, thank and adore, the Lord God omnipotent in trinity and unity . . . be of penitent heart, bring forth
fruits meet for repentance, for know ye that we shall soon die.
Give and it shall be given you, forgive and ye shall be forgiven,

---

[1] Thode, Franciskus v. Assisi und die Anfänge der Kunst der Renaissance 1885.
[2] See Müller, l.c. pp. 19 ff., 185 ff.

and if ye forgive not, the Lord will not forgive you your
trespasses. Blessed are they who die in penitence, for they
shall be in the Kingdom of Heaven," etc.[1] But the power of
this love had its source in the example of Christ and of His
devoted disciple, St. Francis, who reproduced ever more deeply
in his experience the life and suffering of his Master. More
and more his feelings became merged in one alone—in love.
This feeling, which in him was so strong that it often over-
powered him, so that he was forced to retire to lonely churches
and forests to give it full vent, was love to Christ ; but it
wedded itself ever more closely to unlimited devotion to his
neighbour, to concern for his spiritual and bodily well-being, tc
warm compassion and self-abasement in the service of his
brethren. So out of humility and love he made of his life a
poem—he, the greatest poet who then lived ; for, after fiery
conflicts, the sensuous element in his ardent nature appeared—
not destroyed, but subdued and glorified, nay, transformed into
the purest organ of the soul's life.[2]

A great work of *home missions* was not contemplated by St.
Francis, but begun ; he was not the first to undertake it, but he
was the first through whom the whole Church derived benefit
from it : Christendom has certainly the right faith ; but it is
not what it ought to be. It is subject to priests and sacraments ;
*but now the individual must be dealt with. He must be laid hold
of, and guided to repentance.* The gospel must be brought home
to every man : the world must be again shaken, and rescued
from its old ways, by a mighty call to repentance : he who has
tasted the sweetness of the love of Christ will turn with
gladness to repentance and poverty. Yet it is not for the
monks and priests alone that there must be concern, but for
individual Christians, for the laity ; they, likewise, must be won
for a penitent and holy life. The " Brothers of Penitence," of
whom St. Francis formed visions, and whom he brought into
existence, were, in spite of their continuing in family life, really
ascetics, who were required to maintain strict separation from
the world and from civic life, and, above all, to take no part in

---

[1] The Rule of 1209. See Müller, p. 187.
[2] See the beautiful characterisation in Thode, l.c. p. 59 ff.

military service. The great saint had not yet made terms with
the world ; the later Tertiaries were as little his creation as the
later Franciscans.[1]

From the monks to the secular priests, from the secular
priests to the laity—this was the course by which Christianity
was to be delivered from secularity ; it is at the same time the
history of the awakening of religious individualism in the West.
And in the measure in which religion became, extensively and
intensively, more world-renouncing, it acquired (paradoxical,
it may seem, but intelligible enough) a higher social and political importance, penetrated more deeply into the life of the
people, and developed itself out of the aristocratic form (in
which, as Roman, it had come to the barbarian nations) into a
form that was popularly social.[2] The further the monachising
proceeded, the more did the virtuosi in religion see themselves
compelled to engage in practical tasks. When the new factor
of *apostolic* life was introduced into the ideal of poverty and
ascetic self-denial, the ideal acquired an enormous immanent
power for *propagandism*, a power such as monachism had never
before possessed, and which does not belong—either formerly
or now—to its distinctive nature. Where "apostolic life"
becomes the watchword, there monachism is at once seen to
apply itself to positive work among the people. In the eleventh

---

[1] See Müller, pp. 117-144. An excellent description of the aim of St. Francis in
Werner (Duns Scotus, p. 2) : "The original designs of the order founded by St.
Francis were the restoring of the original Christian Apostolate, with its poverty and
renunciation of the world, that through the force of this restoration there might be
restored to the Church itself the apostolic spirit ; the awakening in Christian souls
everywhere of a striving after holiness and perfection ; the keeping the example of a
direct following of Christ before the eyes of the world as a continuous living
spectacle ; the comforting of all the suffering and wretched with the consolation of
Christian mercy ; and, by self-sacrificing devotion, the becoming all things to those
spiritually abandoned and physically destitute."

[2] Cf. Thode, l.c. p. 521 f. : "The beggar of Assisi is the representative of the
third estate, the great lower mass of the people, in their combined upward striving
towards a position self-sustained and independent ; but at the same time also the
representative of each individual out of this mass, as he becomes conscious of himself,
and of his rights in relation to God and to the world. With him, and in him,
mediæval humanity experiences the full power of the emotional force that dwells in
each individual, and this inner experience brings with it a first knowledge of one's
own being which emancipates itself from dogmatic general conceptions."

and twelfth centuries what engaged attention was the great
political problem of releasing Church from State ; the question
was, how to break down the great forces, the power of the
Princes, the power of purely secular national bishops, in short,
the title to exist of all unpliant political factors. At the close
of the twelfth, and in the thirteenth centuries, there followed
immediately upon this undertaking the *positive* evangelising of,
and giving ecclesiastical character to, all relationships, to the
whole of civilisation and the individual life, this being done
under the dominating idea of the apostolical. Monachism, as
apostolic life, entered upon this new work as formerly in the
days of Clugny it entered upon the work of freeing Church
from State. And how powerfully did religious individualism
assert itself in Francis, when he ventured to place before himself
and his disciples the example of *the Apostles*, and did not
hesitate to say to the brothers that they could, and should, be
what the Apostles once were, and that to them everything that
Christ had said to the Apostles applied !

He was not the first who awakened this " apostolic life." We
know of powerful phenomena in the twelfth century in which
the new impulse had already found expression.[1] But these
older movements, tenaciously as they survived (and to some

[1] See the history of sects in the twelfth century, especially the Waldensian, cf.
Müller, Die Waldenser und ihre einzelnen Gruppen bis zum Anfang des 14. Jahr-
hunderts (1886), and the older fundamental work of Dieckhoff. The ground-thought
of the Waldensian movement is unquestionably " to imitate the apostles, and therefore to observe literally the instructions which the Lord gave to his wandering
disciples in the missionary address, Matth. 10. The undertaking, therefore, displays
everywhere the same features as, thirty years later, the similar attempt of Francis in
its initial stages : distribution of all property among the poor and renunciation of all
further possessions, according to Matth. 19, 21, 29 ; then, the apostolic preaching,
in constant itineracy, and the particulars as to apostolic garb and methods of
travelling. They go two and two, without shoes, only sandals of wood on their feet,
in simple woollen garments, without money. They move from place to place, seek
shelter and support among those to whom they preach the gospel—for the workman
is worthy of his hire—and despise all settled life and private householding, in imitation of the Son of man, who had not where to lay His head." The Waldensians
seem to have exercised an influence on St. Francis ; but as to how, and by what
means, nothing is known. On this account it will always be possible to believe in
an entire independence, in a resemblance merely in fact ; but this is not probable,
especially as relations have been ascertained between St. Francis and Southern
France.

extent survived as Catholic, in spite of being condemned), came
too early ; the clergy were not yet strong and matured enough
to tolerate them, and, besides, there was lacking to them the
element of unconditional submission to the Church, or more
exactly, to the secular clergy, and of renunciation on principle
of criticism of the Church.[1]

[1] The "Poor" were already excommunicated by Lucius III. (1184). On their
spread in Northern Italy, where they had precursors in the Order of the Humiliates,
but were only brought into existence by Waldes, on the relation of the Lyonnese
Poor to those of Lombardy, and on the breach between the latter and Waldes, see
Müller, l.c. pp. 11-65. The view that the efficacy of the Sacraments depends on the
worthiness of the celebrator—a revolutionary principle under then existing conditions
—appeared again among the Poor of Lombardy before 1211. Of itself the view was
fitted to sever entirely the connection with the ancient Church, and was perhaps one
of the causes of the ultimate breach between the Lyonnese and Lombard poor. The
former were not so sharply opposed to the Roman Church as the latter. They did
not regard it as Antichrist, but included it rather in the great community of the
baptised, and recognised its administration of the Sacraments. But they made it a
grave reproach against the Roman Church that its hierarchy exercised apostolic powers
without adopting the apostolic life of poverty and homelessness (see the demand of
the Didache regarding the qualities of apostles and prophets). They did not contest
the *full authority* of the duly ordained bishops, who derived their dignity from the
apostles ; but they looked upon it as a deadly sin that they refused to live as did the
apostles. A certain wavering in their attitude towards the Roman Church was the
result. The judicial and legislative authority of the hierarchy was certainly disputed,
or at least held as needing restriction. But as the "Brothers" did not organise into
communities the "Friends" (the "believers") won over by them, but rather left
them in the old relationships, the position of the reigning Church towards the Brothers
and their adherents was much more definite and decided than was their position
towards it. The French kinsmen of the Waldensians were not a new evangelical
community, based on the idea of the universal priesthood, but "the sect itself is
nothing but a hierarchy, which, founded on the thought of the apostolic life and the
demand for a special ethical perfection, places itself alongside the Roman hierarchy,
that, in an organisation which partakes at least of the fundamental forms of the latter,
it may carry on preaching, dispense sacramental penance, and in its own innermost
seclusion celebrate the Eucharist. So little is there the idea of the universal priesthood that the laity do not belong at all to the sect, membership being conferred
rather only by consecration to one of the three hierarchical grades." (See Müller, p.
93 ff. and cf., as a parallel, the way in which the Irvingites now carry on their propaganda, and relate themselves to the communitas baptizatorum). Nor was the old
traditional Church doctrine assailed by the Waldensians. They diverged only in
respect of certain doctrines which bore upon practice, and which, besides, had not
yet been formulated. Thus they rejected purgatory, and disapproved therefore of
the Church practice that was connected with the idea of it (*i.e.*, of all institutions
that were meant to extend their influence into the world beyond). The rejection of
oaths, of service in war, of civil jurisdiction, of all shedding of blood, seemed to them,

For this is the third element in the piety of St. Francis—
childlike confidence in the Church and unconditional obedience
to the secular clergy. "Let all the Brethren," so it runs in the
Rule of 1209, "be Catholics, live and speak as Catholics . . .

as to so many mediæval sects, simply to follow from the Sermon on the Mount. On
the other hand, the branch in Lombardy (which carried on a propaganda in Germany)
took up a much more radical attitude towards the Roman Church (see Müller, p. 100
ff.) Although in what was cardinal it adhered to the standpoint of the French group
of the stock (close communion, but only of men and women living *apostolically ;*
administration of the sacrament of penance ; instruction of the " Friends" by preaching), it nevertheless saw in the Roman Church only apostasy, which at a subsequent
time it traced to the benefactions of Constantine (cf. the Spirituales). This Church
appeared to them accordingly as the synagogue of evil-doers and as the whore, its
priests and monks as Scribes and Pharisees, its members as the lost. And so all
regulations, orders, sacraments, and acts of this Church were to be rejected. Everything without exception, above all, the Pope and the mass, then also all legal
regulations for worship fell under the adverse judgment. We can therefore gather
testimonies here to the full for the "evangelical" character of these Lombards, who
rejected all ecclesiastical differences of rank within the Christian community, all
pomp, riches, lights, incense, holy water, processions, pilgrimages, vestments, ceremonies, etc., and in place of these required support of the poor, who would have
nothing to do with the worship of Mary and the saints, who disbelieved as much in
miracles of saints as in relics, who—at least originally—rejected the entire sacramental
system of the Church, and both limited the number of sacraments and only recognised
their validity on condition that the priest was free from mortal sin. But from the
beginning onwards this attitude towards the reigning Church was really in many
respects only "academic," for the great mass of the " Friends," *i.e.,* of adherents, by
no means actually so judged the Roman Church, but remained within the sacramental
bonds. Further, the extremely defective vindication of this radical opposition on the
part of the Brethren themselves shows that it was more the result of the breach forced
upon them from without, or, say, of the doctrine of poverty, than the product of
a religious criticism dealing with what was essential. Finally, this view is confirmed
by the circumstance that from the beginning the Brethren left themselves, as can be
proved, a convenient alternative, by means of which they might be able to recognise
the celebration of the sacraments by one guilty of mortal sin (they said that in that
case the worthy Christian receives *directly from the Lord* in the dispensation of
sacramental grace). Moreover, in the time following they approached always more
closely to the Church and its sacramental celebration, partly on practical grounds (to
avoid detection), partly because confidence in their own "apostolic" powers always
became feebler, and the Catholic orders were viewed with longing and with greater
trust. The whole movement, therefore, was at bottom not dogmatic. It was on the
one hand—if we would draw the conclusions without hesitation—too *radical* to play
a part in the history of dogma (Christianity is the apostolic life), on the other hand
too *conservative,* as it set aside absolutely *nothing* that was Catholic with good
conscience and clear insight. It is a phenomenon in the history of Catholic *piety,*
though it may be worth considering in connection with the history of dogma that

and let us regard the clergy and all religious persons as masters
in those things which relate to the salvation of the soul, and do
not deflect from our religion, let us reverence in the Lord both
their rank (ordinem) and their office and their administration."
(See the Rule of 1221, c. 19).[1] That a nature like St Francis
felt oppressed by nothing *external*, if only free scope was given
him for his ideal,[2] that he could maintain his inner freedom and

the whole hierarchico-sacramental apparatus of the Church was called in question.
Had the movement come a generation later, the Church would no doubt have found
means for incorporating it into itself, as it did the Franciscan.   Such an attempt was
even made with the "Catholic Poor" of the converted Durandus of Huesca, formerly
a French Waldensian (acknowledged by Innocent III. a year before St. Francis
stood before him), and of the converted Lombard, Bernhard Primus, also one of the
"Poor"; but there was no more success in leading the whole movement back to the
channel of the Church by means of such approved Poor ones (Müller, p. 16 ff.)   Only
in the Mendicant Orders did the powerful counter-movement become organised and
permanent (cf. Müller's excellent directions for finding the connection between the
approvals of the Societies of Durandus, Dominic, and Francis (Waldenser, p. 65 ff.);
also the same author's Anfänge des Minoritenordens (pp. 43, 69 f.), and the perhaps
anti-Waldensian passage on the Rule of 1209 (p. 187): "Nulla penitus mulier ab
aliquo fratre recipiatur ad obedientiam"). The Mendicant Orders naturally,
particularly that of Dominic, set themselves in opposition, not only to the unsanctioned
"Poor," but to sectarianism as a whole. On this latter there is no reason to enter in
the history of dogma, for however high its importance may have to be estimated in
connection with Church politics and social life, and however clearly it indicates that
piety felt itself straightened within the tyrannical structure of the Roman Church and
among its priests and ceremonies, it is equally certain that the mediæval sects continued entirely without influence as regards the development of dogma.   It cannot
even be said that they prepared the way for the Reformation; for the loosening
which, to some extent, they brought about, was no prior condition of that movement.
In the controversies rather which prevailed between the Roman Church and the
dualistic (or pantheistic) sects, the Reformation placed itself entirely on the side of
the former.   What prepared the way for the Reformation in the domain of theology
(keeping out of view the development of the ideas of the State and of natural rights)
was always only the revived Augustinianism and the subjectivity of mysticism allied
with it.   As long, therefore, as it is regarded as expedient that the history of dogma
should not be treated as history of culture, or as universal history, attention must be
withdrawn from such phenomena as the Cathari, Albigenses, etc.

1 But in the year 1210, and later, Francis would not be induced to connect himself
with an already existing Order, or to conform to the older Monachism, and in this
obstinacy towards the Pope and the cardinals he showed that he knew the greatness
of his cause.

2 This was not done indeed, and it led to sore distress on Francis' part; yet
Sabatier seems to me to have exaggerated this strain in relationship (see Mariano, and
especially Hegler); the Cardinal to whom the movement was chiefly due also did the
most to make it political.   The relation of St. Francis to the Curia and to the Church

pure cheerfulness of soul, even under quite other burdens than
the Church then imposed, that he must have emptied himself of
his very essence if he had undertaken to " abolish " anything,
are things that are manifest.   For him, obedience to all existing
ordinances was as much a need as humility, and never assuredly
did the shadow of a sceptical reflection as to whether the
hierarchy was as it should be, or as to whether it should exist
at all, fall upon the soul of this pure fool.   But how could it
fail to come about that the ideal of poverty and the ideal of
obedience should come into conflict ?   We cannot here unfold
the history of St. Francis and of the Minorite Order.   It is well
known against what mistrust he had to contend on the part of
the secular clergy (even the curia), especially in France (but
even on the part of the older Orders), and how the conditions
reproduced themselves here which we have observed at the
establishment of monachism in the end of the fourth, and
beginning of the fifth, centuries, as well as in connection with
the Cluniacensian reform in the West.   It is well known also
that " poverty " was the great theme in the history of the
thirteenth and fourteenth centuries ; that there was as much
stubborn and passionate controversy over it as in the fourth
and fifth centuries over the natures of Christ, and that in this
controversy as artful and clever formulæ made their appearance
as at Chalcedon and Constantinople.   For thousands, the controversy about poverty was a controversy about the gospel
itself.   By this conflict the formulæ of the old dogmatic were
little or in no way touched ; but they, so to speak, sank into the
ground.   The question about the nature of the gospel was
narrowed down to a *practical* question about life-conduct.
Even when we keep out of view the pedantic mode of treatment,
the way of stating the question appears to us strangely inadequate.   Yet " poverty," certainly, was only the final expression for the whole sum of the virtues involved in imitating
Christ.   What the watchword " poverty " denoted was an
immense step of advance from dead faith, and from a barren
service of ceremonies and works to spiritual freedom in religion,

politicians, or rather the relation of these to him, still needs a thorough investigation.
Excellent discussions in Hegler, l.c. 436 ff.

and to an earnest personal Christianity. The new Order soon broke up into different sections. In the one principal section, the last to submit, it certainly wrought invaluable results in the first generations of its existence. Its preaching kindled an earnest Christian life, indeed in many regions it was the first thing that produced an individual Christianity at all among the laity—so was it in Germany. Yet as everything was brought by it into closest connection with the confessional, the sacraments and the Pope, as all greater freedom was repressed as sectarianism, or crushed out—just by the Mendicant Orders—only an inferior kind of existence was allowed to this individual piety of the laity. For what the Minorites were obliged to sacrifice to the hierarchy—it was nothing less than the chief part of their original ideal, only the shadow remaining—they, so to speak, indemnified their conscience by the unparalleled energy with which they served the Church in its plans for ruling the world, and won for it the interest and allegiance of the laity. Here, at this final stage, therefore, the enemy the Church had in her own midst was once more vanquished ; the enormous force of world-forsaking Christianity, which threatened the political supremacy of the Church, became visibly her servant ; the " exempted " Order became, along with the Order of Preachers, her surest support.

But in other sections the obedience was not powerful enough to control that force.[1] " Poverty " turned itself against the rich and worldly Church, and when there was to be threatening and forced silence, it threw off restraint. It called upon the Church to serve ; it united itself with the old apocalyptic ideas, that had already been long exercising their power in secret ; it adopted the critical attitude of the " Lombard Poor " ; it joined hands readily with the new social, and even the new territorial, ideas, the conceptions that were taking shape of the inherent rights of nations and individuals, of States and Princes.[2] While

[1] Of course many personal elements entered also, such as we can study in the most interesting of the earlier Franciscans, Elias of Cortona.

[2] See the writings of Joh. de Oliva and Ubertino de Casale (both were under the influence of the writings of Joachim of Fiore). The view of history friendly to the State as against the Secularised Church appears already in the middle of the thirteenth century (and even among the Dominicans) : see Voelter in the Ztschr. f. K.-Gesch.

it declared the Church to be Babylon, and hierarchy Anti-Christ, it was not fastidious about its partnership. It left the dogmatic of the Church unassailed ; but against the Church itself it declared war, an undertaking so full of contradiction that it was only possible in the Middle Ages, the period of contradictions and illusions ; for did not this Church possess in its system of dogma the surest and most definite title for its existence ? Only in one branch (the Fraticelli) did the contradiction become so radical that the fences dividing from the heretical sects (Apostolic Brethren, Beghards) became frail.

From these last-mentioned sections nothing permanent developed itself.[1] The importance for universal history of the vast movement of the Mendicant Orders is not to be seen at all in new doctrines or institutions, though these were not entirely wanting, but lies rather in the religious *awakening* that was produced by them during a period of 150 or—if a time of slackened

IV., H. 3. On the "Spirituales," and the "Fraticelli" (the latter are not to be identified with the former), as well as on the conflicts in the time of John XXII. and Louis of Bavaria, see Ehrle in the Archiv. f. Litt.-u. K.-Gesch. des Mittelalters, Vol. I. and II., Müller, Kampf Ludwig's des Bayern 1879 f., the same author in the Ztschr. f. K.-Gesch. VI., part 1, Gudenatz, Michael von Cesena, 1876.

[1] At a later time Hussism incorporated and wrought over a great part of the Fianciscan and Joachimic-Franciscan elements (see Müller, Bericht uber den gegenwärtigen Stand der Forschung auf dem Gebiet der vorreformatorischen Zeit, in den Vorträgen der theol. Conferenz zu Giessen 1887 S. 44), and as it spread widely, even beyond Bohemia, among the lower orders it prepared the way for the great Baptist movement and the social revolutions of the sixteenth century. Yet creations of a lasting kind appeared here as little as permanent influences on the Church generally. But from the point of view of Church history and the history of culture, the study of the powerful movement, essentially one throughout, which began with Joachimism and culminated with the Hussites and Baptists, is of the deepest interest. Like the "Illuminism" (Aufklärung) in the eighteenth century, and the Romantic ideas in the nineteenth, Joachimism spread over Europe in the thirteenth century, not as a new system of dogma, but as a new mode of viewing history and the highest problems, comforting to the seriously disposed, because it flattered them ; cf., *e.g.*, the Chronicle of Salimbene (Michael, Salimbene und seine Chronik., Innsbruck 1889). Strange that this movement should have begun in the hills of Calabria, the most out-of-the-way district of Southern Europe ! It is still too little studied, while it certainly belongs to a period more open to our inspection than any in which prophetism played a part. Where prophets appear and are welcomed, fabrications are the immediate sequel. But the history of Joachimism is the typical history of all prophetism. Of the way in which it succeeds in adjusting itself in the world, Salimbene also furnishes some beautiful examples.

effort on the part of the Orders is overlooked—of 300 years.
" The individual began to reflect on the saving truths of the
Christian religion, to enter himself into a personal relation to
them." That is the highest significance of the Mendicant
Order movement. In this sense the Orders were a prior stage
of the Reformation. But when religion passed into the circles
of the laity, and independent religious life was awakened there,
it was a natural result that redoubled vigilance should be exercised lest the old dogma should be injured. So long as dogma
is in the hands of priests and theologians, it can maintain a
certain freedom ; this is here natural to it, indeed. But as soon
as the laity become thoughtfully interested in ecclesiastical
Christianity, dogma becomes extraordinarily sensitive. Those
who are entrusted with the care of the religio publica must—as
the Mendicant Orders did—guard it with jealousy, if the result
of the general interest is not to be a general running wild of
religious speculation. The criterion of what is firmly fixed
ecclesiastically must everywhere be applied without hesitation,
especially if the Church practice of the present is to be corrected. On the other hand, the ecclesiastically pious laymen
themselves demand that the dogma shall continue as a *rocher
de bronze*, and they feel every movement or alteration of it to be
an injury to their personal Christianity. This was the situation
that was always becoming more firmly established in the three
centuries before the Reformation. The larger the number grew
of those who sought to become really familiar with religion, the
larger became also the number of sectaries of all kinds ; but the
more inviolable also did dogma appear to the ecclesiastically
faithful, and the greater were the efforts of the hierarchy to put
down all "heresy." Besides, dogma had come from the beginning, and indeed chiefly, to the mediæval nations, as a
series of legal ordinances. This character it must retain,
all the more if the spiritual life had a more vigorous and
manifold development ; otherwise the unity of the Church was
lost. There must at least be an imperative demand for fides
implicita, *i.e.*, for respectful obedience. Thus the awakening,
which in Germany seems to have gone on continually increasing
from the middle of the thirteenth century, contributed to main-

tain the unalterable character of dogma. Ideally dogma had always been immutable ; but now to the reality of this unchangeable thing there attached itself a profoundly practical interest.

The history of piety in the centuries immediately preceding the Reformation consists of a series of sermons on repentance and of *revivals*, of reforms with a view to a deepening of spiritual life that was to extend through the whole of Christendom. Only in its leading points have we to take a survey of it. What comes first under our notice here is the alliance of the Mendicant Orders with Mysticism.

By Mysticism, as has been explained above, there is to be understood nothing but *theological piety* (contemplation), having a reflex aim, modelled on Augustine and the Areopagite, and fertilised (though not thoroughly) by Bernardine devotion to Christ. That this theology should have been found congenial to the temper of the Mendicant Monks, as soon as they at all took to do with theology, is easily understood. Bonaventura, Albertus, and Thomas Aquinas were the greatest Mystics, not although, but because, they were *theologians* and Mendicant Monks.[1] The same is true of David of Augsburg and Theodoric of Freiburg. Widely-extended investigations have been instituted with the view of classifying the Mystics, and it has been thought possible to distinguish between a Scholastic, a Romanic, and a German, a Catholic, an Evangelical, and a Pantheistic Mysticism. But at bottom the distinctions are without importance. *Mysticism is always the same ; above all there are no national or confessional distinctions in it.* The differences never have to do with its essence, but only either with the *degree*, the *way* and the *energy* with which it is applied, or with its being predominantly directed upon the *intellect* or upon the *will*. Even as regards this last point it is only a question of difference of degree, and, at the same time, this last-mentioned distinction shows again very plainly the complete alliance of

[1] Herrmann remarks very correctly (Verkehr des Christen mit Gott 1. Aufl., p. 100) : " The (present day) lovers of Mysticism present on a diminished scale the same spectacle as the great Schoolmen ; they seek repose from the work of their faith in Mystic piety."

Mysticism with objective theology; for it is from this alliance that distinction springs. *Mysticism is Catholic piety in general, so far as this piety is not merely ecclesiastical obedience, that is, fides implicita.* Just for that reason Mysticism is not *one* form among others of pre-reformation piety—perhaps the latent evangelical—but is the Catholic expression of *individual* piety in general. The Reformation element that is ascribed to it lies here simply in this, that Mysticism, *i.e.*, Catholic piety, when developed in a particular direction, is led to the discernment of the inherent *responsibility* of the soul, of which no *authority* can again deprive it; and that it is thereby, at the same time, brought face to face with the question of the certitudo salutis (assurance of salvation), a question which can never again pass out of its view till it is solved in the act of faith. But where that question is determined, *Mysticism points beyond itself; for the entire scheme of thought in which it moves always admits only of a perpetually increasing approach to the Deity, and never allows the constant feeling of a sure possession to arise.* That, as a Christian, one must always be growing, was rightly discerned by the Catholic piety; but it never arrived at a clear and peaceful vision of the truth, that this growth can, and must, have its sure and inalienable basis in firm confidence in the God of grace, that is, in salvation. As for Catholic Christianity to-day, the Evangelical faith, described as " trust-faith " (" Fiduzglaube "), is a stumbling-block and foolishness, so also before the tribunal of Mediæval Mysticism it was a thing of which there was no understanding. For these Mystics, who framed and saw through so many sacred paradoxes, there was *one* paradox that remained hidden, namely, that in the spiritual life one can only *become* what he already is in faith. Only where they arrived at the discernment of this can they be described as precursors of the Reformation.

If Mysticism is withdrawn from the Catholic Church and set down as " Protestant," then Catholicism is emptied of its character, and evangelical faith becomes deteriorated. Is there then to be no living and individual Catholic piety? But where should we have to seek it, if not in Mysticism? In the three centuries before the Reformation, where can we find even a single

manifestation of truly religious life that had not its source in
" Mysticism " ?   Or is Mysticism to be denied to Catholicism,
because the latter requires, above everything else, devotion to the
Church and the Sacraments, and because the history of Mysticism
is the history of continual conflicts between it and sacramental
and authoritative ecclesiasticism?   But when did it become
permissible to regard such conflicts as showing that one of the
two factors is illegitimate?   Is there not a conflict also between
the unquestionably Catholic ideal of asceticism, and the equally
unquestionable Catholic ideal of world supremacy?   Are the
great Mystics not the great Saints of the Church?   Or shall it
be held, against all that appears, that this Church cannot produce
and tolerate independent piety *within its own lines?*   Now, no
Evangelical Christian, certainly, would ever think of confounding
his delight in the warm spiritual life which Catholic Christianity
exhibits in the centuries before the Reformation [1] with full
approval of it, if—one must, unfortunately, add it—he had made
clear to himself what evangelical faith is.   The inability to fight
one's way to such faith produces the craving for Mysticism
which is *then,* as one is of course a Protestant, claimed for
Protestantism.   The fondness, it is true, for " German "
Mysticism has received a severe check from records that have
shown that if one is enthusiastic about Master Eckhart, etc., and
derives edification from him, one must be still more enthusiastic
about St. Thomas, or about the Areopagite and Augustine.
But still more powerful checks will be needed if a view of
history is to be got quit of, which seems the proper one to all
fragmentary natures that deal in a dilettante way with religion,
theology and philosophy—a Mystic that does not become a
Catholic is a dilettante.   For one, what is of value in the

---

[1] Herrmann (Verkehr des Christen mit Gott 3 Aufl., p. 21) justly emphasises the
following also : " We must confess to ourselves that if we Evangelicals think we have
another kind of religion, we are in any case still far from having reached the thoroughness of culture which Catholicism possesses in that Mysticism . . . it is a wonderfully
perfect expression of a particular kind of religion.   The speculations of Catholic
Mysticism are of ancient date.   Apart from Neoplatonism, it has little peculiar to it in
this respect.   But in the capacity to make personal life the subject of observation
and delineation, it represents a height of attainment which Protestantism has not yet
reached."

Mystics is their "individualism," as if everything were already
implied under this form; for another, it is their feeling, no
matter what the "feeling" is for; for a third, it is the
pantheistic metaphysic, which, without much trouble, can be
abstracted from Mysticism; for a fourth, it is their ascetic views
and their resolution of Christology into the Ecce Homo, or into
the endless series of men travailing in birth with the Christ; for
a fifth, it is the light of "illuminism" (Aufklärung) which broke
forth from Mysticism.   What historian, with clear vision, will be
able to pass by these fruits of Mysticism without sympathy, or
with amused indifference?   What Christian will not draw with
heart-felt delight from the spring of fresh intuitions which flows
forth here?   Who, as an investigator of history, will not readily
acknowledge that an Evangelical Reformation was as impossible
about the year 1200 as it was prepared for about the year 1500?
But if Protestantism is not at some time yet, so far as it means
anything at all, to become entirely Mystical, it will never be
possible to make Mysticism Protestant without flying in the
face of history and Catholicism.[1]

[1] The right conception of Mysticism as Catholic piety has been taught—in opposition to Ullmann's "Reformers before the Reformation"—by Ritschl (Rechtfert. und
Versöhn. vol. I., Geschichte des Pietismus, vols. I.-III., Theologie und Metaphysik)
who has also given hints for further investigation (connection of the Mystics with the
Anabaptists, Hussites, etc.).   He has been followed by a large number of more
recent investigators.   Besides the works named above, p. 25, among which those of
Denifle are epoch-making, as having shown that Master Eckhart is, in his Latin
writings, entirely dependent on Thomas, and even in other respects owes his best to
him (Archiv f. Litt.-und K.-Gesch. des Mittelalters II., pp. 417-640; preparatory
work had already been done here by Bach in his monograph on Eckhart), see Lasson,
Meister Eckhart, 1866, also the more recent works on Tauler and the Friends of God
(Denifle), Pfeiffer's edition of the German Mystics (2 vols., 1845-57), Suso's Works,
edited by Denifle (1877), still further, Ritschl in the Zeitschr. f. K.-Gesch. IV., p.
337 ff., Strauch, Marg. Ebner und Heinrich v. Nördlingen, 1882.   On the earliest
German Mystics see Preger, Vorarbeiten z. einer Gesch. der deutschen Mystik (Ztschr.
f. die hist. Theol. 1869, and several essays in the Abhandl. der hist. Klasse d. bayer.
Akad. d. Wissensch., which, along with his comprehensive history of Mysticism, are
rich sources of material).   On Ruysbroek cf. Engelhardt, Rich. v. St. Victor und R.
1838; on Thomas à Kempis "de imitatione Christi" the literature is voluminous, cf.
Hirsche, Prolegomena z. einer neuen Ausg. 2 vols. 1873-83, the same author on the
Brothers of the Common Life in the R.-E². In general: Denifle, Das geistliche
Leben. Blumenlese aus den deutschen Mystikern und Gottesfreunden. 3. Aufl. 1880,
A very full delineation of Mysticism is also given in Thomasius-Seeberg, D.-Gesch.
2 Aufl. II. 1 pp. 261 ff., cf. also Seeberg, Ein Kampf um jenseitiges Leben. Lebens-

In the three pre-Reformation centuries, the individual Catholic piety, which we call Mysticism, had in it only the difference represented by varieties. It was rooted in the Neoplatonic-Augustinian view of the first and last things, as this has been described above, Vol. V. p. 106 f. : God and the soul, the soul and its God ; the one and the many, God and the creature. The soul that has departed from God must return to Him by *purification*, *illumination*, and essential *unification ;* it must be " unformed," " formed," and " transfigured " (" entbildet," " bildet," " überbildet "). With their more definite and richer vision of the inwardly experienced, Mediæval Saints spoke of the retirement of the soul within itself, of the contemplation of the outer world as a work of God, of the poverty and humility to which the soul must dispose itself, of conversion and return to God, and the school of suffering. But they also described the whole process in the most exact way. It begins with longing ; there follows the renunciation of the *creaturely*, but also of al self-righteousness and all self-conceit. That is the purification of the soul for true Christian poverty. What the Church offers in the shape of means—the Sacraments—must be used ; but all things must be taken up into the inner life. It is as signs of the

---

bild eines mittelalterlichen Frommen., 1889. I give no extracts from the writings of the German Mediæval Mystics, because I should like to avoid even seeming to countenance the error that they expressed anything one cannot read in Origen, Plotinus, the Areopagite, Augustine, Erigena, Bernard and Thomas, or that they represented religious progress, while in respect of intrinsic Christian worth, their tractates really stand for the most part lower than the writings of Augustine and Bernard. The importance of those works rests in this, that they were written in *German*, and that they were intended for the *laity*. They are therefore of inestimable value within the history of the *German* church and dogma. But in general history we may, and must, content ourselves with a characterisation. Whether, perhaps, they represent a considerable advance in the history of epistemology and metaphysic, is a question I do not trust myself to answer, nor does it fall to be considered here. As to the idea of regeneration, which is strongly emphasised in many Mystic writings, we must take in connection with it the silence on forgiveness of sins, that we may see how even this idea stood under the ban of intellectualism. The " clarification " which the Mysticism of the fourteenth century underwent in the fifteenth certainly related very specially to that aggressive intellectualism, so that the piety which expresses itself, for example, in the famous book de imitatione Christi (Thomas à Kempis) may be described as essentially Bernardine without Neoplatonic admixture, but yet only as Bernardine. A new, powerful element of joy in God, who forgives sin, and bestows faith, is sought for in vain.

love of God that they must be contemplated.   And as formerly
in Neoplatonism (cf. also Origen, and again the Areopagite)
everything sensible on which the lustre of a sacred tradition
rested, was highly esteemed as a *sign* of the eternal, and, therefore, as a means of spiritual exaltation, so by this piety also,
sacred signs were not discarded, but were multiplied and
increased.   As the more recent investigations have shown us,[1] in
the centuries before the Reformation a growing value was
attached, not only to the Sacraments, but to crosses, amulets,
relics, holy places, helpers of the needy, saints, etc.   As long as
what the soul seeks is not the rock of assurance, but means for
inciting to piety, it will create for itself a thousand holy things.
It is, therefore, an extremely superficial view that regards the
most inward Mysticism and the service of idols as contradictory.
The opposite view, rather, is correct ; such piety seeks for holy
signs, and clings to them.   It can at the same time hold
redemption by Christ as the supreme, all-embracing proof of the
love of God ;[2] but the sovereignty of Christ has not dawned
upon it, because it really regards the supreme proof of love as
the means by which the *possibility* of individual salvation is
given, that is, the impulse towards *imitation* is strengthened.
Just as little does the inward purification conflict with the
sacramental, as mediated by the sacrament of penance.   The
Mystics rather, with dwindling exceptions, always directed
attention, not to contrition merely, but to the whole confessional,
and to perfect repentance, that is, to the sacrament of penance.
After purification, there follows illumination.   Here the
Bernardine direction now comes in : there must be a being
formed in Christ, and after Christ's image.   In one's own
experience, Christ's life of poverty and His suffering humanity
must be reproduced, with a view to attaining to his Deity.   It
is well known how, in this direction, the tenderest training of the

[1] See the works of Gothein, Kolde, Kawerau, Haupt, and above all v. Bezold
(Gesch. der deutschen Reformation) on the inner state of Catholicism at the close of
the fifteenth century.   Succinct accounts in Lenz, Martin Luther, 1883 (introduction)
and Karl Müller, Bericht uber den gegenwärtigen Stand, etc., 1887.

[2] There are several Mystics of the fourteenth century who, in many passages of their
devotional writings, find their sole ground of comfort, as definitely as St. Bernard, in
the sufferings of Christ.

soul is combined with a distressingly sensuous presentation of
the sufferings of the "man" Jesus.   The *following* of Christ that
is prompted by compassion, the *imitation* of Him that has its
spring in love—these are required to a degree that can be
reached only by long practice, and by the most anxious strain-
ing of every thought.   Not unfrequently, this imitation then
becomes changed into the idea that one must become a
Christ one's self, must travail anew in birth with Christ.   There
were nuns, indeed, who fancied that they bore Christ in
their womb.   The highly-trained *imagination*, and *theory*, had
equal parts in the production of this idea.   The former—
inasmuch as it actually experienced what it passionately
contemplated ; the latter—inasmuch as in the Neoplatonic-
Augustinian tradition there was contained that idea of God and
the spiritual creature, according to which the appearance of the
Logos in Christ was only a special case in a long series; with Him
the indwelling of God in man took its beginning ; and, besides
this, all love of God is something so sovereign that it does not
admit of the intermingling of a third in the relation to which it
gives life.   But, on the other hand, this view of Christ as the first
in a series stood in agreement again with the view of His death
as an extraordinary event that is the basis of reconciliation with
God ; for, as this piety sacrifices no outward visible sign, so it
surrenders also no part of the sacred history ; only, it allows no
weight to it at the highest stage.   Yet, at countless times in the
case of the most distinguished Mystics, as already in the case of
St. Bernard, it is just at the highest stages of religious feeling
that confidence in Christ asserts itself ; for, as they derived
everything from divine grace—especially where the theology of
St. Thomas exercised its influence—so this grace is discerned in
the Christ who is our righteousness.   Further, there was added
here the trinitarian speculation, as it was developed from the
thought of *love*.   Thus the piety shown by Richard of St. Victor in
the earlier period, by Bonaventura and others in the later, was able
to attach itself most intimately to this intractable dogma of the
Trinity, and also to the other dogma of the Incarnation.   The
infinite love must be contemplated in the Mystery of the Trinity,
and the highest point of the spirit's enlightenment is reached

when in prayer, in knowledge, and in vision, man becomes
absorbed in the great mystery of the union of deity and
humanity, and contemplates the indifference of opposites
(indifferentia oppositorum), seeing how the Creator and the
creature, the lofty and the lowly, the being and the not-being
coalesce in one. From all these speculations, in which the old
formulas are placed in the light of omnipotent love, in which the
boldest and most complex theology is finally led back to the
All-One, and converted into *feeling*, there resulted an intense
deepening of inner life. This inner life was again discovered,
and there was given to it the place of central command. But
it found much richer expression still than in the days of
Neoplatonism ; for, in those centuries before the Reformation,
in conjunction with the most frightful self-torturing, nay in the
midst of them (think of St. Elizabeth), and in conjunction with
whimsical or insane ideas, the elevating power of suffering, and
the purifying influence of pain, were proved by experience and
preached. What an ennobling of feeling, and what a deepening
of the life of the soul issued from this—a Renaissance before and
alongside of the Renaissance—cannot be described. One must
read the writings in poetry and prose, for example the verses
of Jacopone,[1] or the treatises and sermons of the German
Mystics, to see how even the language here underwent a
regeneration. A lyric poetry that awakens a response in us
exists only from the thirteenth century, and what force the Latin
and German tongues are capable of developing in describing the
inner life we have been taught by the Mendicant Monks. From
the discernment that lowliness and poverty, scorn and contempt,
shame and misery, suffering and death, are aids to the saint's
progress, from the contemplation of the Man Jesus, from compassion, and pain, and humility, there sprang for Western
Christianity, in the age of the Mendicant Monks, that inner
elevation and that enrichment of feeling and of moral sensibility
which was the condition for all that was to grow up in the time
that followed. One speaks of the Renaissance and the
Reformation, and comprehends in these words, taken together,

---

[1] See Schlüter u. Storck, Ausgewählte Gedichte Jacopone's, 1864. Thode, l.c. pp.
398 ff.

the basis of our present-day culture; but both have a strong common root in the elevation of religious and æsthetic feeling in the period of the Mendicant Monks.

But the Catholic character of this elevation shows itself most plainly in this, that with repentance, faith, and love to Christ, the process is not concluded : man must become entirely nothing ; he must pass out of himself, in order, finally, to be merged into the Godhead. There is meant by this, certainly, the highest spiritual freedom also (see, *e.g.*, the " Deutsche Theologie "); but as the freedom is enfolded in the metaphysical thought that God is all and the individual nothing, freedom can only be conceived of as absorption into the deity. He alone can experience this union with God who has followed the way of the Church, and has been an imitator of Christ. But how can the command be given to adhere to the historical, when all the powers of the imagination have been let loose, and it has been declared the organ for coalescing with the Godhead. The Church Mystics made earnest attempts to check the pantheistic, " extravagant," wild-growing piety ; but they themselves frequently were at least incautious with their final directions, nay, to these the ardent application was wanting, so long as they had still respect to something that lay outside of God and the soul (even the Trinity here was felt to be something disturbing ; the God with whom the soul has to do at this supreme height of exaltation is the solitary One). Thomas himself, " the normal dogmatic theologian," gave the strongest impulse to this restoration of the most extravagant Mysticism. He was followed by Eckhart and others.[1] According to Thomas, the soul can already here on earth so receive God into itself that it enjoys in the fullest sense the vision (visio) of His essence. It itself already dwells in

---

[1] Although, shortly before his death, Eckhart had retracted everything unecclesiastical in his writings, two years after his death a process was instituted against him, *i.e.*, twenty-eight of his propositions were condemned, partly as heretical, and partly as open to suspicion (Bull of John XXII., 1329). On this condemnation, and on the relation of Suso to Eckhart, see Denifle in the Archiv. f. L.-u. K.-G. des Mittelalters II. and Seeberg, Ein Kampf um jenseitiges Leben. 1889, p. 137 ff. Even Suso could not quite escape the reproach of polluting the land with heretical filth. It was always the Ultra's, who, by making an appeal to them, brought discredit upon " Church " Mystics.

heaven. The earthly, that still clings to it, is, as it were, as un-
substantial as the earthly in the consecrated elements. But if
the soul is capable, through rapture (per raptum), of such a
flight from its nothingness to God, if God can enter into its innermost depth, then—here is the necessary inversion of view—the
soul itself includes, in its innermost being, a deeply hidden
divine element. Pantheism is transformed into self-deification.
The divine is at bottom the capacity of the soul to abstract and
emancipate itself from all that is phenomenal; it is the pure feeling of spiritual freedom and exaltedness above all that is and
can be thought. In this feeling, which arises as an act of grace,
and is only guarded by this co-efficient in its mood from the
pride of self-assertion, the soul has the sense of being one with
the divine Being, who, in the Catholic view, is Himself best described by negative definitions. In these negative definitions
the Mediæval Mystics went much further than Augustine and the
Areopagite.[1] We must go back to Valentinus and Basilides, to
the Βύθος (abyss), to the Σιγή (silence) and the Οὐκ ὢν θεός (the
God that is not), to find the fitting parallels to the "Abysmal
Substance" ("Abgründlichen Substanz"), the "Waste Deity"
("Wüsten Gottheit"), the "Silent Silence" ("Stillen Stillheit").
In this hot forcing-house of thought, religion was not really
matured, but the Mediæval man had his sense of self-importance
awakened. In the Thomist Mysticism, which, of course, always
insists on principle that the essential distinction between God
and man must be recognised, both the whole process and the
supreme attainment are intellectually conditioned. *Knowledge*
is the means of reaching spiritual freedom, and the highest state
attained is nothing but the natural result of the *absolute* knowledge given in vision. Here Thomas and his disciples adhere
strictly to Augustine, who also admitted no progress in religious
life without advancing knowledge, and for whom the highest
fellowship with God had also no other content than that of the
visio dei, *i.e.*, of essential knowledge. The contemplation that
rises to intuition suffers thereby no qualitative change; for intuition is simply that form of knowledge in which every medium
has fallen away, in which the subject, having become wholly in-

---

[1] Cf. especially Eckhart and Suso.

tellect, apprehends the purely spiritual object, and so, also, as there is no longer any hindering restriction, coalesces with it. Yet in this conception of the contemplated end there was presupposed the Anselmic conviction, that all objects of faith here below can be made rational, so that the whole ascent to the Supreme end can take place through the intellect. Where this conviction, however, became uncertain, then, if the final end of union to God was to be held as attainable in this world, it could no longer be contemplated as enjoyment of God and eternal life *through the intellect*. But this latter idea was unsatisfactory also for this reason, that the Thomists had to admit that the end thus described could always be reached only per raptum, *i.e.*, intermittently and seldom. Hence we see how, after the appearance of Duns Scotus, and after the development of Nominalism, the end is otherwise described. The confidence in the rationality of the objects of faith threatens to disappear, *on the other hand the religious impulse towards constant supreme fellowship with God grows stronger*—therefore the enjoyment of God and eternal life came to be placed in the *will*, which, in general, indeed, had increased attention directed to it in Nominalist science.[1] *Salvation consists in union of will with God*, in the rest which the creaturely will finds in the will of God, that is, in surrender and repose. That this way of viewing things likewise found an eccentric expression was unavoidable from the monastic character of all Catholic piety. Yet a very marked advance was certainly made here, which directly prepared the way for the Reformation; for, first, piety was now delivered from intermixture with those speculative monstrosities, which really served only to stupefy simple devout feeling (of course the speculative philosophers will always prefer Thomas to Duns); second, a way was indicated by which the soul might attain to the feeling of *constant* fellowship with God. This "Nominalist" Mysticism tended more and more to supplant the Thomist in the 15th century.[2] *One must give up his own will to the will of God.*

[1] To this distinction between the Thomist and the Quietist (Nominalist) Mysticism Ritschl was the first to point, see Gesch. des Pietismus I., p. 467 ff., and Zeitschr. f. K.-Gesch. IV., p. 337 ff; also already in the first vol. of Rechtfertig. u. Versöhn.-Lehre.

[2] About 1500 it seems to have gained the ascendency; cf. the attitude of Staupitz

The Nominalists themselves, certainly, failed to see clearly where
the divine will is to be sought for, and what it is, and just on
that account much wild growth still developed itself even here.
But only within Nominalist piety could the question about
assurance of salvation (certitudo salutis) arise, because there
was no longer a building upon the intellect, because the pointing
to bare authority was bound, in the course of time, to be felt unsatisfactory, and because the problem was correctly stated, as
being the question, namely, about the power that is capable of
breaking self-will and leading the will to God.[1]

This revival of piety from the thirteenth century to the fifteenth
would not be perfectly described were not a fact, at the same time,
strongly emphasised, which, on first view, seems very paradoxi-

and Thomas Münzer.   Even the "German Theology," of which Luther was so fond,
is quietistic.

[1] In the section on the history of theology the characteristics and significance of
Nominalism will receive a still further illustration.   Meanwhile, however, let it be
noted here, that by its "positiveness," based on mere authority, Nominalism purchased its truer insight into the nature of religion at a heavy cost.   Here Anselm and
Thomas undoubtedly hold a higher position ; but these men were hindered by their
intellectualism from doing justice to the Christian religion as a *historic magnitude and
force.*   What I have set forth in these pages (p. 97 ff.) has been keenly assailed by
Lasson and Raffaele Mariano.   Plainly enough they put before me the alternative of
irreligious criticism or blind faith (Köhlerglauben), when on their side they claim for
the Thomist Mysticism that it is the only form of religion in which faith and thought,
history and religious independence, are reconciled.   It must be the endeavour of each
of us to find something in his own way.   What we have ultimately to do with here is
the great problem as to what history and the person of Christ are in religion, and
then there is the other problem also as to whether religion is contemplation or something more serious.   That the end to which our striving is directed is the same—the
seeking, finding, and keeping hold of God—may be confidently granted on both sides.
But my opponents have an easier position than I have : they can prove—and I recognise this proof—that the piety that culminates in Mysticism and the old ecclesiastical dogma hang together, *and they can at the same time let the question rest as to
what reality of fact answers to the dogma.*   That is to say, the dogma renders them
the best services, just when they are at liberty to contemplate it as a mobile and
elastic magnitude, which hovers between the poles of an inferior actuality and that
"highest," which can never have been actual as earthly : out of the darkness there is
a pressing forward to the light ; *luminous clouds show the path !*   But I seek in the
dogma itself of the Christian Church for something concrete, namely the Gospel of
Jesus Christ as the Lord.   The tradition which the dogma represents is treated with
more respect when it is criticised and sifted, than when one takes it as it is, in order
ultimately to bid it a secret farewell, *i.e.*, to substitute for it something quite different
—namely the idea.

cal, namely, *the revival of a life of practical activity in the service of one's neighbour.* We should think that where Catholic
piety, *i.e.,* Mysticism, flourished, monastic contemplation and asceticism would repress everything else.[1] In point of fact, there
was a weighty problem for that piety here. Yet the way in
which it was solved shows again most distinctly that in the
Mendicant Order movement we have to do with a reformation of
the Church. This movement strengthened, theoretically, the
old Catholic position, that the contemplative life is higher than
the practical. But as it presents itself in St. Francis as a movement born of love, so also from the first, as " imitation of the poor
life of Jesus," and as " Apostolic life," it recognised in *loving
activity the highest sphere for its exercise.* In this way the old
Monasticism was superseded, which rendered services of love
only to the hierarchy, the princes and the papal policy, but
otherwise retired within itself, and felt service to a poor brother
to be a work of supererogation. It was the Mendicant Orders
and their theologians who first gave a conspicuous place again
to the command, " Love thy neighbour as thyself." They
praised the contemplative life; they still continued always to
maintain the distinction between it and the practical; but they
drew this distinction in such a way that one living in contemplation (that is, the monk) was, nevertheless, required to
serve his neighbour with all his powers, while the Christian occupied with the affairs of life, was never justified in leaving out
of account concern for his brother. Thus there came to exist
between the contemplative and active lives a wide neutral province, so to speak, which belonged to both, to the former as well
as to the latter—the province of self-denying love. The love of
God on the part of monk and layman could prove its existence
only in the love of one's neighbour. Hence it is to be understood how enthusiastic Mystics used expressions that sound like
an exaltation of the active life above the contemplative; what
they had in their mind was unfeigned brotherly love, mercy,
gentleness, the spirit that returns good for evil, and active

---

[1] On the relation of Metaphysic to Asceticism, or, say, of Mysticism to Asceticism,
see the dissertation of Bender in the Archiv. f. Gesch. der Philos. vol. 6, pp. 1 ff.,
208 ff., 301 ff.

ministration to need. Neither their " intellectualism " nor their
" quietism " hindered them in their powerful preaching of mercy,
but rather strengthened them in it ; for they would no longer recognise any monachism, or any service of God, that disregarded
the service of one's neighbour. The obligation to make one's self
every man's servant in love was first plainly asserted again by
Francis, and after him it was repeatedly enforced as *the highest
attainment of Christian life* by Thomas and Bonaventura, by
Eckhart, Suso, Tauler, Thomas à Kempis, and all the hundred
active witnesses to Christian piety in the centuries before the
Reformation.[1] The simple relation of man to man, sanctified by
the Christian command of love and by the peace of God, issued
forth from all the traditional corporations and castes of the
Middle Ages, and set itself to break them up. Here, also, the advent of a new age, in which, certainly, only a few blossoms developed into fruit, was brought about by the history of *piety*.
But this piety, although it always continued to call more loudly
for reform in the affairs of the Church, still remained under the
ban of the idea that God gives grace in the measure in which a
man progresses in love. How this state of things was to be
remedied, no one had any inkling.

In what precedes it has already been indicated several times
that, while maintaining the line of distinction, the Mendicant
Orders brought about inwardly (to some extent even outwardly) a
mutual approximation of monks and laity. The activity of the
former among the people on the one hand, and the awakening
of a strong religious life among the laity on the other, brought
them together. But it was in general the characteristic of the
period under review, that the laity always came more to the
front, and in the fifteenth century they took their place in their free
religious associations alongside the monks in theirs, though,
no doubt, as a rule, there was dependence on the monastic
unions. The period from 1046 to 1200 was the period of the
monachising of the priests ; that from 1200 to 1500 brought the
monachising of the laity (notice, also, the participation of women
in the Mystic and charitable movements) ; but *the latter* process

[1] With Eckhart the direction originated to let even ecstacy go, though it should be
as great as that of Paul, if one can help a poor man even with a sop.

was not carried out without a deeply penetrating alteration of
Monachism, and it is to be observed that the *charitable* element
was here determinative. When, in spite of earnest reforms, the
Mendicant Orders were now, nevertheless, unable (from the end
of the fourteenth century) fully to recover the position and confidence
they had once enjoyed, the free Christian associations came quite
into the foreground. But they secured, if I see aright, a large
measure of influence only on *German* soil. What they did for
the German was done for the Romanic peoples, naturally more
mobile, but less susceptible of abiding impressions, by the great
Preachers of Repentance, of whom there was no lack among them
at any period, from the time of Francis to that of Savonarola,
and who, along with their preaching of repentance, knew also
how to stir national and political feeling. But it was only the
Anglo-Saxons and the Czechs, hitherto kept in subjection and
poverty by other nations, who understood, at this period, how to
derive from the Franciscan doctrine of poverty a politico-national
and an ecclesiastical programme, and among whom a great
movement took place, in which the rise to independent piety
united itself with a national rise and emancipation. In both
countries the result, certainly, did not correspond with the first
steps. In England, the movement ran its course comparatively
quickly, and in Bohemia deeper religious motives were unable to
hold their ground alongside the national and political aims im-
periously asserting themselves, and at first, at least, were overborne by motives of an ecclesiastical, a social revolutionary, and
an anti-hierarchical character, though afterwards the religious
element wrought its way to the front again.

Any one, therefore, wishing to describe the stages in the history of piety during this period, must begin, by way of introduction, with a view of the Lyonnese, Lombard and Catholic
" Poor."   Then follows the establishment of the Mendicant
Orders, who, by developing the principle of poverty, the apostolic life and repentance, as well as by preaching love (caritas)
raise monachism to its highest point, and free it from its restrictions, but at the same time impart to it a most powerful
influence upon the lay world. The Church succeeds in taking
this movement into its service, in creating by means of it an

interest in Church institutions among the aspiring lay Christianity, and in placing a check upon heresy. The Mendicant
Orders made themselves masters of all the forces of the Church ;
above all, they developed more deeply the individual Mystic
piety, by grasping more firmly its old fundamental elements,
poverty and obedience, adding to these love, and gave it a
powerful force of attraction, which united itself to the aspiring
individualism and trained it. By urgent preaching of repentance, which pointed to future judgment, even the widest circles
were stirred, and the new movement settled down, in part, into
monk-like associations (the third Order). But the principle of
" poverty " embraced not only an ascetically religious, but also
a social and anti-hierarchical, nay, even a political ideal, for the
neutral state could be regarded as the power that had to deprive the Church of her property, or, in the event of her being
recalcitrant, to execute judgment upon her. The new movement united itself therefore with the apocalyptic ideas, which,
in spite of Augustine, had never died out in the West, and
which had received a new development from Joachim and his
following.[1] Partly within the Order, and partly beyond it, an
apocalyptic socio-political excitement grew up, asserting itself
in a hundred different ways. Its relative justification over
against the rich worldly hierarchy was furnished by the wide
hold which it everywhere secured for itself : it made its appearance in all lands, and it continued to exist, always again gathering new strength, till far on in the period of the Reformation.
In the second half of the thirteenth century the Mendicant
Orders reached, at least in the Romanic lands, their highest
point of influence. From that time they began to decline :
after the close of the century the movement as a whole was
broken up and distributed among the efforts of individual men.
The great struggle about poverty in the age of John XXII.
had, so far as it was *religious*, only a limited importance. In
Germany, on the other hand, there began, from the end of the

[1] See Wadstein, Die eschatologische Ideengruppe in den Hauptmomenten ihrer
christlich-mittelalterlichen Gesammtentwickelung, 1896. The details of these ideas
scarcely belong to the history of theology, not to speak of the history of dogma ; but
as was the case with the ideas about the devil, they exercised a very strong influence.

thirteenth century, the "German" Mystic movement, *i.e.*, the introduction of the impassioned individual piety of the monastic theologians into the circles of the laity. For a century and more, the work of bringing about an inward conversion of the laity in Germany was carried on, and it was quite specially by Mendicant monks, chiefly Dominican, that this service was rendered. (David of Augsburg, Theodoric of Freiburg, Master Eckhart, Tauler, Merswin, the "Friends of God," Suso, Henry of Nördlingen, Margaret Ebner, Ruysbroek, etc.)

While in the Romanic lands the Mendicant Orders grew weaker, and in Germany the religious life, still through their influence partly, slowly advanced, the world-ruling Church pursued a course of complete self-abandonment at Avignon, and seemed to have the deliberate wish to subject the ecclesiastical fidelity of the already imperilled piety to the severest test. Nay, how firmly the papacy and the Church as an institution still held together souls and the world is shown by the confusions and complaints which, when the great schism ensued, became still more numerous. Under the impression produced by frightful elemental calamities, the apocalyptic, anti-hierarchical ideas became the real danger, especially as even Mendicant monks were regarded as enemies of the papacy. But only in England did a great movement at that time result. The law of God, poverty, the Augustinian theology—these were the dominant ideas under which Wyclif undertook his Catholic reform and preached to the reigning Church judgment and repentance—a second Francis, of more understanding but less resolute, more cautious but less free. Beyond England at first no similar movement was anywhere to be traced ; but it was everywhere apparent that the world had entered upon a religious age, in which the multiplicity of aspirations testified that the dissolution of what existed at the time was felt to be the signal for a new construction—the ridicule and frivolity of some Italian poets and novelists of an inferior order have no claim whatever to be considered. In its greatest representatives, the Renaissance, especially the German, which was much more important in the realm of thought than the Italian, felt that it had outgrown neither the Catholic Church nor the Christian religion.

What was really breaking up was mediæval *society*, mediæval *institutions*, the mediæval *world*.[1] So far as the Church was interwoven with this last, nay, constituted the chief part of it, and in this form had hitherto been held as holy—a state of things on which the Mendicant Orders had been able to work no change—the crisis was already prepared. But there was no proclaiming of separation from the Church ; there was a seeking for means for politically reforming it (this almost alone was the question at the Reform Councils), and monachism also took itself seriously to task.[2] From the end of the fourteenth century till the time of the Reformation there was a continuous succession of efficient reforms in the older Orders and in the younger, of course on the basis already laid. If the signs do not mislead, the Mendicant Orders in particular rose higher again in the course of the fifteenth century and gained an always increasing influence on popular circles, in the Romanic lands through the occasional appearing of preachers of repentance, in Germany through earnest, steady work. But it is certainly unmistakable that all this did not yet give satisfaction and rest. The proof of this lies—apart from other sectarian agitations—in the fact that the Wyclifite movement, which in literary form had crept in among the Czechs, who were already deeply infected with apocalyptic excitement and Franciscan fanaticism, could strike its roots so deeply in Bohemia under Huss, and could occasion so terrible a revolution, a revolution that shook the half of Germany. From the confused intermingling of "religious, social, national, Joachim-apocalyptic, chiliastic, specifically Wyclifite and Waldensian tendencies, thoughts, hopes and dreams," individuals gathered out what appealed to them. All shades were represented, from the wild

---

[1] See Lamprecht, Zum Verständniss der wirthschaftlichen und Socialen Wandlungen in Deutschland vom 14. zum 16. Jahrh., in der Ztschr. f. Social-und Wirthschaftgesch. I., 2. 3, pp. 191-263. The significance of the state of the towns is specially to be observed (see the works by Schmoller).

[2] Höfler, Die Romanische Welt und ihr Verhältniss zu den Reformideen des Mittelalters, 1878. Maurenbrecher, Gesch. d. Kathol. Reformation I., 1880. Kolde. Die deutsche Augustiner-Congregation, 1879. Dittrich, Beiträge z. Gesch. der Kathol. Reform im 1. Drittel des 16. Jahrh. I. u. II. (Görres-gesellsch.-Jahrbuch V. 1884, p. 319 ff., VII. 1886, p. 1 ff.).

warriors of God, who inflicted judgment with fire and sword on the Church and on all despisers of divine law, to the quiet brothers, who really judged the Church as hardly, and clung to as utopian hopes regarding the adjustment of human relationships, but who were willing to wait in patience and quietness.   In the fifteenth century the currents of all foregoing attempts at reform flowed together; they could converge into *one* channel; for *all* of them sprang originally from one source — the doctrine of poverty, wedded to apocalyptic and to certain Augustinian thoughts, that is, Catholicism. " Silent and soft is poverty's step," Jacopone had once sung in his wonderful hymn. That was truly no prophecy of the future.

Even after the papacy, by an unparalleled diplomacy, had released itself from the oppressive requirements of the Reform Councils, when the nations were defrauded of the sure prospect of a reform of the Church, when the Popes, with their great undertaking of securing a sovereign state, descended to the lowest depths of degradation and spoke of reform with scorn, piety as a rule did not lose faith in the *Church*, but only in her representation at the time, and in her corrupt order.   It is a mistake to conclude from the contempt for priests and for lazy monks to the existence of an evangelical spirit.   There can express itself in such contempt the purest and most obedient Catholic piety.   This piety displayed in the second half of the fifteenth century a strength of vigorous impulse, in some measure even a power, greater than ever before.   And it remained immovably the *old* piety.   It attracted the laity more powerfully ; it became richer in good works and in the spirit of love; it united clergy and laity in common religious undertakings ; it wrought for the deepening and strengthening of the inner life.   But just on these grounds it attached higher value to outward signs, sought for them, increased their number, and gave itself up to them.   One may detect in this something of unrest, of dissatisfaction ; but we must not forget that this is just what belongs to Catholic piety.   This piety seeks, not for a basis of rock, but for *means of help*, and even where it is most inward, and seems to have bidden farewell to everything ex-

ternal, it must confess that, openly or secretly, it still uses the
narcotics and stimulants.

An enormous revolution, ever again retarded, was preparing
in the fifteenth century. *But this revolution threatened institutions, political and ecclesiastical ;* threatened the Church, not its
gospel, the new dogma-like doctrines, not the old dogma.
That a reformation of piety in the sense of *faith* was preparing,
is suggested by nothing whatever that is historically apprehensible ; for the most radical opponents, and the most faithful
supporters, of the dominant Church, were at one in this, that
the forces for a reform of the ecclesiastical life were bound up
in Augustine and Francis. The Church doctrines that became
the subject of controversy were really no Church doctrines as
yet ;[1] and then again—even the most radical Church programme had its strong roots, and its justifying title, in elements
of the vulgar Church doctrine. Thus dogma remained substantially unassailed. How could anyone imagine, in the age
of Nominalism, that the salvation by reform must come from
doctrine, so long as the authority of the dogmatic tradition
remained untouched ? And yet, certainly, it would be a very
childish view that would regard the Reformation as something
absolutely new, because no direct preparatory stages of it can
be pointed out. Individualism, the force of personal life, the
irresistible demands for a reconstruction of civil life and social
order, the needs of a piety always growing more restless, the
distrust of the hierarchy, the rising consciousness of personal
responsibility and craving for personal certainty, the conviction
hat Christ is in His Church, and yet that He is not in ecclesiasticism—all these things could not have reached the ends
contemplated by them without a Reformation, which, to outward
view, appeared less radical than the programme of the devastating and burning Hussites, but in reality left that programme far
behind it. And the piety, *i.e.*, the ecclesiastical faith itself, had,
among the manifold elements it included, the new element implanted within it, in the shape of words of Christ and doctrines

---

[1] The doctrines of indulgence, of the hierarchy, of free will, etc. Certainly there
was opposition also to some old traditional doctrines (eternal damnation, purgatory,
etc.), but it was not thorough-going.

of Paul, in the life displayed by every Christian who, through trust in the grace of God in Christ, had found inward deliverance from the law of grace-dispensations and merit, and from the law of the letter.

Under a theology that had degenerated into a tangled brake, from the hundreds of new religious-ecclesiastical institutions, societies, and brotherhoods, from the countless forms in which the sacred was embodied and sought after, from the sermons and the devotional literature of all kinds, there was to be heard *one* call, distinct and ever more distinct—the call to vigorous religious life, to practical Christianity, to the religion that is really religion. " Say unto my soul, I am thy salvation "—this prayer of Augustine was the hidden force of the unrest among the nations, especially the Germanic, in the fifteenth century. Dogmatically expressed : there was a seeking for a sure doctrine of salvation ; but one knew not himself what he sought for. The uncertain and hesitating questions got only uncertain and hesitating answers. Even at the present day we cannot escape the charm that clings just to such questions and answers ; for they let us see into the living movement of the heart ; but he for whom religion has become so serious a matter that he seeks, not for charms, but for nourishment, will not be inclined to exchange Luther's Smaller Catechism and his hymns for all the wealth, beauty, and freshness of the German devotional literature of the fourteenth and fifteenth centuries.[1]

1 What is here said applies also to Gothic architecture. It is certainly the greatest, most perfect, and most harmonious product of architectural art since the time of the Greek temple ; indeed, it is the only style that is all-pervasive, and that embraces all in unity, as the Greek temple style does. In itself it proves that the mediæval period at its highest point of attainment possessed a harmonious culture which of its kind was perfect. But just on that account the Gothic is the style of mediæval Catholic Christianity, the style of Mysticism and Scholasticism. It awakens exactly the feelings, emotions, and sensations of awe which the Catholic piety, of which it is born, seeks to produce ; just on that account also it is of *Romanic* origin, and the history of its spread is simply a parallel to the history of the spread of Romanic piety. Perhaps the deepest thing that can be said about the Gothic, about its ineffable charm and its æsthetic impressiveness—though at the same time it suggests the inevitable reaction of Protestant piety against it—has been put into words by Goethe in his Wahlverwandschaften (Hempel's edition, XV., pp. 143, 137, 173) : " . . . She sat down in one of the seats (in a Gothic chapel), and it seemed to her, as she looked up and around, as if she was, and yet was not, as if she realised

2. *On the History of Ecclesiastical Law.—The Doctrine of the Church.*

" In the fifty years that elapsed between the appearing of the Gratian book of laws (which contains, besides the Isodorian, numerous forgeries of the Gregorian Deusdedit, Anselm and Cardinal Gregorius) and the pontificate of Innocent III., the papal system achieved for itself complete supremacy. In the Roman Courts justice was dispensed according to Gratian's law, in Bologna the teaching was regulated thereby, even the Emperor Frederick I. already had his son, Henry VI., instructed in the Decretum and in Roman law. The whole decretal legislation from 1159 to 1320 was framed on the basis of Gratian, and presupposes him. The same holds good of the dogmatic of Thomas in the relative material, while the scholastic dogmatic in general was made entirely dependent in questions of Church constitution on the favourite science of the clergy at the time, namely, jurisprudence, as it had been drawn up by Gratian, Raymund, and the other collectors of decretals. The

her identity and yet realised it not, as if all this that was before her was to vanish from her and she from herself, and only when the sun passed from the hitherto very brightly illumined (stained glass) window did she awake." " From all figures there looks forth only the purest existence ; all must be pronounced, if not noble, at least good. Cheerful collectedness, ready recognition of something above us to be reverenced, quiet self-devotion in love and expectant waiting, are expressed in all faces, in all attitudes. The aged man with the bald head, the boy with the curly locks, the sprightly youth, the grave-minded man, the glorified saint, the hovering angel, all seem to know the bliss of an innocent satisfaction, of a devout expectancy. The commonest thing that happens has a touch of heavenly life about it, and an act of divine service seems perfectly adapted to every nature. For such a religion most men look as for a vanished golden age, a lost paradise." But on the other hand : " As for myself, this mutual approximation and intermingling of the sacred and the sensuous is certainly not to my liking ; I am not pleased when people set apart and consecrate and adorn certain special places, that thereby alone they may foster and maintain the feeling of piety. No surroundings, not even the commonest, should disturb the feeling in us of the divine, which can accompany us everywhere, and make every place a consecrated temple. I would like to see an important religious service held in the saloon, where people usually take food, gather for social inter-course, and enjoy themselves with games and dancing. The highest, the most excellent thing, in man is formless, and we must guard against giving it shape in anything save noble deeds."

theory, as well as the texts and proofs relating thereto, were
derived by the theologians from these collections of laws."[1]
With regard to the nature of the Church, while the Augustinian
definition was firmly retained, that the Church is the community
of believers or of the predestinated, the idea was always gaining
a fuller acceptance that the hierarchy is the Church, and that
the Pope, as successor of Peter, and episcopus universalis, unites
in himself all the powers of the Church.   The German Kings
themselves were in great part to blame for this development, for
while they, and, above all, the Hohenstaufens, led the struggle
for the rights of the State against the papacy, they left the
latter to its own irresponsible action in the ecclesiastical domain.
Only when it was now too late did Frederick II. point out in
his address to the Kings of the Franks and Angles (ad reges
Francorum et Anglorum) that the hierarchy must be restored
by an inner reform to its original poverty and humility.[2]   In its
development to autocratic supremacy *within the Church* and
the Churches, a check was put upon the papacy from the
beginning of the fourteenth century only from France.[3]

We cannot be required to show here what particular conclusions
were drawn by the Popes and their friends from the idea of the
Church as a civil organism of law in the thirteenth century and
in the first half of the fourteenth, and in what measure these
conclusions were practically carried out.   The leading thoughts
were the following :   (1) ·*The hierarchical organisation is
essential to the Church, and in all respects the Christianity of
the laity is dependent on the mediation of the priests* (" properly
ordained "), *who alone can perform ecclesiastical acts.*   When
we pass from Cyprian to Gregory I., from the latter to
Pseudoisidore and Gregory VII., we might conclude on superficial consideration that the principle just stated had long been
determinative.   But when we enter into detail, and take into

---

[1] See Janus, p. 162 f.

[2] See the passage in Gieseler II., 2, 4 ed. p. 153.

[3] The "pragmatic sanction" of Louis the Holy is a forgery of the year 1438 (or
about this time), as Scheffer-Boichorst has shown in the Kleinere Forsch. z. Gesch.
des Mittelalters (Mitth. des Instituts f. österreich. Geschichtsforschung VIII., Bd. 3
part ; published separately, 1887).   In the first edition of this work I had still treated
this sanction as genuine, but my attention was immediately directed to the mistake.

account the ecclesiastical legislation from the time of Innocent
III., we observe how much was still wanting to a strict application of it in theory and practice till the end of the twelfth
century. Only from the time of the fourth Lateran Council was
full effect given to it, expressly in opposition to the Catharist
and Waldensian parties.[1] (2) *The sacramental and judicial
powers of the priests are independent of their personal worthiness.*
This also was an old principle ; but after having been long
latent, it was now strongly emphasised, asserted in opposition
to all "heretical" parties, and so turned to account that by it
the hierarchy protected themselves against all demand for
reform, and, above all, evaded the appeal to resume the
apostolic life. Whoever returned from the "heretical" parties
to the bosom of the Church was required to declare that he recognised the celebration of Sacraments by sinful priests.[2]
(3) *The Church is a visible community with a constitution given
to it by Christ (even as such it is the body of Christ* [corpus
Christi]) ; *as a visible, constituted community it has a double power,
namely, the potestas spiritualis and the potestas temporalis*
(spiritual and temporal power). *Through both is it, as it shall
endure till the end of the world, superior to the transitory states,
which are subordinate to it. To it, therefore, must all states and
all individuals be obedient de necessitate salutis* (as a necessary
condition of salvation) ; *nay, the power of the Church extends
itself even to heretics* [3] *and heathen.*[4] Even these principles [5] have
their root in the Augustinian doctrine of the Church ; [6] but

---

[1] See especially the first and third decrees of the Synod ; Mansi XXII., p. 982 sq.,
Hefele V., p. 879 ff. It was not, however, carried out to its full logical issue, as is
shown by the admission of the right of the laity to baptise in case of emergency, by
the recognition of absolution by a layman in casu mortis, and by the treatment of
the sacrament of marriage.

[2] See *e.g.* the confession of Durandus, Innocent III., ep. XI. 196.

[3] On the Inquisition, see Janus, p. 254 ff., and Thomas, Summa Sec. Sec. quæst.
11 art. 3 conclusio : " Hæresis est peccatum, per quod meruerunt per mortem a
mundo excludi " ; art. 4 concl.

[4] Augustinus Triumphus (ob. 1328), Summa de potest. eccl. ad Johannem XXII.,
Quæst. 23 art. 1 : " Pagani jure sunt sub papæ obedientia." Yet this continued a
controverted question in spite of the Bull " Unam sanctam."

[5] The hierarchy together with the monks are held as properly the Church.

[6] There were certainly also passages to be found in Augustine that could be

from the logical expression and thorough-going application which they received between 1050 and 1300, they present the appearance of an unheard-of innovation. They obtained their complete formulation from Boniface VIII.;[1] but long before him the Popes acted according to these principles. The worst consequence was not the undervaluing,[2] repression and serious deterioration of civic life (here, on the contrary, there can be discerned also many salutary effects in the interests of popular freedom), but the inevitable profanation of religion, inasmuch as all its aims and benefits were perverted and falsified through the light being foreign to them in which they presented themselves from the standpoint of *Church law ;* and obedience to an external human institution, that was subject to all errors of human passion and sin, was raised to the first condition of Christian life. " It was this Church on which there fell that heaviest responsibility that has ever been incurred in history : by all violent means it applied as pure truth a doctrine that was vitiated and distorted to serve its omnipotence, and under the feeling of its inviolability abandoned itself to the gravest immorality ; in order to maintain itself in such a position, it struck deadly blows at the spirit and conscience of the nations, and drove many of the more highly gifted, who had secretly withdrawn from it, into the arms of unbelief and embitterment."[3]

(4) *To the Church has been given, by Christ, a strictly monarchical constitution in His representative, the successor of Peter, the Roman Bishop. Not only is all that is valid with regard to the hierarchy valid in the first instance of the Pope, but*

employed against the Gregorian claims of the Church, v. Mirbt. Die Stellung Augustin's in der Publicistik des Gregor. Kirchenstreits, 1888.

[1] See note 2 on p. 122.

[2] Gregory VII. carried to the furthest extreme the opposition to the evangelical doctrine that the powers that be are ordained of God ; see epp. VIII. 21 : "Quis nesciat, reges et duces ab iis habuisse principium, qui deum ignorantes, superbia, rapinis, perfidia, homicidiis, postremo universis pæne sceleribus, mundi principe diabolo videlicet agitante, dominari cæca cupiditate et intolerabili præsumptione affectaverunt." But even according to Innocent III., the State arose "per extorsionem humanam." On the other hand, even the strictest papalists, indeed Gregory VII. himself, were not clear as to the limits between civil and ecclesiastical power.

[3] Burckhardt, Kultur der Renaissance, 3. ed. 2. vol., p. 228.

to him all powers are committed, and the other members of the hierarchy are only chosen in partem solicitudinis (for purposes of oversight).   He is the episcopus universalis (universal bishop); to him belong, therefore, both swords, and as every Christian can attain salvation only in the Church, as the Church, however, is the hierarchy, and the hierarchy the Pope, it follows that de necessitate salutis all the world must be subject to the Pope.   In numerous letters these principles had already been maintained by Gregory VII. in a way that could not be out-vied (cf. also the so-called dictatus Gregorii).   Yet in his case everything appears as the outflow of a powerful dominating personality, which, in a terrible conflict, grasps at the extremest measures.   In the period that followed, however, his principles were not only expressed, but were effectively applied, and, at the same time, as the result of a marvellous series of forgeries, were believingly accepted even by those who felt obliged to combat the papacy. At the time when the papacy saw itself confronted with a weak imperial power in the West, and with a still weaker Latin Empire in the East, this view of things established itself (from the time of Innocent III. onward) in the souls and minds of men.   So far as I know, Thomas was the first to state the position roundly in the formula : " (ostenditur etiam), quod subesse Romano pontifici sit de necessitate salutis " (it is also shown that to be subject to the Roman pontiff is essential to salvation).[1]   Then the whole theory was summed up in a form not to be surpassed in the Bull " Unam sanctam " of Boniface VIII. (1302), after the Popes for a whole century had strictly followed it in hundreds of small and great questions (questions of Church policy, of civil policy, of diocesan administration, etc.), and were in a position for daring to disregard all protests.[2]

[1] Opusc. c. err. Græc. fol. 9.   The Roman law was in general paraded in an extravagant way before the weak Greeks in the thirteenth century, and that had a reflex influence on the West.

[2] The most important sentences of the Bull ran thus : " Unam sanctam ecclesiam Catholicam et ipsam apostolicam urgente fide credere cogimur et tenere.   Nosque hanc firmiter credimus et simpliciter confitemur, extra quam nec salus est nec remissio peccatorum (the Church is now spiritually described with its head, Christ). Igitur ecclesiæ unius et unicæ unum corpus, unum caput, non duo capita, quasi monstrum, Christus videlicet et Christi vicarius Petrus Petrique successor (there

The setting up of strict monarchical power and the destruction of the old Church constitution is represented in three stages by Pseudo Isidore, Gratian, and the Mendicant Orders; for the latter, through the special rights which they received, completely broke up the local powers (bishops, presbyteries, parish priests), and were subject entirely to papal direction.[1] All the premises from which there necessarily followed the infallibility of the

follows John XXI., 16 ; here the oves universæ were entrusted to Peter). In hac ejusque potestate duos esse gladios, spiritualem videlicet et temporalem, evangelicis dictis instruimur. Nam dicentibus apostolis : ecce gladii duo hic (Luke XXII. 38) in ecclesia scilicet, cum apostoli loquerentur, non respondit dominus nimis esse, sed satis. Certe qui in potestate Petri temporalem gladium esse negat, male verbum attendit domini proferentis ; converte gladium tuum in vaginam (Matt. XXVI. 52). Uterque ergo est in potestate ecclesiæ. spiritualis scilicet gladius et materialis. Sed is quidem pro ecclesia, ille vero ab ecclesia exercendus. Ille sacerdotis, ille manu regum et militum, *sed ad nutum et patientiam sacerdotis.* Oportet autem gladium esse sub gladio et temporalem potestatem spirituali subici potestati, nam cum dicat apostolus (there follows Rom. XIII. 1) . . . non ordinatæ essent, nisi gladius esset sub gladio (the spiritual power trancends in dignity and nobility *all* earthly power as much as the spiritual the earthly). Nam veritate testante *spiritualis potestas terrenam potestatem instituere "* (is it literally institute? or institute in the sense of religious consecration ? or instruct ? In view of the immediately following "judicare," and of the sentence of Hugo St. Victor, which is here the source, the first meaning is the most probable ; Finke [Röm. Quartalschrift 4. Supplementheft, 1896, p. 40] is inclined to adopt the second) " *habet et judicare, si bona non fuerit* (there follows Jerem. I. 10). Ergo si deviat terrena potestas, judicabitur a potestate spirituali, sed si deviat spiritualis minor, a suo superiori, si vero suprema, a solo deo, non ab homine poterit judicari, testante apostolo (1 Cor. II. 25). Est autem hæc auctoritas, etsi data sit homini et exerceatur per hominem, non humana sed potius divina, ore divino Petro data sibique suisque successoribus in ipso quem confessus fuit petra firmata, dicente domino ipsi Petro (Matt. XVI. 19). Quicunque igitur huic potestati a deo sic ordinatæ resistit, dei ordinationi resistit, nisi duo *sicut Manichæus* fingat esse principia, quod falsum et hæreticum judicamus, quia testante Mose non in principiis sed in principio coelum deus creavit et terram. *Porro subesse Romano pontifici omni humanæ creaturæ declaramus, dicimus, definimus [et pronuntiamus] omnino esse de necessitate salutis.*" As can be understood, the Bull at the present day gives trouble to not a few Catholics, and the attempt is made to strip it to some extent of its dogmatic authoritative character, or to find help in interpretation. A collection of the more important papal pronouncements from the time between Gregory VII. and Alexander VI. is given by Mirbt, Quellen z. Gesch. des Papstthums, 1895, p. 47 f.

[1] Janus, p. 166 : " Ready everywhere to interpose and take action as agents of the papacy, entirely independent of the bishops, and of higher authority than the secular priests and the local clergy, they really formed churches within the Church, laboured for the honour and aggrandisement of their orders, and for the power of the Pope, on which their privileged position rested."

Pope had been brought together ; they were strictly developed,
too, by Thomas, after new forgeries had been added.[1] Nevertheless, though the doctrine had long been recognised, that
through a special divine protection the Roman Church could not
entirely fall from faith, and was the divinely appointed refuge
for doctrinal purity and doctrinal unity, beyond the groups that
stood under the influence of the Dominican Order, the doctrine
of infallibility did not command acceptance. The history of the
Popes was still too well known ; even in the canonical law-book
there were contradictory elements, and [2] Popes as great as
Innocent III. admitted the possibility of a Pope falling into sin

---

[1] There are specially to be considered here the Pseudocyrillian passages ; see the
valuable inquiry by Reusch, Die Fälschungen in dem. Tractat des Thomas v. Aquin
gegen die Griechen, Abhandl. d. k. bay. Akad. der Wissensch. III., Cl. 18, Bd.
3 Abth., 1889. On Thomas as the normal theologian for the doctrine of infallibility,
see Langen, Das Vatic. Dogma, 3 Thl., p. 99 ff. ; Leitner, Der hl. Thomas über das
unfehlbare Lehramt des Papstes, 1872, Delitzsch, Lehrsystem der römischen K., I.,
p. 194 ff. Thomas, Summa Sec. Sec. qu. 11 art. 2 : " Sic ergo aliqui doctores
videntur dissensisse vel circa ea quorum nihil interest ad fidem utrum sic vel aliter
teneatur, vel etiam in quibusdam ad fidem pertinentibus, quæ nondum erant per
ecclesiam determinata. Postquam autem essent auctoritate universalis ecclesiæ
determinata, si quis tali ordinationi pertinaciter repugnaret, hæreticus censeretur.
Quæ quidem auctoritas principaliter residet in summo pontifice." Sec. Sec. qu. 1 art.
10 (" utrum ad summum pontificem pertineat fidei symbolum ordinare ? "). Here,
as usual, the thesis is first denied, then follows : " editio symboli facta est in synodo
generali, sed hujusmodi synodus auctoritate solius summi pontificis potest congregari.
Ergo editio symboli ad auctoritatem summi pontificis pertinet." Further : " Nova
editio symboli necessaria est ad vitandum insurgentes errores. *Ad illius ergo auctoritatem pertinet editio symboli, ad cujus auctoritatem pertinet finaliter determinare ea
quæ sunt fidei, ut ab omnibus inconcussa fide teneantur.* Hoc autem pertinet ad auctoritatem summi pontificis, ad quem majores et difficiliores ecclesiæ quæstiones referuntur
(there follows a passage from the decretals). Unde et dominus (Luke XXII. 32)
Petro dixit, quem summum pontificem constituit : ego pro te rogavi, etc. Et hujus
ratio est : quia una fides debet esse totius ecclesiæ secundum illud 1 Cor. I. 10 : Id
ipsum dicatis omnes, et non sint in vobis schismata. *Quod servari non posset nisi
quæstio exorta determinetur per eum, qui toti ecclesiæ præest, ut sic ejus sententia a
tota ecclesia firmiter teneatur, et ideo ad solam* auctoritatem summi pontificis pertinet
nova editio symboli, sicut et omnia alia quæ pertinent ad totam ecclesiam, ut con-
gregare synodum generalem et alia hujusmodi." The tenet, that to every Pope
there belongs personal holiness (Gregory VII.), was no longer reasserted, because,
as Döllinger (Janus, p. 168) supposes, the danger existed of arguing from the
defective holiness of a Pope to the illegality of his decisions.

[2] See the canon in Gratian ascribed to Boniface " Si Papa," dist. 40, 6. On the
whole question see Mirbt, Publicistik im Zeitalter Gregors VII., p. 566 ff.

in matters of faith, and, in that case, acknowledged the competency of the judgment of the entire Church.[1]   It was thus possible that at the University of Paris a decided opposition should establish itself, which led, *e.g.*, to the Pope being charged with heresy in connection with a doctrine of John XXII.   The indefiniteness in which many Church doctrines (and theories of practice, *e.g.*, in regard to ordination) still stood, and the hesitating attitude which the Popes assumed towards them, also prevented the dogmatic authority of the papacy from being taken as absolute.[2]   Although the falsification of history, by the publication of historic accounts that painted over in an incredible way the great conflict between the papacy and the Empire, reached its climax about 1300,[3] and the principles of the Thomist policy[4] always received a fuller adoption, the decisive question of the infallibility remained unsolved.   From about the year 1340, indeed, the literature in which the papal system was delineated in the most extravagant way,[5] ceased entirely to be

---

[1] See the admission in Eymerici Director. Inquis., p. 295 (cited in Janus, p. 295).

[2] See the question of reordination in connection with " Simonists."

[3] Martin of Troppau and Tolomeo of Lucca.

[4] Thomas, de regimine principum, continued by Tolomeo.

[5] The most extreme works are those of Augustinus Triumphus, Summa de ecclesiast. potest. (ob. 1328) and of the Franciscan Alvarus Pelagius, De planctu ecclesiæ (ob. 1352).   From the Summa de potestate eccl. of the former, and from the work de planctu ecclesiæ of the latter, Gieseler II., 3, 2 Aufl., p. 42 ff. and 101 ff., gives full extracts, which show that the glorification of the Pope could not be carried further in the nineteenth century.   Augustinus asserted generally : " Nulla lex populo christiano est danda, nisi ipsius papæ auctoritate ; " for only the papal power is immediately from God, and it embraces the jurisdictio et cura totius mundi. Alvarus carried the identifying of Christ with the Pope to the point of blasphemy, and at the same time declared the Pope to be the rightful possessor of the imperium Romanum from the days of Peter.   At bottom, both distinguish the Pope from God only by saying that to the earthly "dominus deus noster papa" (see Finke, l.c., p. 44 ff. ; observe that I have placed the word " earthly " before the expression, which indicates the trope here employed, so far as there is one), adoration is due only " ministerialiter."   (Finke, l.c., pp. 40-44, has objected to this last sentence, and believes he has refuted it from the source, Augustinus Triumphus.   That, according to Augustinus, there belongs to the Pope the servitus summa [*i.e.*, the Latreia, full divine worship] I have not asserted.   But certainly Augustinus teaches that the Pope possesses participative and exercises ministerialiter the summa potestas [the dominatio, the divine power of rule] ; in accordance with this therefore must the dulia also be defined which belongs to the Pope.   Instead of the somewhat short expression " ministerialiter," which it would be better not to use, I should have

produced. Only after 120 years did it re-appear, when it was a
question of rescuing and asserting the old claims of the papacy
against the Council of Bâsle. It was then that Cardinal
Torquemada wrote that defence of the papal system,[1] which,
resting on a strict Thomistic foundation, was still regarded at
the period of the Reformation as the most important achievement of the papal party. But from the middle of the fifteenth
century the papal system, as a whole, was again gathering
power, after the storm of the Councils had been happily
exorcised by the brilliant but crafty policy of Eugene IV. Only
the French nation maintained what ground of freedom was
already won in opposition to the Pope (Bourges 1438). The
other nations returned, through the Concordats, to their old
dependence on the Autocrat in Rome;[2] indeed, they were, to
some extent, betrayed just by their own local rulers, inasmuch
as these men saw it to be of advantage in hastening their attainment to full princely power to take shares with the Pope in the
Church of the country.[3] This fate overtook, in the end, even the
French national Church (through the concordat of Dec. 1516),
and yet in such a way that the king obtained the chief share of
the power over it. While, as the fifteenth century passed into
the sixteenth, the Popes were indulging wildly in war, luxury,
and the grossest simony, Cajetan and Jacobazzi wrought out
the strictest papal theory, the former including in it the doctrine
of infallibility.[4] The hopes of the nations in the Council were

said : "The adoration" belongs in the way in which it is due to him who shares in
the divine power of rule, and exercises it as an instrument of God.)

[1] De Pontifice Maximo et generalis concilii auctoritate ; see also his Summa de
ecclesia and the Apparatus super decreto unionis Græcorum.

[2] Rome, however, always understood these concordats as acts of grace, by which
only the party admitted to partnership was bound. Even at an earlier time this
view was maintained by Roman canonists, and was deduced from the supreme
lordship of the Pope over all men.

[3] Think of the develoⁿment of the territorial-prince system in the fifteenth century.
Great rulers (Emperor Frederick III.) and small literally vied with each other, till
far on in the sixteenth century, in injuring the independence of their national churches.
The local princes derived a passing, but the Pope the permanent, advantage.

In the period of conflict between the Popes and the Councils the question about
the infallibility of the Pope in matters of faith had retired into the background. At
the Union Council at Florence it was not mentioned. Even Torquemada admitted
the possibility of a Pope falling into a heresy ; from this, however, he did not conclude

quenched, the old tyranny was again set up; it was complained, indeed, that the ecclesiastical despotism was worse than that of the Turks, but, nevertheless, men submitted to the inevitable. About the year 1500 the complaints were perhaps more bitter than at any other time; but the falling away was slight, the taking of steps less frequent. Heresy seemed to have become rarer and tamer than in the thirteenth and fourteenth centuries, especially after the Hussite movement had exhausted itself. The "heretics" — so it appeared — had really become the "silent in the land," who shunned an open breach with the Church; their piety appeared less aggressive. "It was pretty generally felt that it had happened to the Church with the Reformation, as formerly it had happened to the King of Rome with the Sibylline books; after the seed of corruption sown by the Curia had, for fifty years, borne a much larger harvest, and the Church itself made no more effort to save it, the Reformation had to be purchased at a much heavier price and with still smaller prospect of success."[1] The Lateran Council at the beginning of the sixteenth century, which treated with scorn all wishes of the nations and promulgated the papal theory in the strictest sense,[2] as if there had never been councils at Constance and Bâsle, was tacitly recognised. But it was the lull before the storm—a storm which the Pope had yet to experience, who had entered upon his office with the words: "Volo, ut pontificatu isto quam maxime perfruamur." (It is my wish that we may enjoy the pontificate in the largest measure possible.)[3]

Before the time of Thomas *theology* took no part in this im-

---

that the council was superior to him, for a heretical Pope was ipso facto deposed by God. This impracticable, imbecile assumption was first rejected by Cajetan, who reverted to the doctrine of Thomas, which was based on fictitious passages from the Fathers, while he added himself a new falsification by suppressing the proposition laid down at Constance : "error est, si per Romanam ecclesiam intelligat universalem aut concilium generale." With him also originated the famous proposition, that the Catholic Church is the born hand-maid of the Pope.

[1] Janus, p. 365.

[2] The Pope, it is said in the Bull "Pastor aeternus," has the "auctoritas super omnia concilia"; he alone may convene, transfer, and dissolve them.

[3] On the handing down of this saying, see Janus, p. 381, n. 407.

posing development of the papal theory; even after him the
share taken by it was small. *The development was directed by
jurisprudence,* which founded simply on external, mostly forged,
historic testimonies, and drew its conclusions with dialectic art.
The meagre share of theology is to be explained on two
grounds. First, Rome alone had a real interest in the whole
theory; but in Rome theology never flourished, either in
antiquity or in the Middle Ages. There was practical concern
in Rome neither with Scripture exposition nor with the
dogmatic works of the Fathers. Whoever wished to study
theology went to France. For the Curia, only the student of
law was of any account; from the time of Innocent IV. a school
of law existed in Rome; the great majority of the Cardinals
were well-equipped jurists, not theologians, and the greatest
Popes of the Middle Ages, Alexander III., Innocents III. and
IV., Boniface VIII., etc., came to the papal chair as highly-
esteemed legal scholars.[1] When it was now much too late, men
with clear vision, like Roger Bacon, or pious patriots, like
Dante, saw that the ruin of the Church was due to the decretals,
which were studied in place of the Church Fathers and
Scripture. The former, in particular, demanded very loudly that
the Church should be delivered from the secularised Church law
which was poisoning it. In the fourteenth and fifteenth
centuries there were complaints constantly made about the
papacy, and about the corrupted Church law ("Jurists bad
Christians") as being the real source of all evil. It was the
spirit of ancient Rome that had settled down on the Mediæval
spirit, that Roman spirit of jurisprudence, which had now, however, degenerated into a spirit of tyranny, and used as its means
audacious forgeries. But the slight share of theology in the
development of the hierarchical conception of the Church is to
be explained not merely from the lack of theology, but, second,
from the fortunate incapacity of theology (till past the middle of
the thirteenth century) to lower itself to this notion of the
Church. Anyone who reflected as a *theologian* on the Church,
instituted researches into the works of the Church fathers, especi-

[1] See Döllinger, Ueber das Studium der deutschen Geschichte (Akad. Vorträge II.,
pp. 407 ff., 418 f.

ally Augustine. But here the spiritual conception of the Church (*i.e.*, the Church as corpus Christi [body of Christ], as multitudo fidelium [multitude of the faithful], as universitas Christianorum [entire mass of Christians]) came so clearly to view that for the time it riveted reflection, and there was failure to force one's way with any confidence to the hierarchical, not to speak of the papal, conception, or it was only touched on. This explains how all the great theologians before Thomas, from Anselm onwards, even those of Gregorian tendency, achieved as *theologians* very little in promoting the development of the hierarchical conception of the Church. They taught and wrote like Augustine, indeed they still remained behind him in precise definition of the Church as an external society.[1] *Theology did nothing for the development and establishment of the papal system till far on in the thirteenth century*, and it may here be said at once in its honour, that with a single, and that even not a perfect, exception (Thomas), it did only half work in the time that followed, leaving the most to be done by the Post-Tridentine theology.[2] So far as I know, there is nothing to be found in the theological writings of the Schoolmen in the shape of rounded off formulæ for, nothing of strictly systematic exposition of, the conception of the Church (as in the case of the doctrine of the Sacraments). On the other hand, both in Hugo St. Victor, and in the later Schoolmen also, not a few fundamental lines of proof with regard to the notion of the Church can be pointed to which were directly and without change taken over by the

[1] See Hugo of St. Victor, de Sacr. II., p. II., c. 2 sq. In his Sentences the Lombard made no mention whatever of the papacy ! So far as others dealt with the Church at all, even the firmness of Cyprian in apprehending the hierarchical notion of the Church was not reached. Numerous proofs in Langen, Das Vaticanische Dogma, 2. Theil. If Hugo differs from the other earlier theologians in entering more fully into a description of the Church, this has a connection with his interest in the Sacraments. What he says about the hierarchy and the Pope falls behind the Gregorian ideas, and therefore does nothing to advance them. Even about the relation of the Church (the Pope) to the State he has still evangelical ideas. And yet here, as elsewhere also, he must be held as in many respects the precursor of Thomas.

[2] It is amazing that in Thomasius-Seeberg (p. 196) the sentence : " As in general, so also with regard to the Church, Scholasticism set itself the task of proving that what exists ought to exist," is followed at once by the other : " It must be emphasised here first of all, that Scholasticism does not know of a dogma of the Church."

"heretical" parties, and by men like Wyclif.[1] What most
simply explains this is that the patristic, and especially the
Augustinian, expositions still determined theology. Yet it is
not to be denied, that from the middle of the thirteenth century
theology took a certain share in developing the conception of
the Church. It was just the Mendicant Monks—to the shame
of St. Francis—who, even as theologians, began to be enthusiastic
for the papal theory, after there had been conferred upon them
such excessive privileges as could only be held legal if the Pope
was really the Lord of the Church. There was added to this,
that in the thirteenth century, in the course of the negotiations
with the Greeks, theology saw that it had to face the task of
ingratiating them into the papal system also. *It was in connection with this task that there was awakened the interest theology
took in the hierarchical conception of the Church which formed the
presupposition of the papal system,*[2] and the great thinker, Thomas
Aquinas, now developed at once the hierarchical and papal
theory, together with a bold theory of the state.[3] But he was far

---

[1] The agreement of the "heretics" with the fundamental Catholic notion of the
Church was not unfrequently substantiated by their Catholic opponents. These men
were still naïve enough to hold the conception of the Church as societas unitatis fidei
as their own basis ; see correct statement by Gottschick (Zeitschr. f. K.-Gesch. VIII.,
p. 348 f.).

[2] The Council of Lyons in 1274 was of epoch-making importance here. The
vigorous re-awakening of interest in the theoretic statement and proof of the papal
system in the middle of the fifteenth century likewise finds an explanation in the
transactions with the Greeks. In this way the relation of the Greeks to the West
came to be of sinister omen. There was a wish to win them for the papacy, and this
became the occasion for developing "scientifically" for the first time—mostly by
means of forgeries—the papal theory !

⎩homas develops the chief attributes of the Pope (summus pontifex, caput
ecclesiæ, cura ecclesiæ universalis, plenitudo potestatis, potestas determinandi novum
symbolum). The discussions on the distribution of hierarchical power may here be
left aside (on the development of the notion of the Church as a monarchy Aristotle's
influence was at work). We have only to note how entirely the second conception
of the Church, *i.e.*, the hierarchical, is dominated by the doctrine of the Sacraments.
The particulars of the Thomist conception of the Church were not dogma in his day,
but they afterwards became the norm for dogmatic construction. That Thomas,
moreover, does not place the hierarchical notion of the Church side by side with the
spiritual without indicating a relation has been shown by Gottschick, l.c. pp. 347-
357. Yet it must not be forgotten that such tenets as those of Augustine regarding
the Church (taken in connection with predestinarian grace) continued to exercise
their own influence even when they were subordinated to alien thoughts. Thomas

from surrendering, at the same time, the spiritual conception of
the Church, or—as was done in the Post-Tridentine period—
from correcting it throughout by means of the hierarchical.
With all his logical consistency in the development of the papal
system, he certainly did not derive the powers of the bishops and
priests entirely from the papal ; in his " Summa " he still works
to a great extent with the notion of the " Ecclesia " as having
the force of a central conception, and in doing so has no thought
of monarchy.   For him it is no figure of speech that the

(Explanation of the Apostolic Symbol ; see also " Summa " III., qu. 8) begins by
representing the Church as a religious community (congregatio fidelium, corpus
mysticum) whose head is Christ.   But while so describing it—as the community of
those who are united to Christ by the love that proceeds from God—he at the same
time accentuates the moral character of the community, as an entire whole ruled by
the divine law, which embraces the earth, heaven, and purgatory, and which has its
end in the vision and enjoyment of God.   In more precisely defining the compass of
the Church, Thomas's process of proof is affected by all the uncertainties which we
already observed in Augustine, and which were due to regard on the one hand to
predestinarian grace (in accordance with which all particulars are determined), and on
the other hand to the empirical circumstances.   Even the reprobi, according to him,
are in the Church de potentia, that is to say, so long as they stand under the influence
of the virtus Christi or still through their free will hold a connection with him.   Now, so
far as the Church imparts to the individual the love of God, and thereby sanctification,
it is an external community like the state, is discernible by external marks, is defined
by an external limit (excommunication) and requires the hierarchical organisation ;
for this last is the presupposition of sacramental celebration.   If, until felicity is
reached, the life of the individual as a believer proceeds by stages of faith (*i.e.*, of
holding true upon authority) and is regulated by the several sacraments which contain
the saving grace, this implies that it is of the essence of the Church that it is the
authority on doctrine and the administrator of the Sacraments.   But this it can only
be as a community with a strictly legal and hierarchical organisation.   In this way
the second conception of the Church is brought by Thomas into closest connection with
the first, and Gottschick (p. 353) is quite correct in further pointing out that " faith
in the objective sense is part of the commands of *the law* by which (see above) the
Church must be guided."   The Church as a legal authority on doctrine, and as a
priestly sacramental institution, is therefore the " exclusive organ by which the Head
of the Church, Christ, forms its members."   One sees then that a very spiritual conception of the Church, nay, even the predestinarian, can be brought into combination
with the empirico-hierarchical (Summa III., qu. 64, art. 2 : " per sacramenta dicitur
esse fabricata ecclesia Christi.")   As salvation is a mystery that cannot be experienced,
i.e., as a certainty regarding its possession can never be reached, inasmuch as it consists of forces that mysteriously operate in the human sphere that is inaccessible to
reflection, nothing remains but simply to surrender one's self to the sacramental
saving institution, which, again, involves the graded priesthood.   In this way the
authority of the clergy necessarily became absolute, and the spiritual (predestinarian)

individual bishop "is called specially the bridegroom of the
Church as also Christ" (specialiter sponsus ecclesiæ dicitur sicut
et Christus).[1]   But, so far as the influence of Thomas extended,
the result was unquestionably a mingling of jurisprudence and
theology in this department and the acclimatising of the
hierarchico-papal notion of the Church.[2]   Yet his influence
must not be over-rated.   The Franciscan (Nominalist) dogmatic
took little to do, so far as I know, with this development of the
conception of the Church.   Even at the beginning of the Reformation, the whole hierarchical and papal theory had no sure
position in dogmatic—*it was Romish decretal law*.   But it had
attained more than a place in dogmatic.   From about 1450 it
was again energetically acted upon from Rome, and the opposition to it appeared no longer so powerful as a century before.[3]

   This opposition we have still to review.   Here it is to be
observed, above everything else, that the imperfect public
development of the conception of the Church was a matter of
little importance, because in the *doctrine of the Sacraments* all
was already acquired as a sure possession which could be expected from a formulation of the conception of the Church in
hierarchical interests.   From this, again, it followed still further,
that the opposition to the hierarchical papal notion of the Church
necessarily continued—in spite of all fostering—without danger,

notion of the Church, so far from correcting, necessarily aided this advance of view.
Hence follows the tenet of the infallibility of the Church, which was bound to
issue in the infallibility of the Pope ; for some kind of rock to build on must be sought
for and found.   If this does not lie in an overmastering certainty which the subject-
matter itself brings with it, inasmuch as it transforms the absoluteness of the moral
imperative into the absolute certainty of the grace of God in Christ, it must be given
in something external.   This external thing, certainly, the infallibility of the priesthood in teaching and administering the Sacraments, can never guarantee to the individual the *possession* of salvation, but only its possibility.

   [1] Summa, III. suppl. qu. 40 art. 4 fin.

   [2] The attitude to the State was involved in the position that only the priest is able
rightly to teach the law of God, but that even the States have no other task than to
care for the salvation of the souls of their subjects by promoting the virtus that corresponds to the law of God.

   [3] No good Catholic Christian doubted that in *spiritual things* the clergy were the
divinely-appointed superiors of the laity, that this power proceeded from the right of
the priests to celebrate the Sacraments, that the Pope was the real possessor of this
power, and was far superior to all secular authority.   The question, however, as to
the Pope's power to rule was certainly a subject of controversy.

so long as the doctrine of the Sacraments was not objected to. But the latter again rested on the peculiar view of salvation, as the sanctification that leads to the visio dei, as active holiness (measured by the standard of the law of God). Here we must go back to an earlier point.[1]

Augustine combined the old Catholic notion of salvation, as the visio et fruitio dei (vision and enjoyment of God), with the doctrine of predestination on the one hand and with the doctrine of the regnum Christi (kingdom of Christ) and the process of justification on the other. As contrasted with the Greek view, both combinations were new ; but the union of the idea of salvation with the process of justification and sanctification was easily effected, because this process was taken as regulated entirely by the *Sacraments*, while the Sacraments, as the Greek development shows, formed the necessary correlate to the idea of salvation. If in salvation, that is to say, the supramundane *condition* in which one is to find himself is mainly emphasised, then there answer to the production of this condition, means that operate as holy natural forces. When Augustine conceived of these natural forces as forces of love working for righteousness, a very great step of progress was taken; but no difference was made thereby in the general scheme, since love was regarded as infused. But certainly he made it possible that there should *also* be given to the whole process a very decided tendency towards morality—which had dropped out of the Greek view as held within the lines of dogma. The forces of love, that is to say, bring it about that here on earth the *law* of Christ, which is summed up in the commandment to love, can be fulfilled. In this way there arises from the forces of love, which are transmitted through the Sacraments as channels, the *kingdom* of Christ, in which righteousness reigns according to the

---

[1] A full understanding of the Catholic conception of the Church can only be reached by starting from the conception of the Sacraments, which, as has been observed, is dependent on the view taken of salvation. But from this point of view it can also be said that the Catholic notion of the Church forms the necessary supplement to the imperfect idea of faith. That which is lacking to faith, taken in the Catholic sense, namely, the certitudo salutis, is supplied by the doctrinal authority of the Church on the one side and by the Sacramental Church institution on the other, and yet in such a way that it is obtained only approximately.

example and law of Christ. The Sacraments have therefore the
double effect, that of preparing for, and conducting gradually to
the visio et fruitio dei, and that of producing on earth the
Church in which the law of Christ reigns and by which the
" bene vivere " (right-living) is produced. By the latter of these
two views the position of the State is determined—as the bene
vivere is its end, it must submit itself to the sacramental institution. But by the whole idea the priesthood as the teaching and
sanctifying corporation is legitimised ; for the administration of
the Sacraments is tied to a particular order, whom Christ has
appointed, and this order, at the same time, is alone empowered
to interpret the law of Christ with binding authority. To them,
therefore, there must be subjection.

This whole view, which, certainly, had not received a clear and
precise expression from Augustine, obtained clearness and
precision in the period that followed—less through the labours
of the theologians than by the force of the resolute Roman
policy. Because this policy aimed, above all, at monarchy in
the Church, *it had, as the result of its victorious exercise, brought
out clearly for the first time, and at the same time created, the
general hierarchical conditions requisite for the existence of such a
monarchy.* Yet, in spite of many forgeries, it could not bring it
about that the factor of *hierarchical gradation*, comparatively insignificant from a dogmatic point of view, but extremely
important from the point of view of practice, should obtain the
support of an imposing tradition ; for from Augustine and the
Fathers in general it was as good as absent. But still further,
Augustine, as we have noted above, combined with the dogma
of salvation as the visio dei the doctrine of predestination, and
developed from the latter a doctrine of the Church that held a
neutral relation to hierarchy and sacrament. No doubt it can
easily be shown that the predestinarian and the sacramental
hierarchical notions of the Church are not necessarily mutually
exclusive, nay, that in a certain sense they require each other,
inasmuch as the individual's uncertainty of his own election,
affirmed by Augustine, necessarily forces him to make a diligent
use of all the means furnished by the Church, and the explanation very naturally occurs that God effectuates the fulfilment

of the predestinating decree only through the empirical Church
with its Sacraments. But Augustine himself did not assert that;
and although in the time that came after, this mode of adjusting
things came to be very much in favour, yet, as there was no
allowing the doctrine of predestination to drop out, there was
involved in this doctrine an element that threatened, like an
overhanging mass of rock, to destroy the existence of the structure beneath. Finally, Augustine had no doubt carried on a
victorious conflict with Donatism; but there was still one point
at which it was not easy to deny entirely the correctness of the
Donatist thesis, and that was the sacrament of penance. It
could certainly be made credible that baptism, the Lord's supper,
confirmation, ordination were valid, even when an unworthy
priest dispensed them; but how was such a man to be able to
sit in judgment upon the holy and the unholy, to apply the law
of Christ, to bind and loose, if the load rested on himself of
ignorance of sin? It was surely more than paradoxical, it was an
inconceivable thought, that the blind should be able to judge
aright as to light and darkness. Was excommunication by such
a man to be held valid before God? Was his absolution to have
force? There was no doubt an escape sought for here, also, by
saying that it is Christ who binds and looses, not the priest, who
is only a minister; but when flagrant unrighteousness was practised by the priest, when such cases increased in number, what
was then to be done?[1]

[1] Let it be distinctly noted here that it was just the strict papal system that had
widely given rise in the period of the great conflicts (eleventh and twelfth centuries)
to the greatest uncertainty about ordinations, seeing that the Popes cancelled without
hesitation "simonistic" orders, and likewise orders of the imperial bishops, nay,
even ordinations at which a single simonist had been present. Innocent II.,
indeed, at the second Lateran Council, pronounced invalid all ordinations of the
schismatics, *i.e.*, of the bishops who adhered to Pope Anaclete II. ("From him
whom he hath ordained we take away the orders" [evacuamus et irritas esse
consemus]; the curialist theologians are disposed to see in this only a suspension of
the exercise of office; Hefele, Concil. Gesch. V.², p. 438 f., leaves the passage unex-
plained; Friedrich [in his edition of Janus, 2 Aufl., pp. 143, 456] holds to the
cancelling of the orders.) Thus it was the Popes who were the instructors of those
sects that spread the greatest uncertainty as to the most important Catholic question,
the question regarding the validity of orders. At the time of the Schism it was laid
down by the papal Secretary, Coluccio Salutato, that as all Church power emanates
from the Pope, and as a wrongly elected Pope has himself no power, such an one can

In a way indicating the greatest acuteness, Thomas combined the predestinarian (spiritual) and the hierarchical conceptions of the Church, and tried to eliminate the points from
which a "heretical" conception could develop itself; but it is
apparent from what has been stated *that one could accept substantially the Augustinian-Thomist notion of the Church with its
premises (doctrines of salvation and the Sacraments), and yet,
when tested by the claims which the Mediæval Church set up at
the time of its greatest power, could become "heretical," in the
event, namely, of his either* (1) *contesting the hierarchical gradation of the priestly order; or* (2) *giving to the religious idea of
the Church implied in the thought of predestination a place superior
to the conception of the empirical Church; or* (3) *applying to the
priests, and thereby to the authorities of the Church, the test of the
law of God, before admitting their right to exercise, as holding the
keys, the power of binding and loosing.*
Certainly during the whole of the Middle Ages there were
sects who attacked the Catholic notion of the Church at the
root ; but however important they may be for the history of
culture, they play no part in the history of dogma ; for as
their opposition, as a rule, developed itself from dualistic or
pantheistic premises (surviving effects of old Gnostic or
Manichæan views), they stood outside of ordinary Christendom,
and, while no doubt affecting many individual members within
it, had no influence on Church doctrine.[1]   On the other hand, it
may be asserted that *all* the movements which are described as
"reformations anticipating the Reformation," and which for a
time resisted not unsuccessfully the introduction of the Romish

give none ; consequently the bishops and priests ordained since the death of Gregory
XI. were incompetent to dispense the Sacraments.   If, accordingly, says Coluccio, a
believer adores the Eucharist that has been consecrated by a bishop ordained in the
Schism, he worships an idol (in a letter to Jost of Moravia in Martene, Thes. Anecd.
II., p. 1159, quoted by Janus, p. 318).

[1] There are referred to here sects like the Catharists and Albigenses, "Patarenes,"
"Bulgarians," as also the adherents of Amalrich of Bena, the Ortliebists (allied to
the Waldensians), the sect of the New Spirit, the sect of the Free Spirit, and many
similar movements ; see Hahn, Gesch. der Ketzer im Mittelalter, 3 Bdd., Reuter,
Aufklärung Bd. II., the different works of Ch. Schmidt, Jundt, Preger, Haupt ;
Staude, Urspr. d. Katharer (Ztschr. f. K.-Gesch. V. 1) ; Döllinger, Beiträge z.
Sectengesch. des Mittelalters, 1890.

conception of the Church, set out from the Augustinian conception of the Church, but took exception to the development of
this conception, from the three points that have been defined
above.   Now whether we look at the Waldensian, the Lombard,
the Apocalyptico-Joachimic, the Franciscan opposition to the
new conception of the Church, whether at that of the Empire or
the Councils, of Wyclif or Huss, or even, indeed, at the humanist,
we have always the same spectacle.   On the first view the
opposition seems radical, nay, expressly antagonistic.   Angry
curses—Anti-Christ, Babylon, Church of the devil, priests of
the devil, etc.—catch the ear everywhere.   But if we look a
little more closely, the opposition is really much tamer.   That
fundamental Catholic conception of the Church, as a sacramental institution, is not objected to, because the fundamental
conception of salvation and of blessedness remains unassailed.
Although all hierarchical gradation may be rejected, the conception of the hierarchical priesthood is allowed to stand ; although the Church may be conceived of as the community of
the predestinated, every Christian must place himself under the
influence of the Sacraments dispensed by the Church, and must
use them most diligently, for by means of these his election is
effected ; although the sacramental acts of unworthy priests
may be invalid, still priests are needed, but they must live according to the law of Christ ; although the Church as the
community of the predestinated may be known only to God,
yet the empirical Church is the true Church, if the apostolic
life prevails in it, and a true empirical Church of the kind is
absolutely necessary, and can be restored by reforms ; although,
finally, all secular rights may have to be denied to the Pope
and the priesthood, yet secular right in general is something
that has gradually to disappear.   The criticism of the Romish
conception of the Church is therefore entirely a criticism *from
within*.

The criticism must not on that account be under-estimated ;
it certainly accomplished great things ; in it the spiritual and
moral gained supremacy over the legal and empirical, and
Luther was fortunate when he came to know Huss's doctrine of
the Church.   Yet we must not be deceived by this as to the

fact that the conception of the Church held by all the opposing parties was only a form of the Augustinian conception of the Church, modified by the Waldensian-Franciscan ideal of the apostolic life (according to the law of Christ). The ways in which the elements were mingled in the programmes of the opposition parties were very different; at one time the predestinarian element preponderated, at another time an apocalyptic-legal, at another the Franciscan, at another the biblical (the lex Christi), at another they were all present in equipoise. Especially on the ground that these opposition parties, starting from the doctrine of predestination, enforced the conception of the "invisible Church," and applied the standard of *Scripture* to everything, they are praised as evangelical. But attention has very rightly been drawn of late to the fact [1] that they by no means renounced the conception of an empirical, true Church, a conception to which they were driven by individual uncertainty about election, and that their standpoint on the ground of Scripture is the Catholic-legal, as it had been adopted by Augustine, Bernard, and Francis.

Under such circumstances it is enough to delineate in a few of their features the conceptions of the Church held by the several parties. The Waldensians contested neither the Catholic cultus nor the Sacraments and the hierarchical constitution in themselves, but they protested (1) as against a mortal sin, against the Catholic clergy exercising the rights of the successors of the Apostles without adopting the apostolic life; and (2) against the comprehensive power of government on the part of the Pope and the bishops, hence against the Romish hierarchy with its graded ranks. But the French Waldensians did not, nevertheless, contest the validity of the Sacraments dispensed by unworthy priests, though this certainly was done by those of Lombardy.[2] Among the Waldensians, then, the conception of the *law of Christ*, as set forth in Scripture and as prescribing to the priests the apostolic life, rises above all other marks of the Church (among those in Italy the Donatist

---

[1] See Gottschick in the dissertation cited above and K. Muller, Bericht, etc., p. 37 f.

[2] See above, p. 90, and Müller, Waldesier, p. 93 ff. and passim.

element developed itself from this). The same applies to a part of the Franciscans, who passed over to the opposition. In the sharp polemic against Rome on the part of the Joachimites, the apocalyptic element takes its place side by side with the legal : clergy and hierarchy are judged from the standpoint of emancipated monachism and of the approaching end of time.[1] No wonder that just this view gained favour with not a few Franciscans, that it extended itself to far in the North among all sections of the people,[2] and that it came to take up a friendly (Ghibelline) attitude towards the State. As thus modified it freed itself up to a certain point from the wild apocalyptic elements, and passed over to be merged in the imperialist opposition. Here also they were again Franciscans who passed over also, and to some extent, indeed, conducted the resistance to the papal power (Occam). In this opposition the dispute was by no means about the Church as a sacramental institution and as a priesthood, but simply about the legitimacy of the hierarchical gradation of rank (including the Pope, whose divine appointment Occam contested), and about the governing powers of the hierarchy, which were denied. But these powers were denied on the ground of the Franciscan view, that the Church admits of no secular constitution, and that the hierarchy *must* be poor and without rights. The assigning of the entire legal sphere to the State was at bottom an expression of contempt for that sphere, not indeed on the part of all literary opponents of the papacy in the fourteenth century, but yet on the part of not a few of them.[3] The imperialist opposition was

---

[1] See Reuter., l.c. II., p. 191 ff., and Archiv. f. Litt.-und K.-Gesch. des Mittelalters I., p. 105 ff.

[2] In greater numbers than before protocols of processes against heretics have been published in recent years ; see Wattenbach in the Sitzungsberichten der Berliner Academie, 1886, IV., and Döllinger, l.c., Bd. 2. We can very easily understand how, above all, the charge was brought against the heretics that they did away with the Sacraments.

[3] Besides Occam, Marsilius of Padua and John of Jandun are specially to be named here ; cf. Riezler, Die lit. Widersacher der Päpste z. Z. Ludwig's des Bayern, 1874, K. Müller, der Kampf Ludwig's d. B. mit der röm. Curie, 2 Bdd., 1879 f., Friedberg, Die Grenzen zwischen Staat und Kirche, 1882, the same author, Die mittelalterlichen Lehren über d. Verh. v. St. u. K., 1874 ; Dorner, Das Verhältniss von

dissolved by that of the Councils. Reform of the Church in
its head and members was the watchword—but the professors
of Paris, who, like the German professors in the fifth and sixth
decades of the present century, gave themselves up to the
illusion that they sat at the loom of history, understood by
this reform merely a national-liberal reform of the ecclesiastical
constitution (after the pattern of the constitution of the
University of Paris), the restriction of the tyrannical and
speculative papal rights, the giving to the Council supremacy
over the papacy,[1] and the liberating of the national Churches
from papal oppression, with a view to their possessing independence, either perfect or relative. The importance of these
ideas from the point of view of ecclesiastical policy, and the
sympathy we must extend to the idealism of these professors,
must not lead to our being deceived as to the futility of their
efforts for reform, which were supported by the approval of
peoples and princes. They attacked at the root the Gregorian
(Pseudo-Isidorian) development of the ecclesiastical constitution
and of the papacy ; but they did not say to themselves, that
this development must always again repeat itself if the root, the
doctrines of the Sacraments and of the priesthood, be left untouched. But how could these doctrines be assailed when there
was agreement with the Curialists in the view taken of salvation
and of the law of Christ ? In face of the actual condition of

K. u. St. nach Occam (Stud. u. Krit. 1885, IV.). How powerfully the idea of the
State asserted itself in the fourteenth century (cf. even Dante earlier) is well known.

[1] Cf. the famous decrees of the fourth and fifth Sessions of the Council of Constance :
" Every legally-convened Œcumenical Council representing the Church has its
authority directly from Christ, and in matters of faith, in the settlement of disputes
and the reformation of the Church in its head and members, every one, even the
Pope, is subject to it." Even the cardinals did not venture to refuse their assent.
The Thomist conception of the Church was as yet no dogma ; by the decisions of
Constance it was tacitly—unfortunately only tacitly—described as error ; but at the
Council, so far as is known, no voice was raised on its behalf, and though Martin V.
took his stand at the beginning on the newly acquired ground, it was only for a
minute. That the Council of Bâsle, on an understanding with the Pope, gave a fresh
declaration of the decrees of Constance, is well known. But thereafter Eugene IV.
himself, and wisely, brought about the breach. On the Council of Constance we shall
shortly be able to judge much better than before, when the great publication of Finke,
Acta concilii Constanciensis will be before us, of which the first volume (Acten z.
Vorgeschichte) has already appeared (1896).

things, which had developed throughout many centuries in the Church, the idea that the Church's disorders could be healed by paralysing the papal system of finance, and declaring the Council the divinely instituted court of appeal in the Church, was a Utopia, the realisation of which during a few decades was only apparent. It is somewhat touching to observe with what tenacity in the fifteenth, and beginning of the sixteenth, centuries, men clung to the hope that a Council could heal the hurt of Israel, and deliver the Church from the tyranny of the Pope. The healing indeed came, but in a way in which it was not expected, while it was certainly the only healing which a Council could permanently bestow—it came at the Councils of Trent and the Vatican.[1]

Even before the beginning of the great opposition movement of the Councils against the papal system, the most important mediæval effort towards reform had been initiated—the *Wyclifite*, which continued itself in the *Hussite*. In spite of wild extravagances, the movement under Wyclif and Huss, in which many of the earlier lines of effort converged, must be regarded as the *ripest* development of mediæval reform-agitation. Yet it will

[1] On the conception of the Church held by the Paris theologians and their friends— they thought of themselves, not without reason, as restoring the old Catholic view, yet under quite changed circumstances the old thing became a new—see Schwab, Gerson, 1858, Tschackert, d'Ailly, 1877, Hartwig, Henricus de Langenstein, 1858, Brockhaus, Nicolai Cusani de concilii univ. potest. sentent., 1867. Also the works on Clemange and the Italian and Spanish Episcopalists. In particular matters the representatives of the conciliar ideas, at that time and later, widely diverged from each other, and more especially, each one defined differently the relation of the Pope to the Council and to the Church : there were some who held the papacy to be entirely superfluous, and some who only wished for it, so to speak, a slight letting of blood. The great majority interfered in no way with its existence, but aimed merely at purifying and restricting it ; see the good review of the Episcopal system in Delitzsch, Lehrsystem der röm. K., p. 165 ff. Janus, p. 314 ff. No doubt it only needs to be recalled here that the Episcopal system arose from the frightful trouble created by the Schism, when the Italians wished to wrest back the papacy from the French. The termination of the Schism was a real, but it was also the only permanent, result of the Councils. Yet it must not be overlooked that in the definitions of the Church which the Episcopalists had furnished, Reformation elements were included, though these certainly were derived almost entirely from Augustine ; for Augustine reiterated the position that the keys are given, not to an individual, but to the Church, and in his dogmatic expositions he always subordinated the constitutional to the spiritual unity of the Church.

appear, that while doing much in the way of loosening and preparing, it gave expression to no *Reformation* thought ; it, too, confined itself to the ground that was Augustinian-Franciscan, with which there was associated only a powerful national element. Yet to Wyclif's theory, which Huss simply transcribed,[1] a high value is to be attached, as being the only coherent *theological* theory which the Middle Ages opposed to the Thomist. All the other mediæval opponents of the Romish Church system work with mere measuring-lines or with fragments.

When we look at what Wyclif and Huss challenged or rejected, we might suppose that here a radical criticism of the Catholic conception of the Church was carried through, and a new idea of the Church presented. Everything must be determined by Holy Scripture ; the practice in regard to worship and the Sacraments is everywhere represented as perverted and as encumbered by the traditions of men; the doctrine of indulgence, the practice of auricular confession, the doctrine of transubstantiation (Wyclif), the manducatio infidelium (communicating of unbelievers), the priests' absolute power of the keys, are as zealously opposed as the worship of saints, images, and relics, private masses, and the many sacramentalia. For the worship of God there are demanded plainness, simplicity, and *intelligibility ;* the people must receive what will be inwardly and spiritually edifying (hence the preference for the vernacular).[2] With the thorough reform of worship and of sacrament celebra-

---

[1] Wyclif's works are only now being made fully accessible ; cf. the Trialogues edited by Lechler, the controversial writings published by Buddensieg, and especially the treatise de ecclesia edited by Loserth (Wyclif Society from 1882). Monographs by Lechler, 2 vols., 1872 (and in Herzog's R.-E.) and by Buddensieg, 1885. The discovery that Huss simply, and to a large extent verbally, adopted the Wyclifite doctrine, we owe to Loserth (Hus und Wiclif, 1884), see also the same author's Introduction to the treatise de ecclesia. The results of Gottschick's discussion of Huss's doctrine of the Church (Ztschr. f. K.-Gesch. VIII., p. 345 ff.) apply therefore throughout to Wyclif. I do not venture an opinion as to how far Wesel and Wessel were influenced by Huss. Savonarola continued the opposition of the Mendicant Monks in the old style.

[2] The translation of the Bible was a great achievement of Wyclif ; but it must not be forgotten that the Church also of the fifteenth century concerned itself with Bible translation, as more recent investigations have shown.

tion there must be a corresponding reform of the hierarchy.
Here also there must be a reverting to the original simplicity.
The papacy, as it existed, was regarded as a part of Anti-
Christ, and this was not less true of the secularised Mendicant
Monk system (as Lechler has shown, it was only towards the
end of his life that Wyclif entered upon a vigorous conflict with
both ; his original attitude towards the Mendicant Monks was
more friendly). The Pope, who contravenes the law of Christ,
is the Anti-Christ, and in the controversial treatise " de Christo
et suo adversario Anti-Christo," it is proved that in twelve matters
the Pope has apostatised from the law and doctrine of Christ.
The head of the Church is Christ, not the Pope ; only through
Constantine has the latter, as the bishop of Rome, become
great. Therefore the Roman bishop must return to a life of
apostolic service. He is not the direct and proximate vicar of
Christ, but is a servant of Christ, as are the other bishops as
well. The entire priestly order exists to serve in humility and
love ; the State alone has to rule. The indispensable condition
of priestly service is imitation of the suffering man Jesus. If a
priest disregards this and serves sin, he is no priest, and all his
sacred acts are in vain.

But behind all these positions, which were for the most part
already made familiar by older reform parties, there lies a distinctly defined conception of the Church, which is not new,
however, but is rather only a variety of the Thomist. Wyclif's
conception of the Church can be wholly derived from the Augustinian (influence on Wyclif of Thomas of Bradwardine, the
Augustinian), when the peculiar national and political conditions
are kept in view under which he stood,[1] and also the impression
which the Franciscan ideal—even to the length of communism
indeed—made upon him. Huss stood under quite similar conditions, and could therefore simply adopt Wyclifism.

Wyclif sets out from the Augustinian definition of the Church

---

[1] This has been observed especially by Buddensieg, l.c. In dealing with Wyclif,
as with all the opposition movements from the thirteenth century to the fifteenth, the
great national economical revolution in Europe must be remembered. At the same
time the Anglo-Saxon type in Wyclif, as contrasted with the Romanic, must not be
overlooked.

as the entire sum of the predestinated in heaven and on earth. To this Church the merely præsciti (foreknown) do not belong; they do not belong to it even at the time when they are righteous; while, on the other hand, every predestinated one is a member of it, even if at the time he is still not under grace, or, say, is a heathen or Jew. No one can say of himself without special revelation (revelatio specialis) that he belongs to this Church. This momentous proposition, which dominates the whole of the further discussion, is a clear proof that Wyclif and Huss stood on Catholic ground, *i.e.*, that the significance of *faith* was entirely ignored. As a fact, the definition of the Church as congregatio fidelium was a mere title; for, as we shall immediately see, faith was not what is decisive; it comes to view rather within the conception of the Church as merely an empirical mark (equivalent to community of the baptized). Further, as it is an established fact that no one can be certain of his election—for how can one surrender himself here on earth to the *constant* feeling of felicity which springs from the vision and enjoyment of God after all other feelings have been quenched? how is it possible to attain to this state of heart even now?— then there is either no mark at all by which the existence of the Church may be determined, or we may rest assured that the Church of Christ exists where the legacy of Christ is in force— the *Sacraments* and the *law of Christ*. The latter, not the former, is the opinion of Wyclif and Huss. *The true Church of Christ is where the law of Christ reigns,*[1] *i.e., the law of love, humility,* and *poverty*, which means the apostolic life in imitation of Christ, and where, accordingly, the Sacraments also, which prepare for the life beyond, are administered in the Spirit of Christ. *The predestination doctrine is not brought into service therefore with the view of making room for faith over against the Sacraments, or in order to construct a purely invisible Church*—what interest would Wyclif and Huss have then had in the reform of the empirical Church?[2]—but it is brought into

---

[1] "Lex Christi" and "lex evangelica" were the terms constantly applied to the contents of the New Testament even by the Reformers of the fourteenth and fifteenth centuries, see Otto Clemen, Pupper von Goch (Leipzig, 1896), p. 120 ff.; but at the same time it is in some way to hold good that that law is a "lex perfectæ libertatis."

[2] See Gottschick, l.c., p. 360 ff.

service *that it may be possible to oppose the claims of the hierarchy as godless pretensions and to set up the law of Christ as the true nota ecclesiæ catholicæ.*   For from what has been shown it follows that there can be no rights in the Church which do not originate from the acknowledged supremacy of the law of Christ.   The question is entirely one of establishing this law. A leap is taken over faith.   The important matter is fides caritate formata (faith deriving form from love), *i.e.*, caritas, *i.e.*, the law of the Sermon on the Mount (consilia).[1]   What is contested is not only the hierarchical gradation, but the alleged *independent* right of the clergy to represent the Church and administer the means of grace without observing the law of Christ.[2]   How can such a right exist, if the Church is nothing but the community of the predestinated, and as such can have no other mark save the law of Christ?   How, again, can acts of priests be valid, when the presupposition of all action in the Church, and for the Church, is lacking to them—obedience to the law of Christ? But this law has its quintessence in the Sermon on the Mount and in the example of the poor life of Jesus; nevertheless (this feature is genuinely Augustinian) the whole of Scripture is at the same time the law of Christ.   This standard then must be applied to all ecclesiastical practice.   And yet in its application, which of course must become entirely arbitrary as soon as the attempt is really made to follow the thousand directions literally, everything is to be subordinated to the law of love that ministers in poverty and—to the reigning dogma.   With the exception of the transubstantiation doctrine, which Wyclif alone objected to, both Reformers left dogma entirely untouched, nay, they strengthened it.   What they aimed at reforming, and did reform, were the ordinances relating to worship and Sacraments, which had originated in the immediately preceding centuries, and were justly felt by them to be restrictions on the

---

1 See Ritschl, Rechtfertigung und Versöhnung, 2 ed. I., p. 134.

2 Huss adhered firmly to the Catholic distinction between clergy and laity.   Wyclif regarded laymen called directly by Christ as capable of priestly acts.   But that a direct appointment by Christ is valid could scarcely be contested even by a Romish opponent of Wyclif.   The only question, therefore, must be as to whether such an appointment can be established.   Hence the assertion that Wyclif and Huss opposed the universal priesthood to the priestly order is incorrect.

full and direct efficacy of word and Sacrament. At the same
time they did not renounce the view that the numerus predes-
tinatorum (number of the predestinated) may find its earthly
embodiment in a true, empirical Church. It certainly could
not but come about, that in the Hussite movement, when once
the watchword had again been emphatically given forth that
everything must be reformed according to the law of holy
Scripture, there should be introduced into the Church the disorder and terror connected with Old Testament socialist and
apocalyptic ideas ; but such things seldom last beyond the
third generation, nor did they last longer then. There was a
falling back upon patience, and the once aggressive enthusiasm
became changed into silent mistrust and reserve.

How this Wyclifite conception of the Church, which really
came into conflict with the Romish only about the Pope and
the sacrament of penance, and arose from an over-straining of
the good Catholic principle of the lex Christi (law of Christ),
can be called evangelical, is difficult to understand. Equally
with Thomas's conception of the Church it leaves *faith* aside, as
Luther understood it ; and it has as its presuppositions, in
addition to the predestinarian doctrine, the Catholic conception
of salvation, the Catholic conception of the Sacraments, and the
Catholic ideal of poverty. It puts an end to the priests who
govern the world ; but it does not put an end to the priests
who dispense the Sacraments, who expound the law of God, and
who alone—by the apostolic life—perfectly fulfil it. Will these
world-ruling priests not return, if it must really be the highest
interest of man to prepare himself for the life beyond by means
of the Sacraments, seeing that that life is not attainable by faith
alone, and a clear, certain and perfect faith does not fall to the
lot of every man ? [1] But however certain it is that this question

---

[1] See Gottschick, l.c., p. 364 f. : "Huss has no other view of salvation than the
ordinary Catholic one. Man's goal is union with God through visio dei and the love
dependent thereon. There is preparation on earth for this by means of faith and the
meritorious fulfilment of the law of love. By faith is understood throughout the
theoretic assent to a quantum of doctrines ; there suffices for a good part of this
quantum the fides implicita. Faith having value only as fides caritate formata, it
follows that the chief matter is fulfilment of the law. But the qualification for this
is dependent on the infusion of grace on the ground of the merit of Christ, a grace

can only be answered in the affirmative (as long as the Sacraments play the chief part in the Church, the priest will be a man of power on earth, and as long as the letter of scripture is regarded as the law of Christ, the official interpreters will be the ruling authorities in the Church) it is equally certain that the Wyclifite conception of the Church represented a great advance. The attempt was here made to separate the religious from the secular; moreover, the value of the law of Christ, as something spiritual, was placed on a level with the value of the Sacraments, nay, the efficacy of all ecclesiastical acts was derived from inward Christian disposition ; the whole " objective " right of a hierarchy in the Church was shaken ;[1] Christians were most urgently reminded that the gospel has to do with life.   And this did not take place outside theology, as if these were personally-formed notions, but on the ground and in the name of the truly ecclesiastical theology.

About the year 1500 Hussitism, as a great movement, had run its course.   But it exerted an incalculable influence : it loosened the hold of the hierarchical papal conception of the Church on the hearts and minds of men, and helped to prepare the way for the great revolution.   No doubt at the beginning of the Reformation the greatest vagueness of view prevailed among the really pious in the land : there was no wish to part with the Pope, but episcopalist (conciliar) and

whereby sin is abolished.   And Huss never mentions any other way in which this takes place than by preaching and the Sacraments, more particularly baptism and the Eucharist or the sacrifice of the mass."   Cf. the passages quoted by Gottschick, l.c., from the treatise de ecclesia, among which those upon fides implicita are specially instructive.   I. 38 : " Christianus debet fidem *aliqualiter* cognoscere."   62 : " Quantum oporteat *fidelem* de necessitate salutis *explicite* credere, non est meum pro nunc discutere, cum deus omnipotens suos electos secundum gradum fidei *multiplicem* ad se trahit."   259 : " Quicunque habuerit fidem caritate formatam . . . in communi sufficit cum virtute perseverantiæ ad salutem. . . . Non exigit deus, ut omnes filii sui sint continue pro viatione sua in actu cogitanti particulari de *qualibet fidei particula* (so always quantitatively estimated), sed satis est, quod post posita desidia habeant fidem in habitu formatam."   Wyclif had a similar opinion (" omnia sacramenta sensibilia rite administrata [but for this there is requisite also, and above all, the priest who lives like the apostles] habent efficaciam salutarem ").

[1] The Council of Constance contested the Wyclifite-Hussite propositions that were adverse to the Pope, as also the exclusive definition of the Church as universitas prædestinatorum.

Waldensian-Hussite ideas were widely disseminated.[1] A distinct settlement was necessary : either the establishment of
the papal system, or a new view of the Church that should be
able to furnish a firm basis for the numerous and heavy assaults
upon that system.   The *empirico-monarchical* conception of the
Church was challenged by the Episcopalists, the *juristic* by
Wyclif and Huss—in this lies the chief importance of these
men.   But for the juristic conception they substituted a
moralistic.   From the latter the former will always develop
itself again.   What was lacking was the conception of a Church
to which one belongs through living faith.   The mere criticising
of the hierarchy, however much courage that might imply, was
not all that was needed.   Nor was it enough that the legal
ordinances of the Church should be traced back to their moral
conditions.   For having done this Wyclif and Huss cannot be
too highly praised.   But it must not be forgotten that the
Church of Christ has to take the criteria for judging what she
is from Romans V.-VIII.   One thing, however, and for our
purposes the most important, will be made apparent from this
whole review, namely, that the manifold development of the
conception of the Church in this period, so far from threatening
the old dogma, gave it an always firmer lodgment—not, indeed,
as a living authority, but as a basis and boundary line.   Where
would the Waldensians and the Hussites, with their appeals to
the lex Christi, to Scripture and the Apocalypse, have arrived at,
if they had not been held fast by the quiet but powerful force of
the ancient dogma ?

But at this point we may extend our observations still a step
further.   Is it the case, then, that the so-called " Reformers
before the Reformation " were the only reformers before the
Reformation, or is it not apparent rather that this designation
has only a proper meaning when it is applied, not to any *one*
phenomenon in the Mediæval Church, but to the Mediæval
Church as a whole ?   For the highest level of observation, there
lies between the Christianity of the Ancient Church and the

---

[1] Besides the works on the history of the spread of Hussitism (especially von Bezold,
Zur Gesch. des Husitenthums 1874, and the Studies of Haupt), see the works of
Keller, which, however, must be used with caution.

Christianity of the Reformation, the Christianity of the Middle
Ages as the intermediate stage, *i.e.*, as the Pre-Reformation.
None of its leading tendencies can be dispensed with in the
picture, not even the hierarchical.   The very conception of the
Church shows that.   For those opposing the " Pre-Reformers"
represented with their Church ideal the certainty that Christ
has left behind Him on earth a *kingdom*, in which He, as the
exalted One, is present, and the holiness of which does not
depend on the moral goodness of its members, but on the
grace which God gives them.   This thought they no doubt disfigured and secularised, yet it must not be said that it had
value for them only in its disfigured form.   No, even it was for
many really an expression of Christian piety.   They thought of
the living and reigning Christ when they thought of the Pope
and his power, of the bishops and the Church, who reduced the
whole world to their rule.   In this form their faith was a necessary complement to the individualistic Christianity of the Mystics,
and the Reformation with its thesis of the holy community and
the kingdom of God, which have Christ in their midst, connected
itself directly with the Catholic thoughts of Augustine and the
Middle Ages, after it had learned from Paul and Augustine to
judge spiritual things spiritually.

3. *On the History of Ecclesiastical Science.*

In connection with the history of piety we have been already
obliged to enter upon the history of theology ; for piety and
theology are most intimately related in the Middle Ages.   In
the former chapter also (p. 23 ff.) a sketch of the history of
science till the close of the twelfth century has been given.
From the immense amount of material in the thirteenth to the
fifteenth century only some cardinal points shall be brought
more prominently to view.[1]

1 See the histories of philosophy by Erdmann, Ueberweg-Heinze (where are the
fullest lists of literary works), Stöckl and Werner (Monograph on Thomas v. Aqu.,
various dissertations on Duns Scotus, Die Scholastik des spateren Mittelalters in 3
vols., 1881 f. : (1) Johannes Duns Scotus.   (2) Die Nachscotistische Scholastik.   (3)
Der Augustinismus des späteren Mittelalters).   Baur, Vorles. über die christl. Dog-

The great advancement of mediæval science from the beginning of the thirteenth century was occasioned (1) by the
immense triumph of the Church and the papacy under Innocent
III. and his successors; (2) by the intensification of piety in
consequence of the Mendicant Orders movement;[1] (3) by the
enrichment and extension of general culture, which was partly
a consequence of inner developments, and partly arose from
contact with the East, in Palestine, Constantinople, and Spain.[2]
Here the acquaintance, now obtained for the first time, with
the *true* Aristotle, the teacher of logic, physics, ethics, and
politics, became of supreme importance. His philosophy,
understood as dogmatism,[3] was hailed as a gospel, or at least as

---

mengesch. 2 Bd., p. 199 ff.   We owe to Bach a beautiful dissertation on Albertus M.,
distinguished by thorough knowledge and abundant points of view.

[1] On the entrance of the Minorite Order into the scientific movement, see Werner,
Duns Scotus, p. 4 ff.

[2] Cf. Books 6-8 of the History of the Aufklärung by Reuter, especially the
sections on the Averrhoistic Aufklärung, as well as on the importance of the
Arabic and Jewish middle-men, also on the influence of the Natural Sciences and
on the University of Paris in the thirteenth century.   The Arabs Avicenna (ob. 1037)
and Averrhoes (ob. 1198), the former supranaturalistic, the latter pantheistic, in his
tendency, were the most important commentators on Aristotle, whose works became
known to the West by means of Spanish Jews.   But by Averrhoes, who exercised a
powerful attraction, Aristotle was in the first instance discredited, so that several
Church interdicts were issued against him.   But it was soon observed that Aristotle,
so far from favouring pantheism, really refuted it.   Scotus Erigena and Averrhoes—
his system meant for the Church of the thirteenth century what Gnosticism in the
second century, Manichæanism in the fourth, Socinianism in the seventeenth, meant
for Church Christianity, and so Renan, Averroes et l'Averroisme—were now regarded as
the real enemies of Church dogma.   Naturalistic pantheism in general now became
the chief object of persecution ; to oppose it, the supranaturalistic elements were derived from Aristotelianism, and this Aristotelianism had the widest scope given to it
(see Schwane, Dogmengesch. des Mittelalters, p. 33 ff.).   Among the Jewish scholars it
was chiefly Maimonides who influenced the Schoolmen of the thirteenth century.
Thomas owed very much to him, and in part transcribed him (see Merx, Prophetie
des Joel, 1879).   In this way the juristic-casuistic element in Scholasticism was still
further strengthened, and pharisaic-talmudic theologoumena crept into mediæval
theology, which are partly traceable to the Persian age of Judaism.   But besides this,
Neoplatonic and Aristotelian material found its way to the schoolmen from the
translations of the Jews, who had rendered the Arabic versions of the Greek philosophical writings into Latin ; see Bardenhewer, Die Schrift de causis, 1882.

[3] In the sense in which Kant exposed and refuted dogmatism.   It was only Roger
Bacon who stoutly fought his way out of these fetters in the thirteenth century ; see
Reuter, II., p. 67 ff.

the necessary introduction to one ("præcursor Christi in naturalibus") and through him the science of the thirteenth century received an almost incalculable amount of material, and, above all, impulses to master the material.

The two new forces of commanding importance in the period, the Mendicant Orders [1] and Aristotle, had first to achieve a position for themselves.   At the beginning they met with hostility from the old Orders, and from the teachers and universities that were in alliance with them.   An attitude of self-defence was assumed towards both.   The new Aristotelianism, indeed, came under ecclesiastical proscription, and there was a wish to exclude theologians of the Mendicant Orders from university chairs.   There were always some, too, who still were influenced by the attacks in general on the scientific-dialectic theology, which had been made by such men as John of Salisbury and Walter of St. Victor.[2]   But the new movement asserted itself with an irresistible energy, and the opposition was silenced.

Yet this was only possible because the new factors really furnished nothing new, but completed the triumph of the *Church* over everything spiritual.   The new Aristotle, as he was understood, taught the theory of knowledge, metaphysics and politics, which admitted of a surer vindication of dogma against such opposition as had formerly appeared, *e.g.*, in William of Champeaux and Roscellin, and offered a defence against the

---

[1] Among all the Orders the Dominican was the first to adopt into its rules directions as to study (see Denifle, Archiv. fur Litt.-u. Kirchengesch. des Mittelalters I., p. 165 ff.

[2] Cf. *e.g.*, for the period about 1250 the Chronicle of Salimbene and Michael l.c., p. 39 f.   That in the Dominican Order itself a tendency had at first to be checked, which, after the style of the older Orders, emphasised asceticism so strongly that no room was left for study, which indeed described science (including theology) as dangerous and pernicious, has been convincingly proved by Wehofer O. P. from the book of the Dominican Gérard de Frachet, "Vitas Patrum" (published not long after 1256, issued in the Monum. Ord. Frat. Prædic. Historica. Löwen, 1896), and from the attitude of Humbert of Romans (General of the Order from 1254 to 1263 ; Görres-Jahrbuch f. Philos. Bd. IX., 1896, p. 17 ff.)   That "propter philosophiam" one goes to hell or at least—after a great example—receives here already on earth a sound cudgelling from angels, was never forgotten in the Catholic Church.   The founder of the Trappist Order simply attempted to bring into force again an old monastic tradition : "study, *i.e.*, philosophy is sin."

dangers both of an eccentric realism and of an empirical mode of thought. If it is permissible, nay necessary, to conceive of the universals on the one hand, as the archetypes that express the cosmos of ideas in the thought of God, then they exist *ante rem* (before the thing); if on the other hand they must be regarded as simply realised in things (categories and forms) then they are *in re* (in the thing); if, finally, it is undeniable that it is only by the observation of things that they are obtained, that accordingly the intellect derives them from experience, then they are *post rem* (after the thing). In this way it was possible to apply to every dogma the epistemological mode of view which seemed best fitted to defend it. The "qualified" realism, which could assume the most different forms, and which had been already represented by Abelard, certainly more in a spirit of sceptical reserve than with a view to speculative construction, became dominant in the thirteenth century. But what was of most importance was that the great theologians who developed it showed even greater energy than their predecessors in subordinating the whole structure of thought to the principle that all things are to be understood by tracing them back to God.

But the tracing back to God was equivalent to subjecting all knowledge to the authority of the Church. The same science which displayed an astonishing energy of thought, and through such scholars as Thomas made a really important advance upon antiquity in the ethical and political sciences, appeared in many respects still more fettered than the science of the eleventh and twelfth centuries; *for in its view, not only the old dogma* (" articuli fidei "), *but the entire department of ecclesiastical practice,* the principles of which were traced back to the articuli fidei, *was absolutely authoritative, and it proceeded much more frankly than before on the principle that in particular questions every instance of authority had as much weight as a deliberate reflection of the understanding.*

It was only in the thirteenth century—and by the theologians of the Mendicant Orders—that the whole existing structure of ecclesiasticism was theologically vindicated, and its newest and most questionable parts, as well as the oldest and most important, declared inviolate by "science"; it was only in the thirteenth century that there was introduced that complete inter-blending of faith on authority and of science which means that at one and the same level there is a working at one time with the "credo," at another time with the "intelligo"; such interblending is not yet found in Anselm, for example.   Certainly it was still theoretically held that theology, resting on revelation, is a (specula-tive) science.[1]   But it was not held as required, nor even as possible, to rear on the basis of faith a purely rational structure: there was rather an alternating between authority and reason ; they were regarded as parallel methods which one employed. The object in view indeed continued to be the knowledge that culminates in the visio dei ; but there was no longer the wish always to eliminate more fully as knowledge advanced the element of faith (authority) in order to retain at the last pure knowledge ; at all stages, rather, the element of authority was held as justifiable and necessary.   Nay, there was now the conviction that there are two provinces, that of natural theology, and that of specific (revealed).   The two, certainly, are thought of as being in closest harmony ; but yet the conviction has been obtained that there are things known, and these, too, the most important, which belong simply to revealed theology, and which can be inter-related certainly, but not identified with natural theology.   Natural theology, moreover, must subordinate itself to revealed, for theology has its foundation in revelation.   In point of fact, however, the dogmatic theologian alternated between

---

[1] See the first question in Part I. of the Summa of Thomas ; Art. I. : " Utrum sit necessarium præter philosophicas disciplinas aliam doctrinam haberi." Art. II : " Utrum sacra doctrina sit scientia."   Answer : " Sacram doctrinam esse scientiam. Sed sciendum est quod duplex est scientiarum genus.   Quædam enim sunt, quæ procedunt ex principiis notis lumine naturali intellectus sicut Arithmetica ; quædam vero sunt quæ procedunt ex principiis notis lumine superioris scientiæ, sicut Perspectiva procedit ex principiis notificatis per Geometriam. . . . Et hoc modo sacra doctrina est scientia, quia procedit ex principiis notis lumine superioris scientiæ, quæ scil. est scientia dei et beatorum.   Unde sicut Musicus credit principia revelata sibi ab Arith-metico, ita doctrina sacra credit principia revelata sibi a deo." Art. III. : " Utrum sacra doctrina sit una scientia?"   Conclusio : "Cum omnia considerata in sacra doctrina sub una formali ratione divinæ revelationis considerentur, eam unam scientiam esse sentiendum est."   Artic. IV. : " Utrum s. doctrina sit scientia practica?" Conclusio : " Tametsi s. theologia altioris ordinis sit practica et speculativa, eminenter utramque continens, speculativa tamen magis est quam practica," etc.

reason and revelation, and his structure derived its style from the former ; for in particular questions the content of revelation is not derived solely from the thought of redemption—however truly this, as the visio dei, may be the contemplated end—but is set forth also in a thousand isolated portions, which are nothing else than heterogeneous fragments of a real or supposed knowledge of the world.   It was the effect of holding that very conception of the goal of redemption as visio dei that the view of the content of revelation threatened to become broken up into an incalculable number of *things known,* and, in spite of the still retained title, acquired the character of a natural knowledge of supernatural things.   Accordingly there was now introduced also the idea of articuli mixti, *i.e.,* of such elements of knowledge as are given both in a natural way and by revelation, only in the latter way, however, in perfection.   What appeared outlined already in Tertullian (see Vol. V. c. ii.) as the distinctive character of Western theology, now came to its fullest development.

From the newly-discovered Aristotle the scholars derived courage to advance from the compilation of mere " sentences " to the rearing of entire doctrinal systems.   The imposing form of the Church also, with the unfolding of its uniform power, may have been a co-operating influence here ; for the Scholasticism of the thirteenth century presents the same spectacle in the sphere of knowledge, which the Church of which it is the servant presents in the sphere of human life generally.   In the one sphere as in the other everything is to be reduced to subjection ; in the one as in the other everything is to be brought into a harmonious system ; in the one as in the other the position is held, tacitly or expressly, that the Church is Christ, and Christ is the Church.   Thus the theological science of the thirteenth century can be described as *the submitting to dialectic-systematic revision of ecclesiastical dogma and ecclesiastical practice, with the view of unfolding them in a system having unity and comprehending all that in the highest sense is worthy of being known, with the view of proving them, and so of reducing to the service of the Church all the forces of the understanding and the whole product of science.*   But most intimately connected with this end is the other, namely, the theologian's attaining in this way to the *visio (fruitio) dei ;* these two ends, indeed, *are mutually involved ;* for all knowledge of Church doctrine and of Church practice is knowledge of God—this was taught by the Church itself.   Now, if the gradual knowledge of God is the only means whereby the individual can attain to salvation (visio dei), then in theology the objective and subjective aims simply coincide ; one serves the Church in serving himself, and the converse is equally true.   The great Schoolmen by no means felt that they wrought as slaves, labouring under compulsion for their masters. The only end indeed that was clearly before them was their own advancement in the knowledge of God ; but, standing as faithful sons within the Church, to which all power was given in heaven and on earth, their speculations necessarily served, with more or less of intention on their part, to glorify the Church's power and give a divine character to all that it did.   And yet how many things did they come to know, the truth of which is entirely independent of the truth of Church theory and practice; how necessary and how helpful was even this period in the general history of science and theology ; and how many seeds were sown broadcast by the great Schoolmen, of the develop- ment of which they did not allow themselves to dream !   Never yet in the world's history was any science quite fruitless which served God with true devotion.   Theology has at any time become a hindrance, only when it has lost faith in itself or become vacillating.   We shall see that this was verified also in mediæval theology.

For all that has been stated up to this point applies only to the pre-Scotist Scholasticism ; it applies above all to Thomas. He exercised, moreover, an enduring influence on the period that followed, and his influence is still at work at the present day.   His predecessors and contemporaries have passed out of view in him.   The Thomist science, as embodied above all in the " Summa," is characterised by the following things: (1) by the conviction that religion and theology are essentially of a speculative (not practical) nature, that they must therefore be imparted and appropriated spiritually, that it is possible so to appropriate them, and that ultimately no conflict can arise between reason and revelation ; (2) by strict adherence to

Augustinianism, and in particular to the Augustinian doctrines of God, predestination, sin and grace,[1] but on the other hand by contesting on principle Averrhoism; (3) by a thoroughly minute acquaintance with Aristotle, and by a comprehensive and strenuous application of the Aristotelian philosophy, so far as Augustinianism admitted in any way of this (under the conception of God the Areopagitic-Augustinian view is only slightly limited); (4) by a bold vindication of the highest ecclesiastical claims by means of an ingenious theory of the State, and a wonderfully observant study of the empirical tendencies of the papal ecclesiastical and sacramental system. Aristotle the politician and Augustine the theologian, two enemies, became allies in Thomas; in that consists the importance of Thomas in the world's history.   While he is a

---

[1] Thomas shows himself an Augustinian by his estimation also of Holy Scripture. *Scripture alone was for him absolutely certain revelation.* All other authorities he held as only relative.   Very many passages can be quoted from Thomas to prove that the "formal principle of the reformation" had a representative in the great Schoolman.   Cf. Holzhey, Die Inspiration d. hl. Schrift in der Anschauung des Mittelalters, 1895.   This book, which did not necessarily require to be written, gives an account of the estimation of Holy Scripture on the part of the mediæval theologians and sectaries from the period of Charles the Great till the Council of Trent. The author remarks very correctly (p. 164 f.) that the view of Holy Scripture, or the mode of apprehending the notion of inspiration, does not pass beyond what is furnished by the Church Fathers, and that even among the theologians from the time of Alcuin till the beginning of the sixteenth century the greatest agreement regarding Holy Scripture prevailed.   But when the author says further, that the doctrine of the absolute perspicuity and sufficiency of the Bible finds no confirmation in the mediæval Church—for even if expressions of the kind were to be met with among the mediæval theologians, yet the living union with the Church and tradition is at the same time presupposed—then that is in *one* respect a platitude.   It is such also (but only in *one* respect) when the author remarks that the Middle Ages always recognised the exposition of Holy Scripture as an attribute of the Church.   But on the really interesting problem Holzhey has scarcely touched, namely whether even in the Middle Ages a unique importance does not belong to Scripture as rule for the *vita Christiana* and whether it was not held by very many in this respect as absolutely clear and sufficient.   That this question is to be answered affirmatively is to me beyond doubt.   To the sentence of Duns Scotus: "Sacra scriptura sufficienter continet doctrinam necessariam *viatori*," many parallels may be adduced.   Besides, there is still another question on which Holzhey has scarcely entered : since when was the decision of the Church in matters of faith placed as *another kind of authority* alongside Scripture as of equal weight?   Certainly not yet since Thomas, scarcely only since Duns, but, as Ritschl likewise (Fides implicita, p. 31 f.) remarks, only since Occam, and even since his time not yet generally.

theologian and an Augustinian, he is still always an absolute
thinker full of confidence ; and yet it must not be overlooked
that in him there are already recognisable the seeds of the
destruction of the absolute theology. Although hidden, arbitrary and relative elements have already found a place for themselves in him. It is still his aim to express all things in the
firm and sure categories of the majesty of the deity whose
pervasive power controls all things, and to prove the strict
necessity of all theological deliverances : the Christian religion
is believed in and demonstrated from principles ; but yet at not
a few points the strength failed, and the thinker was obliged to
fall back upon the authority which supports the probable,
although he understood how to maintain for the whole the
impression of absolute validity.[1]

[1] Anselm proves in part the articuli fidei ; in principle Thomas refuses to do so
(Pars. I., Quæst. I., Art. 8) ; yet the ratio bases itself on the articuli fidei in order to
prove something else. We shall see how, as the development proceeded, Scholasticism always relied less on ratio in divine things. This may be an appropriate place
for a short description of the "Summa" (see Portman, Das System der theol. Summe
des hl. Thomas, Luzern 1885). The 1. Part (119 Quæst.) treats of God and the issue
of things from God, the 2. Part (1. Sect.) of general morality (114 Quæst.), the
2. Part (2. Sect.) of special morality (189 Quæst.) from the point of view of the
return of the rational creature to God, the 3. Part of Christ and the Sacraments (90
Quæst.) As a supplement there has been added, from the commentary on the
Lombard, the concluding part of the doctrine of the Sacraments, and the eschatology
(102 Quæst.) Every Quæstio contains a number of articuli, and every articulus is
divided into three parts. First the difficultates are brought forward, which seem to
answer in the negative the question propounded, then the authorities (one or more,
among them here and there also Aristotle), then follows the speculative discussion,
dealing with principles, and thereafter the solution of the particular difficulties (the
conclusiones are not formulated by Thomas himself, but by his commentators). The
scheme corresponds with the Pauline-Augustinian thought : " From God to God."
The introduction (Quæst. 1) comprises the questions on theology as a science, on
the subject (object) of theology—God and all else sub ratione dei,—on the methods
(auctoritas and ratio, theology as doctrina argumentativa, sed " hæc doctrina non
argumentatur ad sua principia probanda, quæ sunt articuli fidei, sed ex eis procedit
ad aliquid aliud probandum . . . nam licet locus ab auctoritate quæ fundatur super
ratione humana sit infirmissimus, locus tamen ab auctoritate quæ fundatur super
revelatione divina est efficacissimus. Utitur tamen sacra doctrina etiam ratione
humana, non quidem ad probandam fidem [*quia per hoc tolleretur meritum fidei*], sed
ad manifestandum aliqua alia, quæ traduntur in hac doctrina. Cum enim gratia non
tollat naturam, sed perficiat, oportet quod naturalis ratio subserviat fidei, sicut et
naturalis inclinatio voluntatis obsequitur caritati. . . . Sacra doctrina utitur
philosophorum auctoritatibus quasi extraneis argumentis et probabilibus, auctoritatibus

But was this strict necessity of any service at all to the
Church? Should the Church not rather have been gratified,
when the understanding perceived its incapacity to follow up
the decisions of authority, and therefore abandoned further

autem canonicae scripturæ utitur proprie et ex necessitate arguendo, auctoritatibus
autem aliorum doctorum ecclesiæ quasi argumentando ex propriis sed probabiliter.
*Innititur enim fides nostra revelationi apostolis et prophetis factæ, qui canonicos libros
scripserunt, non autem revelationi, si qua fuit aliis doctoribus facta*"), on the
exposition of Holy Scripture, etc. Quæst. 2-27 of the I. Part treat of God's existence
(five proofs for God), the nature of God (primum movens, ens a se, perfectissimum,
actus purus), His attributes, His unity and uniqueness, His knowableness, the name
of God, further of the inner life-activity in God (of His knowledge, His world of
ideas, His relation to truth, His life, His will, the expressions of His will, providence
and predestination); lastly, of the outer activity of God or the divine omnipotence,
and of the divine blessedness.   Then follows in Q. 27-44 the investigation de
processione divinarum personarum (Trinity); lastly, Q. 44-119, the doctrine of
creation, and here (1) the origination of things (creation out of nothing, temporality
of the world); (2) division of creation (doctrine of angels, doctrine of the world of
bodies, doctrine of man, here minute investigations into the substance of the soul, the
union of body and soul, the powers of the soul, human knowledge; then concerning
the creation of man, the divine image in man, paradise and the original state); (3)
the doctrine of the divine government of the world (on angels as means of providence,
etc.).   The II. Part (1 sect.) is grounded entirely on the Aristotelian Ethics.   It
begins with an introduction on man's end (the bonum = beatitudo = deus ipse = visio
dei), and proceeds to treat of freedom, the nature of free acts of the will, the
goodness and badness of acts of the will (to the goodness belongs the rationality of
the act of the will), merit and guilt (Q. 6-21).   Thereon follow investigations into
the emotional life of man (passiones), which is minutely analysed (Q. 22-48).   Now
only comes the account of the principles of moral action, of "habitus" or of the
qualities of the soul.   After an introduction (Q. 49 sq.) the doctrine of virtue is
discussed (divided according to the object into intellectual, moral, and theological
virtues), the cause of the virtues, their peculiarities (virtue as moderation or the
"middle" course between two extremes) and the culmination of the virtues in the
gifts of the Holy Ghost (the eight beatitudes and the fruits of the Spirit).   This is
followed by the doctrines of the nature of sin (contrary to reason and nature), of the
division of sins, of the relation of sins to one another, of the subject (the will), the
causes (inner and outer) of sin, of original sin and its effects (the deterioration of
nature, darkening = macula, the reatus poenæ, mortal sins and venial sins).   All this
belongs to the inner principles of moral conduct.   This part concludes with the
discussion of the outer principles, namely, the law and grace.   The "law" is
discussed on all sides, as eternal law (that is, the law according to which God
Himself acts, and whose reflected rays are all laws valid for the creatures), as natural
law, as human law, as Old Testament and New Testament law, and as law of
"counsels" for special perfection.   But the New Testament law, as it is inward, and
infused by grace, is the law of grace, and thu the way is prepared for passing to the
second outer principle of moral acts—to grace which gives man aid for the good.   Grace
is the outer principle of the supernatural good; in the intellectual sphere it is not

effort ?   To this question the reply must not be absolutely affirmative, but still less must it be negative.   The Church, as it then already was, and as it still is to-day, needs both things ; it

necessary for the knowledge of natural truths, but it is so for the knowledge of the supernatural ; it is likewise requisite for ability to do the supernatural good.   Here there is a keen polemic against Pelagianism : man cannot by naturally good acts even prepare himself sufficiently for grace ; he can neither convert himself, nor continue always steadfast in goodness.   An inquiry into the nature, division, causes, and effects of grace (doctrine of justification, doctrine of the meritoriousness of good works), forms the conclusion.   The II. Part, 2. section now contains special ethics, namely, first, the precise statement of the theological virtues (faith, hope, and love), the commands corresponding to these virtues, and the sins against them, then the discussion of the cardinal virtues, wisdom, righteousness (here in Q. 57-123 the most exhaustive account is given, inasmuch as religiousness as a whole is placed under this term), courage, and moderation ; lastly, the discussion of the special virtues, *i.e.*, of the gifts of grace and duties of station (Q. 171-189).   Under this last title there are dealt with (*a*) the charisms, (*b*) the two forms of life (the contemplative and the active), (*c*) the stations of perfection (namely, the station of the bishops as the virtuosi in neighbourly love, and the station of the monks, with special reference to the Mendicant monks).   The III. Part now aims at showing by what provision and means the return of the rational creature to God has become possible by way of faith, hope, and love, namely, through Christ and the Sacraments.   To this there is the intention to add eschatology.   Hence there is a treatment here (1) of Christ, in particular of His incarnation and His natures.   After a discussion of the necessity of the incarnation (on account of sin, and since a satisfactio de condigno was requisite) for the removal of original sin, the personal unity, the divine person, of Christ, and His human nature are set forth (in which connection, Q. 8, there is reference to the Church as the mystic body of Christ, and the thought of "Christus" as the head of mankind is strongly accentuated) ; then the consequences of the personal union (communicatio idiomatum) and all bearings of the constitution of the Godman are explained.   On this follows (2) a section on the work of Christ, which, however, contains almost no speculation whatever, but illustrates in an edifying way the history of Christ from his entrance into the world (Q. 27-31, the doctrine of Mary).   In connection with the suffering and death of Christ, the point of view of the "conveniens" as distinguished from the "necessarium" has special prominence given to it.   Immediately after the work of Christ the doctrine of the Sacraments is added (Q. 60 sq.) ; for redemption is imparted to individuals only through the Sacraments, which have their efficacy from Christ, and through which men are incorporated into Christ.   The statement begins with the general doctrine of the Sacraments (nature, necessity, effect, cause, number, connection) ; then follows the discussion of baptism, confirmation, the eucharist, and penance.   Here Thomas was obliged to lay down his pen.   It was not granted to him to complete his "Summa."   What was still wanting, as has been remarked, was supplied from his other works ; but in this supplement we miss somewhat of the strictness marking the expositions given by himself in the Summa, since it was mainly constructed out of notes and excursus on the text of the Lombard.   Observe lastly, that in the Summa repetitions are not only not avoided, but occur to an incalculable extent.

is indispensable to it that its articuli fidei and modes of practice
be *also* proved, and their rationality brought to view ; but it is
still more needful to it that there be a blind surrender to its
authority.

In this respect there was still obviously too little done by
Thomas. In him, the determination of the relation of ratio to
auctoritas is, indeed, marked by a quite special amount of confusion, the claims of faith (as faith on authority) and of knowledge receive no elucidation whatever, not to speak of reconciliation, and he stated not a few propositions in which there was a
complete surrender to authority, that " faith " might not be
deprived of its " merit " (see the sentence quoted above :
" Sacred doctrine, however, uses human reason also, not indeed
for proving faith, for through this the merit of faith would be
lost " [Utitur tamen sacra doctrina etiam ratione humana, non
quidem ad probandam fidem, quia per hoc tolleretur meritum
fidei]).   Yet his real interest in theology is still the same as
that of Augustine.   Theology is cognition of God in the strict
sense ; the necessity, which is accentuated in God, must also
pervade the whole cognition of Him.   The articuli fidei, and all
results of world-knowledge, must be merged in the unity of this
knowledge which truly liberates the soul and leads it back to
God.   At bottom the imposing and complicated system is
extremely simple.   Just as the perfect Gothic Cathedral, from
its exhibiting what is really an organic style, expresses a single
architectural thought, and subordinates all to this, even making
all practical needs of worship serviceable to it, so this structure
of thought, although all ecclesiastical doctrines are submissively
and faithfully taken account of, still proclaims the *one* thought,
that the soul has had its origin in God, and returns to Him
through Christ, and even the Augustinian-Areopagite turn
given to this thought, that God *is* all in all, is not denied by
Thomas.

But this attitude is dangerous.   There will always be a fresh
development from it of the " Spurious Mysticism," as the
Catholics call it, in which the subject is eager to go his own
way, and avoids *complete* dependence upon the Church.   Nevertheless, the course of scientific development came to be helpful

CHAP. II.]   HISTORY OF ECCLESIASTICAL SCIENCE.   161

to the Church, and we may almost say that the Church here
gathered figs of thistles.   The assiduous study of Aristotle, and
the keener perception gained through philosophy and observation, weakened the confidence of the theologians regarding the
rationality and strict necessity of the revealed articles of faith.
They began to forego revising them by means of reason, and
subordinating them as component parts of a system to a
uniform thought.   Their scientific sense was strengthened, and
when they now turned to the revealed tenets, they found in
them, not necessity, but arbitrariness.   Moreover, the further
they advanced in psychology and secular science and discovered
what cognition really is, the more sceptical they became towards
the "general": "latet dolus in generalibus" (deception lurks
under general conceptions).   They began to part with their
inward interest in the general, and their faith in it.   The "idea,"
which is to be regarded as "substance," and the "necessity" of
the general, disappeared for them ; they lost confidence in the
knowledge that knows everything.   The particular, in its concrete expression, acquired interest for them : will rules the
world, the will of God and the will of the individual, not an incomprehensible substance, or a universal intellect that is the
product of construction.   This immense revolution is represented
in mediæval science by Duns Scotus, the acutest scholastic
thinker ;[1] but only with Occam did it attain completion.

We should expect that the result of this revolution would
have been either a protest against the Church doctrine, or an
attempt to test it by its foundations, and to subject it to critical

[1] See Baur, l.c. II., p. 235 : "The thorough reasonableness of the ecclesiastical
faith, or the conviction that for all doctrines of the ecclesiastical system some kind of
rationes can be discovered, by which they are established even for the thinking
reason, was the fundamental presupposition of Scholasticism.   But after Scholasticism
had risen to its highest point in Thomas and Bonaventura, it became itself doubtful
again of this presupposition.   This very important turning-point in the history of
Scholasticism, after which it tended increasingly to fall to pieces, is represented by
Duns Scotus."   (Doctrine of double truth as consequence of the Fall !)   Besides
Duns Scotus, and after him, it was chiefly the doctor resolutissimus Durandus who,
at first a Thomist, passed over to Nominalism and obtained currency for its mode
of thought (see his commentary on the Lombard).   He worked in the first third of
the fourteenth century ; on him see Werner in the 2. vol. of the "Scholastik des
späteren Mittelalters."

162 HISTORY OF DOGMA. [CHAP. II.

reconstruction. But it was 200 years before these results followed, in Socinianism on the one hand, and in the Reformation theology on the other. What happened at first was quite different : *there was a strengthening of the authority of the Church, and, along with full submission to it, a laying to its account of responsibility for the articles of faith and for the principles of its practice.*[1] What was once supported by reason in league with authority must now be supported by the latter alone. Yet this conversion of things was felt to be by no means an act of despair, but to be an obviously required act of obedience to the Church, so complete was the supremacy of the latter over the souls of men, even though at the time it might be in the deepest debasement.

When Nominalism obtained supremacy in theology and in the Church, the ground was prepared for the threefold development of doctrine in the future : Post-Tridentine Catholicism, Protestantism and Socinianism are to be understood from this point of view.[2]

Nominalism exhibits on one side a number of outstanding excellences : it had come to see that religion is something different from knowledge and philosophy ; it had also discovered the importance of the concrete as compared with hollow abstrac-

---

[1] Even the sufficiency of the Bible was doubted by Duns (against Thomas).

[2] Nominalism only achieved its position in the Church after a hard struggle. From the days of Roscellin it was viewed with suspicion, and the appearing of Occam in its support could not be in its favour (Occam's writings prohibited in 1389 by the University of Paris). But from the middle of the fourteenth century it established itself, and even Dominicans — although the controversy between Thomists and Scotists continued — became advocates of it. Indeed, when Wyclif and other Reformers (Augustinians) again adopted realism, a new chapter began. Realism now, from the close of the fourteenth century, became ecclesiastically suspected (on account of the spiritualism, the determinism, and the intellectualistic mysticism, which seemed to endanger ecclesiasticism). The most important representatives of Post-Scotistic Scholasticism are Petrus Aureolus, John of Baconthorp, Durandus, and Occam. On the "theological mode of thought and the general mental habit" of these scholars, see Werner, Nachscotist. Scholastik, p. 21 ff. On the Thomist scrutiny applied by Capreolus to Post-Scotistic Scholasticism, see ibid., p. 438 ff. That Nominalism, in spite of its dogmatic probabilism, did not, at least at the beginning, weaken dogma, is best illustrated by the fanatical attack on the peculiar doctrine of Pope John XXII.

tions, and to its perception of this it gave brilliant expression,[1] *e.g.*, in psychology ; through recognising the importance of will, and giving prominence to this factor even in God, it strongly accentuated the personality of God, and so prepared the way for the suppression of that Areopagite theology, from which the danger always arose of its causing the world and the reasonable creature to disappear in God ;[2] finally, by placing restrictions on speculation it brought out more clearly the positiveness of historic religion.   But this progress in discernment was dearly purchased by two heavy sacrifices : first, with the surrender of the assurance that an absolute accordant knowledge could be attained, there was also surrendered the assurance of the categorical imperative, of the strict necessity of the moral in God, and of the moral law ; and secondly, among the historic magnitudes to which it submitted itself, it included the Church with its entire apparatus—*the commands of the religious and moral are arbitrary, but the commands of the Church are absolute.*   The haven of rest amidst the doubts and uncertainties of the understanding and of the soul *is the authority of the Church.*

Neither the latter nor the former was, strictly speaking, an innovation.[3]   Through the institution of penance an uncertainty about the moral had for long become widely diffused : it was only a question of expressing in theory what had for centuries been the fundamental thought in practice—*the sovereign right of casuistry.*[4]   Moreover, the contradictory mode of procedure,

---

[1] See Siebeck, Die Anfänge der neueren Psychologie in der Scholastik, in the Zeitschr. f. Philos. u. philos. Kritik, 1888, 1889.

[2] Duns also rejected the Thomist idea that in created things the absolute divine original form is pictured forth, and, under the direction of Aristotle, passed over to a naturalistic doctrine of the world.

[3] Still less, as frequently happens, is the Jesuit Order, with its casuistic dogmatic and ethic, to be made accountable here, as if it was the first to introduce the innovation.   This Order simply entered into the inheritance of mediæval Nominalism.

[4] For the speculative Scholasticism there was substituted the empirico-casuistic. The Nominalists sought to show, with an immense expenditure of acuteness and *speculation*, that there could not be a speculative Scholasticism.   When they had furnished this "proof," there remained over purely hollow forms, which were bound to collapse, or could be maintained only through the compulsory force of a powerful institution.   What was *not* brought within the view of Nominalism, in spite of all its progress, was *the idea of personality* (see for the first time the Renaissance), and consequently the *person of Christ* (see the Reformation), and above all, *history* (see

which the great Schoolmen (Thomas at the head of them), in
obedience to the spirit of jurisprudence, applied to each particular
dogma and each ethical position, necessarily had the effect of
shaking the conviction that there is something absolutely valid.
If, as any page of Thomas will suggest, from two to twelve
grounds can be adduced for every heresy and for many immoral
assertions—if, *e.g.*, there are a dozen grounds on which it may
be alleged that simplex fornicatio is *no* mortal sin (Thomas),
how can the belief be firmly maintained in face of this that it
must nevertheless be regarded as such?

From the conflict between yes and no will there always result
certainty on behalf of the answer which the dogmatic theologian
prefers? How can certainty be reckoned on at all, so long as
there is still *one* ground only for the counter position, and so
long as the *one* ground cannot be shown which alone is valid?
Nominalism only continued here what Realism had begun; it
merely did still more in the way of differentiating and distinguishing; it extended the recognised method of the acute
advocate to ever new fields, to the doctrine of God, to the
doctrines of creation and providence, to the holiness and the
honour of God, to sin and reconciliation, and it always came to
the conclusions, (1) that all is relative and arbitrary—but even
in Thomas's dogmatic already much that is very important in
the doctrine of religion is only "conveniens"; (2) that the
doctrines of revealed religion conflict with natural theology, with
the thought of the understanding about God and the world
(doctrine of double truth). Finally, when Nominalism taught
that, since belief (credere) and understanding (intelligere) cannot
be reconciled, there must be a blind surrender to the authority
of the Church, and that it is just in this blind obedience that
both the nature, and also the *merit*, of faith consist, here also it
only wrought out fully a general Catholic theorem; for Tertullian
had as little doubt as Thomas that all faith begins with sub-

the eighteenth and nineteenth centuries). For it the place of history was still occupied
always by the *rigid Church*. It is not otherwise still to-day with the science of the
Jesuits. They consistently trifle with history, and can treat it, in the tone of a man
of the world, with a certain amusement and easy scorn, when once they have established the things which the conception of the Church requires to be established.

mission. Though afterwards—from the time of Augustine—many
considerations had been adduced for modifying the original
theorem and changing faith into inward assent and love, nevertheless the old position remained the same, that faith is originally
obedience, and that in this it has its initial merit. But if it is
obedience, then it is *fides implicita, i.e.*, submission is enough.
*When the later Nominalism declared with increasing distinctness
the sufficiency of fides implicita, or laid it at the foundation of its
theological reflections*, because many truths of faith, taken in
general, or as dealt with by individuals, do not admit of being
accepted in any other way, *it only gave to an old Catholic thought
a thoroughly logical expression* ;[1] for the danger of transforming

----

[1] The juristic Popes from Gregory VII. onwards, especially the Popes of the
thirteenth century, anticipated the Nominalist doctrine of fides implicita : " In his
commentary on the Decretals (in lib. I., c. 1 de summa trinitate et fide Catholica)
Innocent IV. laid down two momentous rules. First, that it is enough for the laity
to believe in a God who recompenses, but with regard to everything else, of dogma
or moral doctrine, merely to believe implicitly, that is to think, and to say, I believe
what the Church believes. Second, that a cleric must obey even a Pope who issues
an unrighteous command " (Döllinger, Akad. Vorträge II., p. 419). The latter
position does not interest us here ; there is interest, however, in the more precise
definition of the former given by Innocent, (1) that the lower clergy, who cannot
carry on the study of theology, are to be regarded as laymen ; only they must believe
in transubstantiation ; (2) that an error with regard to Christian doctrine (the doctrine
of the Trinity even) does not do harm to a layman, if he at the same time believes
(believes erroneously) that he holds to the doctrine of the Church. Ritschl (Fides
implicita, 1890) has dealt more minutely with this important doctrine. He shows
that it originated from a passage of the Lombard (l. III., dist. 25). But the terminology, the range and the validity of the fides implicita remained uncertain among the
theologians and Popes till the end of the thirteenth century. The great teachers of
the thirteenth century (above all Thomas) confined it within narrow limits, and in
this contradicted the Popes (even Innocent III. comes under consideration ; see
Ritschl, p. 5 f.). Even Duns differs little from Thomas (p. 20 ff.). But Occam
reverted to the exposition of Innocent IV. (p. 30 f.); nay, although he is a doctor, he
claims fides implicita for himself (with regard to the doctrine of the Eucharist) :
" quidquid Romana ecclesia credit, hoc solum et non aliud vel explicite vel implicite
credo." Occam wishes to get free play for his doctrine of the Eucharist, which
diverges from the traditional view ; he saves himself therefore by roundly acknow-
ledging the Church doctrine, that he may then make his divergence appear as a
theological experiment. Here therefore the fides implicita is turned to account for
another purpose. It is remarkable that in its original purpose it was rejected (no
doubt on account of Thomas) by Gregory XI. (against Raymund Lullus); but by
Biel it is again accepted, and treated apparently with reserve, but in the end there is
seen just in it the proof of fides as infusa (as the work of God). Neither Occam nor
Biel wishes by this to treat dogma ironically, on the contrary they show their want

religion into an ecclesiastical regime was at no time absent from
Western Catholicism.[1]

What has already been briefly hinted at above may be distinctly stated here—the problem was *the elimination of Augustinianism from the ecclesiastical doctrine.* The whole turning from
Realism to Nominalism can be represented *theologically* under
this heading. Augustine falls and Aristotle rises—ostensibly
not in theology indeed, but only in the field of world-knowledge,
yet as a fact in theology as well; for no one can keep

of inner freedom in relation to dogma ; but when Laurentius Valla winds up his
critical supplementings with the assertion that he believes as mother Church does, the
irony is manifest. In what way the fides implicita extended into the period of the
Reformation has been shown by Ritschl, p. 40 ff., who also traces out the doctrine
among later Catholic teachers. That there is an element of truth in the recognition
of the fides implicita is easily seen ; but it is not easy to define theologically what is
right in it. Where value is attached to the mere act of obedience, or where, for that
part, there is also something of merit attributed to it, the limit of what is correct is
transgressed.

[1] Into the philosophy of Duns Scotus (see Werner, l.c., and the summary in the
article by Dorner in Herzog's R.-E., 2 ed.) and of Occam (see Wagemann in the
R.-E.) I cannot here enter further. Important theological doctrines of both will fall
to be spoken of in the following section. It is well known that Duns Scotus himself
was not yet a Nominalist, but prepared the way for applying this theory of knowledge
to dogmatics. He already emphasised the independence of the secular sciences
(even of metaphysics) as over against theology, while in general he brought out much
more clearly the independence of the world (in continual discussions with Thomas)
as over against God. To balance this he gives wide scope to the arbitrary will of
God as over against the world. Yet that this opinion may not lead to everything
being plunged in uncertainty, the knowledge of God derived from revelation (as distinguished from rational knowledge) is strongly accentuated. In Duns we still
observe the struggle of the principle of reason with the principle of arbitrariness
tempered by revelation and made conceivable ; in Occam the latter has triumphed.
To the understanding, which Occam brings into court against dogma, the task is
assigned of showing that logic and physics cannot be applied to the articles of faith,
and to the supernatural objects that answer to them. All doctrines of faith are full of
contradictions ; but so also it must be, according to Occam ; for only in this way do
they show themselves to be declarations about a super-sensible world, which to the
understanding is a miracle. This theologian has been misunderstood, when his
criticism of dogma has been taken as suggesting the irony of the doubter. If, after
proving the doctrine of transubstantiation impossible, he finally holds it as more
probable than any other doctrine, because the Church has fixed it, and because the
omnipotence of God appears in it most unlimitedly, *i.e.*, because it is the most
irrational doctrine that can be thought of, in this he is severely in earnest, however
much he might like to maintain his own dialectic doctrine on this point. And what
holds good of the doctrine of the Supper holds good also of all other cardinal

metaphysics and theology entirely asunder, and the theological doctrines of the Nominalists prove that, while they have reverently called a halt before the old dogmas, after having shown them irrational, on the other hand they have revised in a new-fashioned way the circle of the new, and really living, doctrines (Sacraments, appropriation of salvation). This work directed itself against Augustine, in its directing itself against Thomas.

We have frequently pointed out already, that the history of Church doctrine in the West was a much disguised history of struggle against Augustine. His spirit and his piety undoubtedly rose far above the average of ecclesiasticism, and the new discoveries which he made were in many ways inconvenient to the Church as an ecclesiastical institution, and did not harmonise with its tendencies. No doubt the Church had accepted Augustinianism, but with the secret reservation that it was to be moulded by its own mode of thought. We have seen to what extent there was success in that in the period that ends, and in the period that begins, with Gregory the Great. Gottschalk already experienced what it costs in Catholicism to represent Augustinianism. In the time that followed there was developed in the sacramental and penance systems a practice and mode of thought that was always the more plainly in conflict with Augustinianism; all the more important was the fact that the Dominican Order, and especially Thomas, sought to rejuvenate the theology of Augustine. Duns Scotus and the Nominalist theology directed themselves in the first instance against Augustine's philosophy of religion, against those doctrines of the first and last things, which gravitated so strongly to pantheism. But in controverting these doctrines, and shaking confidence in the doctrine of God as the All-One, they also

doctrines of the Church. Unreasonableness and authority are in a certain sense the stamp of truth. That is also a positivism, but it is the positivism whose sins have fully developed. Here, too, it applies, that one abyss calls up another. The Pre-Nominalist theology had loaded reason with a burden of speculative monstrosities, and at the same time required it to bear the whole weight of religion ; the sobered ratio abandoned entirely the thought of a λογικὴ λατρεία, became always more prepared to recognise the faith of ignorant submission as religion, and fell back on knowledge of the world. On Biel, see Linsenmaun in the Tüb. Quartalschr., 1865.

shook confidence, for themselves and others, in the Augustinian
doctrines of grace and sin, which certainly had the closest
connection with his doctrine of God.   These Nominalists, who
(following Duns Scotus) always insisted that reason relates to
the realm of the worldly, and that in spiritual things there must
simply be a following the traditional authority of revelation,
that the understanding, therefore, must be left out of play, really
wrought in a most vigorous way, and with the utmost use of the
"understanding," within the lines of the Church doctrine.
Under certain circumstances " not to speculate " leads also to a
metaphysic, or at least does not hinder a traditional speculation
from being corrected and transformed in many of its details, and
so also in its entire cast.   At any rate this principle did not prevent the Nominalist theologians from revising the existing dogma
under the protection of authority.   But not only did this work
now acquire an entirely external, formalistic character, but there
were also introduced into everything the principles of an
arbitrary morality, of the "conveniens" too, the expedient and
the relative.   One might say, that the principles of a cosmopolitan
diplomacy in matters of religion and morals were applied to
objective religion and to subjective religious life.   God is not
quite so strict, and not quite so holy, as He might be imagined
to be ; sin is not quite so bad as it appears to be to the very
tender conscience ; guilt is not immeasurably great ; redemption
by Christ, taken as a whole, and in its parts, is very serviceable,
but not really necessary ; faith does not require to be full
surrender, and even of love a certain amount is really enough.
That is the "Aristotelianism " of the Nominalistic Schoolmen,
which Luther declared to be the root of all mischief in the
Church; but that is also the "Aristotelianism" which must be
most welcome to the hierarchy; for here they hold the key of
the position, seeing that they determine how strict God is, how
heinous sin is, etc.   That at the same time they neither can nor
will part entirely with Augustinianism (Thomism) was remarked
above.   But they determine where it is to come in, and they
showed that they watched jealously the extent to which it was
applied.
    In the Pelagianism and Probabilism of Nominalism there lies

the express apostasy from Augustinianism.[1] But just because
the apostasy was so manifest, there could not fail to be a certain
reaction—though certainly no longer a strong one—in the
Church. Not only did the Dominican Order, in their defending
the theology of their great teacher, Thomas, persistently defend
Augustine also (though not, as a rule, in the most important
points), but men also appeared in the fourteenth and fifteenth
centuries who observed the *Pelagian* tendency of Nominalism,
and strenuously resisted it in the spirit of Augustine.[2]   Here
Bradwardine must first be mentioned (ob. 1349) who placed the
entire Augustine, together with the predestination doctrine, in
strong opposition to the Pelagian tendency of the period.[3]   On

[1] Also from the ancient Church and from dogma in its original sense as a whole.
Whoever transforms all dogmatic and ethic into casuistry, thereby proves that he is
no more inwaidly, but only outwardly, bound.

[2] Werner has the credit of having described the reaction of Augustinianism in the
third vol. of his " Scholastik des Späteren Mittelalters." Yet his account is by no
means complete.   In pp. 1-232 he treats of "the representation of the Scholastic
Augustinianism given by the mediæval Augustinian-Hermit School," *i.e.*, almost exclusively of the doctrines of Ægidius (ob. 1315), the great defender of Thomas, and
of Gregory of Rimini ; then, in pp. 234-306, of Bradwardine's doctrine.   Stöckl also
goes into the Augustinianism of the fifteenth century, but in his own way.   Moreover, Werner will not admit a rejuvenated Augustinianism.   "The earlier and later
attempts to obtain a specific Augustinianism fall under different points of view,
according as they signify a reaction against the enfeebling and externalising of the
Christian ecclesiastical thought of salvation, or the opposition, supported by the name
of Augustine, of a resuscitated one-sided Platonism to Aristotelianism, or, finally, as
they arose from a vague fusion of the respect for Augustine in the Church generally,
with the authority of the head and leader of a particular school.   It was to such a vague
fusion that the Mediæval Order-theology of the Augustinian Hermits (?) owed its
origin, which came into existence as schola Ægidiana, and, under many changes,
continued to exist till last century " (p. 8 f.).

[3] See Lechler, Wiclif I. Bd., and the same author's monograph on Bradwardine,
1863.   Bradwardine made a further endeavour to create a philosophy adequate to the
Christian conception of God, and on that account went back on the Augustinian
Anselmic speculation as regards an absolutely necessary and perfect being, from which
all that is and can be is to be deduced.   But yet he shows himself to be dependent
on Duns in this, that he represents God and the world exclusively under the contrast
of the necessary and the contingent (see his book de causa dei adv. Pelag., Werner
pp. 255 ff. 299), while in other respects also very strong influences of Nominalism are
discernible in him.   Yet these influences disappear behind the main tendency, which
is directed to showing the "immediate unity and coincidence of theological and
philosophical thought," and to restoring Augustine's doctrine of grace together with
Determinism.   ("All willing in God is absolute substance.")   Werner will have it

him Wyclif was dependent as a theologian, and as Huss took all
his theological thoughts from Wyclif, and introduced them into
Bohemia and Germany, Bradwardine is really to be signalized
as the theologian who gave the impulse to the Augustinian
reactions that accompanied the history of the Church till the
time of Staupitz and Luther, and that prepared the way for the
Reformation.   In the fifteenth century the men were numerous,
and some of them influential too, who, standing on the shoulders
of Augustine, set themselves in opposition to Pelagianism.   But
they neither overthrew, nor wished to overthrow, the strong
basis of the Nominalist doctrine, the authority of the Church.
Moreover, Augustinianism exercised an influence in many ways
on the reform parties and sects ; but as no new theology
resulted, so also all these efforts led to no Reformation.   The
Augustinians still allowed a wide scope to the fides implicita
and the Sacraments, because even they believed in the idol of
Church authority.   The reigning theology remained unshaken
so long as it was not assailed at the root.   Even attacks so
energetic as those of Wesel and Wessel passed without general
effect.[1]   But the fact is unmistakable, that in the course of the
fifteenth century the Nominalist Scholasticism fell steadily into
disrepute.   While the period revelled in new, fresh impressions
and perceptions, that theological art became always more
formalistic, and its barren industry was always the more keenly
felt.   While the rediscovered Platonism was being absorbed
with delight, that art still lived under the impulses of the
Aristotle who had arisen 250 years before.   The spirit of
the Renaissance and of Humanism was in its innermost nature
alien to the old Scholasticism ; for it had no wish for formulæ,

that he has proved that Bradwardine is no Thomist, but that he reverts to the pre-
Thomist Scholasticism.   That is right in so far as Bradwardine is a logical Augustinian.
But Werner has an interest in emphasising as strongly as possible the peripatetic
elements in Thomas ; for only when these are emphasised in a one-sided way can
Thomas continue to be the normal theologian.   " According to the 'universal feeling'
the Aristotelian basis was indispensable for the ends of a methodically conducted theological scholastic science, and as a rational restraint upon giving a false internal
character to the Christian ecclesiastical religious consciousness " (p. 305).

[1] Even the rejection of all philosophy and of the whole of Scholasticism, of which
we have an instance in Pupper of Goch (O. Clemen, l.c. p. 135 ff.)—whom Luther
described as " Vere Germanus et gnosios theologus "—changed nothing.

syllogisms, and authorities ; it wished neither the darkness nor
the illumination of the "Aristotelian" Scholasticism, but was
eager for *life*, that can be *reproduced in feeling*, and for
perceptions that elevate above the common world and the
common art of living.[1]   For the poets and humanists—though
not for all, yet certainly for the most of them—the ecclesiastical
theology, as represented in the Scholastic labours of the Schoolmen, was like stagnant, filthy water.   But still there was always
the endeavour to find the redeemers in antiquity.   *Plato*, at
length the true Plato, was discovered, revered and deified.   It
was not by chance that the Platonic reaction coincided with the
Augustinian in the fifteenth century ; for the two great spirits
of ancient times had an elective affinity—Plato's Dialogues and
Augustine's Confessions are not incapable of being united.   The
influence of Plato and Augustine guided all the movements in
the fields of science and theology in the fifteenth century that
rose against a Scholasticism which, in spite of its rich perceptions,
had become fossilised and hollow, and had lost touch with the
needs of the inner life and of the present time.   The reflection
of the Germans was more serious than that of the Italians and
French.   In the last third of the fifteenth century Germany took
the lead in thought and scholarship.   The Romanic nations did
not produce in the fifteenth century a man like Nicolas of Cusa.[2]
Nicolas was the precursor and leader of all the distinguished
men who, in the following century, starting from the Platonic
view of the world, brought so strong and fresh a current of real
illuminism into the world.   Though fantastical in many ways
and even greatly interested in magic and ghosts, some of them
at once discoverers and charlatans, these men laid, nevertheless,
the basis for the scientific (even experimental) observation of
nature, and were the restorers of scientific thought.   Assurance
of the unity of all things and the bold flight of imagination—both
of which had been lost by scholastic wisdom—made the new

[1] Burckhardt, Die Cultur der Renaissance in Italien. 4. Aufl., 1885.   Voigt,
Wiederbelebung des class. Alterthums. 2 Aufl. 2 Bde., 1880 f.

[2] See Stöckl, l.c., Janssen, Gesch. des deutschen Volkes Bd. I., Clemens, Giordano
Bruno u. N. v. K., 1847.   Storz, Die specul. Gotteslehre des. N. v. K. in the theol.
Quartalschr., 1873, I.   Laurentius Valla is superior to Nicolas as a critic, but other-
wise not on a level with him.

science possible. This science by no means arose because Nominalism, or the philosophy of the great student of nature, Aristotle, as it was then treated, was always growing more empirical, and gradually developed itself into exact science, but a new spirit passed over the withered leaves of Scholasticism, scattered them boldly to the four winds, and derived confidence and power for gathering out of nature and history their secrets, from the living speculations of Plato that grasp the whole man, from the original historic sources now discovered, and from converse with the living reality.

By theology little advantage, certainly, was derived from this in the fifteenth century. The Italian Humanists, the fathers of this European movement, practically took nothing to do with it —at the most they instituted some historical investigations, with the view of annoying the priests and monks (Laurentius Valla : favours from Constantine, origin of the Apostolic Symbol, writings of the Areopagite)—and even the Germans made no real contributions to progress.[1] One could help all other sciences by going back upon antiquity, but not theology. What it could learn from Plato and the Neoplatonists it had learned long before. When men like Nicolas of Cusa sought to release it from the embraces of the Schoolmen, they themselves knew of no better form for it than that which had been given to it by Augustine and Mystics like Eckhart. But trial had been made of this form of long time. Just because it appeared unsatisfactory, and there was an unwillingness any longer to breathe in this fine fog, there had been, in course of time, a passing over to Nominalism. Now, there must be a reverting to the beginning —though it might be better understood. Another prescription was not offered. Theology seemed doomed to move helplessly in a circle ; fundamentally it remained as it was ; for the iron ecclesiastical authority remained. Then came the help, not from Aristotle, nor even from Plato and Augustine, but from the conscience of a Mendicant Monk.

But what the Renaissance and Humanism did *indirectly* for theology[2] must not be ignored. While it was not really

[1] Yet, "German patriotism effected a union in many ways of the anti-Romish traditions with Humanistic Illuminism" (Loofs).

[2] Drews, Humanismus und Reformation, 1887.

demolished by them, and still much less re-shaped, yet for the future re-shaping they certainly rendered most valuable services. The sources of history were gradually disclosed for it also, and the Humanist Erasmus not only laid the foundation of textual criticism of the New Testament and scientific patrology, but carried them at once to a high state of perfection. From a taste for the original, criticism grew up. What had died out in the Church with Origen, nay, in some measure even before Origen, or what—keeping out of view a few Antiochians—had never really developed themselves strongly, namely, historic sense and historic exegesis, developed themselves now. The Reformation was to reap the benefit of them ; but by the Reformation also they were soon to be swallowed up again. For the history of theology, and of dogmas, in the strictest sense of the term, Humanism was otherwise quite unfruitful. Theology was put aside by it with a respectful recognition, or with an air of cool superiority, or with saucy ridicule. Scarcely anyone approached it with serious criticism. Erasmus aimed at giving it a humanistic ennoblement and freeing it from restrictions. When the Reformation dawned, he pronounced, among other things, the controversy about indulgences to be a monks' quarrel, or a delightful dilemma for causing stir among the parsons. When things then grew serious and a decision had to be made, it became apparent that the Franciscan ideal, in peculiar combination with antique reserve and humanistic worldliness, with silent hatred of dogma and Church, and external submission, had a stronger hold on many aspiring souls than a liking for the gospel.[1] The scholar, besides, would not let himself be disturbed by the din of the " Lutheran rogues." Theological doctrine was held to be something indifferent : " Quieta non movere "—(let things that are at rest not be stirred)—or, at least, only in the form of a learned passage of arms. The avenger was at the door ; the following 150 years showed the terrified scholars to a frightful extent that theology will not be mocked.

[1] Dilthey (Archiv. f. Gesch. d. Philos. 5 Bd., p. 381 ff.), in a way that seems to me substantially correct, but somewhat forced, has described Erasmus as the founder of theological Rationalism with accommodation to the Church. Erasmus was too many-sided, and too uncertain of principles, to found anything beyond methods.

4. *The Moulding of Dogma in Scholasticism.*

In the Scholasticism of the thirteenth century the Latin Church attained what the Greek Church attained in the eighth century—a uniform systematic exhibition of its faith. This exhibition had as its presuppositions, *first*, Holy Scripture and the articuli fidei, as these had been formulated at the Councils ; *second*, Augustinianism; *third*, the ecclesiastical (papal) decisions and the whole development of ecclesiasticism from the ninth century ; *fourth*, the Aristotelian philosophy.

We have shown in the third and fourth chapters of Vol. V. how the old scheme of Christian doctrine had undergone a trenchant modification at the hands of Augustine, but how, in its ultimate basis—as regards the final aim of religion and theology—it did not lose its recognised validity, its form, rather, having only become more complicated. While Augustine described the influences of grace that operate in the Sacraments as the influences of *love*, he allowed the old view of the Sacraments to remain, namely, that they prepare for, and help to secure, the enjoyment of God. But he at the same time gave the most powerful impetus to a dual development of piety and ecclesiastical doctrine ; for the forces of love that operate in the Sacraments establish also the " kingdom of righteousness " on earth, produce in this way the life in love that corresponds with the " law of Christ," and qualify the individual for those good works which establish merit before God and create a claim for salvation.

In this last turn of thought Augustine had subordinated (by means of the intermediate idea, " nostra merita dei munera " [our merits gifts of God]), his new view of divine grace as a gratia gratis data (grace freely given) to the old, chiefly Western, view of religion, as a combination of law, performance, and reward, and in the period that followed this subordinating process always continued to be carried further. *Grace (in the form of the Sacraments) and merit (law and performance) are the two centres of the curve in the mediæval conception of Christianity.* But this curve is entirely embedded in faith in the Church ; for since to the Church (as was not doubted) the Sacraments, and the power of the keys dependent on them, were entrusted, the Church was not merely the authority for the whole combination, but was in a very real sense the continued working of Christ Himself, and the body of Christ, which is enhypostatically united to Him.   In this sense mediæval theology is *science of the Church* (Ecclesiastik), although it had not much to say about the Church.   But on the other hand, at least till Nominalism triumphed, this theology never lost sight of the fundamental Augustinian aim : " Deum et animam scire cupio.   Nihilne plus ?   Nihil omnino " (I desire to know God and the soul. Nothing more ?   No, nothing whatever), *i.e.*, it never discarded the view that in all theology what is aimed at ultimately is *exclusively* the cognition of God and of the relation of the in-dividual soul to Him.[1]   It was the intermingling of theology as ecclesiasticism with theology as nourishment for the soul that produced within mediæval theology its internal discords, and lent to it its charm.   From this intermingling also there is to be explained the twofold end here set before the Christian religion, although to the theologians only one of the ends was consciously present : religion and theology must on the one hand lead the individual to salvation (visio dei or surrender of the will), but it must on the other hand build up on earth the kingdom of virtue and righteousness, which is the empirical Church, and bring all powers into subjection to this kingdom.[2]

---

[1] In Nominalism this became otherwise.   The exhibition of the ecclesiastical doctrine became more and more an end in itself, and was detached from the philosophy of religion.   That on this account the originality and independence of the Christian religion as a historic phenomenon came to view again more plainly, is not to be denied.

[2] In their definition of salvation or of the finis theologiæ, the Schoolmen exhibit a Mystic, *i.e.*, an Augustinian, *i.e.*, an old Catholic tendency.   The fruitio dei is held to be the final end, whether it is realised in the intellect or in quiescence of the will in God.   For this individualistic mode of viewing salvation, which is indifferent to the moral destiny of man, the Church is either not taken into account at all, or is taken into account simply as a means, and as an auxiliary institution.   Only in so far as man con-ceives of himself as a being that is *earthly*, bound to time, and must train himself, are all his ideals, and the forces that render him aid, included for him in the Church (salva-tion in time is salvation in the Church), and he must reverence the Church, as it is, as the mother of faith, as the saving institution, nay, as the regnum Christi.   But this regnum has in the world beyond a form totally different from its present form.

Augustine utilised in quite a new way the articuli fidei ; for him they are no longer faith itself, but, re-shaping them in many ways, he builds up faith by means of them.   Yet their authority was not thereby shaken, but in a certain way was still further increased, inasmuch as the *external* authority became greater in the degree in which the internal—that faith identified itself *exclusively* with them—became less.   This was exactly how things continued to move on in the Middle Ages.   It was solely the articles of faith of ecclesiastical antiquity that were, in the strict sense, dogmas.   Only the doctrine of transubstantiation succeeded in winning for itself equal dignity with the old dogmas,[1] by the quid pro quo that it is implied in the doctrine of the incarnation.   When in this way the doctrine of transubstantiation took its place side by side with the old dogmas, everything really was gained ; for by this link of attachment the whole sacramental system might be drawn up to the higher level of absolute Christian doctrine.   This, too, afterwards took place, although, prior to the Council of Trent, the distinction was never made in detail between what belongs to dogma and what is simply a portion of theology, and even after the Council of Trent the Church wisely avoided the distinction.   It is thus explained how, about the year 1500, no one except the most decided papists could affirm how far the province of necessary faith in the Church really extended.

The task of Scholasticism, so far as it was dogmatic theology, was a threefold one.   Following Augustine, it had to shape the

---

In this whole view Scholasticism nowhere passed beyond Augustine.   The relation is not drawn between the aim to be realised in the earthly, and the aim to be realised in the heavenly Church.   *In the last resort* Roman Catholicism was then, and is also to-day, no phenomenon with but one meaning, as the Greek Church is, and as Protestantism might be.   At one time it points its members to a contemplation that moves in the line of knowledge, love, and asceticism, a contemplation that is as neutral to the Church as to every association among men, and to everything earthly ; at another time it directs men to recognise in the earthly Church their highest goods and their proper aim.   These directions can only be followed alternately, not together.   In consequence of this, Roman Catholics maintain two notions of the Church, which are neutral towards each other, the invisible communion of the elect and the papal Church.

[1] See the Symbol of 1215.

old articuli fidei so that they would adjust themselves to the
elliptic line drawn round the sacrament and merit; it had to
revise the doctrine of the Sacraments, which had come to it
from Augustine in an extremely imperfect form;[1] and it had
to gather from observation the principles of present-day Church
practice, and to bring these into accord, on the one hand with
the articuli fidei, raised to the level of theology, and with the
doctrine of the Sacraments, and on the other hand with
Augustinianism.   This task became more complicated from the
fact that the Schoolmen—at least the earlier—uniformly combined dogmatics with philosophy of religion, and thus introduced into the former all the questions of metaphysics, as
rising out of the general state of knowledge at the time.   But
*this great task was really faithfully carried out by mediæval
theology.*   That theology fulfilled the claims that were made
upon it; indeed, there has probably never been a period in
history when, after hard labour, theology stood so securely in
command of the situation, *i.e.*, of its age, as then.   At the same
time it knew how to maintain for itself until the fifteenth
century the impression of a certain roundedness and unity, and
yet left room, as the contrast between the Franciscan and
Dominican dogmatists shows, for different modes of development.   Yet on the other hand it must not be denied that the
opinion here expressed by no means applies when we deal with
the relation between piety and theology.   In the case of
Thomas, it is true, the claims of the latter and former still
coincide, although not so perfectly as in the Greek Church at
the time of the Cappadocians and of Cyril.   But from the close
of the thirteenth century piety and theology manifestly held an
increasingly strained relation to each other.   The former
recognised itself always less clearly in the latter.   They were
one, it is true, in their ultimate ground (finis religionis, authority
of the Church); even the most devoted piety was not really able
to free itself from these bonds.   But starting from the common
basis, theology unfolded a tendency to treat the holy as something authoritative, external and made easy by the Church, and
this tendency piety viewed with growing suspicion and annoy-

[1] In this lies the greatest importance of Scholasticism within the history of dogma.

ance. In the doctrines of the Sacraments and of grace, as
Scholasticism gave fuller shape to them—developing germs which
were not wanting even in Thomas—the strain between theology
and piety reached clearest expression. The Augustinian
reactions from the middle of the fourteenth century, at one time
noisy in their course, at another time moving on silently and
steadily, were the result of this strain. *The official theology of
the fifteenth century must be recognised only in a relative way as
the expression of the true Catholic piety of the period.* This
applies even to Tridentine Catholicism, and holds true to the
present day. The doctrine, as it is, is not the sphere in which
vital Catholic faith lives. But because its foundations are also
the foundations of this faith, the faith lets itself in the end be
satisfied with this doctrine.

As we have not to do with the philosophy of religion, we
must confine ourselves in what follows to describing the
scholastic revision of the old articuli fidei, the scholastic doctrine
of the Sacraments, and the scholastic discussion of Augustinianism as related to the new Church principles, which led
finally to an entire dissolution of the Pauline Augustinian
doctrine. With regard to the first of these points the statement
can be quite brief, seeing that in the revision of the old articuli
fidei theological doctrines were dealt with which, as scientifically
unfolded, never acquired a universal dogmatic importance,
and seeing that this revision leads over at many points into the
philosophy of religion.

A. *The Revision of the Traditional Articuli Fidei.*

1. The article " de deo " (on God) was the fundamental and
cardinal article.[1] In the strictly realistic Scholasticism the
Areopagitic Augustinian conception of God was held as valid :
God as the absolute substance. Where this conception was
adhered to, its absolute necessity for thought was also asserted
(Anselm's ontological proof,[2]) and a high value was ascribed to

---

[1] See the excellent selection of passages from the sources in Münscher-Coelln II.,
I, § 118, 119. Schwane, l.c., p. 122 ff.

[2] Anselm's discussions of the conception of God, in which there is the first step of

the proofs for God.   Through the acquaintance with Aristotle, however, the Areopagite conception of God was restricted, which had developed itself in Scotus Erigena, Amalrich of Bena and David of Dinanto, as well as among the adherents of the Averrhoistic Aristotelianism, into pantheism.   The cosmological proofs, to which preference was more and more given,[1] led also to a stricter distinguishing between God and the creature, and Thomas himself, although the Areopagite Augustinian conception of God is still for him fundamental, stoutly combated pantheism.[2]   Following Anselm, Thomas also linked the conception of God as the absolute substance with that of self-conscious thought, adopted, still further, from Aristotle the definition of God as actus purus, and thus gave the conception a more living and personal shape.   But he had at the same time the very deepest interest in emphasising absolute sufficiency and necessity in God ; for only the necessary can be known with certainty ; but it is on certain knowledge that salvation, *i.e.*, the visio dei, depends.   Thomas accordingly now conceived of God, not only as necessary being, but also as an end for Himself, so that the world, which He creates in goodness, is entirely subordinated to His own purpose, a purpose which could realise itself indeed even without the world.[3]   Yet Duns already combated (against Richard of St. Victor, see also Anselm, Monolog.,) the notion of *a necessary existence due to itself*, and thereby really abandoned all proofs of God : [4] the infinite is not cognisable by demonstration, and hence can only be

advance beyond the Areopagite conception, are not taken note of at all by the Lombard, who adhered simply to the patristic tradition. Thomas is the first to adopt Anselm's speculations.

[1] See Thomas, P. I., Q. 2, Art. 3, where the cosmological argument appears in a threefold form.

[2] Ritschl, Gesch. Studien z. christl. L. v. Gott, Jahrbb. f. deutsche Theol., 1865, p. 277 ff., Joh. Delitzsch, Die Gotteslehre des Thomas, 1870. Ritschl has shown (see also Rechtfert. u. Versöhnungslehre, Bd. I., 2 Aufl., p. 58 ff.,) that the Aristotelian conception had already a strong influence on Thomas.

[3] Summa, P. I., Q. 19, Art. 1, 2.

[4] In Sentent. Lomb., I. Dist. 2, Q. 2, Art. I.   On Duns' doctrine of knowledge and of science, see Werner, Duns Scotus, p. 180 ff.; ibid., p. 331 ff., on his doctrine of God, which only admits of an a posteriori ascertainment of the qualities of the divine Being.

believed in on authority. Occam made as energetic an attack
on the "primum movens immobile" (prime immovable mover)
and likewise fell back on authority. But with the impossibility
of demonstrating the infinite, and of giving life by speculation
to the notion of the "necessarium ex se ipso," there disappeared
also for Nominalism the conception of the necessity of the inner
determinedness of the infinite Being, of whom authority taught.
God is not summum esse (supreme being) and summa intelli-
gentia (supreme intelligence) in the sense in which intelligence
belongs to the creature, but He is, as measured by the understanding of the creature, the unlimited almighty will, the cause
of the world, a cause, however, which could operate quite otherwise from the way in which it does. God is thus the absolutely free will, who simply wills because He wills to, i.e., a
cognisable ground of the will does not exist. From this point
of view the doctrine of God becomes as uncertain as, above all,
the doctrine of grace. Occam went so far as to declare
monotheism to be only more probable than polytheism ; for
what can be strictly proved is either only the notion of a single
supreme Being, but not His existence, or the existence of
relatively supreme beings, but not the one-ness. Accordingly
the attributes of God were quite differently treated in the
Thomist and in the Scotist schools. In the former they were
strictly derived from a necessary principle, but only to be
cancelled again in the end, as identical in the one substance,
in the latter they were relatively determined ; in the former—
in accordance with the thesis of the summum esse—a virtual
existence of God in the world was assumed, and in the last
analysis there was no distinguishing between the existence of
God for Himself and His existence for the world, in the latter—
as the world is a free product of God's will, entirely disjoined
from God—only an ideal presence of God is taught. As can
easily be seen, the contrast is ultimately determined by different
ideas of the position of man and of religion. For the Thomists,
the idea is that of dependence on *God Himself*, who comprehends and sustains all things, for the Scotists the idea is that of
independence in relation to God. It certainly meant an
important advance upon Thomas when God was strictly con-

ceived of by Duns as will and person, and was distinguished
from the world; but this advance becomes at once a serious
disadvantage when we can no longer depend upon this God,
because we are not permitted to think of Him as acting according
to the highest categories of moral necessity,[1] and when, accordingly, the rule holds, that the goodness of the creature consists
in surrender to the will of God, of which the motives are inscrutable, while its content is clearly given in revelation (so
Duns).[2] The view that contemplates God as also arbitrariness,
because He is will, becomes ultimately involved in the same
difficulties as the view that contemplates Him as the all-
determining substance, for in both cases His essence is shrouded
in darkness. But the narrow way that leads to a sure and
comforting knowledge of God, the way of faith in God as the
Father of Jesus Christ, the Schoolmen would not follow.
Therefore their whole doctrine of God, whether it be of a
Thomist or of a Scotist cast, cannot be used in dogmatic. For
on this point dogmatic must keep to its own field of knowledge,
namely, the historic Christ, and must not fear the reproach of
"blind faith" (" Köhlerglaubens," collier's faith,) if it is blind
faith that God can be felt and known only from personal life—
and, in a way that awakens conviction, only from the personal
life of Christ. This does not exclude the truth that Thomistic
Mysticism can warmly stir the fancy, and gently delude the
understanding as to the baselessness of speculation. How far,
as regards the conception of God, mediæval thought in
Nominalism had drifted from the thought which had once given
theological fixity in the Church to the articulus de deo, can best
be seen when we compare the doctrine of God of Origen,

---

[1] Werner, l.c., p. 408 : " It is a genuinely Scotist thought that the absolute divine
will cannot be subjected to the standard of our ethical habits of thought (!) "

[2] In contrast with this, Thomas had taught (P. I., Q. 12, Art. 12) that indeed " ex
sensibilium cognitione non potest tota dei virtus cognosci et per consequens nec ejus
essentia videri," but that both the existence of God and " *ea quæ necesse est ei
convenire*" can be known. Duns and his disciples denied this ; but, on the other
hand, they asserted that God is more cognisable than the Thomists were willing to
grant. The latter denied an adequate (essential) knowledge of God (cognitio
quidditativa) ; the Scotists affirmed it, because it was not a question at all about the
knowledge of an infinite intelligence, but about the knowledge of the God who is
will, and who has manifested His will.

Gregory of Nyssa, or John of Damascus with that of Duns or Occam.[1] But the whole of dogmatic is dependent on the conception of God ; for that conception determines both the view of salvation and the view of reconciliation.[2] Finally, it must be pointed out, that mediæval theology strongly emphasises the conception of God as *judge*, though this conception was not introduced by it into speculations as to the nature of God.

2. Stormy debates on the right way of understanding, and the right way of mentally representing the doctrine of the Trinity,[3] had already run their course, when the Mendicant Orders made their appearance in science. The bold attempts to make the mystery more intelligible, whether by approximating to tritheism (Roscellin),[4] or by passing over to Modalism (Abelard), were rejected in the period of Anselm and Bernard (against Gilbert).[5] Where Augustine's treatise De trinitate was studied and followed, a fine Modalism introduced itself everywhere,[6] and it was easy for any one who wished to convict another of heresy to bring the reproach of Sabellianism against his opponent who was influenced by Augustine. Even the Lombard was charged with giving too much independence to the divina essentia, and with thus teaching a quaternity, or a species of Sabellianism.[7] The lesson derived in the thirteenth

---

[1] On this, and the acute criticism of the Aristotelian doctrine of God, see Werner, Nachscotistiche Scholastik, p. 216 ff.

[2] It is a special merit of Ritschl that in his great work in the department of the history of dogma he has shown everywhere the fundamental importance of the conception of God.

[3] See Münscher, § 120, Schwane, l.c. p. 152 ff., Bach, Dogmengesch. Bd. II., Baur, L. v. d. Dreieinigkeit, Bd. II.

[4] Application of the Nominalist mode of thought ; against him Anselm ; see Reuter I., p. 134 f. ; Deutsch, Abelard, p. 256 f.

[5] There was a disposition to detect even tritheism in Abelard ; on his doctrine of the Trinity, see Deutsch, p. 259 ff. Abelard's wish was to reject both the Roscellin conception and strict Sabellianism, yet he does not get beyond a fine Modalism (see Deutsch, p. 280 ff.). It is noteworthy that, like Luther at Worms, he stated in the prologue to his Introductio in theol., that he was ready to be corrected, " cum quis me fidelium vel virtute rationis vel auctoritate scripturæ correxerit " (see Münscher, p. 52).

[6] Thus it was with Anselm and the Victorinians, especially Richard, who reproduced and expounded the Augustinian analogies of the Trinity (the powers of the human spirit).

[7] Joachim of Fiore made it a reproach that the 4th Lateran Council, c. 2, took

century from these experiences was to guard the trinitarian dogma by a still greater mustering of terminological distinctions than Augustine had recourse to. The exposition of the doctrine of the Trinity continued to be the high school of logic and dialectic. In Thomism the doctrine still had a relation to the idea of the world, in so far as the hypostasis of the Son was not sharply marked off from the world-idea in God. Thomism was also necessarily obliged to retain its leaning to Modalism, as the conception of God did not at bottom admit of the assumption of distinctions in God, but reduced the distinctions to relations, which themselves again had to be neutralised. The Scotist School, on the other hand, kept the persons sharply asunder. But this school, especially in its later period, could equally well have defended, or yielded submission to, the quaternity, or any other doctrine of God whatever. But before this the whole doctrine had already come to be a mere problem of the schools, having no relation to living faith. The respect that was paid to it as the fundamental dogma of the Church was in flagrant contrast with the incapacity to raise it in theological discussion above the level of a logical mystery. Like Augustine in his day, the mediæval theologians let it be seen that they would not have set up this dogma if it had not come to them by tradition, and the decree of the Lateran Council (see page 182, note 7,) which places behind the persons a "*res* non generans neque genita nec procedens" (*a thing* not begetting nor begotten nor proceeding) really transforms the persons into mere modalities κατ᾿ ἐπινοίαν (existing for thought), or into inner processes in God. Or is it still a doctrine of the Trinity, when the immanent thinking and the immanent willing

---

the Lombard under its protection and decreed : "Nos (*i.e.*, the Pope) sacro et universali concilio approbante credimus et confitemur cum Petro (scil. Lombardo), quod una quædam summa res est, incomprehensibilis quidem et ineffabilis, quæ veraciter est pater et filius et spiritus, tres simul personæ, ac singulatim quælibet earundem. Et ideo in deo trinitas est solummodo, non quaternitas, quia quælibet trium personarum est illa res, videlicet substantia, essentia sive natura divina, quæ sola est universorum principium, præter quod aliud inveniri non potest. Et illa res non est generans neque genita nec procedens, sed est pater qui generat, filius qui gignitur, et spiritus sanctus qui procedit, ut distinctiones sint in personis et unitas in natura."

in God are defined and objectified as generare and spirare
(begetting and breathing)? But in Nominalism the treatment
of this dogma grew no better.   The Thomist School was certainly still regulated by a concrete thought, when it sought to
make the Trinity more intelligible by means of analogies; for
according to these the finite world, and especially the rational
creature, show traces of the divine nature and the divine
attributes. But this idea Scotism had set aside, emphasising
the threefold personality as revealed fact. Its "subtle investigations," even Schwane confesses,[1] "went astray too much into
a region of formalism, and came to be a playing with notions."

3. The doctrine of the eternity of the world [2] was universally
combated, and the creation from nothing adhered to as an
article of faith.   But only the Post-Thomist Schoolmen expressed the temporality of the world, and creation out of nothing,
in strict formulæ.   Although Thomas rejected the pantheism
of the Neoplatonic-Erigenistic mode of thought, there are still
to be found in him traces of the idea that creation is the
actualising of the divine ideas, that is, their passing into the
creaturely form of subsistence. Further, he holds, on the basis
of the Areopagite conception of God, that all that is has its
existence "by participating in him who alone exists through
himself" (participatione ejus, qui solum per se ipsum est). But
both thoughts obscure the conception of creation.[3]   Hence it is
characteristic of Thomas, who elsewhere, as a rule, finds strict
necessity, that he refrains from showing that the world's having
a beginning is a doctrine necessary for thought ; Summa., P. I.,
Q. 46, Art. 2 : "It is to be asserted that the world's not having
always existed is held by faith alone, and cannot be proved
demonstratively : as was asserted also above regarding the
mystery of the Trinity . . . that the world had a beginning is

[1] L.c., p. 179.
[2] See Münscher, § 121, 122, Schwane, pp. 179-226.
[3] For a pantheistic view of creation in Thomas an appeal, however, can scarcely
be made to the expression frequently employed by him, "emanatio" (processio)
creaturarum a deo ; for he certainly does not employ the expression in a pantheistic
sense. If he says, P. I., Q. 45, Art. 1 : "emanationem totius entis a causa universali,
quæ est deus, designamus nomine creationis," just for that reason he shows in what
follows, that "creatio, quæ est emanatio totius *esse*, est ex *non ente*, quod est *nihil*."

credible, but not demonstrable or knowable. And it is useful
to consider this, in case perhaps some one, presuming to demonstrate what is of faith, should adduce reasons that are not
necessary, thus giving occasion for ridicule to infidels, who
might think that on the ground of such reasons we believe what
is of faith." If only Thomas had always taken to heart these
splendid words, which, moreover, were directed against Bonaventura and Albertus Magnus, who undertook to prove the beginning of the world in time a doctrine of reason ! Duns Scotus
and his school naturally followed Thomas here, in so far as they
held the temporality of the world as guaranteed simply by the
authority of faith.[1] Yet the view of Albertus certainly survived
at the same time in the Church. The purpose of the creation of
the world was taken by all the Schoolmen to be the exhibition
of the love (bonitas) of God, which seeks to communicate itself
to other beings. Even Thomas, correcting the Areopagite conception of God, declared the creation of the world no longer a
necessary, but only a contingent, means, whereby God fulfils
His personal end. Yet he certainly represented the personal
end of God, which is freely realised in creation, as the supreme
thought : "divina bonitas est finis rerum omnium "[2] (the divine
love is the end of all things), *i.e.,* God's willing His own blessedness embraces all movements whatever of that which exists, His
willing it by means of creation of the world is His free will ; but
as He has so willed to create, the end of the creature is entirely
included in the divine end ; the creature has no end of its own, but
realises the divine end, which is itself nothing but the actualising of
the love (bonitas). In this way the pantheistic acosmism is certainly not quite banished, while on the other hand, in the thesis of
Thomas, that God necessarily conceived from eternity the *idea*
of the world, because this idea coincides with His knowledge
and so also with His being, the pancosmistic conception of God
is not definitely excluded. In the Scotist school, the personal

---

[1] Scotus holds the possibility of a divine creation from eternity as not unthinkable,
but disputes the arguments by which Thomas sought to corroborate the position that
a beginning of creation in time cannot be proved ; see Werner, Duns Scotus,
p. 380 ff.

[2] P. I., Q. 44, Art. 4 ; see also Q. 14, 19, 46, 104.

end of God and the end of the creature are sharply disconnected.[1]
As regards divine providence, from the time of Anselm and
Abelard onwards, all the questions were again treated which were
formerly dealt with by Origen ; but from the time of Thomas
they were added to in an extraordinary degree, so that quite new
terminology was here created.[2] To the question whether this
world is the best, Thomas gave a negative answer, after Anselm
had answered it in the affirmative ; yet even Thomas thinks this
universe cannot be better ; God, however, could have created
other things, which would have been still better.[3] As a consequence of his fundamental view, Thomas assumes that God
directs all things immediately ; yet the greater the independence
was that was attributed to the world, the stronger became the
opposition to this thesis.   In the theodicy, moreover, which was

[1] Here would be the place to deal with the doctrine of angels held by the Schoolmen ; but as the material relating to this subject—the fencing and wrestling ground
of the theologians, who had here more freedom than elsewhere—is very loosely connected with dogma, and is at the same time unworthy of serious consideration, it may
be passed over ; see Thomas, P. I., Q. 50-65 ; Schwane, pp. 194-217.

[2] See Summa, P. I., Q. 103-117 : de gubernatione rerum, divided according to the
points of view of finis gubernationis, conservatio and mutatio rerum.   Under the
first point of view it is established speculatively that the finis rerum must be " quoddam bonum extrinsecum," because the finis universalis rerum as the ultimate goal
must be the " bonum universale," but this latter cannot be included in the world,
since the world, in virtue of its created quality, can never include more than a
participative bonum ; hence God Himself is the finis gubernationis (see above).
Further, in the general doctrine of government the questions are treated, whether
there is a gubernatio at all, whether it proceeds from *one*, whether its effect is uniform
or manifold, whether *everything* is under it, whether it is everywhere *direct*, whether
anything can happen præter ordinem gubernationis, and whether anything " reniti
possit contra ordinem gubernationis dei."   The " conservatio" is defined (q. 104,
art. 1) as only a continued creating, and so it is said at the close of the article (ad. 4) :
"conservatio rerum a deo non est per aliquam novam actionem, sed per continua-
tionem actionis quæ dat *esse*, quæ quidem actio est sine motu et tempore, sicut etiam
conservatio luminis in aëre est per continuatum influxum a sole."   This not unobjectionable definition is applied in many different ways.   Thus miracle is declared
impossible, in so far as the ordo rerum depends on a prima causa, while on the other
hand it is admitted in view of the causæ secundæ (art. 6).   But according to Thomas
the real miracles, although they are not so designated, are the creation of the world
and of souls, and also the justificatio impiorum ; for they are præter ordinem
naturalem.   The miracle of all miracles is God, quod habet causam simpliciter et
omnibus occultam.

[3] P. I., Q. 25, Art. 6.

vigorously revised in the thirteenth century in opposition to the
dualistic sects, Thomas attached himself more closely to
Augustine. He did not shrink from the thought that God produces "quasi per accidens" (as it were accidentally) the corrup-
tiones rerum (corruption in things); for the "perfection of
things in the universe requires that there shall be not only
incorruptible, but also corruptible entities" ("perfectio rerum
universitatis requirit, ut non solum sint entia incorruptibilia, sed
etiam corruptibilia"); but from this it follows that the perfectio
universi requires beings that *can* fall from the good, "ex quo
sequitur ea interdum deficere" (from which it follows that they
are sometimes defective).[1]   In these doctrines, too, greater
caution came to be exercised, as the distinction came to be more
sharply drawn between God, and the creature as endowed with
its own volitional movement.[2]

4. The history of Christology was similar to that of the
doctrine of the Trinity.   In the twelfth century there was still
much keen discussion with regard to the former, as the satisfaction was not general with the Greek scheme that had been
framed in opposition to Adoptianism (Abelard's Nestorian
Christology was a protest against the doctrine of John of
Damascus and of Alcuin, and continued to extend its influence).[3]
Even the Lombard, although, with Alcuin, he denies that the
Logos assumed a human *person*,[4] still gravitated—certainly in a
very peculiar way—to a Nestorian thought, in so far as he
denied, in the interest of the *immutability* of God, that by the
incarnation God "became" something, the humanity rather
being for him only like a garment.[5] But against this doctrine,

---

[1] P. I., Q. 48, Art. 2.

[2] Very worthy of notice is Duns' criticism of Augustine's and Anselm's doctrines of
malum ; see Werner, l.c., p. 402 ff.

[3] See Deutsch, l.c., pp. 289-318. Abelard's doctrine is a very vigorous attempt
to give full justice to the humanity of Christ within the lines of the traditional dogma.
But there was the feeling that this attempt was heretical, and it is, in fact, questionable, if we consider that it threatens the unity of the person of Christ, on which
all depends, but which, of course, at that time could only be expressed in the
impracticable categories of the natures.

[4] Sentent. III., dist. 5 C.

[5] Sentent. III., dist. 6. Yet it was only the disciples that utilised the thought
thrown out by the Master. Besides, the doctrine asserts nothing else than what

described as Nihilianism, and adopted by the dialecticians
(Christ was, as man, non aliquid [not something]), a strong opposition was raised in the period of Alexander III., especially
by German scholars (Gerhoch); there was asserted, in opposition
to it, the most complete and real interpenetration of deity and
humanity in Christ (see Alcuin), and the Lombard's doctrine
was even publicly described as dangerous.[1] With this "nota"
against "Nihilianism," the doctrine of the two natures came to
the great Schoolmen, and the problem of the "hypostatic union"
now became as much the field of contest for the acutest thought
as the problem of the Trinity.[2] At the same time the view
all took of the communicatio idiomatum implied that the
thought must be excluded of a human person as existing for
himself in Christ.   But here, also, there resulted important
differences between the Thomists and Scotists; for Thomas
made the greatest effort to give such predominance to the divine
factor that the human became merely something passive and
accidental; as he was influenced by the Areopagite, he continued
also, in a very real way, the Greek Monophysite Christology;
nor was there wanting to him the Areopagite background, that
the Logos entered into just the same relation to human nature
as a whole, into which he entered with the human nature of
Jesus. Against this Scotus made an effort, in a very modest
way, and with a profusion of confusingly complicated terminology, to save something more of the humanity of Christ.
But in return for this, he has to hear the verdict of modern
Catholic theologians of dogma, that "he won for himself no
laurels; that what he did, rather, in this field, with his critical
censures (of the Angelic Doctor) was mostly a fiasco."[3] His
effort to attribute existence even to the human individual nature

Cyril had expressed regarding the incarnation of the Logos with the μεμένηκεν
ὅπερ ἦν.

[1] See Bach, l.c., Bd. II., Hefele, Conciliengesch. V.², p. 616 ff. (Synod of Tours,
1163), and p. 719 f. (3rd Lateran Synod, 1179).

[2] See Schwane, pp. 251-296.

[3] Schwane, p. 288; compare the full account in Werner, l.c., p. 427 ff. Duns
taught a double filiation, and in the Report. Paris. expressly professed belief also in
the probability of Adoptianism; see p. 439 f. On the similar Christology of Post-
Scotist Scholasticism, see Werner II., p. 330 f.

of Christ was disapproved. His mild attempts, likewise, were repudiated to fix certain limits to the human knowledge of Christ, and to deduce the sinlessness of the human will of Jesus, not from the hypostatic union, but from the "plenissima fruitio quam habuit Christus" (fullest enjoyment that Christ had), *i.e.*, from his perfect surrender of will.[1] On this field Thomism continued victorious. The Scotists did not succeed in securing the recognition of a special mode of being for the individual human nature of Christ.[2]

The victory of the Monophysite doctrine of Christ concealed under the Chalcedonian formulæ,[3] was all the more surprising from no practical religious use whatever being made of it, the real interest in Christ finding expression rather, on the one hand, in the idea of the poor life of Jesus and the Ecce homo, on the

---

[1] See Werner, p. 440 ff.

[2] The doctrine of the Holy Spirit did not receive a further development in Scholasticism. From the days, certainly, of the Latin Empire in the East till the Synod of Florence there was controversy and negotiation with the Greeks in numberless treatises about the procession of the Holy Spirit. The negotiations for union lasted, with interruptions, for almost 250 years, and for a time they furnished a certain prospect of success, because from the thirteenth century there was a small Latin party in the East, which, however, in the end was disowned by the whole Eastern Church. At Lyons in 1274 (can. 1) Greeks made admission that the Holy Spirit proceeds from the Father and the Son ("non tamquam ex duobus principiis, sed tamquam ex uno principio, unica spiratione"), and at Florence (Mansi XXXI., p. 1027 sq.) there was a coming to terms in a complicated formula, which, however, expressly justified the "filioque." But as early as 1443 the Florentine Council was condemned at a Jerusalem Synod by the Patriarchs of Antioch, Alexandria, and Jerusalem. The Greeks with Latin sympathies either confessed penitently their "betrayal of the faith," or preferred to remain in Italy and become Roman dignitaries.

[3] This victory, it is true, came about not in Scholasticism but in the Church. Scholasticism was led on rather by Occam to a complete dissolution of the God-Manhood of Christ, so that for Socinianism there remained nothing more to do (see Werner II., p. 353 ff.). In Certilog., concl. 6, Occam writes: "Est articulus fidei, quod deus assumpsit naturam humanam. Non includit contradictionem *deum assumere naturam asininam;* pari ratione potest assumere lapidem vel lignum." Also (l.c. concl. 62): "To Christ the predicate Son of God can only be attributed in so far as in Him the Verbum divinum appears united with *the human nature;* of a filiation relation of the Verbum divinum in itself the reason of man knows nothing"; so also the doctrine of the Trinity is contrary to reason (I., Dist. 9, Q. 1). If as over against this there is a pointing to fides, it is simply submission to authority that is meant. If, now, from any cause, this authority fell away, Socinianism was ripe.

other hand, in the doctrines of reconciliation and of the Sacraments.[1]   But it is only apparently that the doctrine of reconciliation has the Greek Christology, together with the doctrine of the two natures, as its presupposition.   This has been shown already above in connection with the reconciliation doctrine of Anselm, Abelard, and the Lombard.[2]   It still remains to us here to specify concisely the thoughts of the later Schoolmen on the work of Christ.[3]

The Lombard had brought the *merit* of Christ into the foreground, and at the same time had given expression to all possible thoughts about redemption by Christ—the Anselmic theory excepted—and had attached himself closely to Augustine and Abelard ("reconciliati sumus deo *diligenti nos*" [we are reconciled to God, *who loves us*]).   The modification in the thirteenth century consisted now in this, that, in opposition to Abelard, and with a certain adherence to Anselm, objective redemption (in its bearing upon God) was brought into the foreground, but at the same time, the point of view of *merit*, which Anselm had only suggested, was strongly emphasised.   This turn of things appears already in Alexander of Hales and Albertus ; but Thomas was the first to furnish a full, strictly-thought-out doctrine of redemption.   Certainly even he alternates between the points of view, which is always a sign that *the* point of view is not firmly got hold of ; for, where the sufficient reason is wanting, reasons tend to accumulate.   But the sufficient reason was really wanting to Thomas ; for P. III., Q. 46, Art. 1-3, the

---

[1] There was repeated here what we have already observed in connection with the doctrine of the Trinity.   In regard to both dogmas theoretical speculation strikes out paths which are scarcely any longer united with the paths along which faith moves. There can scarcely be conceived of a greater contrariety than is implied, when in the doctrine of the person of Christ the "homo" is almost entirely eliminated, 'and then in the doctrine of the work of Christ this "homo" takes the commanding place. No doubt by means of words and terminologies all chasms can be bridged over ; but they are still only words.

[2] See p. 54 ff.

[3] See Ritschl, Vol. I., p. 55 ff.; Münscher, § 135 ; Schwane, pp. 296-333.   The passio Christi dominates the whole Western theology.   If John of Damascus (see Vol. III., p. 288) calls the incarnation the only new thing under the sun, Walter v.d. Vogelweide expresses the general conviction of the West, when in one of his best-known poems he exalts the suffering of Christ as the miracle of all miracles.

necessity of the death of Christ is explicitly rejected—God could also have simply remitted sin in the exercise of His free will,—the chosen way of deliverance by the death of Christ (liberatio per mortem Christi) is only the most fitting, because, by it, more and greater things are imparted to us than if we were redeemed solely by the will of God (sola voluntate dei).

There were three points of view especially which Thomas applied. First, he stated (Q. 46) a large number of arguments that were intended to prove that the death of Christ, with all the circumstances of His suffering, was the most fitting means of redemption. Within the lines of this idea many points of view are already suggested that deal with the facts. But above all the infinite pain which He endured is taken into account. His suffering (during His whole life and in death) is represented as being the sum of all conceivable suffering, in the sense too of its being His own pain and the pain of sympathy on account of our sin. Here justice is done to the Abelardian-Augustinian tradition, *viz.*, that the suffering of Christ, the Mediatorial *Man*, is redemptive, inasmuch as it brings God's love home to our hearts, becomes an example to us, recalls us from sin, and stirs as a motive responsive love. But on the other hand, the convenientius (more fitting) in an objective sense is also already brought out here, inasmuch as the death of Christ was the most fitting means for winning for men the gratia justificans (justifying grace) and the gloria beatitudinis (glory of beatitude).[1]

---

[1] Q. 46, Art. 3 : " Tanto aliquis modus convenientior est ad assequendum finem, quanto per ipsum plura concurrunt, quæ sunt expedientia fini. Per hoc autem quod homo per Christi passionem liberatus, multa concurrerunt ad salutem hominis pertinentia *præter liberationem a peccato :* Primo enim per hoc homo cognoscit, quantum hominem deus diligat, et per hoc provocatur ad eum diligendum, in quo perfectio humanæ salutis consistit. Unde Apostolus dicit : ' *Commendat* suam caritatem deus,' etc. Secundo quia per hoc nobis dedit exemplum obedientiæ et humilitatis et constantiæ, justitiæ et ceterarum virtutum in passione Christi ostensarum, quæ sunt necessaria ad humanam salutem. Unde dicitur, I., Pet. 2 : ' Christus passus pro nobis, nobis relinquens exemplum, etc.' Tertio quia Christus per passionem suam non solum hominem a peccato liberavit, *sed etiam gratiam justificantem et gloriam beatitudinis ei promeruit,* ut infra dicetur (Q. 48). Quarto, quia per hoc est homini inducta major necessitas, se immunem a peccato conservandi, qui se sanguine Christi redemptum cogitat a peccato, secundum illud I., Cor. 6 : ' Empti estis pretio,' etc. Quinto quia hoc ad majorem dignitatem hominis cessit, ut sicut homo victus fuerat et deceptus a diabolo, *ita etiam homo esset qui diabolum*

In Q. 408, new points of view are now introduced under
the heading "de modo passionis Christi quantum ad effectum"
(on the mode of Christ's suffering as regards its effect). The
hypothetical character here passes into the rear behind the necessary result of the suffering. But the whole inquiry is dominated
by the fundamental thought : "Christus non est passus secundum divinitatem, sed secundum carnem," (Christ did not suffer
as to His divinity, but as to His flesh), with which the divinity
associated itself. Here the death of Christ is placed under the
points of view of merit (Art. 1), satisfaction (Art. 2), sacrifice
(Art. 3), redemption (Arts. 4 and 5), and "efficientia" (Art. 6).
This is succeeded, in Quest. 49, by an inquiry as to how far the
death of Christ has freed us from sin (Art. 1), from the power of
the devil (Art. 2), and from liability to penalty (a reatu pœnæ)
(Art. 3), and again, as to whether by it we are reconciled to God
(Art. 4), whether by it entrance to heaven is secured for us
(Art. 5), and whether by it Christ was exalted (Art. 6). Among
these points of view there stand out prominently (secondly)
that of satisfaction and (thirdly) that of merit as specially
important.

The conception of satisfaction is obtained by taking (against
Anselm) in the strictest sense the voluntariness of Christ's sufferings, and then defining this voluntary suffering according to
the particular rule, that satisfaction always consists in a gift for
which the party injured has more love than he has hatred for
the injury. This is shown in the suffering of Christ, which is
described (see above) as not only suffering in death but suffering in life,[1] and which has its value in the divine-human life of
the Mediator. Just on that account the satisfactio is not only
sufficient but superabundans ;[2] i.e., it is not only æqualis omni-

---

vinceret, et sicut homo mortem meruit, ita homo moriendo mortem superaret. Et
ideo convenientius fuit quod per passionem Christi liberaremur, quam per solam dei
voluntatem." In Q. 47 the treatment of redemption from the point of view of the
convenientissimum is continued.

[1] It is a step in advance on the part of Thomas that he does not confine himself to
the death of Christ, but embraces in his view His whole life as suffering.

[2] Q. 48, Art. 2 : "Respondeo dicendum, quod ille proprio satisfacit pro offensa,
qui exhibet offenso id quod æque vel magis diligit, quam oderit offensam. Christus
autem ex caritate et obedientia patiendo *majus* aliquid deo exhibuit, quam exigeret

bus peccatis humani generis (equal to all the sins of the human race), but positively in excess of them.   In this way an idea is obtained which, though apparently unobjectionable and worthy, was to give occasion to the most unhappy speculations.   A vicarious penal suffering, in the strict sense of the terms, is not recognised even by Thomas, because on the whole question he allowed only a limited range to the justitia dei.[1]   Still, some lines of exposition in Quest. 49 touch on that thought.[2]

recompensatio totius offensæ humani generis ; primo quidem propter magnitudinem caritatis ex qua patiebatur, secundo propter dignitatem vitæ suæ quam pro satisfactione ponebat, quæ erat vita dei et hominis ; tertio propter *generalitatem* passionis et magnitudinem doloris assumpti, ut supra dictum est (Q. 46, Art. 6).   Et ideo passio Christi non solum sufficiens, sed etiam *superabundans satisfactio* fuit pro peccatis humani generis."

[1] To this satisfactio superabundans Thomas returns in the 4 Art. [redemptio : "respondeo dicendum, quod per peccatum dupliciter homo obligatus erat, primo quidem servitute peccati, quia qui facit peccatum, servus est peccati. . . . Quia igitur diabolus hominem superaverat, inducendo ad peccatum, homo servituti diaboli addictus erat.   Secundo, quantum ad reatum pœnæ, quo homo erat obligatus secundum dei justitiam.   Et hoc etiam est servitus quædam ; ad servitutem enim pertinet quod aliquis patiatur, quod non vult, cum liberi hominis sit uti se ipso ut vult.   Quia igitur passio Christi fuit sufficiens et superabundans satisfactio pro peccato et reatu pœnæ generis humani, ejus passio fuit *quasi quoddam pretium* per quod liberati sumus ab utraque obligatione.   Nam ipsa satisfactio qua quis satisfacit, sive pro se sive pro alio, *pretium quoddam dicitur*, quo seipsum vel alium redimit a peccato et a pœna. . . . Christus autem satisfecit non quidem pecuniam dando aut aliquid hujusmodi, sed dando id quod fuit maximum, seipsum scil. pro nobis.   Et ideo passio Christi dicitur esse nostra redemptio."   There is a not unimportant turn of thought (Q. 47, 2 ; 48, 3), where the suffering of Christ is looked at from the point of view of sacrifice.   Here it is not merely love in general that is described as that which has efficacy in the voluntary sacrifice, but still more precisely *obedience :* "Convenientissimum fuit, quod Christus ex obedientia pateretur . . . obedientia vero omnibus sacrificiis antefertur . . . miles vincere non potest nisi duci obediat, et ita homo Christus victoriam obtinuit per hoc quod deo fuit obediens. . . . Quia in morte Christi lex vetus consummata est, potest intelligi quod patiendo omnia veteris legis præcepta implevit : moralia quidam, quæ in præceptis caritatis fundantur, implevit in quantum passus est et ex dilectione patris et etiam ex dilectione proximi, cæremonialia vero præcepta legis, quæ ad sacrificia et oblationes præcipue ordinantur, implevit Christus sua passione, in quantum omnia antiqua sacrificia fuerunt figuræ illius veri sacrificii, quod Christus obtulit moriendo pro nobis. . . . Præcepta vero judicialia legis, quæ præcipue ordinantur ad satisfaciendam injuriam passis, implevit Christus sua passione, permittens se ligno affigi pro pomo quod de ligno homo rapuerat contra dei mandatum."

[2] See Art. 3 and 4 : "Respondeo dicendum, quod per passionem Christi liberati sumus a reatu pœnæ dupliciter.   Uno modo directe, in quantum scil. passio Christi fuit sufficiens et superabundans satisfactio pro peccatis totius humani generis ; *exhibita*

With regard to *merit*, a distinct idea is to be got under this term as to how far Christ's suffering really profits individuals. It is a circumstance of value that Thomas sets aside, and ceases to employ, the Greek thought which dominates his doctrine of the *person* of Christ, namely, that the humanity of Christ is in itself human nature in general. With this mechanical idea of the matter he was not satisfied. Here also we see that between his doctrine of the person of Christ, and his doctrine of His work, there is quite a chasm. Only once [1] does he touch on

autem satisfactione sufficienti tollitur reatus pœnæ (this is, of course, no taking over of penalty). Alio modo indirecte, in quantum scil. passio Christi est causa remissionis peccati, in quo fundatur reatus pœnæ." To the objection that on the liberati pœnæ satisfactoriæ are still imposed by the Church, he replies thus : "Ad hoc quod consequemur effectum passionis Christi, oportet nos ei configurari. Configuramur autem ei in baptismo sacramentaliter, secundum Rom. 6, 4 : 'Consepulti sumus ei per baptismum in mortem.' Unde baptisatis nulla pœna satisfactoria imponitur, quia sunt totaliter liberati per satisfactionem Christi. Quia vero Christus semel tantum pro peccatis nostris mortuus est, ut dicitur I. Pet. 3, 18, ideo non potest homo secundario configurari morti Christi per sacramentum baptismi. Unde oportet quod illi, qui post baptismum peccant, configurentur Christo patienti per aliquid pœnalitatis vel passionis quam in se ipsis sustineant (!) Quæ tamen multo minor sufficit, quam esset condigna peccato, cooperante satisfactione Christi." A wonderful illustration of satisfactio superabundans ! Even in the 4 Art. the reconciliatio dei is traced, not to the endurance of the penal suffering, but to the "sacrificium acceptissimum." God is reconciled (1) because the passio Christi peccatum removat, (2) because it is sacrifice ; "est enim hoc proprie sacrificii effectus, ut per ipsum placetur deus"; for as man propter aliquod obsequium acceptum forgives the injury, "similiter tantum bonum fuit, quod Christus voluntarie passus est, quod propter hoc bonum *in natura humana inventum* deus placatus est super omni offensa generis humani, quantum ad eos qui Christo passo conjunguntur." With a change of disposition on God's part Thomas will have nothing to do, although he expresses himself more cautiously than the Lombard. "Deus diligit omnes homines quantum ad naturam quam ipse fecit, odit tamen eos quantum ad culpam . . ., non dicendum, quod passio Christi dicitur quantum ad hoc, deo nos reconciliasse, quod de novo nos amare inciperet, sed quia per passionem Christi sublata est odii causa, tum per ablationem peccati tum per recompensationem *acceptabilioris beneficii*." In the 5 Art. the passio Christi is expressly related both to the peccatum commune totius humanæ naturæ (et quantum ad culpam et quantum ad reatum pœnæ), and to the peccata propria singulorum, qui communicant ejus passioni per fidem et caritatem et fidei sacramenta. Yet in connection with the latter the removal of the reatus pœnæ is not expressly emphasised. The clearest passage on the penal worth of the death of Christ is in Q. 47, Art. 3 : "in quo ostenditur et dei severitas, qui peccatum sine pœna dimittere noluit." But a connected view is not outlined from this as a starting-point, while such a view can be shown in Bernard.

[1] See the foregoing note.

the thought that God is reconciled because He has now found the good in human *nature*. Elsewhere he has quite a different view, with which indeed he crowns his discussion (Q. 48, 1), and of which as his discussion proceeds he never loses sight. It is the view hinted at by Anselm, that by His voluntary suffering Christ *merited* exaltation (Q. 49, 6), that the exaltation, however, cannot be conferred upon Him, but passes over from Him to the Church of which He is the Head.[1] The fulness with which Thomas stated and repeated this thought is a guarantee that for him it was an extremely valuable one. It has also been expressed by him thus (Q. 48, Art. 2): "The head and the members are, as it were, one mystical person, and thus the satisfaction of Christ belongs to all *believers*, just as to His own members" (caput et membra sunt quasi una persona mystica, et ideo satisfactio Christi ad omnes *fideles* pertinet, sicut ad sua membra). Here, finally, the conception of the *faithful* (fideles) also (as the ecclesia) is introduced into the question about the effect and bearings of redemption; but only in the 1st Art. of Quest. 49 has Thomas come to deal more closely with *faith*—simply however to pass over at once to love: "It must be affirmed that by faith also there is applied to us the passion of Christ, with a view to its fruit being seen, according to the passage Rom. 3: 'Whom God hath set forth as a propitiator through faith, etc.' But the faith by which we are cleansed from sin is not fides informis, (unformed faith), which can exist even along with sin, but is fides formata per caritatem (faith deriving form from love), so that in this way the passion of Christ is applied to us, not intellectually merely,

---

[1] Q. 48, Art. 1 : "Christo data est gratia non solum sicut singulari personæ, sed in quantum est caput ecclesiæ, ut scil. ab ipso redundaret ad membra. Et ideo opera Christi hoc modo se habent tam ad se quam ad sua membra sicut se habent opera alterius hominis in gratia constituti ad ipsum. . . ." Q. 49, Art. 1 : "Passio Christi causat remissionem peccatorum per modum redemptionis, quia enim ipse est caput nostrum, per passionem suam quam ex caritate et obedientia sustinuit, liberavit nos tam quam membra sua a peccatis, *quasi* per pretium suæ passionis, sicut si homo per aliquod opus meritorium, quod manu exerceret, redimeret se a peccato quod pedibus commisisset. Sicut enim naturale corpus est unum ex membrorum diversitate constans, ita tota ecclesia, quæ est mysticum corpus Christi, computatur quasi una persona cum suo capite, quod est Christus," and other passages, especially P. III., Q. 8.

but also effectually." (" Dicendum quod etiam per fidem applicatur nobis passio Christi ad percipiendum fructum ipsius,
secundum illud Rom. 3 : ' Quem proposuit deus propitiatorem
per fidem, etc.' Fides autem per quam a peccato mundamur
non est fides informis, quæ potest esse etiam cum peccato, sed
est fides formata per caritatem, ut sic passio Christi nobis ap-
plicetur, non solum quantum ad intellectum, sed etiam quantum
ad effectum.")

When we review the exposition given by Thomas, we cannot
escape the impression created by confusion (multa, non multum,
[many things, not much]). The wavering between the hypothetical and the necessary modes of view, between objective and
subjective redemption, further, between the different points of
view of redemption, and finally, between a satisfactio superabundans and the assertion that for the sins after baptism we
have to supplement the work of Christ, prevents any distinct
impression arising. It was only a natural course of development when Duns Scotus went on to reduce everything entirely
to the relative. It is what always happens when an attempt
is made to find a surer hold for the actual in what is assumed to
be the metaphysically necessary ; this actual presents itself in
the end only as the *possible*, and so, very soon also, as the irrational. No one thought of the moral necessity of penalty.

Duns Scotus draws the true logical conclusion from the
theory of satisfaction (as distinguished from the idea of vicarious
penal suffering), by tracing everything to the " acceptatio " of
God. All satisfaction and all merit obtain their worth from the
arbitrary estimation of the receiver. Hence the value of Christ's
death was as high as God chose to rate it. But in the strict
sense of the term infinity cannot at all be spoken of here ; for
(1) sin itself is not infinite, seeing that it is committed by finite
beings (it is, at the most, quasi infinite, when it is measured,
that is to say, though this is not necessary, by the injury done
to the infinite God) ; (2) the merit of Christ is not infinite, for
He suffered in His human (finite) nature [1] ; (3) in no sense is

[1] In Sent. III., Dist. 19, n. 7 : "Meritum Christi fuit finitum, quia a principio
finito essentialiter dependens, etiam accipiendo ipsum cum omnibus respectibus, sive
cum respectu ad suppositum Verbi, sive cum respectu ad finem, quia omnes respectus
isti erant finiti."

an infinite merit needed, because God can estimate any merit as highly as He pleases; for nothing is meritorious in itself, because nothing is good in itself, but the sovereign divine will declares what it wills to be good and meritorious. And so Duns has not hesitated to assert that an angel, or even a purus homo who should have remained free from original sin and been endowed with grace, could have redeemed us. It is a question merely of receiving the first impulse; the rest every man must acquire for himself together with grace. Grace must only raise him, so to speak, above the point at which he is dead. Of course, Duns made the further effort to show the conveniens of the death of the God-man, and here he works out essentially the same thoughts as Thomas. But this no more belongs, strictly speaking, to dogmatic. For dogmatic, it is enough if it is proved that in virtue of His arbitrary will God has destined a particular number to salvation; that in virtue of the same arbitrary will He already determined before the creation of the world, that the election should be carried out through the suffering of the God-man; and that He now completes this plan by accepting the merit of the God-man, imparting the gratia prima to the elect, and then expecting the rest from their personal efforts. Here the reason at bottom for Christ's having died is its having been prophesied (see Justin), and it was prophesied because God so decreed it. Everything " infinite "—which is surely the expression for what is divine and alone of its kind—is here cleared away; as a fact, human action would have been enough here, for nothing is necessary in the moral sense, and nowhere does there appear more than a quasi-infinity.[1] This

[1] See Ritschl, I., pp. 73-82; Werner, p. 454 ff. In Sentent. III., Dist. 19, Q. 1. The 20 Dist. is entirely devoted to the refutation of Anselm. Let us quote some leading sentences here: " Sicut omne aliud a deo ideo est bonum, quia a deo volitum, et non e converso, sic meritum illud tantum bonum erat, pro quanto acceptabatur et ideo meritum, quia acceptatum, non autem e converso quia meritum est et bonum, ideo acceptatum." . . . " Christi passio electis solum primam gratiam disponentem ad gloriam consummatam efficaciter meruit. Quantum vero adtinet ad meriti sufficientiam, fuit profecto illud finitum, quia causa ejus finita fuit, vid. voluntas naturæ assumptæ et summa gloria illi collata. Non enim Christus quatenus deus meruit, sed in quantum homo. Proinde si exquiras, quantum valuerit Christi meritum secundum sufficientiam, valuit procul dubio quantum fuit a deo acceptatum, si quidem divina acceptatio est potissima causa et ratio omnis meriti. Omne enim

theory, the product of thought on the uncontrollable, predestinating arbitrariness of God (and on legal righteousness), stands
side by side with an explicit doctrine of two natures![1]   But it is
quite distinctly irreligious in this respect, that it confines the
work of Christ to the procuring of that " gratia prima " (primary
grace), which is nothing but the creating of a kind of *possibility*,
in order that man may himself take concern for the *reality* of his
redemption.[2]

By Scotus it was brought about that this doctrine also became severed from faith, and was entirely transformed into a
dialectic problem.   In this lies the disintegration of dogma
through Scotism.   The doctrine of the Trinity, Christology, and
the doctrine of redemption, were now happily withdrawn from
the domain of the *inwardly* necessary, comforting faith that
saves.   Thus it continued to be in the Nominalist school.   Only
in the one particular, which, however, was constantly brought
under the category of the conveniens—namely, that the love of
God shown in the death of Christ becomes a motive to reciprocal love—did there survive a meagre remnant of an inspiring
thought.   While in the fourteenth century the Scotist theory of
satisfactio secundum acceptationem (satisfaction on the ground
of acceptance) gained always more adherents, was here and

---

aliud a deo ideo est bonum quia a deo dilectum, et non e contrario . . . deus non
acceptat opus idcirco quod sit meritorium aut bonum.   Tantum ergo valuit Christi
meritum sufficienter, quantum potuit et voluit ipsum trinitas acceptare.   Verum
tamen ex sua ratione formali et *de condigno* non potuit in infinitum seu pro infinitis
acceptari, quia nec illud in se fuit formaliter infinitum.   Nihilosecius si spectes
supposito merentis circumstantiam et dignitatem, habebat *quandam* extrinsecam
rationem, propter quam *de congruo* in infinitum extensive, id est pro infinitis, potuit
acceptari.   Sed quid meruit Christus?   Meruit sane *primam gratiam* omnibus qui
eam recipiunt, quæ et absque nostro merito confertur.   Nam licet in adultis qui
baptizantur non desideretur aliqua dispositio, nihilominus non merentur illam gratiam
per suam dispositionem . . . nullus actu ingreditur regnum cœleste, nisi cooperetur,
si habuerit facultatem, et utatur prima gratia, quam sibi Christus promeruit."

[1] Certainly this doctrine of two natures, from its Nestorianism, has already the
tendency in it to do away with the deity of Christ.

[2] The redemption theory of Scotus, which, dialectically considered, is superior to
the Thomist through its completeness, is very severely criticised even by Schwane,
who, however, does not bring out its Pelagian feature (p. 327 ff.).   He speaks of
" shallow apprehension of the incarnation, and a weakening of the conceptions of
righteousness and merit."

there carried even to the point of blasphemy by the formalism of dialectic, and had an influence even on the Thomists, traces are not wanting in the fifteenth century that more serious reflection, dealing with the essence of the matter, had begun to return. This had undoubtedly a connection with the revival of *Augustinianism*, perhaps also with a renewed study of *St. Bernard*, and it is to be met with more in the practical religious, than in the systematic expositions ; indeed, in the former the thought of Christ's having borne the penalty of guilt in the interests of the righteousness of God seems never to have entirely disappeared. Ritschl points to Gerson.[1] " Gerson declares sin to be the crime of high treason, and finds God's righteousness so great that in mercy He surrenders His innocent Son to penalty, evidences, in this way, the harmony between His righteousness and His mercy, and removes sin on condition that the sinner unites himself to Christ by faith, *i.e.*, by obedience and imitation.[2] In the Nominalist school the same view is still to be met with in Gabriel Biel.[3] In the end, even John Wessel comes back to it." But Ritschl is inclined to think that the idea of the penal value of Christ's death, which, from the time of Athanasius, had ever again appeared sporadically in the Church, did not pass from Biel and Wessel to the Reformers.[4]

[1] L.c. I., p. 85.

[2] Expos. in pass. dom. (Opp. ed. du Pin III. pp. 1157, 1187, 1188) : " Per læsæ majestatis crimen morti est obnoxius. Rex tamen adeo justus fuerit, quod nec ullo pacto crimen tuum dimittere velit impunitum, altera vero ex parte tam benignus et misericors, quod proprium filium suum innocentem doloribus committat et morti, et quidem sponte sua, ut justitiam concordet cum misericordia fiatque criminis emendatio. . . . Nunquam deus malum impunitum permitteret, eapropter omnia peccata et delicta nostra Jesu Christo supposuit. Ideo ipse est justitia et redemptio nostra, modo nos junxerimus ei et per fidem gratiamque ei adhæserimus."

[3] See Thomasius, Christi Person und Werk, III., 1, p. 249 ff.   Seeberg, l.c., p. 147.

[4] In dealing with the history of dogma, we are not required to enter on the history of the doctrine of Scripture, for that doctrine underwent no change, even the uncertainties about the Canon were not removed, and the slight differences in the way of understanding the notion of inspiration have no weight attaching to them. The history of Bible prohibition, or of the restriction of the use of the Bible among the laity, does not fall to be considered here (see above, p. 156).

B. *The Scholastic Doctrine of the Sacraments.*[1]

The uncertainty of the Schoolmen regarding the doctrine of redemption, and the fact that the treatment of it could be as easily relegated by them to the School as the doctrines of the Trinity and of the natures in Christ, are explained from the circumstance, that in the doctrine of the Sacraments it was definitely set forth what *faith* in the divine *grace in Christ* needed. In the Sacraments this grace is exhibited, and in the Sacrament of the Eucharist particularly it is clearly and intelligibly traced back—through the doctrine of transubstantiation—to the incarnation and death of Christ. That was enough. Those facts now form merely the *presuppositions;* faith *lives* in the contemplation and enjoyment of the Sacraments. But the Sacraments are committed to the Church, and are administered by the *hierarchy* (as servants, priests, and as judges). Thus the connection with Christ, which is effected only through the Sacraments, is at the same time mediated by the *Church.* Christ and the Church indeed are really made one, in so far as the same Church which administers the Sacraments is also, as the mystical body of Christ, so to speak, *one* mystical person with Him. This is the fundamental thought of Mediæval Catholicism, which was adhered to even by the majority of those who opposed themselves to the ruling hierarchy.

The Schoolmen's doctrine of the Sacraments has its root in that of Augustine; but it goes far beyond it (formally and materially). Above all, there was not merely a passing out of view in the Middle Ages of the connection between verbum and sacramentum, on which Augustine had laid such stress, but the verbum disappeared entirely behind the sacramental sign. The conception became still more magical, and consequently more objectionable. On the other hand, it cannot be denied that in its seven Sacraments Catholicism created a very efficient and impressive institution of an educational kind, the service of

[1] Münscher, § 138-152. Hahn, Lehre v. d. Sacramenten, 1864: same author, Doctr. romanæ de num. sacram. septennario rationes hist. 1859. Schwane, l.c., pp. 579-693.

which, however, for the individual, did not consist in giving him certainty of salvation, but in training him as a member of the Church. And yet the mediæval doctrine of the Sacraments must be regarded, at least in its Thomist form, as the *logical* development of the Old Catholic fundamental view ; for the definition of grace given by Thomas (P. III., Q. 62, Art. 1) : "*grace is nothing else than the communicated likeness of the divine nature*, according to the passage II Pet. 1 : he hath given to us great and precious promises, that we may be partakers of the divine nature " (gratia nihil est aliud quam participata similitudo divinæ naturæ secundum illud, II Pet. 1 : Magna nobis et pretiosa promissa donavit, ut divina simus consortes natura), *allows of no other form of grace than the magical sacramental.* Augustine's view, which, however, does not at bottom contradict the one just stated, is here thrust aside, and only comes under consideration so far as a link with it is found in the " participata similitudo divinæ naturæ " (communicated likeness of the divine nature). Hence the further suppression of the verbum, to which even Augustine, though he has the merit of having taken account of it, had not done full justice.

A strictly developed doctrine of the Sacraments could not exist, so long as the *number* of the Sacraments was not definitely fixed. But on this point, as antiquity had handed down nothing certain, the greatest vacillation prevailed for centuries, so difficult was it to determine anything which had not already been determined by the tradition of ancient times. The doctrine of the Sacraments was accordingly developed under the disadvantage of not knowing for certain to what sacred acts the general conceptions were to be applied. Still, theology had already wrought for long with the number seven, before the number was officially recognised by the Church.

The number seven developed itself in the following way : As sacred acts in a pre-eminent sense, there had been handed down from ecclesiastical antiquity only baptism and the Eucharist, but baptism included the Chrisma (anointing). This last could be counted separately or not. At the same time, there was an indefinite group of sacred acts which were enumerated quite variously (the reckoning of the Areopagite was not determinative). Bernard, *e.g.*, speaks of many Sacraments, and himself mentions ten.[1] Even Hugo of St. Victor gives quite a special place to baptism and the Eucharist.   Yet it was just he who contributed to a widening of the conception.   By him,[2] as well as by Abelard,[3] there are reckoned as the sacramenta majora or spiritualia baptism, the Eucharist, confirmation, unction [4] and marriage.[5] How this combination arose is unknown.   It continued to exist, however, in the school of Abelard, *i.e.*, there was no reduction again made, only additions followed.   Robert Pullus may have exercised an influence here,[6] who in his Sentences counts along with the other three Sacraments, not unction and marriage, but confession [7] and ordination.[8] From the combination of these reckonings the number seven as applied to the Sacraments may have arisen.[9] No doubt the sacred number also gave fixity to this particular enumeration.[10] It is first found in the Sentence Book of Alexander III., when he was still Master Roland,[11] and then in the Lombard.[12] The latter however represents it, not as a recognised tenet, but as his own view, without

---

[1] See Hahn, p. 103 f., and in general the copious proofs, pp. 79-133.

[2] Summa sentent. tract., 5-7.

[3] See Deutsch, Abälard, p. 401 ff.

[4] Extreme unction cannot be traced back under the term " Sacrament " further than to Innocent I. (ep. ad Decent).

[5] Marriage of course is very often named a sacrament from the earliest times, on the ground of the Epistle to the Ephesians.

[6] Sentent. V. 22-24 ; VII. 14.

[7] How gradually the "sacrament of penance" arose our whole account in the foregoing chapters has shown ; see Steitz, Das Römische Buss-sacrament, 1854. Gregory I. called the reconciliatio of the sinner a sacrament.   From the time of Petrus Damiani (69. orat.) confession was often so described, *e.g.*, even by Bernard.

[8] Since Augustine's time ordination had very frequently been styled a " sacrament " ; but even the anointing of princes, and the consecration of bishops and of churches, etc., were regarded as Sacraments.

[9] In a passing way the number six also occurs.   In the twelfth century, moreover, the considerations connected with the Sacraments have a very close connection with the struggle against the heretics (Catharists).   It may be that subsequent investigation will succeed in showing that the fixing of the number seven was the direct consequence of this struggle.

[10] See Hahn, p. 113 f.

[11] Denifle in Archiv. f. Litt.-u. K.-Gesch. d. Mittelalters, vol. I., pp. 437, 460, 467.

[12] Sentent. IV., dist. 2 A.   The former view, that Otto of Bamberg already has the number seven, is disproved ; see Hahn, p. 107.

specially emphasising it. The vacillation continued to exist
even in the period that followed. The decrees of the great
Councils of 1179 and 1215 imply that there was still nothing
fixed as to the number of the Sacraments. But the great
Schoolmen of the thirteenth century, who followed the Lombard, all accepted seven as the number of the Sacraments, and
although special stress was laid by them on baptism and particularly the Eucharist, which was described, *e.g.*, by Thomas as
the most potent of all the Sacraments (" potissimum inter alia
sacramenta sacramentum,")[1] they already made some attempt
to vindicate the number on internal grounds.[2] For the first

---

[1] P. III., Q. 65, Art. 4 : " Sacramentum eucharistiæ est potissimum inter alia
sacramenta. Reasons : (1) because in it there is contained Christus substantialiter,
not merely a virtus instrumentalis participata a Christo : (2) because all other Sacraments look to this Sacrament sicut ad finem (this is then proved in the case of each
separately) ; (3) because almost all Sacraments in eucharistia consummantur."

[2] In l.c. the Sacraments are graded according to their value : " Aliorum sacramentorum (*i.e.*, the Euchaist is previously assumed to be the chief Sacrament) com-
paratio ad invicem potest esse multiplex. Nam in via necessitatis baptismus est
potissimum sacramentorum, in via autem perfectionis sacramentum ordinis ; medio
autem modo se habet sacramentum confirmationis. Sacramentum vero pænitentiæ et extremæ unctionis sunt inferioris gradus a prædictis sacramentis, quia,
sicut dictum est, ordinantur ad viam Christianam non per se, sed quasi per
accidens, scil. in remedium supervenientis defectus. Inter quæ extrema unctio
comparatur ad pænitentiam, sicut confirmatio ad baptismum ; ita scil. quod pænitentia est majoris necessitatis, sed extrema unctio est majoris perfectionis." But in
Q. 65, Art. 1, the number seven is justified at length. The Sacraments are instituted
" ad perficiendum hominem in his quæ pertinent ad cultum dei secundum religionem
Christianæ vitæ et in remedium contra defectum peccati. Utroque modo convenienter ponuntur VII. sacramenta. Vita enim spiritualis conformitatem aliquam
habet ad vitam corporalem." In the bodily life of the individual there is taken into
consideration his individual weal and his weal as a social being. This is then set
forth scholastically in several sub-sections, and it is then shown that in the spiritual
life baptism means birth (regeneration), confirmation the augmentum (robur), the
eucharist, nourishment ; penance, healing of the maladies that have super-
vened ; extreme unction, the taking away of the " reliquiæ peccatorum." These
five Sacraments relate to the individual. To man as animal sociale there relate also
in spiritual things ordo and marriage. Proof : the potestas regendi multitudinem et
exercendi actus publicos is necessary in the spiritual life, and marriage provides for
the propagatio tam in corporali quam in spirituali vita. In the same way it is now
shown that each separate Sacrament has also its meaning contra defectum peccati,
and that the number seven is conveniens (*e.g.*, ordo contra dissolutionem multitudinis
and marriage in remedium contra concupiscentiam personalem et contra defectum
multitudinis, qui per mortem accidit). Thomas also mentions another view, which
he had found entertained by others : " fidei respondet baptismus et ordinatur c.

time at Florence (1439) was there a definite ecclesiastical declaration made as to seven being the number of the Sacraments.[1]

The technical revision of the conception of the sacrament
begins with Hugo of St. Victor.   He sets out from the
Augustinian definition : "sign of a sacred thing" ("visible form
of invisible grace"), but it appears to him unsatisfactory, because
too wide.   He adds to it two things : first, that the sacrament
must have a natural resemblance to the sacred thing which it
represents ; second, that it is also the vehicle of this sacred
thing, and communicates it to the receiver of the sign.   Hence
(de sacram, Christ. fid. I. 9, 2): "A sacrament is a corporeal or
material element set forth sensibly to view, representing by resemblance, signifying by institution, *and containing by consecration some invisible and spiritual grace*" (sacramentum est
corporale vel materiale elementum foris sensibiliter propositum
ex similitudine repræsentans, ex institutione significans et ex
sanctificatione continens aliquam invisibilem et spiritalem
gratiam), or (Summa tract. IV. 1): "a sacrament is a visible
form of invisible grace conveyed in it, *i.e., which the sacrament
itself conveys,* for it is not only the sign of a sacred thing, but
also its efficacious operation" (sacramentum est visibilis forma
invisibilis gratiæ in eo collatæ, quam scil. confert ipsum sacramentum, non enim est solummodo sacræ rei signum sed etiam

culpam originalem, spei extrema unctio et ordinatur c. culpam venialem, caritati
eucharistia et ordinatur c. pœnalitatem malitiæ, prudentiæ ordo et ordinatur c. ignor-
antiam, justitiæ pænitentia et ordinatur c. peccatum mortale, temperantiæ matrimonium et ordinatur c. concupiscentiam, fortitudini confirmatio et ordinatur c.
infirmitatem." We may smile at these attempts ; but yet we shall not be able to
deny the serviceableness of this combination of the seven Sacraments which accompany life. The inclusion particularly of orders on the one hand, and of marriage on
the other, was a master-stroke of a perhaps unconscious policy.

[1] Eugene IV. in Bull "Exultate deo" (Mansi XXXI., p. 1054): "(sacramentorum
septem novæ legis) quinque prima ad spiritalem uniuscujusque hominis in se ipso
perfectionem, duo ultima ad totius ecclesiæ regimen multiplicationemque ordinata
sunt (quite according to Thomas, see above); per baptismum enim spiritualiter
renascimur, per confirmationem augemur in gratia et roboramur in fide, renati autem
et roborati nutrimur divina eucharistiæ alimonia. Quod si per peccatum ægritudinem
incurrimus animæ, per pænitentiam spiritualiter sanamur, spiritualiter etiam et corporaliter, prout animæ expedit, per extremam unctionem ; per ordinem vero ecclesia
gubernatur et multiplicatur spiritualiter, per matrimonium corporaliter augetur."

efficacia). The sacrament has, further, the similitudo from nature, the significatio from institution, the efficacia through the consecrating word of the priest, or the first from the Creator, the second from Christ,[1] and the third from the dispenser (!). This German "Mystic" was therefore the first to give fixed form to the mischievous definition which so sadly externalised the sacrament and eliminated the word. The Augustinian distinction between the sacrament and the saving benefit in the sacrament (res sacramenti or res cujus sacramentum est) Hugo retained.

Hugo's definition passed over to the Lombard, and was never again set aside in the Church. By it the Sacraments, in the stricter sense of the term, were raised above the field of the "sacramentalia": the Sacraments are not merely signs; they are vehicles and "causes" of sanctification. The Lombard defines thus (Sent. IV., Dist. 1 B): "That is properly called a sacrament which is a sign of the grace of God, and a form of invisible grace in such a way that it bears the image thereof, and exists as a cause (et causa existat). Sacraments, therefore, are instituted for the purpose, not merely of signifying, but also of sanctifying. For things that are merely instituted for the sake of signifying are only signs and not sacraments, as were the carnal sacrifices and ceremonial observances of the old law." But, further, Sacraments are "signa data" (signs given, not "natural" signs), in the sense, namely, that they rest on free divine institution. The Lombard differs, accordingly, from Hugo in his regarding as necessary, not a corporeal or material element, but only some kind of sign, which may therefore consist also in an *act;* and also in his not saying that the Sacraments *contain* grace, but only—with greater caution—that they effect it *causally.*

In general, this definition of the Lombard lies at the foundation of the later definitions. But the more firmly it came to be held that the number of the Sacraments was seven, the more distinctly was the difficulty felt of applying the definition given to all the Sacraments individually. Hence it is not to be wondered at that the Nominalist theologians abstained more and

---

[1] But Hugo still refrained from tracing all Sacraments to institution by Christ.

more from giving a general definition that dealt with the
essence.[1]

Thomas begins (III., Q. 60) his statement of the doctrine
of the Sacraments with the words : " After consideration
of those things which relate to the mysteries of the incarnate
Word, there are to be considered the Sacraments of *the
Church*, which have *efficacy* from the incarnate Word Himself."[2] By these terms, the unguarded definition of Hugo
is set aside. He then proceeds, down to Quest. 65, to state the
general doctrine of the Sacraments. Here it is worthy of note
that Thomas, going still further than the Lombard, modifies the
cruder conception of Hugo ("continet"). Indeed, he will not
accept, without guarding clauses, the "causa existit" of the
Lombard. He rejects, certainly, the opinion of Bernard and
others, that God only works "adhibitis sacramentis" (with employment of sacraments). This would not lead beyond an interpretation of them as signs ; but he then shows that it can be said
of the Sacraments that "in some way" (per aliquem modum) they
"cause grace." The "*causa principalis*" of grace, rather, is God,
who works as the fire does by its warmth, that is, *communicates
in grace His own nature.* The Sacraments are the "causa
instrumentalis" ; but this latter cause "does not act by virtue of
its own form, but only through the impulse it receives from the
principal agent" (non agit per virtutem suæ formæ, sed solum
per motum quo movetur a principali agente). "Hence the effect
does not derive its character from the instrument, but from the
principal agent ; as a couch does not derive its character from

---

[1] Biel, Sentent. IV., Dist. 1., Q. 1, dub. 1 (see Hahn, l.c., p. 18 f.) : "Sciendum
quod duplex est definitio.—Una est oratio exprimens quid rei, alia est oratio exprimens
quid nominis. Primo modo nihil definitur, nisi sit res una h. e. terminus significans
unam rem (that is logical Nominalism). Definitione quid nominis potest omnis
terminus categorematicus definiri, quicquid significet in recto vel in obliquo. Nam
pro omni nomine possunt poni plura nomina distincte significantia illa, quæ
significantur per illud unum nomen tam in recto quam in obliquo. Ad propositum
dicitur, quod sacramentum non potest definiri primo modo h. e., definitione quid rei
quia sacramentum non res una, sed *aggregatum ex pluribus* . . . sed tantum definitur
definitione quid nominis."

More exactly, Q. 62, Art. 5 : " Sacramenta novæ legis habent virtutem ex passione
Christi." Hence also the incorporatio in Christo is the effect (Q. 62, Art. 1).

the axe, but from the design which is in the mind of the artificer (unde effectus non assimilatur instrumento sed principali agenti ; sicut lectus non assimilatur securi, sed arti, quæ est in mente artificis). And in this way the Sacraments of the new law cause grace, for they are applied to men by divine appointment (ex divina ordinatione) for the purpose of causing grace in them (ad gratiam in eis causandam). . . . It is to be asserted that the causa principalis cannot properly be called the sign of an effect that may be hidden (effectus licet occulti), though the cause itself is sensible and manifest ; but the causa instrumentalis, if it be manifest, can be called the sign of a hidden effect, because (eo quod) it is not only cause, but also *in a certain way* (quodammodo) effect, in so far as it is set in motion (movetur) by the principal agent. And according to this, the Sacraments of the new law are at the same time causes and signs, and hence it is that it is commonly said of them, that they *effect what they symbolise* (efficiunt quod figurant)." The "causæ et signa" is in the style of Old Catholic thought ; but the opposition of a spiritual to a coarse Mysticism is quite specially apparent here. In the period that followed, the loosening of grace from sacrament, in the sense of regarding the latter as merely associated with the former, was carried still further, but not because a more spiritual view was advocated (as by Thomas), or because weight was laid on the "word,"[1] but because the conception of God, which indeed exercised its influence even upon Thomas, only in another way, allowed only of a conjunction by virtue of divine arbitrariness.[2] Bonaventura already had denied, both that the Sacraments contain grace substantially (substantialiter), and

---

[1] This laying of weight on the word would, on the other hand, have necessarily led to the recognition of a closer union of sacrament and grace ; for the word, as the word of forgiveness of sin, isitself the grace. The mistake therefore of Thomas and the Lombard does not lie in their uniting the Sacraments too closely with grace by calling them causæ (indeed the position, rather, of Hugo is correct—" continent gratiam ") ; their mistake lies in their defining grace as " participata similitudo divinæ naturæ " ; for to describe a grace so conceived of as the content or the effect of the Sacraments amounts to changing the Sacrament into a magical means. We can understand the relative title which the Nominalists had as over against this, to regard the grace so conceived of as merely *accompanying* the Sacrament ; but by this again the certainty and comforting power of God's offer of grace were imperilled.

[2] Brevilog., p. VI., c. I.

that they effect it causally (causaliter); God has not bound His grace to the Sacraments, but has appointed by decree ("ex decreto") that it shall be derived "per sacramenta" from the supreme physician, Christ. In this direction Scotus went further. He defines the Sacrament [1] as "a sensible sign, which efficaciously signifies, by divine appointment, the grace of God, or the gracious effect of God, and is ordained for the salvation of man the pilgrim" (signum sensibile, gratiam dei vel effectum dei gratuitum ex institutione divina efficaciter significans, ordinatum ad salutem hominis viatoris). But the ambiguous formula, which he employs elsewhere also, "significans efficaciter effectum dei gratuitum" (signifying efficaciously the gracious effect of God), really means that God's grace works *side by side* with the Sacraments; for the cause of grace is exclusively the divine will, while this cause is represented by the Sacrament, in the Sacrament's accompanying it (concomitatur). There does not lie in the Sacraments an "intrinsic supernatural virtue," [2] but (in Sentent. IV., Dist. 1, Q. 5) "the receiving of the Sacrament is an appointment binding in order to the effect which the Sacrament signifies (dispositio necessitans ad effectum signatum per sacramentum), not, indeed, through some intrinsic form, . . . but only per *assistentiam dei* (through the aid of God), who causes that effect, not of absolute necessity, but by a necessity that has regard to the power ordained (necessitate respiciente ad potentiam ordinatam). For God has *made the appointment universal* (disposuit universaliter), and has *certified* to the Church (but how?) [3] that on him who receives such a Sacrament, He will confer the signified effect." The same doctrine was taught by Occam and Biel.[4] But this view is directly counter to that of Thomas, who had asserted that in the Sacrament itself there is

---

[1] In Sentent. IV., Dist. 2, Q. 2.

[2] In this there is a gratifying protest expressed against the magical.

[3] Scotus speaks even directly of a "pactum dei initum cum ecclesia," that He will always be present at the Sacraments with His influence.

[4] Yet Biel endeavours, by means of ingenious distinctions, to get beyond the idea of mere concomitance, and to conceive in such a way of the "pactum cum ecclesia" that God is thought of as in virtue of it making the Sacraments causæ secundæ of grace, just as all that happens in the world is caused by causæ secundæ, which have their efficiency from the causa prima ; see Dieckhoff, Ev. Abendmahlslehre, p. 219.

inwardly present "a virtue for producing the sacramental effect" (virtus ad inducendum sacramentalem effectum). The Nominalist thesis wanted inward stability ; for it is quite formalistic, and leaves the *concrete* nature of the gracious effect out of account. This point being reached, a threefold development was possible ; either that there should be a turning back to the Old Catholic realism of Thomas (Biel already entered upon this course, and later Catholicism followed him), or that the Sacraments should be conceived of strictly as signs (thus many mediæval sects and Zwingli), or that the content of the gracious will of God should be defined anew, namely, as the word of the gospel, and it should be shown that this word forms also the content of the Sacrament, that the two therefore coincide. Of one thing, at any rate, there can be no doubt, *viz.*, that the motive of the so-called "evangelical" opposition on the part of many sects and "Earlier Reformers" to the reigning view of the Sacraments, is to be sought for in logical Nominalism, that at bottom the opposition directed itself therefore against the Thomist practice. The "word," so far as my knowledge goes, was not seen to be the content of the Sacrament and of the divine will.

Now there was still an almost countless number of questions of detail regarding the Sacraments,[1] in answering which the Thomists and Scotists were, as usual, of different opinions. First of all, Thomas (following Augustine) distinguished sharply between the Sacraments of the old and new Covenants. The former only prefigured grace, the latter cause it. But already Bonaventura, and after him Scotus, were of opinion that certain Old Testament institutions (circumcision) were real Sacraments. Yet Bonaventura also made the distinction, that only the New Testament Sacraments are efficacious per se (the Old Testa-

---

[1] Hahn has distinguished the following leading points of inquiry : the conception of the Sacraments, their necessity, their serviceableness, their difference at different periods of human history, the conception of New Testament Sacraments, their parts, their institution, the administrators of the several Sacraments, the conditions under which the Sacraments come to exist, their effect (their character indelebilis, their gracious effect (*a*) in its nature, (*b*) relation of the different Sacraments in respect of their gracious effect, (*c*) more precise definition of the gracious effect of the Sacraments severally) origin and conditions of the sacramental efficacy.

ment only "per accidens," that is, by means of the added
faith ! !),[1] while Scotus declared circumcision to be a Sacrament
efficacious ex opere operato ("by effect of Christ's passion").
But at the Council of Florence Thomas's view was approved:[2]
"the Sacraments of the new law differ much from the Sacraments of the old law. For the earlier did *not* cause grace, but
only *prefigured* a grace to be given through the passion of Christ,
while those which we have both *contain* grace, and *convey* it to
those who worthily receive" (complete return to the position of
Hugo and Thomas).

In what follows the chief points of the Thomist doctrine are
stated, since that doctrine finally became dominant:

Generically (in genere) the Sacraments as a whole are necessary to salvation, but specifically (in specie) this applies, in the
strictest sense, only to baptism. The other Sacraments partly
come under the rule "non defectus sed contemptus damnat" (not
omission but contempt condemns), and they are partly necessary
only under particular circumstances (orders, marriage, extreme
unction, even the Sacrament of Penance). But the perplexity

---

[1] Even Thomas makes this distinction in Sentent. IV., Dist. 2, Q. 1, Art. 4, and,
moreover, we find here the expression "ex opere operato," which we look for in vain
in parallel passages of the Summa, although he has the thing it denotes (Q. 61, Art.
IV., and elsewhere). In the commentary on the Lombard the words occur : "Sacramenta veteris legis non habebant aliquam efficaciam ex opere operato sed solum ex
fide ; non autem ita est de sacramentis novæ legis, quæ ex opere operato gratiam
conferunt." On the expression "ex opere operato" see R.-Encyckl.[2] XIII., p.
277 f. It was already used in the twelfth century (not by the Lombard), before it
was applied to the Sacraments. As distinguished from the expression "ex opere
operantis or operante," it denotes that the *act as such* is meant, not the *actor*. An
effect ex opere operato therefore is an effect that is produced simply by the act itself
as performed, independently of all co-operation of him who performs it, or of him
who derives benefit from it. Peter of Poictiers is supposed to have been the first to
use the term in connection with the doctrine of the Sacraments (he adds further " ut
liceat uti.") William of Auxerre says : "Opus operans est ipsa actio (oblatio) vituli,
opus operatum est ipsa caro vituli sc. ipsum oblatum, ipsa caro Christi." Also
Albertus M. on John 6, 29 : " Dixerunt antiqui dicentes, quod est opus operans et
opus operatum. Opus operans est, quod est in operante virtutis opus vel a virtute
elicitum vel quod est essentialis actus virtutis, et sine illo nihil valet virtus ad
salutem. Opus autem operatum est extrinsecum factum quod apothelesma vocant
sancti, sicut operatum legis est sacrificium factum vel circumcisio facta vel tale
aliquid."
[2] Mansi XXXI., p. 1054.

showing itself here appears still greater when the Sacraments are considered in their effects. It is here seen, that is to say, that according to the Augustinian distinction of sacramentum and res sacramenti *all* would require to have a threefold effect, namely, first, a significative (sacramentum); second, a neutral (as compared with the real saving benefit of grace) or preparatory (sacramentum et res)—Augustine called this character, and compared it with the corporalis nota militiæ (corporal mark of military service); and, third, a saving effect (res sacramenti). Now, this distinction Thomas also followed. He shows that those who are set apart to the service of God must, first of all, have a certain *stamp impressed* on them, as in the case of soldiers. Through this process of stamping a certain *capacity* is imparted, *i.e.*, for receptio et traditio cultus dei (receiving and administering the worship of God); hence the character is the "character Christi." This character is not implanted in the essentia (essence), but in the potentia (powers) of the soul, and as participatio sacerdotii Christi (participation in the priesthood of Christ) is engraven on the soul "indelibly," and hence cannot be repeated. Yet all Sacraments do not impart such a character, but only those which qualify the man "ad recipiendum vel tradendum ea quæ sunt divini cultus" (for receiving and dispensing those things which pertain to divine worship), and this holds good of baptism, confirmation, and orders. The objection, that surely all Sacraments make man a "partaker of the priesthood of Christ," and so, must impart a character, is obviated by the ingenious distinction between that formula and the other: "deputari ad *agendum* aliquid vel *recipiendum* quod pertineat ad cultum sacerdotii Christi" (deputed to *do* something or *receive* something that pertains to the worship connected with the priesthood of Christ) (baptism, orders, confirmation).[1] So

---

[1] P. III., Q. 63, Art. 2-6 ; cf. I : "sacramenta novæ legis ad duo ordinantur, vid. ad remedium c. peccata et ad perficiendam animam in his quæ pertinent ad cultum dei secundum ritum Christianæ vitæ. Quicumque autem ad aliquid certum deputatur, consuevit ad illud consignari, sicut milites qui adscribebantur ad militiam antiquitus solebant quibusdam characteribus corporalibus insigniri, eo quod deputabantur ad aliquid corporale." This is then applied to the spiritual, see Art. 2 : "Sacramenta novæ legis characterem imprimunt, in quantum per ea deputantur homines ad cultum dei secundum ritum Christianæ religionis." Also Art. 3 : "Totus ritus

also if the serious objection is urged that "in any Sacrament of
the new law there is something that is only res, and something
that is only sacramentum, and something that is res and sacramentum," and that therefore in every Sacrament a character is
to be assumed, since this character is just res and sacramentum,
the objection is got quit of by saying that that which is at the
same time res and sacramentum does not require always to be
a character.[1]   This whole theory was sanctioned at Florence
(l. c.): " Among the Sacraments there are three which indelibly
impress on the soul character, that is, a certain spiritual sign
distinct from the rest (a cæteris); hence they are not repeated
in the same person.   But the remaining four do not impress
character and admit of repetition."

The question, " What is a Sacrament?"[2] is answered as
follows: it is (1) a sign; (2) not any sign whatever of a sacred
thing (quodvis rei sacræ signum), but such a sign of a sacred
thing as makes man *holy ;* (3) this "making holy" (sanctificare)
is to be looked at under three aspects: "the *cause* of our sanctification is the passion of Christ, the *form* of sanctification consists
in grace and virtues, the ultimate *end* (finis) is life eternal."
Hence now the complete definition: " A sacrament is a sign
commemorative of what went before (rememorativum ejus quod
præcessit), *viz.,* the passion of Christ, and representative
(demonstrativum) of what is effected in us by the passion of
Christ, *viz.,* grace, and anticipatory, that is, predictive (prog-
nosticum, *i.e.,* prænuntiativum) of future glory"; (4) the sacrament must always be a "res sensibilis," for it corresponds with
the nature of man that he should attain to the knowledge of
intelligible, through sensible, things; (5) these sensible signs
must be "res determinatæ," that is, God must have selected and
appointed these things: "in the use of Sacraments two things
can be considered, *viz.,* divine worship and the sanctification of

christianæ religionis derivatur a sacerdotio Christi, et ideo manifestum est, quod
character sacramentalis specialiter est character Christi, cujus sacerdotio configurantur
fideles secundum sacramentales characteres, qui nihil aliud sunt quam quædam partici-
pationes sacerdotii Christi."

[1] The real, at least the original, motive here, is to save the objectivity of the sacrament in view of unbelieving reception.

[2] Q. 60.

man, of which the first pertains to men viewed in their relation
to God (pertinet ad homines per comparationem ad deum), the
second, on the other hand, pertains to God viewed in His relation
to man ; but it does not belong to anyone to determine what is
in the power of another, but only what is in his own power ";
hence "in the Sacraments of the new law, by which men are
sanctified, it is necessary to use things appointed by *divine
institution* (ex divina institutione determinatis)"; (6) it is very
fitting that " words " also are used in connection with the Sacraments, because the Sacraments are thereby in a certain way
conformed (quodammodo conformantur) to the incarnate Word,
and can thus symbolise the sacred things more plainly ; [1] and,
moreover (7) " verba determinata " are necessary, just as " res
sensibiles determinatæ " are necessary, nay, they are necessary
even in a higher degree ; hence he who utters sacramental words
in a corrupt form, if *this is done designedly* (qui corrupte profert
verba sacramentalia, si hoc ex industria facit), does not show
that he intends to do what the Church does, and thus the sacrament is not seen to be perfectly celebrated (non videtur perfici
sacramentum) ; nay, even an unintentional lapsus linguæ, which
destroys the sense of the words (*e.g.*, if one says, " in nomine
matris ") hinders the Sacrament from becoming perfect ; likewise
(8) every addition or subtraction annuls the Sacrament, if made
with the intention of introducing another rite than that of the
Church. Further, the res sensibiles are described as being the
materia, the words as the *forma* (Aristotelian) of the Sacrament.[2]

To the question as to the necessity of the Sacraments,[3] it is
replied (1) that they are necessary on three grounds, (*a*) from
the constitution of human nature (ex conditione humanæ naturæ ;
man must be led through the corporeal to the intelligible) ; (*b*)
from the state of man (ex statu hominis ; " medicinal remedy

---

[1] So it is only for this reason that the word is necessary in connection with the
Sacrament.

[2] Hugo and the Lombard had already described the " words " as the *form*. This
view likewise was fixed ecclesiastically by the Bull of Eugene IV. : " Hæc omnia
Sacramenta tribus perficiuntur, vid. rebus tamquam materia, verbis tamquam forma,
et persona ministri conferentis sacramentum cum intentione faciendi quod facit
ecclesia."

[3] Q. 61.

against the disease of sin "); (*c*) from a tendency in human action (ex studio actionis humanæ ; man clings to the sensible, and it would be too hard to sever him entirely from it). To the objection, again, that the passion of Christ is surely sufficient in itself for salvation, the answer is given, that the Sacraments are not useless, " *because they work in the power of Christ's suffering, and the passion of Christ is somehow* [1] *applied to men by the Sacraments* " (quia operantur in virtute passionis Christi, et passio Christi quodammodo applicatur hominibus per sacramenta); (2) in the state of innocence man neither required the Sacraments as a remedy for sin (pro remedio peccati), nor for perfecting the soul (pro perfectione animæ); (3) in the state of sin before Christ certain Sacraments were necessary " by which man might confess his faith concerning the future advent of the Saviour " (quibus homo fidem suam protestaretur de futuro salvatoris adventu); (4) in the Christian state Sacraments are necessary, " which represent those things which took place before in Christ" (quæ significant ea quæ præcesserunt in Christo). By this change in the Sacraments the unchangeableness of God is not affected, who, like a good father in a home, " gives different precepts to His family to suit different times " (" pro temporum varietate diversa præcepta familiæ suæ proponit"). The fathers were redeemed " by faith in the Christ who was to come," we are redeemed " by faith in the Christ who has now been born and has suffered "; what they had to do with were Sacraments " that corresponded with grace that had to be foreshadowed " (quæ fuerunt congrua gratiæ præfigurandæ), what we have to do with are " *Sacraments that correspond with grace that has to be shown as present* " (sacramenta congrua gratiæ præsentialiter demonstrandæ).[2]

To the question as to the effect of the Sacraments[3] it is replied,

[1] Observe this word ; Thomas is a Mystic.

[2] Cf. on this also Q. 62, Art. 6 : " Sacramenta veteris legis non contulerunt gratiam justificantem per se ipsa, *i.e.*, propria virtute, quia sic non fuisset necessaria passio Christi. . . . Manifestum est, quod a passione Christi, quæ est causa humanæ justificationis *convenienter derivatur virtus justificativa ad sacramenta novæ legis,* non autem ad sacramenta veteris legis. . . . Patet, quod sacramenta veteris legis non habebant in se aliquam virtutem qua operarentur ad conferendam gratiam justificantem, sed solum significabant fidem, per quam justificabantur."

[3] Q. 62.

that we must distinguish between "grace" and "character." The latter has already been treated above ; we have also learned to know the view of Thomas (p. 206) on the Sacraments as "instrumental causes" in addition to the "principal cause" (God). But Thomas has given more precise definitions as to the effect. First, it is laid down (Art. 2) that sacramental grace adds something beyond the "grace of virtues and gifts," namely, "a certain divine help for securing the end of the Sacrament" (quoddam divinum auxilium ad consequendum sacramenti finem).[1] Second, the proposition "sacramenta signant et *continent* (causant) gratiam " (the Sacraments signify and *contain* [cause] grace) is more exactly explained (Art. 3). Third, it is shown that, as there is contained in the Sacraments (Art. 4), and that, too, "in verbis et rebus " (in words and things), "a certain instrumental virtue for conveying grace (which is the effect of the Sacrament) that is proportioned to the instruments" (quædam instrumentalis virtus ad inducendam gratiam, quæ est sacramenti effectus, proportionata instrumento), this virtue originates "from the benediction of Christ and the application of it by the minister to sacramental use," and is to be traced back to the "principal agent." Fourth, the relation of sacramental grace to the passion of Christ is more precisely defined

---

[1] " Gratia virtutem et donorum sufficienter perficit essentiam et potentias animæ, quantum ad generalem ordinationem actuum animæ, sed quantum ad quosdam effectus speciales, qui requiruntur in vita Christiana, requiritur sacramentalis gratia.—Per virtutes et dona excluduntur sufficienter vitia et peccata, quantum ad præsens et futurum, in quantum scil. impeditur homo per virtutes et dona a peccando ; sed quantum ad præterita peccata, quæ transeunt actu. et permanent reatu, adhibetur homini remedium specialiter per sacramenta.—Ratio sacramentalis gratiæ se habet ad gratiam communiter dictam, sicut ratio speciei ad genus, unde sicut non æquivoce dicitur animal communiter dictum et pro homine sumptum, ita non æquivoce dicitur gratia communiter sumpta et gratia sacramentalis." The Protestant polemic had to come in here and show that the gratia virtutum et donorum as gratia fidei is the only grace, and that the sacramental grace in every sense is nothing but the manifestation of the gratia virtutum et donorum, or, say, of the general and only grace. Of this latter it is said (l.c.), " gratia secundum se considerata perficit *essentiam* animæ in quantum participat quandam similitudinem divini ' *esse* ' ; et sicut ab essentia animæ fluunt ejus potentiæ, ita a gratia fluunt quædam perfectiones ad potentias animæ, quæ dicuntur virtutes et dona, quibus potentiæ perficiuntur in ordine ad suos actus." But also : " Ordinantur autem sacramenta ad quosdam speciales effectus necessarios in vita Christiana."

(Art. 5): "The principal cause of grace is God Himself, in relation to whom the humanity of Christ is, so to speak, a conjoined
instrument (ad quem comparatur humanitas Christi sicut
instrumentum conjunctum) (as *e.g.*, the hand is a conjoined
instrument), while the Sacrament is, as it were, a separate
instrument (*e.g.*, like a stick). And thus it is necessary that
saving virtue be derived for the Sacraments from the divinity of
Christ through His humanity (et ideo oportet, quod virtus
salutifera a divinitate Christi per ejus humanitatem in ipsa
sacramenta derivetur). But sacramental grace appears to be
appointed (ordinari) for two things especially, viz., for the
removal of the defects of past sins, in so far as they pass away
as acts (transeunt actu) and remain as guilt (remanent reatu),
and again for the perfecting of the soul in those things which
pertain to the worship of God according to the religion of the
Christian life. But it is manifest from what has been said above,
that Christ has wrought for us, chiefly by His passion, a deliverance from our sins that is not only meritorious and sufficient but
also satisfactory (quod Christus liberavit nos a peccatis nostris,
præcipue per suam passionem non solum sufficienter et meritorie
sed etiam satisfactorie). In like manner also He initiated by
His passion the ritual (ritum) of the Christian religion, yielding
Himself up as an offering and sacrifice to God (offerens se ipsum
oblationem et hostiam deo), as it is declared in Ephes. V.
Whence it is manifest that the Sacraments of the Church have
their efficacy principally from the passion of Christ, of which the
virtue is in some way united (copulatur) to us through receiving
the Sacraments, as a sign of which (in cujus signum) there
flowed from Christ as He hung upon the Cross water and blood,
of which the one relates to baptism, the other to the eucharist,
which are the most potent (potissima) Sacraments."[1]

---

[1] I have quoted the whole passage, because it shows more clearly than any other
that the Catholic doctrine of the Sacraments is at bottom nothing but a reduplication
of the redemption by Christ, or, to put it otherwise, a second structure above the
first, by which the first is crushed to the ground. *As grace was conceived of physically, but this physical grace could not be directly connected with the death of Christ or
derived from it, it was necessary to associate with God the Redeemer, besides the
instrumentum conjunctum* (*the God-man Jesus*), *still another instrumentum separatum*
(*the Sacraments*). If on the other hand the life and death of Christ can be so under-

To the question as to the " causa sacramentorum " (whether per auctoritatem or per ministerium) the reply is as follows :[1] (1) as the "inner effect" of the Sacraments is justification, it appears as if this effect could be produced only by God ; but by way of administering (" per modum ministri ") man also (the priest) can be the "instrumental cause " of the effect. Whether he is more or less good does not come into account here ; the effect of the Sacrament remains always the same, nay, even as regards the "annexa," the priest's prayers, it makes no difference what the character of the priest is ; for they are offered " ex parte ecclesiæ " (on the part of the Church), not on the part of an individual person. (2) God alone is the "institutor sacramentorum," from whom alone also their "virtus" proceeds. Hence it follows : "those things which are done in the Sacraments by appointment of men (per homines instituta) are not necessary to the sacrament (de necessitate sac.), but have to do with a certain solemn observance of it (pertinent ad quandam solemnitatem) . . . but those things which are necessary to the Sacraments *are instituted by Christ Himself*, who is God and man. And although all things are not handed down in Scripture, yet the Church has these things from a well-known (familiari) tradition of the Apostles, as the Apostle says, 1. Cor. XI. : The rest will I set in order when I come."[2] To the objection that the Apostles acted as God's representatives (" vicem dei ") on earth, and therefore might also be institutors of Sacraments, it is replied, that they were certainly not allowed to set up another Church, and so also " it was not lawful for them to institute other Sacraments, (for) it is by Sacraments that the Church of Christ is declared to

stood *that these themselves are seen to be the grace and the Sacrament*, the reduplication is useless. This is the evangelical Protestant point of view ; at least it ought to be. Of course it is then no longer possible to conceive of grace *physically;* for in that case the Catholic doctrine of the Sacraments must again return, which is, however, a pure invention of men, and has nothing to support it in the gospel history. This holds true notwithstanding the institution of the Supper by Jesus ; for where is it found written that the consecrated elements " causant et continent gratiam ex opere operato " ?

[1] Q. 64.

[2] If the necessaria in sacramentis are all to be traced to Christ the institutor, then the Bible is not enough ; *tradition* must be appealed to ; but where is then the limit ?

be formed (fabricata)." (3) It is laid down that the authority in the Sacraments belongs to Christ as God, but that He as man "had the power of the chief *ministry* or pre-eminence and works meritoriously and effectually (potestatem *ministerii* principalis habuit seu excellentiæ et operatur meritorie et efficienter)." (4) It is shown that Christ could convey this "power of ministering" (not the "authority") to other servants, *viz.*, "by giving them such fulness of grace that their merit would operate for rendering the Sacraments effectual (operaretur ad sacramentorum effectus), that the Sacraments would be consecrated on the invocation of their names (ut ad invocationem nominorum ipsorum sanctifica-rentur sacramenta), and that they would themselves be able to institute Sacraments and, without the ritual of the Sacraments, be able to convey by their power alone the effect of the Sacra-ments (ut ipsi possent sacramenta instituere et sine ritu sacra-mentorum effectum sacramentorum conferre solo imperio)." But this "potestas excellentiæ" He has not conveyed to the servants, in order to avoid the "inconveniens," that is, that there might not be many heads in the Church; "if He had nevertheless communicated it, He would Himself have been the head in the principal sense, and they only in a secondary (ipse esset caput principaliter, alii vero secundario)." (5) It is shown that the Sacraments can be validly celebrated even by bad servants, as these act only instrumentally, and "the instrument does not work by its own form or virtue, but by the virtue of him by whom it is moved (non agit secundum propriam formam aut virtutem sed secundum virtutem ejus a quo movetur);" but of course (6) bad servants commit a mortal sin when they celebrate the Sacraments, though the sin does not extend to the receiver, "who does not communicate with the sin of the bad minister, but with the Church." (7) The "intention" and "faith" of the minister are treated (in Art. 8 and 9). The former he must necessarily have,[1] but not the latter: "as it is not required for

---

[1] More precisely : "Quando aliquid se habet ad multa, oportet quod per aliquid determinetur ad unum, si illud effici debeat. Ea vero quæ in sacramentis aguntur possunt diversimode agi, sicut ablutio aquæ quæ fit in baptismo potest ordinari ad munditiam corporalem et ad ludum et ad multa alia hujusmodi. *Et ideo oportet ut determinetur ad unum*, i.e., *ad sacramentalem effectum per intentionem abluentis.* Et hæc intentio exprimitur per verba quæ in sacramentis dicuntur, puta cum dicit : Ego

the perfection of the Sacrament that the minister have love (sit in caritate), but sinners also can dispense Sacraments, so his faith is not required for the perfection of the Sacrament, but an unbeliever can dispense the true Sacrament, provided other things are present which are necessary to a Sacrament." Thus even heretics can dispense the Sacraments, that is, "sacramentum," not "res sacramenti"; for the "power of administering sacraments pertains to spiritual character, which is indelible (he confers, but sins in conferring)."

These doctrines of Thomas, from which a regard to faith (fides) is obviously lacking,[1] and which altogether pass very rapidly over the question as to the conditions of *saving* reception of the Sacraments, underwent afterwards great modification from the time of Scotus onwards.[2] In many points, moreover, the Thomist theses were novelties, and hence were not forthwith received. Thus Thomas was the first to assert the origination of all Sacraments by Christ. Hugo[3] and the Lombard were frank enough to trace several Sacraments, not to Him, but to the Apostles, or to the pre-Christian Era (marriage), and were satisfied with saying that all Sacraments are now administered in the power of Christ (in potestate Christi). Only with Alexander of Hales begins a more exact investigation of the origin of the Sacraments. But till the time of Thomas we still find much uncertainty. It had been usual to fall back on the general assertion of their divine origin, or a "certain" institution by Christ was taught,[4] while in the case of the different Sacraments

te baptizo in nomine," etc. An instrumentum inanimatum receives "loco intentionis motum a quo movetur," but an instrumentum animatum must have the intentio, scil. "faciendi quod facit Christus et ecclesia." But Thomas now places himself more decidedly on the side of the lax, *i.e.*, he disputes the position that a *mentalis* intentio is necessary. What is enough, rather, as the minister acts in loco totius ecclesiæ, is the intention of the *Church* as *actually* expressed in the sacramental words which he speaks, "nisi contrarium exterius exprimatur ex parte ministri vel recipientis sacramentum.'

[1] Hence the 13th Art. of the Augustana; "Damnant illos, qui docent, quod sacramenta ex opere operato justificent, nec docent fidem requiri in usu sacramentorum, quæ credit remitti peccata."

[2] Yet Scotus himself stands very near Thomas in the doctrine of the Sacraments.

[3] On his want of logical thoroughness, see Hahn, p. 155.

[4] See Hahn, p. 158 ff.

very different hypotheses, attributable to embarrassment, were adopted.   But there always continued to be some (on to the sixteenth century) who traced back individual Sacraments simply to *apostolic* institution.[1]

In addition to the problem as to how far the effect is *bound* to the Sacrament (see above), the chief questions in the period that followed were those as to the " minister sacramenti " and as to the conditions of saving reception.   There was certainly agreement on the points, that there are Sacraments whose minister is not designated in the institution by Christ, and that we must distinguish between Sacraments which only a baptised Christian, a priest, or a bishop can duly celebrate ; yet in making the application to each separate Sacrament, and in defining the relations of the minister and the receiver to the Sacrament, great controversies prevailed (is the priest who blesses the marriage, or are the parties to be married, the minister of the Sacrament of Marriage?   In regard to the Eucharist, also, and other Sacraments, old ideas still continued to exercise their influence, and that not always in the case of declared heretics merely ; further, as to confirmation there was doubt whether the exclusive power of the bishops rested on divine or on ecclesiastical appointment, while in connection with this there arose again the whole of the old dispute as to whether presbyters and bishops were originally identical, etc., etc.).

The controversy as to the conditions of saving reception penetrated more deeply ; for here it was necessary to show in what relation the two poles of the Romish view of Christianity were to be placed, *whether the factor of merit was to have predominance over the factor of sacrament or vice-versa.*   The development in Nominalist theology was such that *merit* always asserted its superiority more decidedly, and the conditions accordingly were always more laxly conceived of, while at the same time the view taken of the depreciated effects of the Sacraments became always more magical.   From this as a starting-point (namely, the conditions), which Thomas had merely touched on, the whole doctrine of the Sacraments really

---

[1] See Hahn, p. 163 f.   By conveying the potestas excellentiæ to the apostles, Christ empowered them to institute Sacraments.

became a subject of controversy again, or received a fresh revision.[1] The chief points are the following :

1. Alexander of Hales and Thomas had not indeed derived from all Sacraments a character, but they had asserted of all that they exercise an influence that is independent of the subjective condition of the receiver. But Scotus and those coming later denied this in the case of penance and extreme unction, teaching that these Sacraments remain without any effect if they are received without the requisite disposition.

2. In the earlier period it was held that for the unworthy recipient the virtue of the Sacraments becomes deleterious in its effect. This the Nominalists denied. In the worthy disposition and in the character, they saw on the contrary, as already existing, a positive dispositio ad gratiam, and declared accordingly that in the case of the unworthy the saving effect ex opere operato is not realised,[2] while the " wrath-effect " is not produced by the Sacrament, but arises from the sin of the receiver, and hence is not ex opere operato, but ex opere operante.

3. That a " disposition " belongs to the saving reception was therefore the general opinion ; but as to *why* it was necessary there was difference of view. Some saw in the disposition, not the positive condition of sacramental grace, but only the conditio sine qua non, *i.e., the disposition is not considered as worthiness ;* the Sacraments, rather, of the new covenant, as distinguished from those of the old, in which the fides was requisite (hence opus operans), work ex opere operato.[3] This

---

[1] See Hahn, p. 392 ff.

[2] What takes place, therefore, is only that the Sacrament is observed as an external adorning of the soul (the unbeliever receives a character, enjoys the body of the Lord, stands in an indissoluble marriage bond, etc.), while the gracious *effect* is not wrought. But this last at once follows subsequently, if the " indisposition " gives way.

[3] In its application to the Sacrament the expression " ex opere operato " itself passed through a history which is too extensive to follow out here ; see Schätzler, Die L. v. d. Wirks. d. Sacr. ex opere operato, 1860. The assertion is certainly false that the expression only denotes that the Sacraments are effectual on account of the work accomplished by Christ, or that Christ works in them, that is, it is an apologetic novelty of Möhler, or, say, of some theologians already in the sixteenth century. The leading thought of Scholasticism was rather this, that the Sacrament itself is the opus operatum, and starting from this point it proceeded to call the *outer* act opus operatum, the inner disposition opus operans.

implied the exclusion, not of the necessity of the dispositio,
but certainly of its causal significance.   In entire contrast with
this view stands the other, which, however, was represented
only by a few, that the Sacraments can only mediate grace
when inner contrition and faith are present, so that all saving
grace is solely the result of penitent disposition and of faith ;
but these as inner motives (interiores motus) are wrought by
God, so that on that ground we must not assume a justification
ex opere operante ; the Sacraments now declare this inner act
of God, make man sure as to the reception of grace, and
strengthen the belief that the reception transmits the effectual
grace to the whole man and makes him the possessor of it.
This view comes very near the evangelical one of the sixteenth
century ; but it differs from it in this, that the idea of grace is
still always the Catholic, as participation in the divine nature,
and that accordingly faith is really held as only something
preliminary, that is, it is not yet seen that the " motus fiduciæ
in deum " (trustful impulse God-wards) is the form and the
essence of grace itself.   Further, it is to be observed that this
view has been expressed clearly and plainly by no Schoolman.[1]

[1] Hahn (p. 401 f.) names as representatives of this view Robert Pulleyn, William
of Auxerre, and John Wessel, and, as holding this view as regards at least the Sacrament of Penance, a large number of theologians, among whom the Lombard,
Alexander of Hales, Bonaventura, and Henry of Ghent are mentioned.   These men
really taught that where there is true contritio, absolution comes directly from God,
not through the Sacrament of Penance only, which in this case only declares.   Karl
Müller (Der Umschwung in der Lehre von der Busse während des 12. Jahrh. in the
Abhandl. f. Weizsäcker, 1892, p. 287 ff.) has shown that this view runs back to
Abelard.   He regards it as something new, and if applied to the common reigning
practice, it would certainly have been something new.   But there was no kind of
change in this practice contemplated by it, and it was only a sign that *theology* again
grappled with the question, and felt itself unable simply to justify theoretically the
conception that prevailed in practice of sacrament and priest.   It went back, therefore, at this point to ideas of the early Church, or to ideas that were Augustinian
and more spiritual (Müller seems to me to overlook this, see further details below).
Alexander of Hales (Summa IV., Q. 14, M. 2, Art. 1, § 3) writes : " Duplex est
pænitentia ; quædam quæ solummodo consistit in contritione, quædam quæ consistit
in contritione, confessione, satisfactione ; *utraque est sacramentum.*   Sed primo modo
sumpta non est sacramentum ecclesiæ, sed secundo modo.   Sacramentum pænitentiæ
est signum et causa et quantum ad deletionem culpæ et quantum ad deletionem
pœnæ.   *Contritio enim est signum et causa remissionis peccati et quantum ad culpam
et quantum ad pœnam* " (the adding of the remission of temporal penalties for sin

According to the third view, which constantly gained more adherents, and always came to be more laxly expressed, the saving grace is a product of the Sacrament and of contrite faith, so that the Sacrament in itself merely raises the soul above the point at which it is dead and plants a seed which develops to saving effect only by the co-operation of contrition and faith. Here first the question now came to be of importance as to what the nature was of this contrition and this faith, or as to what the state of soul must be which puts the receiver into the position for letting the sacramental grace attain to its full effect. To begin with it was generally answered here, with Augustine, that the receiver must not "obicem contrariæ cogitationis opponere" (oppose a barrier of adverse thought.) But what is this "obex"[1] or this "impedimentum"? It was replied that the receiver must not receive the Sacrament "cum fictione" (insincerely). But when is he a hypocrite? The earlier theologians required a "bonus motus interior," that is, a really pious spirit that longs for grace, contrition, and faith, and so, since every "bonus motus" is in a certain way meritorious,

takes place, however, only through the priestly sacrament). With this view of repentance, as is well known, the Reformation formed a connection. That fides and sacramentum are exclusively essential to each other in the case of all Sacraments was emphasised by Robert Pulleyn and Wessel (the former, Sentent. I., octo P. V., c. 13: "quod fides facit, baptismus ostendit; fides peccata delet, baptismus deleta docet, unde sacramentum dicitur." VI. 61: "Absolutio, quæ peracta confessione super pænitentem a sacerdote fit, sacramentum est, quoniam rei sacræ signum est. Et cujus sacræ rei est signum, nisi remissionis et absolutionis? Nimirum confitentibus a sacerdote facta a peccatis absolutio remissionem peccatorum, quam antea peperit cordis contritio, designat. A peccatis ergo presbyter solvit, *non utique quod peccata dimittat, sed quod dimissa sacramento pandat.*" The latter, de commun. sanct. [edit. Groning, 1614], p. 817: "Effectus sacramentorum sunt secundum dispositionem suscipientis et secundum requisitam illi intentioni dispositionem. . . . Dispositio vero requisita huic sacramento, ut efficax fiat, est fames et sitis hujus vivifici cibi et potus. Unde quanto minus eum esurit et sitit, pro tanto minorem etiam effectum consequitur." 818: "Semper sacramenta fidei sunt instrumenta, tanto semper efficacia, quanto est fides negotiosa"). But in view of these valuable sentences, we must remember, as has been remarked above, that to closer inspection a mysterious gratia is placed behind and above the fides, which lowers the fides to a means.

[1] The Greek Scholasticism also knows of the obex. Antonius Melissa quotes in the Loci Comm. (Migne, Bd. 136, col. 823), sermo 16, the saying of a certain Theotimus: ἔοικεν ἡ ἁμαρτία παρακωλύματι, κωλύοντι τὴν εὔνοιαν τοῦ θεοῦ ἐν ἡμῖν γενέσθαι.

certain merits.   The "barrier" is here therefore the lack of such
a positive good disposition.   So it was taught by the Lombard,
Alexander, Thomas,[1] and a large number of theologians, and
they further laid it down that, as all merit is rewarded, the
reception of the Sacrament results in a twofold grace, namely
(1) ex opere operato, (2) but also ex opere operante; the latter
is different from the sacramental grace, but is always added to
it (ex merito, on account of the disposition, and greater or less,
according to the measure of the disposition).   Here already,
then, merit is introduced in a hazardous way.   Yet the later
theologians (among the earlier, Albertus) required only the
absence of an undevout disposition ; what is held by them as a
barrier is simply the presence of a "motus contrarius malus," *i.e.*,
contempt of the Sacrament, positive unbelief, or an unforgiven
mortal sin.[2]   They said that the dignity of the New Testament
Sacraments consists just in this, that they presuppose *no* positive
disposition, while such disposition is to be presupposed in the
case of all other grace.   Hence Scotus defines : "for the first
reception of grace (the non-sacramental) there is required some
kind of merit (aliquis modus meritorius) de congruo ; but for the
second (the sacramental) nothing is required save a reception
of baptism that is voluntary and without insincerity (sine
fictione), *i.e.*, with the intention of receiving what the Church
confers, and without mortal sin in act or will (sine actu vel
voluntate peccati mortalis), so that in the first there is required
some intrinsic work in some way accepted as meritum
de congruo, in the second there is only required an external work
(opus exterius), with putting away of inner hindrance (cum
amotione interioris impedimenti)."   One sees that here the
doctrine of the Sacraments is already quite drawn into the
(Pelagian) doctrine of justification, and subordinated to it, while
apparently the power of the Sacrament is increased, seeing that
it is to be held as effectual even where a tabula rasa exists.

[1] In Sentent. IV., Dist. 4, Q. 3, Art. 2 : " Indispositus reputatur et qui non credi
et qui indevotus accedit . . . in sacramentis præcipue fides operatur . . . ideo
defectus fidei specialius pertinet ad fictionem."

[2] Scotus, in Sent. IV., Dist. 1, Q. 6: "Sacramentum ex virtute operis operati
confert gratiam, ita quod non requiritur ibi bonus motus interior qui mereatur
gratiam, sed sufficit quod suscipiens non ponat obicem."

Yet with the increased power there contrasts the really small saving effect, which passes, rather, into the "acceptance of the merits of man." Between these two views there was still a third, which certainly stands quite near the last mentioned, frequently coalesced with it, and was afterwards to become the predominant one ; it is neither satisfied with the absence of the "malus motus," nor does it require the "bonus motus," but it demands that a "certain" sorrow shall precede the reception of the Sacrament, which does not require to spring from the highest motives, but may arise from lower, *e.g.*, from fear of punishment or something similar. This "sorrow" is described as *attritio*,[1] and it is said of it that, if there is earnest striving, the Sacrament can raise it to contritio. But others now went still further and taught *that the Sacrament changes attritio into contritio ex opere operato.* According to this extremely widely diffused view, the man can be saved *who lets himself stand in dread of hell,* even though otherwise all inner connection with the Christian religion is wanting to him ; he must only assiduously use the Sacrament of Penance, in the opinion that it can protect him against hell. Yet even this "opinion" does not need to be a sure faith ; he may only hold the effect of the Sacrament as not impossible ; "attrition, when the Sacrament is added, is made sufficient by the power of the keys" (attritio superveniente sacramento virtute clavium efficitur sufficiens).[2]

A quite magical view of the Sacraments here competes in a pernicious way with that doctrine of "merit," according to

[1] Scotus was the first to direct his attention to this very correctly observed character of the commoner type of humanity, and began to use it in the way indicated for the doctrine of salvation ; see Hahn, p. 413 f.

[2] Or : "Attritus accedit ad confessionem, ex quo ibi fit contritus, *unde fugatur fictio.* Et sic non habet dubium, quia et sacramentum suscipit et effectum ejus scil. remissionem peccatorum." Numerous passages in Hahn, l.c. From this point of view, indeed, the mere purpose to partake of the Sacrament, or the partaking per se, might come to be regarded as something initially meritorious, and this step was really already taken from the time of the Lombard, the view becoming quite widely prevalent. Nay, as if the conscience and the plain understanding reacted against the sacramental magic, the Lombard declares that the humiliatio before the sensible materials in the Sacrament establishes merit (Sentent. IV., Dist. 1 C.): "propter humiliationem quidem, ut dum homo sensibilibus rebus, quæ natura infra ipsum sunt, ex præcepto creatoris se reverendo subicit, ex hac humilitate et obedientia deo magis placeat et apud eum mereatur."

which God of His good pleasure (per acceptationem) takes as complete what is only a beginning, and indeed is not even a beginning, since the motives of those "meritorious" acts may be religiously neutral.   In connection with the doctrine of justification we shall return to this worst point, which dominated the whole practical and theoretical system of Catholicism at the beginning of the Reformation period.[1]   But certainly it is clear here already, that to hush up rather than to give comfort was the effect of a doctrine of the Sacraments having this form and issue.   This doctrine was originally framed on the exalted idea of the "participatio divinæ naturæ," and it still continues to betray its basis in the first stages of its construction.   But it ends in confirming the man of common spirit in his low-type morality and feeble piety.   The earnest Catholic may not apply these final conclusions to himself; he may confine himself to the original thesis, which is not forbidden to him, but for the careless, the Church has prepared a broad road and opened a wide gate.   In a *relative* way it may work much good with this; for its system is derived from listening to life; it gives pedagogic direction on the question as to how one who is not quite thoughtless, who is not perfectly stolid, who is not entirely sunk in earthly enjoyment, can be aided, and introduced into a better society, with better modes of life.   But as soon as we consider that it is the *Christian religion* we have to do with here, that religion of earnest spirit and comforting power, this structure of opus operatum, attritio and meritum is seen to be a mockery of all that is sacred.[2]

---

[1] Apol. Confess. Aug. 13: "Hic damnamus totum populum scholasticorum doctorum, qui docent, quod sacramenta non ponenti obicem conferant gratiam ex opere operato sine bono motu utentis.   Hæc simpliciter judaica opinio est sentire quod per ceremoniam justificemur, sine bono motu cordis, hoc est, sine fide.   Et tamen hæc impia et perniciosa opinio magna auctoritate docetur in toto regno pontificio."

[2] On Duns Scotus' doctrine of the Sacraments see Werner, Scotus (1881), pp. 462-496; on the doctrine of Post-Scotist Scholasticism see the same author, Die Nachscotistische Scholastik (1883), p. 380 ff.   As specially important characteristics of the Scotist doctrine of the Sacraments note the following : (1) the rejection of the *inner* necessity of the Sacraments, since God can grant the saving grace even without the employment of these outward signs (all the more firmly is the *outer* necessity maintained, on the ground of the positive divine appointment) ; (2) the rejection of

The individual Sacraments. (1) *Baptism.*[1] This Sacrament[2] is the medicine for the consequences of the Fall, and lays the basis of the new life ; it has therefore a negative and a positive effect.[3] The former, in which the " grace " already appears as " most perfect,[4] relates to original sin. In so far as this consists in guilt, penalty, and concupiscence, baptism abolishes all these with the entire sin ; *i.e.*, the guilt (guilt of original sin and of the previously committed sinful deeds without exception)[5] is

an influence of a naturally necessary kind in the media of sacramental grace ; (3) the strong emphasising of the Sacraments as notæ ecclesiæ ; (4) the assertion that since the Fall there have been Sacraments effectual ex opere operato ; (5) the rejection of the virtus supernaturalis in the Sacraments ; (6) the rejection of the position, that the intellect is the vehicle of the sacramental character ; (7) the assertion that only from the positive appointment of God is it to be concluded that baptism cannot be repeated ; (8) the assertion, that the reatus culpæ after the act of sin is no reatio realis, *i.e.*, that there remains nothing in the *soul* of the effect of sin, which would again be sin ; for the habitus vitiosus is not sin, seeing that it remains even in the justified ; hence there stands nothing that is a link between the sinful act and the obligatio ad pœnam ; the latter, therefore, is only a relatio rationis of the divine intellect or will, which has its ground in the "ordering will " of God ; in accordance with this the view of the Sacrament of Penance is formed. Occam emptied the Sacraments of every kind of inner and speculative import ; they have simply an importance because God has so *ordained* them ; but we do not know why. Here also the position of things was such that as soon as the authority of the Church disappeared, there was necessarily a falling away, not only of the doctrine of the Sacraments in every sense—that was no misfortune—but also of every doctrine of grace ; for no one had taken the precaution to secure that the latter should be able to exist independently of the Sacraments.

[1] See the detailed exposition in Thomas, P. III., Q. 66-71. Schwane, pp. 605-622.

[2] According to the general view (something similar already in Ignatius of Antioch) Christ, at His own baptism, imparted to the water consecration and power. Hence the water needs no special consecration, as the material does in the other Sacraments.

[3] According to the Scholastic view, which, however, was not shared by all, an abolition of sin is in itself possible without infusion of saving grace (so Thomas).

[4] Gabriel Biel (according to Hahn, p. 334) : " Licet gratia baptismalis sit incipientium et ita *imperfecta* quantum ad habilitandum ad bonum, tamen quantum ad liberandum a malo habet vim gratiæ perfectissimæ . . . restituit perfectam innocentiam."

[5] On the other hand : "baptismus non est institutus ad delendum omnia peccata futura, sed tamen præterita et præsentia." Hence the rule : "baptismus delet quidquid invenit." This reluctance to relate the sin-cancelling grace of baptism to the future, had originally sprung from regard for the interests of human freedom and for the serious nature of Christian morality. But in the Scholastic period what is aimed at mainly is to protect the Church Sacrament of Penance.

blotted out, the penalty remitted (and that means the eternal
penalty totally, the temporal penalty likewise, so far as it
consists in pœnæ determinatæ ; but so far as it finds expression
in the penal evils of the earthly life, it remains), and the
concupiscence is controlled.   The last point is new, as only in
Scholasticism is a clear distinction drawn between sinful and
innocent concupiscence.   The meaning is this, that through sin
sinful concupiscence has come into existence as disorder of the
lower impulses, or as dominion of these over the higher impulses and over the province of human action, whereby a fomes
peccati (slumbering fire of sin), ever continuing, and working
with a certain necessity, has developed itself.   Baptism, now,
has the effect of so rectifying the disorder of the passions, and
moderating the " fomes peccati," that man is now in a position
for resisting, or for keeping within appointed limits, the concupiscence, which is involved in his earthly nature, and is
therefore in itself innocent.   This view of the natural life, which
is not a religious one, will occupy us again in the next section
(under C).   Here it is enough to note that, in order to give expression to the absoluteness of the negative baptismal influence
as an effectual one, the conception of an innocent concupiscence
was admitted.[1]   The positive effect of baptism is summed up
under the term, " sacramentum regenerationis."   But while here

---

[1] Lombard, Sentent. II., Dist. 32, A. B. : " Licet remaneat concupiscentia post
baptismum, non tamen dominatur et regnat sicut ante, immo per gratiam baptismi
mitigatur et minuitur, ut post dominari non valeat, nisi quis reddat vires hosti eundo
post concupiscentias.   Nec post baptismum remanet ad reatum, quia non imputatur
in peccatum, sed tantum pœna peccati est, ante baptismum vero pœna est et
culpa. . . . Per gratiam baptismi vitium concupiscentiæ debilitatur atque extenuatur,
ita ut jam non regnet, nisi consensu reddantur ei vires, et quia reatus ipsius solvitur."
Thomas defines the fomes (after the Fall) in the 27 Q., P. III., as "rebellio
inferiorum virium ad rationem," or as "inordinata concupiscentia sensibilis
appetitus"; but by grace it is weakened and loses the reatus.   What was still
thought of even then (see Augustine) was almost exclusively the sexual impulse and
generation.   Therefore there can be no thought of removing the concupiscence, and
Thomas asserts : "baptismus non aufert actu infectionem, prout afficit personam,
quod patet ex hoc, quod baptizatus per actum naturæ originale transmittit in prolem."
He says also, P. II., 1, Q. 74, Art. 3 : " Transit peccatum originale reatu et remanet
actu (this is not so strongly expressed afterwards).   Sed talis corruptio fomitis non
impedit, quin homo rationabili voluntate possit reprimere singulos motus inordinatos
sensualitatis, si præsentiat, puta divertendo cogitationem ad alia."

there was in general no occasion to pass beyond the old
ecclesiastical conception (even the special connection of baptism
with faith is still always emphasised), yet misgivings arose on
two points. Is the positive grace in baptism " perfectissima,"
and do the children receive this grace as perfectly as baptised
adults ? Although in general it was declared that baptism is
the sacrament of justification, and that through it the baptised
person receives the gratia operans and cooperans, provided he
does not already possess it (in which case there is only an
increasing), yet, from the time of Nominalism especially,
baptism was in point of fact held to be only the sacrament of
initiation for justification.[1] Hence there was an increased
willingness to assume in the case of children the perfect application of baptismal grace,[2] while it was held at an earlier period,
that to children there is perfectly communicated only purification from original sin, the positive grace being only infused into
them afterwards at successive times.[3] As regards the faith of
children, there was no fixed opinion ; the majority seem to have
held that the faith of the Church (or of the sponsors) intervenes
here vicariously, and that thereby the saving effect is made
possible.[4] Thus baptism only lays the foundation for the
process of justification, or it implants it " in habitu," but not " in
actu " (that Mary was thought of as an exception to this was a
matter of course on the Catholic view ; for to her nothing could

---

[1] See note 4 on p. 227.

[2] As a rule, no doubt, with the addition, that the habitus ligatus est propter
pueritiam, but that as truly is it perfectly imparted as the sleeping man is a living
man. So already Thomas. At the Council of Vienna in 1311, the view was declared
the sententia probabilior and sanctioned, that baptism is the cause in the case of
parvuli, both of the remissio culpæ and of the collatio gratiæ (quoad habitum, etsi
non pro illo tempore quoad usum), i.e., that it communicates the gratia informans et
virtutes (Mansi XXV., p. 411).

[3] Lombardus, IV., Dist. 4 H. : " de adultis, qui digne recipiunt sacramentum, non
ambigitur quin gratiam operantem et cooperantem perceperint . . . de parvulis vero,
qui nondum ratione utuntur, quæstio est, an in baptismo receperint gratiam qua ad
majorem venientes ætatem possent velle et operari bonum ? Videtur, quod non
receperint, quia gratia illa caritas est et fides, quæ voluntatem præparat et adjuvat.
Sed quis dixerit, eos accepisse fidem et caritatem ! "

[4] Following Augustine, Thomas III., Q. 68, Art. 9 : the parvuli sunt in utero
matris ecclesiæ and are thus nourished.

be given by baptism which she had not already possessed before baptism).[1]

Baptism is absolutely necessary (baptism with blood a substitute), conveys a character, cannot be repeated, is valid when it is performed with water (materia) and with the words of institution (forma),[2] and is regularly dispensed by the priest. Yet in an emergency a deacon, and even a layman, can baptise. The considerations regarding the sacramentalia which accompanied baptism do not belong to the history of dogma;[3] just as little do the secondary consequences of baptism, as, *e.g.*, spiritual affinity, etc.

As the Church had to contend, especially from the thirteenth century onwards, against sects and schools who, on different grounds (as a rule out of opposition to the prevailing sacramental system, here and there also from opposition to the sacramental system in general), disputed the rightfulness of infant baptism, or who denied the necessity of baptism altogether, an apologetic, polemical discussion of the Sacrament of Baptism was necessary. Yet there was never nearly so much fulness of statement here as in the account given of the Sacrament of the Eucharist.[4]

2. *Confirmation.*[5] This Sacrament obtained its independent existence simply through Western practice, inasmuch as only the bishop[6] could administer it. Hence it naturally resulted, that it became dissociated from baptism, which, however, forms its presupposition,[7] and with which it shares the quality, that it conveys a character, and therefore cannot be repeated. The

---

[1] Here there were great controversies, which will be briefly dealt with afterwards.

[2] Thomas, P. III., Q. 66, Art. 6, declares (against Hugo) that baptism in the name of Christ alone is invalid; yet the Apostles allowed themselves such baptism.

[3] See Schanz, Die Wirksamkeit der Sacramentalien, Tüb, Theol. Quartalschr. 1886, Part. 4.

[4] See the polemic against the Catharists (Moneta), Petrobrusiani, etc.

[5] Thomas, P. III., Q. 72, Schwane, pp. 622-627.

[6] Because only the Apostles had the power to impart the Holy Spirit by laying on of hands.

[7] Not only its presupposition, " sed est majoris necessitatis," Thomas, l.c., Art. 12. With regard to the presupposition it is said in Art. 6: " si aliquis non baptizatus confirmaretur, nihil reciperet."

material is the Chrisma consecrated by the bishop, the form the sacramental words : " consigno te, etc." The effect, which, of course, as additional to that of baptism, either cannot be definitely expressed, or restricts the importance of the baptismal communication of grace, is *power* (robur) for growth, strength for conflict with enemies of the faith (military), the gifts of the Holy Spirit, or even—as a portion of the process of justification —the gratia gratum faciens (grace that renders well-pleasing).[1] Doubts about this Sacrament, which, according to Thomas,

---

[1] " Robur," or " potestas ad pugnam spiritalem," is the chief conception ; baptism distinguishes believers from unbelievers, confirmation the newly-born from the mature. At the same time Thomas (Art. 7) sought to introduce confirmation into the process of justification, in which, certainly, he had poor enough success : " datur baptisato spiritus sanctus ad robur . . . missio seu datio spiritus s. non est nisi cum gratia gratum faciente. Unde manifestum est, quod gratia gratum faciens confertur in hoc sacramento . . . gratiæ gratum facientis primus effectus est remissio culpæ, habet tamen et alios effectus quia sufficit ad hoc quod promoveat hominem per omnes gradus usque in vitam æternam . . . et ideo gratia gratum faciens non solum datur ad remissionem culpæ, sed etiam ad augmentum et firmamentum justitiæ, et sic confertur in hoc sacramento." But any number of Sacraments might then be forced in ! See the summing up of the chief deliverances on the Sacrament by Eugene IV. (l.c., p. 1055), where it is said of the effect : " datur S. S. ad robur, ut vid. Christianus audacter Christi confiteatur nomen." The Pope will have it, besides, that per apostolicæ sedis dispensationem even ordinary priests have celebrated the Sacrament, yet only with oil which a bishop had consecrated. This continued afterwards to be the Catholic view, or, say, practice. This special linking of confirmation to the power of the Pope goes back to Thomas. He framed the theory, fraught with large consequences, that the Sacraments of the Eucharist and of ordination relate to the true body of Christ, the others to the mystical (the Church). Hence in the celebration of the latter five Sacraments there is to be taken into account, besides the potestas ministerii in general, the power of jurisdiction (in the case of one in a higher, in the case of another in a lower degree) belonging to the Church, that is, the Pope. In consequence of this he has the right, in the case of confirmation, to depute ordinary priests ; in Sentent. IV., Dist. 7, Q. 3, A. 1 : " Sciendum est, quod cum episcopatus non addat aliquid supra sacerdotium per relationem ad corpus domini verum, sed solum per relationem ad corpus mysticum, papa per hoc quod est episcoporum summus non dicitur habere plenitudinem potestatis per relationem ad corpus domini verum, sed per relationem ad corpus mysticum. Et quia gratia sacramentalis descendit in corpus mysticum a capite, ideo omnis operatio in corpus mysticum sacramentalis, per quam gratia datur, dependet ab operatione sacramentali super corpus domini verum, et ideo solus sacerdos potest absolvere in loco pænitentiali et baptizare ex officio. Et ideo dicendum, quod promovere ad illas perfectiones, quæ non respiciunt corpus domini verum, sed solum corpus mysticum, potest a papa qui habet plenitudinem pontificialis potestatis committi sacerdoti."

"etiam a non jejunis dari vel accipi potest"[1] (can be given or
received even by those not fasting), never disappeared; Wyclif
again gave emphatic expression to them; for a reliable proof
from tradition could not be obtained.[2] In the last resort
Thomas is unable otherwise to defend the "conveniens" in the
ritual than by the sentence:[3] "it must be firmly held that the
ordinances of the Church are directed according to the wisdom
of Christ. And for this reason it ought to be certain that the
ritual which the Church observes in this and in other Sacraments
is fitting" (firmiter tenendum est, quod ordinationes ecclesiæ
dirigantur secundum sapientiam Christi. Et propter hoc
certum esse debet, ritus quod ecclesia observat n hoc et in aliis
sacramentis esse convenientes). If we assume, not the dogmatic, but the practical pedagogic point of view, we cannot
deny the serviceableness of this observance, especially when
taken along with infant baptism, both as regards the plebs
Christiana, and as regards the bishop, who in this way comes
close to every member of his diocese.[4]

3. *The Eucharist.*[5] At the beginning of the thirteenth
century, after the conflicts in the eleventh, and many uncertainties in the twelfth, the doctrine of transubstantiation,
together with what was derived from it, or coheres with it,
was substantially settled. The Lateran Council (see above,
p. 53) of the year 1215 had brought the development to a conclusion, and had given to the Sacrament the highest conceivable
place, as was shown by the deliverance regarding it being
introduced into the Symbol.[6] But the "heretical" opposition
had made the deliverance necessary. This opposition never

---

[1] Thomas, l.c., Art. 12.

[2] A passage from Pseudo-Isidore (ep. episc. Melchiadis) played an important part,
as also the Pseudo-Dionysius.

[3] Thomas, l.c.

[4] Its institution by Christ, first asserted by Albertus, even Thomas has only
"proved" by declaring that Christ instituted the Sacrament, John XVI. 7,
"promittendo."

[5] Thomas, P. III., Q. 73-83; Schwane, pp. 628-661; Article, "Transubstantiation," by Steitz-Hauck, Real-Encyclopädie, vol. 15², pp. 803 ff., 815 ff. (a very
thorough-going account).

[6] Baur points out very correctly (Vorles, II., p. 475) that Thomas tries to prove
that Christianity without transubstantiation is not the absolute religion.

became silent ; nay, in the circles of the Church theology itself, there were set forth in later times views of transubstantiation, that, strictly speaking, had the effect of cancelling it.

Here, also, it was Thomas whose view of the Sacrament became classic in Catholicism. The modifications which Nominalism allowed itself to adopt disappeared ; the doctrine of Thomas remained. Thomas put an end to the uncertainties still betrayed by the Lombard at some points,[1] and he applied in perfected form to the Sacrament the dialectic mode of treatment which had once occasioned so much offence. He could dispose of the Sacrament with confidence, for he was a Realist, and Duns Scotus could do so likewise (in some respects in a still more perfect form), because he also readily adopted a realistic theory of knowledge. But this confidence thereafter received a check ; for it is only in a forced way, if at all, that the Nominalist mode of thought can come to terms with transubstantiation. It must either let it drop, or declare it an intensified miracle, by which two impossible things become actual.

In the Sacrament of the Supper and the doctrine regarding it, the Church gave expression to everything that it highly prized —its dogma, its mystical relation to Christ, the fellowship of believers, the priest, the sacrifice, the miraculous power which God had given to His Church, the satisfaction of the sensuous

---

[1] Only the fact of the conversio was a certainty for the Lombard, not the modus ; see Sentent. IV., Dist. 11 A. : " Si quæritur, qualis sit ista conversio, an formalis an substantialis vel alterius generis, definire non sufficio ; formalem tamen non esse cognosco, quia species rerum quæ ante fuerant, remanent, et sapor et pondus. *Quibusdam* videtur esse substantialis, dicentibus sic substantiam converti in substantiam, ut hæc essentialiter fiat illa." Yet that is at bottom the opinion of the Lombard also, for he unequivocally teaches (Dist. 12 A.) that after the transformation the accidents are " sine subjecto." In the doctrine of the Mass the Lombard had not yet reached the height of Realism ; ideas of the ancient Church still exercised their influence on him ; see Sentent. IV., Dist. 12 F. : " Quæritur, si quod gerit sacerdos proprie dicatur sacrificium vel immolatio, et si Christus quotidie immolatur vel semel tantum immolatus sit ? Ad hoc breviter dici potest, illud quod offertur et consecratur a sacerdote vocari sacrificium et oblationem, quia memoria est et repræsentatio sacrificii veri et sanctæ immolationis factæ in ara crucis. Et semel Christus mortuus est in cruce, ibique inmolatus est in semetipso, quotidie autem immolatur in sacramento, quia in sacramento *recordatio*, fit illius quod factum est semel."

impulse in piety, etc., *only not the faith which seeks for certainty and to which certainty is given.*   This appears very plainly from the description of the effects of the Eucharist as a Sacrament and as a sacrifice.   The Sacrament was universally reverenced as the chiefest Sacrament, the sun among the Sacraments, etc., because here res and sacramentum coincide (the matter becomes itself Christ), because the incarnation and the death on the Cross are represented as operative in it, or are repeated in it, and because it embraces the past, the present, and the future.   Yet the effects, which are summed up under the term *nourishment* of the spiritual life of the soul, and are detailed as incorporation into Christ, incorporation into the Church, communion of the members with each other, forgiveness of venial sins, perseverance in faith, strengthening of human weakness, refreshment, foretaste and fore-celebration of the heavenly blessedness, anticipation of eternal fellowship with God, etc., do not attain to the effect of the Sacrament of Penance.   Just as little is specific importance attached to the Eucharist as a sacrifice ; under this term, indeed, personal merit rather is strongly asserted.   In the sacrifice of the Mass one testifies his obedience to God; like every sacrifice it is a performance which can claim a reward.   Thus all effects here are at the same time dependent on the receiver.   These effects *appear* to be estimated most highly ; the sacrifice of the Mass, indeed, is a constant repetition of the death on the Cross; but this constant repetition has respect only to daily sins, to penal evils and bodily need.   It extends, no doubt, in its effect, beyond the earthly life—in practice, the bearing of the sacrifice of the Mass on the penalties in purgatory was almost its most important bearing—yet there are also other means, which are really not less effectual than the Masses.[1]

[1] On the effect of the Eucharist, see Thomas, Q. 79.   In the first Art. he shows that it conveys grace; in the second that it gives aid for eternal life; in the third that it does not blot out mortal sins, seeing that it is given to the spiritually alive, though under certain circumstances it removes an unconscious mortal sin ; in the fourth that it blots out the peccata venalia ; in the fifth that it does not cancel the penalty of sin entirely, but only "secundum quantitatem devotionis sumentium"; in the sixth that it guards men against future transgressions ; in the seventh that as a Sacrament it profits only the receivers, but as a sacrificium the spectators also : "In quantum in hoc sacramento repræsentatur passio Christi, qua Christus obtulit se hostiam deo,

The materia of the Sacrament is wheaten [1] bread and wine.[2]
The appropriateness of these, and, in particular, of this *double*
form, is dealt with very minutely. The very ancient symbolic
idea of the many grains which become *one* bread also reappears
in the Schoolmen.[3] The forma is the words of consecration,
which are spoken in the name of Christ (not in the name of the
minister).[4] In connection therewith, Bonaventura explains the
"hoc" as denoting the bread, Thomas as denoting the accidents
of the bread ("hoc sub his specibus contentum," *i.e.*, that which
is here presented is not bread, but my body). But the forma is
not only an appeal to God (Bonaventura, Duns) that He will accomplish the transubstantiation, but an effectual power, as soon
as the priest has the intention to work the mystery.[5]

But the difficult question was now this, How is the transubstantiation to be thought of? [6]   Here there was, first, a rejection
already by the Lombard of the idea of a new-creation of the
body of Christ, for Christ's body already exists; but, second, the
opinion was also rejected by him that Christ makes the bread
and wine into His body, so that they become the Sacrament,
whether by assumptio or by consubstantiality; there must be
believed in rather a conversio of such a kind that the substances

habet rationem sacrificii, in quantum vero in hoc sacramento traditur invisibilis gratia
sub visibili specie, habet rationem sacramenti . . . hoc sacrificium, quod est memoriale
dominicæ passionis, non habet effectum nisi in illis qui conjunguntur huic sacramento
per fidem et caritatem.   Unde et in Canone Missæ non oratur pro his qui sunt extra
ecclesiam ; illis tamen prodest plus vel minus secundum modum devotionis eorum."
So the Mass profits only those who already have fides and caritas, as securing for them
an augmentum fidei, or a remission of penalty, and always according to the measure
of their desert.   The Eucharist is the Sacrament and sacrifice which accompanies the
process of justification, so far as that process has already begun and is disturbed by
no mortal sin, and which carries the process to its higher stages.

[1] Controversy with the Greeks about leavened bread.
[2] Mixing with water is the rule.
[3] Thomas, Q. 74, Art. 1.
[4] Q. 78, Art. 1.
[5] Thomas, in Sentent. IV., Dist. 8, Q. 2, Art. 3 : " In verbis prædictis sicut et in
aliis formis sacramentorum est aliqua virtus a deo, sed hæc virtus non est qualitas
habens esse completum in natura . . . sed habet esse incompletum, sicut virtus
quæ est in instrumento ex intentione principalis agentis."
[6] There was in possession no traditional doctrine whatever on this point ; indeed,
a proof for the fact itself of transubstantiation could not be derived from earlier times.
Special appeal was made to Pseudo-Ambrosius.

of the elements pass into the substances of the body of Christ, while the accidents remain behind without a subject.[1] What happens to the substance of the elements, whether it breaks up and is destroyed, the Lombard declared that he did not know. Alexander of Hales distinctly rejects consubstantiality and destruction, and speaks of a "passing over." But he at once adds, that after the change, the *whole* Christ is present, inasmuch as the human soul and the deity of Christ always are concomitantly (per concomitantiam) where His flesh is. The continuance of the accidents without a subject he pronounced a miracle.[2] Bonaventura attached weight to the conversio taking place both as regards the materia and the forma of the bread (it would otherwise be imperfect); yet we must not understand by the former the materia prima (matter as the potency [potentia] of all material substances). [3] With regard to the first Eucharist celebration—the treatment of which is the hardest crux of the whole theory—it was universally held, indeed, that Christ partook of Himself in eating (as an example, and with a view to the enjoyment of love, not with a view to being perfected), but while Hales thought that Christ partook then already of His glorified body, Bonaventura taught (Thomas following him) that Christ partook of His mortal body, which, however, as Eucharistic was already present "impassibiliter" (in impassible form). All of them thought of the parallels in creation and incarnation, and sought to explain the mystery from these. Thomas now submitted to a final treatment the accidents, which, as the subject is wanting to them after the conversio, are maintained in existence by God as the first cause (causa prima).[4] But at the

---

[1] Sentent. IV., Dist. 12 A. : "Si vero quæritur de accidentibus, quæ remanent, scil. de speciebus et de sapore et pondere, in quo subjecto fundantur, potius mihi videtur fatendum existere sine subjecto, quam esse in subjecto, quia ibi non est substantia nisi corporis et sanguinis dominici, quæ non afficitur illis accidentibus. Non enim corpus Christi talem in se habet formam, sed qualis in judicio apparebit. Remanent ergo illa accidentia per se subsistentia ad mysterii ritum, ad gustus fideique suffragium, quibus corpus Christi habens formam et naturam suam tegitur."

[2] Summa IV., Q. 38, 40.

[3] It is an opinion peculiar to Bonaventura, that the substance of the bread would return if the accidents were destroyed.

[4] Thomas III., Q. 77. In the first Article the question is discussed : "Utrum accidentia quæ remanent, sint sine subjecto"; it is answered in the affirmative, since

same time, following Bonaventura, he laid the foundation for an extremely complicated doctrine of the form of all matter, which was afterwards spun out by Duns and the Nominalists. As the bread, that is to say, is changed as regards the material *and the form*, both changes must be demonstrated in the transubstantiated result. But as the soul of Christ (form) only appears present concomitantly (per concomitantiam), the body of Christ must have a form for itself.[1] Thus Thomas is led to the idea of a "form of corporeity" (forma corporeitatis), which is identical neither with the soul nor with the outer shape, but appears as the ground of the qualities of the body. Further, in accordance with this, Thomas conceives of the conversio as a *passing over* in the strict sense of the term (*no* destruction = annihilatio of the elements).[2] The miracle is identical with a miracle of creation in so far as in the case of both the two states are not united by a common subject (substance); for the continued existence of the accidents is no real bond. Duns pursued this line further, and came to the adoption of a plurality of forms in matter. He required this assumption, as he assailed St. Thomas with reflections arising from the hypothesis, that the Eucharist was conceivably celebrated during the time when Christ lay in the grave. The Thomist doctrine was not framed to meet this case, as it assumed a forma substantialis for the *living* body. Hence, according to Thomas, only an imperfect transubstantiation would then have taken place—that is, a transubstantiation only into the material of the dead body. Duns himself appealed more confidently to the divine omnipotence, placed in the foreground the general possibility that God can transform everything (even the material into the spiritual, and vice versa), affirmed the existence of a matter without quality which is capable of everything, and came very close to the view, that in transubstantiation one sub-

they cannot become accidents of the body of Christ. In the second Article it is asked: "utrum quantitas dimensiva sit subjectum aliorum accidentum," etc., etc. Here already the logical investigations into space begin.

[1] Summa P. III., Q. 75, Art. 6: "Forma substantialis panis *non* remanet" (which is elaborately proved). Yet the breaking relates, not to the body of Christ, but to the species sacramentalis ("corpus Christi non frangitur"); see Q. 77, Art. 7.

[2] Even animals, according to Thomas, enjoy the body of the Lord (Q. 80, Art. 3). Bonaventura is in favour of the opinio honestior that this does not happen.

stance is annihilated and another is introduced. Above all,
however, his thesis, that God Himself, as if on the ground of a
contract, always works the conversio, so that the words of consecration only form the *occasion*, influenced all the Nominalists
afterwards. But by a logical process there then followed also
upon this view a modification of the way of understanding transubstantiation, in the direction of impanation and consubstantiality. For it became natural to assume, that if the divine working only *accompanies* the words of the priest (that is, the forma
sacramenti), it only *accompanies*, also, the elements (the materia;
a "moral" conjunction by the free will of Christ). This doctrine
was first suggested as possible, and then asserted as possible. But
when once the idea of the conversio was separated by a logical
distinction into two acts—into annihilation, and entrance of the
body of Christ into the place of the annihilated subject—the
first act could also drop out. The miracle only becomes the
greater when substance stands side by side with substance. At
the same time the signal was now given for investigations
into *space* in its relation to *substance*, investigations which,
from the time of Scotus onwards, did not continue without
fruit for the doctrine of space. Human thought does not
advance without receiving a determining impulse from
the practical sphere: from the doctrine of God there grew
up the doctrines of thought and of will; from the doctrine of the Trinity, the doctrine of the Kosmos; from the
doctrine of the Lord's Supper, the doctrine of space. If the
question as to the relation of the body of Christ to the elements
already led to inquiries into space, still greater was the impulse
in that direction as soon as the question arose as to how
the eucharistic body is related to the glorified body of Christ in
heaven. The thorny discussions on this subject do not belong
to dogma strictly speaking. As new-creation was excluded, the
question was as to the presence in the Sacrament of the body
that is already in heaven. And again, as the body *as a whole*
appears at the same time in each of the independent particles of
the consecrated bread, a space-less presence had necessarily to
be taught. This Thomas began to do;[1] but it was only the

[1] Q. 76, Art. 3-6.

Nominalists who treated the question as virtuosi (especially
Occam), though they did not come definitely to the doctrine of
the ubiquity of the body of Christ. On the other hand, it was
they, especially John of Paris and Occam, who anticipated the
Lutheran doctrine of the real presence in the bread.[1] An
energetic opponent of the doctrine of transubstantiation was
Wyclif (but even he did not get clearly beyond impanation, and
if he was incensed by the idolatry that was practised with the
host, yet it was by grounds of reason [the absurdity of accidents
without substance] that he was moved to opposition.)[2] By him
not a few (but not Huss)[3] were constrained to renounce the

[1] John of Paris (de modo existendi corpus Christi, etc., printed in London, 1686)
declared that the interpretation of the real presence as conversio did not come within
his faith, but that he was prepared to retract, if it was proved to him that the Church
(the Pope) had defined it. After then rejecting the Berengarian doctrine, as not
leading to communicatio idiomatum of bread and of body, he holds the following
view as free from objection (p. 86): "ut substantia panis maneat sub accidentibus
suis non in proprie supposito, sed tracta ad esse et suppositum Christi, ut sic sit unum
suppositum in duabus naturis." As Münscher (p. 257) has correctly explained, the
idea here is this, that the bread and the body of Christ become united into *one
substance*, in virtue of a common likeness of their qualities, similar to that which it
was believed must be assumed in the conjoining of the two natures in Christ in the
unity of one person. It may be said, therefore, that the orthodox Catholic view of
the Supper is Monophysite; the Berengarian, Nestorian; and that of John of Paris,
Chalcedonian. Even Occam declared that there is nothing in Scripture on the
question that the substance of the bread does not remain (de sacram. alt. 5), and with
regard to the view of the real presence, according to which "corpus Christi in eodem
loco cum substantia panis et vini manet," he says that it is "multum rationalis, nisi
esset determinatio ecclesiæ in contrarium, quia illa salvat et vitat omnes difficultates
quæ sequuntur ex separatione accidentium a subjecto" (for this contradicts the
Nominalist theory of knowledge). But he falls back ultimately on the wish that the
doctrine of the conversio may be revealed to the Church.

[2] Trial. IV. 2: "Inter omnes hæreses, quæ unquam in ecclesia pullularunt,
nunquam considero aliquam plus callide per hypocritas introductam et multiplicius
populum defraudantem, nam spoliat populum, facit ipsum committere idololatriam,
negat fidem scripturæ et per consequens ex infidelitate multipliciter ad iracundiam
provocat veritatem." In c. 4 he then works out the view that panis and body of
Christ are at the same time present. Yet he scouts the idea that any kind of priest—
even a sinful one therefore—can produce Christ. The doctrine of impanation
receives from him a spiritual turn, though this has not the effect of entirely cancelling
it. Against the coarse form of this doctrine he waged war, and came close to
Berengar.

[3] In his treatise de corpore Christi, written during imprisonment, Huss assents to
transubstantiation. But from his other writings we must assume that he was not of

monstrous doctrine, and in the fifteenth century the opposition
to it is met with not infrequently.¹ Yet it remained the reigning
view ; the hostility of declared heretics could only be in its
favour.²

The consequences of the transubstantiation doctrine were
manifold, and of radical importance ; the following may be
mentioned :—

(1) The discontinuance of child communion.³

(2) The augmentation of the dignity of the priests, by whom
daily Christ was magically produced and offered up.

(3) The withholding of the cup. From the time of the
Lombard it was a settled belief that the whole Christ is contained in each species, and that meant, too (according to the
doctrine developed especially by Thomas),⁴ Christ concomitantly (per concomitantiam) in His body and soul as well as in
His divinity. But that being so, it was permissible, safer indeed
(that the wine might not be spilt, and the Sacrament thereby
profaned), and, with a view to increasing the dignity of the priest,
" conveniens," that the layman should receive only in the form

the opinion that a sinful priest can effect it (see above his conception of the Church,
p. 143).

¹ Wesel was an adherent of the impanation doctrine.

² The decree as to the Lord's Supper in the Bull of Eugene IV. "Exultate deo"
runs : "Tertium est eucharistiæ sacramentum, cujus materia est panis triticeus et
vinum de vite, cui ante consecrationem aqua modicissima admisceri debet (there
follows an elaborate justification of this mixing in opposition to the Armenian
practice). Forma hujus sacramenti sunt verba salvatoris, quibus hoc conficit sacramentum. Nam ipsorum verborum virtute substantia panis in corpus Christi et
substantia vini in sanguinem convertuntur, ita tamen, quod totus Christus continetur
sub specie panis et totus sub specie vini. Sub qualibet quoque parte hostiæ consecratæ
et vini consecrati, separatione facta, totus est Christus. Hujus sacramenti effectus,
quem in anima operatur digne sumentis, est adunatio hominis ad Christum. Et quia
per gratiam homo Christo incorporatur et membris ejus unitur, consequens est, quod
per hoc sacramentum in sumentibus digne gratia augeatur, omnemque effectum, quem
materialis cibus et potus quoad vitam agunt corporalem sustentando, augendo,
reparando et delectando, sacramentum hoc quoad vitam operatur spiritualem, in quo,
ut inquit Urbanus Papa, gratam salvatoris nostri recensemus memoriam, a malo
retrahimur, confortamur in bono et ad virtutum et gratiarum proficimus incrementum."

³ This certainly had also other grounds ; but one ground lay in the extravagant
ideas of the content of the Sacrament.

⁴ P. III., Q. 76, Arts. 1 and 2.

of the bread (sub specie panis), while the priest drank the cup in the name of all.[1]   At Constance this became fixed.

(4) The adoration of the elevated host (elevation is represented as having been already adopted in opposition to Berengar), the procession of the host, and the feast of Corpus Christi (1264. 1311) : for the body of Christ is, of course, not present merely at the moment of enjoyment, but, when once produced by consecration, remains until the accidents are dissolved.[2] Against this idolatry there arose in the fourteenth and fifteenth centuries much opposition, which, however, continued to be lacking in vigour.

It was already pointed out above that as regards the idea of the Eucharist as a sacrifice, the Lombard was still influenced by the old ecclesiastical motive of recordatio (remembrance).   But from ecclesiastical antiquity there was certainly taken over also the idea of the *repetition* of the sacrificial death of Christ (Gregory I.), and on the basis of the doctrine of transubstantiation this idea now necessarily became firmly established.   The Roman Canon of the Mass, which did not originally contain the idea of the bloodless repetition of the death of Christ, and still bears traces to-day of not having contained it, has in its most recent portions the new idea.   At the Lateran Council in 1215 the idea is presupposed, and brief note is taken of it,[3] and the Schoolmen, although they do not here give elaborated doctrines, have no other thought than that the priest offers the body of the Lord.[4]   The Eucharist as a sacrifice, as it formed the central

1 Thomas, P. III., Q. 80, Art. 12: The priest *must* enjoy the sacramentum perfectum, since he celebrates it ; the custom of some Churches is to be approved (Thomas still expresses himself cautiously) of withholding the cup from incautious laymen.   Thereafter there was a rapid advance made in practice ; the history of this process, and of the opposition to it, is not relevant here, as a dogma was not involved.

2 Q. 76, Art. 6 : " Corpus Christi manet, quousque species sacramentales manent."

3 Chap. I.

4 For the Eucharist as a repetition of the sacrificial death of Christ, there could be produced from tradition only a bad, and, to some extent, a forged proof.   Thomas treats the question in Q. 83, Art. 1.   According to his custom he raises at the outset three objections, and they are very telling, against the position that Christ is offered in this Sacrament.   He appeals, first, to the passage in Hebrews about the being once offered ; secondly, to the circumstance that in the Mass Christ is not crucified ; thirdly, to the Augustinian position, that in the sacrifice of Christ " idem est sacerdos

part of divine service, was for the people much more important
than the Sacrament. Although, in strict theory, there were
connected with it only slender results (see above), yet misdirected
piety made this observance entirely its own, and saw in it its real
defence in life and in death. The mischief of low masses and
masses for souls was as much the consequence of violent impor-
tunity on the part of the laity for as many masses as possible, as

et hostia," which does not apply in the case of the Mass. But he then explains that
(1) the *one* sacrifice is not touched by the repetition, for in the repetition it remains
always the same ; (2) that the altar is repræsentativum crucis ; and (3) that the priest
"gerit imaginem Christi," and hence it holds good even for the sacrifice of the mass,
that "*quodammodo idem est sacerdos et hostia.*" The positive exposition is extremely
weak, even when we adopt Thomas's standpoint, and shows plainly that at bottom the
repetition of the sacrificial death of Christ could not in any way be theoretically
justified. But it stands here as it does with the doctrine of the Church. The practice justifies itself by its existence ! What Thomas has submitted is as follows:—
"Duplici ratione celebratio hujus sacramenti dicitur immolatio Christi. Primo
quidem quia, sicut dicit Augustinus ad Simplic. solent imagines earum rerum nomin-
ibus appellari, quarum imagines sunt . . . celebratio autem hujus sacramenti,
sicut supra dictum est (Q. 79, Art. 1. 3), imago quædam est representativa passionis
Christi quæ est vera ejus immolatio. Et ideo celebratio hujus sacramenti dicitur
Christi immolatio (here, therefore, there is an expression only of symbol and remembrance). Alio modo quantum ad effectum passionis Christi, quia scil. per hoc sacramentum participes efficimur fructus dominicæ passionis, unde in quadam dominicali
oratione secreta dicitur : Quoties hujus hostiæ commemoratio celebratur, opus
nostræ redemptionis exercetur. Quantum igitur ad primum modum poterat dici
Christus immolari etiam in figuris Veteris Testamenti . . . sed quantum ad
secundum modum proprium est huic sacramento, quod in ejus celebratione Christus
immolatur." One easily sees that there is not the smallest degree of proof given for the
repetition of the sacrificial death of Christ. Even in other passages in which Thomas
speaks of the Eucharist as a sacrifice, I have found nothing more than bare assertions,
and sometimes an entire uncertainty as to the relation of the Eucharistic to the true
sacrifice. How weak the position is, too, with regard to the effect of this sacrifice, is
shown by Q. 79, Art. 5 : " Sacramentum effectum sacrificii in eo qui offert habet vel
in his, pro quibus offertur." It is really instituted as a sacrament; for "non est
institutum ad satisfaciendum, sed ad spiritualiter nutriendum per unionem ad Christum,"
but "per concomitantiam" a certain remission of penalty also is effected. "In
quantum est sacrificium, habet vim satisfactivam, *sed in satisfactione magis attenditur
affectus offerentis quam quantitas oblationis*. Quamvis ergo hæc oblatio ex sui quan-
titate sufficiat ad satisfaciendum pro omni pœna, tamen sit satisfactoria illis, pro
quibus offertur vel etiam offerentibus, secundum quantitatem suæ devotionis et non
pro tota pœna." It must by no means be regarded as an accident that Thomas has
not repeated the audacious propositions of Hugo and Albertus (the Father first offered
the Son for us, we then offer Him for the Father). Thomas has only allowed the
term vera immolatio to stand, because he held that the "Church" taught it. In the
Bull of Eugene IV., moreover (see above), there is no mention of a repetition.

of priestly self-importance; for in the Mass the priest, who is here not a minister but an originator (autor), appears in a very real sense as the mediator between God and men, and, as priest of the body of Christ (sacerdos corporis Christi), his dignity comes most distinctly to view. The Mass was assailed as unbiblical by Wyclif. On the part of others also opposition arose in the fourteenth and fifteenth centuries against the low masses and masses for souls, which, however, was directed, as a rule, only against the abuse (abusus).

4. *Penance.*[1] Although in theory baptism and the Eucharist were placed together and emphasised as the two principal Sacraments, yet, as a fact, the two chief closely connected Sacraments were baptism and penance (" second plank after shipwreck " [secunda tabula post naufragium]—so first Tertullian, after him many teachers). But inasmuch as baptism is only administered once, while the Sacrament of Penance is administered repeatedly, and as almost every baptised person comes to be in a position for requiring this latter Sacrament, for which no other can be substituted, this Sacrament became practically the *most important means of grace.* Now, as the Church had completely saturated this Sacrament with its hierarchical spirit, and at the same time attached to it its enfeebled doctrines of sin, grace, and merit, the most important means of grace thus became subordinated to the meaner ecclesiastical tendencies.[2]

The hierarchical practice, which the laity themselves demanded as a security for grace, preceded the theory by many centuries. In respect of theory there was a special shyness on this point, and an adhering to the evangelical line of thought, that the genuine contrition of the Christian is in itself "sacramental" (see above).[3] In spite of the attempts

[1] Thomas, Summa, P. III. Q. 84-90, Suppl. Q. 1-28. Schwane, p. 661, ff. Steitz das römische Busssacrament, 1854.

[2] Herrmann remarks correctly (Ztschr. f. Theol. u. Kirche I vol., p. 30): "In the Romish institution of penance the question is not about the way in which the Christian attains to renewal of mind, but about providing security for the Christian as he is.

[3] Karl Müller, in the dissertation referred to above (p. 222), sees in this rather something new. Certainly this thought was for a long time not expressed, because there was entirely wanting a "theologian of penance"; but neither had the prevailing sacramental priestly practiceany normal theologian. In my opinion it was a novelty in

of Hugo to define the Sacrament of Penance in a stricter ecclesiastical sense (the priest *effects* forgiveness; but Hugo still
demands, on the other side, the perfect contritio),[1] the Lombard as the disciple of Abelard, and Master Roland, too,[2]
adhered to the old ecclesiastical theory.[3]   Gratian placed

theology, when Hugo of St. Victor (see Müller, p. 218 f.) declared that man can only
be freed from the sentence of eternal damnation by priestly absolution, that this absolution is perfectly real, and that " sententiam Petri non præcedit, sed subsequitur
sententia cœli." In opposition to this, Abelard, and all those who, following in his
steps (see Müller, p. 308 ff.), emphasised the contritio, and regarded God as the
judex, the priest as the declarator, appear to me to have reproduced an old ecclesiastical thought, which is parallel to the Augustinian " Crede et manducasti," and coincides with the very early idea that sins against God are only forgiven by God. That
—as the practice of penance, as regards the satisfactions, had become quite different
from what it was in the ancient Church—the distinctions of Abelard and his disciples
with respect to this were new, is certain.

1 De sacram. II. 1. 14.   Moreover, Hugo certainly then makes other conditions
still as regards the certainty and sovereignty of the priestly forgiveness of sin with respect to the forgiveness of God.   That at bottom the Sacraments, as a whole, effect
only the *possibility* of salvation—the cardinal thought that lies concealed under the
Catholic doctrine of the Sacraments—is acknowledged by Hugo in the following very
noteworthy sentence (c. 8) : " Ubique magis virtus sacramentorum exprimitur, nec
quod per ea quilibet participantes salvandi sint, *sed quod salvari possint, significatur.*"
A pernicious influence on the shaping of the new theory and practice of penance was
exercised by the Pseudo-Augustinian treatise de vera et falsa pænitentia (Migne T. 40,
col. 1113 sq.), which seems to have appeared in the tenth or in the beginning of
the eleventh century (see Karl Müller, Abhandl. f. Weizsäcker, 1892, p. 292. ff.).
Luther had already recognised its spuriousness before 1517.

2 It has been effectively shown by Müller, that the spiritual view of penance goes
back to Abelard. He says, " the great innovation "; I would say " restoration."
On this account, therefore, he is in disfavour among modern Catholic theologians.
Credit is given to him, indeed, for placing together the three things, contritio (com-
punctio) cordis, confessio oris, satisfactio operis, but his demanding a *perfect* contritio
(caritate perfecta), and his not regarding the priestly absolution as absolutely necessary,
are held to be grave defects. As a fact, he declared the contritio, conjoined with the
votum confitendi, to be sufficient ; this is followed by the divine forgiveness of sins,
the infusion of grace and the remission of the eternal penalty " ante oris confessionem
et satisfactionem " (Sentent. IV., 17 A). Hence the consequent reckoning of the
priestly absolution as a forgiveness merely *declarative*, or as a forgiveness merely
ecclesiastical, as distinguished from the divine forgiveness, 18 E : " Ecce quam varia
a doctoribus super his traduntur, et in hac tanta varietate quid tenendum sit ? Hoc
sane dicere ac sentire possumus, *quod solus deus peccata dimittit et retinet*, et tamen
ecclesiæ contulit potestatem ligandi et solvendi. *Sed aliter ipse solvit vel ligat, aliter
ecclesia.* Ipse enim *per se* tantum ita dimittit peccatum, quia et animam mundat ab
interiori macula et a debito æternæ mortis solvit." 18 F : " Non autem hoc sacerdotibus concessit, quibus tamen tribuit potestatem ligandi et solvendi *i.e., ostendendi*

the old and new views side by side, without coming to a decision himself.[1]

The Lateran Council of 1215 laid here also the basis of a fixed doctrine. This doctrine appears in perfected form, not yet in Alexander of Hales, but certainly in Thomas. Thomas shows first (in Q. 84) that penance is a Sacrament. In the 1st Art. he starts the objections that there are no corporeal things (corporales res) present, that penance is not dispensed "by ministers of Christ," but is inwardly wrought by God, and, finally, that we cannot distinguish between sacramentum, res, and res and sacramentum. But he sets aside these objections by pointing to the visible acts of the penitent and of the absolving priest, and by recognising in the former, which are completed by the latter, the materia sacramenti. In the 2nd Art. he shows that these acts are the materia *proxima* (proximate material), while the sins "to be detested and destroyed" (peccata detestenda et destruenda) are the materia *remota* (remote material). In the 3rd Art. there follows the fatal proof that the words, " I absolve thee " (ego te absolvo) are the form (forma) of the Sacrament, for " this Sacrament receives its full effect from those things which are spoken by the priest " (hoc sacramentum perficitur per ea quæ sunt ex parte sacerdotis) ; but these words of the priest are by appointment of Christ (Matt. 16). Since the Sacraments "effect what they represent" (efficiunt quod figurant), it is not enough in the sacramental absolution to say, " May God have mercy on thee " (misereatur tui deus) ; "yet such language is also premised in the sacramental absolution, that the effect of the Sacrament may not be hindered on the side of the penitent " (præmittitur tamen etiam in sacramentali absolutione talis oratio, ne impediatur effectus sacramenti ex parte

---

homines ligatos et solutos . . . Quia etsi aliquis apud deum sit solutus, *non tamen in facie ecclesiæ solutus habetur* nisi per judicium sacerdotis. In solvendis ergo culpis et retinendis ita operatur sarcerdos evangelicus et judicat, sicut olim legalis in illis qui contaminati erant lepra quæ peccatum significat." In addition to the declaration of forgiveness as an ecclesiastical act (for the congregation), the binding and loosing on the part of the priests consists, according to the Lombard, simply in this, that they impose the works connected with penance, or, abate and remit them. Here, therefore, there still exists a complete understanding of the distinction between inward forgiveness and ecclesiastical reconciliation.

[1] De pænit. P. II., c. 33, q. 3, dist. 1.

pænitentis). The general rule that God alone forgives sin is not violated by the priest's absolution, for the priests are "authorised ministers" (this is a makeshift). In Art. 4 the laying on of the hand at confession is dealt with (it is not necessary, as what is contemplated is forgiveness of sins, not the obtaining of positive grace). In Art. 5 the necessity of sacramental penance for anyone guilty of mortal sin is shown : "the salvation of the sinner—that is, that his sin be removed from him—is not possible without the Sacrament of Penance, in which there operates the virtue of Christ's passion, through absolution of the priest together with the work of the penitent, who co-operates with grace for the destruction of sin." To this there is further added : "When once anyone has fallen into sin (ex quo aliquis peccatum incurrit), *love, faith, and mercy do not deliver the man from sin without penitence* (as if they could exist at all without penitence !) ; for love requires that a man grieve for the offence committed against his friend, and that a man be anxious to satisfy his friend ; faith also requires that he seek to be justified from his sins through the virtue of the passion of Christ, which operates in the Sacraments of the Church ; rightly directed mercy (misericordia ordinata) also requires that a man find a remedy in his repenting for the misery into which his sin has plunged him (ut homo subveniat pænitendo suæ miseriæ, quam per peccatum incurrit) " (but the necessity of *sacramental* penance has not thus been proved). In Art. 6 it is shown that penance is "the second plank after shipwreck." In Art. 8 it is explained that the "pænitentia" does not need to last till the end of life, but only "for a time determined by the measure of the sin" (ad determinatum tempus pro mensura peccati) ; yet "penitence is twofold, *viz.*, internal and external. That is internal penitence in which one grieves over sin committed, and such penitence ought to last till the close of life. . . . That is external penitence in which one shows external signs of grief, and verbally (verbo tenus) confesses his sins to the priest who absolves him, and makes satisfaction according to the priest's judgment (juxta ejus arbitrium satisfacit) ; and such penitence does not need to continue till the end of life, but only for a time determined by the measure of the sin." In Art. 9 it is shown that a penitence continuous in act (continua secundum actum) is impossible, but that a penitence continuous in habit (secundum habitum) is obligatory. In Art. 10 it is proved that sacramental penance can be repeated ; love can be lost through free will ; but God's mercy seeks always to restore it. In Q. 85 there now follows a minute inquiry into penance as "virtue," and in Q. 86 the effect of penance is dealt with "as regards the remission of mortal sins" (quoad mortalium peccatorum remissionem). Here it is explained in Art. 4 that with the forgiveness of guilt and the cancelling of eternal penalty all the "penal liability" (reatus pœnæ) is not blotted out ("potest remanere"). If sin, that is to say, is departure from God as the supreme good, and "a perverse turning to mutable good" (conversio inordinata ad commutabile bonum), then there follows from the former eternal, from the latter temporal guilt and penalty. Now, although penance takes the eternal guilt and penalty, as well as the temporal guilt, entirely away, yet the temporal penalty *may* remain ; for "in baptism a man attains to (consequitur) a remission of his whole penal guilt (reatus totius pœnæ), but in penance he attains to the virtue of the passion of Christ *according to the measure of his own acts* (secundum modum propriorum actuum) (this, then, is the ultimate ground of the strange and objectionable view) which are the material of penance (qui sunt materia pænitentiæ) ; *and so it is not always by the first act of penance, by which blame (culpa) is remitted, that liability to the whole penalty is cancelled, but by all the acts of penance when completed* " (et ideo non statim per primum actum pænitentiæ quo remittitur culpa, solvitur reatus totius pœnæ, sed completis omnibus pænitentiæ actibus).[1] In Q. 87, in which the forgiveness of venial sins through penance is treated, it is shown that to one guilty of

---

[1] Hence, also, in the 5th Article the following exposition : " Peccatum mortale ex parte conversionis inordinatæ ad bonum commutabile quandam dispositionem causat in anima vel etiam habitum, *si actus frequenter iteretur.* Sicut autem dictum est, culpa peccati mortalis remittitur, in quantum tollitur per gratiam aversio mentis a deo. Sublato autem eo, quod est ex parte aversionis, nihilominus remanere potest id quod est ex parte conversionis inordinatæ, cum hanc contingat esse sine illa (!), sicut prius dictum est ; et ideo nihil prohibet, quin remissa culpa remaneant dispositiones ex præcedentibus actibus causatæ, quæ dicuntur *peccati reliquiæ* . . . sicut etiam remanet fomes post baptismum."

mortal sin no venial sins are forgiven, so long as the mortal sin
is not blotted out (Art. 4). With Q. 90 begins the inquiry into
the " parts of penance."

As all these thoughts of Thomas were no doubt already common property in his day, so they continued also to be among
the Schoolmen. The necessity of priestly absolution, hence
also confession before the priest, and, still further, the idea of
the effectual action of the priest in the Sacrament, were settled
matters.[1] The inner contrition was certainly regarded as res
and sacramentum (the res sacramenti is the forgiveness of sins,
the Sacrament is the external acts of the penitent and the priests,
see Thomas III., Q. 84, Art. 1); but it is not enough, and just
because it is not yet enough, the perverse opinion could easily
creep in ex contrario, that perfect contrition is, indeed, essential
to non-sacramental penitence, but that in the case of sacramental
penitence the addition of the Sacrament completes the imperfect contrition. This opinion not merely crept in, it became
actually dominant. But in the definition of the particular parts
of penance (partes pænitentiæ) a general perversion of the
worst kind made its appearance, of which the seeds, indeed, are
to be found already in Thomas.[2]

With respect to *contrition*, no other thought was entertained
till the thirteenth century (see above, p. 221 ff.) than that what is
alone of account before God is a perfect penitent disposition, *i.e.*, a
disposition prompted by love.[3]   Contrition as an inner spirit and
habit was magnified as an essential Christian virtue, and as "virtue"

---

[1] Yet there still continued certainly to be a want of logical consistency, in so far as
many Schoolmen maintained that perfect contrition conjoined with the *votum sacramenti* is immediately followed by the forgiveness of sins—a position which even to-
day is still valid in the Catholic Church.

[2] How seriously even the *fundamental* theory was threatened (though that of
Thomas continued to be held valid) is shown by the proposals of Duns Scotus and
Durandus (see Schwane, p. 665) to call the sacrament not so much " penance " as
" confession." Durandus would only have *confession* and *absolution* described as
material and form of the sacrament ; for *contrition* and satisfaction are not parts of the
Sacrament, but the *preparation* for the forgiveness of sin (Durandus, in Sent. IV.,
Dist. 16, Q. 1).   This proposal is quite logical, but it shows very plainly how
penitence had become externalised in having become a sacrament.   It was inevitable
that this process of externalising should continue.

[3] See Stückert, Die Katholische Lehre v. d. Reue, 1896.

received elaborate treatment.[1]   But it was already pointed out
by Alexander of Hales that God has made entrance into the
Church easier for man,[2] and he distinguishes attritio (timor
servilis [servile fear]) from contritio.   This distinction Thomas
adopted.   He explains, however : " attrition, as is declared by
all, is not a virtuous activity" (attritio, ut ab omnibus dicitur,
non est actus virtutis).   Yet he then defines it in the same article
as " in spiritual matters a certain displeasure over sins committed, which, however, is not perfect, but is an *approach* to
perfect contrition" (in spiritualibus quædum displicentia de
peccatis commissis, sed non perfecta, [quæ est] *accessus* ad perfectam contritionem).[3]   Prior to him Bonaventura had already

[1] Thomas, Summa III., Suppl. Q. 1 : contritio in opposition to superbia, which is
initium omnis peccati.   An extremely artificial and empty distinction between contritio as virtus and contritio as sacramental in Q. 5, Art. 1 : "Contritio potest
dupliciter considerari, vel in quantum est pars sacramenti vel in quantum est actus
virtutis, et utroque modo est causa remissionis peccati, sed diversimode : quia in
quantum est pars sacramenti primo operatur ad remissionem peccati instrumentaliter,
sicut et de aliis sacramentis patet ; in quantum autem est actus virtutis sic est quasi
causa materialis remissionis peccati, eo quod dispositio est quasi necessitas ad justificationem, dispositio autem reducitur ad causam materialem."   To the question, why
then the sacrament is necessary if the contritio is enough, Thomas replies (l.c. Art.
1): "Quamvis possit tota pœna per contritionem dimitti, tamen adhuc necessaria est
confessio et satisfactio, tum quia homo non potest esse certus de sua contritione,
quod fuerit ad totum tollendum sufficiens, tum etiam quia confessio et satisfactio sunt
in præcepto."

[2] Summa IV., Q. 59, M. 2, A. 4 : "*expeditius* et melius liberatur peccator per
sacramentum pænitentiæ quam per *pænitentiæ virtutem.*"

[3] P. III., Suppl. Q. 1, Art. 2.   Without using the word "attritio," he gives already
the thing in P. III., Q. 85, Art. 5, where an exceedingly important statement of the
stages of penance is given, which clearly shows the divergence of the Catholic from
the evangelical view : "De pænitentia loqui possumus dupliciter.   Uno modo
quantum ad habitum.   Et sic immediate a deo infunditur sine nobis principaliter
operantibus . . . alio modo possumus loqui de pænitentia quantum ad actus quibus
deo operanti in pænitentia cooperamur.   Quorum actuum primum principium est dei
operatio convertentis cor, secundus actus est motus fidei, tertius est motus timoris
servilis, quo quis timore suppliciorum a peccatis retrahitur" (take also : "peccatum
prius incipit homini displicere [maxime peccatori] propter supplicia, quæ respicit
timor servilis, quam propter dei offensam vel peccati turpitudinem, quod pertinet ad
caritatem . . . ipse etiam motus timoris procedit ex actu dei convertentis cor").
"Quartus actus est motus spei, quo quis sub spe veniæ consequendæ assumit propositum emendandi.   Quintus actus est motus caritatis, quo alicui peccatum displicet
secundum se ipsum et non jam propter supplicia" (that is the contritio).   "Sextus
est motus timoris filialis, quo propter reverentiam dei aliquis emendam deo voluntarius
offert."

said :[1] " For the Sacrament of Penance it is not necessary that
he who comes to it has love, or an inclination to love that is
sufficient when judged by the standard of truth, provided it be
sufficient when judged by the standard of probability ; but this
disposition is attritio, which, by reason of superadded confession
and absolution of the priest, frequently so receives form from
grace (formatur per gratiam), that it becomes contritio, or that
contritio follows upon it." This thought Thomas did *not* adopt ;
he tacitly rejected it rather, and expressed himself altogether
with strictness and earnestness regarding contritio and its necessity in Q. 1-5. Yet the considerations suggested by Alexander of
Hales[2] and Bonaventura continued to have their influence. It
was especially Scotus who secured currency for the view, that
attrition, in itself inadequate, is sufficient for the reception of
the Sacrament of Penance, since the Sacrament itself makes
the sorrow perfect by " infusion of grace."[3] On this point the
decrees of Trent adopted—though, indeed, only conditionally—
the side of the Scotists.[4]

---

[1] In Sentent. IV., Dist. 17, p. 2, a. 1, q. 4.

[2] Summa IV., Q. 60, A. 3 : "si autem pænitens præparatus quantum in se est
accedat ad confessionem attritus, non contritus . . . confessio cum subjectione
arbitrio sacerdotis et satisfactio pænitentiæ injunctæ a sacerdote est signum et causa
deletionis culpæ et pœnæ, quia sic subjiciendo se et satisfaciendo gratiam acquirit."

[3] See Reportt IV., Dist. 14, Q. 4, schol. 2 (quoted in Schwane, p. 666) : " Dico,
quod bonus motus præcedens sacramentum pænitentiæ tantum est attritio et dispositio de congruo ad deletionem culpæ et infusionem gratiæ, quæ remissio culpæ et
collatio gratiæ sunt in virtute sacramenti pænitentiæ et non in virtute attritionis tantum,
nisi dispositive. Sed hæc attritio post collationem gratiæ, quæ confertur in susceptione sacramenti, fit contritio formata."

[4] Sess. XIV. de pænit., c. 4 : "attritio peccatorum ad dei gratiam in sacramento
pænitentiæ impetrandam disponit." In recent times, following Lämmer (Vortrident.
Theologie), Bratke (Luther's 95 Thesen und ihre dogmenhistor. Voraussetzung,
1884) and Dieckhoff (Der Ablasstreit, dogmengesch. dargestellt, 1886) have very
fully treated the scholastic doctrine of penance in connection with the doctrine of
indulgences, after a controversy on the doctrine of indulgences had broken out,
occasioned by the great work of Janssen (see Kolde, Die deutsche Augustiner-Congregation u. Johann v. Staupitz, 1879, the same author in the ThLZ. 1882, No. 23,
and also dissertations by Kawerau, Köstlin, Schweitzer and Janssen " An meine
Kritiker "). Bratke already placed the doctrine of indulgences in a clearer light in
opposition to Köstlin. But Dieckhof has especially the credit of having traced back
the theory to the lax view of penance, and of having shown that here the seat of the
evil must be sought for. There can be no doubt that the doctrine of attritio more
and more threatened to become the Church's chief *means of producing ease of mind,*

The theologian on *confession* (before the priest) is Thomas, the Lombard having previously, as Catholic scholars express it, thrown obscurity over the connection between confession and

and that it actually became such subsequently in wide circles (especially through the influence of the Jesuit Father Confessors ; but also, prior to them, through the influence of the preachers of indulgences). Opposition certainly was not wanting, and it grew stronger in many circles in the fifteenth century (Augustinian-Thomist reaction, see Bratke, p. 59 ff. and elsewhere) ; but when one reads, *e.g.*, the discussions of John of Paltz, the senior contemporary and Augustinian brother of Luther (Kolde l.c.), one is shocked to see what a withering up of religion and of the simplest morality resulted from the "attritio" ("gallows-repentance"). The priest is here extravagantly dignified (in the book "Cœlifodina") ; for he is the most necessary person, because only very few men are really contrite ; on the other hand, everyone can bring himself in the end to an imperfect contrition ; and now he, the priest, through the sacrament of penance, transforms this imperfect into a perfect sorrow ("paucissimi sunt vere contriti, ergo paucissimi salvarentur sine sacerdotibus ; possunt autem omnes aliquo modo fieri attriti, et tales possunt sacerdotes juvare et eorum ministerio facere contritos et per consequens possunt eos salvare "). Or—everything depends on an experienced priest ; there is nothing lacking to anyone who finds such ("non potest esse peccator adeo desperatus, quia posset consequi indulgentias, si habuerit intelligentem et fidelem informatorem et voluerit facere, quod potest, et habeat *attritionem aliqualem*, quæ tunc in sacramentis sibi succurritur et imperfectum ejus tollitur, et informis attritio, *i.e.*, caritate carens formatur per gratiam sacramentalem ") ; see Kolde, pp. 187, 191 ; Dieckhoff, p. 14 ; Bratke, pp. 53 ff., 111 ff., 128 ff. The last-mentioned gives abundant material, from which it appears that Paltz by no means stood alone. Everywhere the assertion is made that it is *easier*, under the new covenant, to attain salvation on account of the wonderful efficacy of the cross of Christ. At the same time it did not fail to be clearly seen that attritio is something else than contritio, not merely quantitatively, but also *qualitatively*. Gabriel Biel, who certainly thinks more earnestly about contrition than Paltz, knows very well that under some circumstances attritio springs from *immoral* motives, hence is by no means a pars contritionis, and is besides, as a rule, a passing mood (Bratke, p. 46 f.). Others knew that also, and nevertheless built up on this attritio their theories that were to lead to heaven. Indeed some actually gave instructions for deluding God in heaven and His holy law ; entrance into heaven was to be secured by merely guarding against mortal sin for one day in the year or for one hour, and showing for this space of time aliquam attritionem (see Petrus de Palude in Bratke, p. 84 ff., especially p. 87, note 1). Thus the doctrine of attritio, *which dominates the whole Christian life*, is really the radical source of mischief in the Catholic system of doctrine ; for in it both things are at work, the magical, and therefore godless, conception of the efficacy of the Sacrament, and the idea, which is no longer Pelagian, but is pressed to the point of denial of all that is moral, of a " merit " recognised in any kind of motus that is only a turning away from sin. In the fourth extra number of the Röm. Quartalschr. (1896), p. 122 ff., Finke has attempted to combat the exposition given here. *One* proposition of the first edition I have now shaped more precisely. The sentence about the " withering up of religion and the simplest morality " I could not change. I would not have written it, if it said in a general way (so Finke seems to have misunderstood me),

the Sacrament, and over the necessity of the former, an obscurity not yet entirely removed even by Halesius.[1] In Q. 6
that at the end of the fifteenth century religion and the simplest morality had become
a desolate waste.   That was not my thought ; I only said that where attritionism
reigns, as in the case of John of Paltz and others, withering up is a necessary result.
To deal now with the subject itself, Finke asserts (1) that an attritio which has only
the timor servilis, in which the fixed purpose of thorough repentance is not present,
was *never* held to be adequate sorrow.   If the "was held" is not to have the sense
of "was established as an authoritative dogma," or if the notion "adequate sorrow"
is not equivocal (attritio is of course in itself never "adequate sorrow," but it becomes such through the sacrament), then the position is false ; cf. Döllinger and
Reusch, Moralstreitigkeiten (1889), I., p. 69 ff., and many other passages.   Liguori
himself was an attritionist (p. 458 f.) ; what he requires over and above the timor
servilis, does not, from the way in which he has presented it, possess much weight.
Finke asserts (2) : " In the practice of penance, confession, and preaching, that is, in
dealing with the Christian people, it was *always taught* from the seventh century to
the sixteenth, *that contritio is requisite for confession ;* the conception of contritio,
which an Isidore presented in the seventh century and a Rabanus in the ninth, coincides with that which we meet with in the sermons at the close of the Middle Ages."
This thesis the author seeks to prove by furnishing (we are thankful to him for it) on
pages 128-135 of his dissertation, extracts from sermons at the end of the mediæval
period, which are intended to show that sorrow springing from fear was not regarded
as adequate.   Certainly, we reply, how often must the words have been spoken from
the pulpit at that time : " contritio non potest esse sine caritate " !   But how little is
proved by that !   We must question the preachers of indulgences, and observe the
real spirit that was awakened by the confessional and by indulgences.   What the
Reformers relate to us in this regard, what we can ourselves discern from the decrees
of Trent as to the practice disapproved by the Fathers of the Council, what breaks out
again afterwards as attritionism in spite of the Tridentinum, is certainly more important than what was said in sermons and *general* directions as to repentance, which
of course urged to the utmost endeavour.   In sermons it was also said that all good
works are gifts from God ; but did Luther simply misunderstand the temper of his
Church, when, in looking back to his works as a monk, he speaks of his " own
works" with a view to sanctification, which he had wished to practise in the spirit of the
Church ?   Besides the assertion which Finke makes without qualifications, which he
has printed in italics, and which relates to a thousand years, is itself very considerably
restricted when he says (p. 123) : " The question is as to whether attritio was the
form of sorrow in the circles of our people, and not as to the doctrinal opinions of a
Duns Scotus, etc., which remained unknown to the people."   As developed doctrines
of course they remained unknown to the people; but were these doctrines really
without consequences in practice ?   And why should one make so light of the doctrines
of the theologians ?   In view of the worthlessness of attritio as timor servilis asserted
by Finke, observe what Bellarmin (de pœnit. II. c. 17) says as to its value.   Perrone
(de pœnit. c. 2, § 91 f.) has certainly been somewhat more cautious, inasmuch as he
introduces the distinction between the timor simpliciter servilis and the worthless
timor serviliter servilis.

    [1] As the priest, according to Halesius, could still only remit temporal penalties and
could not forgive sins, even on that account the necessity of confession could not be

(P. III. Suppl.) Thomas has dealt at length with the necessity of confession. In Art. 1 its absolute necessity is proved from the nature of the case;[1] in Art. 2 it is shown that confession is divinely enjoined (juris divini); in 3 it is pointed out that though, according to divine law, only those guilty of mortal sin are obliged to confess, yet according to *positive* law all Christians must confess at least once a year;[2] in Art. 4 it is laid down that one may not confess sins of which he does not know himself to be guilty; in 5 it is declared that it is not necessary to salvation (de necessitate salutis) to confess sins *at once*, but that delay is not without danger, and that a regard to Church regulations (times of confession) is advisable; finally in 6 it is proved that a dispensation exempting from confession (for ever) can on no account whatever be given; even the Pope can as little be exempted from confession as he can declare that a man can be saved without baptism.[3]

Q. 7 treats of the "quidditas confessionis," *i.e.*, of its nature, as "disclosure of the latent disease in the hope of pardon" (aperitio latentis morbi spe veniæ); and also as an "exercise of virtue" (actus virtutis)[4] and as an "exercise of the virtue of penitence" (actus virtutis pænitentiæ). Q. 8 is specially important, for it develops the doctrine as to the administrator ("minister") of confession. Here it is at once said in Art. 1: "The grace that is conferred in the Sacraments descends from the head to the members, and so he only is the minister of the Sacraments in which grace is given, who has a ministry in con-

confidently proved yet. Even Bonaventura did not trust himself to represent the order to confess as originating in the institution and command of Christ.

[1] "Sicut aliquis per hoc quod baptismum petit se ministris ecclesiæ subicit, ad quos pertinet dispensatio sacramenti, ita etiam per hoc quod confitetur peccatum suum se ministro ecclesiæ subicit, ut per sacramentum pænitentiæ ab eo dispensatum remissionem consequatur, qui congruum remedium adhibere non potest, nisi peccatum cognoscat, quod fit per confessionem peccantis. Et ideo confessio est de necessitate salutis ejus, qui in peccatum actuale mortale cecidit."

[2] The "positive" law is the decree of the Council of 1215; further, every one of course must know himself to be a sinner; still further, one must confess in order to come with greater reverence to the Eucharist; finally, in order that the shepherd may be able to superintend his flock and protect it from the wolf.

[3] "Sicut non potest dispensari in jure naturali, ita nec in jure positivo divino."

[4] Art. 2: "ad virtutem pertinet, ut aliquis ore confiteatur, quod corde tenet."

nection with the true body of Christ (qui habet ministerium
super corpus Christi verum), which belongs only to the priest
who is able to consecrate the Eucharist, and therefore as in the
Sacrament of Penance grace is conferred, the priest only is
minister of this Sacrament, and therefore to him only must be
made the sacramental confession (sacramentalis confessio) which
ought to be made to the minister of the Church." But in Art. 2
it is conceded, that " in case of necessity a layman supplies the
place of the priest, so that it is possible to make confession to
him " (in necessitate etiam laicus vicem sacerdotis supplet, ut
ei confessio fieri possit).[1] The necessity of confessing venial
sins to the priest is denied (Art. 3), and this view continued to
be held, as even Duns assented to it. Confession must take
place before the Parochus (priest of the parish); only by authority of one of higher rank (" ex superioris privilegio ") and in
case of death (" in casu mortis ") (Art. 4-6) may this be departed
from. In Q. 9, on the " quality of confession," Art. 2, which
treats of the " integrity of the confession,"[2] and Art. 3, which
forbids confession " through another or in writing," are specially
important.[3] Q. 10 deals with the effect of confession, and 11
with the reticence of the minister, which is very strongly accentuated (" God covers the sin of him who surrenders himself in
penitence ; hence this also should be indicated in the Sacrament
of Penance (hoc oportet in sacramento pænitentiæ significari),
and thus it is of *the essence of the Sacrament* (de necessitate sacramenti), that one conceal confession, and he sins as a violator of

---

[1] Yet such confession is not sacramental in the strict sense.

[2] As one must disclose to the physician the whole disease, and this is the presupposition of being healed, so is it also with confession. " Ideo *de necessitate* confessionis est, quod homo *omnia peccata* confiteatur *quæ in memoria habet,* quod si non
faciat, non est confessio, sed confessionis simulatio." Mortal sins that have been forgotten must be confessed in the confession that follows. A voluminous work on the
history of auricular confession has been written by Lea, 2 vols. (English), Philadelphia, 1896. I have not yet been able to look into it.

[3] To describe the qualities of confession the scholastic stanza was framed (see
Art. 4) :

> " Sit simplex, humilis confessio, pura, fidelis,
> Atque frequens, nudo, discreta, libens, verecunda,
> Integra, secreta, lacrimabilis, accelerata,
> Fortis et accusans et sit parere parata."

the Sacraments who reveals confession " (et tanquam violator sacramenti peccat, qui confessionem revelat).

These definitions of Thomas underwent, indeed, many modifications in the Scotist School, but *in substance* they became permanent.

Confession is made before the priest ; it is followed by *absolution*. We have already pointed out how much time elapsed before the new ideas became currently accepted, (1) that confession must be made to the priest,[1] (2) that the priest confers absolution as proceeding from himself (in the exercise of divine authority)[2] and as effectual (Matth. 16, John 20). The power of absolution, which is given to every priest, appears complicated because it is connected with the power of jurisdiction (in its application), which, as is well known, was graded. Here also Thomas was the first to furnish the theory ; for even for Halesius and Bonaventura there are still points of uncertainty, which were due to the continued influence of the older view. In the Summa P. III., Suppl. Q. 17-24, Thomas has developed the doctrine of the power of the keys (potestas clavium), and has shown that the priest's absolution is the " causa instrumentalis " (in a physical sense) of the forgiveness of sin. But in the Scotist School, which in general relaxed the connection between the Sacrament and the res sacramenti, only a moral communication, through absolution, of forgiveness of sin was assumed, the priest being held as moving God by means of his absolution to fulfil his " covenant." The priests' power of jurisdiction has also been dealt with by Thomas, and from his time it was always treated in connection with the theory of absolution, although it leads in a quite different direction, is really calculated indeed to weaken confidence in the power of every priest to absolve. It was asserted, that is to say, by the majority, though not by all, that the power of jurisdiction is also ex jure divino (by divine authority), and that the restrictions therefore on the permissible conferring of absolution were not merely ecclesiastical regulations, but had divine right. But in the Middle Ages there had by this time developed itself an immense system of special per-

[1] On the exception, see above.
[2] Not ex potestate auctoritatis or excellentiæ, but ministerii.

missions, reservations, etc., which had their basis in arbitrary
decisions of the Popes. The position, though vigorously contested, continued to be held as valid, that ecclesiastical superiors
" in conveying judicial power *in foro interno* can by reservation
make any kind of restrictions in respect of duration, place, and
object." Was it not inevitable that by such procedure, in dealing with which it was impossible for the layman to find his way,
confusion and uncertainty should arise about the Sacrament ? [1]

[1] The most important propositions of Thomas regarding absolution are the following : Suppl. Q. 17, Art. 1 : "In corporalibus clavis dicitur instrumentum, quo
ostium aperitur, regni autem ostium nobis per peccatum clauditur et quantum ad
maculam et quantum ad reatum poenæ, et ideo potestas qua tale obstaculum remove-
tur, dicitur *clavis*. Hæc autem potestas est in divina trinitate per auctoritatem, et
ideo dicitur a quibusdam, quod habeat clavem auctoritatis, sed *in Christo homine* fuit
hæc potestas ad removendum prædictum obstaculum per meritum passionis quæ etiam
dicitur januam aperire. Et ideo dicitur secundum quosdam habere clavem excellentiæ.
Et quia ex latere Christi dormientis in cruce sacramenta fluxerunt, ex quibus ecclesia
fabricatur, ideo in sacramentis ecclesiæ efficacia passionis manet, *et propter hoc etiam
ministris ecclesiæ, qui sunt dispensatores sacramentorum, potestas aliqua ad prædictum
obstaculum removendum est collata*, non propria, sed virtute divina et passionis Christi,
et hæc potestas metaphorice clavis ecclesiæ dicitur, quæ est *clavis ministerii*."
Especially important is Q. 18, Art. 1 : "Sacramenta continent ex sanctificatione invisibilem gratiam. Sed hujusmodi sanctificatio quandoque ad necessitatem sacramenti
requiritur tam in materia quam in ministro, sicut patet in confirmatione. Quandoque
autem de necessitate sacramenti non requiritur nisi sanctificatio materiæ, sicut in baptismo, quia non habet ministrum determinatum quantum ad sui necessitatem et tunc
tota vis sacramentalis consistit in materia. Quandoque vero de necessitate sacramenti
requiritur consecratio vel sanctificatio ministri sine aliqua sanctificatione materiæ, et
tunc *tota vis sacramentalis consistit in ministro, sicut est in pænitentia* . . . Per
pænitentiæ sacramentum nunquam datur gratia, nisi præparatio adsit vel prius fuerit.
Unde virtus clavium operatur ad culpæ remissionem, vel in voto existens, vel in actu
se exercens . . . sed non agit sicut principale agens, sed sicut instrumentum, non
quidem pertingens ad ipsam gratiæ susceptionem causandam etiam instrumentaliter,
sed disponens ad gratiam, per quam fit remissio culpæ. Unde solus deus remittit per
se culpam et in virtute ejus agit . . . sacerdos *ut instrumentum animatum*
. . . ut minister. Et sic patet, quod potestas clavium ordinatur aliquo modo ad
remissionem culpæ non sicut causans, sed sicut disponens ad eam ; unde si ante absolutionem aliquis non fuisset perfecte dispositus ad gratiam suscipiendam, *in ipsa confessione et absolutione sacramentali gratiam consequeretur*, si obicem non poneret."
In what follows it is now proved that the priestly clavis cannot possibly relate only to
the remission of penalty ("ut quidam dicunt"). In Art. 2 it is then shown that "ex
vi clavium non tota poena remittitur, sed aliqiud de poena temporali, cujus reatus post
absolutionem a poena æterna remanere potuit, nec solum de poena illa, quam pænitens
habet in confitendo, quia sic confessio et sacramentalis absolutio non esset nisi in
onus, quod non competit sacramentis novæ legis, sed etiam de illa poena, quæ in purgatorio debetur, aliquid remittitur." With regard to the efficacy of the absolution a

Absolution is preceded by the appointment of *satisfactio*, if such has not already been made. Here the priest acts as a skilled physician (medicus peritus) and impartial judge (judex aequus). The practice of satisfactions (Church-penances) is very old (see vol. v., p. 268 f., 324 ff.), the giving it a mechanical form and the over-estimation of it—by putting it alongside contritio as a part of penance—are in theory comparatively new. The idea is now this, that satisfactio, as a portion of the Sacrament of Penance, is the necessary manifestation of sorrow through works that are fitted to furnish a certain satisfaction to the injured God (and thereby become the occasion also for limiting the temporal penalties). In baptism there is forgiveness of the

distinction also of this kind was drawn : God cancels the reatus culpæ, Christ the reatus pœnæ æternæ ; both are effectually wrought by the minister sacramenti in the exercise of plenary divine power, and he has at the same time the right belonging to him to give abatement in his absolving of the reatus pœnæ temporalis. In Q. 19, Art. 3, Thomas shows that the clavis ordinis is given only to the priest, while the clavis jurisdictionis—quæ non clavis cœli est, sed quædam dispositio ad eam !—may be granted also to others. In Q. 19, Art. 5, it is explained that even the bad priest retains the keys ; on the other hand, it is said in Art. 6 of the heretical and schismatic priests that in them "manet clavium potestas quantum ad essentiam, sed usus impeditur ex defectu materiæ. Cum enim usus clavium in utente prælationem requirat respectu ejus in quem utitur, propria materia in quam exercetur usus clavium est homo subditus. Et quia per ordinationem ecclesiæ unus subditur alteri, ideo etiam per ecclesiæ prælatos potest subtrahi alicui ille, qui erat ei subjectus. Unde cum ecclesia hæreticos et schismaticos et alios hujusmodi privet subtrahendo subditos vel simpliciter vel quantum ad aliquid, quantum ad hoc quod privati sunt, non possunt usum clavium habere." In Q. 20, Art. 1, it is explained that only to the Pope, as he possesses the indistincta potestas super omnes, does there fall the application of the power of the keys with respect to all, while it is said of the others that "non in quolibet uti (potestatem clavium) possunt, sed in eos tantum, qui eis in sortem venerunt, nisi in necessitatis articulo." But the priest cannot always absolve even his subditus ; for aliqua peccata—if the power is not conferred upon him—fall to be dealt with by his superior (Art. 2). A priest can absolve even a bishop ; for "potestas clavium, quantum est de se, se extendit ad omnes" (Art. 3). Questions 21-24 treat of excommunication, with which the power of jurisdiction has specially to do (Q. 21, Art. 4 : "Even an unjust excommunication habet effectum suum ; in the case of a mortal sin it must be respected ; sed si quis pro falso crimine in judicio probato excommunicatus est, tunc, si humiliter sustinet, humilitatis meritum recompensat excommunicationis damnum." Q. 22, Art. 1 : "Of the priests only bishops and majores prælati can excommunicate, qui habent jurisdictionem in foro judiciali, ad quod spectat causa, quæ obligat hominem in comparatione ad alios homines" : but even those who are not priests can excommunicate [because it is not a question of gratia], if they have the jurisdictio in foro contentioso).

sin, along with the penalty, without any satisfaction ; but God
requires from the baptised person a certain satisfaction—although
both before and now the merit of Christ is the decisive thing—
partly because the man can render a certain satisfaction, partly
because it serves to make him better, and is fitted to protect him
against further sins.   But this satisfaction is only of real value
when it is rendered in a state of grace (caritas).   Hence the
man guilty of mortal sin must first be absolved, that he may
then furnish the satisfaction which is required of him, and which
he has promised to render prior to absolution.   But there is a
certain value also in works that are not performed in a state of
grace (caritas) ; even they are not without their weight as satisfactions, and can abridge the temporal penalties of sin.   The
satisfying works are especially prayer, fasting, and alms ; for
they deliver man from his natural disposition.   But the Schoolmen also justified the practice that originated in the wilder times
of the Germanic Church, according to which satisfaction can,
under certain circumstances, be rendered by others, because
Christians are united to one another as members of one body.
And this leads us to the subject of indulgences.[1]

[1] Thomas treats satisfactio in Suppl. Q. 12-15.   In Q. 12, Arts. 1 and 2, satisfactio is shown to be actus virtutis et justitiæ ; in Art. 3 the old definition is justified,
that satisfacere is both " honorem debitum deo impendere " and " præservare culpam
futuram."   In Q. 13 it is shown that man is not in a position to satisfy God quoad
æqualitatem quantitatis, but certainly quoad æqualitatem proportionis ("ex hoc
quod per liberum arbitrium agit, deo satisfacere potest, quia quamvis dei sit prout a
deo sibi concessum, tamen libere ei traditum est, ut ejus dominus sit ") ; in Art. 2
there follows the proof that one can render satisfactio for another ; yet the thesis has
its guarding clauses (" Pœna satisfactoria est ad duo ordinata, scil. ad solutionem
debiti et ad medicinam pro peccato vitando."   In the latter regard one can help
another only per accidens, in so far as by good works he can procure for the other an
augmentum gratiæ : "sed hoc est per modum meriti magis quam per modum satisfactionis.   Sed quantum ad solutionem debiti, unus potest pro alio satisfacere,
dummodo sit in caritate, ut opera ejus satisfactoria esse possint ").   In Q. 14 the
quality of the satisfactio is treated ; here the questions as to the necessity for the
man's being in a state of caritas are discussed and answered with still greater strictness ("Quidem dixerunt"—Art. 2—"quod postquam omnia peccata per præcedentem
contritionem remissa sunt, si aliquis ante satisfactionem peractam in peccatum
decidat et in peccato existens satisfaciat, satisfactio talis ei valet, ita quod si in peccato
illo moreretur, in inferno de illis peccatis non puniretur.   Sed hoc non potest esse,
quia in satisfactione oportet quod amicitia restituta etiam justitiæ æqualitas restituatur
cujus contrarium amicitiam tollit.   Æqualitas autem in satisfactione ad deum non est

Indulgences. The doctrine of indulgence stands inwardly in closest relation to the doctrine of attritio ; outwardly it appears as a consequence of the doctrine of satisfactio.[1] Theoretically it has nothing to do with the reatus culpæ (moral culpability) and the reatus pœnæ æternæ (liability to eternal death); in practice there not only arose, in the Middle Ages, serious irregularities, which the Catholics (see the Council of

secundum æquivalentiam, sed magis secundum acceptationem ipsius. Et ideo oportet, etiamsi jam offensa sit dimissa per præcedentem contritionem, quod opera satisfactoria sint deo accepta, quod dat eis caritas, *et ideo sine caritate opera facta non sunt satisfactoria,*" but in Art. 5 it is conceded that bona opera extra caritatem facta diminuunt pœnam inferni, *i.e.*, as Augustine says, moderate damnation and limit the temporal penalties. Q. 15 treats of the means of satisfactio ("satisfactio sive referatur ad præteritam offensam sive ad futuram culpam per *pœnalia* opera fieri asseritur"). Here the following shocking justification of the three penal means of satisfaction is given (Art. 3) : " satisfactio debet esse talis, per quam aliquid nobis subtrahamus ad honorem dei, nos autem non habemus nisi tria bona, scil. bona *animæ,* bona *corporis* et bona *fortunæ,* scil. exteriora. Ex bonis quidem fortunæ subtrahimus nobis aliquid per eleemosynam, sed ex bonis corporis per jejunium. Ex bonis autem animæ non oportet quod aliquid subtrahamus nobis quantum ad essentiam vel quantum ad diminutionem ipsorum, quia per ea efficimur deo accepti, sed per hoc quod ea submittimus deo totaliter, et hoc fit per orationem. . . . *Secundum quosdam duplex est oratio ; quædam quæ est contemplativorum, quorum conversatio in cælis est, et talis quia totaliter est delectabilis non est satisfactoria. Alia est, quæ pro peccatis gemitus fundit et talis habet pœnam et est satisfactionis pars.* Vel dicendum et melius, *quod quælibet oratio habet rationem satisfactionis, quia quamvis habet suavitatem spiritus, habet tamen afflictionem carnis.*" The importance in respect of theory of satisfaction as expiation of temporal penalties of sins that are not remitted does not, for the rest, come specially into view for Thomas, in addition to the other ends which satisfactions contemplate. Indeed, it is even granted in abstracto that contritio can be so perfect that *all* penalty is condoned by God. Yet as a fact satisfactions were regarded almost exclusively from the point of view of expiation of the penalties of sin (and these were chiefly the future penalties of purgatory). It was here that indulgences came in, and it was here that there entered the very pardonable misunderstanding of the laity that satisfactions in themselves deliver from *all* penalties for sin—and it was only with this deliverance that the majority took to do.

[1] For the literature see above (p. 250, note 4). Add also Schneider, Die Ablässe, 7 ed., 1881. Thomas, Suppl., Qs. 25-27. Götz, Studien z. Gesch. d. Buss-sacraments in the Ztschr. f. K.-Gesch., Vol. 15, p. 321 ff., Vol. 16, p. 541 ff. These investigations, which start from an examination of a series of forged Bulls on indulgences, illustrate the history of the development of indulgences, give important disclosures as to the Bulls connected with the Crusades, and treat also the papal cases of reservation in the penance discipline (cf. Hausmann, Gesch. der päpstl. Reservatfälle, 1868). The importance which belonged in the course of the development of indulgences to the peregrinations to the sacred places, or to Rome (imposed as penance works), comes prominently to view in these studies.

Trent) admit, but these irregularities still continue, and nothing is done to check the over-estimation of indulgences.[1]

Scholasticism found indulgences already in existence, a great increase of them having taken place especially in the period of the Crusades.   It simply framed its theory according to the practice.   If the doctrine of satisfaction was already an extremely arbitrary one, which, in spite of all saving clauses, necessarily endangered the importance of repentance, the doctrine of indulgence became arbitrariness intensified, and exercised an extremely ruinous influence on religion and morality.   The practice and theory of indulgences can, no doubt, be idealised, nay, it is possible indeed to justify, in a certain way, the idealised practice.[2]   Were that not possible it would be incredible that so many earnest Christians have defended indulgences.   But the scholastic theology by no means idealised them.

The practice of indulgences has its root in the *commutations*. The exchange of more arduous for easier penitential acts was called indulgence.[3]   The penance performances were here taken into consideration in their significance for the expiation of the temporal penalties of sin.   The heaviest temporal penalties for sin were those of purgatory : for the earthly penalties for sin were, on the one hand, as experience taught, unavoidable, and on the other hand, even though one thought of year-long

---

[1] That even in *theory* there were defects in the Middle Ages is acknowledged by Catholic witnesses themselves (see Schneider, p. 10, note 2) : " Certain letters of indulgence are found which speak at the same time of forgiveness of guilt and of penalty (a culpa et a pœna) ; but, according to the opinion of Benedict XIV., these indulgences are spurious, and must be ascribed to those collectors of alms who proclaimed indulgences and at the same time collected alms previous to the Synod of Trent."   Of course on the Catholic side an appeal is readily made to the circumstance that " peccatum " was also used for " penalty for sin," " atonement for sin." This meaning can really be proved ; but whether it suits all cases in which indulgences and sin are brought into conjunction is more than questionable.

[2] To defend at the same time both the satisfactions and the indulgences is certainly difficult.   If the former are due to the glad eagerness of the heart, delivered from guilt, to exercise the love bestowed on it, the thought of the indulgence will not arise.   On the other hand, if indulgences are the remission of the temporal penalties of sin, they must not be brought into relation with the idealised satisfactions.

[3] Such exchanges were also necessarily introduced, because the old penitential demands were in part exorbitantly high.

penances, they were of no weight as compared with the long and painful penalties in purgatory. It was a refined practice of the Church, which had gradually developed itself, to comfort men in an easy way about hell by means of grace (Sacrament of Penance), and, on the other hand, to terrify them by means of purgatory. Was this purgatory, then, not also a hell? But how skilfully was the whole idea derived from studying the moral feelings of the homines attriti (men practising attrition)![1] They did not really believe in hell, because the gravity of sin had not been disclosed to them, and because, accordingly, they were not to be constrained to a life in God. *Hence the Church shut up hell by means of the Sacrament of Penance.* But that at some period in the future it would, for a long time, go very badly with them, and that one day they must expiate all their sins,—that they believed. Therefore the Church opened purgatory.[2] That this purgatory could be made less severe or briefer, these homines attriti were also very ready to believe; for they lived, all of them, in the thought that good performances simply compensate for delinquencies, and even the "gallows contrition" is not so enduring as to constrain men to practise serious repentance—even in the sense of steady self-denial and heroic action. *Hence the Church discloses indulgences.* In them she shows to the man of lower type her real power; for the magic of the Sacrament of Penance has certainly not yet given him complete rest. He has a remnant of the moral feeling that something must be done on his part in order that forgiveness may become credible and sure. "Faith" and "con-

---

[1] The indulgences were most truly the refuge of the Christians of lower type, although the most pious also made use of them. It is related of Tetzel that when, in the small town of Belitz, near Berlin, no one would buy indulgences from him, he said indignantly, that those in the town must either be "right *pious people* or desperate villains." This is told by Creusing in his "Märkische Fürstenchronik," edited by Holtze, p. 159, the informant being the Miller of Belitz, Meister Jacob (see Heidemann, Die Reform. in der Mark Brandenburg, p. 77).

[2] After these words were long written down, I came across Rousseau's description in his Confessions of the demonic Madame de Warens. It is here said (German edition by Denhard, I., p. 291) : ". . . although she did not believe in a hell, she strangely refused to let her faith in purgatory be taken from her." Rousseau regards it as strange, because, in spite of his change of faith, he was never able to free himself entirely from the Protestant influences of his youth.

trition " he neither can nor will practise, but something he will willingly do.   Here the Church now intervenes, and says to him that his poor performance can be converted and transformed by the power of the Church into something so lofty that by means of it the penalties of sin in purgatory are abolished.   The man wishes to know no more.   What has still to happen can cause him little concern, and the Church itself says to him that if he is well provided with the Sacrament of Penance, what follows will not affect him.[1]   Attritio, sacramentum pænitentiæ, indulgentia,—these form the Catholic triad.   What was to be done for the indulgence was the only burdensome thing here; but even this was made very easy.   Thus the indulgence became a

---

[1] The doctrine of purgatory (purgatorium) was a settled matter for the Schoolmen, and was energetically maintained against the Greeks from the thirteenth to the fifteenth century.   This purgatory, which is for departed souls who are absolved but have not made satisfaction for all sins, exists, according to the Latin view, till the judgment of the world (the Greeks, so far as they recognised it at all, put it after the judgment), or for a shorter time.   The souls of the righteous, who need no further purification, attain at once to the vision of God (the counter doctrine of John XXII. was rejected).   More particularly, the Schoolmen taught that there are five dwelling-places of departed souls : (1) hell, to which those guilty of mortal sin at once pass ; (2) the limbus infantium, *i.e.*, of children who have died unbaptised ; (3) the limbus patrum, *i.e.*, of the Old Testament saints ; (4) purgatorium ; (5) heaven ; see the detailed statement in Thomas, Suppl., Q. 69.   That the souls of the pious have knowledge of what takes place on earth, and intercede for their earthly brethren, has been shown by the Lombard (Sent. IV., Dist. 45 G) : " Cur non credamus et animas sanctorum dei faciem contemplantium in ejus veritate intelligere preces hominum, quæ et implendæ sunt vel non ? . . . Intercedunt ergo pro nobis ad deum sancti, et *merito,* dum illorum merita suffragantur nobis, et *affectu*, dum vota nostra cupiunt impleri. . . . Oramus ergo, ut intercedant pro nobis, *i.e.*, ut merita eorum suffragentur nobis, et ut ipsi velint bonum nostrum, quia eis volentibus deus vult et ita fiet " ; similarly Thomas (Suppl., Q. 73 or 74, Art. 1).   The existence of purgatory is thus established by Thomas (l.c., Q. 69, Art. 7) : " Satis potest constare purgatorium esse post hanc vitam ; si enim per contritionem deleta culpa non tollitur ex toto reatus pœnæ nec etiam semper venialia dimissis mortalibus tolluntur, et justitia hoc exigit, ut peccatum per pœnam debitam ordinctur, oportet quod ille, qui post contritionem de peccato et absolutionem decedit ante satisfactionem debitam post hanc vitam puniatur.   Et ideo illi qui purgatorium negant, contra divinam justitiam loquuntur, et propter hoc erroneum est et a fide alienum (there follows a forged passage from Gregory of Nyssa's Works, representing that the whole Church so teaches).   Quod non potest nisi de illis, qui sunt in purgatorio, intelligi ; ecclesiæ autem autoritati quicunque resistit, hæresim incurrit."   Yet opposition to this doctrine never ceased, and it became very active in the fourteenth and fifteenth centuries.   Wyclif and Wessel strenuously adopted the hostile attitude of the Mediæval sects.

caricature (persiflage) of Christianity as the religion of redemption through Christ.

The theory of the Schoolmen is as follows : After there had been uncertainty till far on in the thirteenth century as to whether the indulgences did not relate merely to the ecclesiastical penalties imposed by the priest, Thomas laid it down that they apply in general to the liability to temporal penalty (reatus temporalis pœnæ) ("on earth and in purgatory"). The righteousness of God demands that no sin shall remain "inordinate" (inordinata), and that man shall also perform what he can perform. He is obliged, accordingly, even as absolved, to discharge the temporal penalties of sin. But what the merit of Christ does not do of itself and directly, inasmuch as in the Sacrament it cancels only the reatus culpæ et pœnæ, *it does outwith the Sacrament as merit.* Christ, that is to say, has done more by His suffering than was required for redemption, and even many saints have acquired for themselves merit which God's grace rewards. This surplus merit (thesaurus operum supererogatoriorum [treasury of supererogatory works]) must necessarily fall to the benefit of the Church as the body of Christ, since neither Christ nor the saints can derive further advantage from it. But alongside the Sacrament of Penance it cannot have another effect than to moderate, abridge, or cancel the temporal penalties of sin. It can be applied only to those who, in penitent spirit, have been absolved after making confession, and it is administered in the first instance by the Pope as the head of the Church. Yet by him a partial power of administration can be conveyed to others. The regular mode of making the application is by requiring for the indulgence a comparatively very small performance ("eleemosynæ," *i.e.,* penance money.)[1]

---

[1] A thesaurus meritorum which the Church administers was first adopted by Halesius (see the passages in Münscher, l.c., p. 290 ff.). The theory received a fixed construction from Albertus and Thomas. In Suppl. Q. 25, Art. 1, the latter gives the following exposition : "Ab omnibus conceditur indulgentias aliquid valere, *quia impium esset dicere, quod ecclesia aliquid vane faceret.* Sed quidam dicunt, quod non valent ad absolvendum a reatu pœnæ, quam quis in purgatorio secundum judicium dei meretur, sed valent ad absolvendum ab obligatione qua sacerdos obligavit pænitentem ad pœnam aliquam vel ad quam etiam obligatur ex canonum statutis. Sed hæc opinio

Now this theory—keeping practice quite out of view—still
admitted in detail of very different modifications (nuances).   It

non videtur vera.   Primo quia est expresse contra privilegium Petro datum cui dictum
est, ut quod in terra remitteret, in cœlo remitteretur.   Unde remissio, quæ fit
quantum ad forum ecclesiæ valet, valet etiam quantum ad forum dei.   Et præterea
ecclesia hujusmodi indulgentias faciens magis damnificaret, quam adjuvaret, quia
remitteret ad graviores pœnas, scil. purgatorii, absolvendo a pænitentiis injunctis.   Et
ideo aliter dicendum, *quod valent et quantum ad forum ecclesiæ et quantum ad
judicium dei, ad remissionem pœnæ residuæ post contritionem et confessionem et
absolutionem*, sive sit injuncta, sive non.   Ratio autem, quare valere possint, est
unitas corporis mystici, in qua multi in operibus pænitentiæ supererogaverunt ad
mensuram debitorum suorum . . . quorum meritorum tanta est copia, quod omnem
pœnam debitam nunc viventibus excedunt *et præcipuæ propter meritum Christi, quod
etsi in sacramentis operatur, non tamen efficacia ejus in sacramentis includitur, sed
sua infinitate excedit efficaciam sacramentorum.*   Dictum est autem supra, quod unus
pro alio satisfacere potest ; sancti autem, in quibus superabundantia operum sanctificationis invenitur, non determinate pro isto qui remissione indiget, hujusmodi opera
fecerunt, alias absque omni indulgentia remissionem consequerentur, sed communiter
pro tota ecclesia, sicut apostolus ait (Coloss. I.), et sic prædicta merita sunt communia
totius ecclesiæ.   Ea autem quæ sunt alicujus multitudinis communia, distribuuntur
singulis de multitudine *secundum arbitrium ejus qui multitudini præest.*"   Note also
the cautious remarks : " Remissio quæ per indulgentias fit, non tollit quantitatem
pœnæ ad culpam, quia pro culpa unius alius sponte pœnam sustinuit."—" Ille qui
indulgentias suscipit, non absolvitur, simpliciter loquendo, a debito pœnæ, sed datur
ei, unde debitum solvat."—" Non est in destructionem indulgentias dare, nisi
inordinate dentur.   Tamen consulendum est eis qui indulgentias consequuntur, ne
propter hoc ab operibus pænitentiæ injunctis abstineant, ut etiam ex his remedium
consequentur, quamvis a debito pœnæ esse immunes, *et præcipue quia quandoque
sunt plurium debitores quam credant.*"   In Art. 2 those are confuted who assert that
the indulgences "non tantum valent, quantum pronuntiantur," only so far avail for
the individual "quantum fides et devotio sua exigit."   It is proved, "indulgentiæ
simpliciter tantum valent quantum prædicantur, dummodo ex parte dantis sit auctoritas et ex parte recipientis caritas et ex parte causæ pietas."   Also : "quæcunque
causa adsit, quæ in utilitatem ecclesiæ et honorem dei vergat, sufficiens est ratio
indulgentias faciendi . . . (nam) merita ecclesiæ semper superabundant."   It is
further shown that indulgences belong to the clavis jurisdictionis (are not sacramental),
and therefore "effectus ejus arbitrio hominis subjacet" (also authorised legati non
sacerdotes can dispense indulgences).   To the question whether indulgences can be
dispensed pro temporali subsidio, it is answered in Art. 3 that this is not possible
simpliciter, "sed pro temporalibus ordinatis ad spiritualia, sicut est repressio inimi-
corum ecclesiæ, qui pacem ecclesiæ perturbant, sicut constructio ecclesiarum et
pontium et aliarum eleemosynarum largitio."   Q. 26 treats of those who can dispense
indulgences ("papa potest facere prout vult"), Q. 27 of the receivers of indulgences.
Here in Art. 1 the thesis is contested of those who assert that to those guilty of mortal
sin indulgences are of benefit, not for forgiveness of sins, but yet ad acquirendum
gratiam : "in omnibus indulgentiis fit mentio de vere contritio et confessis."   In Art.
3 it is shown that the indulgence does not avail for one who has not done what the

could also be conceived of more strictly or more laxly. In particular, the demand that one must be in a contrite frame of mind could be lowered to an extraordinary degree.[1] But not

indulgence is given for. Compare with this also Q. 74, where in Art. 10 the question is answered whether indulgences are of use for the dead. The answer is that they are of no direct use, as the dead cannot do what the indulgences are given for. On the other hand they are of indirect use, that is, if the indulgence formula runs thus : " Quicumque fecerit hoc vel illud, ipse et pater ejus vel quicumque alius ei adjunctus in purgatorio detentus, tantum de indulgentia habebit." " Talis indulgentia non solum vivo sed etiam mortuo proderit. Non enim est aliqua ratio quare ecclesia transferre possit communia merita quibus indulgentiæ innituntur in vivos et non in mortuos." The indulgences, moreover, do not work simply per modum suffragii ; they are effectual. Yet arbitrariness on the part of the Pope in rescuing souls from purgatory must be limited by this, that there must always be a causa conveniens indulgentias faciendi ; but such is always to be found. It is furthermore probable that the recognition of a thesaurus meritorum had a long course of historic preparation in the history of religion ; see Siegfried in Hilgenfeld's Ztschr., 1884, Part 3, p. 356 (also Gött Gel. Anz., 1881, St. 12 and 13) : " The doctrine of a treasury of good works from which indemnifications can be derived for the sins of others came originally into Judaism under Iranian influences, as is known to have been the case with so much else in the later Jewish dogmatics. If we compare what appears regarding this in Spiegel's " Eranische Alterthumskunde " with what is to be found in Weber's System der altsynagcgalen paläst. Theol., 1880, p. 280 ff., that this is a fact we shall not be able to doubt. Now as this doctrine, after being first brought forward by Alexander of Hales, owed its recognition within the Catholic Church chiefly to Thomas Aquinas, of whom it is also well known that he transcribed Maimonides (Merx, Die Prophetie des Joel, 1879, pp. 354-367), the suspicion at once arises that this doctrine also was derived from Jewish sources. The more exact proof that this was actually so we reserve, as it would lead us too far afield here." Against this conjecture Güdemann (Jüd. Litr.-Blatt., 21 Jahrg., 29 Oct., 1890) has raised objections, and has tried to show that the "merit of the Fathers" ("Sechus Owaus") is something else and much more harmless. Yet identity no one has asserted, but only a historical connection. The thesaurus meritorum has been developed in directions, and has found applications, of which certainly Judaism did not think. But my conviction that a historical connection exists has not been shaken by Güdemann's objections. For the rest I do not presume to be a judge in this matter, but I would like to point out something akin. In the "History of Joseph" preserved in the Syriac, which is said to have been composed by Basil of Cæsarea, and yet contains only Jewish Haggada, and, so far as I can see, nothing Christian (and so apparently is of Jewish origin), one reads (see Weinberg, Gesch. Josefs, angeblich verfasst v. Basilius d. Gr. Berlin, 1893, p. 53) : " Potiphar's wife said : But if thou art afraid of sin, as thou hast asserted, then take gold and silver, as much as thou wilt, and give to the poor ; and God will forgive thee thy guilt." It is a woman under the devil's influence whom the narrator represents as speaking, and he certainly disapproved of the woman's speech ; but it shows undoubtedly that such reflexions were not far off. The abusus—and that is condemned also by a pious Catholic—is disapproved.

[1] A large amount of material on the lax and strict theories in Bratke, l.c. One

only did that happen ; the practice, as has already been indicated, struck out on quite different paths.   With more or less
of design, it left the question in obscurity as to what really was
cancelled by the indulgence (see the ambiguous expression " for
the salvation of the soul," and others similar) ; it substituted
for the demand for true sorrow and honest resolution to reform
a reference to the Sacrament of Penance, or it was quite silent
upon the demand ; it gave to the indulgence an interpretation in
which the power of the Church and the priest thrust aside the
theoretic basis of the merit of Christ, and, finally, it encouraged the shocking folly of believing that, by the means of
religion, man can provide himself with temporal advantages,
and that beyond this, the spirit and power of religion are
summed up in warding off just punishments.   With all this
there is still unmentioned the ruinous effect that must have
been produced by the frequently shameful use of the indul·
gence money, and by the whole speculative system of the Curia.
The Sacrament of Penance culminated unfortunately in these
indulgences, and without incurring the charge of deriding, one
may state concisely the final word of this system thus:
*Every man who surrenders himself to the Catholic Church, and
who, for some reason, is not quite satisfied with the inner state of
his heart, can secure salvation and deliverance from all eternal
and temporal penalties—if he acts with shrewdness and finds a
skilful priest.*[1]

thing that made a principal difference was the question as to whether indulgences
were not of use even for those guilty of mortal sin ad acquirendam gratiam, or,
whether they could not be given beforehand to such persons, to be used by them
when they felt disposed.   Of course the differences of Scotists and Thomists as to
attritio and contritio are important here also.   The explanations of the Jubilee
indulgence in Bratke, pp. 201 ff., 240 ff., appear to me to be partly based on misunderstanding and partly exaggerated.   The account of the indulgence theory of the
ecclesiastical reform party, p. 234 ff. (Cajetan) is instructive, both as helping us to
understand the earliest position of Luther, and as enabling us to see how poorly armed
this reform party was.

[1] The theory of indulgence is summed up in the Extravagante Unigenitus
of Clement VI. of the year 1349 : " Unigenitus dei filius . . . sanguine nos
redemit quam in ara crucis innocens immolatus, non guttam sanguinis modicam
(quæ tamen propter unionem ad verbum pro redemptione totius humani generis
suffecisset), sed copiose velut quoddam profluvium noscitur effudisse. . . .
Quantum ergo exinde, ut nec supervacua, inanis aut superflua tantæ effusionis

Against this theory there not only was a reaction on the part of the re-invigorated or Augustinian Thomism, in the shape of a strong insistence on the moral and religious requirements for the reception of indulgences, but—keeping the sects out of view—there also arose in the fourteenth century a radical opposition, which had likewise an Augustinian (and biblical) basis. Against no other ecclesiastical practice and theory did Wyclif assume so determined an attitude as against indulgences. He saw in them nothing but arbitrariness, which had only forced its way in of recent times; the Bible knew nothing of indulgences, which encroached upon the prerogative of God, and were therefore positively blasphemous. He also saw clearly the mischief of indulgences in hindering obedience to the law of Christ; still he did not frame a satisfactory theory as to how a *distressed* conscience can be comforted. For him, and for his scholar Huss, the perniciousness of indulgences lies simply in their unbiblical character, in the pretensions of the hierarchy (the Pope), and in the corruption of morals. But indulgences cannot be rooted out by merely quickening conscience and contending against priestly power.[1]

miseratio redderetur, thesaurum militanti ecclesiæ acquisivit, volens suis thesaurizare filiis pius pater, ut sic sit infinitus thesaurus hominibus, quo qui usi sunt dei amicitiæ participes sunt effecti. Quem quidem thesaurum non in sudario repositum, non in agro absconditum, sed per beatum Petrum . . . ejusque successores suos in terris vicarios commisit fidelibus salubriter dispensandum, et propriis et rationabilibus causis : nunc pro totali, nunc pro partiali remissione pœnæ temporalis pro peccatis debitæ, tam generaliter quam specialiter (prout cum deo expedire cognoscerent) *vere pœnitentibus et confessis* misericorditer applicandum. Ad cujus quidem thesauri cumulum b. dei genetricis omniumque electorum a primo justo usque ad ultimum merita adminiculum præstare noscuntur, de cujus consumptione seu minutione non est aliquatenus formidandum (!), tam propter infinita Christi merita quam pro eo quod, quanto plures ex ejus applicatione trahuntur ad justitiam, tanto magis accrescit ipsorum cumulus meritorum."

See Buddensieg, Wyclif, p. 201 ff., Trialogus IV., 32 : "Fateor quod indulgentiæ papales, si ita se habeant ut dicuntur, sapiunt manifestam blasphemiam. Dicitur enim, quod papa prætendit, se habere potentiam ad salvandum singulos viatores, et quantumcunque viantes deliquerint, nedum ad mitigandum pœnas ad suffragandum eis cum absolutionibus et indulgentiis, ne unquam veniant ad purgatorium, sed ad præcipiendum sanctis angelis, ut anima separata a corpore indilate ipsam deferant in requiem sempiternam. . . . Contra istam rudem blasphemiam invexi alias, primo sic : nec papa nec etiam dominus Jesus Christus potest dispensare cum aliquo nec dare indulgentias, nisi ut æternaliter deitas justo consilio definivit.

Not less strenuous than the opposition of Wyclif and Huss
to the indulgences were the attacks of Wesel and Wessel.
Both likewise wrote from the standpoint of Augustine against
the indulgences. They too described the theory as unbiblical
and as unsupported by any tradition, and used as weapons for
overthrowing it the sole efficiency of God, the majesty of the
divine penal righteousness and the gratia gratis data (caritas
infusa). The punishments which God decrees man cannot
avert ; only the penalties of positive law, or the ecclesiastical
penalties, can the Pope remit. God infuses His grace without
merit (sine merito), but only in the case of those who are perfectly disposed for it. At the same time Wesel relaxes the
connection between sacrament and communication of grace
(nominalistically : "propter pactum institutum cum sacerdotibus"
[on account of an agreement instituted with the priests]).
At bottom there is no distinction between his doctrine of the
Sacrament and the vulgar one. He is merely unable, from feeling
more decidedly the majesty of God, to draw the conclusions from
the indulgences, which, along with others, he calls "piæ fraudes." [1]

Sed non docetur, quod papa vel homo aliquis potest habere colorem justitiæ (on this
falls the greatest weight) taliter faciendi ; igitur non docetur, quod papa talem habeat
potestatem. . . . Item videtur quod illa opinio multipliciter blasphemat in Christum,
cum extollitur supra ejus humanitatem atque deitatem et sic super omne quod dicitur
deus. . . . Sed eia, mili es Christi, abicite prudenter hæc opera atque *fictitias
principis tenebrarum* et induimini dominum Jesum Christum, in armis suis fideliter
confidentes, et excutite ab ecclesia tales versutias antichristi, docentes populum, *quod
in ipso solo cum lege sua et membris debet confidere et operando illis conformiter ex
suo opere bono salvari*, specialiter si antichristi versutias fideliter detestetur."

[1] A series of passages from the Disput. adv. indulgentias of Wesel has been re-
printed by Hauck, p. 303 f. Everything in Wesel is really only apparently radical.
He lets the vulgar doctrine of the Sacraments stand, up to the point at which the
Sacrament of Penance does not cancel the temporal penalties of sin. But at this
point he will stop short ; for these penalties cannot at all be cancelled (1) because
God decrees them and means to carry them out ; (2) because there is no one who
could remove them—the priests are in everything only ministri dei in remittendis
culpis—(3) because it is in keeping with piety to endure them ; (4) because there
could be no purgatory at all, if the theory of indulgences were correct ; for the
treasury of indulgences would be enough to compensate for all temporal penalties. If
there mingles already in the polemic of Wesel a Wyclifite-Hussite (Donatist) element,
in so far as it is required that the objective importance of the priests (the hierarchy)
be diminished (by no means abolished), this element is much more recognisable in
Wessel. To the *pious* alone are the keys given. Now as the Popes and priests are

The Church, in spite of these forms of opposition, went on its way.[1]

5. *Extreme unction.*[2] Only from Thomas's time was it asserted that Christ Himself instituted this Sacrament, while the Apostle James (5, 14) only proclaimed it. The Materia is oil blessed by the bishop, while the episcopal consecration was declared " conveniens " by Thomas on the same ground as in the case of confirmation (expression of the higher power of the bishop with respect to the " mystical body of Christ," see above, p. 231, note ; hence the Pope can also give power to ordinary priests to consecrate). The " form " is a deprecatory prayer (the indicative form can at the most be added). The administrator is any priest. The Sacrament can be repeated.[3] The receivers are those under fatal illness and the dying. The purpose (res sacramenti) is the remission of sins (remissio pec-

in many cases not pious, these carnales homines have power at all only in externis, *i.e.*, what they undertake has to do, not with the true Church and grace and sin, but with the empirical Church ; see de sacram. pœnit. f. 51 : " Carnalis homo non sapit, quæ sancti amoris sunt, igitur judicare non potest. Unde judicium ecclesiæ et eorum qui in ecclesia præsident, quia saepe carnales, animales, mundiales aut diabolici sunt et tamen suum officium vere administraut sicut vïïi spirituales est deo pleni, liquet excommunicationes et indulgentias non ad ea quæ caritatis et amoris sunt se extendere sed tantum ad exteriorem pacem et tranquillitatem ecclesiæ. Unde indulgentiæ sunt remissiones de his pœnis quas prælatus injunxit aut injungere potuit." But further, the keys that are given to Peter are not handed over to arbitrary use ; true repentance and *divine* forgiveness go together. Everything rests on grace, and only pious priests are ministri dei, *i.e.*, ministers of the grace which God alone is able to infuse. But Wessel took still another important step. He asked himself whether the temporal *penalties* of sin really remain after forgiveness, and he is inclined to see discipline rather in the penalties of the absolved. (f. 60.) From this point he also assailed the conception of satisfactio operum, and drew a conclusion from Augustinianism which scarcely anyone before him had ventured to draw : satisfaction cannot take place at all, where God has infused His love ; it leads of necessity to a limitation of the gratia gratis data, and detracts from the work of Christ. The plenitudo gratiæ excludes the satisfactio (fol. 61, 62), how much more the indulgences, which he defines thus (l.c.) : " indulgentiarum materia est abusus quæstorum et saepe illorum falsum crimen, nonnumquam impura et corrupta intentio papæ."

[1] At Constance (Mansi XXVII., p. 634, No. 42) the proposition was condemned : " Fatuum est credere indulgentiis papæ et episcoporum."

[2] Thomas, P. III., Suppl. Q. 29-33. Schwane, p. 675-677.

[3] In the earlier period, Ivo and others expressed themselves against repetition. From the Lombard's time repetition is approved, but not in one and the same illness.

catorum), but only of venial sins, or the cleansing away of the
remains of sin, or occasionally (per accidens), that is, if no
hindrance exists, the full forgiveness of sins.[1]   Therefore the
Sacrament is also defined as " completion " of the Sacrament of
Penance, though it remains quite dark why and how far this
Sacrament needs completion.   Here also, as in the case of confirmation, we have to do, not with a Sacrament that is the
product of a dogmatic *theory*, but with an observance, the
value of which is raised so high on grounds of expediency,[2]
while theoretically it is rated very low.   Even bodily healing is
expected, if it please God, from this Sacrament.

6. *Priestly ordination*.[3]   In connection with this Sacrament
the general sacramental theory can be maintained, if at all, only
by artifice, because the hierarchical interest created it, and
introduced it into the sacramental system of grace simply with
a view to self-glorification.   The " form " is the words " accipe
potestatem offerendi " (receive the power of offering); the
" material " cannot be pointed out to the senses with certainty;
but Thomas here made a virtue of necessity, and the others
followed him; from the very uncertainty the hierarchical nature
of the Sacrament is proved.[4]   One thought of the vessels or

[1] Thomas, l.c., Q. 30, Art. 1 : " Principalis effectus hujus sacramenti est remissio
peccatorum, quoad reliquias peccati (what does that mean?), et ex consequenti etiam
quoad culpam, si eam inveniat." Art. 2 : " Ex hoc sacramento non semper sequitur
corporalis sanatio, sed quando expedit ad spiritualem sanationem.   Et tunc semper
eam inducit, dummodo non sit impedimentum ex parte recipientes " ; cf. the comprehensive description of the Sacrament in the Bull of Eugene IV. (Mansi XXXI., p.
1058).

[2] In itself it was, no doubt, very expedient to introduce a Sacrament in connection
with death, and thereby to increase confidence in dying.   This was strengthened by
the rite of anointing the several members, and thereby showing in an impressive way
to the sick, that the members with which he had sinned had been cleansed.   Here,
also, as in the case of confirmation, the Church gave heed to men's need of something
"objective," instead of leading them without any ceremonies to Christ.

[3] Thomas, P. III., Suppl. Q. 34-40.   Schwane, pp. 677-685.

[4] Q. 34, Art. 3 : " Sacramentum nihil est aliud quam quædam sanctificatio homini
exhibita cum aliquo signo visibili.   Unde cum in susceptione ordinis quædam consecratio homini exhibeatur per visibilia signa, constat ordinem esse sacramentum." Art.
5 : " Materia in sacramentis exterius adhibita significat virtutem in sacramentis agen-
tem ex intrinseco omnino advenire.   Unde cum effectus proprius hujus sacramenti,
scil. character, non percipiatur ex aliqua operatione ipsius qui ad sacramentum accidit
sicut erat in pænitentia sed omnino ex intrinseco adveniat, competit ei materiam

symbols by which the hierarchical functions were represented (Thomas), another of the laying on of hands. The former was asserted by Eugene IV. in the Bull "Exultate" (l.c.). The dispenser is solely the bishop. Here there arose, however, many questions, in some respects entering deep into ecclesiastical law and ecclesiastical practice, indirectly also into dogmatic, which will only be noted here; (1) on the seven orders (ordines), and their relation (the Pope can empower even an ordinary priest to ordain to the lower orders); (2) on the relation of the priestly to the episcopal consecration (in how far is the bishop superior to the priest? in respect of divine right? (jure divino); (3)—and this was the most important question— on the validity of orders that have been conferred by schismatic or heretical bishops. From as far back as the Donatist conflict there prevailed a controversy on this point, which was decided in the Church, as a rule, in a liberal spirit, to the effect, namely, that such ordinations are indeed unpermitted, *i.e.*, are null and void as to their practical effects, but yet are not invalid. On the other hand the Lombard asserted that no heretic can duly celebrate confirmation, the Eucharist and ordination to the priesthood. Thereafter there prevailed among the Scholastic theologians great uncertainty; yet there was a growing leaning to the liberal view, the Sacrament of Penance alone being excepted. But in the Middle Ages the Popes very often declared entirely invalid the ordinations of bishops who were under disfavour and of rival Popes. As regards the effect of this Sacrament, the *character* was here the chief matter.[1] It

habere, tamen diversimode ab aliis sacramentis quæ materiam habent. *Quia hoc quod confertur in aliis sacramentis, derivatur tantum a deo, non a ministro qui sacramentum dispensat, sed illud quod in hoc sacramento traditur, scil. spiritualis potestas, derivatur etiam ab eo qui sacramentum dat sicut potestas imperfecta a perfecta. Et ideo efficacia aliorum sacramentorum principaliter consistit in materia, quæ virtutem divinam et significat et continet, ex sanctificatione per ministrum adhibita. Sed efficacia hujus sacramenti principaliter residet penes eum, qui sacramentum dispensat,* materia autem adhibetur magis ad demonstrandum potestatem, quæ traditur particulariter ab habente eam complete, quam ad potestatem causandam, quod patet ex hoc quod materia competit usui potestatis."

[1] Not a saving benefit, therefore, given to an individual; for the ordo serves the Church (Thomas, Q. 35, A. 1). Here, also, the doctrine of sacramental grace (participatio divinæ naturæ) has breaches made in it; nay, Thomas says plainly, Q. 34,

consists in the conveyance of the right to dispense the Sacraments,[1] to forgive sins, to officiate as judge, and to be mediator
between God and men.[2]   But on the other hand, again, all the
seven orders were called Sacraments by some (in the case of
others they are regarded only as sacramentalia), although it
was added, that only the diaconate and the presbyterate have
institution by Christ as their basis.   The episcopate could not
be reckoned as a special ordo, because tradition forbade it;
but efforts were made to assign to it a special position, higher
than the ordinary priesthood, and given to it by Christ, and a
basis was found for it, not in sacramental, but in judicial power.
Duns Scotus, moreover, laid down the lines of the doctrine, that
the episcopal consecration is a special Sacrament.

7. *Marriage*.[3]   Like the former Sacrament, this one also
encroaches, in the particular questions connected with it, on the
field of ecclesiastical law, only that these questions are tenfold
more numerous than in the case of the other.   The expediency
of declaring marriage a Sacrament, and thereby bringing this
foundation of society under ecclesiastical jurisdiction is obvious.
Just on that account it was overlooked also that the declaring
of marriage a Sacrament implied that breaches had previously
been made in the general conception of a Sacrament.   Marriage
was already instituted by God in Paradise for the propagation
of the human race (and therefore as an obligation [ad officium]),
and to be indissoluble too ; but according to Thomas it was
only raised to the position of a Sacrament by Christ, inasmuch
as He made it the picture of His union with the Church, thereby
established anew its indissoluble character, and also united with

---

Art. 2 : "unde relinquitur, quod ipse character interior sit essentialiter et principaliter
ipsum sacramentum ordinis ! "

[1] At the same time the celebration of the Mass is the chief matter ; it alone is mentioned in the formula of consecration.

[2] The Lombard, Sent. IV., Dist. 24 I. : " Sacerdos nomen habet compositum ex
Græco et Latino, quod est sacrum dans sive sacer dux.   Sicut enim rex a regendo
ita sacerdos a sacrando dictus est, consecrat enim et sanctificat."   At the same time
being empowered to teach was also no doubt mentioned, and for the person of the
priest an undefinable " amplius gratiæ munus, per quod ad majora redduntur idonei "
(Thomas, Q. 35, Art. 1).   In the Bull " Exultate " (Mansi, l.c., p. 1058) it is said :
" Effectus augmentum gratiæ, ut quis sit idoneus minister."

[3] Thomas, P. III., Suppl. Q. 41-68.   Schwane, pp. 685-693.

marriage a saving gift.[1] So far as it also provides for propagation within the *Church*, its sacramental character is already
justified ;[2] but besides its sacramental effect, marriage, since the
Fall, has also the character of an indulgence, as "remedium"
against the insurgent passions of the flesh.[3] It is further admitted, that among all the Sacraments marriage has the "mini-
mum de spiritualitate,"[4] hence it stands in the last place, and the
unmarried life is to be preferred. The examination of the
question, whether the "copula carnalis," or, the right to demand
the "debitum conjugale," belongs to the essence of marriage,
was necessarily treated with Joseph's marriage in view. As
there was no wish to exclude that right from the essence of
marriage (the *assertion* of the right does not belong to its
essence), one was led to the interesting question whether
Mary, when she concluded marriage with Joseph, was not
obliged to agree *conditionally* to a *possible* assertion of the right
of marriage on the part of Joseph. The Lombard still answered
this question in the affirmative ;[5] but Bonaventura already
found another way of solving it.[6] As to "material" and "form,"
there prevailed the greatest uncertainty. Yet in the Middle
Ages it was not doubted that the decisive external sign is the
expressed "consensus" of the parties to the marriage,[7] the

---

[1] Thomas, l.c., Q. 41, A. 1 ; 42, A. 2, 3. In the way in which the Lombard
describes the marriage bond as sacramental, a beautiful proof is presented of the
ultimate interest of Western Post-Augustinian Catholicism, in so far as it is determined at the same time by the thought of conformitas naturæ divinæ and by that of
caritas, Sentent. IV., Dist. 26 F. : "Ut inter conjuges conjunctio est secundum
consensum animorum et secundum permixtionem corporum, sic ecclesia Christo
copulatur voluntate et natura, qua idem vult cum eo, et ipsa formam sumpsit de
natura hominis. Copulata est ergo sponsa sponso spiritualiter et corporaliter,
i.e., caritate et conformitate naturæ. Hujus utriusque copulæ figura est
in conjugio. Consensus enim conjugum copulam spiritualem Christi et ecclesiæ,
quæ fit per caritatem, significat ; commixtio vero sexuum illam significat, quæ fit per
naturæ conformitatem."

[2] Thomas, P. III., Q. 65, A. 4.

[3] Thomas, Q. 42, A. 2.

[4] Thomas, P. III., Q. 65, A. 2.
    Sentent. IV., Dist. 30 B.

[6] See Schwane, p. 688.

[7] Thomas, Q. 42, Art. 1 : "Verba quibus consensus matrimonialis exprimitur sunt
forma hujus sacramenti." Also : "Sacramentum matrimonii perficitur per actum
ejus, qui sacramento illo utitur, sicut pænitentia. Et ideo sicut pænitentia non habet

priest's blessing was held to be only "a sacramental," not the
Sacrament.[1] Many Schoolmen, it is true, sought to extract an
effectual spiritual character, but the majority recognised only a
quite undefined saving grace.[2] On the other hand Durandus
denied entirely the opus operatum (the saving grace), saying
that marriage only *signifies* something sacred (union of the
Church with Christ).[3] That excessive recognition of saving grace
stands in flagrant opposition to the view that was derived from
Augustine, that the "copula carnalis" in marriage, because it is
not materially different from the "copula carnalis fornicatoria,"
is so deeply infected with sin, that sin is committed, not indeed
by the partner who consents, but by the partner who demands,
even when it is done for the purpose of avoiding adultery.[4]
While therefore the Sacrament consists in the expressed "consensus" to enter into marriage with a person of the other sex,
and thereby the right of the "debitum conjugale" is implicitly
laid down, the assertion of this sacramental right is to be held a
sin![5] In the Bull of Eugene IV. (l.c). there is to be found, again,
a short serviceable summing up.[6]

aliam materiam nisi ipsos actus sensui subjectos, qui sunt loco materialis elementi, ita
est de matrimonio."

[1] Thomas, Q. 42, Art. 1 : "benedictio sacerdotis est quoddam sacramentale."

[2] Thomas, Q. 42, Art. 3.

[3] See Schwane, p. 689.

[4] So Bonaventura and Thomas, Q. 49, Art. 4-6, especially Art. 5 : "utrum actus
matrimonialis excusari possit sine bonis matrimonii." Here, among other things, it
is said: "si aliquis per actum matrimonii intendat vitare fornicationem in conjuge, non
est aliquod peccatum ; . . . sed si intendat vitare fornicationem in se . . . hoc est
peccatum veniale."

[5] The contradictions on Thomas's part are here very great ; for on the other hand
it is said, l.c., Art. 4, that proles, fides, and sacramentum not only excuse, but
sanctify, the act of marriage. See also in Sentent. Dist. 26, Q. 2, Art. 3 : "Cum in
matrimonio datur homini ex divina institutione facultas utendi sua uxore ad procrea-
tionem prolis, datur etiam gratia, sine qua id convenienter facere non posset."

[6] "Septimum est sacramentum matrimonii, quod est signum conjunctionis Christi
et ecclesiæ secundum apostolum. Causa efficiens matrimonii regulariter est mutuus
consensus per verba de præsenti expressus. Adsignatur autem triplex bonum matrimonii. Primum est proles suscipienda et educanda ad cultum dei. Secundum est
fides quam unus conjugum alteri servare debet. Tertium indivisibilitas matrimonii,
propter hoc quod significat indivisibilem conjunctionem Christi et ecclesiæ. Quamvis
autem ex causa fornicationis liceat tori separationem facere, non tamen aliud matrimonium contrahere fas est, cum matrimonii vinculum legitime contracti perpetuum
sit." How strong still in the fourteenth century was the disinclination of the Scotist

In the doctrine of the Sacraments Thomas was the teacher of determining influence in the Middle Ages, and he has remained such to the present day in the Catholic Church. But, so far as the new ecclesiasticism admitted of it at all, Thomas went back to Augustine. Yet how strongly even in him the doctrine of the gratia gratis data (grace graciously bestowed) is affected by a regard to the doctrine, that God treats with us according to our merits; how this latter view, which Augustine had not entirely eradicated, still exercised its influence, Thomas's doctrine of the Sacraments shows already very plainly. The earnest, truly religious spirit which distinguished him was increasingly weakened and led astray by regard for what was held valid. Yet that, certainly, is not the only weakness. An influence, at least equally pernicious, was exercised by the logical apprehension of grace as a physical, mysterious act, and a communication of objective benefits. That also originated with Augustine, and that also, logically carried out, broke up Augustinianism ; *the breaking up of Augustinianism was really not occasioned from without ; it was in great part the result of an inner development.* The three elements which Augustine left standing in and along with his doctrine of grace, *the element of merit, the element of gratia infusa and the hierarchical priestly element*, continued to work, till they completely transformed the Augustinian mode of thought. But as we have seen, that was already foreshadowed in Gregory the Great, and on the other hand the process did not reach its termination yet in the Middle Ages. The Augustinian reaction of the fifteenth and sixteenth centuries which partly embodied itself in the decrees of Trent, was only fully checked again, after a struggle for three hundred years, in the nineteenth century.

C.   The Revision of Augustinianism in the Direction of the Doctrine of Merit.

That the *grace* springing from the passio Christi is the foundation of the Christian religion, and therefore must be the Alpha

theologians to regard marriage as a full sacrament, may be seen from Werner, II., p. 424 ff. (against Durandus Aureolus).

and Omega of Christian Theology—this fundamental Pauline and Augustinian thought was directly denied by no ecclesiastical teacher of the West.¹ But as in itself it may mean many things, and, without definite interpretation, by no means guarantees the purity of the Christian religion—for what is grace? God Himself in Christ, or divine forces? and what does grace effect? faith, or a mysterious quality?—so also, if the effect of grace is to be held as only "improvement," for this very reason it is capable of being wrought over in a way that ultimately cancels it.

The Lombard—in accordance with his intention to reproduce tradition—confined himself to repeating with precision the Augustinian propositions about *grace*, predestination and justification (faith and love).² But as soon as he brings forward pro-

---

¹ The proposition of Irenæus (III., 18, 6) : " Si non vere passus est, nulla gratia ei, cum nulla fuerit passio," is the firmly adhered to basis of the whole of the Christianity and of the whole of the theology of the West.

² Sentent. II., Dist. 25 P. : " Libertas a peccato et a miseria per gratiam est ; libertas vero a necessitate per naturam. Utramque libertatem, naturæ scil. et gratiæ, notat apostolus cum ex persona hominis non redempti ait : ' velle adjacet mihi, etc.,' acsi diceret, habeo libertatem naturæ, sed non habeo libertatem gratiæ, ideo non est apud me perfectio boni. Nam voluntas hominis, quam naturaliter habet, non valet erigi ad bonum efficaciter volendum, vel opere implendum, nisi per gratiam liberetur et adjuvetur : liberetur quidem, ut velit, et adjuvetur, ut perficiat . . . dei gratiam non advocat hominis voluntas vel operatio, sed ipsa gratia voluntatem prævenit præparando ut velit bonum et præparatam adjuvat ut perficiat." He repeats also correctly the Augustinian doctrine of predestination (I. Dist. 40 D.) : God does not elect on the basis of prescience, but it is only the election that produces the merits. He rejects præscientia iniquitatis quorundam : "reprobatio dei, qua ab æterno non eligendo quosdam reprobavit, secundum duo consideratur, quorum alterum præscit et non præparat, *i.e.*, iniquitatem, alterum præscit et præparat, scil. æternam pœnam." Reprobation rests on the mysterious but just decision *not* to show mercy to some ; its result is hardening. The chief propositions of the Lombard on faith, love, and works are : III. Dist. 23 D. : " Credere deo est credere vera esse quæ loquitur, quod et mali faciunt . . . ; credere deum est credere quod ipse sit deus, quod etiam mali faciunt ; credere in deum est *credendo amare*, credendum in eum ire, credendo ei adhærere et ejus membris incorporari : *per hanc fidem justificatur impius*" (word for word after Augustine). So also he distinguishes in faith, after Augustine, id quod and id quo creditur (l.c. sub. C.). The latter, subjective faith, is to be distinguished according as it is virtus and according as it is not virtus. Faith, so far as love is still wanting to it, is fides informis (not virtue). All deeds without faith are devoid of goodness, II. Dist, 41 A. : "cum intentio bonum opus faciat et fides intentionem dirigat, non immerito quæri potest, utrum omnis intentio omneque opus illorum malum sit, qui fidem non habent? . . . Quod a quibusdam non irrationabiliter astruitur, qui dicunt omnes actiones et voluntates hominis sine fide malas esse . . . Quæ ergo sine fide

positions about free will, these have by no means an Augustinian, but rather a Semipelagian ring ; for they are already dominated by a regard to *merit*.[1] Where this view is taken, that is to say, a point must always be ultimately found, which makes it possible to attribute a value to the *independent* action of man over against God. But the contradiction which plainly comes out in the Lombard, when his doctrine of grace is compared with his doctrine of freedom, is equally prevalent among the theologians before him, nay, in them it comes out more strongly, most strongly in Abelard.[2] There is still to be observed as

---

fiunt, bona non sunt, quia omne bonum deo placet." II. Dist. 26 A. : " Operans gratia est, quæ prævenit voluntatem bonam : ea enim liberatur et præparatur hominis voluntas, ut sit bona bonumque efficaciter velit ; cooperans vero gratia voluntatem jam bonam sequitur adjuvando . . . Voluntas hominis gratia dei prævenitur atque præparatur, ut fiat bona, non ut fiat voluntas, quia et ante gratiam voluntas erat, sed non erat bona et recta voluntas." It is repeatedly said that grace consists in the infusion of fides cum caritate (*i.e.*, the Holy Spirit), and that only with this the merits of man begin ; accordingly justitia as bona qualitas mentis (viitus, qua recte vivitur) is entirely a work of God.

[1] Sentent. II., Dist. 24 C. : " Liberum arbitrium est facultas rationis et voluntatis, qua bonum eligitur gratia assistente vel malum eadem desistente." II. Dist. 27 G. : "Cum ex gratia dicuntur esse bona merita et incipere . . . gratia gratis data intelligitur, ex qua bona merita incipiunt. Quæ cum ex sola gratia esse dicantur, non excluditur liberum arbitrium, *quia nullum meritum est in homine, quod non fit per liberum arbitrium*." II. Dist. 26 G. : " Ante gratiam prævenientem et operantem, qua voluntas bona præparatum in homine, præcedere quædam bona ex dei gratia et libero arbitrio, quædam etiam ex solo libero arbitrio, quibus tamen vita non meretur, nec gratia, qua justificatur." II. Dist. 27 J. : "Cum dicitur fides mereri justificationem et vitam æternam, ex ea ratione dictum accipitur, quia per actum fidei meretur illa. Similiter de caritate et justitia et de aliis accipitur. Si enim fides ipsa virtus præveniens diceretur esse mentis actus qui est meritum, jam ipsa ex libero arbitrio originem haberet, quod quia non est, sic dicitur esse meritum, quia actus ejus est meritum, si tamen adsit caritas, sine qua nec credere nec sperare meritum vitæ est. Unde apparet vere quia caritas est spiritus s., qui animæ qualitates informat et sanctificat, ut eis anima informetur et sanctificetur, sine qua animæ qualitas non dicitur virtus, quia non valet sanare animam." II. Dist. 41 C. : "Nullus dei gratiam mereri potest, per quam justificatur, potest tamen mereri, ut penitus abiciatur. Et quidem aliqui in tantum profundum iniquitatis devenerunt, ut hoc mereantur, ut hoc digni sint ; alii vero ita vivunt, ut etsi non mereantur gratiam justificationis, non tamen mereantur omnino repelli et gratiam sibi subtrahi."

[2] In Anselm (Dialog. de lib. arb.), Bernard (de gratia et lib. arb.), and Hugo the Augustinian propositions regarding grace are repeated, but the explanations of free will are in part still more uncertain than in the Lombard. According to Anselm the rectitudo liberi arbitrii has disappeared indeed, but the potestas servandi rectitudinem remains ; see c. 3 : "liberum arbitrium non est aliud, quam arbitrium potens servare

noteworthy the specific view taken by the Lombard of saving grace, who simply identifies it with the Holy Spirit. His meaning is, that while all other virtues become man's own by means of an infused habit (habitus), love arises directly in the soul through the indwelling of the Holy Spirit, since it is the indwelling Holy Spirit Himself. In this noteworthy view there lies the approach to a more evangelical position ; for " habitus " there is substituted the direct activity of the Holy Ghost. Just on that account this view[1] seldom found followers ;[2] quite as few did the other, that in grace the gratia gratis dans (God Himself) and the gratia gratis data ought to be distinguished.[3] The desire was to have, not God, but divine forces that can become human virtues.

rectitudinem voluntatis propter ipsam rectitudinem." The ratio and the will power remain, and so, after the Fall, men are like those who have eyes and can see, but for whom the object has disappeared (c. 4). The libertas arbitrii is accordingly defined by him (1) formally (ratio et voluntas tenendi), but also (2) materially, in as much as the voluntas *tenendi* remains. According to Bernard (c. 8) there belongs to free will, not the posse vel sapere, but only the velle ; but the latter remains: " manet igitur post peccatum liberum arbitrium, etsi miserum, tamen integrum . . . non ergo si creatura potens aut sapiens, sed tantum si volens esse desierit, liberum arbitrium amisisse putanda erit." In this formal description of free will Hugo diverges still further from Augustine ; for what is characteristic of this fatal development is this, that for Augustine's religious mode of view, for which freedom is beata necessitas, there is substituted an empirico-psychological mode of view, which is of no concern for religion, and which nevertheless now influences religious contemplation. "Voluntas semper a necessitate libera est " : this proposition is again made a foundation in the doctrine of religion. On Abelard's doctrine see Deutsch, l.c., p. 319 ff., who illustrates in particular the dangerous side in the conception of intentio on which Abelard lays stress, and shows how the intellectualism of the theologian is in conflict with the traditional doctrine of original sin.

[1] See II. Dist., 27 J. (see above, p. 277, note 1); I. Dist., 17 B. : " Ipse idem spiritus sanctus est amor sive caritas, qua nos diligimus deum et proximum, quæ caritas cum ita est in nobis, ut nos faciet diligere deum et proximum, tunc spiritus sanctus dicitur mitti ac dari nobis." I. Dist., 17 Q. : " Alios actus atque motus virtutum operatur caritas, *i.e.*, spiritus s., mediantibus virtutibus quarum actus sunt, utpote actum fidei, *i.e.*, credere fide media, et actum spei, *i.e.*, sperare media spe. Per fidem enim et spem prædictos operatur actus. *Diligendi vero actum per se tantum sine alicujus virtutis medio operatur.* Aliter ergo hunc actum operatur quam alios virtutum actus."

[2] Duns contested it ; on the other hand, Pupper of Goch and Staupitz defended it ; see Otto Clemen, J. Pupper von Goch (Leipzig, 1896), p. 249.

[3] Sentent. II., Dist. 27 G. : " Cum ex gratia dicuntur esse bona merita et incipere, aut intelligitur gratia gratis dans, *i.e.*, deus, vel potius gratia gratis data, quæ voluntatem hominis prævenit."

Here lies the fundamental error. In its ultimate basis the mode of view is not a religious but a moral one. That comes out distinctly in the case of the Schoolman who may be styled par excellence the theologian of grace, namely Thomas. It would seem as if one could not value grace more highly than he has done ; *from God to God through grace*—that is the theme of his entire dogmatic. And yet ultimately it is habitual virtue on which all depends. The decisive mistake was already made by Augustine. It lies in the *gratia cooperans*, which is distinguished from the gratia operans (præveniens). The latter does not procure justification and salvation, but the former. But the former is only cooperative, for it runs parallel with the liberated will, and the two together produce merit, which is the matter of importance. But why is merit the matter of importance? Because the theologian cannot conceive of anything else availing before God than *improvement* that exhibits itself in a habitus. That thought, however, is not framed from the standpoint of religion, but from the standpoint of morality, or is a distressed conscience to be comforted by saying that there will gradually be formed a habit of love? Look at it as we will, faith appears important here only in so far as it opens the way for the procuring of virtues ; the gratia præveniens becomes the bridge that leads over to morality. But in the last analysis the cause that led to this scheme of doctrine lies still deeper ; for we must necessarily ask, why is the grace, which is, of course, to dominate the whole process, so narrowly conceived of in respect of its power, that it is unable to effect, alone and perfectly, what it contemplates? The answer to this question must not simply run : in order to set aside the thought of an arbitrary procedure on God's part, for in other connections there was a falling back on the hidden will of God. Nor is it enough to say that the moral principle, that each one shall receive according to his deeds, furnishes the solution here ; this had an influence, but was not the only thing that was at work. *At bottom, rather, it was because the conception itself of God and of grace admitted of no other conclusion.* There was no recognition of *personality*, neither of the personality of God, nor of man as a *person*. If even in earthly relations man cannot be otherwise raised to a higher stage, than by passing into a person who is superior, more mature, and greater, that is, by entering into spiritual fellowship with such an one, and attaching one's self to him by reverence, love, and trust, then the same holds good, but in a way that transcends comparison, of the rising of man from the sphere of sin and guilt into the sphere of God. Here no communications of things avail, but only fellowship of person with person ; the disclosure to the soul, that the holy God who rules heaven and earth is its Father, with whom it can, and may, live as a child in its father's house—that is grace, nay, that *alone* is grace, the trustful confidence in God, namely, which rests on the certainty that the separating guilt has been swept away. That was seen by Augustine as little as by Thomas, and it was not discerned even by the mediæval Mystics, who aspired to having intercourse with Christ as with a friend ; for it was the *man* Jesus of whom they thought in seeking this. But all of them, when they think of God, look, not to the heart of God, but to an inscrutable Being, who, as He has created the world out of nothing, so is also the productive source of inexhaustible forces that yield *knowledge* and *transformation of essence.* And when they think of themselves, they think, not of the centre of the human ego, the spirit, which is so free and so lofty that it cannot be influenced by benefits that are objective, even though they be the greatest perceptions and the most glorious investiture, and at the same time is so feeble in itself that it can find support only in another *person.* Therefore they constructed the thesis : *God and gratia (i.e.,* knowledge and participation in the divine nature), in place of the personal fellowship with God, *which is the gratia.* That gratia, only a little separated from God in the thesis, became in course of time always further removed from Him. It appears deposited in the merit of Christ, and then in the Sacraments. But in the measure in which it becomes more impersonal, more objective, and more external, confidence in it is also impaired, till at last it becomes a magical means, which stirs to activity the latent good agency of man, and sets in motion the standing machine, that it may then do *its* work, and that *its* work may be of account before God. One sees plainly that everythings depends ultimately on the conception of God.   In the gratia cooperans that conception of God comes to view which represents God, not as the holy Lord in relation to guilty man, and as the Father of Jesus Christ in relation to His child, but as the unfathomable power that comes to help man with knowledge and with secret influences of a natural kind, in order that, by love and virtue, man may be able to win independent worth before Him.   In Thomas it is the Augustinian intellectualism, closely conjoined with the doctrine of deification, which ultimately determines the view of God and of grace.   In the later Schoolmen the intellectualism is surmounted, and a beautiful beginning is made to reflect upon will, and thereby upon personality.   But as it is no more than a beginning, grace appears finally in Nominalism simply as emptied of its contents and reduced to a magical force.   Where the simplest and the hardest thing is not taken account of— childship and faith in contrast with the guilt of sin—piety and speculation are condemned to treat *physics* and *morality* (the natura divina and the bonum esse [the divine nature and the being good]) in endless speculations, to see grace in the conjunction of these two elements, with the result that, when the understanding has awakened and discovered its limits, there is an ending up with a bare aliquid (something) and with a morality that underbids itself.   This conclusion is in keeping with the God who is inscrutable self-will, and who, just on that account, has set up an inscrutably arbitrary institution of grace as an establishment for the insurance of life.

The fundamental features of Thomas's doctrine of grace are the following : [1] the *external* principles of moral action are the law aud grace (Summa II. 1, Q. 90): " The exterior principle moving to goodness is God, who both instructs us by the law and aids us by grace."   In Qs. 90-108 the law is treated, and in Q. 107, Art. 4, it is asserted, that although the new law is easier as respects the external commands, it is more difficult as respects the " repression of the inner impulses " (cohibitio inter-

---

[1] On the general scheme in which Thomas has inserted his doctrine of grace, and especially on the significance of the Church as correlate of redemption, see Ritschl. Rechtfertigung, I. vol., 2 ed., p. 86 ff.   The most wonderful thing in Thomas is that in the whole account no notice is taken of the specific nature of grace as gratia Christi.

iorum motuum).[1]   In Qs. 109-114 there follows the doctrine of
grace. Thomas treats first (Q. 109) of the necessity of grace.
In Art. 1 it is laid down that it is impossible without grace to
know any *truth*. The exposition is extremely noteworthy
because it is very strongly determined by Aristotelian influences.[2] At the same time the intellectualism of Thomas comes
out here most distinctly : grace is the communication of supernatural *knowledge* ; but the " light of grace " (lumen gratiæ) is,
moreover, " *superadded* to nature " (naturæ superadditum). In
both these views a disastrous step forward is taken ; for what
is " superadded " is not necessary to the accomplishment of
man's end, but reaches beyond it, may therefore be wanting, or
establishes, if it is present, a superhuman worth, and hence a
merit. Only now in Art. 2 is the relation of grace to moral
goodness spoken of. Here appears at once the consequence of the "superadditum." To man in his state of integrity
the capacity is ascribed to do in his own strength " the good
proportionate to his nature " (bonum suæ naturæ proportion-

---

[1] " Quantum ad opera virtutum in interioribus actibus præcepta novæ legis sunt
graviora præceptis veteris legis."   The later Schoolmen did not indeed directly
contest this position, but they asserted that through the Sacraments the defective
fulfilment of the commands of the new law is supplemented.

[2] " Cognoscere veritatem est usus quidam vel actus intellectualis luminis ('omne
quod manifestatur lumen est '), usus autem quilibet quendam *motum* importat . . .
videmus autem in corporalibus, quod ad motum non solum requiritur ipsa forma, quæ
est principium motus vel actionis, sed etiam requiritur motio primi moventis.   Primum
autem movens in ordine corporalium est corpus cæleste."   This is now applied to the
motus spirituales, whose ultimate author must therefore be God, " ideo quantumcunque
natura aliqua corporalis vel spiritualis ponatur perfecta, non potest in suum actum
procedere nisi moveatur a deo, quæ quidem motio est secundum suæ providentiæ
rationem, non secundum necessitatem naturæ, sicut motio corporis cœlestis.   Non
solum autem a deo est omnis motio, sicut a primo movente, sed etiam ab ipso est
omnis formalis perfectio, sicut a primo actu.   Sic igitur actio intellectus et cuju;-
cunque entis creati dependet et a deo quantum ad duo.   Uno modo in quantum ab
ipso habet perfectionem sive formam per quam agit, alio modo in quantum ab ipso
movetur ad agendum.   Intellectus humanus habet aliquam formam, scil. ipsum
intelligibile lumen, quod est de se sufficiens ad quædam intelligibilia cognoscenda
. . . altiora vero intelligibilia intellectus humanus cognoscere non potest, nisi fortiori
lumine perficiatur . . . quod dicitur lumen gratiæ, in quantum est naturæ superadditum.   Sic igitur dicendum est, quod ad cognitionem cujuscunque veri homo indiget
auxilio divino, ut intellectus a deo moveatur ad suum actum, non autem indiget ad
cognoscendam veritatem in omnibus nova illustratione superaddita naturali illustra-
tioni, sed in quibusdam quæ excedunt naturalem cognitionem."

atum)—God only comes into view here, as everywhere else, as
"primus movens" (the primary mover); yet divine help was
needed in order to obtain a meritorious "bonum superexcedens"
(surplus goodness). But after the Fall there is need in order to
both these ends of grace, which must first restore man's nature.
Accordingly a twofold grace is required by him here. In this
way the distinction is already drawn between gratia operans
and gratia cooperans, and at the same time *there is contemplated
as man's goal a supernatural state, which can only be reached by
help of the second grace, which produces merits.*[1] In Art. 3 the
question as to whether man can love God above all things without grace is dealt with in the same way : Nature before the
Fall is certainly capable of that; for it is "quiddam connaturale homini" (something congenial to man); but after the Fall
nature is incapable of it.   "Man in the state of unfallen nature
did not need the gift of grace superadded to natural goodness
(naturalibus bonis) for loving God naturally above all things,
though he needed the aid of God moving him to this, but in the
state of corrupt nature man needs also for this the help of grace
that heals nature."[2] In Art. 5 it is said regarding the question
as to whether without grace man can merit eternal life, that
every nature can, by its action, only bring about an effect which
is proportionate to its strength.   "*But eternal life is an end ex-
ceeding the proportions (proportionem) of human nature*; hence
man cannot in his own strength produce meritorious works
which are proportionate to eternal life. *Therefore without grace*

---

[1] "In statu naturæ integræ quantum ad sufficientiam operativæ virtutis poterat
homo per sua naturalia velle et operari bonum suæ naturæ proportionatum, quale est
bonum virtutis acquisitæ, non autem bonum superexcedens, quale est bonum virtutis
infusæ ; sed in statu naturæ corruptæ etiam deficit homo ab hoc, quod secundum
suam naturam potest, ut non possit totum hujusmodi bonum implere per sua
naturalia.   Quia tamen natura humana per peccatum non est totaliter corrupta, ut
scil. tanto bono naturæ privetur, potest quidem etiam in statu naturæ corruptæ per
virtutem suæ naturæ aliquod bonum particulare agere, non tamen totum bonum sibi
connaturale." He must be healed auxilio medicinæ. "Sic igitur virtute gratuita
superaddita virtuti naturæ indiget homo in statu naturæ integræ, quantum ad unum
scil. ad operandum et volendum bonum supernaturale, sed in statu naturæ corruptæ
quantum ad duo, scil. ut sanetur et ulterius ut bonum supernaturalis virtutis operetur,
quod est meritorium."
[2] In Art. 4 the fulfilling of the law of God is treated in the same way.

man cannot merit eternal life." Nothing is said here of merits
de congruo, nay, in Art. 6 it is denied that by natural good
deeds man can prepare for this grace ;[1] no doubt conversion to
God comes about in free will, but the will cannot turn to God
unless God converts it ; for man cannot raise himself independently from the state of sin without grace,[2] cannot even in this
state avoid with certainty mortal sins (Art. 8), nay even the
redeemed man needs grace in order not to fall into sin ;[3] hence
perseverance is also a special gift of grace.[4]

After this, in Q. 110, the *essence* of grace is described. The
inquiry begins very characteristically with the question " whether
grace places anything in the soul" (utrum gratia ponat aliquid

[1] " Quod homo convertatur ad deum, hoc non potest esse nisi deo ipsum con-
vertente, hoc autem est præparare se ad gratiam, quasi ad deum converti . . . homo
non potest se præparare ad lumen gratiæ suscipiendum, nisi per auxilium gratuitum dei
interius moventis."

[2] Art. 7 : " Cum enim peccatum transiens actu, remaneat reatu, non est idem
resurgere a peccato, quod cessare ab actu peccati, sed resurgere a peccato est reparari
hominem ad ea quæ peccando amisit." Sin has three evils as its consequences,
macula, corruptio naturalis boni, reatus culpæ. None of these results can be
removed otherwise than by God.

[3] Art. 9 : " homo ad recte vivendum dupliciter auxilio dei indiget. Uno quidem
modo quantum ad aliquod habituale donum, per quod natura humana corrupta
sanetur et etiam sanata elevetur ad operanda opera meritoria vitæ æternæ, quæ
excedunt proportionem naturæ. Alio modo indiget homo auxilio gratiæ, ut a deo
moveatur ad agendum. Quantum igitur ad primum auxilii modum, homo in gratia
existens non indiget alio auxilio gratiæ quasi aliquo alio habitu infuso, indiget tamen
auxilio gratiæ secundum alium modum, ut scil. a deo moveatur ad recte agendum, et
hoc propter duo. First generally (nulla res creata potest in quemcunque actum
prodire nisi virtute motionis divinæ), second specially, propter conditionem status
humanæ naturæ, quæ quidem licet per gratiam sanetur quantum ad mentem, remanet
tamen in ea corruptio et infectio quantum ad carnem per quam servit legi peccati ;
remanet etiam quædam ignorantiæ obscuritas in intellectu ; propter varios enim rerum
eventus *et quia etiam nos ipsos non perfectæ cognoscimus*, non possumus ad plenum
scire quid nobis expediat, et ideo necesse est nobis, ut a deo dirigamur et protegamur
qui omnia novit et omnia potest. Et propter hoc etiam renatis in filios dei per
gratiam convenit dicere : Et ne nos inducas in tentationem, et fiat voluntas
tua, etc."

[4] Art. 10 (strictly Augustinian, against Pelagius) : " Ad perseverantiam habendam
homo in gratia constitutus non quidem indiget aliqua alia habituali gratia, sed divino
auxilio ipsum dirigente et protegente contra tentationum impulsus . . . et ideo postquam aliquis est justificatus per gratiam, necesse habet a deo petere prædictum
perseverantiæ donum, ut scil. custodiatur a malo usque ad finem vitæ : *multis enim
datur gratia, quibus non datur perseverare in gratia.*"

in anima).   Here it is laid down that gratia has a threefold
meaning = benevolent disposition, free gift without equivalent,
and thanks.   Divine grace is not only benevolent disposition,
but also gift, and therefore " it is manifest that grace places
something in him who receives grace."   Now the definition:
" Thus, therefore, by man's being said to have the grace of God,
there is signified something supernatural in man proceeding
from God.   Sometimes, however, the grace of God is a designation for God's eternal love itself, as it is also called the grace of
predestination, in so far as God has predestinated or chosen
some gratuitously, and not on the ground of merit " (sic igitur
per hoc, quod dicitur homo gratiam dei habere, significatur
quiddam supernaturale in homine a deo proveniens.   Quandoque
tamen gratia dei dicitur ipsa æterna dei dilectio, secundum quod
dicitur etiam gratia prædestinationis, in quantum deus gratuito
et non ex meritis aliquos prædestinavit sive elegit).[1]   But as
grace "places something in the soul," *it is also a quality of the
soul, i.e.*, in addition to the help by which God in general moves
the soul to good action, He *infuses into it a supernatural quality.*[2]
In the two following articles (3 and 4) it is now proved that
grace is not only the being filled with this or that quality (not
only with love even), but that it is related to the infused virtues
as the natural light of reason (lumen rationis) to the acquired
virtues (virtutes acquisitæ), and that it is to be regarded therefore as participation in the divine nature by means of an
illumination penetrating the whole being, whereby the true
sonship to God comes to exist.[3]

---

[1] Art. 1.

[2] Art. 2: " . . . multo magis illis quos movet ad consequendum bonum supernaturale æternum, *infundit aliquas formas seu qualitates supernaturales, secundum
quas suaviter et prompte ab ipso moveantur ad bonum æternum consequendum.*"

[3] Art. 3: " Sicut lumen naturale rationis est aliquid præter virtutes acquisitas, quæ
dicuntur in ordine ad ipsum lumen naturale, ita etiam ipsum lumen gratiæ, *quod est
participatio divinæ naturæ*, est aliquid præter virtutes infusas, quæ a lumine illo derivantur et ad illud lumen ordinantur."   Hence because grace is not a mere virtue,
but aliquid virtute prius, it is not placed in aliqua potentiarum animæ, but in the
essence of the soul itself.   " Sicut enim per potentiam *intellectivam* homo participat
cognitionem divinam per virtutem *fidei*, et secundum potentiam *voluntatis amorem*
divinum per virtutem *caritatis, ita etiam per naturam animæ participat secundum
quandam similitudinem naturam divinam, per quandam regenerationem*" (Art. 4).

From this point, in Q. 111, the division of grace is sketched. And, first, a distinction is drawn between gratia gratum faciens (by which man is united to God [qua ipse homo deo conjungitur]), and gratia gratis data (the priestly official grace, by which the man himself is not justified, but the justification of another is contemplated [qua non homo ipse justificatur, sed justificatio alterius comparatur]). It is worthy of note that Thomas begins with this distinction (Art. 1). Then follows the separation of grace into gratia operans and gratia co-operans (that by which He moves us to good volition and action—gift of habit divinely imparted to us [illa, qua nos movet ad bene volendum et agendum—habituale donum nobis divinitus inditum]); it is justified by the proposition : " the operation of any *effect* is not attributed to that which moves, but to the mover " (operatio alicujus effectus non attribuitur mobili, sed moventi). In the effect, so far as our soul is mota non movens (the moved, not moving) the gratia operans appears ; in the effect, so far as it is mota movens (the moved, moving) the gratia cooperans appears (Art. 2).[1]   Parallel with this is the division into gratia præveniens and gratia subse-

---

[1] Note also : "Est autem in nobis duplex actus ; primus quidem interior voluntatis ; et quantum ad istum actum, voluntas se habet ut mota, deus autem ut movens, et præsertim cum voluntas incipit bonum velle, quæ prius malum volebat.   Et ideo secundum quod deus movet humanam mentem ad hunc actum, dicitur gratia *operans*. Alius autem actus est exterior qui cum a voluntate imperetur consequens est quod ad hunc actum operatio attribuatur voluntati.   Et quia etiam ad hunc actum deus nos adjuvat et interius confirmando voluntatem, ut ad actum perveniat, et exterius facultatem operandi præbendo, respectu hujusmodi actus dicitur gratia *cooperans*.   (There follows a proof-passage from Augustine).   Si igitur gratia accipiatur pro gratuita dei motione, quia movet nos ad bonum meritorium convenienter dividitur gratia per operantem, et cooperantem.   Si vero accipiatur gratia pro habituali dono, sic est duplex gratiæ effectus, sicut et cujuslibet alterius formæ, quorum primus est *esse*, secundus est *operatio*. . . . Sic igitur habitualis gratia, in quantum animam sanat vel justificat sive gratam deo facit, dicitur gratia *operans*, in quantum vero est principium operis meritorii, quod ex libero arbitrio procedit, dicitur *cooperans*."   At an earlier point Thomas had already made an analogous distinction with regard to righteousness (justitia) ; see II., 1 Q. 100, Art. 12 : " Si loquamur de justificatione proprie dicta sic considerandum est, quod justitia potest accipi prout est in *habitu* vel prout est in *actu*, et secundum hoc justificatio dupliciter dicitur.   Uno quidem modo secundum quod homo fit justus adipiscens *habitum justitiæ*.   Alio vero modo, secundum quod *opera justitiæ* operatur, ut secundum hoc justificatio nihil aliud sit quam *justitiæ exsecutio*.   Justitia autem, sicut aliæ virtutes, potest accipi et *acquisita et infusa*.   Acquisita quidem causatur ex operibus, sed infusa causatur ab ipso deo per ejus gratiam, et hæc est *vera justitia*, secundum quam aliquis dicitur justus apud deum."

quens (Art. 3).[1] In Art. 4 the gratia gratis data, *i.e.*, the grace
with which one helps others (for the edification of the community, official grace), is subjected to a further division according to 1 Cor. xi., and in Art. 5 it is shown that the gratia gratum
faciens is to be valued much more highly than the gratia gratis
data.

In Q. 112 the causæ gratiæ (causes of grace) are now considered. That God alone can be the cause is deduced in a
genuinely Old Catholic way from the conception of grace as
deifica (making divine).[2] Hence man cannot even prepare
himself for this grace, the preparation rather, *which is necessary*,
must be effected by grace itself,[3] therefore the act of preparation
for gratia infusa is not meritorious, for although every forma
presupposes a materia *disposita* (prepared), yet it holds good
even in the things of nature that "the preparedness of the
material does not necessarily secure form save by virtue of the
agent who causes the preparedness" (dispositio materiæ non ex
necessitate consequitur formam nisi per virtutem agentis, qui
dispositionem causat).[4] This gratia gratum faciens can be
smaller in the one, greater in the other, just because it is a free

---

[1] " Sicut gratia dividitur in operantem et cooperantem secundum diversos affectus,
ita etiam in prævenientem et subsequentem, qualitercumque gratia accipiatur. Sunt
autem quinque effectus gratiæ in nobis, quorum primus est ut anima sanetur, secundus
est, ut bonum velit, tertius est, ut bonum quod vult efficaciter operetur, quartus est, ut
in bono perseveret, quintus est, ut ad gloriam perveniat. Et ideo gratia secundum
quod causat in nobis primum effectum, vocatur præveniens, respectu secundi effectus
et prout causat in nobis secundum, vocatur subsequens respectu primi effectus."

[2] "Cum donum gratiæ nihil aliud sit quam quædam participatio divinæ naturæ, quæ
excedit omnem aliam naturam, ideo impossibile est quod aliqua creatura gratiam causet.
Sic enim necesse est, quod solus deus deificet, communicando consortium divinæ
naturæ per quandam similitudinis participationem, sicut impossibile est, quod aliquid
igniat nisi solus ignis " (Art. 1).

[3] The thought is this, that gratia as *habituale* donum dei requires a preparation, because (Aristotelian) " nulla *forma* potest esse nisi in materia disposita ; sed si loquamur de gratia secundum quod significat auxilium dei *moventis ad bonum* (that is, the
gratia prima), nulla præparatio requiritur ex parte hominis, quasi præveniens divinum
auxilium." With this momentous distinction the dissolution of Augustinianism took
its beginning.

[4] Art. 3 : " Præparatio hominis ad gratiam est a deo sicut a movente, a libero autem
arbitrio sicut a moto . . . Secundum quod est a libero arbitrio, nullam necessitatem
habet ad gratiæ consecutionem."

gift;[1] but because it is something supernatural, no one here
below to whom it is not specially revealed can know for certain
whether he possess it.[2]

There follows in Qs. 113 and 114 the inquiry into the effects
of grace. In correspondence with the distinction between gratia
operans and gratia cooperans the effect of grace is twofold—
justification and meritorious good works; but even in justification the will must co-operate. Only the very first point is distinguished by the sole efficiency of grace. This comes out at

___

[1] This also is a momentous, as it is also an Augustinian, proposition, due likewise to
thinking of grace as gratia infusa (habitus). No doubt Thomas further explains, that
ex parte finis the greatness of grace always remains the same ("conjungens hominem
summo bono, quod est deus"). But "ex parte subjecti gratia potest suscipere magis
vel minus, prout scil. unus perfectius illustratur a lumine gratiæ quam alius. *Cujus
diversitatis ratio quidem est aliqua ex parte præparantis se ad gratiam, qui enim magis
se ad gratiam præparat pleniorem gratiam accipit.*" This position was the main source
of disaster for the period that followed : there was naturally the growing tendency to
think more of the præparatio than of the causa, and to overlook the addition which
Thomas had appended : "sed hac ex parte non potest accipi prima ratio hujus
diversitatis, quia præparatio ad gratiam non est hominis, nisi in quantum liberum
arbitrium ejus præparatur a deo. Unde prima causa hujus diversitatis accipienda est
ex parte ipsius dei, qui diversimode suæ gratiæ dona dispensat ad hoc quod ex diversis
gradibus pulchritudo et perfectio ecclesiæ consurgat, sicut etiam diversos gradus rerum
instituit, ut esset universum perfectum." This explanation manifestly leads in quite a
different direction from the one mentioned first, with which it is associated ; for in the
case of the former it is really a question about a more or less, in the case of the latter,
on the other hand, it is a question about *varieties*, which are necessary to the per-
fectness of the beautiful whole. But Thomas could unite the two explanations in
accordance with his ontology, because, like Augustine, he regarded ultimately even
the less good as necessary in the cosmic system, since it is just in this way that the
beauty of the whole comes out in the manifoldness of its parts. Of course this reflection simply cancels the ethical mode of contemplation and transforms it into the
æsthetic. Thus, so far as Thomas does not derive the existence of more or less grace
from the dispositio (præparatio) hominis, but traces it rather to God, *he knows only of
æsthetic ways of justifying it* (Art. 4).

[2] This is the third momentous position (Art. 5): "Nullus potest scire, se
habere gratiam, certitudinaliter; certitudo enim non potest haberi de aliquo, nisi
possit dijudicari per proprium principium." No one is sure of a conclusion, who does
not know the major premiss. "Principium autem gratiæ et objectum ejus est ipse
deus, *qui propter sui excellentiam est nobis ignotus.*" One can only ascertain the
possession of grace conjecturaliter (per aliqua signa). But one can very well *be sure
of possessing scientia and fides*, "*non est autem similis ratio de gratia et caritate.*"
We see here what ruin was wrought by the thought of gratia infusa as a mysterious
habitus which is applied to the soul ! But this habitus, of which one cannot be
certain, corresponds with the deus ignotus !

once in Art. 1 (Q. 113). Thomas raises the question whether
the justification of the sinner is the remission of sins (utrum
justificatio impii sit remissio peccatorum?), and in an extremely
round-about explanation he answers at bottom with no, although
he apparently replies to the question in the affirmative.   He
lays it down, that is to say, that "justification, passively received,
introduces an *impulse towards righteousness*" (justificatio passive
accepta importat motum ad justitiam), but that it comes into
view here "as a certain change (transmutatio) from a state of
unrighteousness to a state of righteousness."   "And because
movement is described rather from the terminus ad quem than
from the terminus a quo, so a change (transmutatio) of this
kind, by which one is changed (transmutatur) from a state of
unrighteousness into a state of righteousness, derives its name
from the terminus ad quem, and is called the justification of the
sinner"; in other words : the actual justification does not yet
take place through the "remission of sins," but only on account
of the *contemplated end* can it be said that forgiveness of sins is
already justification ; in reality, however, justification—as a
translation into a new state—only takes place later.   This
becomes still plainer, when it is affirmed in Art. 2 that even for
the forgiveness of sins the gratia infusa is necessary.   This has
the effect, certainly, of introducing a bad confusion ; for if the
position : "remission of guilt cannot be understood where there
is no infusion of grace" (non potest intelligi remissio culpæ, si
non adest infusio gratiæ) is correct (it is proved by the reflection
that forgiveness of sins *presupposes* "the effect of divine love"
in us, *i.e.*, presupposes that we love God in return), then forgiveness of sins, instead of being the first thing, is the last, and one
must ask himself, what then is really the effect of the gratia
præveniens (in the strictest sense)?   Is it mere vocatio (calling),
or something undefinable?   Thomas here got astray with his
own distinctions, or—in a highly characteristic way—he left in
darkness what man owes to prevenient grace.   In accordance
with this it is pointed out in Arts. 3-5, that for justification there
must already co-operate a movement of free will (motus liberi
arbitrii), a movement of faith (motus fidei) and a hatred of sin
(odium peccati), *i.e.*, we are at once led on to contemplate the

intermingling of grace and self-activity.[1]   Only now does justification take place (Art. 6); for " four things are to be reckoned
(enumerantur) which are required for the justification of the
sinner, *viz.*, the infusion of grace, the movement of free will in
relation to God (in deum) by faith, and the movement of free
will in relation to sin (in peccatum), and the remission of guilt
(this last *follows*, then, from the three other things); the reason
of which is that, as has been said, justification is a certain movement by which the soul is moved by God from a state of guilt
into a state of righteousness ; but in any movement by which
anything is moved by another, three things are required.   First,
the moving (motio) of the mover himself ; second, the movement
as in motion (motus mobilis) ; third, the consummation of the
movement, or the arrival at the goal.   From the side (ex parte),
therefore, of the divine moving there is received the infusion
of grace, from the side of free will the retirement and advance
(recessus et accessus) of movement, while the consummation or
arrival at the goal of this movement is brought about (impor-
tatur) by the remission of guilt.   *For in this justification is con-
summated."* [2]   But although justification culminates in the
forgiveness of sins, yet, as will appear, the whole process does
not yet culminate in justification.   Of this justification of the
sinner it is further taught (Art. 7), that it is effected " originaliter "
at the moment of *infusion,* and that *" it is realised instantane-
ously and without succession "* (in instanti fit absque successione).
The difficulty, that the giving of *form* (infusion) can only take
place in materia disposita (in prepared matter) is set aside by
saying, that " for the infusion of grace into the soul God does

---

[1] Art. 3: "In eo, qui habet usum liberi arbitrii, non fit motio a deo ad justitiam
absque motu liberi arbitrii, sed ita infundit donum gratiæ justificantis, quod etiam
simul cum hoc movet liberum arbitrium ad donum gratiæ acceptandum in his, quæ
sunt hujus motionis capaces." 4: "deus movet animam hominis convertendo eam
ad se ipsum . . . prima conversio ad deum fit per fidem . . . ideo motus fidei
requiritur ad justificationem impii." 5: "recessus et accessus in motu liberi arbitrii
accipitur secundum detestationem et desiderium . . . oportet igitur quod in justificatione impii sit motus liberi arbitrii duplex, unus quo per desiderium tendat in dei
justitiam, et alius, quo detestetur peccatum."

[2] It may be remarked, by the way, that here and there in the Middle Ages it is
related that those specially endowed with grace *detected* (sensibiliter) the infusion of
grace, felt with the sense of taste a sweetness, etc.

not require any disposition save that which He Himself creates. But He creates a disposition of this kind sufficient for the reception of grace, sometimes indeed suddenly, but sometimes gradually and in stages" (ad hoc quod gratiam infundat animæ, non requirit aliquam dispositionem, nisi quam ipse facit. Facit autem hujusmodi dispositionem sufficiēntem ad susceptionem gratiæ quandoque quidem subito quandoque autem paulatim et successive).[1]   In what follows, the order of the process is now inverted in a bold way (Art. 8): from the point of view of time the four things named above coincide, but causally they follow each other thus—(1) the infusion of grace; (2) the movement towards God in love; (3) the turning from sin; (4) the forgiveness of guilt.   The legitimacy of this inversion is not proved by Thomas; the aim in view is manifest; grace must stand at the beginning.   But because he is averse to distinguishing a grace which is not infused, but is simply the awakening of trust (fiducia), he cannot allow validity to the scheme which would really correspond with his mode of thought, namely, (1) a grace that is merely movens; (2) faith (fides); (3) detestation of sin; (4) remission of guilt; (5) infused grace (gratia infusa).   He, therefore, places infused grace first " causally " (causaliter) (from the correct reflection that at all events the precedence belongs to this), but it is a mere assertion, which he himself cannot effectively prove, that this gratia is infusa ; for its effects do not correspond with this.   The confusion which, on closer inspection, we at once see to have been introduced by him here,[2] was not without its influence in the period that followed.   In the concluding view taken of justification (Arts. 9 and 10), it is laid down that it is not only a great work (opus magnum) of God,

---

[1] The exposition is again cosmological (Aristotelian): " Quod enim agens naturale non subito possit disponere materiam, contingit ex hoc, quod est aliqua proportio ejus quod in materia resistit ad virtutem agentis et propter hoc videmus, quod quanto virtus agentis fuerit fortior, tanto materia citius disponitur.   Cum igitue virtus divina sit infinita, potest quamcunque materiam creatam subito disponere, etc. etc."

[2] It shews itself, e.g., in the contradiction Art. 8 ad Primum, where he says: " Quia infusio gratiæ et remissio culpæ dicuntur ex parte dei justificantis, ideo ordine naturæ *prior* est gratiæ infusio quam culpæ remissio.   Sed si sumantur ea quæ ex parte hominis justificati, *est ex converso ;* nam prius est ordine naturæ liberatio a culpa, quam consecutio gratiæ justificantis."   But only the one thing or the other holds good. It is the worst scholasticism to assert that the two views can be held together.

but is really even a miraculous work (opus miraculosum); but at bottom the latter holds good only of sudden conversions: "certain miraculous works, although they are less than the justification of the sinner, so far as the good that comes into existence is concerned, are, nevertheless, beyond the usual order of such effects, and therefore have more of the nature of miracle" ("quædam miraculosa opera, esti sunt minora quam justificatio impii quantum ad bonum quod fit, sunt tamen præter consuetum ordinem talium effectuum et ideo plus habent de ratione miraculi"). This exhausts justification, yet not the whole process; only now, rather, are the effects first considered which are imparted through grace in an increasing measure to *him who is already justified. They are all placed under the head of merit* (Q. 114). First, the question is raised whether man can acquire merit at all before God (Art. 1). The answer runs: not in the absolute sense of strict righteousness, but certainly in virtue of a benevolent arrangement of God.[1] Then in accordance with this it is declared impossible that anyone should merit for himself eternal life, even if he lives in the state of unfallen nature (in statu

[1] This is the religious robe that is thrown over the irreligious "merit." Thomas says that meritum and merces are the same = retributio as pretium of a deed. Justitia in the strict sense exists only inter eos, quorum est simpliciter æqualitas. Where therefore there is simpliciter justum, there is also simpliciter meritum vel merces. In other cases there exists at the most a meritum secundum quid (not justum). But between God and men there is the greatest inequality, and all goodness which man has springs from God; hence there is here, not a meritum simpliciter, but certainly a meritum "*in quantum uterque operatur secundum modum suum.*" But the modus humanæ virtutis is appointed by God; "ideo meritum hominis apud deum esse non potest nisi secundum persuppositionem divinæ ordinationis, ita scil. ut id homo consequatur a deo per operationem *quasi mercedem*, ad quod deus ei virtutem operandi deputavit." Still it is to be noted here, that Thomas does not determine merit purely according to the arbitrary will of God; it is estimated rather by the faculty and end of man. Yet in the period that followed, there was an adhering always more closely, because it was more convenient, and because the conception of God admitted of it to pure arbitrariness as respects meritoriousness, and a relying on the Church's being initiated into the purposes of this arbitrariness. But in this article Thomas has a still further addition that is not without its significance; he continues: "Sicut etiam res naturales hoc consecuntur per proprios motus et operationes, ad quod a deo sunt ordinatæ, differenter tamen, quia creatura rationalis se ipsam movet ad agendum per liberum arbitrium. Unde sua actio habet rationem meriti, quod non est in aliis creaturis." It is implied therefore in the *nature* of free will that it acquires merits; in Art. 4, *e.g.*, in addition to the thesis that the meritorious originates ex ordinatione divina, Thomas has made an independent use of this thesis.

naturæ integræ) (Art. 2); for "eternal life is something good that
exceeds the proportions of created nature" (vita æterna est
quoddam bonum excedens proportionem naturæ creatæ).[1] On
the other hand, to the question, whether the man who is in a
state of grace can merit eternal life "ex condigno," no explicit
answer is given.[2] The decision rather runs (Art. 3), "meritorious
work of man can be looked at in two ways; on the one hand
in so far as it proceeds from free will, on the other hand
in so far as it proceeds from the grace of the Holy Spirit.
If it is looked at with respect to the substance of work and
in so far as it proceeds from free will, there cannot here be
condignity on account of the very great inequality of proportions.
For it appears *congruous*, that man working according to his
virtue should be rewarded by God according to the excellence of
his virtue.   But if we speak of meritorious work with respect to
what proceeds from the grace of the Holy Spirit, it is in this
case meritorious of eternal life ex condigno.   For here the value
of the merit is estimated according to the power of the Holy
Spirit who moves us to eternal life.   The reward also of the
work is estimated by the dignity of the grace by which man,
made a participant of the divine nature, is adopted as a son of
God, to whom inheritance is due in virtue of the very right of
adoption " (opus meritorium hominis dupliciter considerari
potest; uno modo, secundum quod procedit ex libero arbitrio,
alio modo, secundum quod procedit ex gratia spiritus sancti. Si
consideretur secundum substantiam operis et secundum quod
procedit ex libero arbitrio, sic non potest ibi esse condignitas
propter maximam inæqualitatem proportionis.   Videtur enim
congruum, ut homini operanti secundum suam virtutem deus
recompenset secundum excellentiam suæ virtutis.   Si autem
loquamur de opere meritorio secundum quod procedit ex gratia
spiritus sancti, sic est meritorium vitæ æternæ ex condigno.
Sic enim valor meriti attenditur secundum virtutem spiritus
sancti moventis nos in vitam æternam.   Attenditur etiam

---

[1] "Nulla natura creata est sufficiens principium actus meritorii vitæ æternæ, nisi
superaddatur aliquod supernaturale donum, quod gratia dicitur."

[2] " Ex condigno "=in a truly meritorious way, as contrasted with " ex congruo "=
in the way of a performance, to which, when a benevolent view is taken of it, a
certain worth and therefore also a certain merit can be attributed.

pretium operis secundum dignitatem gratiæ, per quam homo
consors factus divinæ naturæ adoptatur in filium dei, cui debetur
hæreditas ex ipso jure adoptionis). The same thing, then, is in
one respect ex condigno, in another respect ex congruo! The
period that followed was not satisfied with this, but attributed to
human merit a higher worth ; but to this Thomas himself gave
the impulse. In Art. 4 it is shown that the meritorious principle
is love, whether we look at merit ex ordinatione divina (by divine
arrangement), or at merit "in so far as man has, beyond other
creatures, the power of acting for himself as a voluntary agent"
(in quantum homo habet præ ceteris creaturis ut per se agat
voluntarie agens). In both cases it can easily be shown, that in
love and in no other virtue merit consists.[1] In view of the
principle "any act of love merits absolutely eternal life"

---

[1] Here in Arts. 5-7, as if by way of giving extra measure, Thomas introduces three
chapters, in which he again expressly shows that one cannot merit the first grace, that
one cannot merit it for another, and that one cannot merit even the reparatio post
lapsum. But the sections are important, for the reason that the decided negative
which Thomas here adopts everywhere was cancelled, or at least modified, in the
period that followed. With regard to the first point, he explains most distinctly that
"omne meritum repugnat gratiæ," hence : "*nullus* sibi mereri potest gratiam
primam." But Thomas did not see that what holds good of the gratia prima holds
good of all grace. Indeed the gratia prima, just because it has nothing to do with
merit, is at bottom an extremely dark phenomenon for him, and this explains his
passing over it so rapidly. He was himself accountable for it therefore, that in the
period that followed even the communication of the gratia prima was attached to
certain merits. The second point is important, because Thomas, in distinction from
the later Schoolmen, here gives Christ the honour, and still keeps Mary and the
saints in the background. He recalls first of all his expositions in Arts. 1 and 3, to
the effect that in the meritorious works of the justified that which free will does is
only a meritum de congruo, and then proceeds : "Ex quo patet, quod merito condigni
nullus potest mereri alteri primam gratiam nisi solus Christus, quia unusquisque
nostrum movetur a deo per donum gratiæ, ut ipsa ad vitam æternam perveniat, et ideo
meritum condigni ultra hanc motionem non se extendit. Sed anima Christi mota est
a deo per gratiam, non solum ut ipse perveniret ad gloriam vitæ æternæ, sed etiam
ut alios in eam adduceret, *in quantum est caput ecclesiæ.* . . . Sed merito congrui
potest aliquis alteri mereri primam gratiam. Quia enim homo in gratia constitutus
implet dei voluntatem congruum est secundum amicitiæ proportionem, ut deus impleat
hominis voluntatem in salvatione alterius." Thus the saints are certainly admitted
by the back-door of meritum de congruo. Regarding the third point it is said :
"Nullus potest sibi mereri reparationem post lapsum futurum, neque merito condigni,
neque merito congrui" ; for the former is excluded, because the grace that might be
the ground of merit is lost by the Fall ("motione prioris gratiæ usque ad hæc [viz.,
the Fall or the mortal sin] non se extendente ") ; the latter becomes in still higher
degree an impossibility through the impedimentum peccati.

(quilibet actus caritatis meretur absolute vitam æternam), it is now asked in Art. 8, whether man can merit the increase (augmentum) of grace or love, and this question is answered roundly in the affirmative ; for "that to which the motion of grace extends falls under merito *condigni*, but the motion of any thing moving extends not only to the ultimate goal of the movement, but also to the whole progress in movement ; but the goal of the movement of grace is eternal life, while the progress in this movement is according to the increase of love. Thus therefore the increase of grace falls under merito condigni" (illud cadit sub merito condigni, ad quod motio gratiæ se extendit, motio autem alicujus moventis non solum se extendit ad ultimum terminum motus, sed etiam ad totum progressum in motu ; terminus autem motus gratiæ est vita æterna, progressus autem in hoc motu est secundum augmentum caritatis. Sic igitur augmentum gratiæ cadit sub merito condigni). On the other hand, the question whether man can also merit *perseverance* in grace is denied in the following article, and thus the ultimate worth of "merit" is cancelled, and a way of return sought for to pure Augustinianism.[1]

In order to form a correct historic estimate of this grace doctrine of Thomas, we must keep in view, in addition to the interest of Christian piety by which he was really guided, and in addition to the practice of the Church, which for him was authoritative, that in the philosophy of religion he was determined by Augustine's doctrines of God and of predestination, and in ethics by Aristotle's doctrines of God and of virtue. Because both were certainties for him, and he therefore made it his business to unite the two, he framed that complicated system of doctrine in which the dexterous, often paradoxical, subtleties of Augustine, the believing sceptic, became as much fundamental tenets as the most direct and confident deliverances of his piety. These fundamental tenets are then placed in connection with the entirely contrasted thoughts of Aristotle, while with wearisome reiteration the definition of God as primum movens is made to

---

[1] "Perseverantia vitæ non cadit sub merito, quia dependet solum ex motione divina, quæ est principium omnis meriti, sed deus gratis perseverantiæ bonum largitur *cuicunque illud largitur.*"

serve as the bridge.   How entirely dependent Thomas is upon
Augustine is shown by the doctrine of predestination, which he
has taken over in all its strictness; [1] how largely dependent he

[1] See Summa I., Q. 23 : Predestination is the providence of God in relation to
creaturæ rationales ; He alone can give them the ultimus finis, *i.e.*, can "appoint
their order." In virtue of His decree, God determines the numerus electorum, and
in so far as it belongs to divine providence "aliquos permittere a vita æterna deficere,"
so also it belongs to it that God should reprobate some. "Sicut enim prædestinatio
includit voluntatem conferendi gratiam et gloriam, ita reprobatio includit voluntatem
permittendi aliquem cadere in culpam et inferendi damnationis pœnam pro culpa"
(Art. 3), nay, l.c., Thomas asserts with chilling sternness that the reprobatio is also
a bonum : "Deus omnes homines diligit et etiam omnes creaturas, in quantum
omnibus vult aliquod bonum ; *non tamen quodcunque bonum vult omnibus. In
quantum igitur quibusdam non vult hoc bonum, quod est vita æterna, diciter eos habere
odio vel reprobare.*" According to this, therefore, there is also a bonum which is no
bonum (for the receiver), and so nothing but the divine will itself : *God loves these
men in hell !* But on the other hand it is also said with Augustine : "Aliter se habet
reprobatio in causando quam prædestinatio. Nam prædestinatio est causa et ejus
quod expectatur in futura vita a prædestinatis, scil. gloriæ, et ejus quod perci-
pitur in præsenti, scil. gratiæ ; reprobatio vero non est causa ejus quod
est in præsenti, scil. culpæ, sed est causa derelictionis a deo (this has not
its source in prescience) ; est tamen causa ejus quod redditur in futuro, scil. pœnæ
acternæ.   Sed culpa provenit ex libero arbitrio ejus, qui reprobatur et a gratia
deseritur." But how shall he not sin if God has forsaken him ?   What does it avail
to add : "reprobatio dei non subtrahit aliquid de potentia reprobati ; unde cum
dicitur quod reprobatur non potest gratiam adipisci, non est hoc intelligendum
secundum impossibilitatem absolutam, sed secundum impossibilitatem condition-
atam"?   It was not easy for Thomas to construe the doctrine of free will, since in the
doctrine of God he had applied throughout the thought of the sole divine causality ;
and in the doctrine of the gubernatio (I., Q. 103) had shown that, just like the
principium mundi, so also the finis mundi is aliquid extra mundum (Art. 2).   But if
the world has no independent end, it follows that the gubernatio must be conceived
of as implying that by Him alone all things are moved, *i.e.*, brought to their goal ;
for they themselves cannot move forward to that, quod est extrinsecum a toto universo.
But by distinguishing the esse and operari, as also the primum movens in things and
the movens ex se, and finally the gubernatio diversa in quantum ad creaturas
irrationales and in quantum ad creaturas per se agentes, Thomas still succeeds in
maintaining free will, which indeed he necessarily requires also, in order to get merit ;
see the discussion of freedom of will, I., 83 (Art. 1 : "Homo est liberi arbitrii,
alioquin frustra essent consilia, exhortationes, præcepta, prohibitiones, præmia et
pœnæ. . . . Liberum arbitrium est causa sui motus, quia homo per liberum arbitrium
seipsum movet ad agendum.   Non tamen hoc est de necessitate libertatis, quod sit
prima causa sui id quod liberum est, sicut nec ad hoc quod aliquid sit causa alterius,
requiritur quod sit prima causa ejus.   Deus igitur est prima causa movens et naturales
causas et voluntarias.   Et sicut naturalibus causis movendo eas non aufert, quin actus
earum sint naturales, ita movendo causas voluntarias non aufert, quin actiones earum
sint voluntariæ, sed potius hoc in eis facit ; operatur in unoquoque secundum ejus
proprietatem "). In accordance with this it is constantly emphasised in the determin-

is upon Aristotle is shown both by his doctrine of God and above all by the Pars Secunda Secundæ, the special doctrine of morals, in which it is demonstrated that virtue consists in the right government of the appetencies and impulses by reason, and is then perfected supernaturally by the gifts of grace. Finally, in order to get a complete view of Thomas's doctrine of grace, we must add his doctrines of the constitution of man, of the primitive state, of the Fall, of original sin and of sin, as they are developed in Parts I., Q. 90-102, and II., 1 Q. 71-89. But we may refrain from presenting these here in fuller detail, partly because Thomas attaches himself closely to Augustine, partly because the chief points have already been specified in the discussion of his doctrine of grace.[1]   Yet his doctrine of the consilia

ing paragraphs on justification that the process of grace realises itself with the *consent* of free will, which consent, however, is at the same time an effect of grace : when God infuses grace, He moves us according to our own proper nature, *i.e.*, in such a way that He moves the free will to the willing acceptance of the gift of grace.   The same thing is said of the virtues ; on the one hand they are likewise infused ; but on the other hand God never acts sine nobis, but always only with the assent of our free will ; for the rational creature is so constituted that in its being impelled by God towards the goal, it must always be impelled consentiente voluntate.

[1] Let us adduce here only a few of the determining positions.   As had been the case already with Augustine, the "primitive state" created a special difficulty for Thomas, inasmuch as on the one hand eternal life was to be regarded as a gift of grace, while on the other hand it was held as certain that it could only be acquired through merit.   It necessarily followed from this that the view taken of the primitive state was indeterminate ; it was not quite conceived of as mere possibilitas boni (in the sense of the highest goodness, quod superexcedit naturam), but neither was it quite thought of as habitus boni.   So Thomas, introducing the idea that the vita æterna is a bonum superexcedens naturam, described the natural equipment of Adam as insufficient for the obtaining of this good, and accordingly assumed that in creation there was given to him over and above the natural equipment a special gratia superaddita, by the help of which his free will should acquire for itself the merit which fits for eternal life ; see I., Q. 95, Art. 1 : Adam received grace at once at creation (not only afterwards)—he was in gratia conditus—for only grace could secure for him the rectitudo, which consists in the subordination of the ratio to God, of the inferiores virtutes to the ratio, of the body to the soul.   But this subordination was not "rationalis" ; for otherwise it would have continued after the Fall ; so it was secundum supernaturale donum gratiæ.   Note also Art. 4 : "Homo etiam ante peccatum indigebat gratia ad vitam æternam consequendam, quæ est principalis necessitas gratiæ."   But this view, still a religious one, had already many breaches made in it before Thomas' time, and these always increased in number ; see below. A further result of this view was that Thomas was not able to identify the *justilia originalis* with the image of God, so far as this image is incapable of being lost, or

evangelica deserves still a special consideration.   This doctrine
forms the conclusion of his discussion of the doctrine of the new
law.   But on the other hand the doctrine of grace also culminates
in the " evangelical counsels," so that in a very real sense these
represent the summit of the whole course of thought.   Thomas
(II., 1 Q. 108, Art. 4) first of all gives the following definition :
" This is the difference between counsel and precept, that precept
introduces (importat) necessity, while counsel is made dependent
on the *option* (in *optione* ponitur) of him to whom it is given, and
so counsels are fittingly (convenienter) added to precepts in the
new law, which is the law of liberty, but not in the old law, which
was the law of servitude (servitutis)."   Thereupon it is remarked
that the " precepts of the new law " are necessary to (but also sufficient for) eternal life, " but there ought to be counsels regarding
those things by which man can attain the appointed end better

say, to unite it with the innate end of human nature, but viewed it as a supernatural
gift, which leads beyond the bonum naturale and the finis naturalis.   The grounds
for this view are easily discovered.   They lie both in the purpose entertained that the
coming into existence of merit shall be proved possible, and in the conceiving of
merit as something supernatural ; in short, in the regarding of asceticism as a state, or
say opus, which is supernatural, meritorious, and which also conducts therefore to
eternal life.   If the supreme good cannot be so described that even the present life
as an end is included in it, then nothing remains but to erect two stories, residence in
the lower story simply serving the purpose of gathering merit for entering the
higher.   The sin which originated with Adam (inherited sin) is loss of the justitia
originalis, and accordingly, as this latter alone effected the ordinatio partium, disorder,
i.e., rebellion of the lower parts against the higher.   On the other hand, the
principia naturæ humanæ continue unaffected by the inherited sin, which is both a
habitus and a culpa, and even the natural capacity of ratio to know and to will the
good is only weakened but not eradicated.   The chief sentences are (II., 1, Q. 82-
89) : " . . . alio modo est habitus dispositio alicujus naturæ ex multis compositæ
secundum quam bene se habet vel male ad aliud . . . hoc modo peccatum originale
est habitus; est enim quædam inordinata dispositio proveniens ex dissolutione illius
harmoniæ, in qua consistebat ratio originalis justitiæ, sicut ægritudo corporalis . . .
unde peccatum originale *languor naturæ* dicitur " (this view is partly æsthetic partly,
pathological, 82, 1).   " Peccatum originale materialiter quidem est concupiscentia,
formaliter vero est defectus originalis justitiæ ;" the former is original sin, because
the " inordinatio virium animæ præcipue in hoc attenditur, quod inordinate convertuntur ad bonum commutabile, quæ quidem inordinatio communi nomine potest dici
concupiscentia " (82, 3).   " Peccatum originale non magis in uno quam in alio esse
potest " (82, 4).   " Anima est subjectum peccati originalis, non autem caro . . . cum
anima possit esse subjectum culpæ, caro autem de se non habeat quod sit subjectum
culpæ, quidquid pervenit de corruptione primi peccati ad animam, habet rationem
culpæ, quod autem pervenit ad carnem, non habet rationem culpæ, sed pœnæ" (83, 1).

and more readily" (consilia vero oportet esse de illis, per quæ
melius et expeditius potest homo consequi finem prædictum).
Then it is explained that here on earth man is placed between the
things of this world and spiritual benefits, and that entire devotion
to the former is removed by the præcepta. Yet on the other hand
man does not require to surrender the things of this world entirely
in order to attain to the goal of eternal life (!), " but he attains
more expeditiously by abandoning (abdicando) totally the good
things of this world, and therefore the evangelical counsels are
given regarding this." But the benefits of this world consist in
the possession of outward goods, in sexual pleasures, and in the
possession of honours, which relate to the lust of the eye, the
lust of the flesh, and the pride of life. To relinquish these
entirely, so far as it is possible—in this consists the evangelical
counsels, and in the adoption of them consists "omnis religio,
quæ statum perfectionis profitetur" (all religion which professes
a state of perfection). The adoption of even one of these
counsels has a corresponding worth, as, *e.g.*, when one gives alms
to a poor man beyond what is obligatory, abstains from marriage
for a long time for the sake of prayer, or does good to his
enemies in excess of what is due, etc. The following of these
counsels is a ground of merit in a still higher degree than the

" Peccatum originale per prius respicit voluntatem " (83, 3). " Cupiditas est radix
omnium peccatorum" (84, 1) ; but, on the other hand, it holds good : " quoniam
inordinate se homo ad temporalia convertens semper singularem quandam perfectionem et excellentiam tamquam finem desiderat, recte ex hac parte superbia, quæ
inordinatus est propriæ excellentiæ appetitus, initium omnis peccati ponitur" (84, 2).
With regard to the consequences of sin : " Principia naturæ (primum bonum naturæ)
nec tolluntur nec diminuuntur per peccatum (empirico-psychological observation, to
which, however, a certain worth also is given for the religious mode of apprehension),
inclinatio ad virtutem a natura insita (secundum bonum naturale) diminuitur per
peccatum (ethical observation, but important for religion), donum originalis justitiæ
(tertium bonum naturæ) totaliter est ablatum " (religious view, v. 85, 1).   That sin can
ever remove totally the inclinatio of the ratio ad bonum is described as unthinkable,
since, according to Augustine, " malum non est nisi in bono " (85, 2). " Omnes
vires animæ remanent quodammodo destitutæ proprio ordine, quo naturaliter ordinantur ad virtutem, et ipsa destitutio dicitur vulneratio naturæ (vulnus ignorantiæ,
malitiæ, infirmitatis, concupiscentiæ" v. 85, 3).   " Mors et omnes defectus corporales
consequentes sunt quædam pœnæ originalis peccati, quamvis non sint intenti a peccanti"
(85, 5). Death is natural to man secundum naturam universalem, non quidem a
parte formæ, sed materiæ (85, 6). Q. 86 treats de macula peccati ; Q. 87 de reatu
pœnæ ; P. 88 and 89 de peccato veniali et mortali.

following of the commands, so that here in a pre-eminent way it holds good, that God gives eternal life to man, not merely in grace, but also by virtue of His righteousness. [1]

Thomas's doctrine of grace, when judged of from the standpoint of religion, presents two faces. On the one hand it looks back to Augustine, [2] on the other hand it looks forward to the dissolution which Augustinianism was to undergo in the fourteenth century. Whoever examines Thomism carefully, will find that its author makes an earnest endeavour, by means of a strictly religious mode of view, to assert the sole efficacy of divine grace ; but on the other hand he will be compelled to note, that *at almost all decisive points the line of statement takes ultimately a different direction*, the reason being that the effect of grace itself is seen in a contemplated end that has a character partly hyperphysical, partly moral ("participation in the divine nature," and "love," conjoined by the thought that love merits eternal life). [3] But as compared with what was presented by Halesius, Bonaventura and others, or, with what was taught at the time, Thomism was already a *religious reaction ;* for those theologians yielded to a much more decided tendency to render

---

[1] See the voluminous exposition in S. II., 2 Q. 184-189, "de statu perfectionis" (bishops and monks), where in Q. 184, Art. 2, the triplex perfectio is described, and it is said of that which is possible here on earth, that it is not indeed attainable that one "in actu semper feratur in deum," but it is attainable that "ab affectu hominis excluditur non solum illud quod est caritati contrarium, sed etiam omne illud quod impedit ne affectus mentis totaliter dirigatur ad deum "; the whole idea of the consilia in particular of virginitas already in Pseudo-Cyprian (= Novatian) de bono pud. 7 : " Virginitas quid aliud est quam futuræ vitæ gloriosa meditatio ?"

[2] It may also be traced back to Augustine that from Thomas, as has been already remarked, the specific nature of grace propter Christum and per Christum never receives clear expression in the whole doctrine of grace. The connection is simply now and again asserted, but is not distinctly demonstrated, *while the whole doctrine of grace is treated completely prior to the doctrine of the person of Christ.* Is that accidental? No, certainly not ! It comes out here again, that in the West, because the Mystic-Cyrillian theory was not maintained (Soterology and Soteriology as identical), there had come to be—in spite of Anselm—entire uncertainty as to how really Christology was to be dogmatically utilised. The only possible solution was not found, namely in adhering, without theoretic speculation, to the impression produced by the person who awakens spirit and life, certainty and blessedness.

[3] Therefore *faith* also, and forgiveness of sins play, in spite of all that is said of them, an insignificant part. Faith is either fides informis, that is, *not yet faith*, or fides formata, that is, *no longer faith*. Faith as inward fiducia is a transitional stage.

the doctrine of grace less effectual by means of the doctrine of merit. By the appearing of Thomas, a development was *checked*, which, apart from him, would have asserted itself much more rapidly, but which in the end, nevertheless (from the middle of the fourteenth century), gained, through the victorious conflicts of the Scotists against the Thomists, the ascendency in the Church, thereby calling forth a new reaction, which seems to have slowly gathered force from the close of the fourteenth century.[1]

At all points, from the doctrines as to the nature of man and as to the primitive state, on to the doctrine of final perfection, there are apparent the dissolving tendencies of the later scholasticism, led by Halesius, Bonaventura and Scotus.

1. Halesius, who was also the first to introduce into dogmatics the expression "supernatural good" as having a technical sense, taught that the justitia originalis belongs to the nature of man itself as its completion, but that there is to be distinguished from this the gratia gratum faciens, which man already possessed in the primitive state as a supernatural good, though this was imparted to him, not *in* creation, but only *after* creation, *while Adam moreover earned it for himself meritoriously by good works ex congruo*.[2] So merit was to begin so early! Thomas knows nothing of this; but Bonaventura repeated this doctrine;[3] it is also to be found in Albertus,[4] and the Scotists adhered to it.[5] The advantage which this doctrine offered, namely the possibility of reckoning to the perfection of human nature itself the justitia originalis, which was distinguished from the gratia gratum faciens, was greatly counterbalanced by the

---

[1] Just in the doctrines of grace and sin did the Scotists gain more and more the upper hand; as regards the other doctrines, their dialectico-sceptical investigations were crowned with a smaller measure of success.

[2] Schwane, l.c., p. 379 f., S. II., Q. 96, membr. 1 : " Alii ponunt, ipsum (Adam) fuisse conditum solummodo in naturalibus, non in gratuitis gratum facientibus et hoc magis sustinendum est et magis est rationi consonum . . . Sic noluit deus gratiam dare nisi præambulo merito congrui per bonum usum natuiæ."

[3] See Schwane, p. 383.

[4] See Schwane, p. 384.

[5] L.c., p. 391. Werner, Scotus, p. 410 ff. Scotus himself says : " Adam conditus fuit sine omni peccato et sine gratia gratum faciente " (Report, Par. III. D. 13, Q. 2, n. 3).

injury involved in introducing the meritum de congruo into
paradise itself, and thus placing merit from the beginning side
by side with the "sole efficacy" of grace. The meritum de
congruo is thus earlier than the meritum de condigno ; for the
latter could only be implanted, and was meant only to be implanted, in Adam after reception of the gratia gratum faciens, in
order that he might merit for himself eternal life.

2. There already appear in Thomas (see above p. 297) approaches towards the breaking up of the Augustinian doctrines
of sin and original sin, in so far as he no longer broadly grants
the proposition, " naturalia bona corrupta sunt " (natural goodness is corrupt), in so far as he defines concupiscence, which is
in itself not evil, as only " languor et fomes " (tinder), emphasizes the negative side of sin more strongly than Augustine, and
assumes, on the ground of the ratio remaining, an abiding inclination towards goodness (inclinatio ad bonum). Yet he certainly taught a stricter doctrine than Anselm, who really only
accentuated the negative side, and began to waver even in
regard to its character as guilt.[1] To him Duns attached himself, in so far as he at bottom separated the question about concupiscence from the question about original sin ; the former is
for him no more the formal in the latter, but simply the material. Thus there remains for original sin merely the being
deprived of the supernatural good, from which there then resulted certainly a disturbing effect upon the nature of man,
while however nothing was really lost of the natural goodness.[2]

[1] De conceptu virg. 27 : "Hoc peccatum, quod originale dico, aliud intellegere
nequeo in infantibus nisi ipsam, factam per inobedientiam Adæ, justitiæ debitæ
nuditatem, per quam omnes filii sunt iræ : quoniam et naturam accusat spontanea
quam fecit in Adam justitiæ desertio, nec personas excusat recuperandi impotentia.
Quam comitatur beatitudinis quoque nuditas, ut sicut sunt sine omni justitia, ita sint
absque omni beatitudine." C. 22 : "Peccatum Adæ ita in infantes descendere, ut sic
puniri pro eo debeant ac si ipsi singuli illud fecissent personaliter sicut Adam, *non puto.*"
Hence also the idea of the limbus infantium now came always more prominently in
view.   But the rejection of the damnation of infants overturns the whole of
Augustinianism.
[2] Comm. in Sent. II., Dist. 30 Q. 2 : Original sin cannot be concupiscence ; for
the latter is (1) natural, (2) " . . . tum quia non est actualis, quia tunc illa concupiscentia esset actualis, non habitualis, *quia habitus derelictus in anima ex peccato
mortali non est peccatum mortale,* manet enim talis habitus dimisso peccato per
pænitentiam ; *nec etiam ignorantia est,* quia parvulus baptizatus ita ignorat sicut non

3. According to Thomas the magnitude of the first sin (and therefore also of inherited sin) is infinite, according to Scotus it is finite.

4. The Lombard had already taught that inherited sin is propagated simply through the flesh, and that the soul created

baptizatus." One is now eager to hear what original sin then is, and the answer is received (D. 32, with an appeal to Anselm): "*carentia justitiæ debitæ.*" "Et si obicitur, quod aliqui sancti videntur dicere concupiscentiam esse peccatum originale, respondeo : concupiscentia potest accipi vel prout est actus vel habitus vel pronitas in appetitu sensitivo et nullum istorum est formaliter peccatum, quia non est peccatum in parte sensitiva secundum Anselmum. Vel potest accipi, prout est pronitas in appetitu rationali, *i.e.*, in voluntate ad concupiscendum delectabilia immoderate, quæ nata est condelectari appetitui sensitivo, cui conjungitur. *Et hoc modo concupiscentia est materiale peccati originalis, quia per carentiam justitiæ originalis, quæ erat sicut frenum cohibens ipsam ab immoderata delectatione, ipsa non positive, sed per privationem, fit prona ad concupiscendum immoderate delectabilia.*" Very loose also is Dun's conception of the first sin of man (of Adam) as distinguished from the sin of the angels ; it did not arise from uncontrolled self-love, but had its root in uncontrolled love for the partner associated with him (Werner, p. 412) ; this uncontrolled conjugal love, however, was (1) not libidinous, for in the primitive state there was no bad libido ; (2) the act to which Adam allowed himself to be led was not in its nature an immoral act, but only transgression of a command imposed for the purpose of testing. Adam accordingly sinned only *indirectly* against the command to love God, and at the same time transgressed the law of neighbourly love by over-passing, through his pliancy, the proper limit. That is a comparatively slight fault, and is not equal in its gravity to the smallest violation of a *natural* rule of morality. Compare with this empiristic view Augustine's or Anselm's description of the great-ness of the first sin ! In order to see clearly the Pelagianism of Scotus, it must still be added that he disputed the doctrine of Thomas, that in the state of justitia originalis even the smallest venial sin was unthinkable. According to him only mortal sins were impossible ; on the other hand, as man in his original state was just man, such sins were quite well possible as do not entail directly the loss of righteousness, but only occasion a *delay* in arriving at the final goal. How small according to this view, in spite of all assertions to the contrary, is the significance of the first sin and of original sin ! In a disguised way Duns taught, as did Julian of Eklanum, that on the one hand there belongs to the natural will the quality that leads it to turn to the good without effort, while on the other hand, because it is the will of *man*, the possibility of "small sins" was given even in the original state ! Occam draws here again the ultimate conclusions (v. Werner II., pp. 318 f.). As everything is arbitrary, he asserts on the one hand that we must not dispute that it is in God's power to remit to the sinner the guilt of sin, and bestow upon him saving grace without repentance and contrition ; on the other hand, he denies all inner ideal necessary connection between moral guilt and penalty or expiation. "In this way," Werner justly remarks, "theological Scholas-ticism arrived at the opposite extreme to the idea expressed in the Anselmic theory of satisfaction of the *inviolability of a holy order*, whose absolute law of righteousness implies, that God can only remit the reatus pœnæ æternæ at the cost of a supreme atonement, the making of which transcends all the powers of a mere creature." But

for the latter is thereby defiled.[1]   He held, therefore, as many
others did, that inherited sin is inherited sin, in so far as it must
propagate itself as a contagion (contagium) from Adam onwards.
At the same time he also touches, on the other hand, on the
thought of Augustine: "all these had been the one man, *i.e.*,
were in him *materially*" (omnes illi unus homo fuerant, *i.e.*, in
eo materialiter erant), though the emphasis lies on the materialiter, so that the matter is to be understood, not mystically but
realistically.[2]   Now, although Thomas, with the view of giving
expression to *guilt*, and at the same time placing the accent on
the will (not merely on the flesh), affirmed, in opposition to this,
an imputation on a mystical basis,[3] yet the former idea continued
to be the ruling one.   Now, if in spite of this the guilt of the
inherited sin is greatly reduced even in Thomas, it appears in

it was not from laxity that Occam destroyed the principles of Augustinianism; there
met in combination in him rather two clearly recognisable factors, "the absolute lack
of an ideal understanding of the world" (or let us say more correctly, his philosophic
empiricism), and the greatest interest in determining the necessity of the saving grace
of Christ simply from revelation itself.   But—vestigia terrent ; we can learn by studying the historical consequences of Occamism, that thinking humanity will not continue
to be satisfied, if religion is set before it simply as revelation, and all links are severed
which bind this revelation with an understanding of the world.   From Occam it either
goes back again to Thomas (Bradwardine and his spiritual descendants, cf. also the
Platonism of the fifteenth century) or passes on to Socinianism.   But should it not be
possible that the *history* of religion should henceforward render to thoughtful reflection
the service that has hitherto been rendered to it by Plato's and Augustine's and
Thomas's understanding of the world?   We shall not be able certainly to dispense
with an absolute, but it will be grasped as an experience.   The Nominalism that sought
to deliver the Christian religion from the "science" that perverted it made a disastrous
failure in carrying on this rightly chosen task, because it understood by religion
subjection to an enormous mass of material, which, having arisen in history, admits
of no isolation.

[1] Sent. II., Dist. 31, A. B. : "caro sola ex traduce est."   With Augustine the
propagation of inherited sin is derived from the pleasure in the act of generation
"unde caro ipsa, quæ concipitur in vitiosa concupiscentia polluitur et corrumpitur :
ex cujus contactu anima, cum infunditur, maculam trahit, qua polluitur et fit rea, *i.e.*,
vitium concupiscentiæ, quod est originale peccatum."

[2] So, I think, must Anselm also be understood, de conc. virg. 23.

[3] Adam's sinful will (as the will of the primus movens in humanity) is the expression of the universal will ; see II., 1, Q. 81, Art. 1 : "Inordinatio quæ est in isto
homine ex Adam generato, non est voluntaria voluntate ipsius, sed voluntate primi
parentis, qui movet motione generationis omnes qui ex ejus origine derivantur."
Hence inherited sin is not personal sin, but peccatum naturæ, the effect of which
really is that its significance and gravity are greatly lessened.

Duns quite insignificant, notwithstanding all that is said regarding it. Nay, even the consequences of sin are presented by him in another light; for, as inherited sin is simply nothing but loss of the supernatural gift (donum), it has not attacked the nature of man. This remains, even after the Fall, uninjured. Duns really carried on a polemic against the Thomist definition of inherited sin as vulneratio naturæ (wounding of nature).[1] Now, if we add to this, that by hair-splitting over defilement, corruption of nature, moral culpability, and penalty (macula, corruptio naturæ, reatus culpæ, pœna), the subject was quite brought down to the level of casuistry, we must come to be of the opinion that Scholasticism ultimately lost sight entirely of the Augustinian starting-point.

The *religious* view of sin, which even Augustine, indeed, had not strictly wrought out, entirely disappeared. Inherited sin was an external negative character, which is cancelled by the positive character of magical grace. Thus there remained only the wretched dregs of a view that had once been full of life, and had deeply stirred the soul.

5. It is obvious that free will also was now bound to have a higher value attached to it than the Augustinian-Thomist tradition admitted of. When once the fundamental thesis was abandoned, that moral goodness only exists in connection with God (by dependence on Him), when, consequently, the view again prevailed that man can make a parade before God with his independent works, the process of emptying Augustinianism of its contents (for the formulæ durst not be surrendered) necessarily became inevitable. Thomas himself, indeed, had begun, though at first timidly, to assign to free will a special range of action as apart from grace. His mode of procedure, in giving with the one hand and taking with the other, could not continue to be maintained. Bonaventura made predestination dependent on prescience, and limited God as cause in His relation to rational creatures. He is not entire cause (tota causa), but cause along with another contingent cause, *i.e.*, with free will (causa cum alia causa contingente, scil. cum libero

[1] In Sentent. II., Dist. 29. See at the same place the passage showing that the " voluntas in puris naturalibus habet justitiam originalem."

arbitrio). For Duns, and likewise for the leading theologians
till the Council of Constance (and later), the will of the creature
is the second great power next to God,[1] and to what they
correctly lay down in the sphere of empirical psychology, *they
also give a material and positive religious significance.* But in
this way they separate themselves both from Augustine and from
religion ; for, as a dogmatic theologian, Augustine knows of free
will only as a formal principal or as the cause of sin.   It was the

---

[1] Bonaventura (in Sentent. I., Dist. 40, Art. 2, Q. 1) asks : " an prædestinatio
inferat salutis necessitatem ? " He answers : " prædestinatio non infert necessitatem
saluti nec infert necessitatem libero arbitrio. *Quoniam prædestinatio non est causa
salutis nisi includendo merita* (complete apostasy from Augustine), et ita salvando
liberum arbitrium (that is ambiguous). Ad intelligentiam autem objectorum
notandum, quod prædestinatio duo importat, et rationem præscientiæ et rationem
causæ. In quantum dicit rationem causæ, *non necessario ponit effectum, quia non est
causa per necessitatem,* sed per voluntatem, et iterum non est tota causa, sed cum
alia causa contingente, scil. cum libero arbitrio. Et regula est, quod quotiescumque
effectus pendet ex causa necessaria et variabili—a necessaria tamquam ab universali, a
variabili tamquam a particulari—denominatur a variabili (in this way predestination
is set aside), quia denominatio est a causa particulari, *et effectus, quia dependet a
causa contingente, est contingens.* Et præter rationem causæ importat rationem
præscientiæ et præscientia quidem totum includit in cognitione liberum arbitrium et
ejus cooperationem et vertibilitatem et totum. Et præterea non est nisi veri, et
etiam de vero contingente est infallibilis." Duns' doctrine of predestination is very
complicated. It is dependent on his conception of God, which includes a determinism of arbitrariness (see Ritschl, l.c., I., pp. 58 f., 64). But just because the
all-working God is always the contingently working will, the possibility of there
being contingency in the world is disclosed. God embraces this contingency only
with His prescience, and this prescience embraces the possible equally with the
actual. The effect of this is, not only that predestination, as having unity, and as
being inwardly motived, is cancelled, but that God appears no longer as the absolute
Being who wills and can do *one thing,* but as the relative Being who, in an unfathomable way, wills and can do everything possible. Over against such a conception of
God the will of man can assert itself not only as *free,* but also as relatively good, and
so predestination and the grace that is the alone cause vanish, or rather predestination
remains, in so far as absolute contingency and absolute arbitrariness coincide ; see in
Sent. I., Dist. 40, in resol : " Prædestinatio bifariam accipitur. Primo et proprie
pro actu divinæ voluntatis, quo rationalem creaturam ad æternam eligit vitam seu
decernit ac determinat se daturum in præsenti gratiam et gloriam in futuro. *Secundo
accipitur fusius pro actu etiam intellectus divini, pro præcognitione vid. quam habet
deus salutis electorum, quæ quidem præcognitio concomitatur et consequitur electionem.*
Divina autem voluntas circa ipsas creaturas libere et contingenter se habet. Quocirca
contingenter salvandos prædestinat, et posset eosdem non prædestinare. . . . Ex quo
consequitur, quod is qui damnatus est damnari possit, quandoquidem ob ejus prædes-
tinationem non est ejus voluntas in bonum confirmata, ut peccare nequeat."

hereditary fate of mediæval dogmatic, that through the mixing up of knowledge of the world with religion, a relatively more correct knowledge of the world became as dangerous, nay, still more dangerous to faith, than a knowledge that was false ; for every piece of knowledge, in whatever way it was found, was at once introduced into the calculation as having religious worth. Against the Pelagianism, which, with ever decreasing hesitation, made use of Augustinianism simply as "an artistic form of speech," Bradwardine was the first to take again a strong stand, and after his time, the reaction never again disappeared, but slowly gathered strength in the fifteenth century, till the time of Wesel and Wessel, Cajetan and Contarini, till the time of Luther and the Decrees of Trent.[1]

[1] From Bradwardine's preface to his treatise de causa dei c. Pelagium Münscher quotes the following passage : " In hac causa, quot, domine, hodie cum Pelagio pro libero arbitrio contra gratuitam gratiam tuam pugnant, et contra Paulum pugilem gratiæ spiritualem ! Quot etiam hodie gratuitam gratiam tuam fastidiunt solumque liberum arbitrium ad salutem sufficere stomachantur ! aut si gratia utantur, vel per-functorie necessariam eam simulant ipsamque se jactant liberi sui arbitrii viribus pro-mereri, ut sic saltem nequaquam gratuita, sed vendita videatur ! Quot etiam, deus omnipotens, impotentes de sui potestate arbitrii præsumentes tuæ cooperationis auxil-ium in operationibus suis recusant, dicendo cum impiis ' recede a nobis ' . . . Quin immo et voluntati suæ in contingenter futuris omnimodam tribuunt libertatem, in tan-tum ut etiam contra vocem propheticam a tua subjectione exemptionem prætendant . . . Et quot et quam innumerabiles eis favent ! *Totus etenim pæne mundus post Pelagium abiit in errorem.* Exsurge igitur, domine, judica causam tuam et sustinen-tem te sustine, protege, robora, consolare ! Scis enim quod nusquam virtute mea, sed tua confisus, tantillus adgredior tantam causam." It is easily seen that here, as in the case of Gottschalk, the spirit and style of Augustine have exercised an influ-ence. But Bradwardine and all the Reformers after him and previous to Luther simply went back upon Augustine (Wyclif, Huss, Wesel, Wessel, Staupitz, etc.). Just on that account this movement issued, not in the Evangelical Reformation, but in the Articles of Trent, or, in Bajus and Jansen ; see Ritschl, Rechtfertigung, 1 vol., 2. ed., pp. 105-140. Ritschl begins these discussions with the not quite accurate words : " The effort will be fruitless to point out in any theologian of the Middle Ages the Reformation conception of the doctrine of justification, that is to say, the deliberate distinguishing between justificatio and regeneratio." Bradwardine's doctrine of free will has been treated in detail by Werner (III., p. 270 ff.). Conscious in the highest degree that it was a question about the articulus stantis et cadentis ecclesiæ, Bradwar-dine revived Augustine's doctrine of the incapacity of free will. Whether he really contracted the horizon of the Augustinian theology by tracing back its contents to the doctrines of the immutability of the divine thought and will as being its ultimate fundamental import (Werner, p. 282 ff.), is a question I leave undiscussed. Certainly to me also the determinism seems to come out more strongly in Bradwardine than in

6. Most distinct, and fraught with the gravest practical results, was the further development of Scholasticism as regards the doctrine of justification and the meritorious acquirement of eternal life. But how many germs tending to develop into the Pelagian deterioration of these doctrines had already been deposited in his system by Thomas himself? I will not repeat here what must have already come clearly to view above in the account of the Thomist doctrine of grace. The most manifest outcome of the further development in Scotism consists in these things: (1) that the decisive effect of "prevenient grace" became more and more a mere assertion, or, say, a form of speech—"co-operating grace" is the only intelligible grace—(2) that what, for Thomas, was "meritum ex congruo" became "meritum ex condigno," while the "merita ex congruo" were seen in impulses and acts which Thomas had not placed under the point of view of merit at all, and (3) that, as a parallel to the meritoriousness of attritio, the meritoriousness of " fides informis," of the mere obedience of faith, became more highly estimated. *In this point the corruption was perhaps greatest ;* for the fides implicita, the mere self-surrender, now became in a sense a fundamental dogmatic principle.[1]

According to Scotus, the man who does not possess the habit of grace (habitus gratiæ), who therefore is not in union with God, and hence can do nothing really meritorious to earn eternal life, must not be held as having no power to conform his conduct to the divine commands. He *can* still always fulfil these commands (otherwise God would require of him something impossible, and would be partial were He not to save all), and He must fulfil them ; *for he must prepare himself for the first grace.* As it is a natural duty to love God beyond every-

Augustine ; but Werner has an interest in separating Bradwardine as far as possible from Augustine, Anselm, and Thomas, because his doctrine led to Wyclif, and to that Augustinianism which Catholic theology no longer tolerates, though, as a fact, it is the genuine Augustinianism. Yet neither can these theologians, on the other hand, make use of the pure Nominalism of Occam. Hence Bradwardine is recognised, so far as he became " an involuntary witness (?) as it were, for the necessity of a restoration of the ecclesiastical Scholasticism on a Thomist basis."

[1] In germ the fides implicita was contained from the beginning in the Western system as a factor to which religious value was attributed. But only in Nominalism did this germ open into blossom.

thing, it is also a duty that can be fulfilled ; accordingly, even the natural righteousness of heathen and sinners is not without connection with the supernatural virtues ; indeed, it cannot at all be *proved* that a habit of love produced by supernatural grace is always necessary in order to love God above all ; this rather is simply an ecclesiastical tenet.   Before the Fall at least all this held good, and it can be proved, indeed, from Aristotle (!) that it holds good also after the Fall.   It is with this in view that Scotus' doctrines of grace and of merit must be understood.   In point of fact, merit always precedes grace with him, that is to say, first the merit de congruo, then the merit de condigno ;¹ the former entirely neutralises the thought of

---

¹ See Werner I., p. 418 ff.   In Sentent. II., Dist. 28, Q. 1, Question : "How can God forgive guilt without giving grace ? videretur enim esse mutatio in deo, si non ponatur in ipso justificato.   Potest illa opinio confirmari per hoc, quod illud præceptum ' Diliges dominum deum, etc.,' est primum, a quo tota lex pendet et prophetæ.   Ad actum igitur hujus præcepti aliquando eliciendum (actus elicitus dilectionis, rationis) tenetur voluntas ; ita quod non potest esse semper omissio actus hujus præcepti sine peccato mortali.   Quodcumque autem voluntas actum hujus præcepti exsequitur, licet informis, et disponit se de congruo ad gratiam gratificantem sibi oblatam, vel resistet et peccabit mortaliter, vel consentiet et justificabitur."   In the following way the Augustinian position that meritum is the munus dei is justified (Dist. 17, Q. 1 in Resol.) : "in actu meritorio duo sunt consideranda.   Primum illud quod præcedit rationem meritorii, in quo includitur substantia et intentio actus ac rectitudo moralis.   Secundum est ratio meritorii, quod est esse acceptum a divina voluntate, aut acceptabile, sive dignum acceptari ad præmium æternum.   Quantum ad primum, potentia est causa prima et principalis, et habitus causa secunda, cum potentia utatur habitu, non e converso ; alias habens semel gratiam nunquam posset peccare, cum causa secunda semper sequatur motionem causæ primæ, nec possit movere ad oppositum illius, ad quod causa prima inclinat.   *Sed accipiendo actum in quantum est meritorius talis conditio ei convenit principaliter ab habitu et minus principaliter a voluntate.*   Magis siquidem actus acceptatur ut dignus præmio, quia est elicitus a caritate, quam quia est a voluntate libere elicitus, *quamvis utrumque necessario requiratur . . . Actus meritorius est in potestate hominis* supposita generali influentia, si habuerit liberi arbitrii usum et gratiam, *sed completio in ratione meriti non est in potestate hominis nisi dispositive,* sic tamen dispositive quod ex dispositione divina nobis revelata " ; observe here the yes and no which comes out in these distinctions.   Consequently Bradwardine was right in fixing down the following errors in the reigning Scholasticism : (1) While denying that the meritum is causa principalis doni gratiæ, it asserts that it is causa sine qua non ; (2) while denying that man can of himself merit saving grace, it asserts that he can prepare himself for it in a way required of him, and that God then gives His grace, because even in naturalibus the forma is at once given to the materia disposita ; (3) while denying that man can, strictly speaking, initiate the saving process, it asserts that he consents

prevenient grace, the latter cancels the decisive significance of
co-operating grace. Everywhere in words, by means of extremely forced distinctions, Augustinianism is defended, but in
reality it is discarded. The position that was not disputed
even by Thomas and Augustine, that we are not justified unwillingly (inviti), receives from Nominalism a Pelagian interpretation, and the other position, that eternal life is the reward
for the merits one acquires on the basis of infused grace, is so
understood that the accent falls on the will, and not on the
merit of Christ. The divine factor really appears only in the
"acceptance" (acceptatio), which, as it dominates the whole
relation between God and man and is arbitrary, does not allow
merits in the strictest (necessary) sense to be spoken of. *The
Nominalist doctrine is not simple moralism, only in so far as the
doctrine of God does not admit in any case of a strict moralism.*
This comes out most plainly in Occam, who, indeed, taken
altogether, presents the paradoxical spectacle *of a strongly
pronounced religious nature finding refuge simply in the arbitrary
will of God.* It is reliance on this arbitrary will alone that frees
him from Nihilism, and the same applies to the greatest
theologians of the period of the Reform Councils, till Nicolas of
Cusa brought about a change. Faith, in order to maintain
itself, found no other means of deliverance from the inrushing
floods of world-knowledge than the plank of the divine
arbitrariness, to which it clung with intense eagerness. These
theologians were still no moralists—they merely appear such to

and follows ex propriis viribus ; (4) it asserts that man merits divine grace ex congruo
(c. Pelag. 39), "et quia iste error est famosior ceteris his diebus, et nimis multi per
ipsum in Pelagianum præcipitium dilabuntur, necessarium videtur ipsum diligentiori
examine perscrutari." The situation at the beginning of the sixteenth century is
excellently described by Ritschl thus (I., p. 138) : "The state of things in respect of
public doctrine which the Reformation found existing was not apprehended and
represented by the two sides with historical precision and justice. The theological
opponents of the Reformation, who were exclusively Realists, entirely ignore the
fact, that for a century and a half the Nominalist School had maintained the Pelagian
doctrine with regard to merita de congruo, and had over-rated the merita de condigno as compared with the merit of Christ, that as a School they had won equal
public rights with the Realists, and even in respect of science and practice had exercised a far-reaching influence on the latter. The Reformers on the other hand
directed their reproaches and charges of Pelagianism, which should have applied only
to the Nominalist tradition, against Scholasticism in general."

us ;—it was only the Socinians who became that. " According
to Occam the necessity of supernatural habits (habitus) for the
obtaining of eternal life cannot be proved on grounds of reason.
What alone could support the proof would be, that the acts of
faith, love, and hope corresponding to these habits are not
possible without their supernatural habits ; this, however, cannot
be proved.   A heathen living among Christians can come to
hold the articles of the Christian faith as true, on grounds of
purely natural conviction ; a philosophically trained heathen
can live according to the conviction, acquired in a natural way,
that God, who is more excellent than all else, must be loved
above all else.   The acts of faith, hope, and love performed by
such men originate, not from infused, but from acquired habits,
while these latter can exist even among Christians, and really do
exist where there is a certain height of moral and intellectual
development.   The necessity of supernatural habits is established
solely by the authority of traditional Church doctrine.   Thus then
as regards the necessity of supernatural habits, we see Occam
arriving at the most extreme opposition to the necessity of
supernatural habits that is possible within the limits of
Church faith." (? !) So Werner.[1] That here there is still
always a keeping within the limits of ecclesiastical faith is an
instructive assertion of the modern Catholic theologian.   The
truth is, that the displacement of "merits" is here carried so far,
that the distinction between merita ex congruo and merita ex
condigno is entirely neutralised ; man can acquire for himself
in the state of nature merita de condigno ; but God has *willed*,
nevertheless, the necessity of a supernatural habitus and has
appointed the corresponding institutions.[2]   Now although many
theologians, such as Occam himself, might feel their religious
conscience quieted by the reflection that God's arbitrary will is
for us His mercy, yet the only general effect possible from this
kind of theology—especially when we recall the attritio and the

---

[1] II., p. 339 f.

[2] The Catholic precautionary position lies simply in this, that God need give the
vita æterna to no one at all, but that that life is in every case an arbitrary gift, the
source of which is an ordained arrangement. This precautionary position, however, has
nothing to do with the question about sin and guilt, but originates in the general
doctrine of God.

indulgences, was *that there should be recognised in good works the instrumental causes (causæ instrumentales) for the reception of eternal life, that these good works, moreover, should be judged to be meritorious even in their minimised form, and that, finally, self-subjection to the revelation taught by the Church should be held to be a sufficient good motive (bonus motus), which is so completed by the Sacraments that it imparts worthiness.* In this way Nominalism was understood even by the earnest Augustinians of the fourteenth and fifteenth centuries. They saw in it a denial of the grace of God in Christ, and they did not let themselves be led astray from this judgment by the most acute distinctions of the Nominalists: " In vain is much said in the way of repudiation ; what the other hears in everything is only a No."

Perhaps the plainest evidence of the decline of an inwardly grounded doctrine of salvation and of the growing attachment of value to creaturely goodness in the last centuries of the Middle Ages, is *the doctrine of Mary*, as embracing both the doctrine of her immaculate conception and the doctrine of her co-operation in the work of redemption.[1]

1. We have seen above (Vol. V., p. 235) that even Augustine had doubts as to whether Mary was subject to the general law of sin, and Paschasius Radbertus already knows that Mary was sanctified in the womb. Anselm, certainly, who on this point was more Augustinian than Augustine, had distinctly rejected the immaculate conception (Cur deus homo II. 16) ; but a few years after his death we meet with a *festival* in Lyons (1140) in honour of the immaculate conception of Mary, which proves how

---

[1] The Pelagian motives underlying the doctrine of Mary are pretty much concealed in Scholasticism, but they are clearly apparent on closer inspection. The treatment, moreover, of the doctrine of the human soul of Christ by Scotus and the Scotists is also a beautiful demonstration of their Pelagianism, but the description here of this complicated line of doctrinal development would take us too far ; see Werner I., p. 427 ff. ; II., p. 330 ff. What alone reconciles us in the marialogy is the observing that pious faith allows itself utterances about the relationship of Mary to God and Christ which it does not venture to make about its own relationship. In this sense— though it appears paradoxical—there is much that is *evangelical* in the doctrine of Mary. It would be an interesting task to prove this from the doctrine of Mary as taught by the Schoolmen individually.

widely current the superstition had already become in the lower strata of the Church.[1]

Bernard (ep. 174 ad canonicos Lugd.) spoke against the new festival, but used feeble weapons in opposing the idea that was expressed in it : that Mary was already sanctified in the womb, and continued also to be protected against all sin ; but that her conception was not sinless, otherwise that of her parents must also have been so (*i.e.*, if in this way the proof is to be got of the sinless birth of Christ) ; that the sinless conception was a prerogative of Christ. But if general opinion already held as certain what Bernard had laid down as to the sinlessness of Mary,[2] and if, besides this, the act of birth was surrounded with the halo of the miraculous, how could the logic in these fancies be hindered from pressing on to the ultimate extreme? The Pre-Scotist Schoolmen still denied, it is true, the immaculate conception (even Bonaventura); but if Thomas adheres to sanctification in the womb, and accordingly assumes, immediately after the conception, a special influence of grace upon Mary, why shall she not be declared exempt from original sin itself? Thomas answers, because Christ is the redeemer of all men ; but that he would no longer be if Mary had remained free from original sin (S. III., Q. 27). Still—everything is possible, of course, for Scholasticism—why can it not be assumed that Christ's death had a reflex power for Mary? Then, again, original sin is a mere privatio, is it not? Why cannot God,

---

[1] The history of the worship of Mary is throughout a history in which the superstitious religion of the congregations and the monks worked upwards from its dark foundations, and determined theology, which reluctantly submitted ; but, on closer view, this is seen to hold good of almost all specifically Western Catholic practices and doctrines. The παράδοσις ἄγραφος, the tradition, which is now claimed as the papal, that has existed semper, ubique et apud omnes, is *the common superstition, which everywhere and always expressed itself in analogous forms.* In this sense the Catholic position cannot be disputed, that the Romish Church is the Church of stable, and yet at the same time living, tradition. This tradition is stable, because the lower religious instincts, which are compounded of fear and sensuousness, are stable ; it is living, because theology by its devices *gradually* legitimised these instincts. This does not of course imply the denial, that apart from this there was another and higher content in the Catholic tradition. For the literature on the worship of Mary see Vol. IV., p. 314, and Reusch, Theol. Lit. Ztg. 1887, No. 7.

[2] A monk relates that Bernard, who appeared to him in a dream, regretted and retracted his doubts about the immaculate conception (see Werner II., p. 349, f.)

who can do everything, fill Mary from the beginning with grace?
And is this being filled with grace not necessary if she is afterwards to act, not merely a passive, but an active part in the
work of redemption (see sub. 2)? So Scotus then held it as
"probable" that Mary was conceived without sin, and therefore
never possessed the concupiscentia carnis (in Sent. III., Dist. 3,
Q. 1). From that time the Franciscans strenuously maintained
this view against the Dominicans (Thomists). The "reflex
power of redemption" was the fig-leaf to cover the apostasy
from Christ, and—to adopt the artistic form of speech—" her
preservation from contracting original sin was due to its being
fitting that the Mediator, Christ, *should prove Himself in the most
perfect way to be Mediator* by means of some human creature
that was above all others adapted for this (that is, meritum de
congruo on Mary's part, seen ex præscientia [in the exercise of
prescience]). The most perfect kind of mediation is that by
which the injured is anticipated in such a way that he never at
all begins to be angry about the injury done to him, *and therefore lets forgiveness drop as superfluous.*"[1]

This proof is extraordinarily instructive, for it contains implicitly
the admission that Christ is not the perfect Redeemer of all men,
but that He only establishes for them the *possibility* of redemption. That is correctly thought from a Catholic point of view ;
but it is not usually plainly expressed in that quarter—nay, for
good reasons there is a very grave reluctance to express it.
Thomists and Scotists rivalled each other in glorifying Mary ;
but the former magnified in her the power and splendour of the
grace which cleanses and purifies, the latter magnified the grace
itself which originally (ab origine) imparts innocence. But if
grace is able to do that, why does it not do it always? It seems,
then, as if it were not really the glorifying of grace that is aimed
at. Certainly not. "Only with the existence of a perfect
innocence wrought by redeeming grace is a complete representation afforded of *all orders of rank in human beatification.* The
highest stage is represented by the blessedness of the soul of
Christ, which was absolutely blessed even on earth without foregoing merit ; then follows the holy virgin, *whose beatifying merit*

[1] III. Dist. 3, Q. 1, n. 4 sq. Werner I., p. 460.

was her perfect innocence wrought by the grace of redemption ; in
the third rank stand those whose souls were never stained by
actual sins; lastly come those who, from being great sinners,
have become saints."[1]

In this graduated choir it is manifestly not grace that is of
effect, but merit.   Here again there was a connecting of the idea
of consilia evangelica with salvation.   As is well known, the
great controversy about the immaculate conception was not
fought out in the Middle Ages.   But the University of Paris
condemned the rejection of the new doctrine (1387) ; at Bâsle
the " Reform Council" gave its voice for it (36. Sess. 1439), and
Sixtus IV. (Extravag. III., 12, 1) prepared the way for its
adoption as dogma by forbidding, under the penalty of excommunication, the pronouncing it heresy, though at the same time
he declared to the world that the apostolic chair had not yet
decided, *i.e,* could not yet overlook the opposition of the
Dominicans at the time.   Not without ground these latter could
point out that they themselves encouraged the deepest conceivable veneration of Mary, for their great teacher had taught
that there should be paid to the holy virgin, not, indeed, latreia
as to God, nor yet douleia, as to the saints,[2] but hyperdouleia.[3]

2. From as early as the time of Irenæus occasion was furnished,
through the fatal parallel drawn between Eve and Mary, for
attributing to Mary a certain share in the work of redemption ;
from the idea of the graded hierarchy of angels and saints in

[1] III. Dist. 3, Q. 1, n. 7, 12.   Werner I., p. 46?.   On the attitude of the later
Scotists, l.c. II., p. 347 f.   Two sanctifications of Mary were assumed, the first at
the moment of her being conceived (extinction of original sin, *i.e.*, of the fomes
peccati), the second at the moment of her conceiving (impossibilitas peccandi).
Occam adopted this double sanctification also, but made less of its effects, because
he did not rate very highly the peccatum originis itself.

[2] Special proofs of the worship of saints and relics are not necessary, as Scholasticism
added nothing of importance to the practice and theory that prevailed even from early
times.   The doctrine of the saints was attached in the closest way to the doctrine of
the consilia.   The intercession of the saints was proved from the idea of the connection
of the earthly Church with the heavenly; on their merita, see the doctrine of indulgences.
Thomas was here also the ruling authority as a teacher, and by his doctrine of the
merits of the saints he prepared the way for the Pelagianism of the Scotists.

[3] Thomas, S. III., Q. 25, Art. 5.   Thomas claimed latreia for the cross and the
image of Christ, III., Q. 25, Arts. 3 and 4; see also II., 1 Q. 103, Art. 4.

heaven the impulse was received to worship Mary along with
Christ as the Queen of Heaven (" in the midst between the Son,
who is holiest of the holy, and all the saints, royal virgin, gate of
heaven, way, the ladder from sins " [media inter filium, qui est
sanctus sanctorum, et alios sanctos, virgo regia, janua cœli, via,
peccatorum scala]; the most extravagant veneration even on the
part of Bernard in the Sermones II. in adv. dom. : " let us also
strive to ascend *by her* to Him who *by her* descended to us ; by
her to come into the grace of Him who by her came into our
misery ; by thee may we have access to the Son, O blessed
contriver of grace, author of life, mother of salvation, that through
thee He may receive us, who through thee was given to us.
Thy innocence excuses before Him the guilt of our corruption . . .
let thy abundant love cover the magnitude of our sins, and thy
glorious fecundity confer on us fecundity of merits ; our lady,
our *mediatrix*, our advocate, reconcile us to thy Son, commend
us to thy Son, represent us before thy Son ! Grant, O blessed
one, by the grace which thou hast found . . . that He who
through thy mediation deigned to partake of our infirmity and
misery, may, through thy intercession also, make us partakers of
His glory and blessedness " [studeamus et nos ad ipsum per eam
ascendere, qui per ipsam ad nos descendit; per eam venire in
gratiam ipsius, qui per eam in nostram miseriam venit ; per te
accessum habeamus ad filium, O benedicta inventrix gratiæ,
genetrix vitæ, mater salutis, ut per te nos suscipiat, qui per te
datus est nobis. Excusat apud ipsum integritas tua culpam
nostræ corruptionis . . . copiosa caritas tua nostrorum cooperiat
magnitudinem peccatorum, et fœcunditas gloriosa fœcunditatem
nobis conferat meritorum ; domina nostra, mediatrix nostra,
advocata nostra, tuo filio nos reconcilia, tuo filio nos commenda,
tuo filio nos repræsenta ! fac, O benedicta, per gratiam quam
invenisti . . . ut qui te mediante fieri dignatus est particeps
infirmitatis et miseriæ nostræ, te quoque intercedente participes
faciat nos gloriæ et beatitudinis suæ[1]]). From here it was only

---

[1] Bernard is also fond of variations on the thought that the Son will hear the mother,
the Father the Son. " Hæc peccatorum scala, hæc mea maxima fiducia est, hæc tota
ratio spei meæ." The Son cannot refuse to hear the mother ; for the " invenisti

a step to the doctrine of Scotus and the Scotists, that Mary cooperated, not only passively, but *actively*, in the incarnation.

gratiam apud deum" is still in force.   These thoughts passed over in succum et sanguinem of Catholicism ; they were disseminated especially by the Franciscans.

[1] On the proof, see Werner I., pp. 433 f., 435 ff.; II. 352 ff.   In Duns the idea coheres with his general zoological ideas ; yet for him it has also independent significance.

HISTORY OF DOGMA

BY

Dr. ADOLPH HARNACK

Volume VII

TRANSLATOR'S NOTE.

THE Translator deeply regrets that, in preparing this concluding volume for publication, he enjoyed only to a limited extent
the aid of the late lamented Professor Bruce, whose enfeebled
state of health precluded the possibility of close and continuous
scrutiny of the English rendering,—although he was engaged in
examining proof-sheets within a few weeks of his death. In
expressing the hope that the volume will not seriously suffer
from appearing mainly on his own responsibility, the Translator
may perhaps be permitted to bear testimony to the profound
interest Dr. Bruce took in Harnack's great work, to his pains-
taking and unwearied efforts to secure that it would be adequately presented to English readers, and to the singular
geniality of his intercourse with those who had the honour
of co-operating with him in his labours.

CONTENTS.

PART II.

DEVELOPMENT OF ECCLESIASTICAL DOGMA.

BOOK III.

The Threefold Issue of the History of Dogma.

[1] The four chapters which make up this volume answer to Chapters I.—IV., of Part II., Book III., in the Original German Edition.

SECOND PART.

DEVELOPMENT OF ECCLESIASTICAL DOGMA.

THIRD BOOK.

THE THREEFOLD ISSUE OF THE HISTORY OF DOGMA.

" ALSO haben die Sophisten Christum gemalet, wie er Mensch und Gott sei, zählen seine Beine und Arm, mischen seine beiden Naturen wünderlich in einander, welches denn nur eine sophistische Erkenntuiss des Herrn Christi ist. Denn Christus ist nicht darumb Christus genennet, dass er zwo Naturen hat. Was gehet mich dasselbige an? Sondern er träget diesen herrlichen und tröstlichen Namen von dem Ampt und Werk, so er auf sich genommen hat; dasselbige giebt ihm den Namen. Dass er von Natur Mensch und Gott ist, das hat er für sich ; aber dass er sein Ampt dahin gewendet und seine Liebe ausgeschüttet, und mein Heiland und Erlöser wird, das geschieht mir zu Trost und zu Gut." (Luther, Erlang. Ausg. XXXV. S. 207 f.)

" Adversarii, quum neque quid remissio peccatorum, neque quid fides neque quid gratia neque quid justitia sit, intelligant, misere contaminant locum de justificatione et obscurant gloriam et beneficia Christi et eripiunt piis conscientiis propositas in Christo consolationes." (Apologia confessionis IV. [II.] init.)

CHAPTER I.

HISTORICAL SITUATION.

IN the fourth section of Chapter IV., Vol. V. (p. 222 ff.), it has been shown that by Augustine the traditional dogma was on the one hand strengthened, *i.e.*, the authoritative force of it, as the most important possession of the Church, was intensified, while on the other hand it was in many ways expanded and recast. That dogma which, in its conception and its construction, was a work of the *Hellenic* spirit on the soil of the Gospel (see Vol. I., p. 17 ff.), continued to exist ; in thinking of dogma one thought of the knowledge of a supernatural world and history, a knowledge that was revealed by God, that was embodied in unalterable articles of doctrine, and that conditioned all Christian life ; but into its structure there were interwoven by Augustine in a marvellous way the *principles* of Christian life-experience, of the experience which he had passed through as a son of the Catholic Church and as a disciple of Paul and the Platonists, while the Roman Church thereafter gave to dogma the force of a great divine system of law for the individual and for Christian society.

By these foregoing steps, of which the influence continued to be fundamental, the inner history of Western Christianity in the Middle Ages was determined. We have seen that no substantially new element can be pointed to in the period of a thousand years intervening between Augustine and the fifteenth century. Yet the theme which Augustine had given out was not merely reproduced and repeated with a hundred different variations, there was rather a real development and deepening of it. All the elements of that theme passed through a history; they were *strengthened*. Just for that reason a crisis was bound to arise. The unity which for Augustine included dogma, the claims of the understanding, the legal regulations of the Church and the principles of individual Christian life, was destroyed; it could not be maintained. Those claims and these legal regulations and principles betrayed more and more of a centrifugal force, and, as they grew stronger, asserted the claim to sole supremacy. Thomas, indeed, the greatest of the Schoolmen, still set himself to solve the vast problem of satisfying under the heading and within the framework of a Church dogmatic all the claims that were put forward by the ecclesiastical antiquity embodied in dogma, by the idea of the Church as the living, present Christ, by the legal order of the Roman Church, by Augustine's doctrine of grace, by the science of Aristotle, and by the piety of Bernard and Francis. But the great work of this new Augustine certainly did not issue in lessening the strain of the mutually antagonistic forces and in securing a satisfying unity. So far as it aimed at this effect the undertaking was futile; to some degree indeed it produced the opposite result. The wealth of material employed in carrying it out only served to strengthen to the utmost all the forces that were to be kept controlled within the unity of the whole. Thomas was as much looked up to as a teacher by the rational criticism of Nominalism as by the Mysticism of Eckhart and the " Pre-Reformers," and if he undoubtedly laid the foundation for the most extravagant theories of the Curialists, yet on the other hand he strengthened the recollection of the Augustinian dictum, that in religion it is purely a question about God and the soul.

The task is a difficult one, and can scarcely be carried out, of indicating in a few of its characteristic features the inner state of Christian religion in the West at the close of the fifteenth century; for the picture this period presents is almost as com-

plicated as that exhibited by the second century of our era.[1]
After what has been stated in the foregoing Book, it must be
enough for our purpose to specify briefly the most important
currents *in their relation to dogma.*

1. *Curialism.*—About the year 1500 a great party was in
existence that treated Church and religion simply as an
outward form of dominion, and sought to maintain and extend
them by means of force, officialism, and an oppressive system of
dues.   The nations held that the chief seat of this party was to
be sought for in Rome itself, at the papal court, and they were
aware that the secularising of the Church, which had become a
heavy burden, not only on consciences, but on all vigorous
forces of life and on all ideals, was carried on from Rome
without shrinking or shame.   It is a matter of no importance
whether among those who in this way undertook to build up
the Church of Christ there were some who in their hearts had
continued inwardly devoted to the cause for which they
ostensibly laboured ; for we have to do here only with the
results which they had their share in producing.   For this
party of Church politicians there was at bottom only one
dogma—*that the use and wont of the Roman Church was divine
truth.*   The old dogma had only value and importance in so far
as it was of a piece with the usages of the Roman Church.
There is implied in this that this party had the strongest
interest in giving to the modern decisions and verdicts of the
Curia entirely the same value and authority as belonged to
dogma.   As, on the one hand, it could never think of abrogating
anything authoritative (if an old tradition, a passage of Scripture, or a dogmatic distinction was inconvenient, any unwelcome
consequence was obviated by the new rule that had now made
its appearance, *that only the Church, i.e., Rome, had the right to
expound*), so on the other hand it had to see to it that the
nations became accustomed to the startling novelty of attributing the same sacredness to papal decisions as to the decrees
of the great Councils.   About 1500 this quid pro quo had

---

[1] Cf. the introductions to the history of the Reformation by Kolde (Luther), v.
Bezold and Lenz (Luther), and also Müller's Bericht in the Vorträge der Giessener
Theol. Conferenz, 1887.

already succeeded up to a certain point, though the success was
still far from being perfect.   But the spirits of men were
wearied and perplexed after the unhappy course of things
during the period of the Councils (Constance, Bâsle).   Even
the Councils had succumbed, or were rendered powerless.
Somewhere, nevertheless, a fixed point had to be found.
Accordingly, the Romanists succeeded in again persuading
many that it was unquestionably to be found in Rome, and
there alone.[1]   The princes, moreover, intent only on maintaining secular rule over the churches in their own dominions, left the
Curia to act in an irresponsible way in the provinces of faith,
morals, and Church practice, and so on their part strengthened
the presumption with regard to the religious (dogmatic) infallibility and sovereignty of the Roman Chair.   The Curia, of course,
could have no interest in gathering the papal decisions into a
sacred code and placing this as a Church law-book side by side
with the old dogma ; for thereby the idea would only have been
encouraged which there was a wish to combat—that the Pope,
namely, was bound by a strictly defined dogmatic canon.
What was desired rather was to accustom the nations to see
invariably in the papal directions issued *ad hoc*, the decisions
that were necessary and that terminated all discussion.   Just
on that account the Curia was only gratified when there still
remained a certain dubiety about many questions that were
stirred regarding dogma and Church polity ; such dubiety it
deliberately fostered where a definite decision could not be

---

[1] See the Bull of Pius II., "Execrabilis," of the year 1459 (Denzinger, Enchiridion,
5th ed., p. 134): "Execrabilis et pristinis temporibus inauditus tempestate nostra
inolevit abusus, ut a Romano Pontifice, Jesu Christi vicario . . . nonnulli spiritu
rebellionis imbuti, non sanioris cupiditate judicii, sed commissi evasione peccati ad
futurum concilium provocare præsumant. . . . Volentes igitur hoc pestiferum virus
a Christi ecclesia procul pellere et ovium nobis commissarum saluti consulere,
omnemque materiam scandali ab ovili nostri salvatoris arcere . . . hujusmodi pro-
vocationes damnamus et tamquam erroneas ac detestabiles reprobamus."   Bull of
Leo X., "Pastor æternus," of the year 1516 (Denzinger, p. 187): "Solum Romanum
Pontificem pro tempore existentem tamquam auctoritatem super omnia concilia
habentem, tam conciliorum indicendorum transferendorum ac dissolvendorum plenum
jus ac potestatem habere, nedum ex sacræ scripturæ testimonio, dictis sanctorum
patrum ac aliorum Romanorum Pontificum etiam prædecessorum nostrorum sacrorum-
que canonum decretis, sed propria etiam eorumdem conciliorum confessione manifeste constat."

reached without provoking considerable opposition. It had long been learned, too, from experience, that angling is better in troubled waters, and that uncertain souls are more easily ruled than souls that have a clear view of what is valid in the Church and has the support of truth.

Very closely connected with this was the circumstance, that in Rome the advantages were more clearly seen which the once dreaded *Nominalistic* Scholasticism could furnish in Church affairs. A theology which, like the Thomistic, aimed at securing for believers an *inner conviction* of the things they had to be-lieve, could certainly also render the Church the greatest ser-vices, and these services the Church can never quite dispense with, so long as it does not wield an unlimited external power. But every theology that is directed towards awakening inner convictions and producing a unity of thought, will to some ex-tent also train its scholars in criticising what is at the time in force, and will therefore become dangerous to a Church system which forbids all scrutiny of its use and wont. It was other-wise with the Nominalistic Scholasticism. After a development for more than 150 years, it had reached the point of show-ing the irrationality, the (to human view) contingent and arbi-trary character of even the most important Church doctrines. Though an interest of faith might *also* be involved in this great critical process (see above Vol. VI., p. 162), yet its most manifest result was that there was a resolute surrender to the authority of the Church. The Church must know what the individual can never know, and its faculty for understanding reaches further than the intelligence of believers. That this result was bound to be welcome to the Curialists is very obvious; Innocent IV. indeed had been beforehand with the assertion, that the layman may satisfy himself with faith in God as requiting, if only he is obedient to the Church. They had no objection to urge, therefore, against that fides implicita, which is nothing but blind obedience, and specially convenient for them must have been the dissolution of the Augustinian doctrine of grace which Nominalism had effected by laying stress on the miracle of the Sacraments and on merit. But who, then, really *believed* still in the dogmas, and sought life on the ground of his *belief?*

Foolish question! For the most thorough-going Romanism, so far as it rises to the question of salvation at all, the superior excellence of the Christian religion above all others consists just in this, that it is a *system* which, as an apparatus, produces under easily fulfilled conditions sanctification of life, up to the point of a man's being well-pleasing to God and having merit. *Faith*, which had always been regarded in Catholicism as something merely preliminary, is here shrivelled up into submission to an apparatus. During the time immediately before the Reformation many of those who served in working the machine in Rome had a Humanistic smile on their lips; but they never went so far as to express vigorous scorn; for there was too much convenience in the system that had been built up, and those who maintained it had too little thought to admit of their jesting being ever taken seriously.

There can be no doubt that this whole mode of procedure was a way of burying the old dogma; not less doubtful is it that there developed itself here—with an alarming logical consistency certainly—an element that lay in the beginnings of Western Catholicism.[1] Augustine, in his day, had thrown himself into the arms of Church authority,[2] and declared the "credere," as meaning blind submission to what the Church teaches, to be the starting-point in the inner process of the Christian life. But what a wealth of Christian experience he at the same time brought with him, and how well he understood how to make of his Church a home! From this there had been a lapse, or it had come to be treated as a matter of indifference. To obey and submit to be trained!—but the training was provided for by the Sacrament, was provided for by the ludicrously small

[1] It has been repeatedly pointed out in foregoing passages how there are betrayed already in Tertullian the elements of the later Catholicism, and even, indeed, of Scholasticism. It would be a fine piece of work to gather together and estimate all the material relating to this: Tertullianus doctorum Romanorum præcursor. It is a remarkable fact that among the old Catholic Fathers the man who most truly represented primitive Christianity was at the same time the most modern.

[2] He himself could certainly have no inkling of the shocking superstition, a defence of which would one day be sought for in his ill-omened proposition; " Quod universa frequentat ecclesia, quin ita faciendum sit, disputare insolentissimæ insaniæ est " (Ep. 54 ad Januar.), and of the facility with which the proof from the general usus of the Church would be employed.

offerings to which the Church could impart the worth belonging
to moral acts.   Beside this there was no longer a place for
dogma in the old sense of the term, as the definitely outlined
content of what is to constitute the inward conviction of a
Christian and is to be vitalized within him.   As dogma was encumbered by a hundred new definitions of which scarcely any
one could take full account—these new definitions, again, being
differentiated according to the form in which Rome had spoken,
as absolutely binding, qualifying, probable, admissible, etc.—it
also became bereft of its *direct* significance.   It is the *legal
system* of the Roman Church, but a legal system ever taking
new ·shape through ever new arbitrary decisions : it is enough
for the Christian to adhere to the institutions which it has
brought into existence.   If this course of things had gone on
uninterruptedly and been victorious—victory seemed already to
await it about 1500—then dogma would have continued indeed
to exist in an outward way, but inwardly both the old dogma
and dogmatic Christianity in general would have disappeared,
and their place would have been taken by a form of religion
belonging to a lower stage.   For the way in which Curialism
placed itself *above* dogma, merely showing respect to its *formal*
dignity, did not arise from the freedom of the Christian man,
but only indicated the complete *secularising* of religion by politics.   The "tolerari potest " of the Curia and the " probabile "
produce a still worse secularisation of the Church than the
" anathema sit."   And yet there was still inherent in this quite
secularised notion of the Church a Christian element—although
by that time its power to bless had almost entirely disappeared.
That element was faith in the Kingdom of Christ on earth, in its
presence and supremacy in the midst of the earthly and sinful.
In having this faith, those who earnestly resisted all opposition
were superior to their opponents ; for they felt that the men
who opposed, aimed at building up a Church from beneath, that
is to say, from the holiness of Christians.   They represented a
religious thought when they upheld the empire of the Pope ; or
rather, in protecting the Church against Mystics and Hussites,
they involuntarily conserved the truth of the conviction that
the Church of Christ is the reign of the gospel among sinful men.

2. *The opposition to Curialism* was not held together by an
identity of thought; the motives, rather, which had prompted
the opposition were very various. Men were influenced by
political, social, religious, and scientific considerations ; but they
were agreed in the one point, that the usages of the Roman
Church had grown into a tyranny, and that the testimony of
ecclesiastical antiquity was against them. In connection with
the observation of this the theses were maintained, that papal
decisions had not the importance of articles of faith, that it was
not competent to Rome alone to expound Scripture and the
Fathers, that the Council, which is above the Pope, must reform
the Church in its head and members, and that in view of the
innovations in dogma, in cultus and in Church law which had
emanated from Rome, the Church must return to her original
principles and her original condition. These positions were not
only represented in the period before the appearance of Luther
by Conventicles, Hussites, and Waldensians or wild sectaries ;
they found their defenders still more in the ranks of the truest
sons of the Roman Catholic Church. Bishops, theological
faculties and monks of unquestionable orthodoxy gave expression to them, and Luther was justified in appealing to such men
at the beginning of his career as a reformer.[1] Even against
papal pronouncements to a different effect there was held to be
a good Catholic right to maintain, that the basis of the Roman
Catholic Church is to be found only in Scripture and in the dogmatic tradition of ecclesiastical antiquity.[2] With a firmness
that seems strange to us to-day this standpoint is still represented in the Augsburg Confession ;[3] of course it will be impossible to deny that, after what had taken place previous to

[1] From the year 1519 ; see also his speech at Worms.

[2] Hence also Luther's appeal to the Greeks, who were certainly no heretics.

[3] In Art. XXI. these terms are used : " Hæc fere summa est doctrinæ apud suos,
*in qua cerni potest nihil inesse, quod discrepet a scripturis vel ab ecclesia Catholica,
vel ab ecclesia Romana, quatenus ex scriptoribus nota est.*" The cautious mode of
procedure of the Augsburg Confession has been made more apparent by Ficker's
fine book on the Confutatio (Leipzig, 1891). The Confutatores were unfortunately
right in a number of their exposures of the defective candour of the Confession.
Luther also was no longer so well satisfied with the book at midsummer, 1530, as he
had been in May, and he had, to some extent, the same strictures to make as the
Catholics with regard to dissimulation.

the year 1530, it could still be asserted there only from tactical considerations. But even the Emperor himself, as we know, applied the same criterion : in the acceptance or rejection of the "twelve articles," *i.e.*, of the Apostolic Symbol as expounded in the early Church, he saw a profession of orthodoxy or heresy.[1]

How untenable, however, this standpoint was, and what a lack of thought was implied in defending it in all seriousness! In point of fact it was only the circumstance that no crisis of any gravity had as yet exposed its weakness that rendered deception possible as to its having grown frail; and, as the Emperor himself was not really guided in his action by it, so none could maintain it any longer without qualification. Was it not the case, then, that since the time of Augustine there had entered into the iron composition of Western religion an immense mass of theological propositions and Christian experiences, which had never been authoritatively fixed, but which nevertheless everyone regarded as legitimate? How many regulations there were which were generally recognized as salutary and proper, and which rested, notwithstanding, only on papal direc-

---

[1] See the information given by Agricola, as quoted by Kawerau (Johann Agricola, 1881), p. 100 : " It happened that in the Vigils of John the Baptist the Emperor held a banquet in the garden. Now, when Queen Maria asked him what he thought of doing with the people, and with the Confession that had been delivered up, he gave the reply : Dear sister, since my coming into the holy Empire, the great complaint has reached me that the people who profess this doctrine are more wicked than the devil. But the Bishop of Seville gave me the advice that I should not think of acting tyrannically, but should ascertain whether the doctrine is at variance with the articles of our Christian faith. This advice pleased me, and so I find that the people are not so devilish as had been represented ; nor is the subject of dispute the Twelve Articles, but a matter lying outside of them, which I have therefore handed over to the scholars. If their doctrine, however, had been in conflict with the Twelve Articles of our Christian faith, I should have been disposed to apply the edge of the sword." It is to be noted here that both Thomas and Duns (see Ritschl, Fides implicita, p. 15 f., 20) put down the contents of the symbol as the theologia revelata, of which the subject-matter is distributed among two sets of seven propositions—seven upon God and seven upon the Incarnation (the mystery of the Godhead, the vision of whom is blessedness, and the mystery of the humanity of Christ, which is the ground of attaining to the honour of God's sons). Not even is the Church included here. (Biel was the first to add it, without, however, bringing out the main Catholic feature, see p. 34 f.). Everything, on the other hand, that is not included here belongs to Natural Theology, and is subject to an estimate different from that applied to the doctrines of faith.

tions or on the tradition of the immediately preceding centuries!
What a readiness there was on all hands to acknowledge the
decisive title of the Pope to interpret Scripture and tradition, in
cases where his pronouncements coincided with what was regarded by one's self as correct! How much doubt there was
as to how far the Council was superior to the Pope, and what
powers a Council had when it acted without the Pope or assumed
an attitude of opposition towards him! And what uncertainties prevailed as to what was really to be reformed, the *abuses*
or the *usages*, the outward condition of the Church—that is, its
constitution and ritual forms, or the administration of the Sacraments, or the Christian life, or the conception of the Church, as
the kingdom established by God in which Christ reigns. We
derive a clear view of this host of uncertainties even from the
line of action followed by Luther from the year 1517 till the
year 1520. Although by that time he had already laid his hand
on the helm and knew distinctly whither he was steering, what
painful contradictions, compromises, and uncertainties, we at
once see to have marked his course in those years, when we
observe what reforms he then contemplated, and what view he
took of the powers belonging to the Church! At that time he
could almost in one breath acknowledge and repudiate the
authority of the Church of Rome, curse the papacy and profess
submission to it!

And yet what is in itself untenable and full of contradictions
can nevertheless be a power. This was true of the opposition to
Curialism about the year 1500. We should, however, be very
much mistaken were we to assume that the efforts of the
opposition, which appealed to ecclesiastical antiquity against the
innovations of Curialism, exercised, or were even intended to
exercise, any considerable influence on the shaping of *doctrine*
in the direction of a conscious return to the old ecclesiastical
theology. The thought of such a return was almost entirely
absent, because *the period generally was an untheological one.*
This distinguishing feature which characterised the two generations immediately preceding the Reformation—the development of which, moreover, had begun at an earlier date—has had
little justice done to it hitherto in the formation of an estimate

of the Reformation. The case can be briefly stated : about the year 1500 theology as such was discredited ; no one expected anything from it, and it had itself ceased to have any real confidence in its work. Many factors had contributed to this. Nominalist Scholasticism had in a sense declared itself bankrupt, and had buried itself in subtleties that were the result of a systematic abuse of the Aristotelian philosophy. Humanism turned away from theology with complaint or with ridicule—in both cases mainly on the ground of a superficial criticism. The men of piety—they might be pious as Erasmus or pious as Staupitz—sought a remedy for the evils of the times, not in theology, but always still in mystic transcendentalism and in indifference to the worldly conditions that environ the bodily life of men ; that is, they sought it with St. Francis or the holy communists of the primitive Church of Jerusalem. Everywhere in the circles of the religiously awakened, the cry for " practical Christianity " was united—as it is to-day—with a weary dislike of theology. Not that by any means there had as yet been a growing out of theology ; but the anxieties, which were the results of the general revolution in the times, were enough—as they are to-day—to awaken the feeling that nothing more could really be done with doctrine as it was then expressed. Besides all this, the *active* life had for two generations been insisting upon its rights, and accordingly a diminished worth was attached to quietistic contemplation. This was the mightiest revolution in the spirit of the times. Even the Renaissance was only an element in it. For religion and theology a crisis thus arose, a crisis the most severe they could pass through from the time of their origin ; for both of them were embedded in acosmistic Quietism. Either they must disappear along with this, or they must be forcibly severed from it and transferred into a new medium.

Had the ecclesiastical " doctrine " been only science, it would, under such circumstances, have run its course ; it would have been obliged simply to step aside and give place, even outwardly, to another mode of thought. This result really followed among the Anabaptist-Antitrinitarian and among the Socinian groups, with whom all those elements combined found lodgment which

led on to " Illuminism." This will have to be dealt with later
on. But Christian doctrine is not merely "science," and during
the eighteen centuries of its existence Christendom as a whole
has never had the wish to break with history (even the most
radical movement — Calvinism — represents no complete
apostasy). Nay, it has felt as if every break, even with the most
unhappy past, would mean self-dissolution. The past, however,
was dogma and dogmatic theology. If there was neither the
ability nor the will to become severed from these, and if, nevertheless, there was an ever-increasing estrangement from them—
as the cry for practical Christianity and the disregard for the
theological element proved—the necessary consequence was that
dogma was respected as *a system of law*, but put aside. That
was really the state of things that had established itself also
among the ranks of the parties in opposition. Anyone who
attacked dogma exposed himself to the risk of being set down
as an anarchist. But anyone who sought a remedy for the
times in return to dogmatic Christianity and in closer occupation with its contents, and who aimed at getting quit of certain
practical abuses by falling back on the old dogmatic theory, was
regarded as wrong-headed, as a creator of disturbance, nay, as
a man to be suspected. Within the circles of higher-class
science favourable to reform, and even within the circles of the
silent opposition throughout the land, it was apt to be looked on
as an instance of monkish squabbling when an attempt was
made to proceed by means of *theory* against the indulgences, the
unlimited worship of saints, and the ritualistic extravagances of
the Church system. But even such attempts were partial and
infrequent. At the most there was a falling back upon
Augustine—the age tolerated that up to a certain point, nay,
demanded it; but where can we find, in those days, the man
who turned back to Christology and the doctrine of God in order
on the basis of these to revise and recast what was held as
valid ?

The ultimate cause of this lack and this incapacity is not
indeed to be sought for in the desolating effects of Nominalism,
or in the æsthetic spirit of the Humanists ;[1] it lay, rather, in the

[1] Cf. Drews, Humanismus und Reformation, 1887.

enormous disagreement that existed between the old dogma and the Christian intuitions that had taken shape in the Christian life of the time. This disagreement, which we have noted even in Augustine, and which is so plainly perceptible at the beginning of the Middle Ages in Alcuin,[1] had become even greater. Which out of the number of the old ecclesiastical dogmas, then, had still a directly intelligible meaning for piety in its then living form? Which dogma, as traditionally understood, had still a real motive power for Christian thought and life? The doctrine of the Trinity? But we only need to glance at the Scholastic doctrine of God, or at Anselm's doctrine of reconciliation, or at the books of devotion and the sermons of that period, in order to feel convinced that the time was past when the thought of the Trinity might, as in the days of Athanasius and the Cappadocians, form the main basis of edification for the Church. The doctrine of the two natures? But unless we are disposed to lend an ear to the sophists, can we fail to hear the strong protests against this doctrine's power to edify, that came from Bernard's mystic devotion to the Bridegroom of the Soul, from the Jesus-love of St. Francis and Thomas à Kempis, and from the image of the man Jesus, whose sorrow-stricken features were presented to view by every preacher in the fourteenth and fifteenth centuries? Did not the doctrine of grace, whether we think of it in the Augustinian-Thomistic or the Scotistic form, did not the huge apparatus of the Sacraments presuppose quite a different Christ from that sharply-defined intellectual thought-structure of Leontius and John of Damascus, which glorified the triumph of the divine nature in the human, and sought to produce by mere contemplation of the union the feeling of a subjugation and redemption of all flesh? Here lay the ultimate cause of the inward estrangement from dogma. Thought was no longer Greek thought, though speculation might apparently succeed without special trouble in returning to these conceptions. But for speculation the conceptions were now only presuppositions, they were no longer Christianity itself. When, however, the old faith is no more the expression of inner conviction, a new faith shapes

See Hauck, K.-Gesch. Deutschlands II. 1, pp. 132-136.

itself under the envelope of the old.   All spheres in which
Christian thought and life moved lay far apart from those
spheres of thought in which there had once developed itself the
faith that *might* be held.   It had now come to be a faith that
must be held; therein one had the merit of Christ, the
Church, the Sacraments, one's own merit and the indulgences.
Within these faith and Christian life moved.   While one
asserted that he stood on the old ground and had not departed
from it by a hair's breadth, there had been advance—a glorious
advance indeed ; but on the pathway there were gulfs that had
not been avoided, and they led down to the deepest regions.
There were not a few who observed this with terror and strong
displeasure ; but how could it be helped, so long as it was not
clearly seen how the condition had developed in which one
found himself, at what point the error had really arisen, and
where the height lay that one was required to reach ?

We can understand how under such circumstances there
should have been a going back to the authority that had at first
pointed out the path by which one had travelled for a thousand
years, and on which there had been the experience of a
splendidly gratifying progress, but also of a deep fall—a going
back, that is to say, to *Augustine*.   In his works were to be
found most powerfully expressed all the thoughts from which
edification was derived ; and on the other hand it was believed
that the grave abuses and errors were not to be found there
which one lamented at the time.   Hence the watchword :
"Back to Augustinianism, as to the true Catholicism of the
Fathers."   In very different forms this watchword was given
forth; in a comprehensive way by men like Wyclif, Huss,
Wesel, Wessel, and Pupper of Goch ;[1] in the most cautious form
by all those theologians who in the fifteenth century and at the
transition from the fifteenth century to the sixteenth went back,
in opposition to the prevailing Nominalism, to the Thomistic
doctrine of grace.   There seems to have been not a few of them ;

[1] Very thorough work has been carried on by Dutchmen during the most recent
decennia on the Augustinians of the Netherlands.   A very excellent monograph on
Goch has quite lately been produced by Otto Clemen (Leipzig, 1896).   On the relation
of Goch to Augustinianism, see l.c., pp. 209-223.

but if they were few, the distinguished position of those who
reverenced Thomas made up for the smallness of their number;
for some of them were to be found among the highest prelates,
even in Italy.   The importance of this retrograde theological
movement at the beginning of the sixteenth century is not to be
underestimated; it became—no doubt under the strong pressure
of the German Reformation—one of the most influential factors
in the Romish Church, when the question arose in the middle of
the sixteenth century as to the *dogmatic* position that was to be
taken up towards Protestantism.   But Augustine could give to
no age more than he himself possessed.   Even by him an
artificial connection only could be formed with the old dogma,
because he had in many respects inwardly grown out of it; and
on the other hand the germs of the abuses and errors of later
times which there was a desire to discard were already deposited
in him, whether one might observe it or not.   To find in
Augustine a remedy for the evils from which the Catholic
Church suffered would at the best have been to secure a reform
for a few generations.   But the old abuses would inevitably have
returned; for their strong, though hidden, roots lie in Augustinianism itself.   Had the Church been remodelled after his
pattern, there would very soon have been a re-introduction of
everything there was the wish to remove.   This is no airy
hypothesis; it can be proved both from the Christianity of
Augustine himself and from the history of the Catholic Church
in more recent times.   While the grave errors and abuses could
only assert themselves powerfully by means of a disintegrating
process on Augustinianism, yet they must be regarded as active
influences of which the sources lay in Augustine's Christianity.
      But this observation, while it goes to the root of things, must
not prevent our noticing very distinctly that the *genuine* Augustinianism exercised a potent critical influence on what had *become disintegrated*, including Nominalism.   It was a power full
of blessing.   It may very well be said that there never would
have been a Reformation had there not been first a revival of
Augustinianism.   It may of course be asserted, on the other
hand, that this revival would not even have resulted in such
Decrees as those of Trent, had it not been strengthened by a

new force. But at any rate there was so great a gulf between the immoral, the irreligious, and even pagan mechanicalism of the ruling church system, and the piety of Augustine, that one cannot fail to observe the salutary reform that would have resulted, if, for example, the Christianity of Wyclif had become determinative in the Catholic Church.

In addition to all this, there had developed itself, amid the decay of mediæval institutions, and under the great change of existing conditions, *one* element which we find everywhere at the beginning of the Reformation period, and which animated in varying degrees the opposing parties. Along all lines of development there had been an ultimate arriving at it; in all, indeed, it was the secret propelling force, which broke up the old and set itself to introduce something new. It is difficult to describe it in one word: subjectivism, individuality, the wish to be one's self, freedom, activity. It was the protest against the spirit of the centuries that had been lived through, and the beginning of a new attitude to the world generally. On a superficial view it appears most distinctly in the ideals of the Renaissance and Humanism; but it lived quite as much in the new politics of sovereigns and in the indignation of the laity at the old regulations in corporation and community, in Church and State. It was powerful in the Mystics' world of feeling, with their striving after practical activity; nay, it is not undiscoverable even in the Nominalistic Scholasticism, which, in its gloomy work of ruining the traditional theology, was not directed by the intellect only, but wrought from a dim impulse to restore religion to faith, and to bring to view faith's independent right and its freedom. The new element revealed itself everywhere as a two-edged principle: the age of Savonarola was the age of Machiavelli; in religion it comprehended all forms of individual religiousness, from the right of unbridled imagination and of prophetism to the right of liberty belonging to the conscience that is bound by the gospel. Within these extremes lay a whole graduated series of individual types; but at many points in the series the eager endeavour to come to one's self, to be and live and act and work as one's self, awakened the restless feeling: if thou art now thyself, and beginnest thyself to live as a man and as a Christian, where is the rock to which thou must cling ; what is thy blessedness, and how art thou to become certain of it ?　How canst thou be, and continue to be, at once a blessed and a free man ?　In this feeling of unrest the age pointed beyond itself; but we do not observe that even *a single* Christian could clearly understand the question that lay at the basis of this unrest, and give to it the answer.

———————

It certainly repays trouble to consider what would have become of dogma if the development had continued which we observe in the fourteenth and fifteenth centuries, and if no new factor had intervened.　*Issues* of dogma there would assuredly have been ; but the question, of course, does not admit of being decided as to *what* issue would have remained victorious.　We can conceive (1) that Curialism might have rapidly achieved a complete triumph and vanquished all refractory elements; in that case the sovereign papal will would have come to be the court of final appeal even in the domain of faith and morals, and the old dogma would have become a part of the papal consuetudinary law, which would really have been modified ad libitum by arbitrary interpretations and decisions of the Pope.　Under such circumstances, believers would have been obliged to become accustomed to the thought that fides implicita, that is, obedience, was a work of merit, imparting *value* to all their other doings, so far as the sacramental system imposed these upon them.　In a material sense dogma would have come to an end ; the Church would have remained the institution authorised to grant salvation ; even though no one had believed what it taught, yet all would have submitted to its regulations. There would thus have been a sinking to a lower stage of religious development.　But it can also be conceived (2) that from the circles of the parties opposed to it a reform might have been forced upon the Church ; a reform which, within the field of ecclesiastical law, would have consisted in a reduction of the powers of the papacy in favour of an ecclesiastical oligarchy, and, within the field of dogmatic, in an establishment

of the Augustinian-Mystic Christianity. We can very well
imagine that all the Augustinian-Mystic thoughts, which as yet
had received no dogmatic symbolic definition whatever, but
which formed the basis of the piety of the best Christians,
would have come eventually to be strictly formulated. In this
case two things would have been possible : the attempt might
have been made to maintain the connection with the old dogma,
as even Augustine had maintained it (even in that event it
would at any rate have become clearly apparent that those
dogmas were presuppositions that had been transcended), or it
would have been shown that another view of the Godhead and
another view of the God-man must be substituted for the old.
But (3) there might also have been expected at the beginning
of the sixteenth century a *breaking up* of the Church. One
section would have advanced along the path described under 1
or 2, another would have taken its course from the illuminist
directions that were given in the pantheistic Mysticism that
neutralised historic Christianity, in the rationalistic criticism of
dogma by Nominalism, and in the Humanistic conception of
the world. If such a movement had taken shape, it would have
been a question whether it would have stopped short before
Scripture, or whether it would not even have advanced beyond
it. One might be ready to expect both in observing the signs
of the times about the year 1500. In the one case a rationalistic
or an enthusiastic Bible-Christianity would have been the issue,
in the other case developments would have necessarily resulted
which cannot be calculated. But in both cases the old dogma
would have ceased to exist. But, lastly (4), one could have
expected (though it is questionable whether, in view of the
mediæval condition of things, such an expectation could have
arisen had the Reformation not taken place) that out of the
fermenting elements in the fourteenth and fifteenth centuries a
new and deeper type of religion would have developed itself.
That is to say, if we combine things that clearly present themselves to view—that a number of the theologians (Dominican
Mystics) were disposed to labour, even in theology, only at
what was really *for edification*, that the point was being sought
for in the spiritual nature of man that is at the same time the

seat of religion and the *nucleus of the soul's life*, that out of this nucleus there was to be formed by *regeneration* a new inner man, who must become certain of his *blessedness* and *freedom;* if we add to this that Nominalism had taught the lesson that the endless efforts of speculation can produce no certainty, that certainty therefore must be sought for somewhere else; and if we then take into consideration what the general state of mind was—that men were then striving to free themselves from the spirit of the Middle Ages, to return to the sources, and to live henceforth as independent personalities, it is perhaps not too bold to expect in the province of religion, at the beginning of the sixteenth century, a new development that would include an evangelical reformation of all that constituted religion, but that would thereby also uproot and put an end to the old dogma, inasmuch as the new point of departure, the living faith in God as being gracious for Christ's sake, and the right to be free springing from that faith, could only allow what belonged to it to retain its place in theology.

But the actual history did not exactly correspond with these expectations. This time, also, history did not connect the new epoch with the old as logic develops a new position from the refutation of an old. The real issues of dogma rather, in the sixteenth century, continued to be burdened with contradictions, which raised for the period that followed important problems. For that reason one might be in doubt as to whether *issues* can really be spoken of; still, after what has been developed in the Prolegomena to the history of dogma (Vol I., 1 ff.), and what has been stated in the sequel, it will certainly be necessary to use this term.

In the sixteenth century the crisis in the history of dogma took a threefold issue.[1]

----

[1] The crisis *in the history of dogma*—if we review the development in connection with the whole movement of spiritual life we shall not speak of issues, nor shall we be satisfied with the movements in the history of dogma. In that case, rather, the historical reflections would have to be included, which Dilthey has so admirably

1. The old Church developed itself on the one hand more decidedly into the papal Church, and thereby struck out on the path indicated above (sub. 1) ; but, on the other hand, it gave fixity to the Augustinian-Mediæval doctrines, and added them to the old dogmas as equally legitimate portions of the system (see above, sub. 2). Although that took place at Trent in a way clearly indicating that the position taken up was not within dogma, but *above* it, and that on that account there was the decision to regulate it by the practical needs of the Church as an outward institution, yet one was obliged to make *compromises ;* for the Reformation forced even the old Church to judge spiritual things spiritually, or at least to adopt the appearance of a spiritual character. Just for that reason the Decrees of Trent still belong to the history of dogma ; for they are not merely products of the ecclesiastico-political skill of the Curia, although they do very really bear that character. So far, however, as this is not the case, they prepared many difficulties for the Church, and checked its full development into Curialism. The discords and struggles within the Catholic Church during the following three centuries made this sufficiently plain. But these struggles resulted, step by step, in suppressing the elements of opposition, till at last, after the immeasurable service which the French Revolution and Napoleon I. rendered to Curialism, the complete victory of the papacy could be proclaimed in the dogma of Mary and in the Vatican Decrees. In this way that was at last attained which the Curia and its followers already

developed in his dissertations on "The Natural History of the Mental Sciences in the Seventeenth Century" (Archiv. f. Gesch. der Philosophie, Vol. V., p. 480 ff. : Vol. VI., pp. 60-127, 225-256, 347-379, 509-545) ; cf. also his essay on " The Autonomy of Thought, Constructive Rationalism, and Pantheistic Monism, viewed in their connection in the Seventeenth Century " (l.c. Vol. VII., pp. 28-91). Dilthey distinguishes between three great trends in the theology of the sixteenth century, which in some minds, of course, crossed one another : (1) The ecclesiastical theology, which adhered to the system of dogma (though with modifications) ; (2) the transcendental theology (Christianity as the fulfilment of the universal religious striving and struggle that goes on everywhere and at all times in humanity)—the school that deals with the universal that lies behind the religions and their forms ; (3) the ethical rationalism (expressed most definitely in Socinianism). The first tendency has its root in the more or less purified *ecclesiastical* tradition, the second in the intuition and feeling of an All-One that reveals itself in a variety of degrees in all that is individual, the third in the ideas of the Stoa.

sought to reach in the sixteenth century; as the Church became
the handmaid of the Pope, so dogma also became subject to his
sovereign rule. It is at the same time a matter of entire indifference in what speculations Catholic theologians indulged
with regard to the relation of the papacy to dogma, when they
asserted that the Pope was bound by Catholic doctrine; for
anyone who has the right to expound will always be able to
find a way in which a new dogma which he creates can be set
forth by him as an old one. The whole idea of dogma, however, as *the faith* which ought to animate every Christian heart,
and which makes the Christian a Christian, is in reality discarded so far as it is left to each individual to determine whether
or not he can adopt the faith in its whole extent. If he succeeds
(but who could succeed in view of the whole, half, and quarter
dogmas, and the countless multitude of decisions?), so much the
better; if he fails, then no harm is done, if only he has the
intention to believe what the Church believes. That we have
here an *issue* of the history of dogma, whether more new dogmas
are afterwards to be formulated or not, is a matter beyond
doubt.

2. In the sixteenth century Antitrinitarian and Socinian
Christianity developed itself. It broke with the old dogma and
discarded it. In view of the rapid decline of the Socinian communities it might be held that the consideration of their
Christianity does not belong to the general history of the
Church at all, and therefore also does not belong to the history
of dogma; yet, if we take into account with how much certainty
Antitrinitarianism and Socinianism can be connected with the
mediæval development (Nominalism), with what energy the
Protestant dogmatic of the seventeenth century grappled with
them as its worst enemies, and finally, how closely in touch is
the criticism applied to dogma by evangelical theologians in the
eighteenth and nineteenth centuries with the Socinian criticism,
we should be in conflict with history were we to think of ignor-
ing the *issue* of the history of dogma that is presented in
Socinianism.

3. But a third issue is to be found in the Reformation itself,
though certainly it is the most complicated, and in many re-

spects the most indefinite one. Instructed by history itself, the Reformation obtained a new point of departure for the framing of Christian faith in the Word of God, and it discarded all forms of infallibility which could offer an *external* security for faith, the infallible organisation of the Church, the infallible doctrinal tradition of the Church, and the infallible Scripture codex.[1] In this way that view of Christianity from which dogma arose—Christian faith the sure knowledge of the ultimate causes of all things, and therefore *also* of the divine provisions for salvation—was set aside : Christian faith is rather the firm assurance of having received from God, as the Father of

---

[1] With regard to the first point a proof is unnecessary. With regard to the second let Luther's treatise be read, "Von den Conciliis und Kirchen" (1539); but along with this also Form. Concord. P. I. Epitome, p. 517 (ed. Müller): "Reliqua vero sive patrum sive neotericorum scripta, *quocunque veniant nomine*, sacris litteris nequaquam sunt æquiparanda (not even the decrees of the Councils therefore) sed *universa illis ita subjicienda sunt, ut alia ratione non recipiantur, nisi testium loco*, qui doceant, quod etiam post apostolorum tempora et in quibus partibus orbis doctrina illa prophetarum et apostolorum sincerior conservata sit. . . . Symbola et alia scripta non obtinent auctoritatem judicis." Also Art. Smalcald. II. 2, p. 303 : "Verbum dei condit articulos fidei, et præterea nemo, ne angelus quidem." Also "Etliche Artikel, so M. Luther erhalten will wider die ganze Satansschule (1530, Erlanger Ausg. XXXI. p. 122): "The Christian Church has no power to lay down any articles of faith, has never yet done so, nor will ever do so. . . . All articles of faith are sufficiently laid down in Holy Scripture, so that one has no liberty to lay down more. . . . The Christian Church ratifies the Gospel and Holy Scripture as a subordinate ; it displays and confesses as a servant displays his master's livery and coat-of-arms," and see other passages. With regard to the third point, later Protestantism narrowed its position. But, so far as is known, no Lutheran of any standing, with the exception of Kliefoth, has ventured to sever himself publicly from the Luther of the earlier years. If, however, the attitude is *at least justifiable* in Protestantism which Luther took up in his well-known prefaces to the New Testament books (see the remarks on the Epistle of James, the Epistle to the Hebrews, and the Apocalypse), that implies the discarding of the infallible Scripture canon. At the same time, while historically very important, it is essentially a matter of indifference that there are to be found in Luther, especially after the controversy on the Eucharist, many assertions that are to the effect that every letter of Scripture is a foundation of Christian faith, for the flagrant contradiction that something at the same time does not, and does, hold good, can only have the solution that it does not hold good. This, however, necessarily follows also from Luther's view of faith, for the basis of his view is that faith is wrought by the Holy Ghost through the preached Word of God. Moreover, there is a common admission at the present day in the widest circles in Protestantism that historic criticism of Scripture is not unevangelical. No doubt this admission extends only to the "principle." Many forbid themselves the application.

Jesus Christ, the forgiveness of sins, and of living under Him in His kingdom—nothing else.   But from that dogma all supports were at the same time removed ; for how can it be unreformable and authoritative if men, with their limitations and entanglements in sin, sketched and formulated it, and if every security external to it is lacking ?   And yet the Reformers allowed the old dogma to remain ; nay, they did not even submit it to revision.   No doubt it was not as a law of faith over and above faith, a law resting on certain outward guarantees, that they let it retain its force ; their so acting was from the conviction, scarcely ever tested, that it exactly corresponded with the Gospel, the Word of God, and that it attests itself to everyone as the obvious and most direct meaning of the Gospel.   They regarded it as a glorious confession of God, who has sent Jesus Christ, His Son, in order that we, being delivered from sins, may be made blessed and free.   Because they found this witness in dogma, every motive disappeared for inspecting it more closely.[1]   It was not as dogma that it continued to them authoritative, but as a confession of God the Lord, who is hidden from the wise, but revealed unto babes.   But because it *remained in force* at all, *it remained in a sense as dogma.*   The old dogma was certainly not merely an evangelic testimony to the God of grace, to Christ the Redeemer, and to the forgiveness of sins ; indeed it reproduced these thoughts of faith only in an indefinite way ; it was, above all, knowledge of God and the world, and a law of faith.   And the more strenuously the Reformation accentuated *faith*, the more emphatically it represented it as the basis of all, in contrast with the uncertainties of the hierarchical, ritual, and monastic Christianity, the more disastrous did it necessarily become for it that it forced together, without observing it, this faith and that knowledge of faith and law of faith. When in particular there was now added the pressure of the external situation, and, as the result of the storms that had arisen (Fanatics, Anabaptists), the courage disappeared to assert anything "that is at variance with the Catholic Church or the Church of Rome, so far as this Church is known from the writers of Scripture" ("quod discrepet ab ecclesia catholica vel

[1] See Kattenbusch, Luther's Stellung zu den ökumen. Symbolen, 1883.

ab ecclesia Romana, quatenus ex scriptoribus nota est"), the
movement issued in the Augsburg Confession, which does not
indeed deny the principle of evangelical Christianity, but which
at the same time began (yet compare already the Marburg
Articles) to pour the new wine into the old bottles.[1] Did the
Reformation (in the sixteenth century) put an end to the old
dogma? It is safer to answer this question negatively than
positively. But if it is granted that it uprooted the foundations
of dogma—as our Catholic opponents with perfect justice represent—,that it is a powerful principle and not a new system
of doctrine, and that its history, throughout the periods of
Orthodoxy, Pietism, and Rationalism, and down to the present
day, is not an apostasy, but a necessary development, then it
must also be granted that the entirely conservative attitude of
the Reformation towards the old dogma belongs, not to the
principle, but to the history. Therefore, the Reformation, as a
continuously active movement, certainly represents an *issue*
of the history of dogma, and, we hope, the right and proper
issue.[2]

[1] That the gospel of the Reformation found a masterly expression in the Confession
of Augsburg (Loofs, D. Gesch., 3rd ed., p. 399 : he cautiously adds, certainly,
"and in the Apology explaining it,") I cannot admit. The Augsburg Confession laid
the basis for the doctrinal Church ; the blame very really lies with it of contracting
the Reformation movement. Would anyone have so written before 1526, not to say
before 1529? Its arrangement is Scholastic, and, besides, is wanting in clearness ;
its statements at important points are, positively and negatively, intentionally incom-
plete ; its diplomatic advances to the old Church are painful, and the way in which
it treats the sectaries as naughty children, and flings out its " anathemas," is not only
loveless but unjust, dictated not merely by spiritual zeal, but also by worldly wisdom.
Yet it must not be denied that at the most important points it struck the nail on the
head, and that inlaid in this earthen vessel there are precious stones, with a simplicity
and fitness of setting which we find in no other Reformation writing. We can
already develop from the Augsburg Confession the Church of the Form of Concord,
if not the particular doctrinal formulæ ; but we can also, by moving backwards, derive
from it, and maintain, the freer evangelical fundamental thoughts, without which there
never would have resulted a Reformation or an Augsburg Confession. As regards
its author, however, it may be said without hesitation that Melanchthon here undertook—and was required to undertake—a task to which his gifts and his character
were not equal.
[2] It is very instructive here to place together the testimonies of two men who were
as different as possible, but who, in their estimate of the Reformation, as regards its
relation to the past and its relation to the present, are entirely at one. Neander writes

With a view to the delineation of our subject, the duty arises of describing more precisely the threefold issue of the history of dogma briefly sketched here. But just because they are issues, what is required of us is no longer an exhaustive statement : for in the issues of a thing it is no longer the thing itself that is the moving force—otherwise it would not take issue—but new factors intervene and come to occupy its place. For our purpose, therefore, it must be enough that we describe briefly the dogmatic development of the Romish Church till the time of the Vatican Decrees, without entering more minutely into political plans and complications, which must be left to Church history and the history of creeds ; that, further, we bring under notice the

(in his Account of the part taken by him in the Evangel. Kirchenzeitung, 1830, p. 20) : "*The spirit of the Reformation . . . did not attain quite at the beginning to clear self-consciousness.* So it happened that in an unobserved way many errors passed over from the old Canon Law into the new Church practice. To this there was added, on the part of a number of the Calvinistic theologians, a mingling and confusing of the Old and New Testament points of view. Luther—who on so many sides towered above the development of his time—setting out from the principle of the faith that unfolds itself freely and by its own inner divine force, reached here also consciousness of pure evangelicalism, *but owing to the movements connected with the Eucharist controversies, and during the Peasants' War, that pure consciousness became clouded again.*" The same scholarly and truthful man confessed publicly more than once that, although he claimed personally to hold the full evangelical faith, he could by no means entirely identify himself with the Augsburg Confession, and, though with all modesty, yet he clearly indicated that that can be no longer done by any Christian of the nineteenth century who has learned from history. To the same effect Ritschl asserts (Gesch. des Pietismus I., p. 80 ff., 93 ff. ; II., p. 60 f., 88 f.) : " The Lutheran view of life did not continue to run in an open channel, but was hemmed in and obstructed by objective-dogmatic interests, and became less distinctly visible. Protestantism was not delivered from the mediæval womb of the Western Church in its complete power and equipment, as was Athene from the head of Zeus. The imperfect way in which it took its ethical bearings, the breaking up of its comprehensive view of things into a set of separate dogmas, its preponderating expression of what it possessed in rigidly complete form, are defects which soon made Protestantism appear at a disadvantage in contrast with the wealth of mediæval theology and asceticism. . . . The Scholastic form of the pure doctrine is really only the preliminary, and not the final, mould of Protestantism." That Protestantism, or Lutheranism, when measured by the Augsburg Confession, no longer possesses a common pure doctrine is simply a fact, which is not altered by simply casting a veil over it. Of the twenty-one articles of faith in the Augsburg Confession, articles 1-5, 7-10, 17, 18, are in reality subjects of controversy even in the circles of those who still always act "on principle" as if nothing had become changed. In concreto the particular divergences are not only "tolerated" but permitted ; but no one, to

Socinian criticism of dogma ; and that, finally, we come to understand the Reformation in such a way that its distinctive character, as contrasted with the dogmatic inheritance of the past, shall become as clear to us as the dogmatic contraction that was its more immediate issue, and as the main lines of its further development down to the present day. To give a full historic narrative down to the time of the Form of Concord and the Decrees of Dort, and then to break off, I regard as a great mistake, for by such procedure the prejudice is only strengthened that the dogmatic formulations of the Churches of the Reformation in the sixteenth century were their classic expression, while they can certainly be regarded only as points of transition.[1]

use Luther's language, will bell the cat and publicly proclaim, and guide the Church in accordance with, what is unquestionably a fact which can never again be changed. We do not find ourselves in "a state of distress" so far as the public expression of our faith is concerned, but the untruthfulness, the timidity, and indolence with which we confront the changes in knowledge—that is the "state of distress." Luther had first to find the truth, and, when he had found it, he sold all that he had in order to purchase it for himself and Christendom. He sold the most glorious thing which the age possessed—the unity of the Catholic Church ; without regard to the "weak," and at the cost of all his old ideals of heaven and earth, he reduced it to ruins ; but his Epigones are so faint and anxious-minded that they will not even admit to themselves any new thing they have learned, and are in danger of selling themselves to a tradition of yesterday, or, after flinging away all evangelical perceptions, of retiring upon Greek dogma.

[1] Why I do not include the history of old Protestant doctrine in the history of dogma may be gathered from Paulsen, Gesch. des gelehrten Unterrichts, 2nd ed., Vol. I. (1896), pp. 432-450. Add to this that the history of old Protestant doctrine is the German after-bloom of the essentially Romanic Scholasticism. What is of value in it consists in some great fundamental perceptions, which, however, can be better studied at the fountain-head—that is, in the Reformers. The rest is without worth, is even without historical interest of a higher kind, and, in spite of the authority which princes, professors, and consistories have given, and still give, to it, is antiquated, and, as a spiritual force, exhausted. The objection of Dilthey is a serious one (Archiv. f. Gesch. d. Philos., Vol. V., Part 3, p. 353 ff.), that Luther's Christianity is not an issue of the history of dogma because it has the old dogma, and above all the doctrines of original sin and satisfaction as its necessary pre-suppositions. I make the admission to Dilthey that one has to take his choice. There is much, it is true, that would justify us in continuing the history of dogma down to the present day ; but what has run its course in it from the end of the seventeenth century in Protestantism has certainly no longer a resemblance formally, nor to some extent even materially, to the old history of dogma. Now, if we observe that this development in Protestantism is not an apocryphal one, but that it had one of its roots—in my opinion its strongest root—in the Reformation, we shall certainly have a right, in spite of the

Even Seeberg and Loofs break off with the Book of Concord and the Synod of Dort. In the case of the former, the adoption of this terminus is certainly intelligible ; one is only surprised not to find the Confession of Westminster, the most important Confession of the Calvinist Churches at the present day. On the other hand, it is difficult to understand how Loofs follows the view of the rejuvenated Lutheranism, a view of which, nevertheless, he himself disapproves in his closing section (p. 463), " Whoever looks with favour on the Union thereby acknowledges that the present must be so connected with the sixteenth cen-

admission that the old dogma was the necessary pre-supposition of the Christianity of Luther, to regard Luther as himself representing the issue of the history of dogma— in the same way, let us say, in which Christ must be regarded as the end of the law, although the law was not cancelled, but affirmed by Him. And here a further remark must be made about the old dogma as the "necessary pre-supposition of the Christianity of Luther." If it is in no sense admitted that the doctrine of original sin, the doctrine of satisfaction, and the doctrine of the "*person* and work" of Christ in general, have a rightful place in the pure, spiritual religion, then certainly the matter is decided ; one must then say with Dilthey that Luther's doctrine of justification itself exists only as long as these, its pre-suppositions, exist—that is, they cannot be united with the piety that thinks. But these very pre-suppositions, in my opinion, admit of a treatment under which their core is still preserved, and under which they still do what they did for Luther's experience of justification, while their mythological or metaphysico-transcendental form falls away. If that can be proved—the limits of this problem as regards *proof* I am fully conscious of—then it is possible to adhere to Luther's conviction of justification, together with the objective positions that lie at the basis of it, without asserting these positions in the inflexible dogmatic form which they once received. But in that case it is here again made out that Luther represents an issue of the history of dogma. Dilthey's objection is at bottom the same as that of Kübel (Neue Kirchl. Zeitschr. 1891, p. 43, etc.) : Since, according to Luther, the individual experience of faith is unquestionably dependent on the structure of the old dogma, he belongs to the history of the old dogma. But, in point of fact, it depends on a number of important motives, which found in the old dogma an imperfect expression. (Something similar had to be noted already in Augustine, although in a lesser degree.) It will be objected that it is not motives that are in question, but the reality or unreality of alleged facts. That also is correct ; the question then will be, whether to these alleged facts (universal attribution of guilt, θεὸς ἐν σαρκί, sacrificial death of Christ) there does not correspond something real, although not, certainly, as explained and spun out by the Greeks, Augustine, and Anselm. Furthermore, in a second series of essays in the Archiv. f. Gesch. d. Philos., Vol. VI., Parts 3, 4 (see Preuss. Jahrb., Vol. LXXV., Part 1, 1894), Dilthey has so firmly grasped the new religiousness of Luther and the Reformers, and has lifted it so high above the plane previously reached in history, that it can no longer be difficult for him to acknowledge that Luther represents an issue of the history of dogma. On these articles see below.

tury that the period of the Epigones is excluded. Now, as the
orthodoxy of the Epigones in the sixteenth century has its root in
this, that the Reformers still retained a number of Old Catholic
presuppositions and dogmas *which were not in agreement with
their own fundamental thoughts*, a convinced approval of the
Union must lead one to see that it is the problem for the
present to carry through the fundamental thoughts of the
Reformers in a more thorough-going and all-sided way than was
done, or could be done, in the sixteenth century." Very correct ;
but in that case one has only the choice—either to continue the
history of dogma down to the present day, or to content one's
self with setting forth the ground-thoughts of the Reformation.
But the latter is, in my opinion, what is required, and that not
merely because the giving form to Protestantism has, notwithstanding the 380 years during which it has existed, not yet come
to an end—the Augustinian-Roman Church needed still longer
time—but, above all, because, as Loofs very correctly remarks,
"the Reformers still retained a number of Old Catholic presuppositions and dogmas that were not in agreement with their
fundamental thoughts, and in these the theology of the Epigones
has its *roots*." Here, therefore, the distinctive character of the
Reformation principle is recognised in this, that, looked at in its
negative significance, it cancelled not only mediæval doctrines,
but Old Catholic *presuppositions and dogmas*. But there is no
dogma down to the present day which is not Old Catholic, or
derived from what is Old Catholic. *Accordingly the Reformation,
that is, the evangelical conception, faith, cancels dogma*, unless
one puts in the place of the real homogeneous dogma some
thought-construction of what dogma might be. But that being
so, it is a bad and dangerous case of connivance when within the
history of dogma the history of the Reformation Churches is only
considered so far as their doctrinal formulations kept within
the lines of the old dogma, or were in complete dependence on it.
The Reformation is the end of dogma in a sense similar to that
in which the gospel is the end of the law. It shook off the *law*
of faith, not with the view of declaring it to be sin, but as expressing the thought that it increases sin, an assertion that was
made of the Mosaic Law by Paul. It substituted for the demand

for the *act* of faith, which answers to the law, the freedom of the
children of God, who are not under the burden of a compulsion
to believe, but have the joy of a blessing bestowed upon them.
And as the Apostle Paul said with reference to the law, it can
say with reference to dogma, " Do we make void the law of
faith ?—nay, we establish it ; " for it knows and teaches that
the believing heart gives itself as a captive to Jesus Christ, and
renders Him obedience.

As the force and violence of the breach with the past was only
imperfectly expressed in the symbolic formulations of Protestantism in the sixteenth century, we should to-day be witnesses
against ourselves and our Christianity if we were to judge these
formulations finally complete. By this " we" there are to be
understood not only some modern theologians, or the straight-
forward adherents of the Evangelical Union—for them that is
self-evident—but not less, nearly all Lutherans. " The general
habit," Loofs is justified in saying, " is to speak of different
Christian confessions : no man of modern orthodoxy is orthodox
in the sense of the period that produced the last symbols, and
almost nowhere is obligation to the symbols conceived of as it
was then." But what a wretched state of things is the result of
this attitude, when there is an unwillingness to admit to one's
self that it is assumed ! One cannot go back ; neither is he
willing to go forward : and thus the ruling power is exercised
by the fancies with which the theologians of the Romantic
epoch bridged over abysses and closed up gulfs—is exercised by
ecclesiastical æstheticism ; is exercised by the fides implicita of
Nominalism, that is, by ecclesiasticism and anxiety about schism.
Each one regards the fancy of the other as false ; but it is
reckoned to him for righteousness if he has closed up the gulf
at all, no matter by what deceptive means it is done. In view
of this, the history of dogma would find rest for itself were it to
propagate the old prejudice that Protestantism stands to-day
beside the Form of Concord and the Synod of Dort. Even if
what we to-day discern, possess and assert—not in spite of our
Christianity, but on the ground of it—the purity of faith as faith
in the Father of Jesus Christ, the strict discipline of Christian
knowledge, moderation in judging diverging Christian convic-

tions, entire freedom of historic investigation of Scripture, with
a hundred other good things—even if these things could not be
successfully derived by us from the Reformation itself—nothing
else would remain for us but to testify that the Reformation was
not the final thing, and that in the course of history we have
passed through new purifications and received new good things
as gifts. As evangelical Christians we are not bound to the
Reformation, still less to the "entire Luther" and the "entire
Calvin," to whom some, in melancholy despair of the clearness
of the gospel and of their own freedom, in all seriousness point
us, but to the gospel of Jesus Christ. But we do not depart
from the plain testimony of history when we rediscover in the
Christianity of Luther and in the initial positions of the Reformation that to which Protestantism has at the present day, in
weakness and under restriction, developed itself, and when we
hold also that Luther's conception of faith is still to-day the
moving spirit of Protestantism, whether there be many
or few who have made it their own. Just on that account
the steps are to be warmly welcomed towards finding successors to the faith formulæ of the Epigones of the Reformation period in Confessions that do not require to be
submitted to under great distress and to be laboriously maintained, but that can be adhered to with truthfulness as the
evangelical faith. Failure, no doubt, followed the genuinely
evangelical attempt in the year 1846 to introduce a new confession : the Union was too weak to be able to do more than
proclaim itself ; it appeared to collapse at the moment when it
was to confess what it really was. But the problem has
remained unforgotten, and attention has recently been again
directed to it in a very impressive way by an evangelical theologian, who describes himself as orthodox and pietistic. We
do not need to dispute about terms ; he makes the demand for
a new "dogma" (Christliche Welt, 1889, Oct. and Nov.). He
means a new Confession of evangelical faith, emancipated from
dogma. But while among us, owing to a most melancholy
blindedness, such a demand is at once regarded as in itself
suspicious, and is met with scorn and the frivolous cry, "Beati
possidentes," things begin to stir among our brethren across the

Atlantic. Before me there lie a number of notices from the ranks of the earnest Calvinists there, contemplating a revision of the Westminster Confession (the chief symbol), that is, a correction of it in many points that were held in the seventeenth century to be the most important. At the head of this movement stands Professor Schaff (see his article, " The Revision of the Westminster Confession : A paper read before a special meeting, Nov. 4th, 1889, of the Presbytery of New York.") If any name, that of Schaff is a guarantee that nothing will be undertaken here that will not be carried through, and carried through, too, in the most prudent and gratifying way. [I allow these lines to stand, though his Church has been deprived of Schaff.] Schaff, and very many along with him, wish an alteration, or possibly an elimination, of Confess. C. III. 3, 4, 6, 7; VI. 1 ; X. 3, 4; XXV. 6; XXIV. 3. But they desire still more. The following noteworthy words are employed (p. 10) :—" . . . . Or if this cannot be done without mutilating the document, then, in humble reliance upon the Holy Ghost, who is ever guiding the Church, let us take the more radical step, with or through the Pan-Presbyterian Council, of preparing a brief, simple, and popular creed, which shall clearly and tersely express for laymen as well as ministers only the cardinal doctrine of faith and duty, leaving metaphysics and polemics to scientific theology ; a creed that can be subscribed, taught, and preached ex animo, without any mental reservation, or any unnatural explanation; a creed that is full of the marrow of the gospel of God's infinite love in Christ for the salvation of the world. Such a consensus-creed would be a bond of union between the different branches of the Reformed Church in Europe and America and in distant mission fields, and prepare the way for a wider union with other evangelical Churches. . . . In conclusion, I am in favour of both a revision of the Westminster Confession by the General Assembly and an œcumenical Reformed Consensus to be prepared by the Pan-Presbyterian Council. If we cannot have both, let us at least have one of the two, and I shall be satisfied with either." To this height of freedom have those risen whom Lutherans are fond of speaking of as "legalistic " Calvinists ! What would be said among us if a man of honour were to demand a revision of the Augsburg Confession? Of course the Calvinistic Churches of America possess something we do not possess—a freely organised Church, which gives laws to itself, and—courage! So we shall perhaps follow some day, if the Evangelicals in America go before with the torch.

One thing at any rate is made apparent by these steps of progress, though it is clear already from the principle of the Reformation—namely, that the Confessional definitions in Protestantism are not regarded as infallible. There is, it is true, an eager search in Lutheranism for an intermediate notion between reformable and infallible; but, so far as I see, no one as yet has been able to discover it. The old dogma, however, gave itself out as infallible; nay, it was only dogma so far as it advanced this claim. The formulations of Protestantism in the sixteenth century are not dogmas in this sense.

CHAPTER II.

(1) *The Codification of the Mediæval Doctrines in opposition
to Protestantism (Decrees of Trent).*

A CODIFICATION of its doctrines was forced upon the Catholic
Church by the Reformation.   For long the effort was made in
Rome to add to the condemnation of the Lutheran tenets a
positive statement of Romish doctrine, or even to secure that
addition through a Council.   From the strictly Curialistic standpoint both the one thing and the other seemed as unnecessary
as it was dangerous.   That princes and peoples should have
imperatively demanded both, and that a Council should really
have come to be held, which, apart from its decrees for reform,
that necessarily resulted in a considerable improvement in the
state of the Church, gave fixed form to hitherto undefined
doctrines, was a triumph of Protestantism.   As it was understood by the princes, this Council was finally to solve a problem
that had been previously dealt with, not without a real mutual
approximation, at religious conferences, and which, for the time,
appeared to have found a solution in the imperial Interim.
But in point of fact the Curia brought it about that at Trent
the opposition to Protestantism found its keenest expression.
In this way the Curia rendered Protestantism very important
service ; for what would have become of the Reformation after
Luther's death—at least in Germany—if there had been a
greater inclination to come to terms at Trent?
   In framing the Decrees of Trent the best forces co-operated
which the Church then had at its command.   True piety and
pre-eminent scholarship took part in the discussions.   The
renovated Thomism, made stronger in Italy by the Reforma-

tion itself, already held at the Council a place of equality with
every other party. From Humanism and the Reformation the
mediæval spirit of the Church had derived power, had strengthened and steeled itself for the conflict. This spirit, in union
with the Curia, really governed the Council by which a regeneration of the old Church was effected. This regeneration
comes to view within the dogmatic sphere in the breach with
the sceptical, critical elements of Scholasticism, and in the
confidence thereby obtained in *doctrine* and *theology*.[1] Notwithstanding what had happened before at the Council of
Florence, it was unquestionably an immense undertaking to
shape out ecclesiastical dogmas with a firm hand from the
almost unlimited material which Scholasticism and Mysticism
had provided, and to do so after a long period of silence extending over centuries. Such a task would never have been
thought of, and still less could it have been carried out, had not
the Reformation gone before with its Augsburg Confession.
The opposition to the Reformation, by which all schools represented at the Council, otherwise so different in character, were
bound together, determined both the selection of the dogmas to
be defined and their formulation. At many points we can still
see that at Trent the Augsburg Confession was followed ; *in all
the Decrees* the opposition to the evangelical doctrine was the
guiding motive. *The dogmatic Decrees of Trent are the shadow
of the Reformation. That it was given to Catholicism to understand itself, to give expression to its distinctive dogmatic character,
and thereby to rescue itself from the uncertainties of the Middle
Ages, was a debt it owed to the Reformation.*[2]

[1] In dogmatic and ethical Probabilism, it is true, the Nominalistic scepticism
returned, in a form very convenient for the Church.

[2] Loofs (Dogmengesch, p. 333 f.) is right in enumerating the following conditions
and tendencies in Catholicism as presuppositions of Tridentinism : (1) The re-
organisation in strict mediæval spirit of the Spanish Church by the crown under
Ferdinand and Isabella ; (2) the restoration of Thomism (especially in the
Dominican Order) ; (3) the zealous fostering (Mystic) of Catholic piety, especially in
some new Orders and congregations for Reform ; (4) the Humanistic efforts for
Reform and the ennobling of theology due to Humanism (there were even
Humanists who wished to return to Augustine) ; (5) the strengthening of the papacy
and the reappearance of Curialism from the middle of the fifteenth century ; (6) the
ecclesiastical interest of the secular sovereigns.

Yet Roman Catholicism was still not able to give *full* expression to itself in the Decrees of Trent. This must become apparent to everyone who compares the Decrees with the present-day condition and the present-day aims of the Church, and who thoroughly studies the Acts of the Council with the view of seeing what the strict Curialistic party wished even then to reach and did not yet reach. Not merely did the strain between Episcopalism and Papalism remain unrelieved—a cardinal ecclesiastical question for Roman Catholicism, indeed the decisive question—but to the recently strengthened Augustinian-Thomistic School also much greater scope had to be allowed within dogmatics than was permitted by a Church system based on the outward sacrament, on obedience, on merit, and on religion of the second order. The regard to the Augustinian-Thomist School is to be explained on different grounds. First of all, if there was a wish publicly to define dogmas like those of original sin, sin, election, and justification, the authority of Augustine could not be altogether passed by, even though at the time there was not a single voice raised on his behalf ; secondly, the most capable bishops and theologians, men of true piety, were to be seen among the ranks of the Thomists ; finally, the fact could not be concealed that a need for reform, .in opposition to the ecclesiastical mechanicalism, really existed in the widest circles, and that it could be met only by entering into the Augustinian thoughts. So it came about that the Roman Church in the sixteenth century derived more from Augustine to introduce into its dogma than we should be entitled to expect from the history through which it passed in the fourteenth and fifteenth centuries. But the way in which it adopted Augustinianism at Trent was not without an element of untruthfulness. No doubt we ought not to reproach the Fathers of the Council if they laboriously turned and polished the separate Decrees and made constant corrections ; so long as dogmas are not proclaimed by prophets, but constructed by the members of a synod, it will be impossible to invent any other method than that by which the work was carried on at Trent. But the untruthfulness here lies in this, that one of the parties—and it was the party whose influence

was finally determinative—had no wish whatever for Augustinianism, that it sought rather to establish as dogma the use and
wont of the Roman Church, which was compatible only with
Semi-Pelagian doctrine and sacramental mechanicalism. And
yet this does not include all that must be said. The untruthfulness lies still deeper. The ruling party, in league with
Rome, and under direction from Rome, had no wish whatever
for definitions, for it knew very well that its fundamental
dogmatic principles, as they came to view in its practice, did
not admit at all of being framed, and dared not at all be framed.
It had accordingly, throughout the whole Council, the one end
only in view—*to emerge from the purgatory of the Council as far
as possible unchanged, that is, having with it all its customs, practices, pretensions, and sins.* In the formulation of the Tridentine
dogmas this aim was reached by it, though it might be only
indefinitely. Just on that account these dogmas are in part
untrue and misleading,[1] although a keen eye perceives even
here what scope was left to " Probabilism," that deadly enemy
of all religious and moral conviction. But it gained its end
completely when it followed up the Decrees with the Professio
Tridentina, and, at the same time, had it established that to the
Pope alone the right is to be attributed to expound the Decrees.
Thus it gathered figs of thorns and grapes of thistles ; for it
now needed to fear no single turn in the Decrees, and, on the
other hand, it enjoyed the advantage which so imposing a
manifesto of the whole Church against Protestantism necessarily
secured.

How the Curia carried on its work at Trent we know, since
we received the bitter account of Paolo Sarpi. Just for that
reason we must include the Tridentinum within the history of
the issues of dogma ; for a stronger power than the interest of
faith, or the interest of pure doctrine, presided over the efforts
of the Council, and directed them in its own spirit—the interest,

[1] Even the self-designation of the Synod is equivocal : " Hæc sacrosancta,
œcumenica et generalis Tridentina Synodus in spiritu sancto legitime congregata, in
ea præsidentibus (eisdem) tribus apostolicæ sedis legatis " ; compare also the famous
and frequently repeated addition : " salva semper in omnibus sedis apostolicæ
auctoritate." As is well known, there was also obstinate discussion as to whether
there was to be given to the Council the title : " universalem ecclesiam repræsentans."

viz., of the Roman Church to assert itself as the unreformable institution that exercises rule and grants salvation. And if it is undeniable that at Trent, and in the Decrees of the Council, a devout faith also expressed itself, which knew no higher power above itself, yet it passed out of view in the general result. Through his prerogative to be the sole exponent of the Decrees, the Pope really made the whole dogmatic work at Trent uncertain and illusory, and the succeeding centuries proved distinctly enough that one would embrace the gravest errors regarding the practical and dogmatic interests of the Roman Church were he to think of forming a view of the faith of the Roman Church on the basis of the Tridentine Decrees alone (taken as they sound). Indeed, he would only discover here somewhat vaguely what at the present day is the real endeavour of the Roman Church in the region of dogma and was visible at Trent only behind the scenes—*namely, to transform dogma into a dogmatic policy*, to declare all traditions as they sound to be sacrosanct, *while admitting, however, at every point conflicting probable opinions*, and to debar the laity from faith and dogma, in order to accustom them to a religion of the second order—to the Sacraments, the saints, the amulets, and an idolatrous worship of the members of Christ's body.

Under such circumstances there only remains an interest of a secondary kind in considering in detail the Decrees as they sound. If we have once made clear to ourselves the contradictory aims that were to be united in them, and feel certain that it is really a matter of indifference whether a Decree has more of an Augustinian ring or not, general history can only in a meagre way take to do with these laboriously refined and elaborated works of art. In the sequel, therefore, we shall restrict ourselves to what is most important.[1]

---

[1] Authorised edition of the Decrees, 1564 (reproduced in Streitwolf und Klener, Libr. symb. eccl. cath., I., 1846). The Masarellian Acta, edited by Theiner (Acta genuina. Agram, 1874, 2 vols.); numerous reports, etc., relating to the Council published by Le Plat (1781 ff.), Sickel (1870 ff.), Döllinger (1876 ff.), v. Druffel (1884 f.), Pallavicini, (1656), Salig (1741 f.). Illustrations by Ranke (Römische Päpste I., Deutsche Reformation V.), Pastor (1879). An introduction to the Council forms Bd. I. d. gesch. d. Kathol. Ref. by Maurenbrecher (1880). The same author afterwards began an exhaustive account in the " Histor. Taschenbuch," 1886, 1888,

The Synod, assembled to deliberate on "the extirpation of
heresies and reform of morals" (de exstirpandis hæresibus[1] et
moribus reformandis), begins, at the third session, with re-
affirming the Constantinopolitan Symbol, including the "filioque"; this Symbol, moreover, is introduced with the words
"symbolum fidei, quo sancta *Romana* ecclesia utitur" ("Confession of faith which the holy *Roman* Church uses"). It then,
at the fourth session, at once took up the question as to the
sources of knowledge and the authorities for truth. For the
first time in the Church it happened that this question was
dealt with at a Council. Everything that had, from the days of
the struggle against Gnosticism, been either established or
asserted with some uncertainty in the consuetudinary law of
the Church still needed final determination. All the more important is the Decree. In its making the main point of the
whole decision lie in preserving the "purity of the gospel"
(puritas evangelii), it gives positive evidence of the influence
of the Reformation; but in its declaring the Apocrypha of the
Old Testament canonical, in its placing tradition alongside
Scripture as a second source of information, in its proclaiming
the Vulgate to be authoritative, and in its assigning to the
Church alone the right to expound Scripture, it defines most
sharply the opposition to Protestantism.[2]

As regards the first point, the Reformation, by its re-adoption
of the Hebrew canon, had given expression to its general postu-
late, that there should be a going back everywhere to the
ultimate and surest sources. In opposition to this the Triden-

but it was not given to him to carry it further. The chief Protestant work against
the Tridentinum from the dogmatic point of view is Chemnitz, exam. conc. Trid.
1565 f. (extracts in German by Benedixen, 1884), cf. Köllner, Symbolik d. röm.-
kath. Kirche, 1844. On the question of the primacy in the Trid. see Grizar in the
Zeitschr. f. Kathol. Theol., 1884. The number of investigations of points of detail
is very great, and these have not yet been utilised for a new, comprehensive account,
because there is still always new material to be expected, especially from the Vatican,
but also from the archives of the States.

[1] Or, "de confirmandis dogmatibus." See III. 1 fin.

[2] The Lutheran Reformation, besides, had not already expressed itself confessionally
on the sources of knowledge and authorities, and, as is well known, did not even
do so later on.

tinum sanctioned the current traditional view.[1] Yet the act of fixing was in itself of the greatest importance; strictly speaking, indeed, it was only through it that a point of rest was attained in the history of the canon within the Roman Church. Even at that time there were still Bible manuscripts belonging to the Church that contained 4th Book of Esra, Hermas, the Epistle to the Laodiceans, etc. This uncertain state of things was now finally terminated.[2]

As regards the second point, the important words run as follows :—" That truth and discipline are contained in the books of Scripture and in unwritten traditions which, having been received from Christ's own lips by the Apostles, or transmitted as it were manually by the Apostles themselves, under the dictation of the Holy Spirit, have come down even to us "[3] (or, " and also receives with an equal feeling of piety and reverence the traditions relating sometimes to faith, and sometimes to morals, as dictated either orally by Christ or by the Holy Spirit, and preserved in continuous succession within the Catholic Church ").[4]

The entire co-ordination of Scripture and tradition was in many respects a novum (especially as regards discipline). A usage was here sanctioned—no doubt to meet the Protestant criticism, which could not be repelled from Scripture alone—

[1] It is also noteworthy, that in the enumeration of the New Testament books, the Epistle to the Hebrews is counted in as the fourteenth Pauline epistle without remark.

[2] The Tridentine Decree goes back even at this place to the Bulls of Eugene IV., which in general were among the most important parts of the material for the decisions of the Council. In the Bull pro Jacobitis " Cantate Domino " the most of the Apocryphal Books are already without distinction placed in a series with the Canonical Books, while the Epistle to the Hebrews is described as an Epistle of Paul. This reckoning follows the Canon of Innocent I. (Ep. 6 ad Exsuperium Tolosanum c. 7). In approving this the Tridentinum originated the contradiction of on the one hand recognising the Alexandrian Canon of the Bible, and on the other hand following the Vulgate, while Jerome rejected the Apocrypha, or at least treated it quite freely ; see Credner, Gesch. des Kanons, p. 300 f., 320 ff.

[3] " Veritatem et disciplinam contineri in libris scriptis et sine scripto traditionibus, quæ ab ipsius Christi ore ab apostolis acceptæ aut ab ipsis apostolis, spiritu sancto dictante, quasi per manus traditæ ad nos usque pervenerunt."

[4] " Nec non traditiones ipsas tum ad fidem tum ad mores pertinentes tamquam vel oretenus a Christo vel a spiritu s. dictatas et continua successione in ecclesia catholica conservatas pari pietatis affectu ac reverentia suscipit."

that had as yet by no means been fully established in the
Middle Ages, as was made clearly apparent at the deliberations
connected with the framing of the Decree.   Voices were raised
demanding that priority should be given to Scripture; but
they failed to assert themselves.   The defining tradition more
precisely as traditio Christi and traditio apostolorum (spiritu
sancto dictante), without, however, indicating in any way what
the two traditions embraced, and how they were distinguished,
was a master-stroke of dogmatic policy, which clearly shows
that the object in view was not to furnish a strong basis for that
which constitutes Christianity.   But the fact is extremely noteworthy that there is entire silence maintained here as to the
authority of the Church and of the Pope.   In this the untruthfulness of the Decree reveals itself; for the ultimate concern of
the Curia was to see that its arbitrary decisions were regarded
as sources of knowledge and authorities on truth.[1]   It was able
to attain that by the help of this quite indefinite Decree ; but at
that time it was unable as yet to give *direct* expression to
it ; hence there was silence maintained with regard to the Pope
and the Church.

   The proclaiming of the Vulgate ("that it shall be held as
authoritative in public reading, disputation, preaching, and exposition, and that no one shall dare or presume to reject it on
any pretext whatever "[2]) was a violent measure, which could
not be justified even by the law of custom, and was, besides,
directly counter to the age in which one lived.[3]   The same thing
is to be said of the requirement, that everyone shall be obliged
to adhere to the sense of Holy Scripture to which the Holy
Mother-Church adheres (" to whom it belongs to judge of the
true sense and interpretation of the Holy Scriptures "[4]), and

---

[1] Repeatedly at the Council speeches were delivered—especially by Jesuits, but also
by others—the sum and substance of which was, that as the Church could never err
in faith, its theory and practice were correct in all particulars (the Church, however, is
Rome).   But as there was not frankness enough to proclaim this position publicly, it
did not come clearly to view in the decisions.

[2] " Ut in publicis lectionibus, disputationibus, prædicationibus et expositionibus pro
authentica habeatur, et ut nemo illam rejicere quovis prætextu audeat vel præsumat."

[3] "Here the Church for ever broke with its own past, and with all that comes
under the name of science."   Credner, l.c., p. 324.

[4] " Cujus est judicare de vero sensu et interpretatione scripturarum sacrarum."

that no one shall dare to set himself up against the " unanimis consensus patrum." This requirement, it is true, was not in itself new ; but it was new that the whole Church should abolish all historico-exegetical investigation of the foundations of religion.[1] The way in which, in the sequel, the use of Scripture generally is subjected to reservations, is also unprecedented ; the decision, moreover, that the Church alone possesses the right to expound Scripture is ambiguous when there is nothing said as to who the Church is. Here also there was not yet courage enough to represent that the Pope was the Church.[2]

At Sessions V. and VI. the Synod then dealt with original sin and justification. This order was due simply to the opposition to Protestantism, and gives to the two Decrees an importance which does not really belong to them. A better course, therefore, is to consider the following Decrees first (Sessions VII.-XXV.) ; for in them (Sacraments VII., XIII., XIV., XXI., XXIII., XXIV. ; Mass XXII. ; purgatory, saints, images, indulgences XXV.) the determining interests of Catholicism found expression, and there was here no need to give one's self anxiety.

That there was the wish to affirm of the Church that it was the Sacrament-Church is apparent from the proposition which is found in the prologue to the Decree of Session VII., and which fills the place of a whole dogmatic chapter : " by means of the Sacraments all true righteousness either begins, or, having been begun, is increased, or, having been lost, is restored " (" per sacramenta omnis vera justitia vel incipit vel cœpta augetur vel amissa reparatur "). Not a word is said as to how the Sacraments have that power, as to what relation they have to the Word and promises of God, and as to how they are related to faith. This silence is the thing of most significance ; for it shows that just the Sacrament itself as externally applied is to be regarded as the means of salvation. Accordingly, without any determination of what the Sacrament in genere is,

---

[1] " Certainly in this way Scripture becomes consecrated, but it is reduced to a mummy, which can no longer develop any kind of life." Cremer, l.c.

[2] See on the whole Tridentine Decree Holtzmann, Kanon und Tradition, p. 24 ff. ; J. Delitzsch, Das Lehrsystem der Römischen Kirche I., p. 295 ff., 358 ff.., 385.

there is a passing on at once to thirteen anathematisms, it
being previously certified merely that all that follows is derived
from the teaching of Holy Scripture, from the apostolic traditions, the Councils, and the consensus patrum. Consequently the
thirteen anathematisms contain a continuous series of definitions, in which the most recent use and wont in the Church, as
defined by the Schoolmen, is raised to the level of dogma,
while all historic memories pointing in an opposite direction—
whose testimony was certainly audible enough—were suppressed. *These dogmas formulated in the thirteen anathematisms
are really the protest against Protestantism.*

Canon I raises to the position of dogma the doctrine that
there are seven Sacraments—no more and no less—*and that all
the seven were instituted by Christ.*[1] Canon 4 rejects the doctrine
that man can be justified before God without the Sacraments (or
without a vow to receive the Sacraments [votum sacramenti])
by faith alone (per solam fidem). Canon 5 pronounces anathema
on those who teach that the Sacraments are instituted for the
sake of only nourishing faith (propter solam fidem nutriendam),
and thus severs the exclusive connection of faith and Sacrament.
Canon 6 formulates the Scholastic doctrine of the efficacy of
the Sacraments ex opere operato (without, however, applying
this expression here), and thereby excludes more decisively the
necessity of faith, a mysterious power being attributed to the
Sacraments.[2] Canon 7 defines this efficacy of the Sacraments
still more exactly, asserting that where they are received in due

[1] Here, no doubt, the question can still always arise, whether He instituted them
all "immediate"; but in view of the literal terms of the Decree that would be a case
of sophistry.

[2] "Si quis dixerit, sacramenta novæ legis non continere gratiam, quam significant
(see above, the Scholastic controversy, Vol. VI., p. 206 f.), aut gratiam ipsam non
ponentibus obicem (see above, Vol. VI., p. 223 f.) non conferre, quasi signa
tantum externa sint acceptæ per fidem gratiæ vel justitiæ et notæ quædam Christianæ
professionis, quibus apud homines discernuntur fideles ab infidelibus, anathema sit."
It is characteristic that the Canon does not assume a third possibility between the
Sacraments as vehicles and the Sacraments as signs. Such a possibility, too, is hard
enough to conceive of, as is proved by the Lutheran doctrine, which makes the
attempt. The Scotist doctrines with regard to the concomitance of the gracious
divine effects and the rite are not expressly controverted by the Tridentinum; but the
terms employed are unfavourable to them.

form (rite), they communicate grace from God's side (ex parte dei) always, and to *all* receivers too. Canon 8 concludes this survey with the words : " if anyone shall say that grace is not conveyed *ex opere operato* by the Sacraments of the New Law, *but that faith alone in the divine promise is sufficient for obtaining grace*, let him be anathema."[1] The 9th Canon raises to a dogma the doctrine of " character " (baptism, confirmation, and consecration to the priesthood), but is cautious in not defining this " character in anima " more exactly than as " a certain spiritual and indelible sign " (" signum quoddam spirituale et indelibile ").[2] The 10th Canon pronounces anathema on those who assert that all Christians have the power to preach the Word and administer the Sacraments, and thus directs itself against the universal priesthood. The 11th Canon raises to a dogma the doctrine of the intentio of the priest (" intention of at least doing what the Church does "[3]), without which the Sacraments are not Sacraments. Lastly, the 13th Canon gives fixity to all unratified customs of the Church connected with the celebration of the Sacraments, it being declared : " If anyone shall say that the received and approved customs of the Catholic Church, which are usually applied in the solemn administration of the Sacraments, may either be despised or omitted by ministers as they please without sin, or changed into other new ones by any pastor of the Churches, let him be anathema." [4]

As in all these statements the Council adopted only negative definitions, it succeeded in the happiest way in steering clear of all the reefs in Scholastic discussion of the Sacraments. Even in

[1] "Si quis dixerit, per ipsa novæ legis sacramenta ex opere operato non conferri gratiam, sed solam fidem divinæ promissionis ad gratiam consequendam sufficere, anathema sit."

[2] Compare Cat. Roman. II., 1 Q. 19, where, however, little more is said than that the character " veluti insigne quoddam animæ impressum est, quod deleri numquam potest . . . et præstat, tum ut apti ad aliquid sacri suscipiendum vel peragendum efficiamur, tum ut aliqua nota alter ab altero internoscatur."

[3] "Intentio saltem faciendi quod facit ecclesia."

[4] "Si quis dixerit, receptos et approbatos ecclesiæ catholicæ ritus in solemni sacramentorum administratione adhiberi consuetos aut contemni aut sine peccato a ministris pro libito omitti, aut in novos alios per quemcunque ecclesiarum pastorem mutari posse, anathema sit."

the selection of what is negatively defined—how much would still remain to be defined—there is apparent an admirable skill. Generally speaking, what is here marked out is really the basis common to all the Schoolmen. Hence, when the definitions are translated into a positive form, they come closest to Thomism, while at the same time they do not exclude the Scotist positions.

There now follow the Decrees on the Sacraments singly. Here the decretum pro Armenis in the Bull of Eugene IV., " Exultate deo," [1] had so prepared the way with its short and yet comprehensive definitions that the dogmatic determination offered no great difficulty to the Fathers. The character of the definitions of particulars is akin to that of the general definitions ; the most extreme, and therefore disputed, Scholastic theses of the Schools are trimmed down in the interest of unity of faith ; and thus a type is produced, which comes very close to the Thomistic, and yet does not make it impossible for the doctrines to be re-shaped in harmony with dogmatic Probabilism.

Among the propositions relating to Baptism (Session VII.) the 3rd Canon (in introducing which no connection is indicated) is the most important, because by implication it makes all the rest unnecessary : " if anyone shall say that in the Church of Rome, which is the mother and mistress of all churches, there is not the true doctrine concerning the Sacrament of Baptism, let him be anathema." [2] The 9th and 10th Canons restrict the importance of baptism, in opposition to the evangelical view ; the 10th is especially instructive from its putting together remembrance and faith (recordatio and fides) in a way that depreciates faith, as well as from its limiting the effect of baptismal grace to former sins.[3] As regards Confirmation, the history of the development of this observance is now finally expunged —history, that is to say, is transcended by dogma (Can. 1);

---

[1] See Denzinger, Enchiridion, 5th ed., p. 172 f.

[2] "Si quis dixerit, in ecclesia Romana, quæ omnium ecclesiarum mater est et magistra, non esse veram de baptismi sacramento doctrinam, anathema sit."

[3] "Si quis dixerit, peccata omnia, quæ post baptismum fiunt, *sola recordatione et fide suscepti baptismi vel dimitti vel venalia fieri*, anathema sit."

moreover, it is henceforth an article of *faith*, that the bishop alone is the minister ordinarius of this Sacrament (Can. 3).

In dealing with the Eucharist (Session XIII.) the Council was not satisfied with Canons, but rose to a Decree. But this Decree, if one glances over the Scholastic questions of dispute, is certainly seen to be pretty vague. It is likewise known that there was here a coming together of opposing theological parties. In defiance of history it is asserted (c. 1) that it has always been unanimously confessed by all the Fathers that the God-man is present " truly, really, and substantially in this Sacrament under the form of things sensible." [1] In spite of imposing language about it, the effect of the Sacrament is really restricted to deliverance from daily (venial) sins and protection against mortal sins (c. 2). Then it is said (cap. 3), the old definition of the Sacrament in its entirety being adopted : " it is indeed common to the most holy Eucharist with the other Sacraments that it is the symbol of a sacred thing and the visible form of invisible grace ; but there is this point of pre-eminence and distinctiveness found in it,[2] that the other Sacraments only have power to sanctify when someone uses them, while in the Eucharist the Sacrament is itself the author of sanctity previous to the use." [3] It had always (it was asserted) been the Catholic faith that the God-man is present immediately after consecration, and wholly present, too, under both forms, in His Godhead, body and soul ; a more precise definition of this is then given— again as describing the faith that had *always* prevailed in the Church : " that by the consecration of bread and wine a conversion takes place of the entire substance of the bread into the substance of the body of Christ our Lord and of the entire substance of the wine into the substance of His blood. Which conversion is fittingly and properly designated by the holy

[1] "Vere, realiter et substantialiter sub specie rerum sensibilium in hoc sacramento."

[2] Cf. Cat. Rom. II., c. 4, Q. 39 : the Eucharist is the fons of all Sacraments, which flow from it like brooks.

[3] "Commune hoc quidem est sanctissimæ eucharistiæ cum ceteris sacramentis symbolum esse rei sacræ et invisibilis gratiæ formam visibilem ; verum illud in ea excellens et singulariter reperitur, quod reliqua sacramenta tunc primum sanctificandi vim habent, cum quis utitur, at in eucharistia ipse sanctitatis auctor ante usum est."

Catholic Church transubstantiation." [1]   Hence there is required
for the Sacrament (c. 5) the worship of adoration (cultus latriæ)
(including the festival of Corpus Christi), and the self-communi-
cating of the priests is described as traditio apostolica (c. 8).
The appended anathematisms are nearly all directed against
Protestantism.   Anyone is condemned who does not recognise
the whole Christ corporeally in the Sacrament, who believes
that the substance of the elements remains after the consecration,
who denies that the whole Christ is in every part of each element, who regards the Sacrament as being Sacrament only " in
use " (" in usu "), but not also before or after use (" ante vel
post usum "), who rejects worship of the Host and the Corpus
Christi festival, etc.   But the worst Canons are 5 and 11; for
the former condemns those who hold that the forgiveness of
sins is the principal fruit of the Eucharist, and the latter runs:
" if anyone shall say that faith alone is sufficient preparation
for taking the Sacrament of the most holy Eucharist, let him
be accursed." [2]   Many demanded that lay-communion also
sub utraque (under both forms) should be simply condemned,
and a Decree to that effect was really imminent.   But under
the pressure of the princes and of public opinion the question
was for a time delayed, and thereafter, there being influences at
the Council itself that strongly asserted themselves in favour
of granting the cup to the laity, it was decided—but only half-
decided—by a Decree (Session XXI.) that betrays only too
plainly the embarrassment felt.   The granting of the cup to the
laity was not forbidden—indeed the admission was found necessary here that " from the beginning of the Christian religion the
use of both forms had not been infrequent," [3] but an anathema
was pronounced on everyone who should demand the cup ex
dei præcepto (as commanded by God), or who was not persuaded that the Catholic Church denied it to him on good

[1] "Per consecrationem panis et vini conversionem fieri totius substantiæ panis in
substantiam corporis Christi domini nostri et totius substantiæ vini in substantiam
sanguinis ejus.   Quæ conversio convenienter et proprie a sancta catholica ecclesia
transsubstantio est appellata."

[2] "Si quis dixerit, solam fidem esse sufficientem præparationem ad sumendum
sanctissimæ eucharistiæ sacramentum, anathema sit."

[3] "Ab initio Christianæ religionis non infrequens utriusque speciei usus fuisset."

grounds. The Scholastic doctrine of the whole Christ in either kind (totus Christus in qualibet specie) formed the dogmatic basis of the right to deny. From nothing can the perverted state of "science" in the Church be more plainly proved than from the fact that this "science" succeeded in its presuming to correct the institution of Christ. But of course science was really only the pretext ; for the motives were quite different that led the Church to withhold the cup from the laity.[1] A crowd of difficulties threatened to arise in connection with the question of the sacrifice of the Mass (Sessio XXII.). This was the most seriously assailed institution, and a theoretical vindication of it could not be evaded; while on the other hand it was impossible to write volumes. Yet volumes would have been required in order to solve all the problems that had been handed down by Scholasticism, problems that had been much discussed, but had never been settled or reduced to precise formulæ. Indeed the questions regarding the relation of the sacrificial death of Christ to the Eucharist (above all to the first celebration), and again of the Mass to the first Eucharist and to the death on the Cross, were in a pre-eminent degree the real mysteries of the labyrinthine dogmatic, and here every doctrinal statement had only resulted in creating new difficulties ! Besides, there was entire vagueness as to how the significance and use of the Masses were to be theoretically understood. The evil state of practice taught that the Mass was the most im-

---

[1] The Decree concludes with a remark which suggests yielding to necessity : "Duos vero articulos, alias (scil. Sess. XIII.) propositos, hos nondum tamen excussos, videlicet : An rationes, quibus s. catholica ecclesia adducta fuit, ut communicaret laicos atque etiam non celebrantes sacerdotes sub una tantum panis specie, ita sint retinendæ, ut nulla ratione calicis usus cuiquam sit permittendus, et An, si honestis et Christianæ caritati consentaneis rationibus concedendus alicui vel nationi vel regno calicis usus videatur, sub aliquibus conditionibus concedendus sit, et quænam sint illæ : eadem s. synodus in aliud tempus, oblata sibi quamprimum occasione, examinandos atque definiendos reservat." With this is to be compared the Decree of the 23rd Session : "integrum negotium ad sanctissimum dominum nostrum (scil. the Pope) esse referendum, qui pro sua singulari prudentia id efficit, quod utile republicæ Christianæ et salutare petentibus usum calicis fore judicaverit." That the decision could not be come to at Rome and in the Council to grant the cup to the laity was an extremely happy circumstance for Protestantism, for many of those who had the fate of the Protestant cause in their hand would have been induced by that concession to make a compromise.

portant function within religious and ecclesiastical life ; yet
dogmatic theory, which could not surrender the unique importance of Baptism and the Sacrament of Penance, left only the
most meagre room for the efficacy of the Mass.   In a very skilful manner the Decree (c. 1) glides over the gulfs in the historic
proof for the establishment of the Mass (by Christ), while it
defines in a way full of manifest contradictions the effect of the
ordinance, this effect being described in c. 1 as " saving virtue
for the remission of sins which are committed by us daily "
(" salutaris virtus in remissionem peccatorum, quæ a nobis
quotidie committuntur "), in c. 2, on the other hand, as " a truly
propitiatory sacrifice " (" sacrificium vere propitiatorium "), which
cancels also the " crimes and heinous sins" (" crimina et ingentia
peccata ") of the penitent (contriti); indeed the expositions here
given can only be understood as meaning that in a way that is
direct, and that includes all blessings, the Mass applies Christ's
death on the Cross.[1]   For the rest, there is a thorough-going
vindication (c. 4), although in a cautiously veiled form,[2] of the
whole evil practice of the Mass, as also a vindication of the
Masses in honour of saints (in honorem sanctorum, c. 3), and,
finally, of the Roman Mass Canon[3] down to the last word (c. 4).
Even the demand that the Mass shall be in the vernacular is
rejected, nor is any proof given (c. 8).[4]   The Canons pronounce
anathema on everything that contradicts these doctrines, and so
makes a sharp separation between the Church of the sacrifice of
the Mass and the Church of the Word.[5]

[1] "Una enim eademque est hostia, idem nunc offerens sacerdotum ministerio, qui
seipsum tunc in cruce obtulit, sola offerendi ratione diversa.   Cujus quidem oblationis
cruentæ fructus per hanc incruentam uberrime percipiuntur : tantum abest, ut illi per
hanc quovis modo derogetur."

[2] "Quare non solum pro fidelium vivorum peccatis, pœnis, satisfactionibus *et aliis
necessitatibus* (in this way the whole disordered state of things is sanctioned), sed et
pro defunctis in Christo, nondum ad plenum purgatis, rite juxta apostolorum tradi-
tionem (!) offertur."

[3] "Qui constat ex ipsis domini verbis, tum ex apostolorum traditionibus ac sanctorum quoque pontificum piis institutionibus "—notice what are put together here !

[4] "Non expedire visum est patribus"; see on this Gihr, Das hl. Messopfer, 4th
ed., p. 305 ff.   In reading this work even a mild evangelical spirit must admit the
Reformers' title to speak of the Mass as idolatry.

[5] A certain influence of the Reformation is apparent in its being required (c. 8) that
the minister shall explain (in the vernacular) something of what is read in the Mass,

As might have been expected, the Decree concerning Penance (de pœnitentia, Sessio XIV.) is the fullest. As the chief parts of this Sacrament were settled matters for Scholasticism, and as the Tridentinum took over here the whole Scholastic work, it is not necessary to repeat in detail the positive definitions (see Vol. VI., p. 243 ff.). The formulations are distinguished by great clearness ; as we read, we have the feeling that we stand on firm ground, though it is on ground which the Church has created for itself.[1] Everything here, down to the questions as to materia, quasi materia, forma, is developed with precision. It is to be pointed out as specially noteworthy, that the feeling of comfort and of relief of conscience that follows upon the reconciliatio is not described as a regular result of the Sacrament (c. 3). But still more noteworthy, on the other hand, is the influence which the Reformation exerted on the description of the penitent disposition that is requisite. The party which declared attritio to be enough for saving reception of the Sacrament did not succeed in asserting itself ; in opposition, rather, to the teaching and practice of the two foregoing centur es contritio was required, and attritio declared to be merely a salutary preparation ("ad dei gratiam impetrandam disponit," "viam ad justitiam parat "). Yet as attritio is called "contritio imperfecta," as it is described as "a gift of God and an impulse of the Holy Spirit, who, however, is not yet indwelling, but only moving,"[2] as the assertion is also made that the reconciliatio is not to be ascribed to contritio "without a vow to receive the Sacrament" ("sine sacramenti voto"), and as a distinction again is drawn between contr tio and contritio (caritate perfecta) itself, as, finally, in spite of all excellent things said about the feeling of sorrow, this feeling is not conjoined with fides, is not developed from fides, all the attempts to get clear of the mechanical view of penance were in vain, and it was shown by

"ne oves Christi esuriant neve parvuli panem petant, et non sit qui frangat eis." So it is only the clearly-understood *word* that seems to be bread !

[1] It may be noted by the way that in c. 2 the sentence occurs : "Ecclesia in neminem judicium exercet, qui non prius in ipsam per baptismi januam fuerit ingressus," *i.e.*, the baptised are *all* placed under its jurisdiction.

[2] "Donum dei et spiritus sancti impulsum, non adhuc quidem inhabitantis sed tantum moventis."

the subsequent development of the doctrine of penitence in the
Church, that there was no serious intention to expel the
attritio.[1] What the 4th Chap. of the Decree de pœnitentia really
does is to throw dust in the eyes of Protestants. In the 5th
Chap. stands the extravagant statement, that "the whole Church
has always understood that full confession of sins is required of
all *by divine law*, because Christ has left behind him priests,
representatives of himself, as overseers and judges to whom all
mortal offences are to be made known"[2] The old dispute as to
whether the priest only pronounces forgiveness, or bestows it
as a judge, is settled according to the latter alternative (c. 6).
As the position is rejected, that God never forgives sins without
also remitting the whole penalty, room is obtained for the
satisfactiones : without these God accepts heathens, but not
Christians who have lapsed. But in a remarkable way the
satisfying penalties (satisfactoriæ pœnæ) are also presented
under an aspect which is quite foreign to their original establishment within the institution of penance; by these, it is represented,
we are made conformable (conformes) to Christ, who has
rendered satisfaction for our sins, ("having from thence the
surest pledge also, that if we suffer together we shall also be
glorified together").[3] That is an evangelical turn of thought,
which falls outside the framework of the "penance."[4] The 15
Canones de pœnitentia, however, leave nothing to be desired in
the way of rejection on principle of the evangelical view. Let
the 4th only be brought under notice : "If anyone shall deny
that, for full and perfect remission of sins, three acts are required
in the penitent, forming, as it were, the material of the Sacrament of Penance, namely, contrition, confession, and satisfaction,
which are called the three parts of penance, or shall say that

---

[1] That the Tridentinum attempts to idealise the attritio is on good ground pointed
out by Stuckert, Die Kath. Lehre v. d. Reue (1896), p. 63.

[2] "Universa ecclesia semper intellexit, integram peccatorum confessionem omnibus
jure divino necessariam existere, quia Christus sacerdotes sui ipsius vicarios reliquit
tamquam præsides et judices, ad quos omnia mortalia crimina deferantur."

[3] "Certissimam quoque inde arrham habentes, quod si compatimur, et conglori-
ficabimur," c. 8.

[4] Compare also what immediately follows ; the thought is evangelical : "neque
vero ita est satisfactio hæc—per illum acceptantur a patre." All the greater is the
contrast presented by the series of propositions directly succeeding.

there are only the two parts of penance, namely, terror struck home to the conscience through the knowledge of sin, and faith awakened by the Gospel or by the absolution through which one believes that his sins are remitted to him through Christ, let him be anathema." [1]

On the Sacrament of Extreme Unction (S. XIV.) it is not necessary to lose a word. The decisions, also, as to ordination to the priesthood (S. XXIII.) contain the Scholastic theses without any corrections. They begin with the famous words : "Sacrifice and priesthood are so conjoined by the appointment of God that both exist in every law" ("sacrificium et sacerdotium ita dei ordinatione conjuncta sunt, ut utrumque in omni lege exstiterit"). The Church of the sacrificial ritual asserts itself as also the Church of the priests, and it does the latter because it does the former. Along with sacrifice, Christ instituted at the same time the priesthood ; the seven orders (ordines) have been in existence from "the very beginning of the Church" [2] (c. 2). The old question of dispute as to the relation of the bishops to the priests (whether they, properly speaking, form an order), is not definitely decided. It is merely asserted that they are superior to the priests, as they have taken the place of the Apostles (c. 4).[3] All co-operation of the laity at the ordination of the clergy is very strongly disapproved of at the close of the Decree.[4] The Decree as to marriage (Sessio XXIV.) has not understood how to give to this formless Sacrament any better dogmatic shape. A kind of homily must take the place of

---

[1] "Si quis negaverit ad integram et perfectam peccatorum remissionem requiri tres actus in pœnitente, quasi materiam sacramenti pænitentiæ, vid. contritionem, confessionem et satisfactionem, quæ tres pænitentiæ partes dicuntur, aut dixerit, duas tantum esse pænitentiæ partes, terrores scil. incussos conscientiæ agnito peccato et fidem conceptam ex evangelio vel absolutione, qua credit quis sibi per Christum remissa peccata, anathema sit."

[2] "Ab ipso ecclesiæ initio."

[3] The uncertainty as to the position of the bishops is still further increased by the 6th Canon, which is occupied, not with enumerating the seven orders, but with treating of the "hierarchia divina ordinatione instituta, quæ constat ex episcopis, presbyteris et ministris." How is the hierarchy related to the seven orders?

[4] The Canons reject the Protestant doctrine. Above all in c. 1 the opinion is condemned, that there is no sacerdotium externum, and that the office is only the nudum ministerium prædicandi evangelium. The 8th Canon leaves the Pope free to create as many bishops as he pleases.

theological development. Only in the anathematisms do the
interests of the Church find expression.[1]

Purgatory and the Saints were already referred to in passing
in the Decree as to the Mass. They were expressly dealt with
at the 25th Session. The Decree as to purgatory contains the
indirect admission that much mischief had been done in the
Church in connection with it, and that it had led Christendom
into superstition; there is allusion even to " base gain, scandals,
and stumbling-blocks for the faithful " (turpe lucrum, scandala,
fidelium offendicula). But just on that account the " sana
doctrina de purgatorio " shall henceforward be strenuously insisted on. To more precise definitions, which would have had
the spirit of the age against them, the Council did not proceed.
So, likewise, there was only a quite rapid dealing with the
invocation and worship of saints, as also with relics and
pictures. The intercession of saints is established, and the
Protestant view declared "impious." The worship of relics and
pictures is also maintained,[2] an appeal being made to the
second Nicene Council. Anyone who is not acquainted with
the practice of the Church might conclude from these calm
definitions, which are adorned by no anathemas, that unimportant abuses were dealt with, especially as the Church did not
omit here also to lament the abuses ("if any abuses, however,
have crept into these holy and salutary observances, the holy
Synod has the intensest desire that they be forthwith abolished,
etc."[3]), and at the close really gives directions for checking the
disorder—directions, however, which, as subsequent history has
taught, really gave to the bishops, or ultimately, let us say, to
the Pope alone, the title to perpetuate the old disorder, and to
intensify it by his authority. The largest amount of reserve

---

[1] The view is condemned (1) that marriage " non gratiam confert." The Church
reserves to itself in the Canons the entire legislation as to marriage, and sanctions all
that it had previously done in this province. In c. 10, in spite of marriage being a
Sacrament, anyone is condemned who does not regard the unmarried state as better
than the married. But why, then, is there no sacrament of virginity?

[2] Yet with the addition: "Non quod credatur inesse aliqua in iis divinitas *vel*
virtus, propter quam sint colendæ."

[3] "In has autem sanctas et salutares odservationes si qui abusus irrepserint, eos
prorsus aboleri sancta synodus vehementer cupit," etc.

and caution was shown in the way in which *indulgences* were spoken of. The Scholastic theory of indulgences is not in any way touched ; the abuses are admitted, and their removal— "lest ecclesiastical discipline be weakened by too great facility."[1] is strongly insisted on.[2] But with regard to the matter itself there is no yielding, even to the extent of an inch; for indulgences have a saving value for Christendom. What is needed is only that the business of granting holy indulgences be carried on in a pious and holy way on behalf of all believers ; everyone is to be condemned who declares them useless, or denies that it is competent to the Church to dispense them.

Thus the Church completed by the Tridentinum her course of distinct secularisation as the Church of sacrifice, priest, and sacrament.[3] In her declaring to be true, saving, and divine all that the Church of Rome did, all the usages she adopted on her long progress through the Middle Ages, she withdrew from the struggle which Luther's theses conjured up, the struggle to reach a true inward understanding of the Christian religion.

1 " Ne nimia facilitate ecclesiastica disciplina enervetur."

2 " Pravos quæstus omnes pro his consequendis, unde plurima in Christiano populo abusuum causa fluxit."

3 In addition to the indulgences (see Schneider, Die Ablässe, 7th ed., 1881) one must study the theory and practice of the *benedictions* and *sacramentalia*, in order to see how far the Catholic Church had drifted, not only from what is Christian, but even from spiritual religion. The dogmatic expositions of the "benedictio constitutiva" and the "consecratio," as distinguished from the "benedictio invocativa," are a veritable mockery, not only of the Christian, but of all spiritual religion. I gather out a few passages from a work of very high authority, Gihr, Das hl. Messopfer, 4th ed., 1887, p. 220 : " However perfect as regards natural worth, artistic adornment, and beauty, the articles may be that are intended for use in the sacrificial celebration, they are certainly not on that account alone to be forthwith employed in divine service : in addition to these qualities the most of the vessels used in worship require a previous benediction or consecration . . . *they must become something sacred* (res sacra). By the blessing and the prayers of the Church the liturgical vessels become, *not merely sanctified, but also fitted to produce various saving effects in those who use them devoutly and who come into contact with them.* The articles employed in worship which are blessed or consecrated are, as it were, transferred *from the domain of nature to the kingdom of grace* (—so we have a cloth transferred to the kingdom of grace, a flagon transferred to the kingdom of grace, etc. !—) and are the special property of God ; *they thus far bear in themselves something divine, on the ground of which a certain religious veneration is due to them and must be paid to them.*" P. 220, n. 1 : " The consecration (benedictio constitutiva or consecratio, in which holy oil is made use of) is essentially distinct from the invocative

All discussions as to grace, freedom, sin, law, good works, etc.,
were at best relegated to the second place; for they were only
conducted on the assumption that under all circumstances the
Church asserted itself as that which it had become—as the
papal, sacrificial, and sacramental institution.   In the Tridentinum the Roman Church formally embodied its refusal to treat
the question of religion at the level to which that question had
been raised by Luther.   It held firmly to the ancient mediæval
stage.   That is pre-eminently the significance of the great
Council.

But, nevertheless, a discussion of the Reformation conception
of Christianity on its merits dared not be avoided.   That was
demanded even by many Catholic Christians.   Just at that
time, indeed, there was a party influential in Catholicism who
strongly accentuated the Augustinian-Mystic thoughts—they
were a counterpoise to the sacramental system—and who set
themselves to oppose the Pelagianism and Probabilism which
are the co-efficients of the Sacrament Church.   The two

benediction on this ground, *that it impresses upon persons and things a higher, supernatural character, i.e.*, it transfers them permanently into the state of sanctified and
religious objects."   P. 300, n. 2 : "*In the case of the candles that are blessed* there is
still the *sacramental* element to be taken into account.   That is to say, these candles
are not merely religious symbols, which represent something supernatural, *but are
also sacred objects, which—in their own way—produce a certain supernatural effect,
inasmuch as they impart to us on the ground of, and by virtue of the prayer of the
Church, divine blessing and protection, especially against the spirits of darkness.*"
P. 360 : "Incense that *has been blessed* is a sacramental ; as such, it does not merely
represent something higher and mysterious, but *works* also (in its way) *spiritual,
supernatural effects . . . it is the organ* (vehicle) *of divine protection and blessing.*
Through the sign of the cross and the prayer of the Church the incense receives a
certain *power* to drive Satan from, or to keep him from, the soul, etc. . . . *It serves*
(also) *to consecrate persons and objects.*   That is to say, with the incense-clouds there
diffuses itself also the power of the blessing which the Church pronounces and means
to bestow ; the incense-clouds bring all they touch *into a consecrated atmosphere.*"
Let one read also the detestable section on the benediction of the priest's garments
(p. 255 f.) and its allegorical and moral significance.   "The garments used in
worship only lose their benediction from being mended when the new unconsecrated
piece applied or inserted is larger than the consecrated piece, but not when it is
smaller," etc.   As in the indulgence the Church really, *i.e.* in praxi, created for
itself a second Sacrament of Penance, so it created for itself in the "sacramentalia"
new Sacraments, which are much more convenient, because they are entirely in the
Church's power.   In both cases it legitimised in Christianity Rabbinism and the
theory and practice of the Pharisees and Talmudists.

Decrees on original sin and justification are, on the one hand, the precipitate of the discussion with Protestant Christianity, and, on the other hand, a compromise between Thomism (Augustinianism) and Nominalism. The Decree on justification, although a product of art, is in many respects remarkably well constructed ; indeed, it may be doubted whether the Reformation would have developed itself if this Decree had been issued at the Lateran Council at the beginning of the century, and had really passed into the flesh and blood of the Church. But that is an idle reflection. That the Roman Church expressed itself on justification as the terms of that Decree represent, was itself a consequence of the Reformation. Just for that reason the Decree must not be over-rated. It was the product of a situation which never repeated itself, nor ever again will repeat itself, for the Roman Church. At that time this Church stood under the influence at once of Augustinianism and Protestantism, not as regards its Sacraments and institutions, but certainly as regards the spiritual conception of religion ; for it could not simply identify itself with the old Nominalistic Scholasticism ; but as yet the Jesuits had not found the way to adopt the critical and sceptical momenta of Nominalism, to translate them into momenta of Probabilism, and thus to create those elastic loci which adjusted themselves to every pressure and every turn of Church politics. Against the Thomists, therefore, one was, up to a certain point, defenceless at Trent ; the Thomists, on the other hand, as the proceedings at the religious conferences had already shown, were not strongly averse to the Protestant doctrine of justification (looked at as a doctrine by itself), however decided they might be in their opposition to Protestantism. The deep distinction between Protestants and Augustinian Thomists is apparent enough from the fact, that just on account of the doctrine of justification the former combated as heretical the " usages " of the Roman Church, while the latter could not understand why it should be impossible to unite the two. Yet a clear perception of the contrast of position was not arrived at, because even Protestantism was then already beginning to treat the doctrine of justification as a Scholastic doctrine, and in its deriving from

justification the right to religious and spiritual freedom had
become uncertain and narrow.   So it could not but follow that
an effort should be made to express the contrast in *Scholastic*
definitions, which are not without their importance, which,
indeed, are highly important as setting forth the different
fundamental views, but which, nevertheless, rather conceal than
elucidate the real distinction in its full extent.   Or is the
difference between Catholicism and Protestantism really described when it is said that for the former justification is a
process (!), for the latter a once-occurring event ; that by the
former an infused grace (gratia infusa) is taught, by the latter
an imputed righteousness (justitia imputativa) ; that for the
former it is a question about faith and love, for the latter a
question about faith alone ; that the former includes in its thinking the idea of conduct, while the latter thinks only of relationship ?   These are all merely half-truths, although the controversy of creeds—especially later on—was carried on chiefly in
the line of these antitheses.   It would stand hard with Protestantism if its view admitted of being expressed in these sharp
formulæ.

On the other hand, if the Roman Church remains the Roman
Church—and at Trent the decision was formed to undertake no
self-reformation—it is a matter of comparative indifference
what it contemplated teaching with regard to justification and
original sin ; for all the propositions here promulgated, whether
their terms suggest Nominalism or Augustinian Thomism or even
the Reformation,[1] are only minor propositions under the major,
that the use and wont of the Roman Church is the supreme
law.

Having first made these necessary observations, let us
examine the two Decrees.   In the Decree on original sin the
flagrant Pelagianism, or Semi-Pelagianism, of Nominalism is
rejected in strong and gratifying terms ; but the positive propositions are so shrewdly constructed that it is always *possible*
still to connect with them a meaning that widely diverges from
that of Augustine.

---

[1] As is well known there was at one time a near approach in Rome to approval of
the entire first half of the Augsburg Confession.

At the very beginning, in Chapter I., it is said that Adam lost the holiness and righteousness " in which he had been constituted " (" in qua constitutus fuerat "). That is ambiguous : it can be .understood as " creatus " (Thomistic ; increated righteousness) ; but it can also be understood as an added gift (Scotistic ; donum superadditum), and the latter interpretation is perhaps confirmed by the phrase " accepta a deo sanctitas et justitia " (" holiness and righteousness received from God "). So also there is ambiguity when it is said that by the Fall the whole Adam in body and soul was " changed for the worse " (" in deterius commutatus "); for what does " for the worse " mean ? In the 6th Decree there is substituted for this, " lost innocence " (" innocentiam perdidisse " c. 1) ; but immediately afterwards it is declared that free will is by no means destroyed, but " weakened in force and perverted " (" in viribus attenuatum et inclinatum "). This definition teaches that " for the worse " (" in deterius ") is really to be understood as a comparative, and that there was no inclination to approve of Augustine's doctrine of sin and freedom. In the 2nd Chapter (cf. Chap. III.) inherited death and inherited sin are strictly taught, and there is set over against them the sole merit of Christ, communicated in baptism (infant baptism, Chap. IV.), by which merit the reatus originalis peccati, that is, guilt, is completely wiped out, so that there is now no longer anything hate-worthy in the man, and the way to heaven (ingressus in coelum) stands open to him. But the Decree also says indirectly that all sin itself is at the same time abolished : " this holy Synod confesses and holds that concupiscence or slumbering passion remains in the baptized ; when this is exposed to conflict it cannot do injury to those who do not yield to, but strenuously resist it through the grace of Christ Jesus. . . . With regard to this concupiscence, which the Apostle sometimes calls sin, the holy Council declares that the Catholic Church has never understood it to be called sin because it is truly and properly sin in the regenerate, but because it springs from sin and disposes to sin."[1]

[1] "Manere in baptizatis concupiscentiam vel fomitem, hæc s. synodus fatetur et sentit: quæ cum ad agonem relicta sit, nocere non consentientibus viriliter per Christi Jesu gratiam repugnantibus non valet . . . hanc concupiscentiam, quam aliquando

With this very rationalistic Scholastic reflection about evil
desire the religious standpoint for contemplating sin was
abandoned, and room was again made for all questions of doubt
that were bound to lead to Nominalistic (Pelagian) answers.
Because in the whole Decree on original sin what was dealt
with was not faith and unbelief, because therefore forgiveness of
sin appeared as an external act, without mention being made
of the medium in which alone men can win for themselves
assurance of forgiveness, it was inevitable that the definitions—
if there was a wish to avoid the magical—should issue in
Pelagianism. If the process of the forgiveness of sins takes
place outside of faith, evil desire cannot be sin ; for in that case
baptism would be insufficient, since it would not secure what it
is meant to secure, namely, the removal of sin. Further, as
the continued existence of evil desire cannot be denied, nothing
remains but to declare it a matter of indifference. Such an
assumption, however, must necessarily have a reflex influence
on the shaping of the doctrines of the primitive state and of
free will ; concupiscence must be ascribed to the nature of man,
and accordingly holiness cannot express his true nature,[1] but is
a donum superadditum. The Decree, therefore, did not reach
the height of the Protestant view, at which, without regard to
the earthly condition of man and the psychological questions,
the problem of sin and freedom is identical with the problem of
godlessness and trust in God.[2]

The " thorny doctrine of grace," as a modern Roman theologian has in an unguarded moment styled it, occupied the Fathers

apostolus peccatum appellat, s. synodus declarat, ecclesiam Catholicam nunquam,
intellexisse peccatum appellari, quod vere et proprie in renatis peccatum est, sed
quia ex peccato est et ad peccatum inclinat."

[1] It can do so, certainly, only on condition that by holiness there is understood the
divinely produced childlike trust in God and the fear of God.

[2] That in spite of the Augustinianism there was a wish to leave everything in the
old position is shown by the closing sentence of the Decree : "Declarat synodus, non
esse suæ intentionis comprehendere in hoc decreto, ubi de peccato originali agitur,
beatam et immaculatam virginem Mariam, dei genetricem sed observandas esse constitutiones felicis recordationis Xysti papæ IV., sub pœnis in eis constitutionibus
contentis, quas innovat." There could, indeed, be as yet no venturing beyond these
definitions "felicis recordationis," without raising a storm, for the opposition between
Franciscans and Dominicans at this point was still unbroken.

for months. The Decree which finally took shape could—after
all that had been written in the fourteenth and fifteenth centuries—have been gladly welcomed by the Protestants, on many
things an understanding could easily have been come to, and
other things might have been left to the Schools, had it not been
necessary to say to one's self that here language frequently
concealed thought, and that the authors of the Decree, in spite
of their Biblical attitude and their edifying language, did not
really know what *faith* meant, as evangelically understood.   In
spite of all appearance to the contrary, the interest that really
governs the whole Decree is the desire to show how there can
be an attainment to good works that have weight in the sight of
God.

The voluminous Decree, which takes the place of the original
sketch, falls into three parts (1-9, 10-13, 14-16).   Almost every
chapter contains compromises.

Chap. I. describes the entire inability of the children of Adam
to deliver themselves from the dominion of sin, the devil, and
death by means of natural power (per vim naturæ) or by means
of the letter of the law of Moses (per litteram legis Moysis). Yet
there is immediately added as a supplement, "Although free
will is by no means extinguished in them, however it may be
diminished in power and perverted" ("tamesti in eis liberum
arbitrium minime extinctum esset, viribus licet attenuatum et
inclinatum ").   Chap. II. declares that God has sent Christ in
order that all men might receive adoption and become sons of
God (Him hath God set forth as the propitiator through *faith*
in His blood for our sins " ["hunc proposuit deus propitiatorem
per fidem in sanguine ipsius pro peccatis nostris "]).   Here,
therefore, *faith* seems to have its sovereign place given to it.
Yet (Chap. III.)—all do not accept the benefit of the death of
Christ, but only those to whom the merit of His suffering is imparted.   What follows leaves the question in obscurity whether
an eternal election of grace must be thought of.   Yet so it would
appear: those only are justified to whom regeneration through the
merit of Christ's suffering is given by means of the grace through
which they become righteous.   A vague sentence indeed, which
leaves it to everyone to determine the relation between election,

justification, and regeneration.   In Chap. IV. justification is
described in a fundamental way as justificatio impii.   It is a translation from the *standing* of the sinful Adam into the *standing*
of grace and adoption (that has an evangelical ring), and, in the
era of the gospel, is effected simply through baptism ("or the
vow to receive it" [aut ejus voto]).   But in the process of
describing justification more exactly in Chap. V., the thought of
"translation from one standing into another" ("ab uno statu in
alterum") becomes embarrassed and uncertain.   It is here
asserted, that is to say, that the beginning of justification is
wrought by the gratia præveniens, that is, the vocatio (by which
adults are called in the absence of any merits of their own ["qua
adulti nullis eorum existentibus meritis vocantur"]—this in opposition to the lax views of Nominalism) ; but its contemplated
end is, "that those who have been alienated from God by their
sins, *may be disposed* by His inciting and *aiding* grace, to convert themselves *in order to their own justification*, by their freely
assenting to, and *co-operating* with, the same grace."[1]   In this
way the Augustinian-Thomistic view is abandoned in favour of
the laxer view ; but still there is no mention whatever of faith.
With a view, however, to conciliate the Thomists, the Decree
still further proceeds : "in such a way that, when God touches
the heart of man by the illumination of the Holy Spirit, man
neither does nothing whatever himself in receiving that inspiration, since he can also reject it, *nor, on the other hand, can he, of
his free will, without the grace of God, bring himself into a position of righteousness before God."*[2]   But of what avail is this con-
ciliation, if, while a human activity towards the good is asserted,
no thought of faith is entertained?   Even in this "preparation
for the justification" ("præparatio ad justificationem") the
thought of merit must necessarily come in ;[3] for the activity

[1] "Ut qui per peccata a deo aversi erant, per ejus excitantem atque *adjuvantem*
gratiam ad convertendum se ad *suam ipsorum justificationem*, eidem gratiæ libere
assentiendo et *co-operando*, disponantur."
[2] "Ita ut tangente deo cor hominis per spiritus s. illuminationem neque homo ipse
nihil omnino agat, inspirationem illam recipiens, quippe qui illam et abjicere potest,
neque tamen sine gratia dei movere se ad justitiam coram illo libera voluntate possit."
[3] The Decree does not, indeed, say that "the letting one's self be disposed for
grace" is a merit, yet it does not exclude this view.

that knows itself to be entirely in-wrought, and therefore is at the
same time "gift," "virtue," and "reward of virtue" ("donum,
virtus, præmium virtutis"), is faith alone.   But just on that
account also, faith forbids the breaking up of "justification," as
"translation into the state of adoption," into various acts.
Wherein the right "disposition" consists is shown in Chap. VI.
It consists (1) in the "faith through hearing" ("fides ex
auditu"); this is a free movement God-wards, inasmuch as one
believes that the content of divine revelation is *true*, and believes
this in particular of the reconciliation and justification through
Christ, (2) in insight into the fact that one is a sinner, and
accordingly, in fear of the divine righteousness, in reflection on
the divine mercy, in the hope that springs from this that God
will be favourably disposed for Christ's sake, and in incipient
love to Him as the source of all righteousness, from which there
arises "a certain hatred and horror" of sin,[1] (3) in the entering,
in connection with the decision to receive baptism, upon a new
life and course of obedience to the commandments of God.
What has all that to do with justification?   This description is
certainly not sketched from the standpoint of one by
whom justification has been experienced, but by one who
stands without, and reflects on what the course of justification
must be if there is to be nothing to upset thought and nothing
to be unintelligible.   Will the justified man know of anything
he can assert, prior to his experience of justification, regarding
his incipient faith, incipient love, incipient hatred, incipient
repentance?   Will he not rather say with the apostle that he is
dead in sins?   What is an incipient good from the standpoint of
one who has the knowledge of Augustine : "for me the good is
to cling to God" ("mihi adhærere deo bonum est")?   And
what is the idea of faith involved, if it is nothing but the beginning of the beginning, a holding the divine revelation to be
true!   Here everything still belongs to the mediæval mode of
view, which has no capacity for perceiving the personal experience, that religion is a relation of person to person.   Under
the influence of the desire, legitimate in itself, that faith shall
produce *life*, a direct leap is taken by the contemplating mind from

[1] *I.e.*, "per eam pœnitentiam quam ante baptismum agi oportet."

assent to love, after the unhappy distinction has been made
between " preparation for justification " and " justification
itself," while " faith in the promises " (" fides promissionum ") is
dealt with as an empty phrase. In Chap. VII. " justification
itself " is now described in quite a Scholastic way. It is—this is
the first statement made—not only the forgiveness of sins, but
also sanctification and renewal of the inward man ; nay, that
Augustine may not be pronounced too much in the right, there
is added, " renewal by *voluntary* acceptance of grace " (" reno-
vatio per *voluntariam* susceptionem gratiæ "). But how can a
man be sanctified otherwise than by the wonderful assurance
given him of forgiveness of sins ? It is characteristic again of
genuine Mediævalism that beyond thinking of forgiveness as the
mechanical *removal* of sin, there is no ability to form any
thoughts regarding it. But if in the matter of forgiveness
all depends on its being *believed* as such, the question of chief
importance relates to the inward condition and spirit of him
who believes it. If this question is put, then the form of expression " not only forgiveness of sins, but also renewal of the
inner man " is simply absurd—unless forgiveness of sins be
viewed as an act that takes place outside human consciousness
and feeling, and that, certainly, is the presupposition of the
Catholic thesis. There now follow the definitions as to the
" final, efficient, meritorious, instrumental, and formal causes "[1]
of justification, which have little interest. The only thing of
importance is that there is described as the " instrumental
cause," not faith, but (in skilfully chosen words) the Sacrament
of Baptism, " which is the Sacrament of the faith without which
no one has ever come to participate in justification " (" quod est
sacramentum fidei, sine qua nulli umquam contigit justificatio ").
This justification then brings it about that we are not only
regarded as righteous, but are truly described as such, and are
such, seeing that we receive into ourselves righteousness, " everyone according to his measure, which the Holy Spirit apportions
to individuals as He wills, and according to each one's own disposition and co-operation " (" unusquisque suam secundum mensuram, quam spiritus s. partitur singulis prout vult et secundum

---

[1] " Causa finalis, efficiens, meritoria, instrumentalis, formalis."

propriam cujusque dispositionem et co-operationem "). Here
we have the complete contradiction of the evangelical conception
—and even, indeed, a flagrant contradiction of the terms " translation into a new standing" ("translatio in novum statum"); for,
strictly speaking, what is suggested here is not a translation into
a new standing as a divinely-produced effect, but the being filled
with righteousness, as if righteousness were a material, this being
filled, moreover, being first of all gradual and different in the
case of different individuals, and then determined by the measure
of one's own disposition and co-operation. Here, therefore, not
only the doctrine of the "meritum de congruo," but also the anti-
Thomistic doctrine of, the " meritum de congruo ante justificationem," are, by implication, left open at least. With greater
precision the " receptio justitiæ " is then described as "inherent
diffusion of the love of God" (" diffusio caritatis dei inhærens,")
so that, along with the forgiveness of sins, a man receives as
infused all these things—namely, faith, love, hope—through
Jesus Christ, into whom he is engrafted. It is not the term
" gratia infusa " that leads astray here—one might very well so
express himself figuratively—but it is the incapacity again to
get out of faith anything else than assent. Hence the further
statement is forthwith made that without the addition of hope and
love faith cannot perfectly unite with Christ. But are not
" faith," " hope," and " love " together what the evangelical
Christian understands by " faith " alone? Certainly it would be
possible to understand the Decree accordingly, and on this basis
to effect a union with the Tridentine view. But the definite
assertion that now follows—namely, that eternal life is only
imparted to hope and love, shows that the controversy at
this point is no dispute about words ; for the placing together
of " love " and " eternal life " has its ultimate ground in the wish
to derive eternal life *also* from man's own deeds, while that life
is unquestionably given in the faith in forgiveness of sin itself
and in that alone.

In the 8th Chapter there is an embarrassed discussion of the
Pauline principle, that justification is tied to faith and takes
place gratuitously. Here there is a flat contradiction of the
apostle, the principle being represented as meaning " that we are

described as being justified by faith, because faith is the *begin-ning*, foundation, and root of human salvation" ("ut per fidem ideo justificari dicamur, quia fides est humanæ salutis initium, fundamentum et radix"). That is more than am-biguity. Equally lacking in truthfulness is the explanation of the "gratis"; for while it is represented here as meaning that nothing that precedes justification, neither faith nor works, *merits* the grace of justification, yet, according to what has been stated in Chap. V., that foregoing preparation is absolutely neces-sary that justification may be obtained. At the close of this first section there now follows (Chap. IX.) the polemic against the empty "fiducia" of the heretics, the formulating of which gave the largest amount of trouble to the Fathers. Help was sought for in the end by transforming the opposing doctrine into a fictitious object of dread. Although one must believe that sins are, for Christ's sake, gratuitously forgiven by the divine mercy, "yet it must be said that to no one *boasting* of his trust and his assurance of the remission of his sins, and *easily resting* in that alone, are, or have been, his sins forgiven" ("tamen nemini fiduciam et certitudinem remissionis peccatorum suorum *jactanti* et in ea sola *quiescenti* peccata dimitti vel dimissa esse dicendum est").[1] What the real aim of this self-evident statement is only appears from what follows. Here it is affirmed that certainty regarding one's own justification does not necessarily belong to justification, that it is not needful that one should firmly believe in the forgiveness of his sins in order to be really freed from his sins, and that it is an error to assume that forgiveness of sins and justification are effected only in faith ("as if anyone not believing this must have doubt about the promises of God, and about the efficacy of the death and resurrection of Christ"[2]). In order that these propositions, which rob true faith of all meaning—faith means simply nothing else than being, or having the wish to be, a member of the Catholic Church—may not

---

[1] Also the addition, "cum apud hæreticos et schismaticos possit esse immo nostra tempestate fit, et magna contra ecclesiam Catholicam contentione prædicatur vana hæc ab omni pietate remota fiducia."

[2] "Quasi qui hoc non credit, de dei promissis deque mortis et resurrectionis Christi efficacia dubitet."

appear too startling, there is added to them the proof, suggestive
either of want of candour or want of understanding, that when
man thinks of his weakness he must always continue to fear
whether he has received grace, as if that had ever been denied
by any serious-minded Christian, while undoubtedly the conclusion drawn, that certainty of salvation is impossible, is entirely
incompetent!

The 2nd section treats of the "increase of justification"
("incrementum justificationis.") Here it is taught (Chap. X.)
that the justified are renewed from day to day by observing the
commandments of God *and of the Church*, and that accordingly
"they grow in righteousness, *faith co-operating with good works*,
and are *in a greater degree justified*" ("in ipsa justitia *cooperante
fide bonis operibus* crescunt atque *magis justificantur*.") Justification, then, is here conceived of in its progress (not justification itself) as a process resting upon grace, faith, and good
works.   With regard to good works it is taught (Chap. XI.) that
even the justified man is placed under the law of commandments, and that these commandments are by no means incapable
of being fulfilled.   In hesitating terms it is affirmed that they
are easy and sweet rather, because they can be fulfilled, or
because one has to pray with a view to their fulfilment, and God
gives help for this end.   Moreover, the righteous do not cease
to be righteous when they fall into daily sins ; for God does not
forsake those who are already justified, if they do not forsake
Him.   But this view can give rest to no tender conscience, if it
be the case that the maintenance of justification must be
dependent in some way on one's own action.   The Decree
expressly observes that one must not rely on faith alone, but on
faith and the keeping of the commandments (observatio mandatorum), even though the latter be interrupted by small sins.
In order, however, to conceal the laxness of this rule, a μετάβασις
εἰς ἄλλο γένος is employed, and the proposition is constructed
thus :—" Therefore no one ought to flatter himself on the ground
of faith alone, thinking that by faith alone he is made an heir
and shall obtain the inheritance, *even though he does not suffer
with Christ, that he may also be glorified with Him*" (" Itaque
nemo sibi in sola fide blandiri debet, putans fide sola se heredem

esse constitutum hereditatemque consecuturum, *etiamsi Christo non compatiatur, ut et conglorificetur.*") To this it is added, that it is contrary to the teaching of the orthodox religion to say that the righteous cannot do a single good work that is not imperfect ; still less can the assertion be tolerated, that all works deserve eternal penalty, and that there must be no looking at all to the eternal reward. In this last cautious turn the notion of desert, without the term describing it, is introduced. It was necessary for the Fathers to move here very warily, if they were to put matters right with all parties. In the 12th and 13th Chapters it is then taught, that, although justification grows, no one is entitled to become assured of his election and of the "gift of perseverance" ("donum perseverantiæ") "except by special revelation" ("nisi ex speciali revelatione"). Yet here again, in Chapter XIII., there is an ambiguity, since only "the being assured with an *absolute certainty*" ("certum esse *absoluta certitudine*") is forbidden, while it is elsewhere said that one must base the surest hope on the "*help* of God" ("in dei auxilio," so not on grace), and since the Pauline sentence is suddenly woven in, that God works the willing and the performing. Yet "labours, watchings, almsgiving, prayers, offerings, fastings, chastity" ("labores, vigiliæ, eleemosynæ, orationes, oblationes, jejunia, castitas") are requisite, for we are not yet regenerated "in glory" ("in gloria") but "unto the hope of glory" ("in spem gloriæ"). Accordingly the whole penance system is recommended, that there may be progress in assurance. However noteworthy it is that all external legality and merit are here left out of consideration, still the fundamental view is retained, that eternal life and the assurance of justification are dependent also on good works, which, however, on the other hand, are to be regarded as the victorious struggle of the spirit with the flesh. The uncertainty of the whole conception is sufficiently indicated by the threefold view taken of good works : they are = "suffering together with Christ" ("compati Christo") = "keeping the commandments of God" ("observatio mandatorum dei" ; in this sense meritorious, though that is not expressly said) and = "contending with the flesh, the world, and the devil" ("pugna cum carne, mundo et diabolo").

In the last section the restoration of justification when it has been lost is dealt with. The restoration is effected (Chap. XIV.) by means of the Sacrament of Penance ("second plank after shipwreck " ["secunda post naufragium tabula."]) The penance of the lapsed must be different from that of the candidate for baptism ; the description of it follows the well-known scheme. Attritio is not thought of, but it is remarked that the Sacrament of Penance does not always, like baptism, cancel the temporal penalty, along with cancelling guilt and the eternal penalty ; hence satisfactions are needed. But it is not the case, as the opponents think, that justification comes to be lost only through unbelief ; it is lost rather through every mortal sin (Chap. XV.) ; nay, it can be lost through such sin, while faith continues to exist. In no way could the inferior conception of faith entertained here be more plainly expressed. It is only here that the Decree now begins to speak explicitly (ex professo) of merit (Chap. XVI.), and it is roundly asserted that eternal life is at the same time fulfilment of the promise and reward, inasmuch as ultimately all depends only on "good works" ("bene operari ") : "and so to those who *perform good works* on to the end, and who hope in God, there is to be offered eternal life, both as grace mercifully promised to the sons of God through Christ Jesus, and as a reward to be faithfully rendered, in terms of the promise of God Himself, to their good works *and merits*." [1] But in order to remove from this view the appearance of self-righteousness, there follows a highly-pitched explanation which is Augustinian, and even goes beyond Augustine. "For since Christ Jesus continually pours virtue into the branches, a virtue which always precedes, accompanies, and follows their good works, and without which their good works could on no account be well-pleasing and meritorious before God, it must be believed that nothing further is lacking to the justified in order to its being held that by their good deeds, which are wrought in God, they have fully satisfied the divine law as regards their

---

[1] " Atque ideo *bene operantibus* usque in finem et in deo sperantibus proponenda est vita æterna, et tamquam gratia filiis dei per Christum Jesum misericorditer promissa, et tamquam merces ex ipsius dei promissione bonis ipsorum operibus *et meritis* fideliter reddenda."

state in this life, and have truly merited also the attainment of
life eternal in its time, provided only they depart this life in
grace . . . thus neither is our own righteousness set down as of
our own origination, nor is the righteousness of God ignored or
repudiated. For the righteousness that is called our own,
because we are justified through its inhering in us, is at the
same time the righteousness of God, because it is infused into
us by God through the merit of Christ. Nor must it be kept
out of view that although in Holy Scripture there is so much
attributed to good works that even to him who shall give to one
of the least of His a cup of cold water, Christ promises that he
shall not lose his reward . . . yet there must be no thought
whatever of a Christian man's confiding or glorying in himself
and not in the Lord, whose goodness toward all men is so great,
that He wills that what are His gifts should be their merits." [1]
If we might understand the Decree as meaning that all that it
says of justification is to be taken as relating to approval in the
last judgment, or if we might introduce the evangelical notion
of faith where it speaks of " faith " and " good works," we could
very well make it the basis of conference with the Catholics.
The correct interpretation of it, however, is that which lies not
in the direction of Protestantism, but in the direction of the
prevailing use and wont of the Roman Church, as is proved by
the propositions regarding the " disposing of one's self for grace "

---

[1] " Cum enim ille ipse Christus Jesus tamquam caput in membra et tamquam vitis
in palmites, in ipsos justificatos jugiter virtutem influat, quæ virtus bona eorum opera
semper antecedit, comitatur et subsequitur, et sine qua nullo facto deo grata et
meritoria esse possent, nihil ipsis justificatis amplius deesse credendum est, quo minus
plene illis quidem operibus, quæ in deo sunt facta, divinæ legi pro hujus vitæ statu
satisfecisse et vitam æternam suo etiam tempore, si tamen in gratia decesserint, consequendam vere promeruisse censeantur . . . ita neque propria nostra justitia tamquam ex nobis propria statuitur, neque ignoratur aut repudiatur justitia dei.   Quæ
enim justitia nostra dicitur, quia per eam nobis inhærentum justificamur, illa eadem
dei est, quia a deo nobis infunditur per Christi meritum.   Neque vero illud omitten-
dum est, quod licet bonis operibus in sacris litteris usque adeo tribuatur, ut etiam qui
uni ex minimis suis potum aquæ frigidæ dederit, promittat Christus eum non esse sua
mercede cariturum . . . absit tamen, ut Christianus homo in se ipso vel confidat vel
glorietur et non in domino, cujus tanta est erga omnes homines bonitas, ut eorum
velit esse merita, quæ sunt ipsius dona."

("se disponere ad gratiam") and the thirty-three appended anathematisms.[1]

The Decrees had the effect of binding the Catholic Church to the soil of the Middle Ages and of Scholasticism, and, at the same time, of fencing it off from Protestantism ; but as the formulations adopted were ambiguous in all the questions to which the Church itself cannot wish an unmistakable answer, the necessary freedom of development was preserved in spite of the huge burden of dogmatic material. To this there was added, that the important doctrines about the Church and about the Pope were not touched—through stress of circumstances they had to be left aside ; but this compulsory reticence proved in subsequent times to be extremely favourable to the papacy. The mediæval Church went forth from the Council of Trent as still substantially the ancient Church. It still included within it the great discords between world-renunciation and world-dominion, Sacrament and morality, and precisely through these discords it asserted that elasticity and many-sidedness which admitted of its holding within it such Cardinals as Richelieu and Borromeo, and enabled it to retain in connection with itself all obedient spirits. Its view was still so much directed in the last resort to the world beyond, that for it the

---

[1] Of these anathematisms the first three are aimed at Pelagianism and Semi-Pelagianism, as is also the 22nd. The remaining 29 all direct themselves, and that too with the greatest keenness, against Protestantism. What is most characteristic is the rejection of the following propositions :—" Opera omnia, quæ ante justificationem fiunt, quacumque ratione facta sint, vere esse peccata vel odium dei mereri, aut quanto vehementius quis nititur se disponere ad gratiam, tanto eum gravius peccare" (7). " Gehennæ metum, per quem ad misericordiam dei de peccatis dolendo confugimus vel a peccato abstinemus, peccatum esse " (8). " Homines justificari vel sola imputatione justitiæ Christi vel sola peccatorum remissione exclusa gratia et caritate, quæ in cordibus eorum per spiritum sanctum diffundatur atque illis inhæreat, aut etiam gratiam, qua justificanur, esse tantum favorem dei " (11). " Fidem justificantem nihil aliud esse quam fiduciam divinæ misericordiæ peccata remittendis propter Christum, vel eam fiduciam solam esse, qua justificamur " (12). " Hominem a peccatis absolvi ac justificari ex eo quod se absolvi ac justificari certo credat, aut neminem vere esse justificatum nisi qui credat se esse justificatum, et hac sola fide absolutionem et justificationem perfici " (14). " Nihil præceptum esse in evangelio præter fidem " (19). " Hominem justificatum teneri tantum ad credendum, quasi vero evangelium sit nuda et absoluta promissio vitæ æternæ sine conditione observationis mandatorum " (20). " Justitiam acceptam

enthusiast, wearing away his life in voluntary poverty, was the greatest saint : but at the same time it preached to men, that all its ideals lay hid in the visible ecclesiastical institution, and that obedience to the Church was the highest virtue. It had still no other thought than that *believing* is equivalent to "being Catholic," and consists in the willingness to hold as true (or, the willingness not to meddle with) incomprehensible doctrines. The restlessness that still remained here it sought partly to soothe away, partly to stimulate, by means of the Sacraments, the indulgences, the Church service, and the ecclesiastical directions for mystico-monastic discipline.

(2) *The Main Features of the Dogmatic Development in Catholicism during the period between* 1563 *and* 1870, *as preparing the way for the Decrees of the Vatican.*

During the three centuries between the Council of Trent and the Council of the Vatican three great controversies stirred the Catholic Schools, and even became extremely dangerous to the whole Church. At Trent the opposing positions in which they took their rise were concealed ; just for that reason a discussion

non conservari atque etiam non augeri coram deo per bona opera, sed opera ipsa fructus solummodo et signa esse justificationis adeptæ, non autem ipsius augendæ causam " (24). " In quolibet bono opere justum saltem venialiter peccare aut mortaliter, atque ideo pœnas æternas mereri tantumque ob id non damnari, quia deus ea opera non imputet ad damnationem " (25). " Justos non debere pro bonis operibus exspectare et sperare æternam retributionem " (26). "Nullum esse mortale peccatum nisi infidelitatis " (27). " Sola fide amissam justitiam recuperari sine sacramento pænitentiæ" (29). "Justificatum peccare, dum intuitu æternæ mercedis bene operatur" (31). The Canones conclude with the words, " Si quis dixerit, per hanc doctrinam (scil. by this Decree) aliqua ex parte gloriæ dei vel meritis Jesu Christi derogari et non potius veritatem fidei nostræ, dei denique ac Christi Jesu gloriam illustrari, anathema sit." It cannot be denied that to some extent the propositions of Protestantism, which are condemned in the Canons, undergo adjustment ; on the other hand, many weak points in the Protestant *doctrine* are hit upon ; but certainly the clearest impression we receive is that the Tridentine Fathers had no understanding whatever of what Luther meant by the righteousness of God, faith, and the forgiveness of sins. He bore witness of the *religion* which had opened to his view in the gospel, and which governed and blessed him as an indivisible power ; they sought to do justice at once to many points of view, religion, morality, the Sacrament, and the Church.

of them in the times that followed was inevitable.   There was
(1) the controversy between Curialism and Episcopalism, which
parted into two questions, (*a*) whether the bishops had independent, divine rights apart from the Pope (and, in the Council,
rights *superior to* the Pope), (*b*) whether tradition was to be
understood in the sense of Vincentius of Lerinum, or whether
the Pope was to be held as determining what is to be regarded
as tradition ; (2) the controversy between Augustinianism and
the Jesuitic (Scotistic) Pelagianism ; (3) the controversy regarding Probabilism.   These three controversies had the closest
inward connection with each other ; at bottom they formed a
unity, and on that account also the Vatican Council decided all
three at one stroke.   The party distinguished by its Curialistic,
Pelagian, and Probabilistic tendency proved the victor.

    (1) (*a*) The original Curialistic outline of the position of the
Pope in the Church, which made the Pope the lord of the
Church, and declared the bishops assistants, whom Christ's
governor adopts " for purposes of oversight " (" in partem
sollicitudinis ") could not be established at Trent.   The recol-
lections of the Council of Constance were, in spite of the Bull
of Leo X. " Pastor æternus," still too vivid.   But neither could
the contrary doctrine, that the Council stood above the Pope,
and that every bishop, as a successor of the Apostles, had his
power from Christ, be raised to a dogma.   The sharply-opposed
theses, " the Pope is *the* bishop, the universal bishop, the
governor for Christ," and " the bishops have their power origni-
ally from Christ, so that the Pope is only primus inter pares,
representative of the unity of the Church, and custodian of its
external order and uniformity," could in no way be reconciled.
Hence the decision of this question at Trent had to be delayed.
But owing to small observations interspersed throughout the
text of the Tridentine decisions, and owing especially to the
prominence given to the " ecclesia Romana,"[1] a bias was
already given to the question in favour of the Curialists.
But what was bound to have an incomparably greater effect
was that the Council, hurrying in a precipitate way to a close,

[1] See also Sess. 6 de reform c. 1, where the Pope is styled " ipsius dei in terris
vicarius."

not only left entirely in the hands of the Pope the confirmation
of its Decrees and the adoption of measures for carrying them
out, but even quietly accepted the Bull in which the Pope
reserved the exposition of the Decrees exclusively to himself.[1]

The "Professio," which appeared immediately thereafter,
misleadingly styled the "Professio Fidei Tridentinæ," set the
seal to this modification of the Tridentine Decrees, in so far as
it included obedience to the Pope within "faith" itself.[2] The
way in which Rome manipulated the Professio from that time
forward, and by means of it brought all bishops under subjection to itself, was a master-stroke of Curialistic politics. The
Catechismus Romanus also, which the Pope took occasion from
the Council to order and approve, was favourable to Curialism,
although on the ground of its Thomistic doctrine of grace it
was inconvenient to the Jesuits, who, on that account, attempted
indeed to contest its authority.[3] Yet, leaving out of view
isolated steps that were taken in all Catholic countries, there

---

[1] See Köllner, l.c., pp. 116 ff.

[2] See Köllner, l.c., pp. 141-165. The words of the Professio, a confession of
faith (!), run thus : "Sanctam catholicam et apostolicam Romanam ecclesiam omnium
ecclesiarum matrem et magistram adgnosco, Romanoque Pontifici, beati Petri apostolorum principis successori ac Jesu Christi vicario, veram obedientiam spondeo ac
juro."

[3] See Köllner, l.c., pp. 166-190. On the attacks of the Jesuits on the Catechism,
see p. 188, and Köcher, Katech.-Gesch., pp. 127 ff. : they sought to show, not merely
that it was partisan, but that it was heretical also. The result of the attacks has
been that the Catechism has been forced into the background in more recent times.
The sections of it bearing upon the Church are strictly Thomistic, and therefore
favourable to papal autocracy. Thus, in P. I., c. 10, q. 10, the unity of the Church
is proved from Ephes. IV. 5, and then it is further said : "Unus est etiam ejus rector
ac gubernator, invisibilis quidem Christus, quem æternus pater dedit caput super
omnem ecclesiam, quæ est corpus ejus ; visibilis autem is, qui Romanam cathedram,
Petri apostolorum principis legitimus successor, tenet." It would have been impossible to secure general recognition of a proposition of this kind at Trent. In Q. 11
there then follows a wordy statement about the Pope, in which he is not described as
representative of the unity of the Church and as its *outward* guide, but rather :
"necessarium fuit hoc visibile caput ad unitatem ecclesiæ *constituendam et conservan-
dam*." A still further step is represented by the words : "Ut Christum dominum
singulorum sacramentorum non solum auctorem, sed intimum etiam præbitorem
habemus—nam ipse est, qui baptizat et qui absolvit, et tamen is homines sacramentorum externos ministros instituit—sic ecclesiæ, quam ipse intimo spiritu regit,
hominem suæ potestatis vicarium et ministrum præfecit ; nam cum visibilis ecclesia
visibili capite egeat, etc."

arose in France a powerful movement against Curialism, quite independent of Jansenism. France, indeed, never fully recognised the Tridentinum in a formal way, although in point of fact the Tridentine system of doctrine asserted itself among the clergy, and even among the Church authorities. From the end of the sixteenth century (Henry IV.), but, above all, during the reign of Louis XIV., the Church of France, in its most important representatives (Bossuet), went back with decision to " Gallicanism." Yet the positive programme was far from being clear. Some were opponents of Curialism in the interest of the unlimited power of their king, others in the interest of their nation, others, again, from their being Episcopalists. But what did Episcopalism aim at? It had no greater clearness about itself in the seventeenth century than in the fifteenth. There was the admission that there belonged to the Pope a supremacy of rank (" suprematus ordinis "), but there was no common agreement as to whether this " suprematus " meant only the first place inter pares, or whether real prerogatives were connected with it. If there was a deciding for the latter, it was doubtful, again, whether these prerogatives were equivalent to a " cura ecclesiæ universalis " committed to the Pope. If this was certain, the questions had again to be asked, whether he could exercise this cura only while consulting and co-operating with all the bishops, and what measures were to be adopted with the view of guarding the bishops against papal encroachments. The fixed point in the Episcopalist theory was simply this, that the bishops were not appointed by the Pope, that they were therefore not delegates and representatives of the Pope, but ruled their dioceses independently " jure divino," that the Pope consequently could exercise no direct power of jurisdiction in their dioceses. But how that could be united with the " suprematus ordinis " of the Pope remained vague. It was clear also that an autocratic power of the Pope (infallibility, universal episcopy) was rejected, and that the Council was regarded as superior to the Pope ; yet there was a vagueness as to the meaning to be attached to the position that was admitted, that the Pope stands at the head of the Council. These difficulties, however, finally issued in somewhat definite formulæ, namely,

in the four Propositions of the Gallican Church (1862),[1] which
have more of a Church-and-State than an Episcopalist character : (1) In temporal matters the princes are subject to no
ecclesiastical power, and can be neither directly nor indirectly
deposed ; no power over temporal and civil affairs has been
committed by God to the successors of Peter. (2) The Pope
possesses, certainly, the " full power in spiritual things " (" plena
potestas spiritualium rerum "), yet in such a way "that the
decrees of the sacred œcumenical Synod of Constance regarding
the authority of general Councils are at the same time valid
and remain undisturbed " ;[2] the Gallican Church disapproves of
those " who impair the force of those decrees, as if they were of
doubtful authority and were less fully ratified, or who twist
them into being merely deliverances of a Council for a time of
schism."[3]   (3) The Pope, in the exercise of his power, is bound
by the Canons, and must also have respect to the rules, customs
and arrangements adopted in France.   (4) The Pope has, no
doubt, the highest authority (? partes) in matters of faith, and
his decrees apply to all Churches and every Church in particular ;

[1] See Collect. Lacensis I., p. 793.   Art. " Gallikanische Freiheiten " in Wetzer
und Welte's Kirchenlex, 2nd ed. V., p. 66 ff.   A century earlier Pithou (1594) gave
an account of the liberties of the French Church, and already laid down the two fundamental rules, that the Pope (1) has no voice in France in regard to civil and temporal
matters, and that (2) in spiritual matters he is bound by the decisions of the Councils,
and therefore by those of Constance also.   These ideas were brought, as an ecclesiastico-political programme, before King Henry IV., when he ascended the throne,
with the view of inaugurating State-Catholicism.   See Mejer, Febronius (1880), p. 20 :
" Under the protection of the Bourbons, who made the Gallican theory their own,
there flourished throughout the whole of Romanic Europe a rich literature in support
of it : Peter de Marca, Thomassin, Bossuet, are names that will not be forgotten so
long as there is a jurisprudence of ecclesiastical law.   The scientific method of this
Gallican Episcopalism differs from that of the fifteenth century especially in two
things—first, in its deriving its proof from the history of law, a mode of proof that
originated in France with the Humanistic jurisprudence of Cujacius, and set itself to
describe the Church constitution of the first centuries with the view of declaring the
later constitution an abuse ; secondly, in this, that in connection therewith, and also
with the traditional French practice, it vindicated for the French King somewhat the
same ruling ecclesiastical power as the Roman Emperor possessed according to the
Justinian books of laws."

[2] " Ut simul valeant atque immota consistant S. Œcumenicæ Synodi Constantiensis
decreta de auctoritate conciliorum generalium."

[3] " Qui eorum decretorum, quasi dubiæ sint auctoritatis ac minus approbata, robur
infringant, aut ad solum schismatis tempus concilii dicta detorqueant."

"*still, his decision is not incapable of reform, unless the assent of the Church has been added.*"[1]

These propositions were rejected, first by Innocent X., then by Alexander VIII., as entirely worthless and invalid.[2] Yet that would have been of little avail had not the all-powerful king, hemmed in by Jansenists and Jesuits, and ever and anon distressed about his soul's salvation, himself abandoned them. He very really betrayed himself and the Church of his country to the Pope, without formally withdrawing the four articles. In point of fact these rather remained in force during the eighteenth century, that is, the French clergy were for the most part trained in them, and thought and acted in accordance with them. But as the eighteenth century was passing into the nineteenth, a second monarch completed the betrayal of the French Church to the Pope—the same monarch who formally recognised the Gallican Articles and raised them to the place of a State-law—Napoleon I. The way in which the French Church and the French Church-order, really degraded already by the Revolution,[3] was, *with the consent of the Pope*, completely demolished by Napoleon, so that, with a disregard of all traditional order and right, he might reconstruct this Church *in league with the Pope* (Concordat of 1801), was an abandonment of the French Church to Curialism. This was not certainly Napoleon's idea. What he wished was to be master of the Church of his country, and the Pope, whom he had in his grasp, was, as high priest, to be his useful instrument. But he had not considered that Western Catholicism no longer allows any secular ruler to be forced upon it, and he had regarded his own political power as invincible. Of his original intentions, therefore, nothing was realised, save the reducing to ruins of the old, relatively independent, French Episcopal Church. He thus laid the foundation of the French Ultramon-

---

[1] "*Nec tamen irreformabile esse judicium, nisi ecclesiæ consensus accesserit.*"

[2] See the strong condemnation in Denzinger, l.c., p. 239 f.

[3] That this degradation, and the reconstruction by means of the Civil Constitution given to the clergy, were already favourable to the future Curialistic development of Catholicism has been recently shown by Lenz in an able essay on the Catholic Church and the French Revolution (in the Journal Cosmopolis, 1st year, 2nd number).

tane Church (without knowing or intending it, the Assembly
of 1789, in drawing up the Constitution, had prepared the way
for this), and after the tyrant had been overthrown, Pius VII.
knew very well what thanks he owed him. Romanticism (de
Maistre, Bonald, Chateaubriand, Lacordaire, etc.) and the
Restoration, in conjunction with the Jesuits, completed the
work ; nay, even agitations for political freedom had to fall to
the advantage of the Curia.[1] But, above all, the writings of de
Maistre (" On the Pope "), in which the Catholic spirit of the
Middle Ages, the spirit of St. Thomas, learned to speak in new
tongues (even in the language of Voltaire and Rousseau), contributed to bury out of view Gallicanism and Episcopalism.
The great Savoyard, who introduced the Ultramontane
" aperçu " into the writing of history, became the instructor of
Görres ; but he found a follower also in that boldest of all
publicists, L. Veuillot, who understood how to recommend to
the French clergy and their following as divine truths even the
most audacious paradoxes. At the present day France, even
Republican France, is the main support of Catholicism, of the
Catholic propaganda and of Ultramontanism : the French have
become the Normans of the modern papacy.[2]

In Germany the Episcopalist agitations were of little account
till the middle of the eighteenth century. But at that time
they broke out most powerfully in the work of the Suffragan
Bishop, Nicolas von Hontheim (Febronii de statu ecclesiæ et
legitima potestate Romani Pontificis, 1763). Different lines

[1] Yet see the firm rejection of the positions of Lammennais by Gregory XVI. in
the years 1832 and 1834 (Denzinger, l.c., p. 310 f.). Indifferentism and the demand
for freedom of conscience are here placed upon the same level : " Ex hoc putidissimo
indifferentismi fonte absurda illa fluit ac erronea sententia seu potius deliramentum,
asserendam esse ac vindicandam cuilibet libertatem conscientiæ. Cui quidem pesti-
lentissimo errori viam sternit plena illa atque immoderata libertas opinionum, quæ
in sacræ et civilis rei labem late grassatur, dictitantibus per summam impudentiam
nonnullis, aliquid ex ea commodi in religionem promanare."
[2] On the development of the French National Church into an Ultramontane Church,
see Mejer, Zur Gesch. der römisch-deutschen Frage, Vol. I.; Friedrich, Gesch. des
vatik. Concils, Vol I.; Nielsen, Die Röm. K. im 19. Jahrh. Vol. I. (German, by
Nichelsen) ; the same author, Aus dem innerem Leben der Kathol. Kirche im 19.
Jahrh., Vol. I. ; Nippold, Handbuch der nenesten K.-Gesch. 3rd ed., Vols. I.
and II.

converge in this book : Gallicanism, the natural-right theories regarding the State which had originated with Hugo Grotius (and the Roman-law theories regarding the emperor or the sovereign), the Dutch Humanism. Hontheim had studied at Louvain. The teachers there, who were under the influence of Van Espen, had taught him that Catholic and Papist were not the same thing, and that the actually existing state of papacy in Germany could not cancel the original order of things, which was involved in the divinely ordained Episcopal office on the one hand, and in the natural rights of the State on the other.[1] The primacy had only a human-historical development; the Church was really represented and led by the Council, to which the Pope is subject. This state of things, which rested on the divinely ordained apostolicity and equality of all bishops as rulers of the Church, must again be established. In the end Hontheim let himself be forced to retract. But his ideas continued to have influence, though not exactly in the direction he had intended. He was more a Gallican and an Episcopalist than a representative of the natural right of the State, which, in the eighteenth century, was becoming modified into the absolute right of the prince. But the ecclesiastical Electors who adopted his thoughts were interested in them primarily as sovereigns, only in a secondary way as bishops. This turn of things was disastrous. The Ems Punctation (1786),[2] the occasion of which was the grievance about the Nuncios, could not hold out any promise to the emperor and the sovereigns, who did not wish an independent Episcopal church, but a State Church in the strictest sense of the term. The opposition, hitherto concealed, between Episcopalism and State Churchism necessarily came to be all the more strongly expressed, from the great bishops themselves, in their own interest, passing over to adopt the State Church thoughts. Owing to this opposition, and also to the divided state of Germany and the rivalry between Prussia and Austria, what was undertaken at Ems very rapidly proved a failure. Never, certainly, since the days of Constance and

---

[1] See Mejer, l.c., p. 20 f.; cf. also, H. Schmid, Gesch. der Kathol. K. Deutschlands v. d. Mitte des 18 Jahrh. I., p. 1 ff.

[2] On this, see Köllner, l.c. I., p. 430 ff.; Schmid, l.c. I., p. 15 ff.

Bâsle, was the sovereignty of the bishops and the unimportant
position of the Pope more boldly formulated within Catholicism
than by the German bishops at Ems a hundred years ago. But
it was a childish illusion of the "philosophical" age to imagine
that a structure like that of the papacy could be overthrown by
decrees like those of Ems, and it was a vast deception to believe
that Roman Catholicism was really weary of life, and had given
final proof of its weakness by being forced to suppress the
Jesuits. In the storm of the Revolution it became apparent
that the old lion still lived, and in their alarm the princes then
hastened to impart to it on their side still more vigour. The collapse of the Imperial Church, with which the State Church of Joseph
II. also disappeared,[1] was a fortunate occurrence for Rome. How
the Curia succeeded in suppressing what remained of Episcopalist
and State Church thought in Germany, in constructing the
Church anew by means of concordats, and in gradually training
for itself an Ultramontane Episcopate and an Ultramontane
clergy, after the National Church tradition had, as in France,
been abolished ; how in this work there co-operated not only the
Jesuits, but above all the princes, the Romanticists, and the un-
suspecting Liberals—has been fully narrated quite recently.[2]
The Vatican Decrees were the culmination of this development.[3]

(1) (b) Their opposition to the Protestant principle of Scripture, and the impossibility of really furnishing traditional proof

[1] Cf. K. Müller in Herzog's R.-E., 2nd ed., Art. "Josefinismus"; on the Synod
of Pistoja under the direction of Ricci, see in the same work the article by Benrath.
Against the adviser of Joseph II., the Canonist Eybel, who had made a most startling
impression with his book, "Was ist der Papst," see the Breve of Pius VI., "Super
solidate" (Denzinger, l.c. p. 273).

[2] See the accounts by Mejer, Schmid, Nielsen, Friedrich, Nippold. We also possess excellent accounts of the history of the Catholic Church of the nineteenth century in separate German countries. Future historians will compare the advance of
Romanism in our century with that in the eleventh century ; it is more powerful at
any rate than that of the Counter-Reformation. See also Hase, Polemik, 3rd ed.,
1st Book.

[3] How little ability there was even in the year 1844 to forecast on the Protestant
side the development of the papal system into the doctrine of infallibility is shown by
a remark of Köllner (l.c., p. 426), whose "Symbolik" cannot be charged with failing
to do justice to the Roman Church. "Quite unecclesiastical, and suggestive only of the
fanaticism of particular Jesuits, is the view of the Pope in the Confessio Hungarica
Evangelis proposita. '. . . Papam caput esse ecclesiæ *nec errare posse.*'"

for many doctrines and usages, led the Catholic theologians in
the period that followed (1) to subordinate Scripture in an ever
increasing degree to tradition, (2) to utilise more fully the distinction drawn by the Tridentinum between two kinds of
tradition (see above), as a distinction giving a title to regard
some traditions as subject to no higher standard.[1] As regards
the first point, Jesuits in particular had done so much with their
Rabbinic art in the way of planing all round the dogma of
inspiration, and had produced so many different views of that
dogma, that in the end almost nothing remained of it. Perrone,
who enumerates all these forms in his dogmatic, mentions also
the last, according to which inspiration does not imply a
miraculous origination of Scripture, but is to be held as only
meaning that the Holy Ghost has *subsequently* (in the Church)
borne witness to the inerrancy of Scripture.[2] Yet this theory,
maintained by the Jesuits Lessius and Hamel (1586), did not
succeed certainly in establishing itself; nay, the Vaticanum
rejected it by declaring (Constit. de fide c. 2): "But the Church
holds those books as sacred and canonical, not because, having
been composed by human industry alone, they were then
authenticated by its authority, nor only because they contain
revelation free from error, but because, being written under the
inspiration of the .Holy Spirit, they have God for their author,
and have been handed down as such to the Church itself."[3]
This formulation still leaves room certainly for a lax view of
inspiration ("assistentia positiva"); but on the other hand, it

---

[1] Cf. Holtzmann, Kanon und Tradition, 1859. J. Delitzsch, Lehrsystem d. röm.
K., I., p. 295 ff. Hase, l.c., pp. 63 ff. The Professio fidei Tridentinæ had already
taken a great step beyond the Tridentinum, inasmuch as it substituted the following
for the Tridentine distinction between the traditiones a Christo and the traditiones ab
apostolis :—"Apostolicas et ecclesiasticas traditiones reliquasque ejusdem ecclesiæ ob-
servationes et constitutiones firmissime admitto et amplector." There is thus introduced here an entirely new terminology, a circumstance to which Holtzmann was the
first strongly to direct attention (p. 253). It is only after this that mention is first
made in the Professio of Holy Scripture !

[2] Prælect. theol. Romæ (1840-42, Paris, 1842), Chap. II., p. 1082 sq.

[3] "Eos libros vero ecclesia pro sacris et canonicis habet, non ideo, quod sola
humana industria concinnati sua deinde auctoritate sint comprobati, nec ideo dumtaxat, quod revelationem sine errore contineant, sed propterea quod Spiritu s.
inspirante conscripti deum habent auctorem atque ut tales ipsi ecclesiæ traditi sunt."

is assuredly in the interests of Catholicism, apart from its opposition to Protestantism, that all that has been handed down
as in the strictest form holy should be also preserved by it as
such.   The lax view, as is well known, made it possible that
there should be the beginnings of an historic criticism of the
Bible in the seventeenth century (Richard Simon).   Yet the
advantages derived from being able to think of one's self as a
man of science are so seriously counterbalanced by the draw-
backs which even the mildest criticism has for the Church, that
even the most decided traditionalists—who have really no need
for the Bible at all—prefer to content themselves with the mere
appearance of Bible criticism.[1]   What came to have much
deeper influence than this anti-Protestant mock fight about the
Bible, was the further shaping of the notion of tradition in the
post-Tridentine development.   This course of formulation came
to a head in the utterance of the first infallible Pope, the authen-
ticity of which, so far as I know, has not been called in question
—" The tradition is I "—after Mohler had in vain sought to
reconcile the Catholic notion of tradition with history and
criticism.

As early as the seventeenth century the controversialists, in
opposing Chemnitz, who had attacked the Roman " dis-
putationes de traditionibus " as " pandects of errors and super-
stitions," laid special stress on the ecclesiastical traditions.
As a matter of fact, in the time that followed, the Tridentine
distinction between " traditiones a Christo " and " traditiones
ab apostolis " almost entirely disappeared—it was handed over
to the Schools ; on the other hand the distinction of the Professio between " traditiones apostolicæ " and " traditiones
ecclesiasticæ " became fundamental.   Bellarmin was still timid in
turning to account the ecclesiastical traditions ; he still sought
for the most part to reach his point by means of the Tridentine
definition, and treated the ecclesiastical traditions disparagingly ;
yet the future principle of tradition, which quite sets itself above
history, as well as above the Church Fathers, was already for-

[1] Such an appearance is very easily produced at the present day by letting the
tradition about the Bible stand, while there is entwined around it a wreath furnished
by readings in Egyptology, Assyriology, and Greek and Roman literature.

mulated with admirable clearness by Cornelius Mussus, formerly a member of the Tridentine Council: "For my part, to speak frankly, I would have more reliance regarding those things that touch the mysteries of faith upon one supreme pontiff than upon a thousand Augustines, Jeromes, and Gregories."[1] There belongs to this connection also the remark of the Jesuits, which has almost a naïve ring about it, "the more recent teachers are, the clearer they are" ("quo juniores, eo perspicaciores esse doctores").[2] It was the Jesuits entirely who put an end to the old notion of tradition represented by Cyprian and Vincentius, and secured a hold for a new one, which for a long time, certainly, was really dominant, but is the opposite of the old. The unqualified deliverance that the Church receives new revelations through the Pope was certainly avoided by cautious theologians of dogma;[3] yet for such a deliverance there was substituted the simple *assertion*, that "traditio ecclesiastica" is just that which the Church (the Pope) has formulated as an article of faith. How seriously this was held is apparent from the urgent directions, not to be in anxiety about the traditional proof (from history) in support of any more recent dogma ; even that is certain and original Church doctrine for which no proof can be furnished, if it is in force as Church doctrine.[4] In this connection are meant to be estimated the depreciatory judgments on the Councils that were pronounced in the seventeenth and eighteenth centuries by the Jesuits, as also the freedom of the criticism applied to the Church Fathers. The Roman Church cannot, of course, part with the Councils, as little as with any other article of its venerable house-furnishings ; but it has no longer a real interest in them, and although during the course of two centuries

---

[1] " Ego, ut ingenue fatear, plus uni summo pontifici crederem in his, quæ fidei my-steria tangunt, quam mille Augustinis, Hieronymis, Gregoriis."

[2] Passages to be found in Holtzmann, p. 267.

[3] Yet testimonies could be gathered to show that in authoritative quarters there was no hesitation in making such statements as that this or that had *not yet* been revealed to the Church.

[4] Of course the historical proof is a beautiful adornment, but it is nothing more ; nay, the undertaking to prove is even held as not without danger. One who under-takes to prove anything is not sure that the proof will be perfectly successful, and that it will make an impression.

it has called to order more than one Jesuit who has recklessly handled the *real* tradition, it cannot but be pleased when now and again it appears that on closer inspection everything in history shows signs of uncertainty and is full of errors and forgeries. What have the Jesuits and their friends not taught us in this respect for two hundred years! The letters of Cyprian falsified, Eusebius falsified, numberless writings of the Church Fathers interpolated, the Constantinopolitan Symbol falsified by the Greeks, the Councils convoked contrary to the intentions of Rome, the Acts of the Councils falsified, the Decrees of the Councils of no account, the most venerable Church Fathers full of heterodox views and without authority—only one rock in this ocean of error and forgery, *the chair of Peter,* and, making itself heard through history, only one sure note incapable of being misunderstood, the *testimony to the infallibility of the successor of Peter.* And yet—the Pope is infallible even without this testimony; *the Church itself is the living tradition; the Church, however, is the Pope.* Nothing changes in the Church, although it itself continually changes;[1] for when any change is made by the Church (the Pope), it receives at once a certificate of antiquity, which carries it back to the time of the Apostles. The Pope can, at the present day, formulate a new dogma, and this was done by him in the year 1854 with regard to the immaculate conception of Mary, although one of his predecessors had declared that "the eternal wisdom had not yet disclosed the depths of this mystery to the Church." Much, therefore, may still lie hidden in the womb of the future, which the eternal wisdom will reveal to the Popes who are to come— but according to the terms of the Ultramontane dogmatic, new revelations do not take place.

As compared with the conception of tradition that is accepted at the present day, how tame the Tridentine Decree regarding tradition appears! It sounds already in our ears like a legend of the olden time: "that truth and discipline are contained in the Scriptures and in the unwritten traditions which have come

---

[1] See the unguarded saying of Archbishop Scherr, of Munich, in reply to Döllinger, "You know that there have always been changes in the Church and in its doctrines," in Friedrich, Tagebuch, 2nd ed., p. 410 f.

down to us as having been received by the Apostles from Christ's
own lips, or as being transmitted, as it were, from hand to hand
by the Apostles themselves, the Holy Spirit having dictated
them."[1] But unfortunately it cannot be asserted that this
principle has gradually developed itself into the principle accepted at the present day, for the latter was already in full force
in the second half of the sixteenth century. It merely did not
find expression, from the adverse force of circumstances (propter
angustias temporum). Just on that account no *history* of the
Roman conception of tradition from the Council of Trent to the
Council of the Vatican can be written ; there can only be
narratives furnished, which indicate the approaching complete
victory of the revolutionary principle of tradition over the older
principle.[2] In this victory the *de-Christianising* and *secularising*
of the Christian religion in Catholicism became complete. The
Gnostic principle of tradition (secret apostolic tradition) and
the "enthusiastic" principle, against which the Old Catholic
principle was in its day set up, obtained entrance into the
Church, and established themselves there, under cover of the
latter. As judged strictly by the standard of the ancient Church
the doctrine of tradition in force at the present day is *heretical*,
because it is Gnostic and enthusiastic.[3] But it is no longer
attached to an elastic fellowship, in which the conflicting factors
control and correct one another up to a certain point, but to a
single Italian priest, who possesses the authority, and in part
also the power, of the old Cæsars. He is no longer checked by
any restriction that arises from the historic nature of the
Christian religion. Yet, hemmed in as he is by the cordon of
the sacred college, by the traditions of his chair, and by the
superstition of the faithful, he can scarcely formulate as a

---

[1] "Veritatem et disciplinam contineri in liberis scriptis et sine scriptis traditionibus,
quæ ab ipsius Christi ore ab apostolis acceptæ aut ab ipsis apostolis spiritu s. dictitante
quasi per manus traditæ ad nos usque pervenerunt."

[2] See the sections in Holtzmann, p. 31 f., 52 f., 83 f., 224 f., 231 f., 237 f., 250 f.,
260 f., 273 f., 283 f.

[3] Hence there is great accuracy in the Articles of Schmalkald, P. III., a. 8 (p. 321,
Müller) : "Quid, quod etiam papatus simpliciter est merus enthusiasmus, quo papa
gloriatur, omnia jura esse in scrinio sui pectoris, et quidquid ipse in ecclesia sua sentit
et jubet, id spiritum et justum esse, etiamsi supra et contra scriptum et vocale verbum
aliquid statuat et præcipiat."

"traditional article of faith," anything that has against it the
spirit of the thirteenth century or of the Counter-Reformation.[1]

(2) In the Catechismus Romanus, published in 1566 by
Pius V., the Thomist doctrine of grace, which had found only a
fragmentary expression at Trent, was very distinctly stated.
But this statement, so far as it was official, was the last of its
kind. The Catechismus Romanus represents the grave of a
doctrine which was maintained in the first half of the sixteenth
century by the best Catholics. It brought to completion the
Augustinian reaction, inasmuch as that reaction was not merely
tolerated, or, for that part, contested, in the Church, but was
recognised, and contributed very much to the regeneration of
Catholicism. From that time there arose a struggle against
Augustine, in which the "Churchmen" par excellence, the
Jesuits, took the leading part. This struggle was not to cease
till "the last enemy" lay on the field helpless, though not slain,
and the worldly practice of the confessional could prescribe to
dogmatic its law.[2] Yet it would be unjust to assert that on the
one side laxity merely prevailed, on the other side religious
earnestness. In the ranks of the opponents of the Augustinians
there were also men of pure Catholic piety, while many of the
Augustinians struck out on courses which really diverged from
the Catholic ecclesiasticism.

The struggle about Augustinianism was waged, not in
Germany, but on Romanic and Belgian soil. The first stage
was represented by the names of Bajus and Molina.[3] In

---

[1] In this connection the letter of advice is very interesting which Bellarmin addressed
to the Pope in the year 1602, see Döllinger, Beiträge III., p. 83, Döllinger und
Reusch, Selbstbiographie des Cardinals Bellarmin, p. 260. This great Curialist ventured—it was in a dogmatic question, no doubt, which concerned him very closely—
to take the upper hand with the Pope, and to remind him that he might not decide
the controversy on his own responsibility, otherwise there would be trouble both to
the Church and himself.

[2] Protestantism took almost no part whatever in this inner Catholic movement.
Leaving dwindling exceptions out of view, the Catholic Augustinians of the sixteenth
and seventeenth centuries adopted against Protestantism as decided an attitude of
opposition and self-defence as the representatives of the prevailing Church practice ;
nay, Augustine was even utilised with the view of being able to combat the Reformation more strenuously.

[3] Linsemann, Michael Bajus und die Grundlegung des Jansenism, 1867. Schneemann, Entstehung der thomistisch-molinistischen Controverse (cf. also other relative

different writings and in his lectures, Bajus, Professor in
Louvain (1544-1589), without undertaking a strictly systematic
development, presented in a sharply definite way the Augustinian
doctrine of sin and unfreedom, with the view, not of coming to
terms with Protestantism, but of combating it. As early as
1560 the Sorbonne condemned a number of his propositions,
which were submitted to it in manuscript. Thereafter he was
arraigned before the Pope on the ground of smaller writings
which he had made public. Jesuits and Franciscans were his
enemies. They took offence above all at his unconditional
rejection of the doctrine of the immaculate conception of Mary.
In 1567 Pius V. issued the Bull " Ex omnibus afflictionibus,"
which, without mentioning Bajus' name, rejected, or at least
took objection to, 79 of his positions.[1] Only when he raised
difficulties against yielding was the Bull published. Twice over
was Bajus forced to retract, after the new Pope, Gregory XIII.,
had confirmed the adverse judgment of his predecessor. In
Bajus Augustine himself was struck at in the sharpest possible
way, though by means of the sentence, " although some opinions
might possibly be sustained on a certain understanding,"[2] the
Curia had left a back door open for itself. A large number of
the propositions censured were, in form and content, Augustinian,
so that in their rejection the renunciation of the authority of the
great African was apparent. The main thoughts of Bajus were,[3]
(1) that grace is always only grace through Jesus Christ,[4]
(2) that God could only create man good, and did create him
such, that, consequently, everything " naturally " good would
have fallen to him, had he continued in goodness, but that for

works of this Jesuit). Serry, Hist. congreg. de auxiliis, L. Meyer, Hist. controv. de
auxiliis, 2 vols., Döllinger und Reusch, Selbstbiographie Bellarmin's, p. 256 ff.
Scheeben, Wetzer und Welte, 2nd ed., 1st vol., " Bajus."

[1] " Quas quidem sententias stricto coram nobis examine ponderatas, *quamquam
nonnullæ aliquo pacto sustineri possent*, in rigore et proprio verborum sensu ab
assertoribus intento hæreticas, erroneas, suspectas, temerarias, scandalosas, et in pias
aures offensionem immittentes respective . . . damnamus " ; see Denzinger, l.c.,
p. 208.

[2] " Quamquam nonnullæ sententiæ aliquo pacto sustineri possent."

[3] I pass over anything peculiar to him that has no relation to Augustinianism or
that contradicts it.

[4] See Propos. 1 in the Bull " Ex omnibus afflictionibus " ; further, 2-7, 9.

that very reason the Fall entailed not only the loss of a " superadded gift " ("donum superadditum "), but the entire ruin of
human nature,[1] (3) that through sin the will of man has become
unfree, and hence man must necessarily sin, though with his
will, is absolutely incapable of the good, and can produce
nothing good out of himself,[2] (4) that accordingly all works of
unbelievers are sins, and the virtues of philosophers are vices,[3]
(5) that original sin is real sin, and this is not less true of concupiscence,[4] (6) that all human beings, inclusive of Mary, are
sinners, and suffer death by reason of their sins,[5] (7) that in no
sense are there human merits in the sight of God ; God, rather,
anticipates all merit by changing the bad will into a good, and
thus producing Himself all good merits (through the merit of
Christ).[6]   In the doctrines of justification and the Sacraments

[1] See the Propos. 1-7, 9, 11, 21, 23 : "Absurda est eorum sententia, qui dicunt,
hominem ab initio dono quodam supernaturali et gratuito, supra conditionem naturæ
suæ fuisse exaltatum, ut fide, spe et caritate deum supernaturaliter coleret," 24, 26,
78.

[2] See the Propos. 20 : "Nullum est peccatum ex natura sua veniale, sed omne peccatum meretur pœnam æternam."   27 : "Liberum arbitrium sine gratiæ dei adjutorio
nonnisi ad peccandum valet."   28, 30, 35, 37, 39 : "Quod voluntarie fit etiamsi
necessario fit, libere tamen fit."   40, 41 : "Is libertatis modus qui est a necessitate,
sub libertatis nomine non reperitur in scripturis, sed solum nomen liberatis a peccato."
46 : "Ad rationem et definitionem peccati non pertinet voluntarium, nec definitionis
quæstio est, sed causæ et originis, utrum omne peccatum debeat esse voluntarium."
65, 67.

[3] See Propos. 25 : "Omnia opera infidelium sunt peccata et philosophorum virtutes
sunt vitia."

[4] See Propos. 47 : "Peccatum originis vere habet rationem peccati sine ulla ratione
ac respectu ad voluntatem, a qua originem habuit."   48, 49, 51 : "Concupiscentia
et prava ejus desideria, quæ inviti sentiunt homines, sunt vera legis inobedientia."
52, 53, 74, 75, 76.

[5] See Propos. 73 : "Nemo præter Christum est absque peccato originali : hinc b.
virgo Maria mortua est propter peccatum ex Adam contractum omnesque ejus afflic-
tiones peccati actualis vel originalis."   72.

[6] Propos. 8 : "In redemptis per gratiam Christi nullum inveniri potest bonum
meritum, quod non sit gratis indigno collatum."   10 : "Solutio pœnæ temporalis,
quæ peccato dimisso sæpe manet, et corporis resurrectio proprie nonnisi meritis
Christi adscribenda est."   22, 29 : "Non soli fures ii sunt et latrones, qui Christum
viam et ostium veritatis et vitæ negant, sed etiam quicunque aliunde quam per ipsum
in viam justitiæ (hoc est aliquam justitiam) conscendi posse docent."   34 : "Dis-
tinctio illa duplicis amoris, naturalis vid., quo deus amatur ut auctor naturæ, et
gratuiti quo deus amatur ut beatificator, vana est."   36 : "Amor naturalis, qui ex
viribus naturæ exoritur, ex sola philosophia per relationem præsumptionis humanæ

Bajus held substantially to the prevailing ecclesiastical type. But although in accordance with this type he recognised righteousness in real perfection, yet he laid a much greater weight on forgiveness of sin than the Decrees of Trent allowed of ; it is true, no doubt, that for him forgiveness of sin is ideal, and is really *not* righteousness, but in point of fact our active righteousness comes to exist only through constantly having as its complement the forgiveness of sins which God reckons as righteousness.   Forgiveness of sins is for him not only an initial act, but a parallel to the " operation of virtue " (" operatio virtutum ").[1]   That, however, is still Catholic.   Augustine's doctrine of predestination Bajus seems to have rather thrown into the background.

While not intending it, Bajus came close in his teaching to the fundamental evangelical thoughts, though these were strangely mixed up by him with Catholic doctrines.   But owing to his retractation, the effect of his far-reaching propositions was lost.   On the other hand, the opposition between Dominicans and Jesuits continued.   The characteristic doctrines of the opponents were rejected from both sides (the " Directions for Study " of the Jesuit General Aquaviva rejected 17 Thomistic propositions ; the Dominicans carried on an effective opposition against these Directions, and condemned the positions regarding predestination of two specially audacious Jesuits—Lessius and Hamel).   But the controversy was only fanned into full flame when the Jesuit Luis Molina had, in the year 1588, published his work, " Liberi arbitrii cum gratiæ donis, divina præscientia, providentia, prædestinatione et reprobatione concordia."[2]   This work starts with the power of the natural man to dispose himself for grace (see the Tridentine Decree), and with amazing Scholastic energy[3] tries to unite the divine

cum injuria crucis Christi defenditur a nonnullis doctoribus."   65, 77 : " Satisfactiones laboriosæ justificatorum non valent expiare de condigno pœnam temporalem restantem post culpam condonatam."

[1] Remarkable theses on justification are found in 42, 43, 44, 63, 64, 68, 69, 70. It is manifest that irrelevant material is introduced into the theses formulated regarding the Pope.

[2] The second edition, 1595, is substantially unaltered.

[3] The old efforts to find varieties in the knowledge of God were continued by

causality, and even the Augustinian theses, with Semi-Pelagianism, or to subordinate the former to the latter.   That, of course,
could not succeed.   But the mere undertaking was, from his
Church's point of view, meritorious, and everything can be
forced together in words.   In point of fact, Augustinianism was
here discarded (God only *aids*), and that, too, in such an overt
way that even Scotists took offence at the book.   It cannot fall
to us to describe the tragi-comedy which now followed in an
unlimited succession of acts.   Yet it illustrates in a very
instructive way the fact that dogma, as dogma, had long been
buried ; for the way in which this Thomistic-Molinistic controversy was carried through—or was *not* carried through—at
Rome furnishes the clearest evidence that dogmatic interest had
been supplanted by the interest of the holy Chair and of the
various Orders.   There was hesitation, a demanding of silence,
a deciding, and a not deciding in so important a question,
because the matter of main concern was not doctrine at all, but
was the peace of the Church and the gratification of the
ambition and lust of power of the parties.   How far this last
was carried is excellently shown by *e.g.*, the attitude of
Bellarmin.   There was not only a threatening of the Pope and
an endeavour to intimidate him when he seemed to favour the
Dominicans too much ; the most zealous papists even laid
hands on the central supports of the system.   The Commission
at first appointed, which characterised many positions of Molina
as inadmissible, was obliged to give way to a new one, that
famous " Congregatio de auxiliis gratiæ," which continued its
sittings from 1598 to 1607, and could never come to a decision,
because Dominicans and Jesuits were represented on it.   In
this controversy the Scholastic terminology was added to in an

Molina, and he turned them to account in carrying out his task : by help of the
" scientia media " God foresees the possible, which, under given circumstances,
becomes the actual.   Into the details of Molina's style of doctrine I cannot enter.
In judging of it, moreover, it must be kept in view that the Catholic Church was no
longer Augustinian, and that what Molina undertook was to give rational expression
to what was actually held valid.   If Molina is to be reproached for writing *about* the
doctrine—*i.e.*, for writing from the standpoint of the rational critic instead of describing justification as the sinner has experienced it —that is not a reproach that falls on
him alone ; it also falls on the Tridentine Decree, and on official Catholicism in
general.

immeasurable degree ("prædeterminatio physica," "gratia efficax efficacitate connexionis cum consensu," etc.), though there was no success in making a dogma out of the contradictio in adjecto (contradiction in terms).   In the sitting of 28th August, 1607, at which Paul V. himself presided, the Jesuits declared the doctrine of physical predetermination to be Calvinistic and Lutheran, hotly opposed a decision eventually come to to suspend Molina's book ("until it be corrected" ["donec corrigatur"]), and assailed the Dominican dogmatist Bañez as a heretic.   Of the other members of the Congregation almost every one had a different opinion as to what was to be done.   Thereupon, on the 18th September, the Pope, no doubt acting on the advice of the Jesuits, dissolved the assembly, declaring at the same time that he would, at his own time, give a decision ("at a fitting opportunity His Holiness would publicly give the declaration and decision that were expected"[1]) ; till then no party must either "characterise" the other, or "visit it with any censure" ("aut qualificare aut censura quapiam notare").   Thus the controversy, which had really been long before decided—for it was the controversy between Augustine and Pelagius—ended with an admission of complete helplessness. [2]

In purer form than by Bajus, whose general theological position is a problem, Augustinianism was revived by Cornelius Jansen, Bishop of Ypres.   The movement that is connected with his name, or with his work "Augustinus," published in 1640, after his death, entered deeply into French history in the seventeenth century, and carried its influence into the eighteenth and nineteenth centuries ; it has still a living monument at the present day

---

[1] "Foie ut sua sanctitas declarationem et determinationem, quæ exspectabatur, opportune promulgant."

[2] See Döllinger u. Reusch, l.c., p. 273 f.   In the year 1611 the Pope induced the Inquisition to issue the order that all books that treated of the material de auxiliis should first of all be submitted to it for its approbation.   Schneemann, the Jesuit, is quite entitled to be proud of the fact that the Molinistic doctrine of grace really won the victory—the doctrine at which even Bellarmin took offence because it exalted human freedom far too much at the cost of grace, and which was adopted not without alteration even in the Decree of the Jesuit General Aquaviva of the year 1613 (l.c., p. 274 f.).

in the old Catholic Church of Utrecht.[1]   At one time the Huguenots had been the "Friends of Religion" in France, *i.e.*, they
included among them almost all who had a living sense of the
seriousness of religion and who took a stand against the secularised Court - Church.   Through the Counter - Reformation,
Catholicism again became a spiritual power even in France.   It
was restored in such a way that the spirit of piety again found
a home in it, in spite of Ultramontanism and Court Churchism.
But with the lapse of time it became always the harder for this
good Catholic, pious spirit to tolerate the lax morality which
was really justified by the theology of the Jesuits, and which,
through the confessional, poisoned both clergy and people.   It
was observed that this lax morality was a consequence of that
Nominalistic-Aristotelian Scholasticism which had already desol-
ated the Church in the fourteenth and fifteenth centuries, and
which was of one blood with Pelagianism.   But at the same time
the earnestly disposed found it more difficult from year to year to
reconcile themselves to that Court and State Christianity which
again established itself in spite of the frightful struggles of the
sixteenth century.   This Christianity was at bottom the deadly
foe of Jesuitism ; but it excelled it in frivolity and worldliness of
spirit.   Thus the pious Catholics saw the Church of Christ in a
most lamentable position.   Protestantism was threatening from
without; internally, the Church was devastated by two enemies,
united in their immorality and their endeavour to lead forth the
Church into captivity, otherwise standing apart, the one agitating
for a despicable Court Christianity, the other driving Christianity
into blind dependence on the Roman confessional : "Behold the
Fathers, who take away the sins of the world ! " (" Ecce patres,
qui tollunt peccata mundi ! ").

From this state of things the powerful Jansenist movement is
to be understood.   As relates to the impulses of true piety, it

[1] The literature on Jansenism is very abundant; see Ranke, Franz. Geschichte, St.
Beuve, Port Royal, 1840 f., Reuchlin, Gesch. von Port Royal, 2 vols., 1839 f., and
in Herzog's R.-E. the article Jansen; further, the Monographs on Paschal and the
Arnaulds ; Schill, Die Constitution Unigenitus, 1876, Schott, Art. Port Royal in
Herzog's R.-E., Henke, Neuere Kirchengesch. II., p. 87 ff.   For the eighteenth and
nineteenth centuries the Church History of Nippold and Friedrich's Gesch. des Vatik.
Concils.

was far superior to the French Conciliar movement of the 15th century. When it sounded forth the appeal to return to the *ancient Church,* that which it thought of was not only—was, in the first instance, not at all—a change of constitution; it was an *inner* regeneration of the Church through repentance and faith, religious awakening and asceticism, as these were understood by Augustine. Once again in the history of Catholicism there was, in France, a close adherence to the great African, after adverse judgment had been pronounced on Luther and Calvin. With the deepest sympathy we follow the effort, so full of blessing, and yet so devoid of any prospect of success, to emancipate the Church from the Church, faith from a Christianity of use and wont, the moral life from a subtly-refined and lax morality. As if that had been possible by a mere *reaction* in the lines of Augustine! Certainly, if Catholicism could be corrected by Catholicism, this would have taken place at that time in France, when the deepest, most earnest, and noblest spirits in the nation crowded together for reform, and one of the greatest orators and rhetoricians of all ages, Pascal, broke silence to awaken the conscience of the nations against the Society of Jesus. But in the end everything disappeared in the sand. It was not merely that the movement was violently suppressed; the movement itself ended, like every Catholic movement for reform, in the renunciation of opposition and in fanaticism.

The work of describing the course of Jansenism falls to Church history. *New* factors requiring to be considered in the history of dogma did not make their appearance in the controversy; hence in this connection the interest attaches mainly to the answer to be given to the question—In what measure did the official Catholicism see itself compelled, in face of this movement, to repudiate Augustine and to strengthen itself in its Nominalistic-Pelagian attitude? Immediately after the appearing of Jansen's "Augustine," the Jesuits did the shrewdest thing it was in their power to do; though themselves the party assailed, they assumed the offensive. Jansen's book really contained pure Augustinianism, incomparably purer than in the restoration attempted by Bajus, while no concessions were made to Protestantism.[1] Hence the doctrine of predestination certainly occupies a very prominent place in Jansen.[2] Through the influence of the Jesuits with the Curia, Urban VIII., after referring to the censure pronounced upon Bajus, confirmed the prohibition of the book, on the ground of its containing heresies. It was now that the struggle broke out in France—a struggle about *religion*, with, at the same time, the undercurrent of a struggle for the rights of personal conviction over against the despotism of the Pope and the papal Mamelukes. But these last-mentioned succeeded in obtaining from the Pope the Bull "Cum occasione" (1653), in which five propositions were described as subject to condemnation, and were, at the same time, represented—though not with entire clearness—as propositions of Jansen. These are the terms of them :[3]—(1) "Some precepts of God cannot be fulfilled by good men, whose wish and effort are according to the measure of strength they at present possess ; they have the further need of grace that shall render obedience possible." (2) "Inward grace is never resisted in the state of fallen nature." (3) "In order to the existence of merit and demerit in the state of fallen nature there is not required in man a liberty that is the absence of necessity; it is enough if there be the liberty that is the absence of constraint." (4) "Semi-Pelagians admitted the necessity of inner prevenient grace for single acts, also for the origination of faith, and they were heretical in this, that they wished that grace to be of such a kind that it should be possible for the human will to resist or obey." (5) "It is Semi-Pelagian to say that Christ died, or that He shed His blood, for all men without exception."[4] Looked at

---

[1] Jansen's doctrine of justification is strictly Catholic.

[2] What makes an account of Jansenism unnecessary is just that Augustine's doctrines of sin, grace, and predestination are so correctly reproduced in it.

[3] See Denzinger, l.c., p. 212 f.

[4] "Aliqua dei præcepta hominibus justis volentibus et conantibus secundum præsentes quas habent vires sunt impossibilia ; deest quoque illis gratia, qua possibilia fiant." "Interiori gratiæ in statu naturæ lapsæ nunquam resistitur." "Ad merendum et demerendum in statu naturæ lapsæ non requiritur in homine libertas a necessitate, sed sufficit libertas a coactione." "Semi-Pelagiani admittebant prævenientis gratiæ interioris necessitatem ad singulos actus, etiam ad initium fidei, et in hoc erant hæretici, quod vellent eam gratiam talem esse, cui posset humana voluntas resistere et obtemperare." "Semi-Pelagianum est dicere, Christum pro omnibus omnino hominibus mortuum esse aut sanguinem fudisse."

apart from the roots from which they sprang, these propositions
are not Jansenist, even though they can be almost literally
established from Jansen, for dogmatic is not a series of equations
from which one may select as he pleases.   The Jansenists, therefore, had certainly a right to raise the "question du fait,"
and to require proof that Jansen so taught.   The real aim of
their opponents was to separate off the extreme conclusions of
Augustinianism and give them an isolated formulation, that
thereby it might be possible to reject these without touching
Augustine, but that thereby also Augustinianism might be slain.
But the Jansenists were placed in an extremely unfavourable
situation, because their Catholicism did not allow of their openly
questioning the authority of the Pope in matters of doctrine.
Their conceding that the Pope had a *right* to decide whether
the question of *fact* was determined weakened their attitude ;
and where is the line to be drawn between questions of right
and questions of fact ?   As early as the year 1656 the declaration was made by Alexander VII. in the notorious Bull "Ad
sanctam b. Petri sedem " : " *We determine and declare* that those
five propositions extracted from the afore-mentioned book of
Cornelius Jansen, and understood *in the sense intended by the
same Cornelius Jansen, have been condemned.*"[1]   When the Chief
Teacher declared in a cold-blooded way that he had also to
decide *in what sense something had been understood by someone,*
what objection could be raised, if there was the general admission
made of his absolute authority ?   So the same Pope took the
further step (1664) of issuing a formula for subscription, in which
all clerics and teachers were not merely enjoined to reject the
five propositions, but were required to confess upon oath that
these were condemned " as meant to be understood by the same
author " (" in sensu ab eodem auctore intento ").   In this way
the Pope already ventured to lord it over consciences; and yet
two more centuries had to run their course before his infallibility
could be proclaimed.   For the time, certainly, the Curia gave
relief so far to the Jansenists, by remaining satisfied with " sub-
missive silence " (" silentium obsequiosum ") (Pax Clementis IX.,

---

[1] "Quinque illas propositiones ex libro præmemorati cornelii Jansenii excerptas *ac
in sensu ab eodem Cornelio Jansenio intento damnatas fuisse, definimus et declaramus.*"

1668); but when the Crown began to view the Augustinian
party, who certainly did not take the attitude of unqualified
advocates of Gallican liberties, first with indifference, and then
with deepening hatred, and finally made a sacrifice of them to
the Jesuits, Clement XI., in the Bull "Vineam domini Sabaoth"
(1705), gave fresh confirmation to all the severe Bulls of his
predecessors against Jansenism, and again made the demand
that there should be a recognition of the definition of Jansen's
intention given by Alexander VII. Port Royal was now
forcibly broken up.

Yet once again, at the beginning of the eighteenth century,
there was a powerful revival of Augustinianism ; not yet had it
been distinctly indicated that in attacking Augustine, what was
aimed at, and what was inevitably involved, was an attack on
the Apostle Paul also. The Oratorian, Paschasius Quesnel, had
published a "gnomon" to the French New Testament, which
very rapidly found circulation as a book of devotion—inciting
to meditation—and was highly prized on account of its simple
Catholic piety. Even Pope Clement XI. had pronounced the
most favourable judgment upon the book ; the great king, who
was already assuming an unpleasantly pietistic air, had let himself be touched by its warmth and simplicity ; the Cardinal
Archbishop Noailles of Paris had recommended it. But this
very recommendation gave occasion to the Jesuits for preparing
a double blow—for attacking at the same time the Cardinal
whom they hated and the book that was offensive to them from
its inwardness of spirit. Agitations against the book, in which
the secret poison of Jansenism was said to lurk, were got up
among the clergy, and in the end a sketch of a damnatory Bull
was sent to Rome. What seemed incredible succeeded. The
feeble Pope, Clement XI., issued the "Constitution" Unigenitus
(1713), in which Romanism repudiated for ever its Augustinian
past. It was against all precedent to single out from a book
like that under notice 101 propositions, and to place these
emphatically under ban, in a way, too, in respect of form,
extremely maladroit. But for the Church of the Jesuits the
Bull Unigenitus has come to be of incalculable value ; for with
this Bull in its hands it has been able to combat all attempts at

an inner regeneration of the Church, and even in the future this manifesto of the infallible Pope will be capable of rendering the best service, if Augustine and Paul, who can never be quite slain, should venture again to threaten the serenity of the Church.[1] The immediate effect of the movement was to create

[1] See the Constitution in Denzinger, p. 243 ff. This second last great pronounce-ment of the Roman Church is in every respect a miserable production. It reveals above all the levity of the procedure followed with regard to dogma (in the narrower sense), which had now become a corpus vile. It is characteristic that here as elsewhere—for it had already become use and wont—there is only a venturing now upon negative propositions. On the "thorny field of the doctrine of grace" the Church merely goes on to indicate what must *not* be believed. Whether between the contrary propositions that are rejected there still remains anything at all that *can* be *believed*, or is worthy of belief, is a question with which the Church takes little con-cern. As a matter of fact there has found expression in the constitution a system of faith that is no longer *faith*, but a shrewd morality. Among the rejected theses the following may be singled out :—Thesis 2 : "Jesu Christi gratia, principium efficax boni cujuscumque generis, necessaria est ad omne opus bonum ; absque illa non solum nihil fit, sed nec fieri potest." 3 : "In vanum, domine præcipis, si tu ipse non das, quod præcipis" (this is an unqualified condemnation of Aristotle). 4 : "Ita, domine, omnia possibilia sunt ei, cui omnia possibilia facis, eadem operando in illo." Add to this Theses 5-7. Thesis 8 : "Nos non pertinemus ad novum fœdus, nisi in quantum participes sumus ipsius novæ gratiæ, quæ in nobis operatur id, quod deus nobis præ-cipit." 9 : "Gratia Christi est gratia suprema, sine qua confiteri Christum nunquam possumus, et cum qua nunquam illum abnegamus." 26 : "Nullæ dantur gratiæ nisi per fidem." 27 : "Fides est prima gratia et fons omnium aliarum." 28 : "Prima gratia, quam deus concedit peccatori, est peccatorum remissio." 38 : "Peccator non est liber, nisi ad malum, sine gratia liberatoris." 40 : "Sine gratia nihil amare possumus, nisi ad nostram condemnationem." 42 : "Sola gratia Christi reddit homi-nem aptum ad sacrificium fidei." 44 : "Non sunt nisi duo amores" (*i.e.*, love for God and love for one's self). 46 : "Cupiditas aut caritas usum sensuum bonum vel malum faciunt." 49 : "Ut nullum peccatum est sine amore nostri, ita nullum est opus bonum sine amore dei." 60 : "Si solus supplicii timor animat pænitentiam, quo hæc est magis violenta, eo magis ducit ad desperationem." 62 : "Qui a malo non abstinet nisi timore pœnæ, illud committit in corde suo et jam est reus coram deo." 68 : "Dei bonitas abbreviavit viam salutis, claudendo totum in fide et preci-bus" 69 : "Fides est donum puræ liberalitatis dei." 73 : "Quid est ecclesia nisi coetus filiorum dei, manentium in ejus sinu, adoptatorum in Christo, subsistentium in ejus persona, redemptorum ejus sanguine, viventium ejus spiritu agentium per ejus gratiam et exspectantium gratiam futuri sæculi ?" 74 : "Ecclesiæ sive integer Christus incarnatum verbum habet ut caput, omnes vere sanctos ut membra." Theses 79-86 condemn the universal use of Holy Scripture. 91 : "Excommunicationis in-justae metus nunquam debet nos impedire ab implendo debito nostro ; nunquam exi-mus ab ecclesia, etiam quando hominum nequitia videmur ab ea expulsi, quando deo, Jesu Christo atque ipsi ecclesiæ per caritatem affixi sumus," (cf. 92). Thesis 94 : "Nihil pejorem de ecclesia opinionem ingerit ejus inimicis, quam videre illic domina-

a new, great crisis in France—it was the last. All who had
still piety or a sense of shame bestirred themselves. Accept-
ants and Appellants stood face to face with each other. The
Appellants, however, were not Huguenots, but Catholics, whose
conscience was troubled by every rebellion against the Pope.
Thus by the law invariably regulating such change in the Middle
Ages, the opposition was changed—into surrender, and into
fanaticism and ecstacy. The iron fence of Catholicism allowed
of no swerving aside. If one was unable to rise above it, that
despair resulted which submits with wounded conscience or
breaks out into wild fanaticism. As a note appended to the
Bull Unigenitus, we read in Denzinger the dry historic account :
" This dogmatic constitutio was confirmed by Clement XI.
himself in the Bull against the Appellants, ' Pastoralis Officii,' of
date 28th August, 1718, in which he distinctly declares all
Catholics to be aliens from the bosom of the Roman Church
who do not accept the Bull ' Unigenitus ' ; it was adopted by
Innocent XIII., in the Decree of 8th January, 1722, by Benedict
XIII. and the Roman Synod in 1725, by Benedict XIV. in the
Encyclical 'ex omnibus Christiani orbis regionibus,' of 16th

tum exerceri supra fidem fidelium et foveri divisiones propter res, quæ nec fidem
lædunt nec mores." 97 : "Nimis sæpe contingit, membra illa, quæ magis sanctæ ac
magis stricte unita ecclesiæ sunt, respice atque tractari tamquam indigna, ut sint in
ecclesia, vel tamquam ab ea separata sed justus vivit ex fide et non ex opinione hominum." It does not need, surely, to be specially emphasised for the first time, that
even the Jesuits could not have publicly condemned these and similar propositions,
had not Quesnel given expression in some passages to that Augustinianism also according to which the grace of God is merged in His all-pervasive efficiency. In the
light of this view, which is secretly present at the end and at the beginning of Augustinianism, all these propositions could be interpreted, and declared heretical. Indeed,
we may go a step further. Does thorough-going Augustinianism not really disinte-
grate the Church ? It was bound to become evident in the end that the dilemma
presented itself of either building a Church with Luther or with the Nominalistic-
Jesuistic teachers. Augustinianism contains in it an element which demolishes all
that constitutes Church. On that account those doctores perspicuiores triumphed
who proved that Christ has left behind Him an institution, whose most welcome
function consists in this, that it procures even for the feeblest morality, provided the
sacrifice of obedience is offered, the highest merits. In Paschasius Quesnel's book,
for the rest, pure Augustinianism does not find expression. His sharp distinction
between outward and inward grace, and the attitude assumed by him towards the
empirical Catholic Church, carry him beyond Augustine, and bring him closer to
Protestantism.

October, 1756, by the Gallican clergy in assemblies in 1723, 1726, 1730, by councils at Avignon in 1725, and at Ebrène in 1727, *and by the whole Catholic world.*" [1]   The author might have added that these confirmations and acceptances describe the history of the victory of the modern Jesuit dogmatic over the Augustinian, *that they are the last word in the Catholic history of dogma* (in the sense of system of Christian doctrine), and that they represent at the same time the triumph of the Church over numberless consciences—over piety indeed—in France. The Huguenots were expelled, the Jansenists broken or annihilated ; the French people now belonged to Voltaire and the Encyclopædists. They hated the Jesuits; but as the fear of God can very well be driven out, but not anxious concern about God, this nation henceforward belonged to that very Jesuit Church which it hated and ridiculed.   Besides, Benedict XIV. (1756) relaxed the fetters of the Constitution Unigenitus.   Every one was to be regarded as a Catholic who should not offer a *public* resistance to it.   But this concession only came when the Bull had already done its work, and merely served to smooth the way of return for crushed spirits, when it was no longer to be feared that they could be troublesome. Jansenist clerics there have afterwards been in France, as there have been Gallican ; but the former have been of very much less account than the latter.   Jansenism as a factor was already annihilated in the eighteenth, Gallicanism not until the nineteenth century. Under the reign of Pius IX. it was still held necessary to search out and dispose of the last remnants of the two parties.   At the same time the new dogma of the immaculate conception of Mary (Constitution " Ineffabilis deus," of 8th December, 1854) set the seal to the rejection of the Augustinian-Thomistic

---

[1] " Hæc constitutio dogmatica confirmata est ab ipso Clemente XI. per bullam 'Pastoralis Officii' 5. Cal. Sept. 1718, contra Appellantes, in qua quoscumque Catholicos, qui Bullam 'Unigenitus' non susciperent, a Romanæ ecclesiæ sinu plane alienos declarat ; ab Innocentio XIII. decret. d. 8, Jan. 1722, a Benedicto XIII. et synodo Romano, 1725, a Benedicto XIV. per encyclicam 'Ex omnibus Christiani orbis regionibus,' 16. Oct. 1756, suscepta est a clero Gallicano in comitiis 1723, 1726, 1730, a conciliis Avenionensi 1725, ab Ebredunensi 1727, *et ab universo mundo Catholico.*"

doctrine of sin and grace.[1]   Henceforward Augustinianism was
scarcely any longer possible in the Roman Church ; but that
Mysticism cannot certainly be banished which at one time is
called Quietism, at another time " Spurious Mysticism " ; for
the Church continually gives impulses towards the origination
of this kind of Christianity, and can itself in no way avoid
training it, up to a certain point.[2]   Indeed, the Jesuit Order has
made efforts that have not been fruitless to furnish occupation
for the irrepressible tendency to inwardness, contemplation, and
Christian independence by sensible means of all sorts, by play-
things and miracles, as well as by brotherhoods, disciplinary
exercises, and rules for prayer, and thereby to keep it bound to
the Church.   The " Spurious Mysticism " which adapts itself
with painful reluctance to ecclesiasticism seems to become
always rarer, just because there has been a learning to make the
Church more of a home for it, and the Church itself, unfortunately, as Catholic, has an innate tendency towards religious
self-indulgence and towards miracle.[3]   The glorious revival and

[1] The Catholics need have little hesitation in regarding Mary as free from original
sin ; for what is original sin to them ?   On the other hand, there is something that
suggests putting on a bold front, when, a hundred times over, they have recourse to
the apologetic device in dealing with Protestantism : " You modern men have least
occasion to stumble at our dogma, for you do not at all believe in original sin."   The
setting up of the new dogma in the year 1854 had three purposes, (1) to prepare the
way for the Vatican Decrees, (2) to give the final despatch to the Thomistic doctrines
of sin and grace, (3) to glorify Mary, to whom Pius IX. devoted an extravagant
worship.   The new dogma runs in these terms, (Denzinger, p. 324): " Definimus
doctrinam, quæ tenet, beatissimam virginem Mariam in primo instanti suæ concep-
tionis fuisse singulari omnipotentis dei gratia et privilegio, intuitu meritorum Christi
Jesu salvatoris humani generis, ab omni originalis culpæ labe præservatam immunem,
esse a deo revelatam (when ? to whom ?) atque idcirco ab omnibus fidelibus firmiter
constanterque credendam."

[2] It might seem advisable to deal here with the *Quietistic* movement which ran
parallel with the Jansenist, with Molinos, Madame Guyon, with the controversy between Bossuet and Fenelon, the Propositiones LXVIII. M. de Molinos damnatæ ab
Innocentio XI. (" Cœlestis Pastor," 1687), and the Catholic-Mystic movements of
the nineteenth century ; but they have had no palpable result within the history of
dogma.   The Church, too, allows the most disorderly Quietistic courses on the part
of the monks, and even of the laity, provided no sovereign claims are set up in connection with them, and they are pursued ad majorem ecclesiæ gloriam.   So it is not
here a question of principles.

[3] Notice the course of development from Sailer to Clemens Brentano, and—to
Lourdes.

the lofty intuitions of the "awakened" in the present century ended with Anna Katharina Emmerich and the Holy Coat of Trêves.[1]

(3) The controversy with regard to Probabilism belongs to the history of ethics. But ethics and dogmatics do not admit of being separated. The juristic-casuistic spirit of the Roman Church had already in the Middle Ages influenced ethics, and along with it dogmatics, in the most unfavourable way. The Nominalistic theology had one of its strong roots in juristic casuistry, *i.e.*, in Probabilism. This was adopted by the Jesuits, and cultivated in such a way that the Popes at times, and even the members of the Order itself, were filled with alarm.[2] It will perhaps be found impossible to convict the Jesuits of any single moral enormity which had not been already expressed by some mediæval casuist from the Mendicant Orders ; but the Jesuits have offered to hold themselves responsible in the world's history for having systematised and applied in the Church what existed before their time only in the shape of hesitating attempts, and was checked by strong counter influences. By the aid of Probabilism this Order understood how in particular cases to transform almost all deadly sins into venial sins. It went on giving directions how to wallow in filth, to confound conscience, and, in the confessional, to wipe out sin with sin. The comprehensive ethical handbooks of the Jesuits are in part *monstra* of abomination and storehouses of execrable sins and filthy habits, the description and treatment of which provoke an outcry of disgust. The most shocking things are

---

[1] Yet there is blessing even in the Heart-of-Jesus worship, the adoration of Mary, etc., where they are carried on with humility, and with an upward look to the God who redeems. As, apart from the confessional, with its power to foster concern, they are the only embodiments of living piety, even sincere Christian feeling finds a refuge in these things ; for the Church which transacts on equal footing with the States, and makes dupes of them, cannot certainly impart vigour to piety, but only to an undevout arrogance. As the heart that seeks to rise to God is not restrained by doctrinal formulæ, but can transform even what is most alien to it into a means of comfort, this same spirit cannot be quenched by idols, but changes them into gracious signs of the God who, in all signs, reveals nothing but His renewing grace.

[2] See Döllinger u. Reusch, Gesch. der Moralstreitigkeiten in der römisch-catholischen Kirche seit dem 16 Jahrhundert, 2 Bdd., 1889, cf. Theol. Litt.-Ztg. 1889, col. 334.

here dealt with in a brazen-faced way by unwedded priests as
men of special knowledge, not with the view of calling down
with prophetic power upon the burden of horror a heavier
burden of judgment, but often enough with the view of representing the most disgraceful things as pardonable, and of showing to the most regardless transgressors a way in which they
may still always obtain the peace of the Church. We are told
that they were personally blameless, highly honourable, and
even saintly men who gave the most revolting confessionary
advices for ascertaining the most disgusting forms of vice and
for cleverly pacifying conscience regarding fornication, adultery,
theft, perjury, and murder. That may have been so; there
were certainly excellent Christians even connected with this
fraternity. But all the greater appears the confusing influence
of the religious system of which they were the servants, when it
was capable of producing such licentious subtleties and such a
perverse estimate of the moral principles and the meannesses of
their fellowmen! And all this too in the name of Christ, the
soothings of conscience as the fruit of His death upon the cross,
and, what was almost worse still, for the greater glory of the
Church! (in majorem gloriam ecclesiæ), for one of the interests
lying at the basis of this system of immorality—no one can
deny it—was to maintain and strengthen the external grasp and
power of ecclesiasticism. The only excuse, if there can be such
here, is this,[1] that that casuistic mode of procedure had already
had a long history in the Church, when the Jesuits raised it to a
method for the entire guidance of souls, as well as for the
theoretic and practical shaping of religion in general. As a
good thing from becoming customary can thereby deprive itself
of its power, so a bad thing that has become customary may
delude the individual as to the force of error and sin that inheres
in it. It might be said, indeed, that this Jesuit morality belongs
to history and not to the system! Much of what was most

---

[1] Or may we assume in the case of some of the worst propositions that they were
the product of a daring casuistic *sport*, which had never any practical importance?
This solution will not apply, at any rate, to some of the very vile confessionary advices; for history teaches that they were translated into deeds. Or had overdrawn
reports found their way to the Pope? Even this, alas, is not easily proved.

revolting has really disappeared, and that an earnest and philanthropic spirit managed to intermingle itself with the most lamentable secrets of the confessionary directions is not to be denied.   But the method has continued unchanged, and it exerts to-day its ruinous influence on dogmatics and ethics, on the consciences of those who receive, and of those who make confession, perhaps in a worse degree than at any period.   Since the seventeenth century forgiveness of sins in the Catholic Church has become to a large extent a highly refined art ; one learns how to receive confession and give the fitting absolution, as one learns the art of speculation in the exchange.   And yet —how imperishable this Church is, and how imperishable is a conscience that seeks for its God !   God can be found by such a conscience even in the idol, and it hears His voice even where it hears at the same time all the voices of hell ! [1]

---

[1] The severe criticism of the casuistic morality, fostered chiefly by the Jesuits, and of their confessionary counsels, must not hinder the impartial historian from recognising what they have achieved, and still achieve.   What would modern Catholicism be without them ?   *They are the active squad of the Church,* who work and reap the fruit that is produced by all *work*.   With the exception of some outstanding German scholars, the Catholic authors who are not Jesuits are a quantité négligeable.   The sober judgment which Leibniz pronounced upon the Order 200 years ago is still substantially correct : "That the Jesuits have so many enemies within their own communion [how far that still holds good to-day, I leave undiscussed], is due, for the most part, to the fact that they take a more prominent and influential position than others. . . . It is not to be doubted that there are honourable and valiant people among them.   At the same time, however, they are often too hot-headed, and many among them are bent upon serving the Order per fas et nefas.   But it is not otherwise all round ; only it is more noticeable among the Jesuits than among others, because they, more than others, are before the eyes of people."   But Leibniz did not observe that the Jesuits are still, at the present day, "Spanish priests," and are most strongly opposed to the German religious spirit.   Their founder, on whom a German Protestant national economist, Gothein, has undoubtedly written the most impartial and best book (if only the Jesuits would show freedom of spirit enough to write the most impartial book upon Luther, instead of leaving Luther to be scurrilously dealt with by narrow-minded and fanatical chaplains !), Ignatius de Loyola, impressed his Spanish spirit for all time upon the Order.   Nothing great has been done by them in anything they have since added to or subtracted from this.   That Spanish spirit, however, though outrun by the development of spiritual culture in morality, religion, and science, still continues to be a dominant force in public and political life.   In the war of 1870 a celebrated man was right in saying : "We fight against Louis XIV."   That war has come to an end.   But we have also the struggle to wage against the Jesuits and the Counter-Reformation, and the end of this war cannot be foreseen.

The Spanish Dominican, Bartholomäus de Medina, was the
first to describe and defend Probabilism "scientifically," this
being done by him in his Commentary on Thomas's Prima
Secundæ (1577). The thing itself had long existed, but the
formula for it had not yet been found. It ran in these terms :
" If an opinion is probable, it is lawful to follow it, though the
contrary opinion is more probable." [1] Seldom has a saying
shown at once the kindling power of this one, and seldom has a
saying continued to work so mightily : it was the emancipation
of morality from morality, of religion from religion, in the
name of morality and religion. Many Spanish Dominicans—
Thomists, that is to say !—and Augustinians seized on the new
watchword at once, and even in the last decennium of the
sixteenth century several theologians could write, the Jesuit
Gabriel Vasquez being among them, *that Probabilism was the
prevailing view among contemporary theologians.*[2] From that
time onwards, down to the middle of the seventeenth century,
Probabilism spread without opposition through the whole
domain of ecclesiastical life. Within the province of faith it
revealed its destroying influence (1) in "*Laxism*" with regard
to the granting of absolution ; (2) in " Attritionism," that is, in
the view that the fear of hell is enough in itself to secure forgiveness of sins through the Sacrament of Penance, that the love
of God, therefore, is not requisite.[3] With regard to both these
points, Dominicans made common cause with Jesuits in showing that the defence of their Thomistic doctrine of grace was
now only a duty imposed upon them by their Order, and was no
longer the outcome of inward interest in the matter itself.
What the fruits were that ripened from Probabilism—towards
which the attitude of the Popes was that of easy toleration—

[1] " Si est opinio probabilis, licitum est eam sequi, licet opposita sit probabilior."
Döllinger u. Reusch, p. 28 ff.

[2] The watchword was not at once eagerly adopted by all Jesuits ; Bellarmin, *e.g.*,
viewed it with disfavour.   For the attitude the Jesuits assume towards this fact see
l.c. p. 31 f.

[3] Attritionism, again, has itself different degrees, according as it is defined negatively or positively, or according as it relates to temporal or eternal penalties, to
penalties or to strong displeasure against sin itself, etc.; on its history cf. Stückert,
Die Kath. L. v. d. Reue (1896), p. 53 ff., 58 ff., 62 ff.

on to the middle of the seventeenth century, has been recently described to us in a simple but startling way.[1]   Then Jansenism arose in France.   Jesuistic Probabilism, even more than Semi-Pelagianism, was the enemy against which this movement directed itself.   Against it Pascal raised his voice : the Provincial Letters represent the most formidable attack which a *ruling* ecclesiastical party has ever in history had to endure.   It is not hard to convict the great man of the use of rhetorical devices—he was a Frenchman and a Catholic; we must not lay it down that he ought to have written as Luther did in the year 1520 ; but in their way the Letters are perfect.   " That in the beginning of the second half of the seventeenth century a turn of things set in, and Probabilism ceased to be the reigning view, must be placed in the first instance to the credit of Pascal—and of the unskilful attempts of the Jesuits to reply to the Letters, published by him in 1656—and of his friends, especially Arnauld and Nicole." [2]

There now followed a struggle, lasting for more than half a century, that seemed to terminate in a growing suppression of Probabilism.[3]   Even by Innocent X. and Alexander VII. a

---

[1] Döllinger u. Reusch, l.c., pp. 97-120.

[2] L.c., p. 35 f.

[3] A number of varieties now developed themselves.   Beginning with the most lax, and passing on to the most strict, we have the following :—(1) One may follow the less certain opinion, even when it is only tenuiter, nay, even when it is only dubie or probabiliter probabilis, that is to say, when there are only some grounds to be adduced for it, *or when it is not certain that there are no grounds to be adduced for it*, (the laxest Probabilism); (2) one may follow the less certain opinion, even though it is less probable, provided only it can be supported by *good* grounds (genuine Probabilism) ; (3) one may follow the less certain opinion, if it is almost as probable as the contrary opinion (rigorous Probabilism) ; (4) one may follow the less certain opinion when it is as probable as the more certain (Æquiprobabilism) ; (5) one may follow the certain opinion even when it is less probable ; the less certain opinion may be followed only when it is more probable than the contrary opinion (Probabiliorism) ; (6) one may only follow the less certain opinion when it is the most probable of all (lax Tutiorism) ; (7) the less certain opinion is never to be followed, even if it is the most probable, *i.e.*, in the case of doubt all action is to be avoided ; the conscience has always to give the verdict, even when the most probable reasons testify against what appears to be duty (strict Tutiorism) ; see l.c., p. 4. ff.   The last-mentioned view, which alone is moral, is regarded as Rigorism, and was expressly condemned by Alexander VIII. on the 7th December, 1690 (see Denzinger, p. 236 : "Non licet sequi opinionem vel inter probabiles probabilissimam ").   This Probabilistic method

number of books of lax theological morality were proscribed, some of them unconditionally, some of them " until they were corrected " ("donec corrigantur"). The latter even contemplated the publication of a Bull against Probabilism. But he satisfied himself with condemning, in the years 1665 and 1666, a number of the worst positions of the Casuists,[1] and, with regard to Attritionism, with dictating the already familiar course, namely, that the contending parties should not condemn each other, until the Holy Chair had come to some decision in this matter.[2] His successor, Innocent XI., condemned, in the year 1679, sixty-five other propositions of the Probabilists, among which some samples of genuine villainy are to be found.[3]

recalls the monstrous haggling, that is, the Probabilism, of the Pharisees and Talmudists in the expounding of the law.   That is probably not accidental, for the method had its beginning in the thirteenth century, *i.e.*, in a period in which Jewish science probably exercised an influence on the theologians of the Mendicant Orders.   Güdemann (Jüd. Litt.-Blatt, 21 Jahrg., 29th Oct., 1890) has taken offence because in the first edition I had spoken of the "monstrous haggling *about moral principles* among the Talmudists," whereas it was only what was ritual that was in question.   He will find now, in place of the expression objected to, the more general expression "about the law."   But that haggling, moreover, had by no means to do merely with what was ritual, and was the ritual so different in Judaism of the old school from what was enjoined as moral ?

[1] See Denzinger, p. 213 f.   I refrain from reproducing these abominable theses, but direct attention to 1, 2, 6, 15, 17, 18, 24, 25, 26, 28, 40, 41.

[2] Decree of 5th May, 1667, in Denzinger, p. 217 : "de materia attritionis non audeant alicujus theologicæ censuræ alteriusve injuriæ aut contumeliæ nota taxare alterutram sententiam, sive negantem necessitatem aliqualis dilectionis dei in præfata attritione ex metu gehennæ concepta, quæ hodie inter scholasticos communior videtur, sive asserentem dictæ dilectionis necessitatem, donec ab hac sancta sede fuerit aliquid hac in re definitum."

[3] Denzinger, p. 218 f.; one would need to sum up and transcribe the whole of them in order to give a picture of this moral desolation.   I content myself with adducing those relating to faith :—4 : "Ab infidelitate excusabitur infidelis non credens ductus opinione minus probabile."   5 : "An peccet mortaliter, qui actum, dilectionis dei semel tantum in vita eliceret, condemnare non audemus."   6 : "Probabile est, ne singulis quidem rigorose quinquenniis per se obligare præceptum caritatis erga deum."   7 : "Tunc solum obligat, quando tenemur justificari, et non habemus aliam viam, qua justificari and qua justificari possimus."   10 : "Non tenemur proximum deligere actu interno et formali."   11 : "Præcepto proximum diligendi satisfacere possumus per solos actus externos."   17 : "Satis est actum fidei semel in vita elicere."   19 : "Voluntas non potest efficere, ut assensus fidei in seipso sit magis firmus, quam mereatur pondus rationum ad assensum impellentium."   20 : "Hinc potest quis prudenter repudiare assensum, quem habebat, supernaturalem."   21 :

One must study these rejected propositions in order to see that among the Romanic peoples both the "morality" and the immorality of the eighteenth century had one of their strongest roots in the doctrine of the Jesuits. But the doctrine itself was worse than both ; it sought to show that the low-type moral code of cultivated society in the times of Louis XIV. was positive Christianity, provided only one did not renounce connection with the Church (by means of the confessional). Still, the worst extreme seemed to be now averted by the enactments of the Pope, by the complaints of the best Frenchmen, by the protests of many monks, and indeed of entire Orders. Within the Jesuit Order itself Thyrsus Gonzales took his stand against the Probabilist doctrine. And while his confrères succeeded, although Gonzales had become their General (1687), in emasculating his great work against Probabilism before it was allowed

"Assensus fidei supernaturalis et utilis ad salutem stat cum notitia solum probabili revelationis, imo cum formidine, qua quis formidet, ne non sit locutus deus." 22 : "Nonnisi fides unius dei necessaria videtur necessitate medii, non autem explicita remuneratoris." 23 : " Fides late dicta, ex testimonio creaturarum similive motivo ad justificationem sufficit." 56 : ",Frequens confessio et communio, etiam in his qui gentiliter vivunt, est nota prædestinationis." 57 : " Probabile est sufficere attritionem naturalem, modo honestam." 58 : " Non tenemur confessario interroganti fateri peccati alicujus consuetudinem." 60 : " Pænitenti habenti consuetudinem peccandi contra legem dei, naturæ aut ecclesiæ, etsi emendationis spes nulla appareat, nec est neganda nec differenda absolutio, dummodo ore proferat, se dolere et proponere emendationem." 61 : " Potest aliquando absolvi, qui in proxima occasione peccandi versatur, quam potest et non vult omittere, quinimo directe et ex proposito quærit aut ei sei ingerit." 62 : " Proxima occasio peccandi non est fugienda, quando causa aliqua utilis aut honesta non fugiendi occurrit." 63 : " Licitum est quærere directe occasionem proximam peccandi, pro bono spirituali vel temporali nostro vel proximo." 64 : " *Absolutionis capax est homo, quantumvis laboret ignorantia mysteriorum fidei, et etiamsi per negligentiam etiam culpabilem nesciat mysterium sanctissimæ trinitatis, et incarnationis domini nostri Jesu Christi.*" 65 : " *Sufficit illa mysteria semel credidesse.*" If this is not a veritable " issue " of dogma, then there is no such thing at all. What did it matter that this particular thesis was rejected by Innocent if it was nevertheless the expression of a general view that was never rejected by the Popes ? With regard to the 61st thesis, it is to be remarked that Tamburini even imparts the advice to the father-confessor : " If thou observest that the penitent before thee is very much addicted to some sin, do not require of him an act of contrition for this special sin ; for there is a danger that, if he is expressly reminded of it, he will not abhor it from the heart, while he will have little or no difficulty in abhorring it in a general way, and when it is taken together with other sins " (Döllinger u. Reusch, p. 63 f.).

to appear (1694), its power was broken at the beginning of the eighteenth century,[1] especially after Alexander VIII. in his Decree of August, 1690, had rejected two of the worst propositions of the Probabilists (regarding philosophic sin).[2] Yet at bottom Jansenism and Anti-Probabilism were solidarically united. If the former was struck down (Constitutio Unigenitus), it was only a question of time for Probabilism to raise its head again. And as for the doctrine of attritio, the Popes had only reached the point of neutrality regarding it. What did it avail, therefore, that in the first half, and in the middle, of the eighteenth century, Probabiliorism prevailed among the French clergy and elsewhere—except in Spain ? From Attritionism as a source Probabilism was bound to issue forth again. " At the very time when the Society of Jesus was crushed, God raised up a new champion for Probabilism, and ensured for the Society a triumph in the future on which human foresight could not have reckoned." This champion was the founder of the Redemptorists, Alphonso Liguori (1699-1787), the most influential Roman theologian since the days of the Counter-Reformation.[3] Liguori, the Blessed (1816), the Holy (1829), the Teacher of the Church (1871), is the true counterpart to Luther, *and in modern Catholicism he has stepped into the place of Augustine.*[4] Throughout his whole life " a restless man of scruples " and a rigid ascetic, all doubts and all self-mortifications merely involved him more deeply in the conviction, that it is only in the absolute authority of a Father-Confessor—here the absolute comes in then—that any conscience can find rest, but that the Father-Confessor must apply the holy law of God according to the principles of Æqui-Probabilism—as applied by Liguori, it is not different from Probabilism. By Liguori complete ethical

---

[1] The parts referring to Gonzales have been treated with special fulness in the work published by Döllinger and Reusch.

[2] Denzinger, p. 235 f. It is true, on the other hand, that in the Decree of December, 1690, very excellent propositions are condemned (against Jansenism, but they were in favour of the Probabilists) ; see d. 3, 5-9, 10-15 (14 : " timor gehennæ non est supernaturalis "). 26 : " Laus quæ defertur Mariæ ut Mariæ vana est."

[3] Liguori and Voltaire were exactly contemporaries ; among the Romanic nations they became the most influential men, the guides of souls.

[4] Cf. the instructive section in Döllinger u. Reusch, pp. 356-476.

scepticism was again established in the morality, and indirectly in the dogmatics, of the Church. Though Liguori does not go so far as the most shameless Probabilists of the seventeenth century, yet he fully accepted their method, and in a countless number of questions, inclusive even of adultery, perjury, and murder, he knew how to transform the vile into the venial. No Pascal took his stand against him in the nineteenth century ; there was a strengthening rather from decennium to decennium of the authority of Liguori, the new Augustine, and to-day he is supreme in all Orders, in all seminaries, in all manuals of doctrine.[1] Any remnants of Augustinianism that succeeded in surviving till the nineteenth century Liguori suppressed. The casuistic morals, together with Attritionism, have thrown dogmatic entirely into the background. Probabilism and Papalism have broken it up ; it is to-day, as circumstances may require, a rigid or an elastic legal order [2]—a prison from which, if the interests of the Church require it, one is not delivered until he has paid the last farthing, and again a building, into which one need never enter, if he only holds himself under dutiful subjection to the Church.

[1] Cf. the most widely-used manual—that by Gury.

[2] This utilising according to inclination of given factors reveals itself in the numerous decisions of the Curia with regard to theological disputes of the nineteenth century, especially in Germany, but also in France; compare the judicial processes recorded by Denzinger relating to Lammenais (p. 310 f., 311 f.), Hernes (p. 317 f., 321 f.), Bautain (p. 319 f.), the Traditionalists (p. 328 f.), Günther (p. 329 f., 330 f., 331 f.), Frohschammer and other German theologians (p. 332 f., 338 f.). Of greatest interest are the theses against " Traditionalism," *i.e.*, against faith, of 11th June, 1855 (p. 328 f.). Here the following is taught : " Ratiocinatio dei existentiam, animæ spiritualitatem, hominis libertatem cum certitudine probare potest. Fides posterior est revelatione, proindeque ad probandum dei existentiam contra atheum, ad probandum animæ rationalis spiritualitatem ac libertatem contra naturalismi ac fatalismi sectatorem allegari convenienter nequit." " Rationis usus fidem præcedit et ad eam hominem ope revelationis et gratiæ conducit." " Methodus qua usi sunt Thomas, Bonaventura et alii post ipsos scholastici non ad rationalismum ducit neque causa fuit, cur apud scholas hodiernas philosophia in naturalismum et pantheismum impingeret." Reason is brought into service when one needs it, and dismissed when it causes disturbance. The same course is followed with Holy Scripture, tradition, and faith.

(3) *The Vatican Decrees.*

After what has been set forth in the two foregoing sections, the proclamation of Papal Infallibility must appear as the necessary outcome of the development. If all authorities, the authority of the bishops, the authority of the Councils, the authority of tradition, the authority of Augustine, the authority of conscience, are demolished, then in a Church that is based on authority a new authority must arise. That work of abolishing could only be carried on so victoriously because the new single authority was long held *in petto*, and there was an acting in view of it. All that was now required was that by a solemn act—an act of this kind could not, unfortunately, be avoided—the Universal Bishop, the living tradition, the Teacher of faith and morals who could not be deceived, the absolute Father-Confessor, should also be proclaimed as such. Those were mistaken who were strongly of opinion that the period was not yet ripe for such a proclamation; no, the time was fulfilled. All lines of development, those within and those from without, converged upon this goal. The former lines we have taken account of; the latter were given in the Romanticism and the reaction in the first decennia of the new century, in the timidity and weakness of those governing, in the indifference of those who were governed. With scarcely a word our century accepted what dared not have been offered to the spirit of any other century without calling into the lists an armed Europe, Catholic and Protestant.[1]

For students of the history of dogma the preparations for the Council of 1869-70, and the course followed at it, have no interest whatever. There were in Catholicism two parties; the one was in favour of the infallibility of the Pope, the other was opposed to it, but did not know exactly what was to happen if it was rejected. That is the whole. Endless efforts of a political kind were at the same time put forth on both sides,

[1] The way had already been prepared by the Syllabus (Denzinger, p. 345 ff.), which condemned, in addition to many bad things, the good spirit also of the nineteenth century.

instructive for the historian of politics, of no consequence for any one who wishes to follow the history of dogma.[1] The Scheme of Faith of 24th April, 1870, contains in its introduction and four chapters nothing new; faith means the recognition of Scripture and of tradition, the holding all as true that is written therein, and the holding it as true in the sense in which it is understood by the Church, which alone has the right to expound.   What was new was brought forward in the Scheme of the Church (18th July, 1870) " Pastor æternus," or rather the formulating as dogma was new.[2]   Christ has given to Peter a place above all the Apostles, that there may be a real unity in the Episcopate.   The primacy of Peter and his successors is therefore real and direct; it has not been committed to Peter by the Church.   It is, further, a primacy of jurisdiction over the whole Church ; accordingly there belongs to Peter the "ordinary and direct power" (potestas ordinaria et immediata) as "plenary and supreme" (plena et suprema) over the whole Church and over each individual Christian.   This "power of jurisdiction" is also in the full sense Episcopal, *i.e.*, there belong to the Pope everywhere all Episcopal prerogatives (Chap. III.:"if any one shall say that the Roman pontiff has only the duty of inspection or direction, but not the plenary and supreme power of jurisdiction over the whole Church . . . or that he has only the greater part, but not the entire measure of this supreme power, or that this power of his is not ordinary and direct over all the Churches and each one singly, or over all pastors and believers and each one singly, let him be anathema."[3])   Thus the Pope is the

---

[1] The proceedings of the Council have been summed up by Friedberg ; the fullest statement has been given by Friedrich, 3 vols., 1877 ff. ; compare Frommann's, Hase's, and Nippold's descriptions.   Interesting information in Friedrich's Journal, and in Lord Acton's work, "On the History of the Vatican Council," 1871.   For the Council as viewed in the light of the history of dogma, see Janus, Der Papst und das Concil, 1869.   Ultramontane account by Cardinal Manning (German translation by Bender, 1877).

[2] Friedberg, Proceedings, p. 740 ff.

[3] "Si quis dixerit, Romanum pontificem habere tantummodo officium inspectionis vel directionis, non autem plenam et supremam potestatem jurisdictionis in universam ecclesiam. . . . aut eum habere tantum potiores partes, non vero totam plenitudinem hujus supremæ potestatis, aut hanc ejus potestatem non esse ordinariam et immediatam in omnes et singulas ecclesias, sive in omnes et singulos pastores et fideles, anathema sit."

universal bishop; he is the supreme judge, the infallible authority. "We teach and declare it to be a divinely revealed dogma : that the Roman pontiff, when he speaks ex cathedra, *i.e.*, when, in discharging his office as pastor and teacher of all Christians (under what recognisable conditions is that the case ?), he in virtue of his supreme apostolic authority defines, by the divine assistance promised to the blessed Peter, the doctrine regarding faith and morals that is to be held by the whole Church, exercises that infallibility by which the divine Redeemer wished His Church to be instructed in the definition of the doctrine regarding faith or morals, and therefore such definitions of the Roman pontiff are of themselves, but not through the assent of the Church, subject to no amendment. But if any one shall presume to contradict this our definition, which may God forbid, let him be anathema!" (Chap. IV.)[1] The recollection of the past, the preparation of the Church's future, are thereby delivered over to the Pope, or rather to the papal Curia. Even dogma is by this Constitution reckoned, so to speak, to the papal domestic estate. What a victory! All great controversies of the four preceding centuries are at *one* stroke waived aside, or at least condemned as of no importance. There is no longer any Episcopalism, and whoever appeals to the old tradition as against the new is ipso facto condemned! All the conflicts that had at one time made up the life of mediæval Catholicism are set aside, "they make a solitude and call it peace" ("solitudinem faciunt, pacem appellant"). The Church has *one* infallible lord; it need concern itself no more about its history ; *the living man alone is in the right.*

History reaches its ends in strangely circuitous ways. Was this Constitution of the year 1870 perhaps to become in the

---

[1] " Docemus et divinitus revelatum dogma esse declaramus : Romanum Pontificem, quum ex cathedra loquitur id est quum omnium Christianorum pastoris et doctoris munere fungens pro suprema sua apostolica auctoritate doctrinam de fide vel moribus ab universa ecclesia tenendam definit per assistentiam divinam, ipsi in beato Petro promissam, ea infallibilite pollere, qua divinus redemptor ecclesiam suam in definienda doctrina de fide vel moribus instructam esse voluit, ideoque ejusmodi Romani pontificis definitiones ex sese, non autem ex consensu ecclesiæ irreformabiles esse. Si quis autem huic nostræ definitioni contradicere, quod deus avertat, præsumpserit anathema sit."

future the means by which the Church should gradually free
itself from the load of its past, from the Middle Ages and
antiquity? That would be an inversion of development such
as is not unknown in history. Will the Constitution " Pastor
æternus " become perhaps the starting point of a new era of
Catholicism, in which the mediæval dogma that is already condemned as of no importance, will more and more disappear, and
there will develop itself from the Heart-of-Jesus worship and
from the living devotion of believers, a new faith, which, again,
may admit of being formulated without difficulty? On the
basis of the complete reduction of all things to an ecclesiastical
level, which the new dogma represents—for what is a bishop or
archbishop to-day alongside the Pope, and on the other hand
how much importance attaches to-day in Catholicism to a layman who has a warm feeling for his Church!—will there perhaps
develop itself a living Christianity of the congregational order,
such as the Church has never yet possessed? And will the
Pope himself perhaps find a means, at the close of this development, for renouncing again the fictitious divine dignity, as a
means was found in the sixteenth and in the nineteenth
centuries for obtaining deliverance from the most sacred
tradition?[1]

Foolish hopes, one will say; and certainly the signs of the
times point in an entirely different direction. As yet the process does not seem to have run its course ; with infallibility, it
appears rather to have reached only the beginning of the end.
Not to refer to the fact that nothing whatever is said in the
Decree of the *personal* qualities of the Pope [2] (can he not be

[1] To that side of the papal infallibility on which it means the authority of the *personal* element as against the rigid authority of the letter and of tradition, and, at the
same time, represents the factor of progress in the Church, I need surely only advert.
So long as the objective authority of the letter and of tradition is held to be divine,
the personal element also must have the authority of the divine, that concurrence
may be possible.

[2] Gregory VII. already claimed for the individual Popes (not merely for the Roman
Church) infallibility, nay, complete personal holiness ; for they possessed all that Peter
had. According to him the Pope's word is simply God's word (see Mirbt, Publicistik im
Zeitalter Gregor's VII., p. 565 f.). But at that time everything had yet a certain uncertainty attaching to it, and even the absolute assertion had still something about
it that was not binding.

declared to be sinless, to be holy, can there not be ascribed to
him a special miraculous power, can he not be regarded as a
peculiar incarnation of the Godhead, can there not be attributed
to him a connection of a unique kind with the Holy Virgin or
with the Holy Joseph, etc.?)—at all events there lies in the
" when he speaks ex cathedra " and in the " when he defines the
doctrine concerning faith and morals to be held by the whole
Church," a sting of uncertainty which must still be extracted.
Many signs suggest that this is desired in authoritative quarters,
and therefore may very well be done in the future.   It is
possible, nay *necessary*, that the "faith or morals" includes
everything which the Pope according to his opinion needs in
order to be Pope, that there is included, therefore, *e.g.*, the
ecclesiastical State.   Let there be observed what in this regard
the acute Jesuit, Paul Graf Hoensbroech, has stated in his book
" Der Kirchenstaat in seiner dogmatischen (!) und historischen
Bedeutung " (1889), p. 74 f.:[1] " . . . thus the entire teaching
Church, Pope and bishops, solemnly announce : Under the
circumstances of the present time the secular supremacy of the
apostolic chair is necessary for the free guidance of the Church.
To be in doubt of that, namely that this has been announced by
the Pope and bishops, is impossible.   As supreme pastor and
teacher, the Pope addresses himself to the whole Church.   The
bishops of the entire earth accept the word of the teaching
Pope and communicate it to believers ; and on the other hand
as the supreme shepherd and teacher the Pope sanctions what
the bishops have done.   *Hence we are entitled to conclude that
this declaration of the necessity of worldly possession contains
infallible truth ; consequently, every Catholic is forbidden to doubt
this necessity, or to contest it.*"   To one reader or another this
conclusion may perhaps at first sight seem strange.   The
declaration as to the necessity of worldly possession is to contain
infallible truth ?   Does this necessity, then, belong to the treasury
of revealed truth, and will one raise the declarations of the

---

[1] I allow this quotation from the first edition to stand, although the author has
since become a Protestant : in the dissertation there speaks, not Graf Hoensbroech,
but the Order itself, although it does not regard everything as *necessary* doctrine
which the author has set forth.

Pope and the bishops regarding this to a dogma, to a real article of faith? Neither the one nor the other. But yet what we have said still holds true. To the Church of Christ there has been promised by its divine founder infallibility, inerrancy, in the case of all decisions that have as their subject the truth revealed by God by means of Scripture or tradition. To this truth of revelation contained in Scripture or tradition there does *not* belong—we repeat it—the declaration as to the necessity of earthly possessions; and in so far as only a truth of *revelation* can become, properly speaking, an article of faith, a dogma, a decision as to this necessity never forms a dogmatic doctrinal position. *But in order that the Church may be in a position to decide with infallible certainty on what are, properly speaking, truths of faith, it must evidently be able to pronounce its judgment with the same inerrancy upon everything which has an inner, necessary connection with these truths of faith. But the earthly possession of the Popes stands in such a connection with the real truths of faith.* For it is a truth of faith that to the Church, or, in other words, to the Pope, there rightfully belongs perfect freedom in guiding the flock committed to his care. But this freedom is, in its exercise, *dependent* on outward circumstances; it *requires* the use of outward means, and these means have therefore an inward, naturally necessary connection with the freedom itself. *Thus the Church can also with infallible certainty* (note the fine distinction: "infallible certainty," not dogmatic infallibility!) *specify those means which, according to the circumstances of the time, are useful or necessary, as the case may be, for the exercise of its divinely-intended freedom.* Now for the present times the Church has declared earthly possessions to be necessary for maintaining the freedom that ought to belong to it, *and the entire Catholic world honours in this claim unerring truth."* [1]

At the present time this last is not yet really done by the whole Catholic world; but that is a matter of indifference. Unquestionably the "yes and no" of this argumentation leads up to the doctrinal position: "The Church places also the

[1] Thus the "infallible certainty," or the "unerring truth," of papal claims, which is really equivalent to dogmatic infallibility, is here made out even for provinces which are not de fide et moribus.

outward and *temporary* means which it declares necessary for
the exercise of its divinely-intended freedom under the protection of the infallibility proclaimed in the year 1870." In this
way the words "doctrine concerning faith and morals"
("doctrina de fide et moribus") are to be understood. What
perspectives are not only opened up by but included in this interpretation, does not require to be demonstrated: the Pope
declares his politics to be infallible, and the Church-State comes,
in a circuitous way, to be as much a dogma as the Trinity.
This interpretation, which is a perfectly legitimate conclusion
from the principle, has not yet been sanctioned in the highest
quarters; but how much time must elapse ere it, too, shall be
drawn? What significance that has for dogma is quite obvious;
by the declaration of papal infallibility all dogmas are ideally
threatened, by formally placing on a level "temporary" political
requirements and doctrines of faith every dogma is materially
emptied of its meaning. Of course it will always be added from
that side: "The Pope receives no new revelations," "faith and
morals stand at an unattainably high stage," "the tradition and
dogma of the Church remain unchangeably the same," "we
speak only of 'infallible certainty,' not of dogmatic infallibility,
when we declare the papal policy authoritative," etc. But what
person of insight will drink poison for wine, because the labels
of the bottles still retain the old inscriptions? There are still
other dogmas in the air. If one will learn what they are, he
must study the doctrines which the Jesuits foster as probable
opinions of their Order. I am not aware, for example, that the
opinion that all Jesuits will be saved has been departed from.[1]
Nor, so far as I know, has the report been contradicted that
prayers to the Pope have appeared in print.[2]

We must not let ourselves be misled as to the true state of
things by the Catholic systems of dogmatic which are still
being constantly written, and by the general reflections on
dogmas which may be read there. Besides, there constantly
appear even there—in the assumption of implicit and quasi

See Döllinger u. Reusch, Moralstreitigkeiten, I., pp. 524-534.
[2] By the Oratorian, Faber, if I am not mistaken.

implicit dogmas (dogmata implicita et quasi implicita),[1] in the
way in which a distinction is drawn between entire, half, and
quarter dogmas, and, finally, in the scope given to the mere
negation of doctrines—on the one hand scepticism, and on the
other hand dogmatic politics.

[1] See the article "Dogma" by Heinrich (Wetzer und Welter III. 2, Col. 1879 ff.):
"Both in material and formal dogmas, whether these truths be declared or not, other
truths of faith can be contained, and these truths, so long as they are not in some way
divested of their hidden character, or explicated, are called dogmata implicita. They
are taught by the Church and believed by the faithful in the explicated dogmas, that
is, they are taught and believed implicitly. But there are two possible causes of the
hidden character of such so-called enclosed dogmas ; the cause may lie in this, that
while the truth in question is declared in Scripture and ecclesiastical tradition, or is
declared directly in a doctrinal deliverance of the Church, it is not declared with such
clearness that every believer, or at least the well-instructed and discerning believer, is
able to perceive it with ease and certainty. In this case this truth, while immediately
revealed and set forth by the Church, is not revealed and set forth with sufficient clearness.
There is here, as the theologians term it, a revelatio et propositio formalis et immediata,
sed confusa et obscura ; such a truth has also been described as quasi implicita. For
in the strictest and most proper sense implicita dogmata are those truths which are
contained not directly and formally in revelation and ecclesiastical deliverance, but
only as it were in their principle, from which they are . . . deduced by a logical
operation. . . . On the question how far the infallibility of the Church extends in
regard to such conclusions, and whether and how far such deductions drawn by the
Church are the object of fides divina and therefore dogmas in the strictest sense,"
etc. Compare also the distinctions between propositiones hæreticæ, erroneæ, hæresi
vel errori proxima, temerariæ and falsæ.

CHAPTER III.

THE ISSUES OF DOGMA IN ANTITRINITARIANISM AND SOCINIANISM.

1. *Historical Introduction.*

No Protestant Christian will read the prefaces that are prefixed to the Racovian Catechism (1609 lat., cf. the edition : Irenopoli post annum 1659) and to the German edition of that work (Rackaw, 1608, 1612) without being stirred to inward sympathy. The former certainly contains a splendid confession of the freedom of faith,[1] and the latter connects itself with the work

---

[1] "Catechesin seu Institutionem religionis Christianæ, prout eam ex sacris litteris haustam profitetur ecclesia nostra, damus in lucem. Quæ quia in non paucis ab aliorum Christianorum orbita discedit, non est quod quis putet, nos eam emittendo in publicum omnibus diversum sentientibus, quasi misso feciali, bellum indicere aut classicum canere ad pugnandum, atque, ut Poeta ait, ad 'Arma ciere viros, Martemque accendere cantu.' . . . Non immerito et hodie conqueruntur complures viri pii ac docti, confessiones ac catecheses, quæ hisce temporibus eduntur editæque sunt a variis Christianorum ecclesiis, nihil fere aliud esse, quam poma Eridos, quam tubas litium et vexilla immortalium inter mortales odiorum atque factionum. Idque propterea, quod confessiones et catecheses istæ ita proponantur, ut iis conscientiæ adstringantur, ut jugum imponatur hominibus Christianis jurandi in verba atque sententias hominum, utque eæ statuantur pro fidei norma, a qui quisquis vel unquam transversum deflexerit, is continuo anathematis fulmine feriatus et pro hæretico, pro homine deterrimo ac teterrimo habeatur, cæloque proscriptus ad tartara detrudatur atque infernalibus ignibus cruciandus adjudicetur. Absit a nobis ea mens, imo amentia. Dum catechesin scribimus, nemine quicquam præscribimus : dum sententias nostras exprimimus neminem opprimimus. Cuique liberum esto suæ mentis in religione judicium : dummodo et nobis liceat animi nostri sensa de rebus divinis citra cujusquam injuriam atque infectationem depromere. Hæc enim est aurea illa prophetandi libertas, quam sacræ litteræ Novi Instrumenti nobis impense commendant, et in qua apostolorum primitiva ecclesia nobis exemplo suo facem prætulit . . . qui vero estis vos, homunciones, qui, in quibus hominibus deo visum est spiritus sui ignem accendere, in iis eum extinguere ac suffocare connitamini ? . . . An vos soli geritis clavem scientiæ, ut nihil clausum vobis sit in sacris litteris, nihil obsignatum : ut

118

of Luther, and gives a place to the Socinian Catechism in the history of the Reformation movement which began with Luther.[1] But both belong to that epoch in the development of the Socinian Church, during which it was already strongly influenced from without ; that Latin preface shows the influence of Arminianism, and the German preface does not represent the *original* attitude of the Unitarian-Socinian movement.

Socinianism, however, is itself a secondary product, and Faustus Sozzini was an Epigone ; but an Epigone as Calvin and Menno Simons were Epigones. As Calvin was the first to give to the Romanic Reform movement its form, its force, and its attitude, and as Simons formed a Church out of the Baptist movement in the Netherlands and North-West Germany, so there belongs to Faustus Sozzini the great merit of introducing

quicquid occluseritis, recludere nemo queat et quicquid recluseritis, nemo valeat occludere ? Cur non meministis, unicum dumtaxat esse magistrum nostrum, cui ista competunt, Christum : nos vero omnes fratres esse, quorum nulli potestas ac dominium in conscientiam alterius concessum est ? Etsi enim fratrum alii aliis sint doctiores, libertate tamen et jure filiationis omnes æquales sunt." On the Catechism having undergone changes since its first appearing, the redactors express themselves thus : "Non erubescendum putamus, si ecclesia nostra in quibusdam proficiat. Non ubique clamandum credimus 'sto in filo, hic pedem figo, hinc me dimoveri ne tantillum quidem patiar?' Stoicorum enim est, omnia mordicus defendere et in sententia præfracte atque obstinato animo permanere. Christiani philosophi seu sapientiæ illius supernæ venientis candidati est, ὑπειθην esse non αὐθαδη, persuaderi facilem esse, non pertinaciter sibi placentem, paratumque cedere sententia, ubi alia vicerit melior. Hoc animo semper nostra edimus."

[1] Preface addressed to the illustrious University of Wittenberg : " For the further reason that we consider it proper, that the holy truth of the gospel, which originated in this illustrious University with the excellent man, Dr. Luther, and went forth from thence into the whole of Christendom, should return to it with interest and in greater perfection and be laid before it for its consideration. But if anyone thinks that God was to repair in so few years, through Dr. Luther and others helping him, all the injury done by Antichrist during so many centuries, he fails to take account of God's way of acting and of His wisdom in all such matters—that all things, namely, are not revealed by Him at once, but that the revelation is by little and little, that human weakness may not be overturned and crushed by the perfection of His revelation. God revealed so much to men through Dr. Luther that devout hearts received great help. . . . But because beyond this many other doctrines still remained that may be great hindrances to men's obtaining the same salvation, it has been God's will gradually to point out these also through His servants, and in place of the detestable and wearisome error to bring to view more perfectly from day to day His saving truth. We believe, moreover, that in accordance with His deep counsel He has used our congregations in Poland also," etc.

order into the wild, fermenting elements, and reducing them to
the unity of Church life.

Viewed from the standpoint of Church history and the
history of dogma, Socinianism has as its direct presuppositions
the great mediæval anti-ecclesiastical movements. Out of
these it developed itself ; it clarified them, and combined them
into a unity. It had itself, however, its main roots in the most
sober and judicious critical movements of the past. Just on
that account it succeeded in bringing under restraint what was
wild, extravagant, and fanciful. Anyone who examines even
rapidly the characteristic features of the Socinian system of
doctrine will meet at once with a *Scotistic-Pelagian* and with a
critico-Humanistic[1] element. On closer inspection he will perceive also the remnants still of an Anabaptist element ; on the
other hand there is an entire absence of Pantheistic, Mystical,
Chiliastic, and socialistic elements.

That Socinianism represents an *issue* of the history of dogma
will be disputed by no one. All that could be disputed is that
it belongs to the *universal history* of dogma at all. This objection has already been replied to above (p. 23). A movement
that was the precipitate of most of what had been occurring in
vague form alongside the Church throughout centuries, but
above all a movement *in which the critical thoughts of the
ecclesiastical theology of the fourteenth and fifteenth centuries had
come to unfold themselves freely, and which at the same time
gathered into itself the impulses of the newer age (Renaissance)*
dare not be regarded as a movement of secondary importance.
*What is characteristic of the Antitrinitarian and Socinian move-
ments of the sixteenth century lies in this, that they represent that
destruction of Catholicism which could be effected on the basis of
what was furnished by Scholasticism and the Renaissance while
there was no essential deepening or quickening of religion.* In
Antitrinitarianism and Socinianism the Middle Ages and the
newer period stretch forth hands to each other across the
Reformation. That which was regarded in the fifteenth
century as so incapable of being formed, an alliance between

---

[1] Even externally this Humanistic element is shaped in an extremely characteristic
way, *e.g.* in the Latin Preface quoted in part above.

Scholasticism and the Renaissance, here appears concluded—
in extremely different ways as regards particular points.   Just
for that reason there is inherent in these movements a prophetic
element also.   Much is already anticipated in them with
wonderful definiteness, which appears, after brief advances,
entirely suppressed within the Evangelical Churches for the
time, because the interest in *religion* in the form that had been
once adopted here absorbed everything for more than 150 years,
and in an incredibly short time became enveloped in Scholasticism.   Historians of culture and philosophers for whom
religion is a matter of indifference or a disturbing element, have
therefore every reason to be deeply interested in the Antitrinitarians and Socinians, in the " Enthusiasts " and pantheists, and,
in contrast with them, to deplore the melancholy half-measures
of the Reformers.   But it does not follow from this that, on the
other hand, one who recognises in the Reformation the true
progress of history, is entitled to pass by these parties unsym-
pathetically or with disapproval.   The critical elements which
they developed brought profit not only to science, but ultimately
to religion also, and they themselves only disappeared after
Protestantism had included within itself in the eighteenth and
nineteenth centuries all that they could furnish of abiding
substance.[1]

   We give in what follows a sketch *from the point of view of the
history of dogma* of the religious movements which accompanied
the Reformation in the sixteenth century, and conclude with an
account of Socinianism (Unitarianism), which alone issued in the
formation of a distinct Church.[2]   The breach with history, the
despair about the Church as it already existed, the conviction
regarding the divinely-given rights of the individual, were
common to all the parties.   Just on that account they cannot
be sharply separated from each other.   Starting from the most

   [1] The rapid development of the Reformation State Churches and National Churches
—the friendly attitude assumed towards the Lutheran Reformation, first by the Elector
of Saxony, and then by other Princes—also brought it about, certainly, that there was
a rapid keeping clear of all that one was not necessarily obliged to adopt.

   [2] The formation of the Mennonite Church does not belong to the history of dogma,
because in the matter of Christian doctrine—it is otherwise as regards ethics—it fell
back mainly on the definitions of the Ancient Churches.

different points (Chiliasm, Mysticism, Rationalism) they arrived
not infrequently at the same results, because the spirit by which
they were influenced in dealing with history was the same.

I. One group of parties attached themselves to the pantheistic
Mysticism of the Middle Ages, but at the same time to the new
culture of the Renaissance, steeped in Platonism, and by having
it as their aim to study, not words, but facts in religion and
science, represented the extreme opposition to " Aristotle," *i.e.*,
to the hollow Nominalistic Scholasticism of the Church. They
destroyed the old dogma formally and materially. Formally
in so far as they not only abandoned respect for the decisions
of the Church, but also addressed themselves to setting aside
the Bible as a law of doctrine (norma normans),[1] and to adding
to or placing above it the " inner light," *i.e.*, the personally experienced revelation of God and the speculation of the emancipated spirit ; materially, inasmuch as the dogmas of the Church
(Trinity, Christology) began to be pantheistically re-interpreted
by them, or to be allowed to drop as being erroneous. It is
well-known that that was not new; as long as ecclesiastical
dogma had existed, *i.e.*, from the fourth century, such tendencies
had accompanied the Church, partly in concealed, partly in
open, form. But it was new that among those representing
these tendencies, psychological observation, nay, experience in
general, began to play an important part, and that there developed itself a distinctive self-consciousness (in the religious,
the moral, and the secular). In this way they attracted to
themselves elements that raised their work high above what
was merely fanciful. Certainly the most of those who are to be

[1] That Augustine also (see Vol. V., p. 99 f., 125 f. note) exercised an influence
here—at least on Seb. Franck—has been pointed out by Hegler in his Monograph,
p. 283 f., note. The same applies to the view stated by Thamer, that a thing is not
true because it is in the Bible, but *vice versâ*. But I cannot see that the right standpoint against verbal inspiration is found in the perception that "Scripture is an
eternal allegory." That was already the view of very many Mystics of the ancient
and mediæval Churches, and just on their account an evangelical Reformation was
necessary. That proposition, rather, is nothing but the unveiling of the inspiration
dogma. There is more " historical criticism " involved in Luther's position towards
Scripture (" Prefaces ") than in the attitude of the most enlightened enthusiasts who
reject the letter. While saying this, I have no wish to underrate the wonderful greatness of the lonely thinker, Sebastian Franck.

included within this group knew as little as their Catholic opponents did of what evangelical *religion* is. They confounded
it with the lofty flights of metaphysics, and just for that reason
they still stood with one foot within the condemned circle of
the dogma which they contested.[1] But in spite of their hostile
attitude towards ecclesiastical Protestantism, some of them undoubtedly came under the influence of Luther. Determined by
him, but at the same time freed from the burden of the past,
rich and courageous in thought, possessed of strong and warm
feelings, they were able in forward movements to raise themselves
above all their contemporaries. But their religion, as a rule,
lacked the weight of simple and earnest simplicity ; their science
—some of them were discoverers, but at the same time charlatans
—lacked sobriety and restraint, and a restless temperament
made it appear as if they were not to be confided in. With this
group, which has a great importance in the history of philosophy,
there were connected—nay, there directly belonged to it in part
—on the one hand Schwenkfeld, Valentine Weigel, Giordano
Bruno—the last mentioned shows by his appealing to the
"divine" Cusanus, where the ultimate source is to be sought for
—on the other hand, Sebastian Franck, the Reformer, strongly
influenced by Luther, and, for a time, Theobald Thamer,[2] the
former in more than one respect citizen of a future Evan-

---

[1] At the close of his life, Thamer really became a Catholic again, and Schwenkfeld
would rather have become Romish than Lutheran.   That is significant.

[2] Cf. Carriere, Die philosophische Weltanschauung der Reformationszeit, 2 Vols.,
2nd ed., 1887, who deals very fully with Sebastian Franck, Weigel, Böhme, and,
above all, Giordano Bruno.   On Schwenkfeld see Hahn, Schwenkfeldii sent. de
Christi persona et opere, 1847, Erbkam, Gesch. der protest. Secten, 1848, Kadelbach,
Gesch. Sch.'s und der Schwenkfeldianer, 1861, Henke, Neuere Kirchengesch., I.,
p. 395 ff.   On Weigel see the Art. by H. Schmidt in Herzog's R.-Encykl.[2] Vol.
XVI.   On Bruno compare the literature in Ueberweg-Heinze, Gesch. d. Philos.   On
Franck see Bischof, Seb. Franck, 1857, Hase, Seb. Franck, 1869 (Gottfried Arnold
again discovered him) and Latendorf, Franck's erste Sprichwörtersammlung, 1876,
Weinkauff in the Ztschr. Alemannia, 5th Vol. (1877), p. 133 ff., Dilthey, Archiv. f.
Gesch. d. Philos., 5th Vol., p. 389 ff. ; also the Art. by Merz in Herzog's Real.-
Encykl.[2], Vol. IV., Henke I., p. 399 ff., but, above all, the excellent monograph by
Hegler, Geist u. Schrift bei S. Franck, 1892.   On Thamer see Neander, Thamer,
1842.   On the younger spiritual kinsman of Franck, the Dutch Coornhert, Dilthey
gives information : Archiv. f. Gesch. d. Philos., Vol. V., p. 487 ff.

gelical Church that is to discard the Catholic law of the letter.[1]

2. A second group, the limits of which cannot be determined, had its strength in its opposition to political and sacramental Catholicism, and brought into the field against this a new socio-political order of world and Church, Apocalypticism and Chiliasm, or contented itself with discarding everything "external," and adhering to a "Biblical Christianity"—but with a constitutional order for the true Christian communities. This group also simply continued the mediæval opposition to the Catholic Church, while it was evidently the ideal of the Franciscan Spirituales, or the ideals akin to it of the Waldensians and Hussites that were regulative here.[2]   But the spirit of a

[1] Among other things, it is to be conceded to Dilthey that the modern speculative theology (the religious universal theism and pantheistic determinism), which developed itself out of Mysticism, has more distinct precursors in some sectaries of the Reformation period than in Luther with his "positivistic penetration."   But what, in my opinion, has more significance is that they drew practical and theoretical conclusions from their piety to which Luther was unable to force his way.   What was still held in common, the old dogma, he utilised with the view of showing Christians again the way to God.   Of the fact that this common element was just at that time beginning to be broken up through the operation of forces that asserted themselves outside the doctrine of salvation, he had scarcely any inkling, or he shut himself entirely up from the impression of this.   The tragedy of this historical fact is deeply moving; but when did it happen otherwise in history? (see Dilthey, l.c. pp. 385 ff.).

[2] Ritschl has directed attention to this.   The regulative principles that Christianity must be realised as fellowship among the actively holy, that inability to sin may be attained, and that the Church has only a meaning as the product of the actively holy, derive their character from the Middle Ages, or say, from the ancient Church.   In numerous investigations, last of all in the dissertation, "Die Anfänge der Reformation und die Ketzerschulen" (Vortr. und Abhandl. aus der Comenius-Gesellschaft, 4. Jahrg. Stück 1 u. 2, 1897), Keller has endeavoured to show that the Anabaptists and the kindred sects stood in direct and exclusive connection with the Waldensians (only the importance they attributed to late baptism is represented by him as having been a novelty).   Along some lines he has really demonstrated this connection, but not its exclusiveness, and, in my opinion, he has also over-estimated the positive importance of the "Heretical Schools."   A good and very complete sketch of the history of the Baptists has been furnished by A. H. Newman, "A History of Anti-Pedo-Baptism from the Rise of Pedobaptism till 1609," Philadelphia, 1897.   One after another of these strong, worthy, martyr-spirited figures passes before us: most of them contemplate joyfully the sure prospect of a violent death.   Among the numerous monographs of which Newman gives a list, pp. 394-406, the works of Loserth are conspicuous: for the Pre-Reformation period, see the works of Haupt.   Only when we have a history of the Inquisition in Germany, and of the German martyrs from the

new age reveals itself among them, not only in their entertainment in many ways of Reformation thoughts, but also in the
stress they lay on Christian *independence*. It is with this in
view that their opposition to infant baptism is to be understood,
which was a protest of the independent individual believer
against the magic of redemption and the sacramental " character." From the standpoint of the history of dogma this
opposition was the main characteristic of the Anabaptists ; for
all other features do not belong to the whole group. With
regard to dogma some of them are good Catholics, others are
Lutheran or Zwinglian, others again are pantheistic and antitrinitarian. It is very remarkable that the antitrinitarian element was not more strongly developed among them ; for it
would seem as if the sharp antagonism to the reigning Church
should necessarily have driven them to Antitrinitarianism, since
the doctrine of the Trinity and Christology form the chief part
of the old detested Catholicism, and the discarding of infant
baptism involves the dissolution of the Church as understood in
ancient times. In this vastly great group also, which had its
representatives during the sixteenth century in Germany, the
Netherlands, Switzerland, Venice, Moravia, Poland, Livonia,
and Sweden, and had connection with the Waldensians (and
" Bohemians "), the modern spirit displayed itself in close association with the mediæval. Not only did the perception find
frequent expression here also that the use of the Bible as a law-
book is Catholic and a check upon religion—though, on the
other hand, certainly, it was just among the Anabaptists that
the most rigid Biblicism had its fanatical supporters—but even
the simple evangelical spirit, which sought in religion for nothing
but religion, and the conviction of the freedom of conscience,
found a home in Anabaptist communities. We owe it to investigations carried on during recent years that the pictures of
excellent Christians, from the circles of the Anabaptists, have
been presented to us, and not a few of these figures, so worthy of

thirteenth to the seventeenth century, shall we be able to estimate the struggle that
was carried on for well-nigh five hundred years against Christian faith and freedom
by the Confessional Churches.

honour and so full of character, have become more intelligible to us than the heroic Luther and the iron-willed Calvin.[1]

3. A third group—whose representatives are almost entirely men of learning, natives of Italy moreover—brings before us the thorough-going development of Nominalistic Scholasticism under the influence of Humanism.   Only as long as Nominalistic Scholasticism maintained an attitude of submission to the Church, and just on that account sought with the one hand skilfully to rebuild, or to uphold, what with the other hand it had demolished, was a union impossible with the critical culture of the Renaissance.   But as soon as it withdrew from the Catholic Church, and kept simply to its own points of departure, independence of rational thought, theism, and autonomous morality, and thus *really* abandoned what its *rational reflection* had abandoned long before (Catholic Dogma, Sacraments, etc.), modern culture could combine with it.   That culture contributed the historic element, the return to the

[1] After the Anabaptists had sunk into oblivion, and even Gottfried Arnold had not succeeded in awaking interest in, and intelligent appreciation of, their memory, the recollection of them has been revived in our days on different sides and in different ways.   In connection with this exaggerations were inevitable (Hagen, Deutschlands litt. u. relig. Verhältnisse i. Ref.-Zeitalter, 1841 ff. ; Keller, Die Reformation und die älteren Reformparteien, 1885).   But the estimate of them has certainly undergone a change, having become much more favourable than it was in former times, and along with Cornelius, Kampschulte, and especially the historians of the Netherlands, Keller has contributed much to this.   The more closely the history of the Reformation in particular provinces and towns has been studied, the more apparent has it become that these Baptists, entering frequently into alliance with Waldensian and Hussite elements, or falling back on former mediæval movements, formed the soil into which the Reformation was received, and that for many decennia they continued closely inter-connected with it in many regions.   The strict conception of the evangelical principle which Ritschl has emphasised is certainly legitimate from a dogmatic point of view ; but it must not be summarily applied to the phenomena of the Reformation period, otherwise the risk is run of choking the springs from which living water flowed.   Again, we must not treat the " inner word" of the "enthusiasts" as a bugbear to be brought helplessly to the ground by the sword of the " Scripture-principle"; for however certain it is that real "enthusiasm" promoted itself by means of the "inner word," it is equally certain that the "inner word" was also the expression for a religious freedom which Luther in his day knew very well, but of which he never so expressed the title that it became in his hands a dogmatic principle limiting the Scripture-principle.   The testimonium spiritus sancti internum which was left behind to the Epigones did not supply the want ; yet it is an important germ for a future that is still to be looked forward to in Protestantism.

sources, the appreciation of philology, the respect for the *classical* in everything that comes under the category of antiquity. In no period have the Italians distinguished themselves by a high degree of speculative capacity. So it is not to be wondered at that intellectual Humanism formed the means by which they delivered themselves from dogma in the sixteenth century. A real religious interest also was at work in this mode of emancipation ; where religion is not a concern for heart and conscience, there is no endeavour to improve its public expression. But the religious motive, in the strictest sense of the term, the motive that asserts itself within the Christian religion as the power of the living God, before whose Holy Spirit nothing that is one's own retains its independence, was very remote from these Italians. Nor did they succeed in bringing about a popular movement even in their own native country ; they continued to be officers without an army.[1]

---

[1] We have no exhaustive account of this entire school. Reference has still to be made to Trechsel, Die protest. Antitrinitarier vor F. Socin (2 vols., 1839, 1844) and the special studies in Socinianism. Yet see the valuable historic hints which Ritschl has given (Rechtfert. u. Versöhn., 1st ed., I., p. 311) : "The fact that Faustus affirmed of the hypothesis of Duns (God could also have redeemed us through a mere man) that it represented the real and necessary, presupposes a radical breach with the universal faith of the Church. To this breach his uncle (Lelio), as well as himself and many other Italians, were led by the state of Christian society in Italy. Here the empire had not recovered the authority it had lost in dealing with Gregory VII. and Innocent III. ; here the Roman Church appeared as the only possible form of Christian society. The Church dominated the masses of the people, whom no expectation of ecclesiastical reform prepared for receiving the Reformation influences from Switzerland and Germany. It was for the most part only men of literary culture who were accessible to these influences. But owing to the state of public opinion and to the unbroken power of the ecclesiastical organs, these men were almost everywhere hindered from the beginning from making a public appearance in the congregations, and were forced to form themselves into secret societies. Their interest in the Reformation, even if it was originally directed to its ethical core, found there neither the requisite fostering nor the requisite control that are furnished by giving practical expression in public to the general religious consciousness. Hence it was that among so many Italians who attached themselves to the Reformation, what was nourished was not the Church spirit, but, on the contrary, either the Anabaptist Sectarianism or the inclination to subject all dogmas to Scholastic criticism, or both together. For the Scholastic interest finds it as natural to deal critically with the doctrines of the Trinity and reconciliation as to frame the correct notion of justification."

4. The circles described under 1 and 3 represent in many respects contrasted positions, in so far as the former had a strong leaning to speculative Mysticism, the latter to sober intelligent thought. Yet not only did Humanistic interests throw a uniting bond around them, but out of speculative Mysticism there developed itself in connection with *experience*, to which value was attached, a *pure* thinking also ; and, on the other hand, the sober Italian thinkers threw off, under the influence of the new culture, the bad habits of that conceptual mythology in which the earlier Nominalism had indulged. Thus the two schools converged. The most important representative of this coalescence was the Spanish thinker—distinguished also for his deeply pious spirit—Michael Servede. In him we see a union of the best of everything that came to maturity in the sixteenth century, if the Evangelical Reformation be left out of account. Servede had equal distinction as an empirical investigator, a critical thinker, a speculative philosopher, and a Christian Reformer in the best sense of the term. It is a paradox of history that Spain, the country that was least affected in the sixteenth century by the ideas of the newer age, and in which at the earliest date Catholicism was restored, produced this unique man.[1]

Within the history of dogma there are two main points that must be kept in view in order to determine the importance of these movements : (1) their relation to the formal authorities of Catholicism ; (2) their relation to the doctrines of the Trinity and of Christ.[2]

As to the first point, the statement can be quite brief: the authority of the presently existing Church as teacher and judge was renounced by them ; but they contested also the doctrinal power of the Church of former times. At the same

[1] On Servede see the numberless works by Tollin, whose intention was to illustrate the whole Reformation history " Servetocentrically " ; Kawerau in the Theol. Stud. u. Krit., 1878, III. ; Riggenbach in Herzog's R.-Encykl.[2], Vol. XIV. ; Trechsel, l.c. I., p. 61 ff.

[2] It is important also to observe that a large number of the Reformers had a leaning to Apokatastasis, and that they most hotly contested the Catholic notion of the Sacraments.

time the relation to Holy Scripture continued almost everywhere vague.   On the one hand Scripture was ranged against
Church tradition—nay, there was here and there a clinging with
unprecedented legalism to the letter ; on the other hand, the
authority of Scripture was subordinated to that of the inner
revelation, indeed, as a law for faith it was even entirely set
aside.   Nevertheless, it can easily be seen that the efforts that
were made to discard, along with the authority of the Church,
the absolute authority of the Bible, continued without any considerable result.   Even those who brought forward the "spirit"
against the "letter" had no thought in many cases of taking
objection to the unique validity of Holy Scripture, but only
wished to introduce a spiritual interpretation of Scripture, and to
secure recognition for the good title belonging to the free spirit
that is guided by the Spirit of God.   The absolute authority of
Scripture passed forth victorious in the end from all the movements that accompanied the Reformation and the Counter-
Reformation.   After some slight hesitation, Socinianism took
its stand firmly on the ground of Scripture.   There was no
serious attempt made by the Reformers of the sixteenth century
to shake this rock—if we keep out of view some excellent men,
who really understood what the freedom of a Christian man is.[1]
It was not due, or at least not in the first instance due, to them
therefore, if a relation of greater freedom towards Scripture was
subsequently secured in the Evangelical Church.   This was
rather a fruit of the *inner* development of Protestantism ; the
continued influence of the ideas of Franck, Weigel, and Böhme
scarcely had to do with this result.   By their holding to the
Scriptures, as gathered together and made the subject of

---

[1] Here Hans Denck, and above all Seb. Franck, are to be mentioned with honour;
on Denck compare Keller, Ein Apostel der Wiedertaüfer, 1882, p. 83 ff., and elsewhere.   Denck holds fast to the word of God in Holy Scripture, but disputes the legal
authority of the letter, and is of opinion that only the spirit can discern the spirit of
the divine word.   Franck treated the whole question with still greater thoroughness
and freedom, see Hegler, l.c., p. 63 ff., Henke, Neuere K.-Gesch. I., p. 403 : "In
the rejection of the 'formal principle' there was much that was more scriptural than
the doctrine that the Spirit is only given through the verbum externum."   This is
correct ; but Luther did not contend for the historical Christ under the rigid integu-
ment of the verbum externum.   The "inner word" and the Christus ex scriptura
sacra prædicatus are not mutually exclusive.

preaching by the Church, the Reformers gave testimony to
their common ecclesiastical character ; but they certainly
shattered the foundations of the dogma ; for this rests, not on
Scripture alone, but on the doctrinal authority of the Church,
and on the sole right of the Church to expound Scripture.
While the Reformers vindicated this right for themselves and
for every Christian man, yet even on their part there was no
passing (here, certainly, they went hand in hand with early
Protestantism) beyond the contradiction, of asserting the
authority of an extensive collection of books as an absolute
norm, while the understanding of these books was left by them
to the efforts of individuals.

As to the second point : in all the four groups described
above, Antitrinitarianism developed itself, but in different
ways.[1] In the first group it was not aggressive, but rather
latitudinarian.   A latitudinarian Antitrinitarianism of the
kind, however, was not wanting in the ancient Church also, and
even, indeed, among the Fathers of dogma ; it belongs in a
certain sense to dogma itself.   To soften by mystic pantheistic
means the rigid dogma, to reduce the Trinity to " modes "
(" modi ") and to intertwine it with the thought of the world, to
see in Christology a special instance of a constantly repeated
occurrence, to contemplate the union of the divine and human
natures in Christ as a perfect fusion, which has its ultimate
ground in metaphysics, to recognise in all dogmas *encasements* of
truth, etc.—all these things were no novelties.[2]   Therefore even

---

[1] Trechsel, l.c., whose method and classification, however, leave much to be
desired.   The Antitrinitarians are dealt with also by Baur and Dorner in their works
on the history of the doctrines of the Trinity and Christology (cf., also the latter's
Gesch. d. protest. Theol. 2nd ed., 1867).

[2] Even a proposition like that of Seb. Franck, who, by the way, was in no sense an
Antitrinitarian : "The Christ after the flesh has served His time," had no bad meaning
attaching to it, and has not the old ecclesiastical tradition against it (see also St.
Bernard, Vol. VI., p. 13).   Franck, who entered very deeply into speculation about
the " flesh " of Christ, only intended to suggest by this that we must not abide by the
flesh, but must lay hold of the Spirit, the deity (see Hegler, l.c., p. 185 ff., 190 ff.).
Many similar statements are to be found among the Reformers, and it is with injustice
that they are frequently construed as heresies.   That the spiritualistic tendency makes
itself felt also in connection with the Christological dogma is not to be denied, yet
there was really no injury done by this.   Taken as a whole, the criticism of the two-
nature doctrine was cautious and mild ; radical criticism was always the exception.

Schwenkfeld, Weigel, G. Bruno, and their followers were not Antitrinitarians in the strictest sense of the term, although their doctrines, by continuing to work as a ferment, served to break up the old dogma.[1]—Within the second group Antitrinitarianism forms only *one* factor in the opposition to the state of things in the Church—which is entirely identified with Babylon—a factor, moreover, which for long did not make its appearance everywhere, and which, even where it asserted itself in conjunction with the rejection of infant baptism and with spiritualism and the doctrine of the apokatastasis, had very different motives underlying it. Denck, perhaps the most excellent of the Anabaptists, scarcely touched upon Antitrinitarianism in his book, " Ordnung Gottes und der Creaturen Werk " (God's order and the work of His creatures). He was concerned about more important things than the polemic against the doctrine of the Trinity; of the deity of Christ he never had any doubt. If he says in one place : " Omnipotence, goodness, and righteousness—these constitute the threefoldness, unity, and trinity in unity of God," this assertion is certainly not to be understood as directly Antitrinitarian. It was merely his purpose, as it was Melanchthon's in the first edition of his " Loci," to withdraw attention from the Scholastic forms and fix it on the matter itself.[2] His associate, Hätzer, a man of impure life, spoke incidentally of the " superstition of the deity of Christ," God being only one ; but it would seem that he himself afterwards attached little weight to this divergence, and his denial exercised no influence.[3] The doctrine of the

[1] Just as the men to be mentioned in the following group carried on a polemic against the "external" conceptions of reconciliation (the satisfaction dogma); cf. Ritschl, Rechtfert. u. Versöhnung, 1st ed., I., pp. 305-311. Münzer accentuated in a genuinely mediæval way only the example of Christ, but was silent as to what was meant by His being the Reconciler. Denck's misunderstanding of a doctrine of Luther became the occasion of his entirely rejecting the idea of a general reconciliation by Christ. Hence in his circle the doctrine of the deity of Christ became open to question.

[2] See Keller, l.c., p. 90. Trechsel, l.c. I., p. 13 ff. Yet Trechsel's account has come to be out of date since Keller wrote. Henke I., p. 418 ff.

[3] Trechsel, l.c. I., p. 13 ff. Keim in the Jahrbb. f. deutsche Theol., 1856, II., and in Herzog's R.-E.[2], Vol. V. One who shared the views of Hätzer was Kautz of Bockenheim.

Trinity was more strenuously combated by Campanus in his
book, "Wider alle Welt nach den Aposteln" ("With the
Apostles against all the world"), a book that led Melanchthon
to declare that the author deserved to be strung up (des "lichten
Galgens" für würdig erklären). Yet the positive discussion of
the question ("Divine and Holy Scripture restored and
amended"), in which the doctrine of two divine Persons was
maintained, the Son being declared consubstantial with the
Father, and yet subordinate to Him, remained a singular
phenomenon.[1] In connection with a philosophy of history
(three Ages), David Joris subjected the Trinity to a Sabellian
treatment, representing it as a threefold revelation of God.[2]
The restless traveller, Melchior Hoffmann, drew up a system of
Christology resembling that of Valentinian,[3] while the Venetian
Anabaptist, Pietro Manelfi, proclaimed Christ to be the divine
man, the child of Joseph and Mary,[4] and succeeded in securing
acceptance for this doctrine at an Anabaptist Synod (1550).[5]
This happened in Italy; for there alone (in some measure also
in Southern France, under the influence of Servede) was there
really a development of Antitrinitarianism. There alone did
it come to be, not *one* moment in conjunction with other
moments, but the really critical moment. That took place
within the third group described above. *The union of Humanism
with the Nominalistic Pelagian tradition in theology gave a place
in Italy to Antitrititarianism as an actual factor in the historic
movement.*[6] Here the doctrine of the Trinity was broken up;
indeed, the discarding of it was regarded as the most important
means for securing purity and freedom for religion. Its place
was taken by the doctrines of the *one* God and the created

[1] Trechsel, l.c., pp. 26-34.
[2] Nippold, in the Zeitschr. f. d. histor. Theol. 1863, 1864. Henke, I., p. 421 f.
[3] Zur Linden, M.H., ein Prophet der Wiedertaüfer, 1885.
[4] On the gospel in Venice see Trechsel II., p. 32 ff. Benrath in the Stud. u.
Krit., 1885, I.
[5] Manelfi ultimately became a Catholic again.
[6] Cf. the entire 2nd Vol. of Trechsel's work. In his estimate of Socinianism
Dilthey lays stress on the Humanistic element, the product of the new Hermeneutics,
while not denying the presence of the Scotistic element (Archiv. f. Gesch. der Philos.,
Vol. 6, p. 97 ff.).

Christ. There remained uncertainty about the latter doctrine :
it assumed at one time an Arian, at another time an Adoptianist
form ; nor was a Sabellian element entirely absent. A noteworthy parallel to the history of the old Adoptianists in the
Church presents itself here. Like the old Theodotians in
Rome, these new Theodotians also were equally interested in
the Bible and in sober philosophy ; like the old Theodotians,
they formed only a school, in spite of all attempts to found a
Church ; like the former, they worked with grammar, logic, and
exegetical methods, and, as the former probably gave a subordinate place to the consciousness of redemption, so the latter
were interested chiefly in religious illuminism (Aufklärung) and
in morals. The more one enters into details (compare also the
proof from Scripture) the more striking does the kinship appear.
Italy produced a whole crowd of Antitrinitarians in the middle
of the sixteenth century.[1] Mention is chiefly to be made of
Camillo Renato, Gribaldo, Blandrata, Gentilis, Occhino, and the
two Sozzinis.[2] This is not the place to give the history of these
men, but the general course of the Antitrinitarian movement
deserves consideration. These Reformers were not able to hold
their ground in Italy ; they were obliged to leave their native
land, and they accordingly endeavoured to secure a settlement
on the borders of it, in the Grisons, and in Southern Switzerland.
Here they were brought into contact with what had been produced through Calvin's influence. It was a time of great
importance in Church history when Antitrinitarianism, coming
from Lyons in the person of Servede, from the South and from
the Grisons in the persons of the men named above, sought to
obtain the rights of citizenship in Geneva, where a large Italian
colony existed, and in Switzerland. The decision lay in the

---

[1] I do not enter into Servede's doctrine, for although this Spaniard was the most
outstanding Antitrinitarian in the sixteenth century he did not succeed in exercising
a permanent influence. What distinguishes him from most of the Italian Antitrinitarians is that his opposition to the doctrine of the Trinity was ultimately based
on pantheism. Modalistic, Gnostic, and Adoptian elements furnished him aid in
building up his Christology, which was constructed on Neoplatonic premises. Henke,
I., p. 423 ff.

[2] Only the most important names are given here ; see many others in Trechsel, II.,
p. 64 ff. On Occhino see the Monograph by Benrath, 1875.

hands of Calvin,[1] and Calvin had allowed himself at one time to speak very disparagingly about the Niceno-Constantinopolitan Creed.[2] Nevertheless, he certainly did not act against his conviction when he took up the most antagonistic attitude towards the Antitrinitarians. Although a narrowing of his standpoint was forced upon him by his opposition to the Genevese "libertines," yet the logical carrying out of his system of faith itself required him to adopt the sharpest measures. He had Servede burnt, and by his powerful words the other Swiss Cantons, where there was originally (especially in Bâsle) a more liberal judgment, were kept from showing toleration and were

---

[1] From the beginning the Reformed congregations did not take their stand so strongly as the Lutheran on the doctrine of the Trinity and the Chalcedonian Christology, the reason being that they thought of the *Reformation* not as merely distinguishing them from the Catholic Church, but as meaning a *breach* with the Church. Just on that account it was much more difficult there to find sufficient grounds for a strict adhesion to ecclesiastical antiquity, especially when some passages of Scripture were allowed to create the conviction that the matter was not so plainly and unquestionably contained in the Bible. How many men there were in Switzerland about the middle of the sixteenth century who, along with the other Catholic doctrines, gave at least a subordinate place to those about the Trinity also ! Among the Reformed enormous weight was attached to the argument that it does not befit a Christian to use expressions that are not to be found in Scripture. Even men like Vergerio were favourably disposed towards the Antitrinitarians (see Trechsel, II., p. 117 ff.). It was really the case that in some of the Swiss National Churches Antitrinitarianism came very near being approved. How great the crisis was between the years 50 and 60 is shown by the numerous letters on the Trinitarian question written at that time by Epigones of the Reformation. The pressure brought to bear by the Lutherans would scarcely have been strong enough to drive the free congregations in Switzerland from the path of freedom. The decision lay in Calvin's hands, and he declared Antitrinitarianism heretical. This settled the matter for Geneva, Switzerland, the Palatinate, and indeed for all the regions that were under the iron rule of the great lawgiver. If the question is simply dealt with by itself, it must be deeply lamented that the Reformation, with a great advance immediately before it, did not take the decisive step. Yet if we consider that the most prominent Antitrinitarians had no discernment of Luther and Zwingli's conception of faith, and were satisfied in part with moralism and illuminism, our conclusion must be that the toleration of them in the sixteenth century would probably have meant the dissolution of evangelical faith, in the first instance within the area of Calvin's influence. By his draconian measures against the Antitrinitarians Calvin protected faith—*i.e.*, Luther's faith.

[2] See Köllner, Symbolik, I., p. 48: "patres Nicænos fanaticos appellat—s. Nicænum battologias arguit—carmen cantillando magis aptum, quam confessionis formulam."

brought round to accept his strict principle. The Antitrinitarians had meanwhile found an asylum in Poland and
Transylvania. That the Italians were attracted to Poland
cannot be explained merely from the great freedom that
prevailed there in consequence of the permanent anarchy
(sovereignty of the great landed proprietors); we must rather
remember that there was perhaps no other country in Europe
in the sixteenth century whose towns were so Italian as those
of Poland. Poland did not, like Germany, pass through a
Renaissance of its own ; but the direct intercourse between
Italy and Poland was of the liveliest kind : Italian master
builders erected the splendid structures in Cracow, Warsaw, etc.,
and the more recent publications on Polish Humanists show us
how active an intercourse of a mental kind there was between
Poland and Italy. It was in part owing to these relationships
that the Italian Reformers came to Poland ; they found their
way to Transylvania, no doubt, simply because it lay on the
confines of Christendom, and the general disorder prevailing
there was in their favour. So also they found their way to
England in the days of Édward VI., when the religious state of
things there seemed to be undergoing a complete dissolution.

In Transylvania and Poland there arose Antitrinitarian congregations ; indeed, in Transylvania the energetic Blandrata
succeeded in securing formal recognition for the Antitrinitarian
Confession as the fourth Christian Confession.[1] Within the
anarchy freedom of conscience also found a home. Blandrata's
positive confession, which he had kept concealed so long as he
was in Switzerland and Lesser Poland, was strictly Unitarian.
He did not recognise the eternal Godhead of Christ, but saw in
Christ a man chosen by God and exalted to God. But the
Unitarian Church soon became separated into a right and left.
The latter went on to reject the miraculous birth of Jesus, and
to deny His claim to divine worship (Nonadorantism). Its chief
representative was Franz Davidis.[2] To help in opposing this

[1] In our literature we possess as yet no monograph on Blandrata; his " confessio
antitrinitaria " was re-issued by Henke in 1794, cf. Heberle in the Tüb. theol.
Ztschr. 1840, IV. An Italian monograph appeared in Padua in 1814 : Malacarne,
Commentario delle opere di Giorgio Biandrate, nobile Saluzzese.

[2] He is regarded at the present day as the father of Transylvanian Unitarianism,.and

section, Fausto Sozzini came to Transylvania (1578), and with his aid Nonadorantism was really successfully suppressed. In Poland the Antitrinitarians mingled at first with the Calvinists.[1] Beyond the country where it originated, Calvinism appeared to be the most liberal confession, because it expressed itself in the strongest language against Romanism. Yet even in Poland discussions arose between the Calvinists and the "Arians," especially after the Synod of Petrikau (1562), which led to a definite breach. From that time there existed in Poland what were strictly speaking Unitarian congregations, which had, however, no fixed order. Anabaptist, Socialist, Chiliastic, Libertinist and Nonadorantist tendencies here found room for themselves and sought to assert their influence. At this point Fausto Sozzini made his appearance. With the clearest insight into what was for him the truth, he united the most determined force of will and the gifts of a born ruler. Out of the seriously endangered, unorganised communities he created a *Church*. In Poland arose a counterpart—poor enough, certainly, as a Church —to that Church in Geneva, which had expelled Antitrinitarianism.[2] It was quite especially to the credit of Sozzini that a new Confession developed itself from Unitarianism, the Christian character of which cannot be denied, and which, after a history rich in dramatic incidents, found a place for itself in England and America and produced excellent men.[3]

But with all regard for the personality of Sozzini, it cannot be

as such is held in high esteem even by the English and North American Unitarians ; on him see the arts. in Ersch and Gruber's Encycl. and in the Kathol. Kirchenlex.[2] III. ; also Forck, Socinianism, I., p. 157 ff., 258 ff. The subdivisions which followed, ranging from Nonadorantism to the borders of Judaism, are of no importance historically, though interesting.

[1] As also in Transylvania and England. Within the sphere of Calvin's influence Antitrinitarianism could be checked only by a prohibition supported by force. On Antitrinitarianism in the Calvinistic Palatinate, see Henke, I., p. 433 f.

[2] On the consolidation of Polish Unitarianism into Socinianism see the account of Fock (Socinianism, 1st Vol., 1847) pp. 137-183. Fock's book is an excellent piece of work, which, however, were it to appear to-day, would be branded as heretical. On the elder Sozzini, see E. Burnat, Lelio Socin., Vevey, 1894.

[3] On Socinianism see the Protestant histories of Creeds : Rambach, Hist. u. theol. Einl. i. d. Relig.-Streitigk. d. ev. K. m. d. Soc., 2nd Part, 1753. Besides Fock's work, see also Ritschl, Rechtf. u. Versöhn. 1st ed. I., pp. 311-337.

denied that his faith was very different from the Evangelical,
and that the criticism to which he subjected the Church doctrine shows itself to be a logical carrying out of the Scotistic
theology.[1]   That has been pointed out in a masterly way by
Ritschl.[2]   The Italian Reformer, who only found a field for his
activity beyond the confines of the Roman Empire, placed himself also outside the general ecclesiastical faith and outside the
Church.   He did not merely correct, as on superficial view he
seems to have done, the ecclesiastical doctrine, he ignored the
correct *tendencies* which led the Church to the doctrines of the
Godhead of Christ, the Trinity, and satisfaction.   One can agree
almost everywhere with the formal criticism to which the
Socinians subjected the orthodox doctrine and yet hold that
the representatives of the latter displayed a much surer understanding of the gospel than their opponents.   But the expression
in which this understanding of theirs was embodied—dogma—
no longer satisfied.   It was ripe for dissolution, and the Socinians
put an end to it.   That this refutation of it in the seventeenth
century had a comparatively slight effect was due not only to
the special circumstances of the times, but in a still higher degree to the resistance every religion makes to being driven from
its positions by a criticism arising from without.

2. *The Socinian Doctrine.*

We have a comprehensive and detailed account of the doctrine
of the Socinians in the Racovian Catechism (1609).[3]   The way
in which this work is laid out and the fulness of its detail are in
themselves characteristic.   Religion is the perfect and correct
knowledge of the saving doctrine.   Here the Socinians are at
one with the Epigones of the Reformation, who also had it in
view to make out of the Church a School.   This principle,

---

[1] Dilthey directs attention to the spiritual connection of the Socinians (and
Arminians) with Erasmus (Archiv. f. Gesch. d. Philos., Vol. VI., p. 87 ff.).

[2] See Gesch. Studien z. Christl. Lehre v. Gott, 3rd Art. in the Jahrbb. f. deutsche
Theol. XIII., p. 268 ff., 283 ff., and in Rechtf. u. Versöhn. I. l.c.

[3] I quote from the edition Irenopoli post annum, 1659.

when logically carried out, leads to denying the Christian religion of all who have not this knowledge. Some Lutherans in the seventeenth century went so far as this. Yet Faustus is willing to assert the thought, that there are other Christian Churches besides his own : *he is tolerant.* Side by side with the definition which restricts the Church to those who have the " sacred doctrine " stands the recognition of the other Churches. But wherein, then, consists that "doctrina salutaris," if the greatest opposition exists between Socinianism and the doctrine of the other Churches? Faustus has omitted to point that out.

The way in which the Catechism is drawn up is as Scholastic as possible. It is a course of instruction for producing theologians. After the definition : "The Christian religion is the way of attaining to eternal life that is pointed out by God through Jesus Christ," [1] it begins with the question as to where we learn this way, and answers : "From the Holy Scriptures, especially of the New Testament." [2] The foremost position is now assigned to the New Testament in the doctrine of religion. All fanatical elements are suppressed. That the New Testament is the sole regulative authority, source, and norm of religion cannot be declared more positively and dryly than by Socinianism. The *Christian religion is the Theology of the New Testament.* In this there is the basis of the positive character which Faustus was led to give to his creation—a positiveness, certainly, which is astounding, as soon as we begin to reflect upon what religion really *is.* All knowledge of the divine is produced from without, and it is *simply* included in the book that has once for all been given. It is not that Christ is the revelation in the book ; but "*in the book* God has made manifest Himself, His will, and the way of salvation " (p. 5). If we recall here the fact that similar expressions are to be found in Calvin, we must not forget that as little as any other of the Reformers did Calvin ever leave it out of view, that the Bible is given to *faith.* But of this we find nothing in Faustus. There

[1] "Religio Christiana est via a deo per Jesum Christum monstrata vitam æternam consequendi."
[2] "Ex sacris litteris, præsertim Novi Testamenti."

is not even an approach made to discovering lines of connection
between the outward revelation contained in the Bible and the
nature of religion ; what we have, rather, is—on the one hand
the book, *on the other hand the human understanding.* The
latter is really the second principle in the Socinian dogmatic,
which has been not incorrectly described therefore as Supra-
natural Rationalism.   There is set over against the revelation
contained in the Bible—not the man who longs after God, who,
sunk in sin and guilt, has no peace or blessedness—but simply
man, as a mortal, but rational being, who is on the outlook for
eternal life. *Religion is a matter of interest for rational man.*
Faustus does not carry his conception of religion beyond this
undoubtedly correct, though extremely general perception.   In
this, and in his Biblicism, he reminds us of the Antiochene
theologians.

Section I. of the Catechism is entirely devoted to Holy
Scripture.   In the first chapter the " certitude of Holy Scripture " (" certitudo sacrarum litterarum ") is treated of (pp. 1-10).
Here external proofs, some of them of an extremely doubtful
kind, are first adduced for the trustworthiness of Holy Scripture.   Then an appeal is made to its being inconceivable that
God should have allowed the falsifying of a book in which He
revealed Himself, His will, and the way of salvation.   Yet an
attempt is certainly made in the end to prove the credibility of
the book from the truth, rather, of the Christian religion : the
book is true, because it is the only source of the true religion.
But why is the Christian religion true ?   Because its founder was
divine (divinus).   How can that be proved ?   From His
miracles, which are attested even by the Jews, and which cannot
have been demonic, because Christ was an enemy of the devil,
and from His resurrection.   The resurrection, again, is to be
established on the testimony of those who saw Him and went
to death for this faith.   We have only the choice—of regarding
the disciples and all Christians who have lived afterwards as of
unsound mind—or of believing in the Resurrection of Christ.
But, further, the history of the Christian religion furnishes a
proof of its truth ; how could so many, relinquishing all earthly
goods, and with the sure prospect of distress, shame, and death

before them, have adopted it, if the Resurrection of Christ were not a truth ? Finally, the truth of the Christian religion is proved by the nature of the religion itself (ex ipsius religionis natura) ; for both the commands and the promises of this religion are so lofty, and so transcend the spirit of man, that they can only have God for their author ; " for the former contain the heavenly sanctity of life, the latter the heavenly and eternal good of man." [1] Hereupon still further grounds for the truth of this religion are derived from its " beginnings, progress, power, and effects " ("initiis, progressu, vi et effectis ").   But with regard to its " power and effect " the Catechism knows of nothing else to say than this : " first, because it has been impossible to suppress this religion by any counsel or craft, by any power or might of men; then because it put an end to all the old religions, with the exception of the Jewish, in which it recognised a character showing that it had proceeded from God, although it was appointed to flourish only till the advent of Christ, the Master, so to speak, of a more perfect piety." [2]   All this applies only to the New Testament.   The trustworthiness of the Old Testament is proved in the briefest way in the last paragraph : the genuine writings of the New Testament attest the Old Testament, therefore it is equally trustworthy.   In the whole of this abstract line of statement, there is almost nothing that has religious worth save the distinguishing between the Old and New Testaments.   But even this is cancelled again in the end.   Evidently Faustus had not the courage openly to reject the Old Testament ; neither had he the capacity to show how Old and New Testaments represented different stages.   On closer inspection, however, the *rational* demonstration of the absolute worth of Holy Scripture is extremely uncertain and therefore irrational.   It is the first, and therefore it is an important attempt to establish the authority of Holy Scripture, *without making an appeal to faith :* the " service " (λατρεία) is to

---

[1] "Nam illa quidem cælestem vitæ sanctimoniam, hæc vero cæleste et æternum hominis bonum comprehendunt."

[2] " Primo quod hæc religio nullo consilio nec astu, nulla vi nullaque hominum potentia supprimi potuerit ; deinde quod omnes priscas religiones sustulerit, excepta Judaica, quam illa pro ejusmodi agnovit quæ a deo profecta fuerit, licet ad Christi tamquam perfectioris pietatis magistri adventum solummodo vigere debuerit. "

show itself as " reasonable " (λογική), but unfortunately *only* as
" reasonable." What an undertaking it was for a Church to
provide itself with such a Catechism : we must go back to the
times of Abelard, nay, even, of the Apologists, to find something
similar in Church history ! Only to our age does this wisdom
appear trivial, after its having reproduced itself in manifold forms
in the eighteenth century. It was certainly not trivial at the
beginning of the seventeenth century ; but it was devoid of all
religious spirit, and at bottom not more " logical" than the
Catechisms of those on the other side.—The two following
chapters (" on the sufficiency and perspicuity of Holy Scripture,"
pp. 11-17) are treated according to the same method. Scripture
is sufficient, because the faith which worketh by love is contained in it " as far as is sufficient " (" quantum satis "). To the
question, how far that applies to faith, the reply is given :
" In Scripture the faith is most perfectly taught, *that God exists
and that He recompenses. This, however, and nothing else is the
faith that is to be directed to God and Christ.*" Who does not
recall here the Nominalistic theologians, and those Popes
(Innocent IV.) who asserted that the Christian only needs to
have faith in God as the recompenser, while with regard to the
rest of the doctrines fides implicita is enough! The fides
implicita is thrown aside—Socinianism has reached its maturity!
In what follows the commands regarding love are entirely
co-ordinated with faith ; but then the question is raised, whether
reason is necessary in religion, if the Bible contains everything
in perfect form. To this the reply runs : " Yes, indeed, the use
of right reason is great in things that pertain to salvation, since
without it it is impossible either to grasp with certainty the
authority of Holy Scripture, or to understand those thing that
are contained in it, *or to deduce some things from other things*, or,
in fine, to recall them that they may be applied. *Therefore when
we say that Scripture is sufficient for salvation, we not merely do
not exclude right reason, but we altogether include it.*" [1] In what

---

[1] "Immo vero magnus rectæ rationis in rebus ad salutem spectantibus usus est, cum
sine ea nec sacrarum litterarum auctoritas certo deprehendi, nec ea, quæ in illis con-
tinentur, intelligi, *nec alia ex aliis colligi*, nec denique ad usum revocari possint.
*Itaque cum sacras litteras sufficere ad salutem dicimus, rectam rationem non tantum
non excludimus, sed omnino includimus.*"

a childlike way clear understanding is here introduced into religion ! Certainly it belongs in some way to it, and it means an advance in theology that has significance for the world's history, when there is the desire to throw off all the burdens that had been heaped up by the old world on the Christian religion, its mysticism, its Platonism, its total-world-knowledge, in order to justify the religion—as it is to be derived from its classic source —before the human understanding alone. But a more naïve form of expression cannot be used than that employed in the Catechism : " We include reason." With what do we include it ? what kind of reason is it which must not be excluded ? where does it come in ? and what scope must be allowed to it ? It is only since Kant's time that men have begun to answer these questions. Previous to that time the controversy between the Socinians and their opponents was a nyktomachy (battle in the dark). After this the Catechism discards the " traditions," and at the same time carries on a polemic against the Romish Church. In the section on the perspicuity of Holy Scripture, there is importance in the distinction drawn between what is essential to salvation and what is not. Altogether there appears here the advantage of reasonable reflection.[1]

Section II. (pp. 18-23) treats of the way of salvation. In spite of his reason man was unable to find out this way of himself, *because he was mortal* (here the element characteristic of the ancient Church appears in unconcealed form). The Catechism places the greatest weight upon the fact (compare the Nominalist doctrine) that Adam was created as a mortal man, subject to all ills. The image of God consisted simply in dominion over the lower creatures (the strongest opposition here to Augustine, Thomas, and Luther, at the same time a view which sets aside every religious thought). The Scripture passages which represent death as having come into the world through sin were got quit of by a process of exegetical juggling :

[1] On religion, Holy Scripture, and reason, see Fock, l.c., pp. 291-413. Because the Bible and reason (the latter as a receptive and *critical* organ) are represented as the foundations of the Christian religion, it was a current dictum among the Socinians that Christianity is supra, not contra rationem. The Nominalistic doctrine had taught the " contra rationem."

Rom. V. 12. treats, not of mortality, but of *eternal* death. Only in the second place is attention directed to the Fall: man is also *made liable to death* for the reason that Adam transgressed a manifest commandment of God. "Whence it further came about that he involved his entire posterity along with himself in the same sentence of death, there being added, however, in the case of each adult, his own sin, the gravity of which is then increased owing to the manifest law of God which men had transgressed." [1] The exposition is not clear here. To the question, again, why then man, though he be mortal, could not himself find out the way of salvation, an answer is given which betrays at once the Scotistic conception of God: "because both so great a reward and the sure method of attaining it *depended entirely on God's judgment and counsel;* but if God Himself does not reveal them, what man can search out and know with certainty His counsels and decrees?" [2] This answer has a very religious ring; but the great moralists left quite out of sight here the moral law: *the way of salvation is simply determined by the absolute will of God.* But what is the nature of this way? [3] The Catechism answers quite evangelically with John XVII. 3. But wherein consists the knowledge of God and Christ? "By that knowledge we understand, not some bare knowledge of God and Christ, consisting only in speculation, but the knowledge *conjoined with its effect, i.e.,* with the life conformed to and agreeing with it"; [4] for so it is taught in 1st John II., 3 f. Compare with this Luther's exposition of this passage, in order to

---

[1] "Unde porro factum est, ut universam suam posteritatem secum in eadem mortis jura traxerit, accedente tamen cujusvis in adultioribus proprio delicto, cujus deinde vis per apertam dei legem, quam homines transgressi fuerant, aucta est."

[2] "Quia et tantum præmium et certa illud consequendi ratio ex solo dei arbitrio ac consilio pependet ; dei autem consilia ac decreta ipso non revelante quis hominum indagare ac certo potest cognoscere?"

[3] The way of salvation has as its goal the vita æterna ; as man is by nature mortal, God has led him by the Christian religion into a new mode of being. That would have been necessary, even if sin had not entered. We have here a perfect reproduction of the doctrine of Theodore (of Mopsuestia) of the two Katastases; see Vol. III., p. 280 f.

[4] "Per cognitionem istam non nudam aliquam et in sola speculatione consistentem dei et Christi notitiam intelligimus, sed—*cum suo effectu,* h. e. vita illi conformi ac conveniente conjunctam."

feel convinced that Socinianism has nothing in common with the Reformation. It is Ultra-Catholicism that it here teaches; there is nothing whatever said of *faith* (of fear, love, and trust); everything applies simply to the knowledge of God and Christ (notitia dei et Christi) and a holy life.

Section III. (pp. 23-45) treats of the knowledge of God as "the Supreme Lord of all things" ("supremus rerum omnium dominus"). Here we meet everywhere with Scotistic thoughts. The idea that God is the absolutely arbitrary One, and that this attribute is the highest that can be asserted of Him, cannot be more strictly formulated than in the sentence (p. 23): "The right, and the supreme power, to decree whatsoever He wills, as concerning all other things, so also concerning us, even in those matters with which no other power has to do, as, for example, our thoughts, hidden as these may be in the innermost recesses of our hearts, *to which He can give laws and appoint rewards and penalties according to His own judgment.*"[1] How much higher is Thomas's position with regard to the conception of God! The thought that God is the Being in whom we may confide was unknown to the Socinians. On the other hand, the doctrine of the *Unity of God* is very distinctly wrought out— although with Tertullian's (see the Treatise adv. Prax.), or the Arian limitation, which is meant to prepare the way for the Socinian Christology (p. 25): "Nothing renders it impossible that that one God should share that dominion and power with others, and has shared it, though Scripture asserts that He alone has power and dominion."[2] The attributes of God are then dealt with in quite an external way, *i.e.*, apart from any relation to faith. Here the old Scholastic method has become

[1] "Jus et potestas summa, ut de ceteris rebus omnibus, ita et de nobis quicquid velit statuendi, etiam in iis, ad quæ nulla alia potestas pertingit, ut sunt cogitationes nostræ, quamvis in intimis recessibus cordis abditæ, *quibus ille pro arbitrio leges ponere et præmia ac pœnas statuere potest.*"

[2] "Nihil prohibet, quominus ille unus deus imperium potestatemque cum aliis communicare possit et communicaverit, licet Scriptura asserat, eum solum esse qui sit potens ac dominator." See also p. 32, where it is correctly shown that in Scripture the word "God" has a double meaning, (1) as principle and Lord of all things, (2) "eum denotat, qui potestatem aliquam sive cælestem sive in terris inter homines summam, aut qui potentiam virtutemque omni humana majorem ab uno illo deo habet t sic deitatis unius illius dei aliqua ratione particeps est."

entirely without substance : God's eternity is His being without beginning or end ; His omnipotence has its limits merely in
contradictions in terms (contradictio in adjecto) (p. 26). To
the question, how far the knowledge (notitia) of the divine
attributes is essential to salvation, a number of answers are
given, all of which are only loosely related to faith. It is a
poor—indeed an objectionable—thesis that is laid down when
it is said (p. 27), that to believe that God is "supremely just"
("summe justus") is necessary to salvation, because thereby we
are persuaded that He will hold to His promises, or when (p. 28)
the belief in God's higher wisdom is held necessary "that we
may have no doubt that even our heart, than which nothing is
more difficult to explore, *from which, moreover, our obedience is
chiefly estimated*, is forthwith and without ceasing scrutinised
and known by Him."[1]   On the other hand the doctrine of the
Trinity is held as not necessary, but only as "extremely useful"
("vehementer utile") for salvation—a bad concession (p. 30).[2]
The proof that is brought forward against this doctrine is in the
first place rational proof (essentia = persona), in the second place
scriptural proof.   Here the Socinians did excellent work, and
delivered exegesis from the ban of dogma. The arguments,
especially the exegetico-polemical, are for the most part un-
answerable. But on the other hand, the Socinians entered as
little into the fundamental confession which dominates the
utterances of Scripture, as into the religious tendencies which
determined the ecclesiastical doctrine.[3]   The concluding line of
proof, which aims at showing that the ecclesiastical doctrine of
the Trinity is dangerous, and the Socinian doctrine of God
"very useful for salvation," is not invalid, but very pithless.[4]   In

[1] "Ut nihil dubitemus, etiam cor nostrum, quo ad perscrutandum nihil est difficilius,
illi prorsus et semper perspectum atque cognitum esse, e quo etiam obedientia nostra
potissimum æstimatur."

[2] See also p. 40 : "hæc opinio (the doctrine of the Trinity) damnare non videtur
eum, cui nulla erroris suspicio mota est."   That is also a Catholic thought (not the
material heresy, but only the formal, condemns).

[3] See Fock II., pp. 454-477, whose criticism, however, of the ecclesiastical doctrine
and of Socinianism were determined by Hegel's philosophy.

[4] "Ista opinio primum unius dei fidem facere convellere et labefactare potest . . .
secundo gloriam unius dei, qui tantum pater Christi est, obscurat, dum eam ad aliud,
qui pater non est, transfert ; tertio ea quæ deo illi uno et summo sunt indigna continet,

the short chapter immediately following, on "the will of God," the placing together of what men knew of the divine will prior to the law (ante legem) and what they knew through the law (per legem) is instructive. Prior to the law they already knew (1) the creation of the world by God, (2) the providence of God with regard to particular matters (!) (providentia dei de singulis rebus), (3) the rewarding of those who seek Him (remuneratio eorum, qui ipsum quærunt). "Under this third point there is included a certain knowledge of those things which are well-pleasing to God, and by attending to which He is obeyed, while it is fitting that no one of those things that were known of old and prior to the law should have been omitted from the law of Moses" (p. 42 sq.).[1] Through the law (per legem) they became acquainted with the decalogue. Thus faith in the providence of God was included by the Socinians also in Pre-Christian knowledge.

In Section IV. (pp. 45-144) there follows the knowledge of the person of Christ. On this much-disputed point the Catechism goes most into particulars. What the Nominalists had spoken of as hypothetical—that God could also have redeemed us by a man—is regarded, now that the authority of ecclesiastical tradition has disappeared, as actual. In point of fact Socinianism has no ground in its own premises for recognising the Godhead of Christ, and if the gospels are brought in to determine the alternative, was Christ a God or a man, the answer cannot be doubtful. But Socinianism did not go on to deal with a deeper inquiry—namely, whether Christ does not so bring us to God that it is implied "that God Himself acts," and whether He has

deum scil. illum unum et altissimum alicujus esse filium vel spiritum et sic habere patrem et sui auctorem, etc. . . . denique alienis a religione Christiana magno est ad eam amplectandam impedimento" (pp. 38 sq.).

[1] "In hoc vero tertio membro comprehenditur cognitio quædam eorum, quæ deo grata sunt et quorum observatione ipsi obeditur, quorum olim et ante legem cognitorum nullum in ipsa lege Mosis fuisse prætermissum consentaneum est." To the question why it is necessary to know that God created the world the brief and curt answer is given : (1) *quod deus velit*, ut id credamus eaque res ad summam dei gloriam pertineat,* (2) "quod nisi certo id nobis persuasum esset, nullam causam haberemus credendi, talem esse de rebus omnibus dei providentiam, qualem ante diximus atque ea ratione animum ad ei obediendum non induceremus." The first is Scotistic ; the second is at all events not spoken from the standpoint of faith.

not become that One in whom God has made Himself
apprehensible in human history. Besides, in this section upon
Christ it has not drawn up its positions from the standpoint of
the community redeemed by Christ from death and sin. The
negative criticism is here again almost at every point unanswer-
able, in some places masterly ; the positive assertions as to what
Christ is to His own fall short in respect of substance of the
most attenuated doctrines of the most arid Scholastics : Christ
is a mortal man, who has become immortal, but no ordinary
man ; for from the beginning He was, through the miraculous
birth, the only begotten Son of God, was sanctified by the
Father and sent into the world, endowed with divine wisdom
and might, raised again ("thus, as it were, begotten anew,
especially as in this way He issued forth like unto God in His
immortality "),[1] and finally invested with a power equal to God's.[2]
Even while dwelling on earth He was "God" (by reason of
the divine might and power the radiance of which appeared in
the mortal); but He is God now in a much higher degree. It is
evident that these declarations, so far as they are a description
of Jesus, coincide pretty much with the biblical testimonies ; but
it is equally manifest that they are entirely worthless, because
they lay down simply the product of exegesis, and are imposed
upon faith as a law. The much shorter and much simpler
testimony of Paul, " No one can call Jesus *Lord* but by the Holy
Ghost," is of immeasurably greater value, because it knows only
of a confession of Christ that is *divinely wrought*, and thereby
assigns to Christology its proper place. Socinianism, however,
proceeds as the old School did. It establishes the doctrine of
the person of Christ chiefly from Scripture ; for this the old
School used Scripture and tradition, and therein had an
advantage ; for from tradition it obtained guiding lines.
Socinianism merely occupied itself with bringing out the

---

[1] "Sic denuo veluti genitus, præsertim cum hac via immortalitate deo similis
evaserit."

[2] Dilthey (Archiv. f. Gesch. d. Philos., Vol. VI., p. 90) : "The Socinian Christology
is conditioned by the religious horizon of the Humanistic system of culture, according
to which messengers of God of different degrees of dignity are to be recognised as
witnessed to by reports of ancient history."

Scripture doctrine exegetically and with avoiding at the same
time too sharp a conflict with reason.

If we take a combined view of the Socinian doctrines of the
person and work of Christ, it may be expressed briefly as
follows: By virtue of a free decree God has determined that
mortal men shall be raised to a new condition, foreign to their
natural being ; that is, that they shall be guided to eternal life
(second katastasis). For this, likewise by a free decision, He
has raised up the man Jesus, whom He equipped through the
miraculous birth with divine powers. This man has, as *Prophet*,
brought the perfect divine legislation, inasmuch as he explained
the decalogue and gave it a deeper meaning ; he further distinctly announced the promise of eternal life, and, finally, gave
the example of the perfect moral life, which he ratified in his
death. " He transcends the limits of the Old Testament, inasmuch as he reformed the Mosaic law, added to it new moral
precepts and sacramental appointments, gave a strong impulse
to the observance of these by the promises of eternal life and
the Holy Spirit, and assured men of the general purpose of
God to forgive the sins of those who repent and seek to reform
themselves. It is admitted that no man can perfectly fulfil the
divine law ; and justification, therefore, results not from works,
but from faith. *But faith means that trust in the law-giver
which includes in itself actual obedience to Him, so far as that is
practicable to men.* Now Christ, by his resurrection, by his
having obtained divine power, guarantees to all those who in
faith as thus meant attach themselves to him, in the first instance actual liberation from sin according to the measure in
which they follow the impulse he gives them to newness and
betterness of life, and, further, the attainment of the supernatural
end set before them ; and also by the Holy Spirit, which he
bestows, the previous assurance of eternal life, while with the
commencement of this life the forgiveness of sins of the individual is complete."[1]

[1] Ritschl, l.c., I., p. 315 f. Ritschl very correctly goes on to say : " In this we
have a palpable indication of the practical antithesis between Socinianism and Church
Protestantism. In the latter the forgiveness of sin is regarded as the primary
principle, in the former as the more remote result of the Christian life. The

The following particulars are worthy of note: (1) In the doctrine of the person of Christ the divinity of Jesus is asserted, His divine *nature* rejected (p. 48: "if we understand by the terms divine nature or substance the divine essence itself, we do not in this sense recognise the divine nature in Christ "[1]) and the ecclesiastical view is argued against on the ground of reason and Scripture. The Socinians found special difficulties here in the passages of Scripture which assert pre-existence of Christ. They sought to show that many passages when looked at closely do not contain pre-existence, and that others can be explained by assuming that Christ (like Paul) was caught up during his earthly life into heaven, and there beheld the eternal life and heard the perfect commands, so that John could say of Him that he came from heaven; finally, it is to be observed that much is said in Scripture "figuratively" ("figurate") (see pp. 48-144, in particular p. 146 sq.).[2]

2. The doctrine of the three offices lies at the basis of the Socinian account of the work of Christ. The prophetic office, however, is dealt with most fully (Section V. and VI., pp. 144-316). In fact, the whole work of Christ, so far as it was clear to the Socinians, was placed under this heading, and we can easily see that it was an accommodation to the old doctrine when they added the kingly and high-priestly offices. Socinianism can really gather up everything in the proposition, that Christ has perfectly revealed to us the divine will. The scheme

opposition of Socinianism to the doctrine of Christ's satisfaction, which lies at the foundation of the former view, thus admits of explanation from this point; but this Socinian estimate of the forgiveness of sins as an accident of the Christian life is at the same time an indication that in Christ the founder merely of an ethical school is discerned, and not the founder of a religious fellowship. And if this contrariety does not always show itself with clearness, if rather it must be allowed that Socinianism nevertheless establishes peculiar religious aims, regulative principles, and conditions, the circumstance is to be accounted for from the fact that Socinianism, as being the first attempt at the exhibition of Christianity as an ethical school, was still exposed to the influences of a view of Christianity, which up to that time had exclusively prevailed, and from which it had in principle withdrawn itself."

[1] "Si naturæ seu substantiæ divinæ nomine ipsam dei essentiam intelligimus, non agnoscimus hoc sensu divinam in Christo naturam."

[2] It should always be remembered that the Socinians were the first to liberate themselves in dealing with the Christological passages of the New Testament from the ban of the Platonising dogmatic.

of the high-priestly office is mainly made use of for controverting the Church doctrine.

3. For the prophetic office of Christ the following scheme is
obtained (p. 148): " it comprehends, first, the precepts, then the
perfect promises of God, then, finally, *the way and manner in
which we ought to conform ourselves both to the precepts and
promises of God.*"[1] This is at the same time regarded as the
content of the New Covenant, so that faith is not even
mentioned. The first chapter now treats of the commands
which Christ has added to the law (pp. 149-209).; for the divine
commands consist of the decalogue and the commands which
Christ and the apostles added to it after discarding the ceremonial law. This discarding is looked upon as the transformation of the severity and rigour of the law (severitas et
rigor legis) into grace and mercy (gratia et misericordia). Yet
the commands that relate to the rightfulness of civil government are still kept in force; " nay, even the Church of Christ
implies the State, since it is nowhere congregated save in the
State."[2] But it is quite certain that Socinianism did not yet
rise above the mediæval suspicion of the State and its legal
ordinances, as can be seen especially from p. 194 sq. After this
the decalogue is now expounded (p. 154 sq.), into which (under
the first commandment) an exposition of the Lord's prayer is
introduced. Christ added the Lord's Prayer to the first
precept; and he still further added to this precept the injunction
that he should himself receive divine worship. The worship of
Christ as divine is vindicated at length (pp. 164-176) in opposition to Nonadorantism.[3] In the second chapter (pp. 209-221)

[1] "Comprehendit tum præcepta, tum promissa dei perfecta, tum denique *modum
ac rationem, qui nos et præceptis et promissionibus dei conformare debeamus.*"

[2] "Quin et ipsa Christi ecclesia rempublican supponit, cum non alibi quam in
republica congregetur" (p. 153).

[3] "Ipsum etiam dominum Jesum pro eo, qui in nos potestatem habeat divinam,
istoque sensu *pro deo agnoscere* ac porro ei confidere ac divinum honorem exhibere
tenemur." The honour that is to be given to Christ consists (p. 165) both in adoratio
and invocatio. This is established from Holy Scripture, and from the conviction of
faith that he is our Lord, who can and will help us. The section relating to this is
among the best the Catechism contains. Of those who are not willing to worship
and invoke Christ it is said on p. 172 sq. : "eos, qui id facere nolunt, Christianos
hactenus non esse, quamvis alioqui Christi nomen profiteantur et doctrinæ illius se

there follows the statement of the special commands of Christ,
so far as these have a *moral* character. The Catechism distinguishes here three commands: (1) trustful and constant joy
in God, unceasing prayer in the name of Christ with the sure
belief in the divine help, and hearty thanksgiving, (2) abstaining
from love of the world, *i.e.*, from the lust of the eye, the lust of
the flesh, and the pride of life, (3) self-denial and courageous
patience. Especially regarding the commands of the first class
the Catechism understood how to say beautiful things ; but
what it sets forth here was placed in no definite connection with
Christ and with faith. In the third and fourth chapters (pp.
221-228 ; 228-243) there follows the statement of the special
commands of Christ so far as these have a *ceremonial* character,
that is, of the commands connected with Baptism and the
Lord's Supper. This mode of view decides at once as to the
meaning Socinianism attributes to these observances. Baptism
is defined (p. 221) as " the rite of initiation by which men, after
obtaining knowledge of the doctrine of Christ and acquiring
faith in him, become bound to Christ and his disciples or are
enrolled in the Church, renouncing the world . . . *professing*,
besides, that they will regard the Father, Son, and Holy Spirit
as the only guide and master in religion, and in the whole of
their life and conversation, and by their ablution and immersion
and emersion, *declaring*, and as it were *exhibiting*, that they lay
aside the defilement of sin, that they are buried with Christ,
that they desire henceforth to die with Him and to rise to newness of life, and pledging themselves that they will really carry
this out, *receiving* also at the same time at which this profession
is made and this pledge taken *the symbol and sign* of the
remission of sins, *and even the remission itself*." [1] The words

adhærere dicant." There then follows a repudiation of the Catholic Mary and saint
worship.

[1] " Ritus initiationis, quo homines, agnita Christi doctrina et suscepta in eum fide,
Christo auctorantur et discipulis ejus seu ecclesiæ inscribuntur, renunciantes mundo
. . . *profitentes* vero se patrem et filium et spiritum sanctum pro unico duce et
magistro religionis totiusque vitæ et conversationis suæ habituros esse ipsaque sui
ablutione et immersione ac remersione *declarantes* ac veluti *repræsentantes*, se peccatorum sordes deponere, Christo consepeliri, proinde commori et ad vitæ novitatem
resurgere velle, utque id re ipsa præstent sese obstringentes, simul etiam hac pro-

that are added quite at the end—entirely unexpectedly and with nothing to introduce them—indicate an accommodation.[1] Baptism is in reality a confession, an undertaking of obligation, and a symbol. Infant baptism is rejected, but tolerated.[2] Its toleration was due to the fact that little importance generally was attached to all that was ceremonial. It is a serious error to associate regeneration with baptism. Socinianism therefore resolved to have nothing to do with the Sacrament as Sacrament. As in baptism immersion was accentuated, so the greatest stress was laid in the Eucharist on the *breaking of bread*, and it cannot be denied that Socinianism made a praiseworthy attempt to restore to this sacred observance its original meaning. But here also it avoided in a latitudinarian way uttering the last word; or, it avoided a complete separation between the ceremony and the forgiveness of sins, which are united in the words of institution.[3] Of the *word* in the Sacrament it took no account; here also, under the influence of its Biblicism and its obedience to the arbitrary commands of God and Christ, it was ready to believe and do what was *prescribed*. Thus the Socinians appear here also as mediæval Christians, although they have struck out the Sacraments. The definition of the "breaking of bread" is as follows (p. 228):

fessione et obligatione facta *symbolum* et *signum* remissionis peccatorum *ipsamque adeo remissionem accipientes*."

[1] The suspicion can scarcely at all be suppressed that many Socinians expressed themselves more positively than they had a right to do. Did they really estimate the formal authority of Holy Scripture so highly that they held everything as true that was contained in Scripture, even when it threw ridicule on their exegetical skill? I cannot persuade myself that this assumption is true, and believe that the "illuminist" element was more strongly developed among them than their writings would lead us to suppose. The philologist, Justus Lipsius, a man of no character but of keen insight, has in his famous characterisation of the Christian Confessions of his day described the Socinians as "hypocritæ docti." Faustus at all events was an exception.

[2] See p. 222: it is not according to the mind of the Apostles; but it is also no true baptism, for the form is not immersion; "quem tamen errorem adeo inveteratum et pervulgatum, præsertim circa rem ritualem, Christiana caritas tolerare suadet in iis, qui certeroquin pie vivant et alios, qui huic errori renuntiarunt, non insectentur, donec veritas magis magisque patescat."

On the words "for the forgiveness of sins" the Catechism is simply silent. In the case of baptism they are at least referred to.

" It has been appointed by Christ the Lord that those believing in Him shall together break and eat bread and drink of the cup, with the view of remembering Him or of proclaiming His death : and this must continue until He returns." [1] Christ instituted this rite, because the remembrance of His death is the remembrance of the most arduous part of His saving work. The Catholic, Lutheran, and Calvinistic doctrines of the Supper are expressly characterised as erroneous (p. 231), are controverted at length, and in opposition to them the symbolic doctrine is shown to be the correct one (p. 238 f.). Nowhere is any prominence given to a religious element ; the ceremony of breaking of bread is the confession of Christ and the remembrance of Him. There now follow—still under the head of the prophetic office—the two chapters on the promise of eternal life (pp. 243-248) and the Holy Spirit (pp. 248-259). The forgiveness of sins here occupies only a subordinate place ; for it is simply *a result* of the Christian life. The proposition : " in eternal life there is included at the same time forgiveness of sins " [2] (p. 243) corresponds with ancient Christianity as it developed itself from the days of the Apologists, but it is opposed to the Pauline-Lutheran thought : " Where forgiveness of sins is, there is life and peace." On the other hand, it is a *primitive Christian* thought, for the assertion of which great credit is due to Socinianism, that the obtaining of the Holy Spirit (consecutio spiritus s.) precedes eternal life (vita aeterna) and produces it. Faustus re-discovered this thought as a biblical theologian, and gave an excellent formal unfolding of it. But how can the meaning of this "obtaining of the Holy Spirit" be correctly and impressively stated, if forgiveness of sins is still left entirely out of view, or is taken account of only as a factor in eternal life? [3] This life itself is described (p. 245) in the most super-

---

[1] " Est Christi domini institutum, ut fideles ipsius panem simul frangant et comedant et ex calice bibant, ipsius commemorandi seu mortem ejus annunciandi causa : quod permanere in adventum ipsius oportet."

[2] " In vita aeterna simul comprehensa est peccatorum remissio."

[3] Certainly at p. 244, and previous to the description of eternal life, a definition of forgiveness of sins is given, which seems to embrace very much. But, first, it quite hangs in the air (it is given without any indication of the connection with what precedes or what follows) ; and, secondly, it entirely omits any reference to Christ

ficial way—it appears as the dregs of the old ecclesiastical dogmatic : "a life that is at no time to come to an end, that is to be spent evermore in delight and divine happiness in heaven itself with God and Christ and the blessed angels."[1]   Eternal life cannot be described otherwise, if it is not estimated by the dread and unrest of the soul which, without Christ, finds in the thought of God only death.   Instead of entering into the religious meaning of eternal life, the Catechism occupies itself with the juvenile Scholastic questions, whether eternal life was already promised in the Old Testament, whether even the men living before Christ could attain to blessedness, etc.   On the other hand, in the section on the gift of the Holy Ghost, there is pointed out by Faustus in the New Testament much more than he was himself in a position to understand.   There is an infringement of his scheme—"the outer word of Scripture and reason"—when it is said (p. 251) that even the former can indeed give rise to a certain confidence in God, "nevertheless for implanting in our souls a firmer and more certain hope, in the power of which we shall be able to continue unsubdued amidst all temptations, it seems required that the promise set before us from without by the Gospel shall be sealed within by God through the Holy Spirit."[2]   But how disillusioned we are by what immediately follows, which shows *that the Holy Spirit is only given to him who already believes the Gospel* (p. 252). Faith therefore is man's own peculiar work, and is always something preliminary : for faith the Holy Spirit is not necessary. Here again we have the clearest evidence that the fundamental spirit of the Socinians is Catholic, and this impression is not weakened when immediately afterwards a keen polemic is

---

and to faith.   We can only conclude from this that the "gratuita a reatu ac pœnis peccatorum liberatio" has nothing to do with the *work* of Christ, but is an unmotived decision of God, of which Christ, among others, has imparted knowledge.   That this is really so, see below.

[1] "Vita nullo tempore finienda, gaudio ac voluptate prorsus divina in ipsis coelis cum deo et Christo beatisque angelis agenda."

[2] "Verumtamen ad inserendam animis nostris firmiorem et certiorem spem, cujus virtute in omnibus tentationibus invicti subsistamus, videtur requiri, ut ea promissio exterius per evangelium proposita, interius a deo in cordibus nostris per spiritum sanctum obsignetur."

carried on against Catholicism on the ground of its regarding
the Holy Spirit as a person (p. 253 sq.).

Very loosely attached to these discussions of the commands
and promises of Christ, as forming the content of His prophetic
office, are five excursus, "on the confirmation of the divine will"
(pp. 259-261), "on the death of Christ" (pp. 261-288), "on
faith" (pp. 288-293), "on free will" (pp. 293-316), and "on
justification" (pp. 316-319).[1] We see here distinctly the effort
to bring the whole material under the head of Christ's office as
Teacher. The corroboration of the revelation of the divine will
is to be sought for (1) in the sinlessness of Jesus, (2) in His
miracles, (3) in His death. The necessity for His death is
proved (p. 261 f.) on various grounds, from which—Scripture
being followed—there are not absent His "having died for our
sins" ("mortuum esse pro peccatis nostris"), the establishment
of faith in the forgiveness of sins, and the preservation of men
from the heaviest penalties. But the chief thing is, that Christ
had to demonstrate His doctrine under the most difficult circumstances, and on that account sealed it by the most igno-
minious death. But from this point the line of argument passes
at once to the resurrection ; the death of Christ yields "confirmation of the divine will" ("confirmatio divinæ voluntatis"),
only because the death was followed by the resurrection. To
the objection, "I perceive that in the work of our salvation
more depends on the resurrection than on the death of Christ,"[2]
the reply is given (not without ground in Scripture), "to this
extent, certainly, that the death of Christ would have been
useless and ineffectual, unless it had been followed by Christ's
resurrection."[3] But why, then, does Scripture frequently derive
everything from the death ? "Because even the death of
Christ, the Son of God, in itself, when the re-awakening by
resurrection takes place, has henceforth a pre-eminent and
unique power in procuring for us salvation, as we have shown

---

[1] "De confirmatione divinæ voluntatis," "de morte Christi," "de fide," "de
libero arbitrio," "de justificatione."

[2] "Plus in resurrectione quam in Christi morte situm esse in nostræ salutis negotio,
perspicio."

[3] "Hactenus sane, quatenus mors Christi inutilis et inefficax futura fuisset, nisi eam
consecuta fuisset Christi resurrectio" (p. 267).

(but that has been shown only very vaguely).   Then, because it
was the way to the resurrection and exaltation of Christ ; for
the former could not be attained by Him without death, owing
to the nature of the case, nor could the latter, owing to the
counsel and arrangement of God.   And, lastly, because among
all the things which God and Christ did for the sake of our
salvation, Christ's death was by far the most arduous work, and
the most evident token of the love of God and of Christ for
us."[1]   This solution is by no means obvious ; why is death a
proof of love?   The Catechism does not enter more minutely
into this, but now directs itself against the doctrine of penal
satisfaction (p. 268 sq.).   It is well known that this point was
brought out in the keenest light by the Socinians.[2]

In his " Prælectiones theologicæ," Faustus has contested in
an exhaustive way the necessity and possibility of satisfaction,
i.e., he has controverted the thought in the same way in which
it had been formerly framed.   Just here, however, he only required to continue the work of the later Scholasticism, to which
nothing had become more uncertain than the rational interpretation of the value of Christ's death by the thought of a strictly
necessary equivalent.   Faustus contested the necessity of
satisfaction from the basis of his Scotistic conception of God :
God is by no means required by His nature to punish sin, and
on that account to impose a penalty in all cases, even though it
be on the innocent ; He stands, rather, above all compulsion,
and in virtue of His absoluteness can act as He will.   Even
Scripture says that He is sometimes wrathful, sometimes pitiful,
but in the New Testament His unfathomable mercy is proclaimed.   Least of all can we deduce satisfaction from His

[1] " Propterea quod et ipsa per se Christi filii dei mors, resurrectione animata,
eximiam prorsus et singularem vim habeat in comparanda nobis salute, ut ostendimus.
Deinde quod via fuerit ad resurrectionem et exaltationem Christi.   Ad illum enim
per rei naturam, ad hanc per dei consilium et constitutionem sine morte pervenire
non poluit.   Denique quod ex omnibus, quæ deus et Christus nostræ salutis causa
fecit, mors Christi opus fuerit maxime arduum et caritatis erga nos dei et Christi
evidentissimum argumentum."

[2] See Fock, l.c., p. 615 ff.   Ritschl, l.c., p. 316 ff.   In his system of Christian
doctrine, Strauss adopted almost all the arguments of the Socinians.   In more recent
times Philippi especially has tried to controvert in detail the Socinian theses.

righteousness ; for to punish the innocent for the guilty is unrighteous.   Neither can a necessity for penalty be derived from
the nature of sin ; for in relation to God sin is an injury done to
His honour ; but such injury can be unconditionally overlooked.
But the idea of satisfaction is, further, an impossible one, as it
leads to pure contradictions ; for (I.) remission and satisfaction
are mutually exclusive ; if God has remitted sin, He requires no
satisfaction ; if He accepts satisfaction, there is no need of remission, since, in this case, the debtor is only under an illusion ;
(II.) but even assuming that remission and satisfaction could
exist together, yet in this case satisfaction in the sense of
substitution is excluded ; for (1) one can take over fines imposed
on another, but not penalties that are personal, and that culminate in the penalty of death ; in this case transference is unrighteousness.   No doubt innocent persons frequently suffer
with the guilty ; yet if that has not been brought about through
being involved in the sin of the guilty, such suffering is not
penal suffering.   But neither can it be asserted that Christ
suffered as the representative and head of humanity ; for He
did not as yet bear that character during the period of His
earthly life, nor has His suffering death exempted anyone from
death ; (2) Christ's positive fulfilment of the law can have no
substitutionary worth, for to this Christ was morally bound, and
His fulfilment of the law secures exemption for no one ; (3) the
supposition that Christ both suffered substitutionally, and fulfilled the law substitutionally, contains contradictory elements,
for if the one thing took place, there was no further need of
the other taking place ; (III.) but even if the vicarious penal
suffering were possible, it would not attain its end, *i.e.*, it would
not provide an actual equivalent ; for (1) an individual equivalent
can always have validity only for an individual case, not for the
guilt of all men ; a single death is a substitute only for one
death ; (2) it was necessary that the representative should
really die the eternal death, but Christ was raised up ; (3) if it
is urged against this that Christ was God, and therefore His
suffering has an infinite worth for God, it must be said that on
that assumption there was no need that God should subject
Him to so much distress, because even the smallest suffering of

the God-man would in that case have been enough ; but the appeal to the Godhead of Christ is lacking in force, because the Godhead is not capable of suffering. If the Godhead of Christ is nevertheless taken into the calculation, yet we may not on that account deify also the suffering itself, which was displayed in temporary and finite acts. This suffering must be estimated as finite, and hence it would have been necessary that the God-man should take upon Him an infinite number of satisfactions ; (IV.) the notions of vicarious satisfaction and of imputation are mutually exclusive ; that is to say, where the former has been rendered, everything further is excluded, the acceptance (acceptatio) is itself implied in the satisfaction ; if the orthodox doctrine asserts in reply to this, that God accepts the work of Christ on our behalf by an act of grace (acceptilatio), then His work is no satisfaction ; for there is "acceptilatio" only where no equivalent work is offered. Therefore the doctrine that God reckons the satisfaction of Christ only to faith destroys the whole scheme of vicarious penal suffering ; for Christ by no means wrought a perfect satisfaction, if it has only conditional validity ; (V.) the doctrine of vicarious penal suffering blunts the conscience, leads easily to moral laxity, and checks the efforts of the will to fulfil the divine law ; (VI.) this doctrine is not contained in Scripture, and is in antagonism to clear passages of Scripture (Cat. p. 270 : " The Scriptures testify everywhere, but especially in the New Testament, that God gratuitously remits to men their sins ; but nothing is more opposed to gratuitous remission than a satisfaction of such a kind as they wish "[1]). On the other hand, Faustus, like Duns and the Nominalists, will not exclude the thought of the *merit* of Christ as bearing upon our guilt. This merit, however, does not come within the system of duty and action which is imposed upon us.[2] Faustus was not confuted by the orthodox, in so far as

[1] " Scripturæ passim deum peccata hominibus gratuito remittere testantur, potissimum vero sub novo fœdere : at remissioni gratuitæ nil adversatur magis, quam ejusmodi qualem volunt satisfactio."

[2] See Ritschl, l.c., p. 319, whom I have followed also in reproducing the criticism of the satisfaction doctrine by Faustus : " If the strict sense of the conception of duty is to have its validity maintained, then—for Faustus—all merit of Christ for Himself and for us is excluded. ' Nihil fecit, quod ipsi a deo injunctum non fuisset. Ubi

he demonstrated the worthlessness of the *juristic* thought-material with which they worked.   But even in other respects his contemporaries were unable to controvert him, because they themselves did not clearly discern the tendencies of the form of doctrine that had come to them traditionally, and hence were as little able to correct the mistakes in their mode of building up doctrine as to bring its excellences successfully to view.   In falling back upon the position that the qualities of righteousness and mercy exist in God with equal claims, they guarded, indeed, the holiness of the law of the good, but did not find escape from contradictions.

The appended section *on faith* is introduced with the idea, that, now that the commands and promises have become known, a statement must follow on the way in which one has to "adjust" himself to them.   This way, it is said (p. 288), is *faith*, "by which we both embrace with our soul the promises of Christ, and henceforth seek, to the best of our ability, to keep His precepts." [1]   Yet the Catholic notion of faith forthwith appears in what is added : "*which faith both makes our obedience more acceptable and well-pleasing to God, and supplies the defects of our obedience, provided it is sincere and earnest, and brings it about that we are justified by God.*" [2]   Thus it is the *actual* obedience

debitum, ibi nullum verum et proprium meritum.'   Thus it is only in a sense different from the proper one that the conception can be applied, what is presupposed being a particular divine decree and divine promise.   Now as the latter adds nothing to what is understood as dutifulness of action, it can only give rise to the conception of merit when in estimating action, not the dutifulness, but—by way of exception—the voluntariness is taken into account.   This thought comes to coincide substantially with the definition of the conception given by Duns and by Calvin.   And although Faustus opposes the latter, in so far as he relates—as Thomas did—the proper conception of merit to the legal estimation of an action, yet he was at one with Calvin in actually admitting the merit of Christ.   This is a new proof that the conceptions of the merit and of the satisfaction of Christ are derived from quite different modes of view.   Satisfaction is derived from the presupposition of a reciprocal relationship that rests upon a purely legal order ; merit from a reciprocal relationship which is moral, but is not conceived of from the highest point of view of law and duty."

[1] "Per quam et promissa Christi animo complectimur et porro præcepta ejus pro virili exsequimur."

[2] "Quæ fides et obedientiam nostram deo commendatiorem gratioremque facit et obedientiæ defectus, modo ea sit vera ac seria, supplet, utque a deo justificemur efficit."

that is the matter that mainly decides. This view is carried out
in the strictest possible way. No trace is to be found of the
evangelical attitude ; for the appended remark, that God over-
looks the deficiency of obedience for the sake of faith, also
contains a good Catholic thought. Catholicism puts in place
of this, submission to the Church, the fides implicita. This was
discarded by Socinianism ; but it, too, substitutes for it a
performance—the performance, namely, of faith. Thus it does
not pass beyond the Catholic system of things. This system it
endorses even in the details of its doctrinal deductions ; *e.g.*
(p. 288) ; "faith in Christ is taken in a two-fold sense ; for
sometimes it denotes that faith on which alone, *unless something
still further is added*, salvation does not follow ; sometimes that
faith on which alone salvation follows." [1] In the first case there
is meant faith without obedience, in the second case faith and
the works of love. The section on free will is here inserted, in
order to place over against the God of absolutism man with his
empty freedom, and in order to abolish the Augustinian-
Thomistic doctrines of predestination and original sin. [2] In

[1] "Fides in Christum duplici ratione sumitur ; interdum enim notat eam fidem,
quam solam, nisi adhuc aliquid aliud accedat, salus non consequitur ; interdum eam
quam solam salus consequitur."

[2] See p. 294 : "Lapsus Adæ, cum unus actus fuerit, vim eam, quæ depravare ipsam
naturam Adami, multo minus vero posterorum ipsius posset, habere non potuit . . .
non negamus tamen assiduitate peccandi naturam hominum labe quadam et ad
peccandum nimia proclivitate infectam esse, sed eam peccatum per se esse negamus."
As in the case of the Nominalists, the divine factor is only admitted as divinum
auxilium, as exterius (Holy Scripture), moreover, and interius. The way in which
the doctrine of the ordo salutis is wrought out quite resembles the way strenuously
maintained at that time by the Jesuits in opposition to Thomism. Of the doctrine
of predestination it is affirmed (p. 300): "totam religionem corruere facit et deo
multa inconvenientia attribuit." The chief passages usually appealed to in support
of predestination are minutely treated in the Catechism, and got rid of in the desired
way by exegetical art. The criticism of the Calvinistic doctrine of predestination
became everywhere the starting-point during the last third of the sixteenth century,
when what was contemplated was to weaken the confessional system of doctrine and
to make the demand for a real toleration arising from the nature of the subject itself.
See Coornhert's criticism as quoted by Dilthey (Archiv. f. Gesch. d. Philos., Vol. 5.
p. 491 ff.), Arminius and his disciples, etc. Yet it must not be forgotten that even
the consciousness of election itself gave rise, in one branch of the believers in it, to
the idea of toleration, or of the rights of the individual. Only the former, however,
saw it to be demanded that religious peace should be established "through setting
up universal principles of right and providing a simplified, general church theology."

the section on justification it is not the Catholic conception that makes its appearance, though that was necessarily to be expected after the explanation given of faith, but—strikingly enough—an evangelical view, deteriorated in the direction of laxity, and sadly perverted (p. 316): "there is justification when God regards us as righteous, or deals with us as if we had been quite righteous and innocent (!). But His way of doing this under the new covenant is by remitting our sins, and giving us eternal life."[1] This definition seems to fall entirely out of the lines of the fundamental Socinian view. Yet we must remember here, that even Pelagius paid reverence to the special character of the Christian religion. The Socinian proposition can only be understood when we (1) consider that the Socinians could not entirely break with Paulinism, and (2) take into account that justification meant very little for them. The chief thing is the obedience which gives proof of itself in fulfilment of the law. Side by side with this stands—as a special feature of the Christian religion—the promise of God to overlook certain defects in that obedience on the part of Christians. At this point the contact with Paulinism is sought for, and the *term* justification, as denoting forgiveness of sins, is introduced. More than this, however, is not done by the Catechism. It is satisfied when in three lines it has in a way included justification in its inventory. To say anything more regarding it is deemed unnecessary ; for the two pages which are elsewhere devoted to justification, deal with the unimportant question as to whether even the Pre-Christian fathers were justified.

4. The brevity of the chapters that still follow (" on the priestly office of Christ," pp. 320-331, " on the kingly office of Christ," pp. 331-339, " on the Church," pp. 340-355),[2] is in itself a proof that the religious doctrine has been virtually concluded when there has been explained the prophetic office of Christ (" praecepta et promissa dei "). But as these headings had to be taken up (according to holy Scripture), much is set forth

---

[1] " Justificatio est, cum nos deus pro justis habet seu ita nobis cum agit, ac si justi et innocentes plane fuissemus. Id vero ea ratione sub novo fœdere facit, ut nobis et peccata remittat et nos vita aeterna donet."

[2] " De munere Christi sacerdotali," " de munere Christi regio," " de ecclesia."

which does not fit into the doctrine, but as Biblical material
traverses it. This is especially apparent in the section on the
high-priestly office. Here the Catechism has not only emphasised the perpetual priesthood of Christ on the ground of
the Epistle to the Hebrews (p. 320 f.), but has also adopted the
thought of the perpetual "expiation of sins by Christ in
Heaven "[1] (p. 321 sq.) : "Jesus carries on in Heaven the expiation of our sins, inasmuch as He liberates us from the
penalties of sins by the virtue of His death, which he endured
for our sins according to the will of God. For a victim so precious, and an obedience so great as that of Christ, have the
perpetual power before God of defending from the penalties of
sins (as in Catholicism, the penalty, not the guilt, is the heaviest
burden) us who believe in Christ and who have died with Christ
that we may not live unto sin ; further, inasmuch as He perpetually guards us by His power, which He obtained in its fulness and absoluteness from the Father, and by His intercession
wards off from us the wrath of God, which was wont to be
poured out upon the wicked, this being what Scripture designates
His appearing for us ; then He frees us from the slavery of sin
itself, inasmuch as He binds us over to Himself, partly by that
same death which He suffered for us, partly by showing us in
His own person what is obtained by him who has avoided sin."[2]
It is expressly emphasised that only through His rising again
has Christ become the heavenly Priest in the full sense. In the
section on the kingly office it is first shown that Christ did not
raise Himself (p. 333 sq.). This proof claims—very suggestively
—the largest space ; it is followed only by unimportant explanations as to the nature of the resurrection body of Christ, the

---

[1] "Expiatio peccatorum per Christum in cælis."

[2] "Jesus in cælis expiationem peccatorum nostrorum peragit, dum a peccatorum
pœnis nos liberat virtute mortis suæ, quam pro peccatis nostris ex dei voluntate
subiit. Victima enim tam preciosa tantaque Christi obedientia perpetuam coram deo
vim habet, nos qui in Christum credimus et Christo commortui sumus, ne peccatis
vivamus, a peccatorum pœnis defendendi ; porro dum potestate sua, quam a patre
plenam et absolutam consecutus est, perpetuo nos tuetur et iram dei, quam in impios
effundi consuevit, intercessione sua a nobis arcet, quod scriptura interpellationem pro
nobis appellat ; deinde ab ipsorum peccatorum servitute nos liberat, dum nos sibi
mancipat, partim morte itidem illa sua quam pro nobis perpessus est, partim in sua
ipsius persona nobis ostendendo, quid consequatur is qui a peccando destitit."

ascension, and the sitting at the right hand of God. In a few words the dominion of Christ over all beings and things is then described. Finally, the last section—on the Church—falls into four short chapters. In the first, the *visible* Church is defined (p. 340) as " the community of those men who hold and profess the saving *doctrine*," *i.e.*, as a School.[1] Every other mark is expressly set aside; " there is no reason why thou shouldst inquire into the marks of the Church " (with the exception of the saving doctrine.) [2] The question as to what the true doctrine is, is answered by pointing to this Catechism with all that it contains.[3] In the second chapter the government of the Church is dealt with (p. 342), " that order rests on the offices of persons to whom the Church of Christ is committed, and on carefully seeing and observing that individual persons fulfil their offices." [4] There are now distinguished, in accordance with Scripture, Apostles, Prophets, Evangelists, Teachers, Pastors (Bishops), Presbyters and Deacons. In the course of exposition the offices of Teachers, Bishops and Presbyters are dealt with as *one*, and it is said of the Apostles, Evangelists, and Prophets, that with its cause their existence has ceased. Hence only Pastors and Deacons remain. The doctrine of Episcopal succession is combated (p. 346) ; nothing is said of Ordination. In the third chapter (" de disciplina ecclesiae Christi ") follows a statement of the main principles of ecclesiastical discipline, well established from the Bible, which ends by showing that the power to bind and loose is to be regarded as the " right of declaring and announcing according to the Word of God, who are, and who are not worthy to be in the Church, or to be members of it " (p. 351).[5] The Catechism closes with the chapter

---

[1] " The Italians have a liking for free unions and academies of a socio-scientific character." During the whole time of its existence Socinianism had mainly the form of a theological academy.

[2] " Nihil est, cur de notis ecclesiæ quæras " (excepta salutari doctrina).

[3] The current orthodox idea of the Church in Protestantism, and the Socinian, are therefore identical.

[4] " Ordo is situs est in officiis personarum, quibus ecclesia Christi constat, et in accurata animadversione et observatione, ut singulæ personæ officiis suis fungantur."

[5] " Jus declarandi et denunciandi secundum dei verbum, qui sit dignus, qui non, ut sit in ecclesia seu membrum ecclesiæ."

" on the invisible Church " (p. 352 sq.).   Here again the Catholic
mode of ·view is very striking.   The exposition begins by saying,
that Holy Scripture " scarcely anywhere " distinguishes a company of truly pious men (" coetus vere piorum hominum ") from
the visible Church, since all truly pious men also belong to the
visible Church ; yet it is to be admitted that the latter is often
spoken of as being everything it ought to be, while really it is
not.   Therefore we can frame the *conception* of a Church
as denoting " a certain multitude of truly pious men, together
with the union that is among them, *which, in a certain figurative
and metaphorical sense may be legitimately called a Church,* for
truly pious men, scattered here and there or even remaining hid,
if indeed true piety allows them to be hid (!),[1] can only in an
improper sense be called a Church." [2]   Taken in this guarded
way, the conception of the invisible Church is accepted.   With
regard to it the assertion is made, that by it, that is by all who
truly believe in Christ and obey Him, is represented in the most
perfect way the body of Christ.   This Church, however, is
invisible, because faith and true piety cannot be seen with the
bodily eye ; but even from " outward actions " (" factis exterior-
ibus ") it can only be established that one is not a member of
Christ, but not that he is.   With this the Catechism concludes,
there being added the exhortation (p. 355) : " I have now set
before thee all things that could concisely be said by me regarding this matter ; what remains for thee is that, having honestly
come to perceive them and know them, thou shalt fix them in
thy mind and regulate thy life in the way prescribed by
them." [3]

    [1] Of course if every vere pius must be a schoolmaster it is unlikely that he will
remain hidden.
    [2] " Quædam hominum vere piorum multitudo ac eorum inter sese conjunctio, quam
per similitudinem quandam et metaphoram ecclesiam appellare liceat, nam vere pii
hinc inde dispersi vel etiam latentes, si modo vera pietas latere sinat, nonnisi im-
proprie ecclesia dici possunt."
    [3] " Jam omnia quæ a me compendio dici hac de re potuere tibi exposui : tuum est
ut iis probe perceptis atque cognitis ei menti infigas et secundum eorum præscriptum
vitam instituas."

In modern Catholicism we have the neutralising, in Socinianism the *self-disintegration* of dogma ; the preceding course of exposition will have shown that in its fundamental nature the latter is nothing else than the Nominalist doctrine, with its principle logically carried out.   As the Anabaptists and the pantheistic mystics of the sixteenth and seventeenth centuries are mediæval phenomena, though they are not unaffected by the spirit of a more modern age, the Socinians are not the " Ultra's of the Reformation," but the successors of the Scotists.

But the development of dogma along Nominalistic lines has here come to its conclusion ; dogma is dissolved.   Certainly as in every case of disintegration there are not wanting residuary products.   Adoptian, Arian, Pelagian motives and doctrines, which seemed to have been subdued by dogma, make their appearance again, and the strict holding to Scripture as the source and authority for faith and for the system of Christian doctrine, makes it seem even as if Socinianism held a very conservative attitude.   Nevertheless the breach with history, and with what had hitherto been called dogma is evident. Nominalism adhered to the living authority of the Church, *indeed in this adherence it gave expression to its religious conviction*, even though the validity of this conviction had to be purchased by renouncing a homogeneous view of God and the world. Socinianism overcame the scepticism of Nominalism that sprang from religious requirements ; it is no longer, like Nominalism, divided within itself—it is *dogmatistic* indeed—; but while throwing off the authority of Church and tradition, it at the same time greatly lost power to understand and to feel what religion is : its "doctrines of faith," so confidently proclaimed, are, so far as they are homogeneously and strictly drawn up, nothing else than the dogmatism of the so-called sound human understanding, to which the Bible commends itself, when it is dealt with rationally.

And yet Socinianism is by no means simply a mediæval, or, for that part, only a pathological phenomenon ; it is seen also, rather, to be a product of the fifteenth and sixteenth centuries and represents a powerful advance in the history of religion, though it is only an indirect one.   We can sum up what it

accomplished in the following theses : (1) it acquired the laud-
able courage to *simplify* the question as to the nature
and import of the Christian religion, to throw off, in spite of
Catholics, Lutherans and Calvinists, the burden of the past, to
reduce to fragments by means of the understanding the system
of dogma, itself the work of mis-directed understanding,[1] and to
restore to the individual the freedom to interrogate in the controversy about the Christian religion simply the classic records
and himself; (2) it relaxed the close relationship between
religion and world-knowledge which had been formed by the
tradition of the ancient Church and sanctioned by dogma, and
sought to substitute ethics for metaphysics as a foil for religion.
Certainly it had poor enough success in that ; metaphysics as a
matter of fact was only attenuated, not improved or checked by
it. Nevertheless it was certainly a powerful antagonist of the
Platonism of the Church doctrine, and made its own contributions towards breaking the supremacy of that system ; (3) it
helped to prepare the way for its being perceived that religion
may not find its expression in unintelligible paradoxes and contradictions, but that it must reach the point of well-defined and
approved declarations, which derive their force from their clearness ;[2] finally (4) it delivered the study of Holy Scripture from
the ban of dogma and itself made a good beginning with a
sound, historical exegesis. It is not difficult, certainly, in view
of all these merits of Socinianism enumerated here to prove also
the opposite, *i.e.*, to show how through the same tendencies
it rather strengthened old errors. But it is enough to reach
the certitude that all these merits really belonged to it. Its
having restricted, and in some measure cancelled, their power,
must not hinder us from attributing them to it. Chiefly through
the medium of Arminianism, but also directly, it helped to

[1] The history of dogma cannot, as a history of "illuminism" may do, stop short with
the negative achievements of a school. Were that allowed, then Socinianism, with
its methodical criticism and its freedom from prepossessions regarding all Church
tradition, could not be too highly praised.

[2] Dilthey, l.c., Vol. 6, p. 88 f. : "What was epoch-making in Socinianism lies in
the clear, sharp, and distinct carrying out of the principle, that the new Protestant
Christianity must *justify* itself before the Humanistic, Erasmic, historico-critical,
formal and moral reason of the great century eager for progress."

introduce Illuminism (Aufklärung), in the good, and in the bad sense of the word, into Protestantism.

In the history of religion—taking the expression in the strictest sense—Socinianism was on the other hand simply a step backwards. For so far from its having to be placed here alongside Protestantism, it was rather a further under-bidding of Catholicism, even of the poorest form of it. That the Christian religion is *faith*, that it is a relation between person and person, that it is therefore higher than all reason, that it lives, not upon commands and hopes, but upon the power of God, and apprehends in Jesus Christ the Lord of Heaven and earth as Father—of all this Socinianism knew nothing. Along with the old dogma *Christianity as religion* was well-nigh completely set aside by it; guilt and repentance, faith and grace were conceptions that were not entirely discarded, merely from a happy want of logical thoroughness—and on account of the New Testament. It is in this logical inconclusiveness that the Christian quality of Socinianism mainly lies.

CHAPTER IV.

THE ISSUES OF DOGMA IN PROTESTANTISM.

(1) *Introduction.*[1]

AT the close of the first chapter of this Book (E.T. Vol. V., Chap. I.) it has been pointed out in what sense, and to what extent, the Reformation has to be treated within the lines of the history of dogma; it must be dealt with as the *issue* of dogma, and as its *legitimate* issue too. In the two issues brought under notice up to this point, the real religious interests which co-operated in giving an outline and shape to dogma had serious injury done to them—in Catholicism, in so far as they were completely overborne by the domination of the empirical church—in Socinianism, in so far as they were almost absorbed by moralism. In the one case the dogma was conserved, but the personal, conscious faith, which was to correspond with it, was weakened by submission to the Church; in the other case dogma was discarded, but there was at the same time a failure

---

[1] In the Neue Kirchliche Zeitung, 1891, Part I., Kübel (†) has subjected to a keen criticism the sketch of the Christian and theological position of Luther that was given in the first edition of this book. I have found no reason on that account to alter my statement, but herewith refer readers to that criticism. On the details of Luther's doctrines I shall not enter, partly because that would not be in keeping with the aim of this work, partly because my theological interest does not lead me so far as to follow all these discussions with personal sympathy, or with criticism. Besides, I see that Luther's decisive importance easily becomes lost to view, when an effort is made to describe all his "doctrines." The concise and accurate way in which Loofs, in his History of Dogma, has delineated a number of Lutheran doctrines in their growth, is worthy of all admiration. In Herrmann's Book, "The Communion of the Christian with God, described on the lines of Luther" (1886, 1st ed.; 1896, 3rd ed.), and in Thieme's work, "The Impulsive Moral Power of Faith, an Inquiry into Luther's Theology" (1895), we have two model instances of the way in which the details of Luther's thought can be made intelligible and suggestive when looked at from a comprehensive point of view.

to recognise the peculiar character of religious faith.   Post-Tridentine Catholicism and Socinianism are in many respects *modern* phenomena ; but this is not true of them when we deal with their *religious kernel*; they are rather the further con-clusions of *mediæval* Christianity.   *The Reformation on the other hand, as represented in the Christianity of Luther, is in many respects an Old Catholic, or even a mediæval phenomenon, while if it be judged of in view of its religious kernel, this cannot be asserted of it, it being rather a restoration of Pauline Christianity in the spirit of a new age.*[1]

In making this statement there is assigned to the Reformation (the Christianity of Luther) its position in history, while at the same time its relation to dogma is determined.   From here also we can see why the Reformation cannot be estimated simply by the results which it achieved for itself during the two first generations of its existence.   How can any one deny, then, that Catholicism, after it had roused itself to become a counter-Reformation, and that Socinianism stood, for more than a century, in a closer relation to the new age than Lutheran Protestantism did?[2]   They worked in alliance with all the culturing influences of the period ; and poets, humanists, men of learning, discoverers, kings, and statesmen, soon felt where their proper place was if they were nothing else than scholars and statesmen.   At the cradle of the Reformation, certainly, it was not sung that it would one day lag behind the times.   It was rather greeted at its birth with the joyful acclamations of the nation, encircled with the shouts of humanists and patriots.   But this its *more immediate* future was already foreshadowed in him from whom alone its future was to be expected—namely,

[1] " In the spirit of a new age "—this also means that primitive Christianity was not copied, nay, that there was a passing beyond its lines at important points.

[2] Hence, too, the numerous instances of Protestants, especially of *learned* Pro-testants, reverting to Catholicism, down to the days of Christina of Sweden, and indeed after that time.   The first Continental Protestant who had the distinct feeling that the Confession had become seriously marred was Calixtus of Helmstadt, who had travelled much.   But even the mystics among the Lutherans in the first half of the seventeenth century make it apparent that they felt the Scholastic narrowing of the Confession to be burdensome (see Ritschl, Gesch. des Pietismus, Vol. II.).   But neither they nor Calixtus found the right means of deliverance.

in Luther. It is not the furthest possible advance beyond the average of an age that makes the truly great man, but the power with which he can awaken a new life in existing society.[1]

What is at least a very one-sided and abstract view of Luther is taken, when we honour in him the man of the new time, the hero of an aspiring age, or the creator of the modern spirit. If we wish to contemplate such heroes, we must turn to Erasmus and his associates, or to men like Denck, Franck, Servede, and Bruno. In the periphery of his existence Luther was an Old Catholic, a mediæval phenomenon. For a period, certainly—it was only for a few years—it seemed as if this spirit would attract to itself and mould into a wonderful unity all that at the time had living vigour in it, as if to him as to no one before the power had been given to make his personality the spiritual centre of the nation and to summon his century into the lists, armed with every weapon.

Yet that was only a splendid episode, which for the time being came rapidly to an end. Certainly those years from 1519 till about 1523 were the most beautiful years of the Reformation, and it was a wonderful providential arrangement that all that was to be achieved, the whole task of the future, was taken in hand forthwith by Luther himself and was close on being accomplished by him. Still, this rich spring-time was followed by no abundant summer. In those years Luther was lifted above himself, and seemed to transcend the limits of his peculiar individuality—he was *the* Reformation, inasmuch as he summed up in himself what was at once implied in the return to Pauline Christianity and in the founding of a new age. At that time the alliance also was concluded between Protestantism and

---

[1] The complement of this observation is to be found in the beautiful words Dilthey has applied to Luther (Archiv. f. Gesch. der Philos., Vol. V., Part 3, p. 355 f.) : " Nowhere as yet has history spoken in favour of the ideal of a morality without religion. New active forces of will, so far as we observe, have always arisen in conjunction with ideas about the unseen. But the fruitful novelty within this domain always arises from the historical connection itself, on the basis of the religious-ness of a departing age, just as one condition of life emerges from another. For it is only when dissatisfaction arises for the genuinely religious man from the innermost and deepest religious and moral experience within the existing union, on the basis of the altered state of consciousness, that an impulse and direction are given for the new. So it was also with Luther" (see also l.c., p. 368).

Germany. It is true, no doubt, that evangelical Christianity
has been given to mankind, and, on the other hand, that the
German spirit is even to-day far from having surrendered itself
yet to Protestantism ; nevertheless, Protestantism and Germany
are inseparably connected. As the Reformation saved the
German Empire in the sixteenth century, so it still continues
always to be its strongest force, its permanently working
principle and its highest aim.

But it is given to no man to accomplish everything, and every
one whose work is lasting and who does not merely blaze forth
like a meteor, must retire within the limits appointed to his
nature. Luther also retired within those peculiar to him.
Those limits were not merely slight integuments, as some
would have us believe, so that for his having become narrowed
we should have to throw the whole blame on Melanchthon and
the Epigones with their want of understanding ; Luther felt
them to be with other things the roots of his power, and in this
character allowed them to have their effect.

But when the problem is contemplated of giving a picture of
this peculiar individuality of Luther, and reckoning up as it
were the sum of his existence, it must be said that no one as
yet has perfectly fulfilled this task. A representation of Luther
can only be given when he is allowed himself to speak and to
express himself in every line of his spiritual constitution : this
Luther can be *reproduced within us in sympathetic feeling*, so
far as this is possible for more limited spirits ; but the attempt
to analyse seems to involve us in insoluble contradictions. Yet
the attempt must be made, if the complicated and in part confused legacy he has left behind is to be rightly understood, and
if we are to master the problem that is forced upon those coming
after him by his appearing in an age in many respects foreign
to him.

He was only in *one* thing great and powerful, captivating and
irresistible, the master of his age, marching victoriously ahead of
the history of a thousand years with the view of inducing his
generation to relinquish the paths that were being followed and
to choose paths that were new—*he was only great in the re-discovered knowledge of God which he derived from the gospel, i.e.,*

from Christ. What had once been *one* of the motives in building up dogma, but had become unrecognisable in dogma, what
had thereafter, from the time of Augustine on through the
Middle Ages, accompanied dogma, vague in its expression, and
with a vaguely recognised title, namely, the living faith in the
God who in Christ addresses to the poor soul the words : " I am
thy salvation " (" Salus tua ego sum "), the firm assurance that
God is the Being on whom one can place reliance—that was the
message of Luther to Christendom. The old Lutheran theologians introduced into their voluminous systems a chapter " on
the vocation of Luther" ("de vocatione Lutheri"). For that
they have been severely handled. But if we must read in a
system of Christian theology about Adam, Abraham and David,
we have a much greater right to welcome a paragraph about
Luther.[1]

For what he restored was nothing less than the religious way
of understanding the gospel, the sovereign right of religion in
religion. In the development that had preceded him there had
not been merely the making a mistake here and there ; there
had been a betrayal of religion to its enemies and to its friends.
Luther spoke himself of a Babylonian captivity, and he was

[1] At lofty moments of his life Luther spoke like a prophet and evangelist. All intermediate conceptions and intermediary persons were transcended : "Your worshipful
Highness the Elector knows, or if he does not know, let it be hereby declared to him,
that I have the gospel, not from men, but only from heaven through our Lord Jesus
Christ, so that I might very well have gloried in being, and written myself down as,
a servant and evangelist, which I mean henceforward to do." Such self-consciousness
almost awakens misgivings ; but it must not be overlooked that it is united with the
greatest humility before God ; it did not arise suddenly, much less in a visionary way,
but it slowly developed itself from dealing with scripture and the religious possessions
of the Church ; it only makes its appearance, finally, in connection with the spirit,
"If God is for us, who can be against us ?" and does not intrude into the empirical
ecclesiastical sphere to dictate laws there. It must be recognised, therefore, as the
genuine expression of a religious freedom, of the kind described by Clement of Alexandria as the temper of the true Christian, and of the kind which the mystics of all
ages have sought in their own way to reach. But we search in vain throughout the
whole of church history for men who could write such letters as that one to the
Elector, and for writings like those composed by Luther in Coburg. I can very well
understand how Catholic critics should find in those letters an "insane arrogance."
There really remains only the alternative that we pass this judgment upon Luther, or
that we acknowledge that there belonged to him a special significance in the history
of the Christian religion.

right in seeing this captivity both in the domination of an
earthly, self-seeking ecclesiasticism over religion, and in the
clinging around religion of a moralism that crushed its life.   It
may be remarked here at once, that he did not with equal
distinctness perceive the deplorableness of that captivity into
which religion had been brought by the Old Catholic theology.
That was not merely because his historic horizon extended only
to about the time of the origin of the Papal Church—what lay
beyond blending for him at many points into the golden line of
the New Testament—*but above all because dogma, the historic
legacy of the period between the second and seventh centuries, was
no longer the more immediate source from which there had flowed
the wrong conditions he had to contend with in the present.*   In
his day the old dogma was a thing lying dead, as has been
sufficiently shown in the account we have already given.   No
one vitalised it for faith.   When Luther therefore attacked the
errors of theology, he directed himself almost exclusively
against the *Schoolmen* and the Mediæval Aristotle.   When he
rated and ridiculed reason, it was these people as a rule whom
he had in view;[1] when he severed the baleful bond between
religious doctrine and philosophy, he was turning his weapons
against the Jesuits.   In combating theology he combated the
theology of the Middle Ages, and even this he combated only
in so far as it ignored the honour of God and of Christ, the
rights of God and the wrong done by the creature.   Keeping
out of view his controversy with the Anabaptists, he knew of
no other controversy with reason than the controversy with
self-righteousness, and with the shifts of the man who makes
use even of religion to escape from his God.

What a wonderful linking together of things!   The same
man who delivered the gospel of Jesus Christ from ecclesiasticism
and moralism *strengthened its authority in the forms of the Old
Catholic theology, nay, was the first to impart again to these forms
meaning and importance for faith, after they had for long centuries remained inoperative.*   From the time of Athanasius there
had been no theologian who had given so much living power

---

[1] See Fr. Nitzsch's valuable study, Luther and Aristotle (1883).   Pupper of Goch
was a precursor of Luther in the radical rejection of philosophy and Scholasticism.

for faith to the doctrine of the Godhead of Christ as Luther did ; since the time of Cyril no teacher had arisen in the Church for whom the mystery of the union of the two natures in Christ was so full of comfort as for Luther—" I have a better provider than all angels are : He lies in the cradle, and hangs on the breast of a virgin, but sits, nevertheless, at the right hand of God, the almighty Father" no mystic philosopher of antiquity spoke with greater conviction and delight than Luther of the sacred nourishment in the Eucharist. The German Reformer restored life to the formulæ of Greek Christianity ; he gave them back to faith. It is to be attributed to him that till the present day these formulæ are in Protestantism a living power for faith—yes, *only* in Protestantism. Here there is a living in them, a defending or contesting of them ; but even those contesting them understand how to estimate their relative title. In the Catholic Churches they are a lifeless possession.

There is certainly injustice done to the "entire Luther" when this side of his significance as a Reformer—which to his own mind was knit in an indissoluble unity with the evangelical side— is dropped out of view or under-estimated. *Luther was the restorer of the old dogma.* He forced the interests of this on the teaching of his time, thereby also compelling it to desert the lines of the Humanist, Franciscan and political Christianity : the Humanist and Franciscan age was obliged to interest itself in what was most foreign to it—*in the gospel and the old theology.*[1]

Indeed we may go a step further : Luther would at any moment have defended with fullest conviction the opening words of the Athanasian Creed : "Whosoever will be saved, before all things it is necessary that he hold the Catholic faith"

---

[1] There is, in my opinion, no difference to be found in Luther at different periods. What he wrote (1541) in his pamphlet "Wider Hans Worst" (Erl. ed., Vol. 26, p. 15) in full agreement with the mediæval view of the "Twelve Articles" he could have written twenty years earlier : "No one can deny that we hold, believe, sing, and confess all things that correspond with the Apostles' Symbol, the old faith of the old Church, that we make nothing new therein, nor add anything thereto, and in this way we belong to the old Church and are one with it. . . . If anyone believes and holds what the old Church did, he is of the old Church." See also p. 35 : "So the life here can certainly be sinful and unrighteous, nay, unhappily is all too unrighteous; *but the doctrine must be certainly and absolutely without all sin.*"

("Quicunque vult salvus esse, ante omnia opus est, ut teneat Catholicam fidem.")   Not only does the Confession of Augsburg ratify the old dogma in its first article, the Smalcaldic Articles also begin with it : "regarding these articles there is no controversy between us and our opponents, since we confess them on both sides" ("de his articulis nulla est inter nos et adversarios controversia, quum illos utrinque confiteamur") ; and if in the immediately succeeding article "on the office and work of Jesus Christ" ("de officio et opere Jesu Christi") it is then stated :   "To depart from this article, or to condone or permit anything against it, is not possible for any of the pious" ("de hoc articulo cedere aut aliquid contra illum largiri aut permittere nemo piorum potest"), the article is not meant to be raised by an addition of the kind above those formerly named : the former were regarded by Luther so much as settled matters that he did not think of such a remark regarding them as being at all necessary.   Of this also there can be no doubt—that the gospel was for him "saving *doctrine, doctrine* of the gospel" ("*doctrina* salutaris, *doctrina* evangelii"), which certainly included the old dogmas ; the attempt to represent the matter otherwise has in my opinion been a failure : the gospel is sacred *doctrine*, contained in the Word of God, the purpose of which is to be learned, and to which there must be subjection.[1]

How is it to be explained that in an age which had thrown dogma into the background, and in which the spirit of science and of criticism had grown so much stronger that it was already combated from various sides, Luther appeared as a defender of dogma and restored it to life again?   To this question more than *one* answer can be given ; one has been already stated : Luther fought against the abuses and errors of the *middle ages.* This answer can be still further expanded ; Luther never contended against wrong theories and doctrines as such, but only against such theories and doctrines as *manifestly* did serious injury to the purity of the gospel, ("puritas evangelii") and to its

---

[1] One of the strongest passages is to be found in the " Kurzes Bekenntniss vom hl. Abendmahl " (1545. Erlangen Edition, XXXII, p. 415) : " Therefore there must be a believing of everything, pure and simple, whole and entire, or a believing of nothing" (he refers to his doctrine of the Eucharist).

comforting power. The statement of this carries with it the
other thing—namely, that there was no alliance between him
and the bright-visioned spirits whose aim was to amend
theology, and thereby to introduce a truer knowledge of the
world and its causes. There was entirely wanting to him the
irrepressible impulse of the thinker that urges him to secure
theoretic clearness : nay, he had an instinctive dislike for, and
an inborn mistrust of every spirit who, guided simply by knowledge, boldly corrected errors. Any one who thinks that here
again he can at the present day be a defender of the "entire
Luther," either does not know the man, or throws himself open
to the suspicion that for him the *truth* of knowledge is a matter
of small importance. That was the most palpable limitation in
the spiritual nature of the Reformer,—that he neither fully made
his own the elements of culture which his age offered, nor perceived the lawfulness and obligation of free investigation, nor
knew how to measure the force of the critical objections against
the "doctrine" that were then already asserting themselves.
There may seem to be something paltry, or even indeed pre-
sumptuous in this remark ; for Luther has indemnified us for
this defect, not only by being a Reformer, but by the inexhaustible richness of his personality. What a wealth this
personality included ! How it possessed, too, in *heroic shape*
all we have just found wanting at the time—a richness of
original intuition which outweighed all the "elements of culture"
in which it lacked, a certainty and boldness of vision which was
more than "free investigation," a power to lay hold upon the
untrue, to conserve what could stand the test, as compared with
which all "critical objections" appear pointless and feeble ;
above all, a wonderful faculty for giving expression to strong
feeling and true thought, for being really a *speaker*, and for
persuading by means of the word as no prophet had done
before ! Yet all these powerful qualities were still incapable of
securing for the coming generation a pure culture, because in
Luther's own case they were not produced by the impulse to
know things as they are. Certainly he had greater things to
do than to correct science and promote general culture in the
full breadth of its development ; and we may be devoutly

thankful that we have had experience of such a man, who made all his activity subservient to the knowledge of the living God. But it is pure Romanticism and self-delusion when one devoutly admires the limitations of Luther's special individuality as being the best thing in him, and it is something worse than Romanticism and self-delusion when what was allowed in a hero, who did not reflect, but did what he *was obliged to do*, is raised to a general law for an age which, when it frankly and without hesitation applies itself to know the truth, likewise does what it is under obligation to do.   And then—who really ventures to restore again the "entire Luther," with the coarseness of his mediæval superstition, the flat contradictions of his theology, the remarkable logic of his arguments, the mistakes of his exegesis and the unfairness and barbarisms of his polemic?   Shall we forget, then, all that has been learned by us, but that was unknown to Luther—the requisite conditions of a true knowledge that is determined only by the matter dealt with, the relativity of historic judgment, the proportion of things and the better understanding of the New Testament?   Is it not the case that the more strictly Christianity is conceived of as *spiritual* religion, the greater is its demand that it shall be in accord with the whole life of our spirit, and can it be honestly said that this accord is secured by the Christianity of Luther?

Yet it was not only his defective theoretic interest that led Luther to stop short before the old dogma, nor was it only his vague knowledge and imperfect understanding of the old Catholic period; *the old dogma itself, rather, joined hands with the new conception of the gospel which he enunciated.*[1]   Here also,

---

[1] It has also been pointed out, that from the time of Justinian the old dogma introduced the book of civil law, that the legal protection which it promised was extended only to orthodoxy, and that, accordingly, every attack on the Trinity and Christology was at that time necessarily regarded as anarchism and threatened with the heaviest penalties.   That is certainly correct, but I cannot discover that Luther ever thought of the serious consequences that would have followed for himself and his followers from opposition to the old dogma.   So far as I see, he never went so far as to feel concerned about this, seeing that he adhered to the old dogma without wavering. Had the case been otherwise, he would certainly have shown the courage that was exhibited by Servede.   The same thing, unless I am mistaken, cannot be said of Melanchthon and Calvin.   As to the former, it was *also* anxious reflections about matters of ecclesiastical and civil polity that led him to avoid those whose attitude

therefore, as everywhere, he was *not regulated merely by external authorities*; the inward agreement, rather, which he thought he found between his faith and that dogma prevented him becoming uncertain about the latter. In "faith" he sought only the honour of God and Christ; that was also done by the old formulæ of faith. In "faith" he would hear nothing of law, work, achievement and merit; the formulæ of faith were silent regarding these. For him the forgiveness of sins, as creating a holy Church and securing life and peace, was the main part of religion; he found these things holding a commanding place in the old formulæ. Jesus Christ was apprehended by him as the mirror of the fatherly heart of God, and therefore as God, and he would know of no other comforter save God Himself, as He appeared in Christ and as He works through the Holy Spirit; the old formulæ of faith bore witness to the Father, Son and Spirit, to the *one* God, who is a Triunity, and said nothing of Mary, the saints, and other helpers of the needy. His soul lived by faith in the God who has come as near to us in earthly form as brother to brother; the old formulæ of faith testified to this by their doctrine of the two natures in Christ. Like Paul he armed himself against the assaults of the devil, the world and sin with the assurance that Christ by His death has vanquished the powers of darkness and cancelled guilt, and that He sits now as the exalted Lord at the right hand of God; the old formulæ of faith bore witness to the death on the cross, the resurrection and exaltation of Christ. While, under the rubbish-heaps of the middle ages, he rediscovered the old faith of Paul in the New Testament, he discovered this faith also in the old dogma: the Church possessed it, confessed it daily, but no longer paid regard to it, knew no longer what it had imported into the mutterings of its priests, and thus in the midst of its possessions forgot what it possessed. *Over against this Church,* why should he not honour, along with the New Testament, the

towards the old dogma was open to suspicion; and Calvin can scarcely be freed from the reproach that he would have taken a different attitude towards the old dogma, and would have treated the Antitrinitarians otherwise, if he had been less political. See information about the civil and political side of the question in Kattenbusch, Luther's Stellung zu den ökumenischen Symbolen, p. 1 ff.

old dogma which witnessed to the Word of God! And in *one* very important respect he was certainly entirely in the right— this old dogma was really an expression of *the religion of ancient times: that which those times maintained together with this, and by means of which they delimited dogma, was not intro- duced into dogma itself.* Only in the middle ages did law, merit and achievement find a place among the doctrines of faith and in worship. As compared with the mediæval, the Old Catholic Church had impressed on it more of a *religious* character ; in its faith and in its worship it confessed what God has done, and what He will do, through Christ.

But was he not altogether right? Was there not really the most beautiful harmony between his faith and the old dogma? This is still asserted at the present day, and an appeal is made in support of it to the apparently strongest witness—to Luther himself, who had no other idea in his mind. According to this view, the shaping of dogma in the ancient Church, down to the sixth and seventh centuries, was " sound "; the only thing lacking to it was justification by faith. This supplement was added by Luther, while at the same time he purified—or can- celled—the false development of the Middle Ages. Over and above this there is a talk about a " reconstruction," a " re- modelling " of dogma, that was undertaken by Luther; but there is difficulty in explaining what such terms are intended to mean : additions and subtractions are not equivalent to recon- struction.[1] Hence the terms are not employed seriously ; they

---

[1] See Thomasius-Seeberg, l.c., II., p. 748 : " The third Period gives us the *re- modelling of dogma* by the Reformation. Here the evangelical faith in justification is taken as the centre. Proceeding from this the mediæval conception of Christianity is broken through at its most determinative points, and from this centre, while the results of foregoing dogma-constructions that are *sound* and that are guaranteed by the records of original Christianity are *retained*, a *reconstruction* of dogma is under- taken." The expression "guaranteed by the records of original Christianity" is, moreover, in the first place quite modern, and hence from Luther's point of view extremely objectionable, and in the second place it represents a renunciation of all that the Church has learned during the last 150 years with regard to the New Testa- ment and the earliest history of dogma. Still more distinctly has Kahnis expressed his view as to the relation of the Lutheran Church to the Roman (Die Sache der Luth. Kirche gegenüber der Union, 1854, p. 90). After taking note of the fact that both Churches recognise the Œcumenical Symbols, and that the Lutheran Church assumes

suggest rather the admission that Luther's notion of faith in some way modified dogma as a whole. How that took place there is, of course, difficulty in stating, for the moulding of dogma in the ancient Church was "sound." From this point of view the whole development of Protestantism from the end of the seventeenth century till the present day must necessarily appear a mistaken development, nay, an apostasy. It is a pity, only, that almost all thinking Protestants have apostatised, and, for the most part, differ from each other only according to the clearness and honesty with which they admit their apostasy.

We have to inquire whether or not Luther's conception of faith, *i.e.*, what admittedly constituted his importance as a Reformer, postulates the old dogma, and therefore, also, is most intimately united with it.[1]

With this in view, we shall first gather together the most important propositions in which he set forth *his Christianity*. Then we shall adduce the most decisive *critical* propositions which he himself stated as conclusions from his religious conception of the Gospel. On the basis of these investigations it will then appear whether, and to what extent, the general attitude which Luther assumed towards the old dogma was free from contradictions. If this can be determined, the final question will arise, whether it is still possible for the Church of the present day to take up the same attitude.

(2) *The Christianity of Luther.*[2]

In the cell of his convent Luther fought out the spiritual battle, the fruit of which was to be the new and yet old evan-

---

a tolerant attitude towards Rationalists and the Schleiermacher School, he continues: " Shall we then have no toleration for our Roman brethren, who adhere to these truths, *and only have a plus, against which we protest.*"

[1] What is dealt with here is simply the question as to the *inner* connection between Luther's Christianity and the old dogma. As to his having cancelled the validity of the *external* authority of dogma, see above, p. 23.ff.

[2] Full accounts of the theology of Luther have been given us by Köstlin, Theod. Harnack, and Lommatzsch. From the point of view of the history of dogma Plitt's " Einleitung in die Augustana " is of importance. For Luther's theology in its initial shapings the works of Köstlin, Riehm, Seidemann, Hering, Dieckhoff, Bratke,

gelical knowledge.[1]   Inward unrest, anxiety about his salvation, had driven him into the convent.   He had gone there in order that—in a genuinely Catholic way—he might, through multiplied good works, propitiate the strict Judge, and " get for himself a gracious God."[2]   But while he used all the means the mediæval Church offered him, his temptations and miseries became more intense.   He felt as if he was contending with all the powers of darkness, and as if, instead of being in the society of angels in the convent, he was among devils.   When in after days at the height of his active career depression came upon him, all that was required in order to regain strength was to remember these convent horrors.[3]   In the system of Sacraments

Ritschl, Kolde, and Lipsius claim special consideration.   A reliable account—though presented in the light of the theology of the Epigones—has been furnished by Thomasius-Seeberg, l.c., II., p. 330-394.   In what follows, my lecture : " M.L. in seiner Bed. f. d. Gesch. d. Wissenschaft u. d. Bildung," 1883, is made use of.

[1] Loofs makes the very accurate remark, l.c., p. 345 : " Luther's development in itself teaches that the Lutheran Reformation did not spring from a criticism of the ecclesiastical doctrine, that it was more than a revision of the ecclesiastical doctrinal system."

[2] Compare very specially the " Brief Answer to Duke George's latest book " (Erl. Ed. XXXI., p. 273) : " If ever a monk got into heaven by monkery, I too would have found my way there ; all my convent comrades will bear me out in that." According to Catholic opinion, of course, Luther made an entirely false beginning in the convent, and proved by his pride that he was not in his proper place.   But his pride consisted simply in this, that he was more in earnest about the matter than his companions.

[3] See one of the most characteristic passages, l.c., p. 278 ff. : " And after I had made the profession I was congratulated by the Prior, convent, and Father-confessor on the ground of being now an innocent child, returning pure from baptism.   And certainly I could most willingly have rejoiced in the glorious fact that I was such an excellent man, who by his own works (so that was the popular view in spite of all the dogmatic warnings against it), without Christ's blood, had made himself so beautiful and holy, and that so easily too, and in such a short time.   But although I listened readily to such sweet praise and splendid language about my own deeds, and let myself be taken for a wonderworker, who in such an easy-going way could make himself holy and could devour death and the devil to boot, etc., nevertheless there was no power in it all to sustain me.   For when even a small temptation came from death or sin I succumbed, and found there was neither baptism nor monkery that could help me ; thus I had now long lost Christ and His baptism.   I was then the most miserable man on earth ; day and night there was nothing but wailing and despair, so that no one could keep me under restraint. . . . God be praised that I did not sweat myself to death, otherwise I should have been long ago in the depths of hell with my monk's baptism.   For what I knew of Christ was nothing more than that He was a stern judge, from whom I would have fled, and yet could not escape."

and performances to which he subjected himself he failed to find the assurance of peace which he sought for, and which only the possession of God could bestow.   He wished to base his life for time and for eternity upon a rock (the mystic's fluctuation between rapture and fear he had no experience of, for he was too strict with himself), but all supports that were recommended to him fell to pieces in his hands, and the ground trembled beneath his feet.   He believed he was carrying on a conflict with himself and his sin ; but he was in reality contending against the religion of his Church : the very thing that was intended to be to him a source of comfort became known to him as a ground of terror.   Amid such distress there was disclosed to him—slowly and under faithful counsel—from the buried-up ecclesiastical confession of faith (" I believe in the forgiveness of sins "),[1] and therefore also from Holy Scripture (Psalms, Epistles of Paul, especially the Epistle to the Romans), what the truth and power of the gospel are.   In addition to this, Augustine's faith-conception of the first and last things, and especially his doctrine of " the righteousness which God gives,"[2] were for him in an increasing degree guiding stars.[3] But how much more firmly he grasped the essence of the matter.[4]   What he here learned, what he laid hold of as *the one thing*, was *the revelation of the God of grace in the gospel, i.e.*, in the incarnated, crucified, and risen Christ.   The same experience which Paul had undergone in his day was passed through by Luther, and although in its beginning it was not in his case so stormy and sudden as in the case of the Apostle,[5] yet he, too,

---

[1] As far as we can follow back Luther's thoughts in connection herewith—that is, to the first years of his academic activity in Wittenberg—we find that for him the gratia of God is forgiveness of sins, which God grants sine merito.

[2] See Luther's Lectures and Annotations on the Psalms, of the years 1513-1515, cf. Loofs, D. Gesch., 3rd ed., p. 346 f.

[3] Especially also Augustine's doctrine of the entire incapacity of fallen man for the good, and accordingly also his predestination doctrine (see the information Luther gives of himself from the year 1516 to the year 1517).

[4] For Augustine there is ultimately in the salvation which grace bestows something dark, indescribable, mysteriously communicated ; Luther sees in it the forgiveness of sins—that is, the God of grace Himself ; and he substitutes therefore for a mysterious and transforming communication the revelation of the living God and "fides."

[5] The way in which Luther gave expression to his faith during the first period shows

learned from this experience *that it is God who gives faith :*
" When it pleased God to reveal His Son in me." In Luther's
development down to the year 1517, there was an entire
absence of all dramatic and romantic elements : that is perhaps
the most wonderful thing in this wonderful character, and is the
seal of its inward greatness. From Mysticism, to which he
owed much, and the speculations of which he not unfrequently
followed in connection with particular questions, he was separated by the entirely unmystical conviction that trust in God
" on account of Christ " (" propter Christum ") is the real content of religion, which nothing transcends, and the limitations
of which can be removed by no speculation. Trust in the
" truth " of God and in the work of Christ formed for him a
unity, and he knew no other way of approaching the Being who
rules heaven and earth than by the cross of Christ (per crucem
Christi).[1]

That, however, which he had experienced, and which, with
ever-increasing clearness, he now learned to state, was, in comparison with the manifold things which his Church offered as
religion, above everything else an immense *reduction*, an
emancipating *simplification.* In this respect he resembled
Athanasius[2]—with whom in general he had the most noteworthy
affinity—and was very unlike Augustine, who never controlled
the inexhaustible riches of his spirit, and who stimulated, therefore, rather than built up. *That reduction meant nothing else
than the restoration of religion :* seeking God and finding God.
Out of a complex system of expiations, good deeds and
comfortings, of strict statutes and uncertain apportionments of
grace, out of magic and of blind obedience, he led religion forth
and gave it a strenuously concentrated form. The Christian
religion is living assurance of the living God, who has revealed

us plainly that he learned not only from Augustine but also from the mediæval
mystics (from Bernard onwards). The linking together of surrender to God with
surrender to Christ is for the first time clearly apparent in them ; for Augustine it
was much more vague. In this sense Luther's faith stands in a distinct historic line ;
yet the originality and force of his experience as a believer is not thereby detracted
from. Even in the domain of religion there is no generatio æquivoca.

[1] See Loofs, l.c., p. 348.
[2] See Vol. III., p. 140.

Himself and opened His heart in Christ[1]—nothing else. Objectively, it is Jesus Christ, His person and work ;[2] subjectively, it is faith ("faith is our life" ["fides vita nostra est"]) ; its content, however, is the God of grace, and therefore the forgiveness of sins, which includes adoption and blessedness. For Luther, the whole of religion was contained within this circle. The living God—not a philosophical or mystical abstraction—the God manifest, certain, the God of grace, accessible to every Christian. Unwavering trust of the heart in Him who has given himself to us in Christ as our Father, personal assurance of faith, because Christ with His work undertakes our cause—this became for him the entire sum of religion. Rising above all anxieties and terrors, above all ascetic devices, above all directions of theology, above all interventions of hierarchy and Sacraments, he ventured to lay hold of God Himself in Christ, and in this act of his faith, which he recognised as God's work, his whole being obtained stability and firmness, nay, even a personal certainty and joy, such as no mediæval man had ever possessed.[3]

From perceiving that "with force of arms we nothing can,"

---

[1] Larger Catechism II., 3 (p. 460, Müller) : "Neque unquam propriis viribus pervenire possemus, ut patris favorem ac gratiam cognosceremus, nisi per Jesum Christum dominum nostrum, *qui paterni animi erga nos speculum est*, extra quem nihil nisi iratum et truculentum videmus judicem."

[2] It has been very specially shown by Theod. Harnack in his work, Luther's Theologie (see particularly the 2nd Vol.), that Luther's whole theology is Christology.

[3] The fullest, most distinct, and truest account of Luther's *religion* is to be found in Herrmann's book referred to above, " The Communion of the Christian with God ; a discussion in agreement with the view of Luther," 3rd ed., 1896. Dilthey also makes the excellent remarks (l.c., p. 358) : " The justification of which the mediæval man had inward experience was the descending of an objective stream of forces upon the believer from the transcendental world, through the Incarnation, in the channels of the ecclesiastical institutions, priestly consecration, sacraments, confession, and works ; *it was something that took place in connection with a supersensible régime.* The justification by faith of which Luther was inwardly aware was the personal experience of the believer standing in the continuous line of Christian fellowship, by whom assurance of the grace of God is experienced *in the taking place of a personal faith*, an experience derived from the appropriation of the work of Christ that is brought about by the *personal election* of grace." What Dilthey adds is correct : "If it necessarily resulted from this that there was a change in the conscious attitude towards dogma and in the basing of faith thereon, *this change did not touch the matter of the old ecclesiastical dogma.*"

he derived the utmost freedom and force ; for he now knew the
power which imparts to the life steadfastness and peace ; he
knew it, and called it by its name.   *Faith*—that meant for him
no longer adherence to an incalculable sum of Church doctrines
or historical facts ; it was no opinion and no action, no act of
initiation (actus initiationis) upon which something greater
follows ; it was the certainty of forgiveness of sins, and therefore
also the personal and continuous surrender to God as the Father
of Jesus Christ, which transforms and renews the whole man.[1]

That was his confession of faith : faith is a living, busy,
active thing, a sure confidence, which makes a man joyous and
happy towards God and all creatures,[2] which, like a good tree,
yields without fail good fruit, and which is ever ready to serve
everyone and to suffer all things.   In spite of all evil, and in
spite of sin and guilt, the life of a Christian is hid in God.
That was the ground-thought of his life.   As included within
this, the other thought was discerned and experienced by him—
the thought of the *freedom* of a Christian man.   This freedom
was not for him an empty emancipation, or a licence for every

[1] Compare August. c. 20 : "Admonentur etiam homines, quod hic nomen fidei non
significet tantum historiæ notitiam, qualis est impiis et diabolo, sed significet fidem,
quæ credit non tantum historiam, sed etiam effectum historiæ, videlicet hunc articulum,
remissionem peccatorum, quod videlicet per Christum habeamus gratiam, justitiam et
remissionem peccatorum."   Compare the exposition of the 2nd Main Article in the
"Kurze Form" (manual for prayer) : "Here it is to be observed that there are two
kinds of believing : first, a believing about God, which means that I believe that
what is said of God is true.   This faith is rather a form of knowledge or observation
than a faith.   There is, secondly, a believing in God, which means that I put my
trust in Him, give myself up to thinking that I transact with Him, and believe
without any doubt that He will be and do to me according to the things said of Him.
Such faith, which throws itself on God, whether in life or in death, alone makes a
Christian man."

[2] Preface to the Epistle to the Romans (Erl. Ed. LXIII., p. 124 f.) : "Faith is a
divine work in us, through which we are changed and regenerated by God. . . . O,
it is a living, busy, active, powerful thing faith, so that it is impossible for it not to
do us good continually.   Neither does it ask whether good works are to be done,
but before one asks it has done them, and is doing them always.   *But anyone who
does not do such works is an unbelieving man*, gropes and looks about him for faith
and good works, and knows neither what faith is nor what good works are. . . .
Faith is a living, deliberate confidence in the grace of God, so certain that for it
it could die a thousand deaths.   And such confidence and knowledge of divine grace
makes joyous, intrepid, and cheerful towards God and all creation."

kind of subjectivity ; for him freedom was dominion over the world, in the assurance that if God be for us, no one can be against us ; for him that soul was free from all human laws which has recognised in the fear of God and in love for and trust in Him its supreme law and the motive principle of its life. He had learned, certainly, from the old Mystics ; but he had found what they sought for. Not unfrequently they remained imprisoned in sublime feelings ; they seldom attained to a lasting sense of peace ; while at one time their feeling of freedom rose to oneness with God, at another time their feeling of dependence deepened into psychical self-annihilation. On Luther's part there was a struggle issuing in active piety, and in an abiding assurance of peace. He vindicated the rights of the individual in the first instance for himself ; freedom of conscience was for him a personal experience. But for him the free conscience was a conscience inwardly bound, and by individual right he understood the sacred duty of trusting courageously to God, and of rendering to one's neighbour the service of independent and unselfish love.

Of trusting courageously to God—because he feared nothing, and because, in his certainty of God, his soul overflowed with joy : " It is impossible for one who hopes in God not to rejoice ; even if the world falls to wreck, he will be overwhelmed undismayed under the ruins." [1] Thus he became the Reformer, because through his joyous faith he became a hero. If even in science knowledge is not enough, if the highest things are achieved only where there is courage, how should it be otherwise in religion ? What Christian faith is, revealed itself to the Germans in Luther's person. What he presented to view was not new doctrine, but an experience, described at one time in words strongly original, at another time in the language of the Psalms and of Paul, sometimes in that of Augustine, and sometimes even in the cumbrous propositions of the scholastic theology. The critical application of his faith to the state of things existing at the time, to the Church as it was, Luther

---

[1] " Impossible est, ut non laetetur, qui sperat in domino, etiam si fractus illabatur orbis, impavidum ferient ruinæ." Operat. in Psalm (1519-1521), Weimarer Ausgabe T.V., p. 182.

never desired ; it was forced upon him because his opponents
observed much sooner than himself the critical force of what he
declared.

In Luther's view of faith there was implied his view of the
Church. For him the Church was the community of the saints,
i.e., of believers, whom the Holy Spirit has called, enlightened
and sanctified through the Word of God, who are continually
being built up by means of the gospel in the true faith, who
look forward confidently and joyfully to the glorious future of
the sons of God, and meanwhile serve one another in love, each
in the position in which God has placed him. That is his
whole creed regarding the Church—the community of believers
(saints), invisible, but recognisable by the preaching of the
Word.[1] It is rich and great ; and yet what a reduction even
this creed is found to contain when it is compared with what
the mediæval Church taught, or at least assumed, regarding
itself and the work assigned to it ! Luther's creed was entirely
the product of his religious faith, and it rests on the following
closely united principles, to the truth of which he constantly
adhered. *First,* that the Church has its basis in the Word of
God ; *second,* that this Word of God is the preaching of the revelation of God in Christ, as being that which creates faith ;
third, that accordingly the Church has no other field than that
of faith, but that within this field it is for every individual the
mother in whose bosom he attains to faith ; *fourth,* that because
religion is nothing but faith, therefore neither special performances, nor any special province, whether it be public worship,
or a selected mode of life, nor obedience to ecclesiastical injunctions, though these may be salutary, can be the sphere in
which the Church and the individual give proof of their faith,
but that the Christian must exhibit his faith in neighbourly
service within the natural relationships of life, because they
alone are not arbitrarily chosen but *provided,* and must be
accepted therefore as representing the order of God.

With the first principle Luther assumed an antagonistic
attitude towards the received doctrine both of tradition and of

---

[1] One easily sees that this definition has an Augustinian basis, and that it is modified
by the determinative position given to the factors " word " and " faith."

the power belonging to the bishops and the Pope. He saw
that previous to his time, the question as to *what is Christian
and what the Church is* had been determined in a way quite
arbitrary and therefore also uncertain. He accordingly turned
back to the sources of religion, to Holy Scripture, and in
particular to the New Testament. The Church has its basis in
something fixed, something given, which has never been wanting to it—in this he distinguished himself from the " enthusiasts "
—but this thing that is given is not a secret science of the
priesthood, nor is it a dreary mass of statutes under the protection of the holy, still less papal absolutism ; but it is something which every simple-minded Christian can discern and
make proof of : it is *the Word of God as dealt with by the pure
understanding*. This thesis required the unprejudiced ascertainment of the really literal sense of Holy Scripture. All arbitrary
exposition determined by authority was put an end to. As a
rule Luther was in earnest in complying with this demand, so
far as his vision carried him. He could not, certainly, divine
how far it was to lead. Yet his methodical principles of
" interpretation," his respect for language, laid the foundation
for scripture-science.

The second principle distinguishes Luther both from the
theologians and from the ascetics and sectaries of the Middle
Ages. In thinking of the Word of God they thought of the
letter, of the inculcated doctrines, and the miscellaneous
promises of Holy Scripture ; he thought of what formed the
core. If he speaks of this core as being " the gospel according
to the pure understanding," " the pure gospel," " the pure Word
of God," " the promises of God " (" promissiones dei "), but,
above all, as being " Jesus Christ," all these expressions as
understood by him are identical. The Word of God which he
constantly had in his mind, was the testimony of Jesus Christ,
who is the Saviour of souls. As faith has only to do with the
living God and Christ, so also the authority for faith and for the
Church is only the *effectual* Word of God, as the Christ who is
preached.[1] Accordingly the Church doctrine also is nothing

---

[1] Here, according to Luther's view, *office* also has its place in the Church ; it is the
"ministerium" in word and sacrament, instituted in the Church (not the

but the statement of the gospel, as it has created and holds
together the Christian community, the sum of the " consolations
offered in Christ " (" consolationes in Christo propositæ ").

But if the Church has its basis simply in these "consolations"
and in the faith that answers to them, it can have no other
sphere and no other form than those which the Word of God
and faith give to it.   Everything else must fall away as disturbing, or as at least unessential.   In this way the third
principle is obtained.   The conception of the Church is greatly
reduced as compared with the mediæval conception, but it has
thereby gained in inner force, and has been given back to faith.
Only the believer sees and knows the holy Christian community; for it is only he who perceives and understands the
Word of God; he *believes* in this Church, and knows that
through it he has attained to faith, because the Holy Spirit has
called him through the *preached* Word.[1]

individual congregation) with a view to leading the individual to faith.   The
creator of this office is, of course, God, not the Church, much less the
individual congregation, and it has its field simply in the administration of the means
of grace with a view to the establishment and maintenance of faith.   (See Art. 5 of
the Confession of Augsburg: "Ut hanc fidem consequamur, institutum est ministerium
docendi evangelii et porrigendi sacramenta ").   That it is occupied exclusively with
this aim is shown in the subsequent part of the article.   But in order to obviate a
false fanatical conclusion it is said in Art. 14: " De ordine ecclesiastico docent, quo I
nemo debeat in ecclesia publice docere aut sacramenta administrare, nisi rite vocatus."
The vocatio legitima is of course a function that is tied to legal ordinances, and thereby
is withdrawn, both from the order of salvation and from arbitrary self-determination.

[1] See the Larger Catechism (Müller, p. 455): "Spiritus sanctus sanctificationis
munus exsequitur per communionem sanctorum aut ecclesiam Christianorum, remissionem peccatorum, carnis resurrectionem et vitam æternam ; hoc est primum nos
ducit spiritus s. in sanctam communionem suam, ponens in sinum ecclesiæ, per quam
nos docet et Christo adducit. . . . Ecclesia est mater et quemlibet Christianum
parturit ac alit per verbum, quod spiritus s. revelat et prædicat et per quod pectora
illuminat et accendit, ut verbum accipiant, amplectantur, illi adhærescant inque eo
perseverent." See also the Kirchenpostille, Predigt am 2. Christtage (Erl. Ed. X.,
p. 162): "The Christian Church keeps all words of God in its heart, and revolves
them, maintains their connection with one another and with scripture.   Therefore
anyone who is to find Christ must first find the Church.   How would one know
where Christ is and faith in Him is, unless He knew where His believers are?   And
whoever wishes to know something about Christ must not trust to himself, nor by the
help of his own reason build a bridge of his own to heaven, but must go to the Church,
must visit it and make inquiry.   Now the Church is not wood and stone, but the
company of people who believe in Christ ; with these he must keep in connection,

Finally, the fourth principle had, outwardly, the most far-reaching consequences; if everything depends upon faith, both for the individual and for the Church, if it is God's will to transact with men only through faith, if faith alone is acceptable to Him, there can be no special fields and forms of piety and no specific pious ways of life as distinct from other ways. From this it followed that the demonstration and practical exercise of faith had to be within the great institutions of human life that have their origin in God (in marriage, family, state, and calling). But all that was included in worship now appeared also in quite a different light. If it is an established fact, that man has neither power nor right to do anything in the way of influencing God, if the mere thought of moving God to alter his feeling means the death of true piety, if the entire relation between God and man is determined by the believing spirit, *i.e.*, by

and see how those believe, live, and teach who assuredly have Christ among them. For outside of the Christian Church there is no truth, no Christ, no blessedness." Into Luther's view of the congregation I do not enter, partly because what is dogmatic in it is simply an application of his conception of the Church, partly because the application was by no means a definite one, Luther having expressed himself very differently on the relation of the particular congregation to the Church, on the powers of the particular congregation, and on the latter as empirical and as representing the true Church. Sohm's able exposition (Kirchenrecht, 1892, I., p., 460 ff.) has been justly described as one-sided. There is correspondence with a frequently expressed thought of Luther in what Sohm writes, p. 473 : "Christian *faith* knows of *no* congregations within the Ecclesia (Christendom) in a legal sense, but only of *gatherings* of believers, which do not as such exist in a legal capacity, but are subject to change in their existence; but which, nevertheless, have this quality, that they represent entire Christendom, the Church of Christ, with all its power and gifts of grace." But besides that this conception is not the only conception of Luther that bears on this matter, when Sohm (p. 479) represents Luther as distinguishing between "human order" and "legal order" ("there may be human order in the Church of Christ, *but it is never legal order*, and can therefore be instituted in any case only as an order simply to be voluntarily observed, never as an order to be enforced by outward compulsion"), this distinction I would not be disposed to regard as in accordance with Luther's views, and the rigid definition also of law by which Sohm is everywhere guided ("enforced by outward compulsion") I regard as overstrained in its application to ecclesiastical law. There is surely still a third thing that lies between "voluntary" and "outward compulsion"—namely, the *dutiful* recognition of a salutary order, and the sum of what is to be recognised in the Church as dutiful has always been described as being *also* ecclesiastical *law*.—The general priesthood of all believers (see especially the Address to the Christian Nobles) was never surrendered by Luther ; but in its application to the empirical congregations he became very much more cautious.

firmly established trust in God, humility and unceasing prayer, if, finally, all ceremonies are worthless, there can no longer be exercises which in a special sense can be described as "worship of God."[1] There is only *one* direct worship of God, which is faith ; beyond this there is the rule that cannot be infringed, that God must be served in love for one's neighbour. Neither mystic contemplation nor an ascetic mode of life is embraced in the gospel.

The inherent right of the natural order of life was for Luther as little an independent ideal as was freedom from the law of the letter. Like every earnest Christian he was eschatologically determined, and looked forward to the day when the world will pass away with its pleasure, its misery, *and its institutions.* Within it the devil in bodily form continues to ply his daring and seductive devices ; therefore there can be no real improvement of it. Even in one of his most powerful treatises, " On the freedom of a Christian man," he is far from making the religious man, the man of faith, feel at home in and be contented with this world, and far from saying to him that he must find his satisfaction and ideal in building up the Kingdom of God on 'earth by ministering love. No, the Christian awaits in faith the glorious appearing of the Kingdom of Christ, in which his own dominion over all things shall be made manifest ; meanwhile, during this epoch of time, he *must* be a servant in love and bear the burden of his calling. Yet whether we are disposed to regard this view of Luther as a limitation or as the most correct expression of the matter, it is certain *that he transformed, as no Christian had done before him since the age of the Apostles, the*

---

[1] See the exposition of the 2nd and 3rd Commandments in the Larger Catechism (p. 399) : " Hic enim rectus nominis divini cultus est, ut de eo omnem nobis omnium malorum levationem et consolationem polliceamur eamque ob rem illum imploremus, ita ut cor prius per fidem deo suum honorem tribuat, deinceps vero os honorifica confessione idem faciat." See also the famous passage, p. 401 : " Ceterum, ut hinc Christianum aliquem intellectum hauriamus pro simplicibus, quidnam deus hoc in præcepto (scil. tertio) a nobis exigat, ita habe : *nos dies festos celebrare, non propter intellegentes et eruditos Christianos, hi enim nihil opus habent feriis.*" See also Conf. of Augs. (p. 60) : " Omnis cultus dei, ab hominibus sine mandato dei institutus et electus ad promerendam justificationem et gratiam, impius est." The whole Reformation of Luther may be described as a Reformation of " divine worship," of divine worship on the part of the individual and on the part of the whole community.

ideal of religious perfection, and that at the same time it fell to
him to transform also the *moral* ideal, although it was only on
the religious side that he was able firmly to establish what was
new.[1]   If we will make clear to ourselves the significance of
Luther, his breach with the past, we must keep his new ideal of
the Christian life and Christian perfection as much in view as his
doctrine of faith, from which that ideal originated, and his
freedom from the law of the letter and of Church doctrine and
Church authority.   What an extraordinary reduction is represented also by Luther's new ideal!   That which was hitherto
least observed under the accumulation of fine-spun and complicated ideals—lowly and assured confidence in God's Fatherly
providence and faithfulness in one's calling (in neighbourly
service)—he made the chief matter; nay, he raised it to the
position of the sole ideal!   That which the mediæval period
declared to be something preliminary, knowledge of God as Lord
and Father and faith in his guardianship, he declared to be the
main part of practical Christianity: *those only who belong to*

---

[1] To Ritschl belongs the great merit of having—it may be said for the first time
—clearly and successfully demonstrated the importance of the Reformation from the
transformation of the ideal of religious and moral perfection.   Yet in doing this he
has not, in my opinion, given sufficient weight to the eschatological tendency in
Luther.   But he has restored their significance to the expositions in Arts. (2), 16, 20,
26, 27 of the Augs. Conf. : " Damnant et illos, qui evangelicam perfectionem non
collocant in timore dei et fide, sed in deserendis civilibus officiis, quia evangelium
tradit justitiam æternam cordis.   Interim non dissipat politiam aut œconomiam, sed
maxime postulat conservare tamquam ordinationes dei et in talibus ordinationibus
exercere caritatem." . . . " Jam qui scit se per Christum habere propitium patrem,
is vere novit deum, scit se ei curæ esse, invocat eum, denique non est sine deo sicut
gentes.   Nam diaboli et impii non possunt hunc articulum credere, remissionem
peccatorum.   Ideo deum tamquam hostem oderunt, non invocant eum, nihil boni
ab eo exspectant."   Of the past time it is said, chap. 26 : " Interim mandata dei
juxta vocationem nullam laudem habebant ; quod pater familias educabat sobolem,
quod mater pariebat, quod princeps regebat rempublicam, hæc putabantur esse opera
mundana et longe deteriora illis splendidis observationibus."   27 : " Perfectio
Christiana est serio timere deum et rursus concipere magnam fidem et confidere
propter Christum, quod habeamus deum placatum, petere a deo et certo exspectare
auxilium in omnibus rebus gerendis juxta vocationem ; interim foris diligenter facere
bona opera et servire vocationi.   In his rebus est vera perfectio et verus cultus dei."
A radical and keen criticism was applied to monachism prior to Luther's time by
Pupper of Goch in his Dialogue (see O. Clemen, l.c., pp. 167-181) ; he, however,
could not sever himself from the ideal of evangelical poverty in the form of the vita
communis.

Christ have a God; all others have Him not, nay, know Him not.[1] That which the mediæval age looked upon with mistrust, worldly calling and daily duty, was regarded by Him as the true sphere of the life that is well-pleasing to God.   The effects were immeasurable ; for at *one* stroke religion was now released from connection with all that was foreign to it and the independent right belonging to the spheres of the natural life was recognised. Over the great structure of things which we call the Middle Ages, over this chaos of unstable and inter-blended forms, there brooded the spirit of faith, which had discerned its own nature and therefore its limits.   Under its breath everything that had a right freely to assert itself began to struggle forth into independent development.   Through his thinking out, proclaiming, and applying the Gospel, everything else was to fall to the Reformer. He had no other aim than to teach the world what the nature of religion is ; but through his seeing the most important province in its distinctive character, the rights of all others also were to be vindicated ; *science* no longer stands under the ban of ecclesiastical authority, but must investigate its object in a secular, *i.e.,* in a " pure " way ;[2] the *State* is no longer the disastrous combination of compulsion and need, so constructed as to lean for support on the Church, but is the sovereign order of public social life, while the home is its root ;[3] *law* is no longer

---

[1] Larger Catechism, P. II., 3, p. 460: "Proinde ii articuli nostræ fidei nos Christianos ab omnibus aliis, qui sunt in terris, hominibus separant.   Quicumque enim extra Christianitatem sunt, sive gentiles sive Turcæ sive Judæi aut falsi etiam Christiani et hypocritæ, quamquam unum tantum et verum deum esse credant et invocent, *neque tamen certum habent, quo erga eos animatus sit animo, neque quidquam favori aut gratiæ de deo sibi polliceri audent aut possunt,* quamobrem in perpetua manent ira et damnatione.   Neque enim habent Christum dominum neque ullis spiritus sancti donis et dotibus illustrati et donati sunt."

[2] See *e.g.* the Treatise "On Councils and Churches" (Erl. Ed., Vol. 25, p. 386) : "Of the schools I have . . . frequently written, that we must hold a firm and decided opinion about them.   For although in what the boys learn, languages and arts, we must recognise what is heathenish and external, yet they are certainly of very great service."   The conclusions, it is true, were not drawn by Luther.   He had as yet no independent science confronting him, or at least only approaches to it.

[3] "On Councils and Churches" (p. 387 f.), after a brief sketch of "Home," " State," and " Church " : " *These are three hierarchies, ordained by God,* and there must be no more ; and we have enough, and more than enough, to do in securing that in these three we shall live rightly in opposition to the devil. . . . Over and

an undefinable thing lying midway between the power of the stronger and the virtue of the Christian, but is the independent norm of intercourse, guarded by the civil authorities, and a divinely ordained power, withdrawn from the influences of the Church; marriage is no longer a kind of ecclesiastical concession to the weak, but is the union of the sexes, instituted by God, free from all ecclesiastical guardianship, and the school of the highest morality ; *care for the poor and active charity* are no longer a one-sided pursuit carried on with a view to securing one's own salvation, but are the free service of one's neighbour, which sees in the real giving of help its ultimate aim and its only reward. But above all this—*the civil calling*, the simple activity amidst family and dependents, in business and in office, is no longer viewed with suspicion, as an occupation withdrawing the thoughts from heaven, but is the true spiritual province, the field in which proof is to be given of one's trust in God, one's humility and prayerfulness—that is, of the Christian character that is rooted in faith.

These are the fundamental features of Luther's Christianity. Any one who takes his stand here and becomes absorbed in Luther's conception of faith, will at once find difficulty in holding the view that, in spite of all this, Luther only supplemented the old "sound" dogma by adding one, or one or two, doctrines. He will be inclined rather to trust here the Catholic judgment, according to which Luther overthrew the system of doctrine of the ancient and mediæval Church and only retained portions of the ruins. At the same time it must not be denied that the steps towards constructing on principle a new ideal of life were not developed by critical force to the point of clearness. For this the time was not yet ripe. In an age when life still continued every day to be threatened by a thousand forms of distress, when nature was a dreaded, mysterious power, when legal order meant unrighteous force, when terrible maladies of all kinds abounded, and in a certain sense no one was sure of his life—in such a time there was necessarily no rising beyond

above these three lofty, divine forms of government, over and above the three divine, natural, and secular spheres of law, why should we have to do, then, with the blasphemous, juggling laws or government of the Pope ? "

the thought that the most important earthly function of religion is to give comfort amidst the world's misery. Assuagement of the pain of sin, mitigation of the evil of the world—this Augustinian mood remained the prevalent one, and assuredly it is neither possible nor intended that this mood should ever disappear. But the task that is set to Christian faith to-day is no apocryphal one because it has not on its side a tradition of Church history. It must be able to take a powerful part in the moulding of personality, in the productive development of the dominion over nature, in the interpenetrating of the spiritual life with the spirit, and to prove its indispensableness in these directions, otherwise it will become the possession of a sect, in disregard of whom the great course of our history will pass on its way.

It is advisable that we should submit to a brief treatment the most important of the *particular* doctrines and theological conceptions which Luther made use of, and should present them here in the sense in which they were utilised by him in support of his new way of apprehending faith. We have to consider them, accordingly, only in their newly-moulded, positive significance. Yet it must be said here at the outset that Luther exercised a very great freedom in the use of theological terminology, and Melanchthon followed him in this down to the time of the Apology. That alone which to Luther appeared worth dealing with in theology was the divine action in Jesus Christ and the experience of faith in this action. Just because it was not a mere *doctrine* that occupied his attention, he used very freely the doctrinal formulæ, employed the numerous expressions which Scripture the old Symbols, and Scholasticism furnished, but very frequently treated them as synonymous. Not a few have felt that they have been required by this to draw up complicated schemes for Luther's doctrine, and so at the hands of the Epigones the theology of Luther has assumed the same complicated and unimpressive form which the Pauline doctrine has received in Biblical Theology. It would appear as if theologians alone among historians and biographers were still unaware, that there is the most radical failure in the endeavour to get an entire view of a great man when the effort is made to reduce all his utterances to an artistic unity and to spin them out to a further point of development. From these utterances the movement must be, not forwards, but backwards, *i.e.*, the miscellaneous and divers-coloured propositions must as far as possible be simplified, and run back as far as possible into a few fundamental thoughts. The fact that light breaks into different colours is not to be explained from the light, but from the different media through which it passes. In order to understand, however, the theology of Luther, we must be guided above all by the perception, that for him the Christian doctrine was no jointed puppet, which can be taken to pieces, and have members withdrawn or added. *The traditional theological schemes were dealt with rather by Luther in view of the fact that in each of them, when properly understood, the whole doctrine found expression.* Whether it be the doctrine of the three-one God that is treated, or Christology, or the doctrine of reconciliation, or of justification, or the doctrine of sin and grace, of repentance and faith, or the doctrine of predestination and free will, what he contemplates is *the setting forth of the whole of Christianity.* Kattenbusch has gained merited distinction from having shown and proved this in connection with two cardinal doctrines, the Trinitarian and the Christological (Luther's Stellung zu den oecumenischen Symbolen, 1883). Only by keeping this observation distinctly in view can an account of the theology of Luther be successful, so far as that theology constituted a *whole*.[1] That there were many other things besides which Luther retained as fragments admits of no dispute.

1. Under the *doctrine of God,* a double set of attributes disclosed themselves for Luther according as God was conceived of *apart from Christ* or *in Christ.* But each of these groups is summed up in *one* single thought ; on the one hand there is the awe-inspiring judge, with whom there can be associated nothing but penalty ; on the other hand the gracious Father, who has turned His heart towards us. As they are looked at in Christ, the attributes of God's truth, justice, grace (veritas, justitia,

[1] Compare also Gottschick, Luther als Katechet, 1883.

gratia dei), etc., are all *identical ;* for they are all contemplated from the point of view of the promises of God (promissiones dei); but these latter have no other content than the remission of sins (remissio peccatorum).   As contemplated in Christ, God has only *one* will, which is our salvation; apart from Christ there is no certainty at all with regard to God's will.

2. *God, Jesus Christ, and the Holy Spirit are objects of faith.* But God is Himself an object of faith, *i.e.,* of hearty trust and childlike fear, only in so far as He has revealed Himself outwardly and once for all among men, and continues to *reveal* this revelation through His spirit in Christendom to individuals.[1] A stricter unity cannot be thought of; for it is by no means God in Himself in whom faith believes—God in Himself belongs to the Aristotelians—it is the God revealed in Christ, and presented to the soul through the revelation of the Holy Spirit. For him in whom the Holy Spirit enkindles this faith there is here no mystery and no enigma, least of all is there the contradiction between one and three ; in Christ, " the mirror of the Father's heart," he apprehends God Himself, and he knows that it is God, that is, the Holy Spirit, who has enkindled such faith and creates the comfort of sin forgiven.

3. Thus also the first article of the Symbol is for Luther a statement of the whole of Christianity ; for when man sets his trust on God as his gracious Creator, Preserver, and Father, and in no state of need has any doubt of Him, he can attain to this only because he looks to Christ, and is in the position of one whose sins are forgiven ; but if he is able to do this he is a perfect Christian.[2]

4. Of *Jesus Christ* faith knows, that " all the tyrants and jailers are now driven off, and in their stead has come Jesus Christ, a Lord of life, of righteousness, of all that is good and blessed, and He has snatched us poor, lost men from the jaws of hell, has won us, has delivered us, and restored us to the Father's grace and favour, and has taken us, as His possession, under His guardianship and protection, so that He now rules us

---

[1] Compare the two passages quoted above, p. 184 and p. 189 from the Larger Catechism.
[2] See the splendid exposition of the 1st Article in the Larger Catechism and in the " Kurze Form der 10 Gebote, des Glaubens und des Vater-Unsers " (1522).

by His righteousness, wisdom, power, life, and blessedness." [1]
That is the knowledge of Jesus Christ which alone answers to
faith, and which faith alone can obtain ; for Christ can be
known only from His " office " and " benefactions " ; in these
benefactions the real and true faith in Christ is embraced.[2]
These benefactions are summed up in the *atonement* which He
has made, *i.e.*, in the forgiveness of sins which He has procured
by His life and death : " He was truly born, suffered, and died,
that He might reconcile the Father to us, and be a sacrifice, not
only for original guilt, but also for all actual sins of men." [3]
This is the chief part of the Gospel, indeed it is the Gospel
itself, to which faith directs itself.   The *whole* person of Jesus
falls for faith simply within this view, all deeds of Jesus and all
His words ; Luther indeed would rather do without the former
than the latter, for the former need no exposition.   The heart
can only forget its dread of God, the terrible Judge, when it
looks on Christ, whose death guarantees that the law and justice
of God have been satisfied, and in whose word and lineaments
the gracious God Himself lays hold of us through the Holy
Spirit.   Just for that reason it is certain that Christ is something more for us than merely our brother, that He is a true
helper, who has suffered penalty and wrath for us, and in whom
God Himself offers Himself to us, and becomes so little and
lowly, that we can lay hold of Him and enclose Him in our
heart.   Where there is this knowledge, neither the deity nor the
humanity of Christ is a problem for faith ; nor is the interblending of the two a problem ; there is here rather the clearest and
most comforting certainty : *God's grace is only manifest in the
historical work of the historical Christ.*   On the one hand we see
in Christ, that " God has entirely emptied Himself and kept
nothing which He could have given to us "—so there is the
firmest assurance of the full deity of Christ,—on the other hand

---

[1] Larger Catechism, II., 2, p. 453.

[2] See the motto from Luther's works prefixed to this vol., and Melanchthon's famous
sentence in the Introduction to the first edition of his Loci : " Hoc est Christum
cognoscere, beneficia ejus cognoscere, non ejus naturas, modos incarnationis contueri."

[3] " Vere natus, passus, mortuus, ut reconciliaret nobis patrem et hostia esset non
tantum pro culpa originis, sed etiam pro omnibus actualibus hominum peccatis,"
Conf. of Augs. 3.

we see Him in the manger and on the cross. The two, however, are not side by side with each other, but in the abasement faith sees the glory. Confessing the deity of Christ could never become doubtful for him who knew—in the sense of believing in—no God at all save in Christ.[1] Loofs is right in pointing out (Dogmen-Gesch., 3rd ed., p. 358), that within the history of dogma the old religious Modalism stands nearest to Luther's view. The speculation about natures is here rejected by Luther on principle. It was quite impossible for him to arrive at it

---

[1] On Luther's Christology compare Schultz, Lehre von der Gottheit Christi (1881), p. 182 ff. The great reform which Luther effected, both for faith and theology, was that he made the historical Christ *the sole principle of the knowledge of God*. Only by him were Matth. xi., 27, and 1 Cor. i., 21-25; ii., 4-16 restored to a commanding position, the effect of which, however, was that the roots of the dogmatic Christianity were severed. "We must neither worship nor seek after any God save the God who is the Father of our Lord Jesus Christ; in this true God Christ also is included." "Anything that one imagines of God apart from Christ is only useless thinking and vain idolatry." "When one loses Christ, *all faiths* (of the Pope, the Jews, the Turks, the common rabble) *become one faith* (see passages in Theod. Harnack's Luther's Theologie, I., p. 371 ff.). "Begin by applying thy skill and study to Christ, there also let them continue fixed, and if thine own thoughts or reason or some one else guide and direct thee otherwise, only close thine eyes and say : I must and will know of no other God, save in my Lord Christ. . . . See, there open there to me my Father's heart, will, and work, and I know Him, and this no one will ever see or come upon in any other way, however high he soars, speculating with his own clever and subtle thoughts. . . . For, as I have always said, that is the only way of transacting with God, that one make no self-prompted approach ; and the true stair or bridge by which one may pass to heaven, that one remain below here and keep close to this flesh and blood, ay, to the words and letters that proceed from His mouth, by which in the tenderest way he leads us up to the Father, so that we find and feel no wrath or dreadful form, but pure comfort and joy and peace." On John 17, 3 : "See how Christ in this saying interblends and unites knowledge of Himself and knowledge of the Father, so that it is only through and in Christ that we know the Father. For I have often said that, and will still go on saying it, so that even when I am dead people may think over it and *guard against all teachers whom the devil rides and guides, who begin at the highest point to teach and preach about God, taking no notice whatever of Christ,* just as up to this time there has been in the great schools a speculating and playing with His works above in Heaven, with the view of knowing what He is, and thinks, and does by Himself." In a similar way Melanchthon in the first edition of his Loci (1521) set aside the entire Scholastic doctrine of God. But how much time elapsed before this doctrine returned ? Even in Protestantism there again came to be a speculating like that of "the Pope, the Jews, Turks, and the common rabble," a laying down with Origen two sources of divine revelation, the book of nature and the book of Holy Scripture, and an introduction of Christ into both books as a *section.*

from his view of saving faith ; for when this was the starting
point, neither did the deity of Christ come within his horizon as
" nature," nor did the oneness of Christ admit of speculation as
to the conjunction ; for conjunction presupposes in some way a
being separate.—It is further manifest that Luther's Christology
closes the line of development represented by Tertullian,
Augustine, Bernard, the Franciscan Mystics.

5. Of *sin* faith knows, that it consists supremely and therefore solely in the want of fear, love and trust towards God.
Just on that account all men before Christ and apart from
Christ are sinners, because (through their guilt certainly) they do
not know God, or at least know Him only as an awful Judge—
do not know Him therefore as He desires to be known. No
one before Luther took so serious a view of sin as he did, the
reason being that he measured it by faith, that is to say, took a
religious estimate of it, and did not let himself be disturbed in
this view by looking upon sins as the graduated manifestations
of immorality, or upon virtues as the manifold forms of worldly
morality. He alone seized again on the sense of the Pauline
proposition, that whatsoever is not of faith is sin. Thus also
the opposition between sin and holiness was first strictly reduced
again by Luther to the other opposition—that namely between
guilt and forgiveness. The state of the natural man is guilt,
which expresses itself in dread of God, the state of the new man
is forgiveness of guilt, which shows itself in confidence in God.
As understood by Luther the contrast, however, can be viewed
still more simply : *to have no God, and to have a God.* The sin
in all sin and the guilt in all guilt is *godlessness* in the strictest
sense of the word, *i.e.*, the unbelief which is not able to trust
God.[1] And on the other hand the highest among all forms of

[1] Besides the defectus of faith Luther and the Augs. Conf. mention also concupiscence, but they constantly accentuate in this the pride of the heart, as also the
lust of the world, and the selfishness of the spirit. Luther broke with the idea that
had become acclimatised from Augustine's time—that sexual pleasure is the original
sin, and the root of all sin, and thereby corrected the error that had led to the most
disgusting explanations and to the most dangerous training of the imagination.
These sentences—which appeared already in the 1st ed.—I feel I must adhere to,
notwithstanding Dilthey's objection (Archiv f. Gesch. der Philos., Vol. V., p. 359),
that Luther and Melanchthon's doctrine of original sin (see Art. 2 of Conf. of Augs.)
lays equal stress on concupiscence, and so is not substantially different from the

goodness is confidence in God as a true helper. Inasmuch as man is created to and for God, the "original righteousness" ("justitia originalis") is accordingly fear, love and trust, nothing more and nothing else, and the fall, which had its source in unbelief, had the *entire* loss of original righteousness as its consequence.[1] Hence the original righteousness is by no means a supernatural gift in the sense that it was added to man as being mature, independent within his limitations and for certain ends perfect ; but it is the essential condition, under which and in which alone man can reach the goal set before him by his Creator. As in the beginning only God himself could produce this original righteousness by His revelation, so also He alone can restore it ; but that has taken place through Christ, who has cancelled guilt and brought to men the God of grace.

6. What Luther wrought out here under the scheme of sin and cancelling of sin he expressed also in his doctrines of *predestination* and the *enslaved will*. As contrasted with the mediæval view his fundamental thought is this—that God has not merely brought into existence objective provisions for salvation, to which there must then correspond a subjective line of action that is in a way independent, and of which the evidence is given in penitence and faith, *but that He bestows faith and creates penitence.* The mediæval theology—even that which took the most severely strict view of the thought of predestination—is known to have always relaxed this thought precisely in the really *religious* aspect of it ; for all the definitions, both of the Thomists and of the Scotists, issue in the end in a more or

Augustinian-Mediæval doctrine in so far as by it also original sin and sexual enjoyment are brought into union.   For this opinion a number of passages written by the Reformers can certainly be appealed to—what mediæval doctrines connected with the doctrine of salvation do not find a support in their writings?—yet the view that the physical impulses are in themselves sinful was certainly transcended by them, not only in principle, but in countless different connections.   That Luther's view of "faith" and "unbelief" cancels this view, even Dilthey will not deny, as I do not deny that the historical theory of original sin had necessarily the effect of always leading the theologians back again in a disastrous way to concupiscence as the cognisable vehicle of sin.

[1] Hence original sin is really the chief sin, *i.e.*, this is true of unbelief. Just on that account it is to be believed that Christ cancels *all* sin, because he takes away the guilt lying in original sin.

less refined synergism ; or rather conversely, the divine agency
appears only as an " aid " (" auxilium "). But for Luther the
religious aspect continued to hold its central significance ; it is
God, that is to say, who works faith, who plants the good tree
and nourishes it. That which when viewed *from without*
appears to be something subjective, and is therefore regarded
by reason as an achievement of man, appeared to him, from his
keeping in view the real experience as he had passed through
it, as the really objective thing, produced within him from
without. This is perhaps what gives to Luther his highest
significance in theology, and on this account his work on the
enslaved will (" De servo arbitrio ") is in *one* respect his greatest.
That significance lies in this, that he completely broke with the idea
that the religious experience is composed of historic and sacramental
acts, which God performs and holds in readiness, and of sub-
jective acts, which somehow are an affair of man's. So to
describe this experience meant for him the depriving it of its
force and the handing it over to reason ; for the latter can then
" objectively " register, describe, and reckon upon the divine
acts, and in the same way it can then fix and prescribe what is
to be done by man. That this was the falsely renowned art
of the Schoolmen, the doctrine of reason and of the devil, was
perceived by Luther, and therein consists his greatness as a
theologian. He put an end both to the arrogant pseudo-
theology of " objective " calculations and to the morality that
gave itself out as religion, but that in its deepest basis was
godless. He did away with the severing of the objective from
the subjective, of the divine factor from the human factor in the
experience of faith. *In this way he produced a complete con-*
fusion in religion for every one who approaches it from without,
because such an one must relinquish all thinking if he is forbidden
to take into consideration at one time the acts of God and at
another time the doings of man ; but it was just in this way that
he made religion clear to the believer, and restored to it the view
in which the Christian believer has at the first, and continues to
have, his experience of it. Nothing is more instructive here than
the drawing a comparison between Luther's work mentioned
above, " De servo arbitrio," and the treatise to which it is the

reply, the work of Erasmus. What a fineness of judgment, what a power to look all around, what an earnest morality does the author of the latter develop ! One is justified in regarding his diatribe as the crown of his literary work ; but it is an entirely worldly, at bottom an irreligious treatise. Luther, on the other hand, takes his stand on the fundamental fact of Christian experience. It is here we have the root of his doctrine of predestination as the expression for the sole efficiency of the grace of God. Certainly Luther had not yet recognised in all its consequences the significance of the perception that the objective revelation and the subjective appropriation must not be separated, that accordingly the awakening of faith itself belongs to revelation ;[1] otherwise it would have become clear to him that this perception nullified all the foregoing scholastic efforts of theology, and hence forbade also conclusions such as he drew in his speculations regarding original sin, and in his book " De servo arbitrio.". For when Luther here reflects on what the "hidden God" ("deus absconditus") is, as distinguished from the God who is " preached " (" praedicatus "), when he admits a double will in God, and so on, that is only a proof that he has not yet rid himself of the bad practice of the scholastic understanding of treating theological perceptions as philosophical doctrines, which one may place under any major premises he pleases, and combine in any way he may choose. Yet with his doctrines of predestination and enslaved will he in the main clearly and distinctly discarded metaphysic and psychology as the basis on which Christian knowledge is to be built up. That " hidden God," moreover, who was left to him by Nominalism he allowed to become always vaguer, or he came to identify Him with that dread judge whom the natural man must recognise in God. While in this way he gave back religion to religion, he also vindicated the independence of the knowledge reached through faith, by setting up the experience of the revelation of God in the heart, i.e., the production of faith,

---

[1] See Herrmann's beautiful expositions in the book mentioned above ; it is an important circumstance that Luther himself spoke of the *revelation* through the Holy Spirit (Larger Catechism, p. 460 : " neque de Christo quidquam scire possemus, si non per spiritum sanctum nobis *revelatum* esset ").

as a *noli me tangere*, to the Jews a stumbling-block and to the
Greeks foolishness. But who understood him! In his knowledge there was seen the old predestination doctrine and nothing
else, as a specially intractable doctrine standing side by side
with other doctrines, and soon there began in Protestantism
the huckstering and higgling over this, Melanchthon leading
the way.

7. But Luther was also able to describe the whole of
Christianity under the scheme of *law* and *gospel*; nay, at a very
early date he embodied his new knowledge in this scheme.
Receiving an impulse here from Augustine, but passing beyond
him (for the sovereign place of faith [fides] in the gospel is not
fully recognised by Augustine), he attached himself so closely
to Paul that it does not seem necessary to state his view in
detail ; nor did he shrink even from the Pauline paradoxes, nay
he strengthened them ; the law is given that it may be violated.
Yet by this he only meant to say, that neither the commandments, *nor even the pleasantest doctrines*, can be of help to man ;
they rather increase his godlessness. Help can come only from
a *person*—here the person is Jesus Christ. That was what was
in Luther's mind, when he set down "gospel," "promises of
God," etc. as = Christ. For him the contrast between law and
gospel was not merely the contrast between a commandment
that worketh death and a promise ; in the last resort it was
rather the contrast between a burdensome husk and the thing
itself. If the gospel as it is preached were only an *announcement*
or a *making salvation possible*, according to Luther it too would
be a "law" ; but it is neither the one nor the other, but something much higher, because it is quite incommensurable with
law; *that is to say, it is redemption itself*. Where Luther, undisturbed by any shibboleth, gave expression to what was really
his own Christianity, he never reflected on the gospel "in itself"
—that for him a Jewish or heathenish reflection, similar to
the reflection on God "in Himself," atonement "in itself," faith
"in itself"—but he kept in view the gospel *together with its
effect*, and only in this effect was it for him the gospel : the God
in the heart recovered in the person of Christ, faith. To this
faith there applies : "in an easy, compendious way the law is

fulfilled by faith" ("facili compendio per fidem lex impletur")
Just on that account he was able to teach Christendom again
what a fundamental distinction there is in respect of principle
between law and gospel : it was he who first gave stability to
the work of Augustine here also, as with regard to predestination and the bondage of the will. Hence it was, too,
that he could never have any doubt that it is only the Christian
overmastered by the gospel who can have true penitence and
that the law produces no true penitence : terror and dread
(attritio, or contritio passiva, *i.e.* a sorrow wrung from one,
brought about through being crushed from without) the law
causes (unless it be hypocrisy) ; but should the gospel not intervene, these take the direction only of unbelief and despair,
that is, of the greatest ungodliness. If in not a few passages in
Luther's works that appears to be otherwise, then it is in part
only apparently so—for the gospel takes even the law into its
service (see the Smaller Catechism ; the gospel expounds the
law, and holds to view also its punitive operation ; in this sense
—that is, as embraced within the gospel—it is not cancelled),[1]

[1] Nay, it is necessary for the Christian to measure himself by the law, and to see
daily that through acquaintance with it the old man is being destroyed. This operation of the law precedes also the pœnitentia evangelica and can therefore be described
as "the fundamental experience in connection with the rise of faith." Yet the God
who cheers the broken heart must nevertheless take a part even here ; for otherwise
the effect of pœnitentia legalis would necessarily be either hypocrisy or despair.
Loofs (Dogmengesch., 3rd ed., p. 355): "For him who knows Christ's cross,
contemplation of the law and despair of self are (according to Luther) salutary ;
'opus alienum dei (*i.e.*, the occidere lege) inducit tandem opus ejus proprium, dum
facit peccatorem, ut justum faciat ;' mortificatio et vivicatio run parallel with each
other in the Christian life : the Christian takes upon himself the 'conteri lege'
('contritio passiva') as a cross, so that in this way contritio passiva and contritio
activa merge into each other here. In accordance with his own experiences, Luther
presupposes that every one, before he understands grace, experiences in himself, and
must experience, the 'conteri lege,' the 'alienum opus dei'; but from this condition
of mere 'conteri lege' he with all his energy struggles forth." In these words,
according to my opinion, Luther's normal attitude to the question of repentance (the
efficacy for this of gospel and law) is correctly indicated ; see the controversy between
Lipsius (Luther's Lehre v. d. Busse, 1892) and Herrmann (Die Busse der evang.
Christen, in the Ztschr. f. Theol. u. K., 1891, Part I). Lipsius has convinced me
that in following Ritschl I have not done justice to Luther's doctrine of the law in
its bearing on repentance. But I cannot agree with all that he sets forth, and chiefly
for this reason, that—however clearly we can see what Luther ultimately wished with

and it is in part due to the pædagogic reflection produced by
the very justifiable doubt as to whether the man of common
and coarse type is to be regarded as a Christian or not (see
below).   The Epigones soon came to quarrel about the law, as
they quarrelled about free will, because the main principle of the
new view was no longer recognised by them.   Luther himself
did not find his proper position in these quarrels ; for he always
showed a very remarkable want of resource when controversies
arose within the circle of Protestantism, and in such cases he
was always inclined to regard the most conservative view as the
right one.   A "third use of the law" (usus tertius legis) cannot
be attributed to him ; for the positive relations of believers to
God are, like their whole course of conduct, to be determined
by the gospel.

     8. But the whole of Christianity also presents itself to view,
finally, in *justification*.   Just because it is usual to see Luther's
importance exclusively in this—that he formulated the *doctrine*
of justification, it is of service to point out on the other hand
that Luther's Christianity can be described while this term is
not made use of.[1]   What he understood by justification has

his distinction between law and gospel—the Reformer's expositions are not found
when we go into detail to be harmonious.   Hence on the one hand it is left to the
subjective judgment to select those that may be held as the most important ; on the
other hand Luther himself has in certain connections of thought given special
prominence to ideas that secure for the law a special, independent importance in
perpetuum.   But is it not a duty to represent the Reformer in accordance with his
most original thought?

[1] This, however, means something else than what is conveyed in Dilthey's statement
(Archiv. f. Gesch. d. Philos., Vol. VI., p. 377 ff.) : " I deny out and out that the
heart of the Reformation religion is to be found in the restoration of the Pauline
doctrine of justification by faith."   Yet a mutual understanding is not impossible,
for in the fine analysis of the Christian system of the Reformers with which Dilthey
has followed up his statement (l. c., see also Preuss. Jahrb., Vol. 75, Part I., p. 44 ff.),
the decisive importance of the "breaking up" by Luther of the "egoistic motives,"
which had still a place even in the highest and most refined Catholic religion, is
brought out as distinctly as the emancipation from the hierarchy, and as the fundamental feature of Lutheran faith, as *trust* in God and the firm consciousness of
"being taken up, guarded, and hidden in the unseen connection of things."   If
Dilthey introduces these and other momenta into the history of the general spiritual,
and especially Germanic, development, this is entirely correct ; neither is any objection
to be made even from the point of view of the history of dogma to the repeated
reference to the fact, that what is in question is not merely a rejuvenation of the

indeed found expression everywhere in what has preceded here, not as a single doctrine, but as the fundamental form of the Christian's state.   It was with the view of describing this state that Luther most frequently made use of the Pauline expression ; if any other view is taken, there will be a failure to understand Luther's meaning.   What is new is not that in a scrupulous and scholastic way Luther separated the justificatio and sanctificatio, and regarded the former as a forensic act (actus forensis), taking place once for all;[1] that is the wisdom of the Epigones, who were always great in distinctions ;—what is new lies in this, "(1) that with few exceptions the receiving of life (vivificatio) or justification (justificatio) is seen ultimately in nothing but in the being redeemed from sin without merit (sine merito redimi de peccatis), in the non-imputation of sin (non imputari peccatum) and the imputation of righteousness (reputari justitiam alicui), (2) that in connection herewith grace (gratia) is identified with mercy (misericordia), with grace for the remission of sins (gratia in remissionem peccatorum), or with truth (veritas), i.e. the fulfilment of the promise (impletio promissi) in the historical work of Christ, and (3) that in consequence hereof faith (fides) appears—though a distinct terminology is still wanting—as trust in God's truth (veritas) and in Christ's work for us : faith = believing in God = the wisdom of the cross of Christ (i.e. the understanding that the Son of God was incarnated and crucified and raised again *for our salvation*) = being well-pleasing to God in Christ (fides = credere deo = sapientia crucis Christi [scil. intellegere, quod filius dei est incarnatus et crucifixus et

primitive Christian, Pauline stage, but a passing beyond this to an organisation and practical application of the inwardly experienced in human society and its order, such as primitive Christianity had not known.   But on the other hand, the Pauline doctrine of justification is not to be restricted to Rom. III. and IV.   There must be added Rom. VIII. and Gal. V., 6—VI. 10.   But if that addition is made, then the most decisive momenta which Dilthey singles out for commendation in the higher religion of Luther, as being new stages of the development, are to be found already in Paul—though certainly their further conclusions are not unfolded.

[1] See on this the fine studies of Loofs and Eichhorn (Stud. u. Kritik., 1884, or 1887) ; they deal with the moulding of the thought of justification in the Apology, but they are not less applicable to Luther's doctrine.   The observations made on the other side by Franck (Neue Kirchl. Zeitschr., 1892, p. 846) do not touch the main subject.

suscitatus *propter nostram salutem*] = deo satisfacere in Christo).
On these three equations, as the regulators of religious self-
appraisement, Luther's piety rests."[1] Under the scheme of
justification Luther, accordingly, gives to the following thoughts
pre-eminently a special clearness and the most distinct expression : (1) that for us all attributes of God combine in the
attribute of His righteousness, with which He makes us righteous
(which is therefore at the same time grace, truth, mercy and
holiness), (2) that it is God who works and not man, (3) that our
whole relation to God rests on the " for Christ's sake " (" propter
Christum ") ; for God's righteousness unto salvation (justitia
ad salutem) is His action through the gospel, *i.e.* through
Christ ; it is the righteousness of Christ (justitia Christi), in
which He beholds us and which he imputes to us ("imputes
the righteousness of Christ " [" imputare justitiam Christi "] or
' for the sake of Christ " [" propter Christum "]) ; (4) that the
righteousness of God (justitia dei), as it appears in the gospel,
effects both things—death and life—that is to say, judgment
and death of the old man, and the awakening of the new ;
(5) that justification takes place through faith—that is, through
the producing of faith : the latter is not so much the human
answer to a divine acting, it is the means, rather, by which God
works out justification and carries it home ; (6) that justification is nothing else than the forgiveness of guilt, and that in
this forgiveness everything is included—that is to say, life and
blessedness—because there are in all only two states—that of
conscious guilt and misery and that of gracious standing and
blessedness ; (7) that justification is therefore not the beginning,
but is at the same time beginning, middle and end ; for as it has
existence only in faith, it is subject to the law of faith, which
every day makes a beginning, and is therefore every day new,
because it must always lay hold anew of the gracious remission
(gratuita remissio), but is also the full and entire faith, if in
sincere penitence it finds comfort in its God ; (8) that justification is both in one—namely, a being righteous and a becoming
righteous ; it is the former, inasmuch as by the faith which
attains forgiveness man is really righteous before God ; it is the

[1] Loofs, Dogmengesch., 3rd ed., p. 348 ff.

latter, *inasmuch as the faith that has become certain of its God,* *can alone bring forth good works.* In this sense faith is undoubtedly an act of initiation, *i.e.,* the beginning of the work of the Holy Spirit on the soul ; yet that is not to be taken as meaning that in man inwardly, or by a new process, something has to be added to faith ; faith, rather, is the beginning in the same sense in which the good tree is the beginning of good fruit. Luther never thought of the relationship otherwise when his thoughts were clear to his own mind, or rather he connected faith with good works still more closely than is represented by the metaphor here employed ; for to him faith itself was already regeneration (regeneratio), the latter not being merely a consequence of the former, so that there at once takes commencement along with faith that practical *life* also and that unresting joyous activity, in which one seeks to serve God as a happy child ("good works perform themselves unbidden "). If " fearing, loving, and trusting " are not merely results of faith, but faith itself, therefore to some extent the fruit is already implied in and given with the tree. Luther never thought of a faith that is not already in itself regeneration (regeneratio), quickening (vivicatio) and therefore good work (bonum opus) ; but on the other hand—in all doubt, in all uncertainty and despondency, refuge is found, not in the thought of the faith which is regeneration, but only in the faith which is "nothing but faith " (" nil nisi fides ") ; in other words : " we are justified by faith alone " (" justificamur sola fide "), *i.e.,* only by the faith which lays hold on the forgiveness of sins. That continued to be the *chief matter* for Luther ; for only this faith secures *certainty of salvation.* This expresses the ultimate and highest thing which Luther wished to say in describing the state of the Christian as a state of justification, and which, under no other scheme, he could make the subject of such impressive preaching : man in his poverty, stricken in conscience and therefore godless, can only find rest in what is highest, in possessing God Himself—that was known by Augustine also—but he finds this rest only when he is absolutely *certain* of God, and he becomes certain of God only through *faith*—both these things were unknown to Augustine. What enabled Luther to carry beyond

themselves and bring to finality all the Reform movements of
the Middle Ages, was that he had found what they sought, and
was able to express what he experienced : *the equivalence of
certainty of salvation and faith.*[1]   No other faith, however, than
the faith that fixes itself on the historic Christ can win the
strength of sure faith.[2]   Thus Luther again made the fundamental thoughts in the eighth chapter of the Epistle to the
Romans the rock-basis of religion.   Nowhere, therefore, can we
see more distinctly than here his opposition to Catholic piety
also.   The ultimate question of this piety was always, how is
the sinful man made capable of doing good works in order to
become acceptable to God? and to this it gave long-winded
replies, constructing at the same time an immense apparatus,
made up of the sufferings of Christ, sacraments, the remnants of
human virtues, faith, and love.   Here Luther had *no question at
all to ask*, but described powerfully and joyfully what the
experience consisted in through which the grace of God had
conducted him.   This experience was for him the certainty
that in faith in Jesus Christ he had a gracious God.   He knew
that all that succeeded with him, all real life and blessedness, so
far as he possessed it, was the outflow of that certainty ; he
knew that certainty as the source of his sanctification and his
good works.   Thereby for him the whole question as to the
relation of faith to good works was in its essence solved.[3]   That

---

[1] In this way Luther transcended mysticism ; cf. Hering, Die Mystik Luther's im
Zusammenhang seiner Theologie, 1879.

[2] Justification bases itself, in Luther's view, on satisfaction, *i.e.*, on the *exchange*
between Christ and the sinner.   See Th. Harnack, l.c., II., pp. 288-404.

[3] On the relation of faith and works see especially Thieme's book referred to above
(1895).   Besides the view of faith which is determinative and by which Luther's
thinking is directed—the view that sees in it that which produces good works unbidden,
there are to be found in Luther other views also, which do not, however, claim to
have equal importance.   There is this view in particular—that good works, *i.e.*,
moral conduct, represent *thankfulness* to God, who has awakened faith in us.
Thankfulness is conceived of here, not as requital, but as the conduct that corresponds with the gift, *i.e.*, as the longing that asserts itself for fuller realisation of
fellowship with God, so that this scheme really runs back into the first-named, only
that the free action comes to view here prominently as joyful recognition of duty to
be fulfilled.   On the question as to what scope belongs (according to Luther) in
moral conduct to the contemplation of one's neighbour as a direct end, or, in other
words, to love for one's neighbour, see Thieme, l.c., p. 20, 298, Herrmann, Verkehr

there must be progress in holiness, conflict and struggle, that
also he knew ; but when he grew weary in good works, he broke
into the prayer, Increase my faith ! The exclusive relation of
forgiveness of sins, faith and assurance of salvation is the first
and last word of Luther's Christianity. Where the knowledge
of God is, there is also life and blessedness—that is the old confession of the Church. But what the knowledge of God is that
is here meant—on this there was no clearness of thought :
future knowledge, philosophical knowledge, intuitive knowledge,
mystic-sacramental enjoyment of God, knowledge through the
Logos—all these mistaken ways were adopted, and as no
certainty of God was found, no blessedness was found. Luther
did not seek a knowledge, it was given in his Christian standing,
God in Christ ; "where forgiveness of sins is, there is life and
blessedness." [1] But in this faith he also acquired religious
independence and *freedom* over against all that was not God ; for
only independence and freedom is life. The freedom which his
opponents had left in a place to which it does not at all belong
he did away with ; but as a substitute for the noxious remnant
which he discarded, he reaped the freedom which Paul glories

des Christen, 3rd ed., p. 259 ff. Herrmann remarks that Luther did not fulfil the
task of showing *how* neighbourly love springs from faith (fellowship with God), *i.e.*,
how faith itself gathers up its own impulses in the strenuous resolve to love one's
neighbour, and how there dare be no moral motives that transcend this. Thieme
adheres to a relative independence of moral work and intercourse with the world.
The monistic religious attitude, for which Herrmann is an advocate, will, howevei,
only stand the dogmatic test, if the homogeneous structure (faith working by love)
can be built up also from the side of neighbourly love ; for, according to the gospel
of Jesus Christ, love of one's neighbour is not subordinated to love to God, but is—
owing to the double position of man—the given *whole* under the point of view of
time, while the love to God is the *whole* under the point of view of eternity. But
even in Luther there are passages enough to be discovered, in which ministering love
appears as the supernatural character of man in the same sense as trust in God's
providence and patience.

[1] Loofs, l.c., 2nd ed., p. 230 : "With the Greeks sin fell into the background
behind φθορά. Ruin and redemption were physically conceived of ; Augustine and
Catholicism attached greater weight to sin, but behind sin stood concupiscentia, in
the main conceived of physically, behind righteousness the hyper-physical infusio
dilectionis, etc. ; hence Catholicism culminates in ascetic morality and mysticism ;
for Luther there stands behind sin (in the ethical sense) sin in the religious sense, *i.e.*,
unbelief, behind the being righteous the fundamental religious virtue, *i.e.*, faith ;
Luther re-discovered Christianity as religion."

in at the close of the eighth chapter of the Romans. With their "free will" the former had become slaves of the Church and of men; in his confession of "unfree will," *i.e.*, in his certainty of justification by faith, Luther found freedom and courage to defy an entire world. That which is called the individualism of Protestantism, and to which a high value is justly attached, has its root here: the Christian is through his God an independent being, who is in need of nothing, and neither stands under bondage to laws nor is in dependence on men. He is a priest before God, taken charge of by no priest, and a king over the world.[1]

(3) *Luther's Criticism of the Ruling Ecclesiastical Tradition and of Dogma.*

We shall place together here in brief form the most important critical propositions of Luther, that it may be seen to what extent the Reformer diverged from the ruling tradition.[2]   In

[1] Compare here the Treatise, "De libertate Christiana."

[2] It is well known that the habit increased with him of describing himself and his adherents as the old Church, his opponents as the apostates and as the "new Church"; see "Wider Hans Worst" (Vol. 26, p. 12): "But how if I have proved that we have held by the true old Church, *nay, that we are the true old Church;* you, on the other hand, have become renegades *from us,* that is from the old Church, and have set up a new Church in opposition to the old Church." Luther now enumerates the points in respect of which he and his adherents have maintained the old, and those which his opponents have abandoned: (1) we have the old baptism, (2) we have the Eucharist as Christ instituted it and as the Apostles and primitive Christendom observed it, (3) we have the keys, as Christ appointed them, with the view of binding and loosing sins that are committed against God's commandments (no "New Keys," no commingling with political power), (4) our discharge of the office of preaching and our proclaiming the Word of God are marked by purity and fulness, (5) we have the Apostolic Symbol, the old faith of the old Church, (6) we have the Lord's Prayer and sing the Psalms with the old Church, (7) like those of old we pay respect to the secular authorities and yield them cordial obedience, (8) we praise and magnify the estate of marriage, as the ancient Church did, (9) we are persecuted as it was, (10) like it, we requite the shedding of blood, not with the shedding of blood, but with patience.   From these ten points Luther makes it clear to himself that his reformation was the restoration of the ancient Church.   On the other hand he shows that the papists are the *new,* false Church; for (1) they do not adhere to the primitive baptism, **but** teach rather that baptism is lost through sin, and that then one must

what way, and in what order he arrived at the separate propositions has already been frequently described. The process, too,
is at all the principal points so obvious, and is at the same time
so plainly the result of what he saw *positively*, that it seems unnecessary here to enter more minutely into the history of the
development of the negative theses. But with a view to understanding his criticism three things must be premised : first, that
the Reformer—differing in this from Zwingli—*always* passed
from the centre to the circumference, *i.e.*, from faith to institution ; second, that down to the year 1521 his polemic against
the Church was step by step forced upon him by his opponents ;
third, that his negative criticism was directed, not against
doctrines in themselves, but against such doctrines as had a
pernicious influence upon *practice*—taking the word in the most
comprehensive sense. On this account there would not be
much difficulty in describing the whole Reformation of Luther
under the heading, " Reform of divine service " (see above,
p. 191).

1. Luther's judgment has been reproduced by Melanchthon
in the well-known sentence of the Apology, IV. (II., beginning) :

make satisfaction with his own works, (2) they have brought in the indulgence as a
kind of new baptism, (3) in the same sense they use holy water and salt, (4) and (5) in
the same sense pilgrimages and brotherhoods, (6) they have introduced many detestable and scandalous innovations into the Eucharist, made it a " priests' sacrifice,"
divided it, severed it from faith, changed it by means of the masses into heathen
idolatry and a lumber market (Grempelmarkt), (7) they have made " New Keys,"
which have to do with outward works (eating, drinking, etc.) and with political
jurisdiction, (8) they have introduced new doctrines, human doctrine and lies (after
the profanation of the Eucharist that is the second abomination), (9) over the Church,
which is a spiritual Kingdom, they have placed a secular head (that is the third
specially wicked abomination), (10) they have set up the worship of saints, " so that
in this matter their Church has come to be in no way different from the Churches
of the heathen, who worship Jupiter, Juno, Venus, Diana, and other dead ones ; "
you have a pantheon like the heathen, (11) they slander the estate of marriage, (12)
they have introduced the novelty of ruling and carrying on war with the secular sword.
Here Luther breaks off, but adds (p. 23) : "There are still many more new matters."
The attitude which he here assumes—of contending that the Reformation related
merely to the innovations of the papists—it was by no means possible for him strictly
to maintain, nor did he desire to do so. He knows very well, though he has not
made it connectedly clear to himself, that the mistaken development of the Church
had begun much earlier.

" Seeing that those on the other side[1] understand neither what
remission of sins is, nor what faith is, nor what grace is, nor
what righteousness is, they miserably corrupt the topic of
justification, and obscure the glory and benefits of Christ,
and rob pious consciences of the consolations presented to them
in Christ."[2]   This means a denial of the truth, not of one part
only of the ruling doctrine of salvation, but of that doctrine itself;
and every particular point of that doctrine, indeed, was assailed by
Luther : (1) that doctrine of God which, instead of dealing with
God only as He is in Christ, calculated in a " sophistical " way
about His attributes, and speculated upon His will—the entire
" metaphysical " doctrine of God was often enough denounced
and ridiculed by him as a product of blind reason;[3] (2) the
Christology, in so far as one was content to speculate about the
two natures, the incarnation, the virgin birth, etc., instead of
fixing attention on the office, the commission, and so, on the
benefits of Christ ;[4] (3) the doctrine of the truth, righteousness,
and grace of God, inasmuch as the comfort furnished by these
themes was not recognised, from their being restricted by reason
through a regard to law and to what man does, and deprived of
their evangelical significance; (4) the doctrines of sin and of
free will, because a Pelagian self-righteousness lay hidden behind
them ; (5) the doctrines of justification and faith, because they
did not at all touch the point that is of sole importance—*the
having a God*—there being set up in place of this, uncertainty
and human desert, (6) the doctrine of good works, because, first,
it showed no knowledge of what good works are, and therefore
no truly good works were ever performed, and because, second,

[1] That is, the Scholastic theologians, whom Luther for a long time distinguished
from the official Church and regarded as a kind of sect who had overmastered the
Church : " The Aristotelicans."

[2] " Adversarii quum neque quid remissio peccatorum, neque quid fides neque quid
gratia neque quid justitia sit, intelligant, misere contaminant locum de justificatione
et obscurant gloriam et beneficia Christi et eripiunt piis conscientiis propositas in
Christo consolationes."

[3] See H. Schultz, Luther's Lehre von der Methode u. d. Grenzen d. dogmat.
Anschauungen über Gott (Ztschr. f. K.-Gesch. IV., 1). Compare above p. 196 ff.

[4] Compare the motto placed at the beginning of this vol.

these "good works" were put in the place that belongs exclusively to faith.

2. In closest connection with this Luther attacked the whole Catholic (not only the mediæval) ideal of Christian perfection. In combating monachism, asceticism, special performances, etc., he combated that "foremost lie" ("πρῶτον ψεῦδος") of the moralistic-Pelagian view, that there is something else that can have value before God than Himself. Just on that account he abolished to its last remnants the notion of a double morality, and represented the *faith* ("vivificatio et sanctificatio") that finds comfort in forgiveness of sins to be the Christian perfection. It was just this, however, that enabled him also to rise above the eschatological temper of the old ideal of perfection ; for it was involved in the nature of that ideal that it was only beyond this earth—in heaven—that it could be fully realised. During this present state of existence the angelic life can only consist in first beginnings. This kind of eschatology Luther broke with and put an end to, without surrendering the longing for the life that comes through vision. It was a new conception of blessedness which he set up in opposition to his opponents ; in thinking of blessedness they thought of an *enjoyment* experienced by sanctified senses and sanctified powers of knowledge ; he thought of the comfort experienced by a pacified conscience. They knew only how to speak of it as something fragmentary ; for at the most they had only experienced it for short periods ; he could bear witness of it as a child does of the love of his father by which he knows himself to be wrapped round. In spite of all the flood of feeling that overwhelmed them, they continued poor and unstable and distressed ; he saw in all that only the old hell by which the sinner is pursued, and, convinced of this, he demolished monachism, asceticism, and everything in the shape of merit. As at every other point, so also in connection with the ideal of blessedness, he exterminated the subtle dualism which runs through the whole Catholic view of Christianity.

From these attacks on the doctrine of salvation and on monastic perfection there necessarily followed, for him, his attacks on the sacraments, on priestism and churchism and the

ecclesiastical worship of God; but besides this also, his attacks
on the formal authorities of Catholicism and of the Catholic
doctrine.

3. Luther not merely denied that the number of the Sacraments was seven—that was the matter of least importance—he
cut the root of the whole Catholic notion of the Sacraments by
his victorious assertion of the three following propositions:
(1) that the Sacraments are of service for the forgiveness of sins
and for nothing else, (2) that they do not "become efficacious
in their being celebrated, but in their being believed in" ("non
implentur dum fiunt, sed dum creduntur"), (3) that they are a
peculiar form of the saving *Word of God* (of the self-realising
promise of God [promissio dei]), and therefore have their power
from the historic Christ.   In consequence of this view Luther
reduced the Sacraments to two (three)—nay, at bottom, to
one only, *namely, the Word of God.*   He showed that even the
most enlightened Church Fathers had only vague ideas about
this matter of primary importance—"Augustine has much to
say about Sacrament, but little about Word"—and that by the
Schoolmen the subject was completely obscured.   He directs
himself both against the magic of the "opus operatum" and
against the mistaken transference of the saving effect of the
Sacrament into the human disposition; he puts an end both to
the mystic vagueness that accompanies a revelling in Sacraments,
and to the scandalously godless calculation of their market
value; he annihilates the convenient and yet so meaningless
thought of portions of grace, and places in the Sacrament the
living Christ, who, as the Christ preached (Christus praedicatus),
vanquishes the old man and awakens the new; he reduces to
ruins nothing less than the whole system, and goes back again
to the one, simple, great act, constantly repeating itself in every
Christian life, of the production of faith through the offer of
grace.   It was above everything else by setting aside the
Catholic doctrine of the Sacraments, that Luther abolished in
principle the error originating in the earliest times, that what
the Christian religion concerns itself with is a good, which, however lofty it may be, is still *objective.*   That doctrine had its
root in the fundamental notion that religion is the remedy for

man's finitude—in the sense that it deifies his nature. This thought was no doubt already shaken by Augustine's doctrine, but only shaken. As the fore-runner of Luther, Augustine had already made the Sacraments serviceable to an inner process ; they were to produce, increase, and perfect righteousness. But as with this end before him he contemplated them from the stand-point of "infused grace" ("infused love"), he did not carry his view beyond the point of regarding them as *instruments* of various kinds, in which only a special power resides, and which in the last resort are not what they represent. The Church afterwards followed him upon this track. By moulding itself into the Sacrament-Church, it really deprived the Sacrament of its worth ; for it is not that which it seems to be ; it merely *makes that possible* which it seems to contain ; but in order that this possible thing may become actual, something else must be added. For Luther, on the other hand, the Sacraments are really only the "visible word" ("verbum visibile"), but the word which is strong and mighty, because in it God Himself works upon us and transacts with us. In the last analysis it is a contrariety in the view of grace that comes out with special distinctness here. According to the Catholic view, grace is the power that is applied and infused through the Sacraments, which, on condition of the co-operation of free will, enables man to fulfil the law of God and to acquire the merits that are requisite for salvation. But according to Luther grace is the Fatherly disposition of God, calling guilty man for Christ's sake to Himself and receiving him by winning his trust through the presentation to him of the picture of Christ. What has Sacrament to mean here?

That the particular Sacraments which Luther retained should have to receive a new treatment in accordance with this was a matter of course. How he desired to have *Baptism* and the *Eucharist* regarded he has indicated in the four propositions about the former,[1] and in the parallel propositions about the

---

[1] "Baptism is the water viewed in the light of God's command and united with God's Word." "It works forgiveness of sins." "This is not done, certainly, by the water, but by the Word of God, which is with and beside the water, and by the faith which trusts in such Word of God in the water." "Baptism means that the

latter, which he introduced into the Smaller Catechism. What
lies beyond these propositions, or does not agree with them,
will be dealt with in the next section.[1] Most deeply incisive
is seen to be his conception of repentance—it is nothing else
than the daily return to baptism (reditus ad baptismum)—as
compared with the Catholic Sacrament of penance, the centre
and heart of the mediæval Church. First of all, for the inner
penitent temper, the confession of sin, and the satisfaction, he
substituted repentance alone; not as if he had simply abolished
confession (confessio) and "satisfactio operis" — to the
former he attached great value, and even for the latter he could
allow a certain title,[2] but nothing else must be placed side by
side with sincere repentance ; for only to it belongs value before
God, because He creates it through faith; secondly, true
repentance was strictly conceived of by him as contrition
(contritio), i.e., as the crushed feeling about sin awakened by
faith, or, more correctly, as hatred of sin; that which the law
can work is at most attrition (attritio), but this attrition of the
Schoolmen is, if there is nothing beyond it, of no value, because
it is not wrought by God, and therefore leads to hell. He thus
brought back repentance from the region of morality and of
arbitrary ecclesiastical order into the sphere of religion : "against
thee only have I sinned"; thirdly, he made a demand for
constancy of penitent disposition, as being the fundamental form
of genuine Christian life in general, and thus declared penance
performed before the priest to be a special instance of what

old Adam must be drowned in us day by day through daily sorrow and repentance
. . . and that there must daily come forth and arise a new man." The same in the
case of the Eucharist.

[1] Let it only be remarked here that Luther's original fundamental principle with
regard to the Eucharist—see his treatise De captiv. Babyl. (Erl. Ed. Opp. var. arg.
V., p. 50)—which lays the basis for his doctrine of the Sacraments, is expressed in
these terms : "Jam missa quanto vicinior et similior primæ omnium missæ, quam
Christus in coena fecit, tanto Christianior."

[2] In the sense in which it was understood by his opponents satisfactio was entirely
discarded by Luther; see Erlang. Ed., Vol. 26, p. 17 ("Wider Hans Worst"):
"And this thing, satisfactio, is the beginning and origin, the door and entrance to all
abominations in the papacy; just as in the Church baptism is the beginning and
entrance to all graces and to the forgiveness of sins." See also p. 55 ; "For one
knows now that satisfaction is nothing."

should be a perpetual habit and practice ; fourthly, he therewith cancelled the necessity for priestly co-operation, whether in connection with confession (confessio)—auricular confession as confession of *all* sins is impossible, as self-revelation to a brother it is salutary—or in connection with absolution : one Christian can and should forgive another his sin, and thereby, as Luther boldly expresses it, become to him a Christ ; fifthly, he laid the strongest emphasis on contrition having combined with it absolution ; it is only as belonging to each other that these two exist, and nothing must disturb or interfere with their union ; but they belong to each other because they are both included in faith (fides) ; in faith, however, confession does not, strictly speaking, consist, to say nothing of "satisfaction" ; sixthly, he removed all abuses that had become connected with the Sacrament ; by relating forgiveness exclusively to the cancelling of eternal guilt, he made an end of the calculations of reason, so dangerous to souls, with regard to mortal sins and venial sins, eternal guilt and temporal guilt, eternal penalties and temporal penalties, and in this way also delivered the Sacrament from being mixed up with the regard to temporal profits which had been the necessary result of reflection upon temporal penalties ; by *restricting* the effect of absolution to eternal guilt, he was led, in harmony with his insight into the nature of sin, to deal with this last much more earnestly than the Schoolmen did : the Schoolmen wrought with venial sin and with attrition, and showed great skill in reducing sins in general to the former, and in making attrition acceptable to God ; in this matter he knew only of his infinite guilt and his God ; seventhly, along with those abuses he expressly set aside the subtly refined doctrines of purgatory, of the applied merit of saints and of indulgences.   Between the contrasted opposites of guilt and forgiveness, hell and heaven, there is nothing intermediate, hence there is no purgatory ; merits of saints are a Pelagian invention, and so they can be placed to no one's credit ; just for that reason indulgences are a foolish fancy, while the practice of them is a subversion of Christ's honour and of penitence ;[1] but if

---

[1] It is well known that on the 31st Oct., 1517, Luther had not yet completed his criticism of indulgences.

they merely relate to arbitrary church ordinances, they do not belong at all to religion.—By his overturning the Catholic Sacrament of penance and substituting for it the thought of justification by faith, Luther abandoned the old Church and came under the necessity of building a new one.

4. From the stand-point of faith he likewise overthrew the whole hierarchical and priestly Church System. His negative criticism in this department does not suffer from the slightest want of clearness. Through justification by faith every Christian is a Christian with full rights and privileges; nothing stands between him and his God; the Church, again, is the community of believers, visible through the preaching of the Word—nothing else. To this Church the "Keys" are given, *i.e.*, the application of the divine Word; they are given to it, because they are given to faith. These propositions have the effect of excluding both a spiritual class to whom believers are bound, and the jurisdictional power of the Church. But this strikes at the heart, not merely of the mediæval Church, but of the ancient Church as well, at least from the time of Irenæus. And with what inexorable energy Luther drew the conclusions here, including even the inference that the Pope is Antichrist; what sport he could make with the "grease, tar and butter" with which the Church anointed its sorcerers and hypocrites; in what language he could describe the Church Order, the canonical law, the power of the Pope as the abomination of desolation in the holy place! If it is asked what the power was that here brought the words of wrath to his lips, the answer must be that it was the knowledge the confession of which is felt to be so hard to-day even by keen-sighted Protestant theologians—the knowledge that the power of faith is as much enfeebled by added burdens as by false doctrine. Why should it not be possible that there should exist in Christendom a Pope, a priesthood, an episcopal constitution, a jurisdictional power of the Church extending over all realms? There is nothing that forbids such an order, if it is serviceable, and there is more than *one* cogent reason recommending it. But to demand this order *in the name of the gospel*, or even to let it continue to appear that it is the outcome of the gospel itself, means to impose a

burden on religion that crushes it.   Luther felt and saw that.
The bishops, the councils and even the Pope he would willingly
have allowed to continue, or at least would have tolerated, if
they had accepted the gospel; to what states of things would
not this man of inward freedom have readily adjusted himself,
if the pure Word of God was taught!   But they appealed on
behalf of themselves and their practices to the Word of God,
and declared they were as surely to be found there as the forgiveness of sins; and so he made havoc of them, and pilloried
them as men who sought for all possible things, only not for
the honour of God and Christ.

5. Not less radical was his attitude towards the ecclesiastical
worship of God.   Here also he broke down the tradition, not
only of the mediæval but also of the ancient Church, as this is
traceable by us back to the second century.   The Church's
public worship of God is for him nothing but unity in divine
worship in respect of time and place on the part of individuals.
By this proposition all the peculiar halo—simply pagan, however, in its character—which surrounded public worship was
dissolved; the special priest and the special sacrifice were done
away with, and all value was taken from specific ecclesiastical
observances participation in which is saving and essential.
Not as if Luther failed to recognise the importance of fellowship—yet even on this matter he betrays uncertainty here and
there [1]—; how highly he estimated preaching and divine service
(ministerium divinum)!   But public divine service can have no
other aim, no other course, no other means, than the divine
service of the individual has; for God treats with us simply
through the Word, which is not exclusively attached to particular persons, and He requires from us no other service than
the faith that unfolds itself in praise and thanksgiving, humility
and penitence, firm trust in God's help amidst all need, therefore
also in fidelity in one's calling and in prayer.   What is contemplated therefore in public divine service can be in no way
different from this: *the building up of faith through proclamation of the divine Word and the offering in prayer of the common*

---

[1] It frequently seems as if public divine service were only a provision for training
the imperfect, and this does not in every case merely seem to be the meaning.

sacrifice of praise. In so far, however, as it is the Christian *life*
that is at bottom the true service of God, public worship always
maintains in relation to this the character merely of something
particular. That Luther took up towards the Catholic mass an
attitude of strong repugnance and repudiated the monstrous
irregularities that turned divine service into a means for securing
profane profit, is denied by no one. That he here set aside
numberless abuses is a manifest fact; but the seemingly
conservative attitude he assumed in making his corrections in
the Manual for Mass, and his declinature to undertake an entire
reconstruction of divine service, led many "Lutherans" in the
sixteenth century, as well as in the nineteenth, to fall back on
extremely objectionable views as to a *specific* (religious) value
of public worship, as to the purpose of worship and its means.
How un-Lutheran that is—because it is possible and necessary
here to correct Luther by Luther himself—and how the
evangelical idea of the worship of God differs toto coelo from
the Catholic, has been excellently shown quite recently. The
question is of special importance within the lines of the history
of dogma, because Luther's attitude towards worship has the
most exact parallel in his attitude towards dogma.[1]

[1] See Gottschick, Luther's Anschauungen vom christlichen Gottesdienst und seine
thatsächliche Reform desselben (1887); compare the discussion on p. 3, where at
every point one might substitute for Old Lutheran Liturgy Old Lutheran dogmatic :
" We should less require . . . to be concerned did we find that the old Lutheran
Liturgy was an even relatively genuine product of the peculiar spirit of the Reformation,
the spirit which we cannot throw off without losing our very selves. That could
only be the case, however, if Luther had derived the highest positive, the so to speak
creative principle of his new liturgical ordinances from the new views that had been
acquired by him of Christianity as a whole. But in point of fact Luther attached
himself to the order of the Roman Mass, and reshaped this only in certain particulars,
on the one hand excluding what was directly contrary to the gospel, on the other hand
introducing certain points of detail.—Besides, he had so little interest in liturgy, was
so little guided by the thought of an inner, vital law controlling the arrangement of
divine service, that in connection with nearly every part of the Catholic legacy he
makes the remark, that this is of little importance, and the matter might be equally
well dealt with otherwise. Under these circumstances we do not actually underestimate the merit Luther acquired in connection even with reform of divine worship,
when we do not conceal from ourselves the necessity for our attempting a *really new
construction* in this field, taking the principles lying in Luther's Reformation view
as our guide. But as in other fields so here also the matter stands thus—*that Luther
himself has already developed the really evangelical principles for the reconstruction*

6. Luther annihilated the formal, outward authorities for faith, which had been set up by Catholicism. That here likewise he not merely attacked mediæval institutions, but set aside the old Catholic doctrine, is beyond dispute. As this has already been dealt with above (p. 23 ff.), let us only sum up here what is most essential. Catholicism, whose mode of view always led it in the first instance to separate into parts the religious experience, that it might then submit it to be dealt with by the understanding, had also introduced here the distinction between *the matter itself* and the *authority*. This distinction corresponded with its method of drawing distinctions generally, a method which proceeded by differentiating at one time between necessity, possibility, and reality, at another time between form and matter, at another time between effect and saving effect. All these extremely confusing arts of reason are lacking in Luther's original theses. Neither is there to be laid on him the weight of responsibility for distinguishing between a formal and a material principle;[1] for the matter was for him the authority, and the authority the matter. But the matter is the Christ of history as preached, the Word of God. From this point he gained the insight and courage to protest against the formal authorities of Catholicism as against commandments of men. Thereby, however, he threw overboard the whole system of Catholicism, as it had been elaborated from the days of Irenæus ; for the inviolability of this system rests *simply* on the formal authorities ; the faith that Fathers and Schoolmen appealed to was obedience to the Church doctrine, an obedience that is certain of what it holds, because those authorities are represented as inviolable. But

---

from his fundamental view of religion, and to a much greater extent, too, than can be discovered from his acts as a Reformer and from the writings that bear upon these." The sure proof of this is given in the dissertation itself.

[1] See Ritschl in the Zeitschr. für K.-Gesch. I., p. 397 ff. Following on this article there is an increasing tendency to discontinue recognising in Luther the distinction between a formal and a material principle. Thus it is even said in Thomasius-Seeberg, II., p. 345 : "The principle of Protestantism is faith in Christ as the only Saviour, the faith that justifies, that is witnessed to by Holy Scripture, that is wrought by the Word of God (by the Holy Spirit)." But in what follows there is again a denial in some measure of this perception in favour of the Scripture principle.

Luther protested against *all* these authorities, the infallibility of
the Church, of the Pope, the Councils, and the Church Fathers,
both with regard to Christian doctrine and with regard to
exposition of Scripture, against the guarantee which the constitution of the Church was alleged to furnish for truth, and
against every doctrinal formulation of the past as such—on the
ground that in every case they themselves required to be
proved.   But—when so bravely carrying on his battle against
the authority of the Councils—Luther took up at the same time
an adverse attitude towards the infallibility of Scripture; and
how could he do otherwise?   If only that is authority which is
also matter—the position of the Christian as both bound and
free postulated this—how could there be authority where the
matter does not distinctly appear, or where even the opposite
of it appears?   The content of a person who gives himself to
be our own, never can be coincident with a written word however clear and certain it may be.   Thus Luther necessarily had
to distinguish even between Word of God and Holy Scripture.
It is true, certainly, that a book which represents itself as the
sure word of Christ and as apostolic testimony, makes in the
highest sense the claim to be regarded as the Word of God.
But yet Luther refused to be dictated to and to have his mouth
stopped even by the apostolical—and that exactly at the most
trying time, when the formal authority of the letter seemed to
be most of all required by him.   What limitations and losses
he subsequently imposed upon himself is a question to be dealt
with afterwards ; but there can be no doubt that the position
Luther took up towards the New Testament in his " Prefaces,"
and even in special discussions elsewhere, was the correct one,
i.e., the position corresponding to his faith, and that by his
attitude towards its formal authorities Catholicism was
abolished by him from its historical beginnings.

7. Finally, there is still a very important point to be
adverted to.   In very many passages Luther has indicated
with sufficient distinctness, *that he merely conceded to his theological opponents the theological terminology, and made use of it
himself merely on account of traditional familiarity with it, and
because the employment of incorrect words was not necessarily of*

evil. He so expressed himself with regard to the most important terms.   First of all he had an objection to all the different
descriptions of justification : to justify, to be regenerated, to
sanctify, to quicken, righteousness, to impute (justificare,
regenerari, sanctificare, vivificare, justitia, imputare), etc., etc. ;
he felt very much that the mere number of the terms was a
serious burden upon his conception, and that no single word
completely answered to his view.   Secondly, in a similar way
he objected to the word satisfaction (satisfactio) in every sense ;
as used by his opponents he will only let it pass.   Thirdly, he
stumbled at the term " Church " (ecclesia); for it obscured or
confused what should simply be called Christian community,
gathering, or—still better—a holy Christendom.   Fourthly, he
observed very clearly the objectionableness of the word
" Sacrament "; what he would have liked most would have
been to see that the use of it was entirely avoided, and that for
the ambiguous formula " Word and Sacrament," there was
substituted the *Word* alone, or that if the term Sacrament was
retained there should be a speaking of *one* Sacrament and
several *signs.*[1]   Fifthly, he himself declared such a term as
ὁμοούσιος to be unallowable in the strict sense, because it
represents a bad state of things when such words are invented
in the Christian system of faith : " we must indulge the Fathers
in the use of it . . . but if my soul hates the word homousios
and I prefer not to use it, I shall not be a heretic ; for who will
compel me to use it, provided that I hold the thing which was
defined in the Council by means of the Scriptures ? although
the Arians had wrong views with regard to the faith, they were
nevertheless *very right* in this . . . that they required that no
profane and novel word should be allowed to be introduced
into the rules of faith." [2]   In like manner he objected to and

---

[1] Erlang Ed. Opp. var. arg. V., p. 21 : "tantum tria sacramenta ponenda . . .
quamquam, si usu scripturæ loqui velim, non nisi unum sacramentum habeam et tria
signa sacramentalia."

[2] "Indulgendum est patribus . . . quod si odit anima mea vocem homousion et
nolim ea uti, non ero hæreticus ; quis enim me coget uti, modo rem teneam quæ in
concilio per scripturas definita est ? ets Ariani male senserunt in fide, hoc tamen
optime . . . exegerunt, ne vocem profanam et novam in regulis fidei statui liceret.

rather avoided the terms " Dreifaltigkeit," " Dreiheit," " unitas,"
" trinitas " (threefoldness, threeness, oneness, trinity). Yet, as
is proved by the words quoted above, there is this difference
observable here—*that he regarded the terminologies of the
mediæval theology as misleading and false, the terminologies on
the other hand of the theology of the ancient Church as merely
useless and cold.* But from still another side he objected most
earnestly to all the results of theological labour that had been
handed down from the days of the Apologists ; and here in still
greater degree than in his censure of particular conceptions his
divergence from the old dogma found expression, namely, in
that distinguishing between " for himself (itself) " and " for us,'
which is so frequently to be found in Luther. Over and over
again, and on all occasions, the definitions given by the old
dogmatic of God and Christ, of the will and attributes of God,
of the natures in Christ, of the history of Christ, etc., are set
aside with the remark : " that He is for himself," in order that
his new view, which is for him the chief matter, nay, which constitutes the whole, may then be introduced under the formula
" that He is for us," or simply " for us." " Christ is not called
Christ because He has two natures. What concern have I in
that ? But he bears this glorious and comforting title from the
office and work which He has taken upon Him . . . that He is
by nature man and God, *that He has for Himself.*" [1] In this
" for himself " and " for us " the new theology of Luther, and at
the same time his conservative tendency find clearest expression. Theology is not the analysis and description of God and
of the divine acts from the standpoint of reason as occupying
an independent position over against God, but it is the confession on the part of faith of its own experience, that is, of
revelation. This, however, puts an end to the old theology with
its metaphysic and its rash ingenuity.[2] But if Luther now

Erlang. Ed., Opp. var. arg. V., p. 505 sq. See also the Augsburg Confutation
(Art. 1), whose authors observed very clearly what was heretical in these words.

[1] Erlang. Ed. Ausg. XXXV., p. 207 f.

[2] See Theod. Harnack, Luther's Theologie, I., p. 83 : " Yet revelation guarantees
a true and saving knowledge 'of the essential Godhead in itself.' Nay, Christians
alone are able to speak of this and have this divine wisdom. It is true, no doubt,
that revelation lays down definite conditions for theology and imposes limits upon it,

nevertheless allows those old doctrines to remain under the terms " God in Himself," " the hidden God," " the hidden will of God," *they no longer remain as what are properly speaking doctrines of faith.* About this no doubt can arise. But that they were not entirely rejected by him has its cause on the one hand in his believing they were found in Scripture, and on the other hand in his failure to think out the problems in a comprehensive and systematic way. With this we shall have to deal in the following section.

In view of what has been set forth in the last two paragraphs with regard to the Christianity of Luther and his criticism of the ecclesiastical dogma, it cannot but be held *that in Luther's Reformation the old dogmatic Christianity was discarded and a new evangelical view substituted for it.* The Reformation was really an *issue* of the history of dogma. The positive and negative elements of Luther's Christian doctrine are most intimately connected; the latter are the effect, the former the cause. If he still concurs with this or that formulation of the ancient or the mediæval Church, then, with what we have considered before us, that is partly apparent only, and it is partly a *free* concurrence, which can never have had its cause in an a priori surrender to tradition. The formal authorities of dogma were swept away; thereby dogma itself, *i.e.*, the inviolable system of doctrine established by the Holy Spirit, was abolished. But it is by no means the case that dogma re-emerges in the old form —now, however, as the content of devout faith ; there appears rather the pure doctrine of the Gospel (pura doctrina evangelii) as a new dogmatic opposed to the old ; for there was a setting aside of all those intellectual dividings up of the content of faith, by which that content was separated into metaphysic, natural theology, revealed doctrine, sacramental doctrine and ethic. In

but these do not consist in that arbitrary and comfortless separation between God's essence and His revelation ; they are partly objective, implied in the content, measure and aim of revelation itself, and they partly relate subjectively to the principle involved in the object itself and to the nature and tendency of theological knowledge as thereby conditioned."

this way the revision extended itself back beyond the second
century of the history of the Church, and it was at all points a
radical one. *The history of dogma,* which had its beginning in
the age of the Apologists, nay, of the Apostolic Fathers, *was
brought to an end.*

*Thereby the work of Augustine was finally brought to com-
pletion;* for, as we have shown in our second Book, this great
man, by going back to Paulinism, began the work of breaking
down and powerfully re-casting the ruling dogmatic tradition
and of restoring theology to faith. But the sceptic stopped
short before the formal authorities of Catholicism, and the
Neoplatonists would not cease revelling in the All-One ; besides,
Augustine knew not yet how to enter into sure possession of the
power given through faith in God as the Father of Jesus Christ.
Thus his Church received from him, along with a problem, a
complex and confused inheritance — the old dogma—and,
running parallel with this, a new inward piety, which moved in
thoughts quite different from dogma. This attitude is revealed
at the very beginning of the Middle Ages by Alcuin, and from
the time of Bernard onwards, Augustinianism, augmented in
some degree by valuable elements, continued to exercise its
influence. Certainly Luther stands in many respects closer to
an Irenæus and an Athanasius than to the theologians of the
fourteenth and fifteenth centuries ; but in many respects he is
further removed from the former than from the latter, and this
is a clear evidence that the inner development of Christianity in
the Middle Ages was by no means merely retrograde or entirely
mistaken. If Luther had to break even with a Tauler or a
Bernard, how much more was a break necessary with Augustine
and Irenæus ! The Reformation is the issue of the history of
dogma because it brings about this issue in the line of the
origination of it *within the history of piety* by Augustine, and of
its subsequent preparation during a period of a thousand years.
*It set up the evangelical faith in place of dogma, this being done by
its cancelling the dualism of dogmatic Christianity and practical
Christian self-criticism and life-conduct.*

But what it placed at the centre of practical Christian self-
criticism and life-conduct was just faith itself and its certainty.

Thereby it gave to the theoretic element—if one may so describe the sure faith in revelation, *i.e.*, in the God who manifests Himself in Christ—a direct importance for piety such as was never known by mediæval theology. " Let this be the sum of the matter : our love is ready to die for you, but to touch faith means to touch the pupil of our eye." [1] Hence nothing is more incorrect than the widely prevalent opinion that the cancelling of dogmatic Christianity by Luther was equivalent to a neutralising of all "faith that is believed" (" fides quæ creditur ") : all that is required is simply pious feeling. A more foolish misunderstanding of Luther's Reformation cannot be conceived of ; for precisely the opposite rather is true of it : *it only restored its sovereign right to faith, and thereby to the doctrine of faith*—in the sense of its being nothing but the doctrine of Christ—*after the uncertainties of the Middle Ages, which had reached their highest point at the beginning of the sixteenth century; and to the horror of all Humanists, Churchmen, Franciscans, and Illuminists set up theology, i.e., the true theology of the cross (theologia crucis), as the decisive power in the Church.* Dogma, which always taught merely how religion is possible, and therefore could not at all stand at the centre of piety, was detached from that proclamation of faith which itself produces and builds up faith, and therefore claims as its right the sovereign position in religion. Luther passed back from the Middle Ages to the ancient Church, in so far as he again reduced the immense material forming the system of Christian faith to Christology. But he distinguished himself from the ancient Church in this, that he undertook so to shape faith in the revelation in Christ that the revelation should appear not merely as the condition of our salvation, but—objectively and subjectively—as the sole efficient factor in it.

But if this describes the revolution of things, then it can be very easily understood how the great task, the fulfilment of which was contemplated, could not be carried out in a thoroughly strict way by Luther himself. A superhuman spirit would have been required in order here to think out and arrange everything

---

[1] " Summa esto : charitas nostra pro vobis mori parata est, fides vero si tangitur, tangitur pupilla oculi nostri."

correctly; for there were two tasks in view, which almost seemed contradictory, though this was not actually true of them : to place the importance of faith as the content of revelation in the centre, in contradistinction to all 'opinion and doing, and thus to bring to the front the suppressed theoretic element, and yet on the other hand not simply to adopt that faith which the past had developed, but to exhibit it rather in the form in which it is life and creates life, is practice, but is religious practice. From the greatness of this problem there is *also* to be explained the survival in Luther's theology of those elements which confuse it and have necessarily shaken the conclusion that the Reformation is the issue of the history of dogma.

(4) *The Catholic Elements retained by Luther along with and within his Christianity.*[1]

Whether the Catholic elements contained in Luther's Christianity be few or many, so much at least is certain from what has been already brought to view—namely, that they belong certainly to the "whole Luther," but not to the "whole Christianity" of Luther. Following in the line of Neander Ritschl,[2] and many others, Loofs too expresses this opinion,[3] "So far as the history of dogma is concerned, the Lutheran Reformation would have completed itself otherwise than it

---

[1] Against the misunderstanding that my criticism of Luther in the following section is unhistorical and over-acute I am not able to protect myself. I know as well as my opponents that for Luther's consciousness his faith and his theology formed a unity, and that the greater part of what is represented here as limitation in Luther's doctrine was the necessary result of the historical position he assumed and of the way in which he set about his great task. But by our seeing this we are not forbidden, if the "entire Luther" is set up as a law of faith for the Evangelical Church, to show what there was in the sum of his conceptions that was simply derived from the history of the times or was traditional. It must also be taken into consideration that he clung to a negative attitude towards certain conclusions deducible from his own religious principles, and towards perceptions that already existed or were making their appearance in his age. But here also the question for history is not what ought to have been, but what was.

[2] See above p. 27.

[3] Dogmengesch., 3rd ed., p. 369.

ultimately did, if the conclusions that follow from Luther's fundamental thoughts had been established by him in their *entirety* and by a *thorough-going* comparison with the *whole* tradition. The fragments of the old that remained restricted even for Luther himself the *validity* of the new thoughts, and, in the case of those who came later, impoverished them." The question as to whether between the years 1519 and (about) 1523 Luther did not take a step of advance that had the promise in it of more thorough reforms, has as a rule been answered negatively by the most recent students of Luther, after H. Lang[1] and others had in an incautious and an untenable way answered it in the affirmative. Yet in my opinion the negative answer can only be given with great reservations.[2] What is in question according to my judgment, as was remarked above (p. 169), is not so much whether there were two periods in the reforming activity of Luther, as rather whether there was a great episode in this work of his during which he was lifted above his own limitations. Yet this point need not be further discussed here. In this connection it falls to us in the first instance to discover the grounds that made it possible for Luther to retain so much of the old, nay, to retain even the old Catholic dogma itself, along with the new, and to interweave the one with the other. In aiming at this we can find a point of departure in our discussions above, p. 168 ff. We shall then have to state and illustrate briefly the most important groups of the old dogma doctrines to be found in Luther.

I. 1. Luther took his stand on the side of *faith* as opposed to every kind of work, on the side of the doctrine of the gospel (doctrina evangelii) as opposed to the performances and processes which were represented as making man righteous. Hence he stood in danger of adopting or approving any kind of expression of faith, if only it appeared free from law and performance, work and process (see the proof above p. 177 f). Into this danger he fell. Accordingly confusion entered into his conception of the Church also. His conception of the

---

[1] M.L., ein relig. Characterbild, 1870.

[2] I am pleased to observe from indications in Weingarten's Zeittafeln und Ueberblicke, 3rd ed., pp. 167-170, that he holds a similar opinion.

Church (fellowship in faith, fellowship in pure doctrine) became
as ambiguous as his conception of the doctrine of the gospel
(doctrina evangelii).

2. Luther believed he was contending only against the abuses
and errors of the Mediæval Church. He declared, no doubt, not
infrequently that he was not satisfied with the "dear Fathers,"
and that they had all gone astray;[1] yet he was not clear-sighted
enough to say to himself that if the Church Fathers were in
error, their decrees at the Councils could not possibly contain
the whole truth. In no way, it is true, did he feel himself any
longer *externally* bound by these decrees, nay, we can see brilliant
flashes of incisive criticism, *e.g.* in his treatise on Councils and
Churches; yet these continued on the whole without effect.
He always fell back again upon the view that the wretched Pope
was alone to blame for all the evil, and that all the mischief,
therefore, was connected with the Middle Ages only. Thus
from this side his prepossession in favour of the faith-formulæ
of the Ancient Church—on the ground that they did not take
to do with works and law—was only further strengthened;
indeed there was exercising its influence here, unconsciously to
himself, a remnant of the idea that the empirical Church is
authority.

3. Luther knew too little of the history of the Ancient Church
and of ancient dogma to be really able to criticise them. No
doubt, when all comes to be put together that formed a subject
of careful study for him,[2] we shall be astonished at the amount
he knew; yet he certainly could not know more that his century
knew, and there were many who were his superiors in Patristic
studies. He never entered deeply into the spirit of the Church
Fathers; on the other hand an abstract criticism was at all
times quite remote from him; under these circumstances, therefore, there remained for him only a conservative attitude. This
attitude Luther really definitely renounced only when he saw
the Fathers following the paths of Pelagius.[3]

[1] See the quotation given in Vol. II., p. 7, note.

[2] The wish here expressed has recently been fulfilled in an excellent way by the comprehensive and thorough investigation by E. Schäfer, Luther als Kirchenhistoriker
(Gütersloh, 1897).

[3] I must assume from p. 3 of. Schäfer's work just referred to that he regards him-

4. Luther always includes himself and what he undertook within the *one* Church which he alone knew, within the Catholic Church (as he understood it).[1] He declared that this Church itself gave him the title to be a Reformer. That was right, if it was right that the empirical Church is only the Church so far as it is the fellowship of faith ; but it was wrong, in so far as the Catholic Church was already something quite different—namely a State resting upon definite holy statutes. This Catholic Church, however, was viewed by Luther as a temporary, though already very old malformation, which could possess no rights whatever. So he believed that he could remain in the old Church, nay, that—though it might be only with a few friends— he was himself the old, true Church. This remarkable view, which is to be explained from the idealism of faith, made it possible for Luther to abandon the old Church and reduce it to ruins, but at the same time to assert that he himself stood within the old Church. If in holding this attitude he was so strong in faith that it gave him no concern how large or small the number might be who did not at the time bow the knee to Baal, yet he had the highest interest in its being shown that he represented the Church that had existed from century to century. Hence there arose the duty of proving that he stood within a historic continuity. But from what could that be more definitely proved than from the faith-formulæ of the Ancient Church, which still retained their authority ?

5. Luther never felt strongly impelled to start from the innermost centre of the new view of the whole of Christianity which he had obtained, and from thence to furnish a systematic statement of the whole, indicating exactly what remained and what had dropped away. He assumed a commanding air in theology, as a child does in the home, summoning forth old and new and always having in view merely the nearest practical end. The correction of theoretical errors as such gave him no concern

self as having refuted the judgment indicated above, which is not, however, the case. What he brings forward to illustrate Luther's knowledge and opinions regarding Church history was in the main known to me ; nothing follows from it that conflicts with the view expressed in the text.

[1] See especially his treatises " Von den Conciliis und Kirchen " and " Wider Hans Worst."

whatever; he had no longing whatever for the clearness of a
well-arranged system of doctrine; but on that account his
strength became also his weakness.[1]

6. Luther used the old doctrines in such a way that expression
was given to the *whole* of Christianity under each scheme, *i.e.*, he
interpreted each scheme in the sense of his view of the whole of
Christianity; what was included in the formula beyond this
gave him little trouble though he might let it retain its validity.
This peculiar attitude made it possible for him to adapt himself to what was very foreign. (See above p. 196.)

7. In principle Luther prepared the way for a sound historical
exegesis; but how far the principle was from being really
applied as yet by his century and by himself! In dealing with
particulars he is still almost everywhere a mediæval exegete,
fettered by all the prejudices of this exegesis, by the typology,
and even, in spite of counter-working principles, by the allegorism. Although in principle he demanded that the understanding of Scripture should be free from the authority of ecclesiastical
tradition, he still continues himself firmly bound by this tradition.
He broke through it where justification was in question, but he
then broke through it also in connection with passages containing nothing whatever of the doctrine of justification or of faith,
or containing only something foreign to these doctrines. Under
such circumstances it cannot surprise us that he found the
doctrines of the Trinity, of the two natures, etc., in Holy
Scripture, and even indeed in the Old Testament. But still
more must be said here—he had altogether as little understanding of history as the majority of his contemporaries had.
History in the highest sense of the word was for him a closed
book. He showed no perception either of the relativity of the
historical or of the growth and progress of knowledge within
history.[2] How could it be possible under such circumstances
to ascertain accurately what Scripture contains as a historic
record? But how can a *pure* form of expression for the essence

[1] We have here the strict parallel to his way of estimating worship, which has
already been spoken of above, p. 221 f.

[2] While this opinion is held, it must not be forgotten of course that his genius as a
hero enabled him to see what was correct at decisive points.

of Christianity be expected if this condition is not fulfilled ?

The foregoing considerations have almost in every case indicated limitations that were involved in the peculiar attitude
of the Reformer as a Reformer, or in the spiritual condition of
the age, and which it was therefore absolutely impossible to
transcend. But Luther's entire attitude was also determined by
limitations which by no means come under this view, but were
rather opposed to his attitude as a Reformer. These, if I see
correctly, were chiefly the following : [1]

8. His perception as a Reformer that the *Word of God* is the
foundation of faith was not so clear as to put an end entirely to
Biblicism : he continued, rather, to be involved here in a flagrant
contradiction, for while he criticised Scripture itself, he certainly
on the other hand set up the letter as the Word of God, in so
far as he adopted without test the Rabbinic-Catholic idea ot
the verbal inspiration of Holy Scripture. In many cases, no
doubt, he counterbalanced this contradictory procedure by in-
terpreting the gospel itself into the letter under consideration ;
but apart from this, he certainly as a rule allowed the particular
Bible narrative, the saying selected, whatever it might be, to
have effect, directly and literally, as the Word of God.

9. Just as little did he rise clearly above the view of the
Ancient Church and the Middle Ages in the question of the
Sacrament. It is true, certainly, that he not only took steps
towards breaking through this view, but really cancelled it by
his doctrine of the *one* Sacrament, the Word; yet there still
lingered with him a hidden remnant, a real superstition
(superstitio), with regard to the Sacrament, and therefore also
with regard to the "means of grace," and this superstition had

---

[1] I should prefer not to embrace a reference under the following scheme to the great
extent to which Luther was dominated by coarse superstition, and that, too, in all
possible fields. I do not include within this his belief in the devil, for that belongs
to another sphere, incommensurable for my experience. But in determining his
entire attitude as the founder of a Confession, the fact cannot certainly be left out of
view that he was more superstitious than many of his contemporaries, nay, that in
many respects he was as superstitious as a child. Those who constantly bring
forward the "whole Luther" are responsible for its being necessary to mention such
things.

the gravest consequences for his construction of doctrine. Though with him error and truth lie closely side by side here, yet it cannot be denied that he gave scope for serious errors.

10. No one assailed the *Nominalistic theology* more keenly than Luther ; but his opponents forced him to theologise, and to answer their way of putting the question.   In this connection he adopted the Nominalistic sequences of thought, and developed them more fully as his own.   But even apart from this he did not discard the remnants of Nominalistic Scholasticism ;· indeed they reappeared in great strength, after he had passed in the doctrine of the Eucharist beyond the limit of what were really his own thoughts ; but even in his doctrine of predestination he furnished scope for the errors and over-acuteness of Scholasticism.[1]

11. After Luther had come into conflict with the "Enthusiasts" and Anabaptists, he acquired a distrust of reason, which passed far beyond his distrust of it as a support for self-righteousness. In many respects he really hardened himself into an attitude of bold defiance towards reason and then yielded also to that Catholic Spirit which worships in paradox and in contradiction of terms (contradictio in adjecto) the wisdom of God and sees in them the stamp of divine truth.   Like Tertullian he could harp on the "certum est, quia ineptum est" (" it is certain, because it is absurd "), and take delight in the perplexities in which the understanding finds itself involved.   He never, indeed, revelled in mystery as mystery, and in his paradoxes there was unquestionably an element of religious power, the secret of heroic spirits, and the secret of religion itself, which never lets itself be made perfectly transparent.   Yet no one disparages reason and science with impunity, and Luther himself had to suffer for the obscurations to which he subjected his conception of faith ; still greater, however, was the penalty for those who adhered to him, who degraded to a new Scholastic wisdom what he had defiantly proclaimed.

[1] See the dissertations that deal with Luther's Nominalism in connection with the criticism of his doctrine of predestination : Lütkens, Luther's Prädestinationslehre, 1858 ; Theod. Harnack, L.'s Theologie, I., p. 70, and elsewhere ; Kattenbusch, L.'s Lehre v. unfreien Willen u. v. d. Prädest., 1875; Ritschl, Rechtf. u. Versöhn., Vol. I.

In connection with these reflections what is of greatest importance must not be passed over : the position which the Reformation took up towards the Anabaptists, and towards others who had affinity with them, became most disastrous for itself and for its subsequent history.   At the present day we are passing through a phase of descriptive history of the Reformation, which does little in estimating the weight of this fact, because it is—for good reasons—most immediately interested in what is of primary importance—Luther's faith and Luther's ideal of life.[1]   There are in fact also many considerations that make it fully intelligible why the Reformation simply rejected everything that was offered to it by the " enthusiasts."   Yet, however many more explanations and excuses for this may be brought forward, the fact remains unaffected thereby, that the unjust course followed by the Reformers entailed upon them and their cause the most serious losses.   How much they might have learned from those whom they despised, although they were forced to reject their fundamental thoughts !   How much more decisively did many of these men put an end to the magic of the sacraments, how much more strictly and accurately they defined the significance of the written Word, how much more clearly they frequently discerned the real sense of Scripture passages, advocating at the same time a sounder exegesis, how much more courageously they drew many conclusions regarding the doctrine of the Trinity, Christology, etc , how much more resolutely did some

---

[1] The Confessionalist description of history had little insight into, and little lov for, the "sects" of the Reformation period.   But since at the same time it did no even clearly discern the real importance of the Reformation, it was necessary in the first instance that this should be brought to light.   That was done by Ritschl, and his disciples follow the directions given by him.   And yet even with this done there has not been a passing beyond a very stiff, and almost indeed a narrow view of the Reformation, and little faculty has been shown for understanding the excellences which the "Enthusiasts" unquestionably possessed at peripheral points—some of them by no means merely at peripheral points.   It must be admitted that the way in which many dilettante "historians of culture" have looked at things and shown their blindness to the true nature of the Reformation could not but have a strongly repellent effect ; even such an enthusiast as Keller was unable to produce conviction.   Yet from him much certainly could have been learned, and, above all, the guiding star for the writing of history—even the history of the Reformation—ought not to have been kept out of view—that real truths are never disparaged with impunity.

of them take their stand for outward, as a consequence of inward
freedom ! No doubt one says even here, "timeo Danaos et dona
ferentes" (" I fear the Greeks even when they bring gifts "), and
certainly these people's presuppositions were foreign as a rule
to the evangelical. But no one escapes responsibility for carefully considering a truth, because the adversary brings it, and
recommends it *also* on bad grounds. And there is something
more to be added : not a few of the demands of the Enthusiasts
were already the product of the *secular* culture, science and
insight which had obtained even in the sixteenth century a certain independence. But it is a bad way of developing theological
firmness—though it has again its unshrinking advocates at the
present day—to hold that perceptions of that kind may be simply
ignored. In many respects the Reformers fenced themselves off
from secular culture where this touched the declarations of faith.
In this sense they were mediæval, and did nothing to bring about
an understanding between revelation and reason, leaving that
great task to a succeeding century, which was by no means still
firmly established in evangelical faith, and was thus much worse
prepared for the solution of the problem. Even if one could
succeed in fully justifying this procedure of theirs, and in showing, perhaps, that even the slightest adoption of " Enthusiast "
knowledge would have meant *at that time* the death of the
Reformation, it would in no way alter the fact that the
Reformation buried under injustice and hatred many better
perceptions which the age possessed and thereby made itself
chargeable with the later crises in Protestantism. The French
Church exterminated the Huguenots and Jansenists ; it received
in place of them the Atheists and Jesuits. The German
Reformation banished the " Enthusiasts "; it received in place
of them the rationalists and modern " Positivism."

II. The consequence of holding this attitude was that, so far
as Luther left to his followers a " dogmatic," there was presented
in this an extremely complicated system : not a new structure,
but a modification of the old Patristic-Scholastic structure. But
it is then apparent after what has been already explained, that
in this regard Luther gave no final expression to evangelical
Christianity, but only made a beginning.

First, there rests with him responsibility—not only with Melanchthon—for the inclusion within the doctrine of the gospel
(doctrina evangelii) of all theoretic elements of Christian speculation which it was believed must be retained.   It is true, certainly, that he never ceased regarding these elements as manifold
testimonies to what is alone important in Christian faith ; but at
the same time he undoubtedly gave to them also an independent
value, because he held them to be perfect testimonies, and therefore to be faith itself.   There were causes leading him to adhere
the more firmly to this course, in his opposition to the Enthusiasts, and in the huge task of training a nation in Christianity ; and thus, without observing it, he passed over to the
view, that the Church, because it is the fellowship that is based
simply on God's revelation, and on the faith answering to it, is
just on that account fellowship in the *pure* doctrine, as including
all that is embraced in the correct theology. [1]   The saving faith

---

[1] Correct and false elements lie close together here.   If the Christian is a *positive*
religion, it is above all necessary to see clearly and maintain purely its content :
"Fides si tangitur, tangitur pupilla occuli nostri."   Further, what Luther has
wrought out in the Sermon on the 35th chap. of the 1st Book of Moses (Erlang. Ed.,
Vol. 34, p. 241 f.) with regard to doctrine and life is correct : "Therefore I have
often given the admonition, that one must be far from separating from each other life
and doctrine.   The doctrine is that I believe in Christ, regard my work, suffering,
and death as nothing, and serve my neighbour, and beyond this take no further
account of what I ought to be.   But the life is that I choose this or that course and act
accordingly.   Thus there is not nearly so much dependent on life as on doctrine, so
that, although the life is not so pure, yet the doctrine can nevertheless continue pure,
and there can be patience with the life. . . .   It is true that we ought to live thus ;
but let me live as I may, the doctrine does not therefore become false . . . anything
higher I cannot preach than that one must slay the old Adam and become a new man.
You say : Yes, but it is nevertheless not done by you.   Answer : I certainly ought
to do it, yes, even if God gives it to me ; but no one will ever attain to this height ;
there will still be many defects here.   Therefore let the life remain here below on
earth, raise the doctrine aloft to heaven."   This seemingly objectionable explanation
at once becomes clear when we observe what Luther here introduces into the conception "doctrine" ; it is the *disposition* corresponding to the doctrine.   For that reason
the content given to doctrine here is simply "believing in Christ, regarding my own
work as nothing and serving my neighbour," or "slaying the old Adam and becoming
a new man."   It is obvious that this "doctrine" is nothing but religion itself ; the
life, however, means the constantly defective earthly embodiment.   Yet over and over
again, led astray by the word "doctrine" and by opposition to legal righteousness,
Luther simply identified with this "doctrine" all articuli fidei of the old tradition
(this being due also to the fact that he understood the art of pointing out in each of

which justifies (or, in other words, the right doctrine), and the
sum of the particular articuli fidei appeared almost as identical.
But in this way there was introduced a narrowing of the notion
of the Church, compared with which even the Roman notion of
the Church appears in many respects more elastic and therefore
superior, and as the result of which Lutheranism approximated
to the Socinian view.   The Church threatened to be transformed
into a School—into the School, namely, of pure doctrine.   But
if the Church is a School, then in its view the distinction between those who know and those who do not know comes to be
of fundamental importance, and the resolute aiming at life passes
into the background ; in other words, there arises the Christianity of theologians and pastors and there develops itself a
doctrinairism which becomes lax in sanctification.   So far as
Luther himself was concerned, he ever again broke through this
view, indeed it was never wrought out with entire strictness
even in the sixteenth and seventeenth centuries, as is proved, *e. g.*,
by the sacred poetry.   Yet the fundamental evangelical view of
Christianity as a whole—not as a sum of separate portions of
doctrine—became obscured, and the practical aim of religion
became uncertain.   *Consequently instead of there being given to
the future clear and unambiguous guidance with regard to faith,
doctrine and Church, there was set to it rather a problem,—
namely, of giving a high place to " doctrine" in the Lutheran sense,
while freeing it at the same time from everything that cannot be
adopted otherwise than by means of spiritual surrender, and
of moulding the Church as the fellowship of faith, without giving
it the character of a theological school.*   The incorrect view of
faith (contemplated as assent to a sum of many articuli fidei of
equal value) became especially disastrous for the evangelical
doctrine of justification.   This doctrine necessarily appeared
now as the correct statement of a particular dogma—nothing
more.   As soon as this came about, the doctrine lost its true

them that " doctrine" properly so called).   But if in the explanation quoted above
one applies " doctrine" to all " articuli fidei," while he either does not at all think,
or scarcely thinks any more, of the preaching that requires him " to slay the old
Adam and become a new man," than the necessary consequence is an evil doctrinairism
and a lax feeling about what is moral.   For the fact that this consequence actually
ensued Luther was not really without responsibility.

significance and thereby its practical design. If it was encroached upon from the one side by the " objective dogmas," it
was only natural that from the other side it should be restricted
by a complicated doctrine of sanctification, mystic union (unio
mystica), etc. How much it became impaired and impoverished
under this pressure has been shown to us by Ritschl in his
account of the preparation in history for Pietism. But we need
only glance at the history of the German Confessional, in order
to see what desolation was caused by Lutheranism in narrowing
faith to " pure doctrine." As no earnest Christian can continue
to be satisfied with correct theology as the ideal of Christian
perfection, it was only a natural consequence, nay a real redemption, when Catholic ascetic criteria were again set up in the
practice of Lutheranism. But as time went on there could not
be satisfaction even with this ; for it was the evangelical faith,
of course, that one held, and hence what was attained was only
a feeble imitation of Catholicism. Thus the evangelical ideal of
life also remained a problem for the evangelical Church. [1]

[1] With another main problem that asserted itself from the first within the doctrinal
history of Protestantism I cannot here deal, as it would lead to an entering deeply
into the development of Protestantism—I mean the relation of the new system of
faith, as first formulated in Melanchthon's Loci, to the *system of natural theology*.
This system, after it had been prepared for by Nominalism, introduced and developed
itself almost unobserved as a " natural child " from the union of Classical Humanism
with certain perceptions of the positive theology. The devotion to antiquity showed
itself in this, that the Ciceronianism, which had partly supplanted the worn-off and
misused Aristotelianism, was clothed with the authority of the universally human,
the innate, the reasonable, as there could not of course be given to it the authority of
revelation. This natural " system," having its ultimate source in the Stoa, and used
only unconsciously or sparingly by Luther, was increasingly turned to account by the
Præceptor Germaniæ even in specific theology, and under the hard shell of Confessional systems of faith began even in the sixteenth century the struggle for the sole
supremacy, a supremacy which it was to achieve in the eighteenth century after it
had acquired strength from the new science of nature. So long as it remained in
combination with other modes of thought, it produced, as a universal principle, very
different effects. At one time it strengthened the Scholastic form of the doctrines of
faith, at another time it weakened particular dogmas that were paradoxical or that
were constructed from a strictly religious point of view. At one time it really gave
dogmatic theologians the consciousness of possessing a system of securely founded
truths, and surrounded even particular doctrines of the faith with the halo of universal
human reason, at another time it appeared as the stern adversary of these doctrines.
Taken as a whole it was a transitional phase, absolutely necessary, from the cognition
that was purely ecclesiastical, determined by the world beyond, and dependent on

Secondly, Luther left behind him an unspeakable confusion
as regards the significance of the old dogmas in the strictest
sense of the word.   No bridge leads to them from his justifying,
saving faith, not because this faith does not reach to them, *but
because those dogmas do not describe the being of God in so wonderful and comforting a way as evangelical faith is able to do from
its knowledge.*   This statement can be tested at every point
where Luther gives direct and living expression to his Christianity.   Christ is not to him a divine Person, who has taken to
Himself humanity, *but the man Jesus Christ is the revelation of
God Himself;* and Father, Son and Spirit are not three Persons
existing side by side, *but one God and Father has opened His
Fatherly heart to us in Christ and reveals Christ in our hearts by
His Spirit.*   What has this view of faith to do with the speculations of the Greeks?   How much more akin these speculations
are to the natural understanding, if only it has granted certain
premises, than Luther's view is!   A philosopher is able to provide himself with the means for discerning profundity and
wisdom in the dogmas of the Greek Church; but no philosopher
is in the position for feeling any kind of relish for Luther's faith.
Luther himself failed to see the gulf that separated him from
the old dogma, partly because he interpreted the latter according to his own thoughts, partly because he had a remnant of
respect for the decrees of the Councils, partly because it pleased
him to have a palpable, definite, lofty, incomprehensible cardinal
article with which to oppose Turks, Jews and fanatics.   Only

tradition, to the knowledge that is critical, historical, and psychologically determined,
and for two hundred years it kept alive scientific problems under the most various
forms and modifications, and united the clearest and best heads.   On Melanchthon's
relation to this system and on the influence it exercised on the oldest formulation of
the Protestant system of faith see Dilthey's Article in the Archiv. f. Gesch. der
Philos., Vol. VI., pp. 225-256, 347-379; Tröltsch, Vernunft und Offenbarung bei
Johann Gerhard und Melanchthon, 1891; Paulsen, Gesch. des gelehrten Unterrichts,
2nd Ed., 1st Vol., 1896.   The doctrine of predestination and the "System of
Nature" accompany the development of the Protestant system of faith.   The two
can coalesce, from both there can develop itself a "religious universal Theism" that
directs itself against the positive theology, or that exercises a strongly repressive
influence upon it.   But until the time of Spinoza predestinarian determinism was
rather the protector of the positive theology, while the "System of Nature" wrought
continuously in the direction of broadening it.

when the doctrines of the Trinity and Christology are viewed as
leading articles in Luther's sense is justice done to them; to
him they were not merely loci, to which other doctrinal loci were
attached, they were doctrines from which he knew how to
develop evangelical Christianity: God in Christ. But what
continued to have vitality when dealt with by him and taken in his
sense was not thereby protected for the future; and he himself,
as a mediæval man, could not resist the temptation to speculate
about these formulæ in the direction already indicated by the
way in which they had been framed. Since at the same
time he would not surrender his fundamental thoughts, he became involved in speculations that were no whit behind the
most daring and worst fancies of the Nominalistic Sophists.
They were different from these only in this, that Luther built
up this thought-world with childlike faith, while the former,
half believingly, half sceptically, went in search of dialectic problems. From the doctrine of the Eucharist (see below) Luther
derived a specially strong impulse to reflect in the old style upon
Christology. But as he conceived of the unity of deity and
humanity in Christ with a strictness that had characterised no
theologian before him, it was inevitable that within the lines of
the two-nature doctrine he should find himself in the midst of
those miserable speculations about the ubiquity of the body of
Christ which are carried on at the supreme heights of scholastic
absurdity. The melancholy consequence was that Lutheranism
—as nota ecclesiæ—received at once in Christology the most
fully developed scholastic doctrine ever received by an ecclesiastical community. Owing to this Lutheranism was for almost
200 years thrown back into the middle ages. *Hence the Reformation terminates here also in a contradiction, which furnished
for subsequent times a problem: it gave to the new Church the
faith in God, Christ and the Holy Ghost of which Paul made confession in Rom. VIII. and which was still witnessed to by Paul
Gerhardt in the hymn, " Ist Gott für mich, so trete gleich Alles
wider mich" (If God be on my side, let all things be my foes);
but it gave to it at the same time the old dogma as the unchangeable cardinal article, together with a christological doctrine, which
did not negate the fundamental evangelical interest, but which had*

received an entirely scholastic shape and had therefore the inevit-
able effect of confusing and obscuring faith. The blame rests
upon Luther, not upon the Epigones, if in the Evangelical
Church at the present day every one must still let himself be
stigmatised as a traitor who declares the doctrine of the Trinity
and the Chalcedonian formula to be an extremely imperfect
doctrine, harmonising neither with evangelical faith nor with
reason (the latter was to be true of it, however, as understood
by its authors). This practice was handed down by the same
Luther who otherwise knew very well what unbelief is in the
sense of the gospel. But Luther, as we have shown, had great
excuses for his error; the same cannot be said for those of the
present day, They have, no doubt, other excuses—a regard to
the orthodoxy that already prevails among the congregations,
the traditional custom of fostering piety by means of these
doctrines—what is there that cannot be used for fostering piety
in this or that person? even the Song of Solomon, even amulets!—and ignorance of the history of dogma.[1] How much

[1] How great this last is may be gathered from the fact that there are those at the
present day who simply place their imaginary notions about Christology—the Kenotic
theory for example—under the protection of the ancient dogma, *i.e.*, who really rule
out the latter, but nevertheless play the part of vindices dogmatis. The position of
things is not essentially different as regards the doctrine of the Trinity. A speculation
is evolved from one's inner consciousness, which has in common with the old dogma
the contradiction between one and three, but is otherwise different from it toto cœlo,
and then one describes himself as orthodox, his opponents as heretical. As if it were
not an easy thing for each of these heretics to garnish his criticism of the old dogma
with similar fancies ! If they could produce real satisfaction in this way, they would
certainly be under obligation to do so. But these adornings have supplanted one
another with astonishing rapidity—for a number of years they have almost ceased to
be attempted ; no one of them really gave satisfaction, each one served at the best
to delay the crisis. No further notice is taken to-day as to *how* one comes to terms
with the old dogma, indeed one shrugs his shoulders beforehand in contemplating his
attempt. But that one *does* come to terms, even although it be by the fides implicita
tenuissima, which means that one has no wish to disturb what the Church believes—
that is enough. Thus from the days of Schleiermacher there is a living within the
 ositive theology so to speak from hand to mouth. But even with that we should
have to reconcile ourselves—our knowledge being in part—were it not that the old
dogma has a fettering, burdening, and confusing influence on the faith of the nineteenth
century. Because that is undoubtedly the case, what must be done is to contend
one's self against the whole world for the simple gospel. The strongest argument
urged from the other side is in these terms : " Observe that it is only where the old
dogma is that there is to be found at the present time in Protestantism deep know-

they derive their life, not from the fundamental thought of the Reformation, but from Catholic reminiscences, is most distinctly shown by the fact that when for this or that reason one has once lost confidence in the old dogma, the almost invariable result is that he declares that *doctrine is not after all a matter of so much importance.* Against this Franciscan-Erasmic attitude too strong a protest cannot be made. If it were possible to enter into a compact with truth at all, the old dogma would still be much to be preferred to that indifference towards doctrine; for such indifference leads inevitably to Catholicism, and is as inimical as possible to evangelical Christianity. Everything as a matter of fact depends upon the right doctrines of God as the Father of Jesus Christ and of the old and new man. Just for that reason the alternative: the old dogma, or mere " practical Christianity" must be answered with a neither-nor. Evangelical faith knows only of "doctrines" which are at the same time *dispositions* and deeds; these, however, are for it, with Luther, Christianity.

But Luther not only took over the old Greek dogma as evangelical doctrine (doctrina evangelii) and law of faith (lex fidei); he also took over the Augustinian doctrine of original sin, the doctrine of the primitive state, etc., and thus imposed upon faith a not less oppressive burden, in so far as he imported into faith a view of history made up of questionable exegesis, undiscerning criticism, and varied speculation. These he corrected, no doubt, according to his own principles, and if the factors themselves had remained, one might have been content with this theory for want of a better; but when looked at from

ledge of sin, true repentance, and vigorous ecclesiastical activity." To this objection the following reply must be given: First, that this self-estimation has a pharisaic and evil ring about it, and that the judgment as to knowledge of sin and repentance falls, not to the ecclesiastical press, but to God the Lord; second, that "vigorous ecclesiastical activity" affords no guarantee for unadulterated evangelical faith; were that alone decisive, Luther was wrong when he brought a revolution upon the old Church, for a long time elapsed before the Lutheran Churches were on a level in respect of vigorous activity with the Post-Tridentine Catholic Church; third, that it is no wonder that the others are in a leading position, who take control of the power of tradition and of all means of rule in the most conservative corporation that exists—in the Church. For the rest, the Christian must find out the good and holy, whatever be the quarter in which it may present itself.

the point of view of justifying faith, it was certainly a μετάβασις
εἰς ἄλλο γένος to formulate articles of faith about these things,
and this μετάβασις was and is not without danger. It is true,
no doubt, that from the standpoint of evangelical faith one
comes to see that *all* sin is unbelief and guilt before God, and
that everyone on the first inquiry finds such guilt already resting
upon him. Yet the dogma of original sin contains more and
less than this conviction represents, because it springs from
"reason." It contains more, because it transforms a proposition
based on Christian *self-criticism* into a piece of general historical
knowledge about the beginnings of the human race ; it contains
less, because it will always give one occasion for excusing his
own guilt. To this connection belong also the partly Nominalistic, partly Thomistic view of the doctrine of predestination [1]
and the doctrine of the double will of God, because they pass
beyond the doctrine of faith.

The *third* contradiction which Luther left behind to his
followers is to be found in his attitude towards Scripture. If he
lacked power to free himself entirely from the authority of the
letter, the lack was still greater on the part of those who came
after him.[2] Besides adhering to the Word of God, which was
for him matter and authority, there was an adherence even on
his part to the outward authority of the written word, though
this was certainly occasionally disregarded by him in his
Prefaces to Holy Scripture, and elsewhere as well. It was probably his opposition to the Anabaptists, some of whom admirably distinguished between Word of God and Holy Scripture,
that led him again to hold to the old Catholic identification of

---

[1] Yet see above, p. 223 f. The question with regard to the doctrine of predestination
is as to the relation in which one places it to religion. It is manifest that while
Luther associated it with, and subordinated it to, the doctrine of the gratia gratis
data, he nevertheless allowed it also a range beyond this, in correspondence with a
special "theology" ("deus absconditus") which is not lighted up by faith. That,
though otherwise influenced by Nominalism, he here passes over to Determinism is no
doubt to be explained from his reading Augustine. His reading Thomas and the later
Thomistic Augustinians is scarcely to be thought of here. Yet he may have received
an impulse from Laurentius Valla, to whom his attention had long been directed (see
Loofs, Dogmengesch., 3rd ed., p. 376).

[2] See Gottschick, Die Kirchlichkeit der sog. Kirchlichen Theologie (1890), p. 36 f.

the two.[1] How disastrous this adherence was is a question
that need not be discussed ; for we are still under its effects
to-day ; indeed, it may be said that no other surviving Catholic
element has restricted the development of Protestantism so
much as this. The requirement that the pure sense of Holy
Scripture should be ascertained, was simply deprived of its force
by regarding Scripture as the verbally inspired Canon. On the
one hand the evangelical doctrine of salvation had the burden
of a hundred and one foreign materials imposed upon it ;[2] on
the other hand, there was a disregarding of Scripture even
where it ought to have been made use of, because one necessarily had to find in it, as the infallible authority, simply what
was already held on other grounds to be pure doctrine. In this
way precisely the same state of things came to exist again in
Protestantism which prevailed in Catholicism ; that is to say,
Scripture was subordinated in all points of importance to the
rule of faith (regula fidei), its essential, historical import was accordingly not sufficiently taken account of ; and, on the other
hand, Scripture was made a source of burdens and snares.
This is always the paradoxical, and yet so intelligible, result of
adopting the belief in an inspired Scripture Canon : in what is
of chief moment this inspired Canon subjects the gospel to the
ecclesiastical " rule of faith," and at the same time it produces
incalculable and confusing effects upon faith in matters of
secondary importance. So we see it to be even in Protestantism.
But that which the same Luther taught : " We have the right

---

[1] Loofs' assertion is not correct (Dogmengesch., p. 373) that the placing of Holy
Scripture and Word of God on the same level was nowhere assailed at that time.

[2] It has been correctly pointed out that its being required that the allegorical
exegesis should be departed from only made the thing worse. This kind of exegesis
was able to get quit of the letter should it not stand at the highest level, and thus
corrected the dangerous principle of verbal inspiration. The *literal sense* of Holy
Scripture and *verbal inspiration:* this combination first came to exist as a consequence
of Lutheranism. The absurd thesis could not of course be really applied in a thoroughly
logical way ; besides, there was created—happily, it may be said—by the exposition
of Holy Scripture according to the analogia fidei, *i.e.*, according to the Lutheran
system of doctrine, a new allegorism ; but the number of cases—by no means incon-
siderable—in which the literal sense of particular passages, valuable only as historical,
was treated as furnishing dogmatic guidance created the most distressing difficulties
and burdens for the Lutheran Churches (even for Luther himself indeed).

touchstone for testing all books, in observing whether they witness to Christ or not," could not certainly continue without its influence.   Nevertheless, it was not this that gave rise to the historical criticism of books in Protestantism.   That was a consequence of the advance made in secular culture.   It was because this was its origin that the evangelical Church took up, and still continues to take up, towards it an attitude of strong resistance.   But if the Church has not the courage and the power to carry on criticism with Luther against Luther in *the interests of faith*, it is itself responsible if criticism is forced upon it from without, and if, as necessarily follows, it serves, not to strengthen the Church, but only to weaken it.   *Here also, then, Luther left a problem to the time coming after, as his own attitude was rendered uncertain by a disastrous survival of the Catholic view : along with the other external Catholic authorities the evangelical Church must also discard the external authority of the written Word, regarded as infallible ; but it must at the same time take up its position within the system of Christian doctrine where faith takes it, namely, beside the person of Christ, as luminously presented in the Gospels, and witnessed to by His first disciples.*

Fourthly, in the doctrine of the sacraments Luther abandoned his position as a Reformer, and was guided by views that brought confusion into his own system of faith, and injured in a still greater degree the theology of his adherents.   In his endeavour to withstand the Enthusiasts, while starting from the point that denotes a specially strong side in his conception of faith, he was led by a seemingly slight displacement to very objectionable propositions, the adoption of which resulted in a partial relapse.   In addition to the vagueness that continued to exist regarding the attitude towards Scripture, the falling back in the view taken of the means of grace became the real source of evil for Lutheranism.   If we think of the doctrinairism, the Scholastic Christology, the magical ideas about the Sacrament, etc., that have developed themselves, it is here that we have to seek for the real beginnings of these defects.

From the fixed and exclusive aspect in which Luther set before him God, Christ, the Holy Spirit, faith, and justification (grace), he came to see that the Holy Spirit is bound to the Word of God, *i.e.*, that the Spirit and the Word of God have an inseparable and exclusive relation to each other. What is contemplated by this principle is, first, the establishment of the certain efficacy of the Word ; and, secondly, the distinguishing of revelation as in the strict sense *external*, because divine, from all that is merely subjective. Hence the words occur in the Smalcaldic Articles, P. III., a. 8 : [1] " And in those things that relate to the spoken and external word, it must be steadfastly held that God bestows upon no one His Spirit or His grace except through the Word and along with the Word, as external and previously spoken, that so we may defend ourselves against enthusiasts, *i.e.*, spirits who boast that they have the Spirit prior to the word and without the word and accordingly judge, twist, and pervert Scripture or the spoken word according as they please. . . . Wherefore we must steadfastly adhere to this, that it is not God's will to transact with us except through the spoken word and sacraments, and that whatever boasts itself without the word and sacraments as Spirit, is the devil himself." [2] This equating of Spirit and Word is undoubtedly correct, so long as there is understood by the Word the Gospel itself in the power of its influence and in the whole range of its validity and application. Yet even the exchange of this Word for the narrower conception, " *vocal* word and *sacraments*," is not unobjectionable. When, however, all that is to be held true of the Word is then forthwith applied to the limited conceptions, " vocal word and sacraments," so that these are *in every respect*

[1] Müller, p. 321 f. Compare the treatise " Wider die himmlischen Propheten " (Erlang. Ed. XXIX., p. 134 ff., especially p. 208 ff.), Art. 5 of the Augs. Conf. : " Per verbum et sacramenta tanquam per instrumenta donatur spiritus sanctus, qui fidem efficit " and the principle so often stated by Luther : " Deus interna non dat nisi per externa."

[2] " Et in his, quæ vocale et externum verbum concernunt, constánter tenendum est, deum nemini spiritum vel gratiam suam largiri, nisi per verbum et cum verbo externo et præcedente, ut ita præmuniamus nos adversum enthusiastas, *i.e.*, spiritus, qui jactitant se ante verbum et sine verbo spiritum habere et ideo scripturam sive vocale verbum judicant, flectunt et reflectunt pro libito. . . . Quare in hoc nobis est constanter perseverandum, quod deus non velit nobiscum aliter agere nisi per vocale verbum et sacramenta, et quod, quidquid sine verbo et sacramentis jactatur ut spiritus, sit ipse diabolus."

and in *all their properties* " the Word," the relapse into magical conceptions is inevitable.   Luther wished by his doctrine of the means of grace to offer sure comfort to troubled consciences, and to guard them against the hell of uncertainty about their standing in grace—an uncertainty which the Enthusiasts seemed to regard as of no account.   Therefore he preached without ceasing that it is as certain that the grace of God is given in the *Word* as that Jesus Christ Himself acts ; therefore he contended against the Scotist doctrine of a mere co-existence of forgiveness of sins and sensible (audible) signs ;[1] therefore he attached so decisive a weight to the "objectivity of the means of grace,"[2] and had the anxious desire that it should be declared of them, that even in every part of their administration and in respect of all that Scripture taught, or seemed to teach, regarding them, they were equally important and inviolable. Yet not merely through separating out particular observances as means of grace did Luther retreat within the narrow, for-saken circle of the Middle Ages—the Christian lives, as he himself knew best, not on *means* of grace, he lives through communion with his God, who lays hold of him in Christ—but in a still greater degree by undertaking, first, to justify infant baptism as a means of grace in the strict sense ; second, to con-ceive of penance as *also* the gracious means of initiation ; third, to declare the real presence of the body and blood of Christ in the Eucharist to be the essential part of this Sacrament.   Pro-bably the mere retaining of the term, "means of grace," would not of itself have had a disturbing effect on evangelical doctrine ; for ever again Luther too distinctly emphasised the fact, that the means of grace is nothing else than the Word, which awakens faith and gives the assurance of forgiveness of sins. But that threefold undertaking brought back upon the Church of the Reformation the evils of the Middle Ages, and hindered

[1] Schmalkald. Art. P. III., a. 5 (p. 320): "Non etiam facimus cum Scoto et Minoritis seu monachis Franciscanis, qui docent, baptismo ablui peccatum ex assistentia divinæ voluntatis, et hanc ablutionem fieri tantum per dei voluntatem et minime per verbum et aquam."

[2] See Harless u. Harnack, Die kirchlich-religiöse Bedeutung der reinen Lehre von den Gnadenmitteln, 1869.

it for many generations from effectively expressing along with the *spiritual* character of the Christian religion its deep *earnestness ;* for the earnestness of religion is reduced when the opus operatum makes its appearance and the strict relation between gospel and faith is relaxed or encumbered.

A. As regards the first point—infant baptism—the question is quite clear for anyone who does not believe himself required on "practical" grounds to confuse the matter. If the fundamental evangelical and *Lutheran* principle is valid, that grace and faith are inseparably inter-related (Larger Catechism IV., p. 496 : "In the absence of faith, baptism continues to be only a bare and ineffectual sign"[1]), then infant baptism is in itself no Sacrament, but an *ecclesiastical* observance ; if it is in the strict sense a Sacrament, then that principle is no longer valid. This dilemma can be escaped neither by a reference to the faith of the sponsors, parents, etc. (thus Luther himself at the first)—for that is the worst form of fides implicita—nor by the assumption that in baptism faith is given ;[2] for an unconscious faith is an almost equally bad species of that fides implicita. It would only have been in accordance, therefore, with the evangelical principle, either to do away with infant baptism, as it was only in later times that the Roman Church did away with infant communion, or to declare it to be an ecclesiastical observance, which only receives its true import afterwards (inasmuch as that which is given in baptism has existence at all only on condition of there being the knowledge of sin). Yet neither of these courses was followed ; Luther retained infant baptism rather as the sacrament of regeneration, and while, according to his views, it should have been at the most a symbol of prevenient grace, he conceived of it as an efficacious act. Thus, although there was an unwillingness to observe it, there was a return to the opus operatum, and the relation between gracious effect and faith was severed. If in the time that came after the voice of conscience was too audible against

[1] "Absente fide baptismus nudum et inefficax signum tantummodo permanet."

[2] Larger Catechism IV., p. 494 : "Puerum ecclesiæ ministro baptizandum apportamus, hac spe atque animo, *quod certe credat*, et precamur, ut dominus eum fide donet."

the absurd assumption that there can be a new birth without
the knowledge of this birth, then the solution that was resorted
to was almost worse still than the difficulty from which escape
was sought. Justification and regeneration were separated ; in
the former there was seen the "objective" (the abstract divine
act of justification, the *forensic* justifying sentence, which
declares the sinner [impius] righteous), in the latter the subjective.   In this way the most splendid jewel of evangelical
Christianity became robbed of its practical power—became,
that is, of no effect.   The forcibly effected distinction of justification from regeneration led the evangelical system of faith
into labyrinths, greatly reduced the importance of justification—
as in Catholicism, justification threatened to become a dogmatic
Locus standing side by side with other Loci—and, through the
interpolation of new dogmas, negatived the practical bearing of
justification on the practical moulding of Christian life.

B. This disastrous development was (secondly) still further
strengthened by an erroneous conception of penitence. Here,
also, Luther himself gave the impulse, and therefore quietly
allowed that to happen which contravened his original and
never abandoned ground principles. That the mediæval Catholic
view also continued to have its influence upon him ought not to
be denied. With his whole reforming doctrine and practice,
Luther had on principle taken his stand on the soil of faith ;
within the experience of the believer he had not asked, how do
the heathen and Turk become Christians, but, how have I
attained to faith, and what are the powers by which my faith is
sustained ?   From this point it was certain to him that it is the
gift of faith (or, otherwise expressed, the Gospel) that establishes
and maintains the Christian standing, and that faith works repentance, which is the negative side of faith itself, the "daily
dying."   The two are inseparably related, and yet in such a way
that faith is the logical prius. From this it follows that only
such repentance has value before God as springs from faith
(the Gospel), and that it must be as constant a temper as faith.
Through such faith and such repentance the Christian lives in
the constant forgiveness of sin ; that is to say, this is the sphere
of his existence, whether that be thought of as the continuous

grace of baptism to which one daily returns, or the ever-repeated appropriation of justification (forgiveness of sins). That is a view, certainly, which can easily transform itself into the dreadful opposite—easy security, and a penitent disposition (with the corresponding sanctification of life) that never on any occasion strongly asserts itself.   If men are told that they must constantly repent, and that particular acts of repentance are of no use, there are few who will ever repent.   And yet, the corruption of what is best is the worst corruption (corruptio optimi pessima); the danger that attaches to a truth can never be a reason for concealing the truth.   It is true, no doubt, that training in the truth cannot begin with presenting to view its entire content, its seriousness and freedom ; but the *system of faith* must not on that account be corrupted.   Yet in Lutheranism it became corrupted very soon, and in the end, as is always the case, that was not reached which these corruptions were intended to reach, namely, the checking of laxity and indifference.   These last, rather, only took occasion to derive pleasant comfort for themselves from the new formulation gradually introduced.   This new formulation goes back to thoughts belonging to "natural theology," or, say, to thoughts belonging to the ancient Church, which Luther himself never wished to eradicate.   Its root was the assumption adhered to in spite of certainty of the abolition of the law (as a *demand*, to which there always answers only a performance), that the law contains the unchangeable will of God, and in this sense has its own permanent range of action side by side with the Gospel (as if the latter did not contain this will implicitly !).   If that was once granted, then it was necessary to find room in the Christian state for the law.   This room is first proved to exist from the experience of the terrors of conscience (terrores conscientiæ) which everyone must pass through. Even here much depends on the emphasis that is laid upon this fact and the measure in which it is subordinated to what is properly the act of faith.   Yet the law as the unchangeable will of God does not yet attain here its full expression ; for the " repentance" that arises through the law is to be translated into the true repentance which the Gospel works.   Now that idea of the law would have justice done to it if the Gospel itself

were conceived of as the law divested of the "legal" forms and
clothed over with mercy; yet this thought, which already comes
close to phenomenalism, could at the most be touched on by so
rugged a thinker as Luther. No, the law as law is certainly
abolished for the Christian—he who makes the attempt by
means of the law takes the path to hell—but for God it still
continues to exist, *i.e.*, God's will remains as before expressed in
it, and he must take cognisance of the law's fulfilment. Where
this thought comes in, Luther becomes uncertain as to the
nature of the application and force of the work of Christ (see
Loofs, l.c., 3rd ed., p. 380), *i.e.*, this work ceases to be regarded
as a work once for all done and completed, and receives an
enlargement, in so far as it is subjected to a view that breaks it
up, that view being that for every particular case of sin on the
part of the baptised, Christ must interpose anew with His
obedience, *i.e.*, with a vicarious fulfilment of the law; for otherwise satisfaction is not made to the law of God. This thought
was not transformed into a theory, but it occurs not infrequently
in Luther; for it was the inevitable result of the requirement
imposed upon God that He shall have compensation made to
Him for every particular transgression of the law. The retained
attritio (contritio passiva) and the uncertainties regarding the
nature and result of the work of Christ thus flow for Luther
from *one* source, namely, the idea that the law contains *also* the
will of God, and therefore has an independent place side by side
with the Gospel. The only means of removing this enormous
difficulty would be the decided recognition of the phenomenal
view, namely, that in the law God presents himself to view as
what the sinner for his punishment must feel and think of Him
as being.

To go back to repentance, this view of the law had as its
result that in the course of instruction law was placed before
Gospel. That was the plan adopted by Melanchthon, with the
consent of Luther, in the "Unterricht der Visitatoren" (Directions for those visiting).[1] At the same time there were grounds

---

[1] Corpus. Ref. XXVI., p. 51 sq.: "Although there are some who think that
nothing should be taught before faith, and that repentance should be left to follow
from and after faith, so that the adversaries may not say *that we retract our former*

for earnestly enforcing ecclesiastical confession, that a check
might be put upon the worst forms of sin.   In this lies the
explanation of the fact that theory also became obscure : *within
the lines of this view* (under other conditions the original view
was still retained in force by Luther and Melanchthon) repentance and forgiveness became the conversion of the ungodly,
or of the backsliding *sinner;* as such they were either identified
with justification or placed side by side with it, but in both
cases they were united most closely with the ecclesiastical confessional.   The ungodly attains for the first time or again to
faith, when his sin is forgiven him on the ground of repentance
(but this repentance can no longer be distinguished from the
Catholic attritio), *i.e.,* when God absolves him anew " in foro " ;
unfortunately, there was also an increasing tendency here to
think of the intervention of the minister, whom the " man of
coarse and degraded character" certainly needed.   But what
else is that than a doublette to the Catholic Sacrament of penance,
with this difference only, that the compulsory auricular confession and the satisfactions have been dropped ?   In this way a
most convenient arrangement was come to about the matter,
and how comfortably things were adjusted by the help of this
Catholic Sacrament of penance, minus the burdensome Roman
additions, is suggestively indicated by Lutheran orthodoxy
when at the height of its influence, and by the reaction of
Spener and Pietism.   Under this view the idea of justification,
as has been already pointed out above, was shrivelled up into an
act of initiation and into *an entirely external action of God,* the
natural effect of which was the blunting of conscience.   Here
also it was inevitable that the Catholic doctrine should now
appear to have superior worth ; for according to this view of

doctrine, yet the matter must be (thus) viewed :—Because repentance and law belong
also to the common faith—for one must first *believe,* of course, *that there is a God*
who threatens, commands, terrifies—let it be for the man of coarse and degraded
character that such *portions of faith* (according to this, then, faith has "portions,"
contrary to Luther's view) are allowed to remain under the name of precept, law,
fear, etc., in order that they may understand the more discriminatingly the faith in
Christ, which the Apostles call "justifying faith," *i.e.,* which makes just and cancels
sin, an effect not produced by *faith* in the *precept* and by *repentance,* and that the man
of *low character* may not be led astray by the word faith and ask useless questions."

what takes place, the holding to the "faith alone" ("fides sola")
necessarily resulted in dangerous laxity. What would really
have been required here would have been to lead Christians to
see that only the "fides caritate formata" has a real value before
God. Hence one cannot wonder—it was rather a wise course
under such assumptions—that Melanchthon afterwards abandoned the "sola fides" doctrine, and became the advocate of a
fine Synergism. But by the task of uniting the old evangelical
conviction with this doctrine of repentance, while at the same
time avoiding Melanchthon's synergism, the theology of the
Epigones was involved in the most hopeless confusion. The
question was really that of inter-relating two "justifications,"
the justification of the sinner (justificatio impii) (on the ground
of the law and of repentance), and justification as the abiding
form of the Christian state. To this there was further added as
the third "justification"—it was dependent again on other conditions—the justification of baptised children : one is justified
by repentance, which is produced by the law and then becomes
faith ; one is justified by the faith which the Gospel effects.;
one is justified by the act of baptism ! These contradictions became still more violent as soon as attention was directed to
regeneration, and they led back to the most hopeless scholasticism. And out of this scholasticism, as in the case of the old
scholasticism, out of all kinds of troubles and painful efforts
there arose—under disguise, but in a form quite recognisable by
an eye familiar with Luther's Christianity—the two fundamental Catholic errors, the assumption of an efficacy of the
means of grace ex opere operato, and the transformation of the
evangelical notion of faith *into a meritorious performance ;* for
there must come in somewhere personal responsibility and
personal activity. Now if one has persuaded himself that everything that suggests "good works" must be dropped out of the
religious sequence, there ultimately remains over only the
readiness to subject one's self to faith, *i.e.*, to the pure
doctrine.

Neither the opus operatum nor the meritoriousness of faith,
but certainly the confusion of the decisive question, already
comes to view in the Confession of Augsburg. It has been very

correctly pointed out by Loofs[1] that the twelfth Article is a shadowy companion of the fourth, and his wish in directing attention to this is undoubtedly to show the objectionableness of this reduplication. But the twelfth Article itself is no longer, in its construction, in harmony with the evangelical conception;[2] for it has approximated to the Catholic Sacrament of penance. The reference to the Ecclesia is in this connection an at least misleading concession, and the division of repentance (pœnitentia) into "contrition" and "faith," the former being put first, while only the latter is expressly traced back to the gospel, is very objectionable. But what is most objectionable is, that the Article favours the Catholic view, by suggesting that every time the Christian falls he falls from the state of grace, and must then be restored to it by the sacrament of repentance. If this view were clearly and unmistakably at the basis of this Article, its effect would be to deny what is central in evangelical faith. This faith makes no distinction between sin and sin, as the Catholic doctrine does, and it knows that "every day we sin much." If the cancelling of the state of grace had to be thought of as always united with this, we should be taken back again into the heart of Catholicism, and it would be a matter of entire indifference whether we should adopt the other Catholic doctrines or not. For in the Evangelical Church there must be no departure from the Article, that God forgives *His child*, the justified Christian, his sins, that, accordingly, not merely does forgiveness of sins and justification constitute the "justification" of the sinner, *but the Christian lives upon the forgiveness of sins, and, in spite of sin and guilt, is a child of God.* This cardinal thought, that the Christian does not fall from grace, if he comforts himself in thinking of the God who forgives sins, and accordingly has the feeling of hatred towards sin, has at least

---

[1] Dogmgesch., 2nd ed., p. 262.

[2] "De pœnitentia docent, quod lapsis post baptismum contingere possit remissio peccatorum quocunque tempore, quum convertuntur, et quod ecclesia talibus redeuntibus ad pœnitentiam absolutionem impertiri debeat. Constat autem pœnitentia proprie his duabus partibus. Altera est contritio seu terrores incussi conscientiæ agnito peccato; altera est fides, quæ concipitur ex evangelio seu absolutione, et credit propter Christum remitti peccata, et consolatur conscientiam et ex terroribus liberat. Deinde sequi debent bona opera, quæ sunt fructus pœnitentiæ."

been veiled by the Augsburg Confession in the twelfth Article,
while elsewhere, certainly, the thought forms the basis of many
of its most important expositions. How, then, could all those
things be right which the Confession teaches so impressively
about the constant trust in God, if the Christian might not
comfort himself constantly with the thought of his being God's
child ? But how sadly has this thought been obscured, in order
to escape the danger of laxity, which, however, only comes in
from another side in a worse form ; how obscure it is even yet
in Protestantism, and how difficult it is to persuade the ac-
credited teachers of the Christian people that blunted consciences can have the seriousness of the gospel exhibited to
them only by setting before them the love of God !

     C. The *third* point is Luther's doctrine of the Eucharist.[1]   In
countless passages Luther declared that Word and Sacrament
are the means of grace, because they contain the *forgiveness of
sins,* and that it is in this alone that their value is entirely contained.   " With stern contempt " he often enough discarded all
fanciful ideas that lead astray from what alone can afford the
Christian comfort.   Accordingly, his doctrine of the Eucharist
could only run in these terms :—that the Word of God, which
is in and with the eating, brings forgiveness of sins, and thereby
procures life and blessedness.   Hence the question about the
body and blood of Christ in the Sacrament must not become in
any way a *theological* question—" theology " being taken as
Luther understood it—or, if it does, it must be discussed in
strictest connection with the *historic* Christ ; for only through
the work of the historic Christ is the Word of God the word of
forgiveness of sins.   That being so, no doubt could arise that
the body and blood of Christ was just that which he had yielded
up to death, *i.e.,* his natural, human body.   Only in this way,
too, could His disciples understand Him.   But if the body which
He gave to His disciples to eat was His natural body, then it is
at once clear that as regards His body it was only a symbol

---

[1] See Dieckhoff, Die evang. Abendmahlslehre (1854), p. 167 ff.   H. Schultz, Die
Lehre vom hl. Abendmahl, 1886.   Schmid, Der Kampf der Luth. Kirche um L.'s
Lehre vom Abendmahl, 1868.   Very full treatment in Thomasius-Seeberg, II.,
p. 522 ff.

that was in question, while faith receives the forgiveness of sins by no means merely in a symbolic way. It is then still further clear, that the Christian is not brought into a more intimate, mystical union with Christ through the Eucharist than through the Word, while this Word is not a mere empty sound about Christ, but the power which proceeds from His historic work. But, finally, the idea of a "more intimate, mystical" union of the Christian with Christ is, when viewed in the light of Luther's conception of faith, altogether the worst kind of heresy; for it places in question the sovereign power and adequate efficacy of the Word of God for the sake of a vague feeling, and thereby robs conscience of the full comfort the Word of God can impart. There must, therefore, be the strictest adherence to the position, that while the various sensible signs under which the Word is presented are by no means, it is true, matters of indifference, and while in various ways they bring the work of the historic Christ close to the heart, yet they are unable to add anything to the power of the Word.

If in what follows another view must be stated as having been held by Luther, it must always be remembered that the one just developed was always most strenuously represented by him and never abandoned; for it runs quite clearly even through writings that can be legitimately quoted in favour of another view. No passages require to be brought forward in proof of it; for in the Smaller Catechism, for example, it and it alone finds expression. Certainly an appeal cannot be taken against it to the word "true" in the sentence: "It is the true body," though it may be unquestionable that Luther here had in his mind his opposition to Zwingli. Even as regards the *Word* what is in question is the "true," *i.e.*, the historical Christ, and *not merely* the Word, but the Word *alone* has, according to Luther, the power to give the heart a realising sense of the true Christ who died for sinners.

And yet in contemplating the Eucharist he went on to "supplement" the view of faith, and this supplement he defended in the most obstinate way, and pronounced it an article involving the existence or non-existence of the Church (articulus stantis et cadentis ecclesiæ). In this way he brought in a host of evils connected with the creation he left behind him : the doctrine of the Sacrament in general became confused, a door was opened for the conception of the opus operatum, doctrinairism was strengthened, the evangelical Christology was led into the melancholy paths of the abandoned Scholasticism, and thus an orthodoxy was framed which was bound to become narrow-minded and loveless. These were the grave internal consequences. The outward results are well enough known ; Protestantism was rent asunder. Yet these latter results were not the worst ; indeed it may be said on the contrary here, that the isolating for a time of the Lutheran Reformation was necessary and salutary, if it was not to lose itself in fields foreign to itself. Had Luther yielded in the question of the Eucharist, the result would have been the formation of ecclesiastical and political combinations, which, in all probability, would have been more disastrous for the German Reformation than its isolation, for the hands that were held out to Luther—Carlstadt, Schwenkfeld, Zwingli, etc.— and which to all appearance could not be grasped simply on account of the doctrine of the Eucharist, were by no means pure hands.[1] Great political plans, and dangerous forms of uncertainty as to what evangelical faith is, would have obtained the rights of citizenship in the German Reformation. Under these circumstances the doctrine of the Eucharist constituted a salutary restraint. In its literal import what Luther asserted was not correct ; but it had its ultimate source in the purpose of the strong, unique man to maintain his cause in its purity, as it had presented itself to him, and to let nothing foreign be forced upon him ; it sprang from the well-grounded doubt as to whether these people had not another spirit. In the choice of the means he committed an error ; in the matter itself, so far as what was in question was the averting of premature unions, he was probably in the right.

This gives us already *one* motive for his " completing " the doctrine of the Eucharist, and perhaps the strongest. Luther

---

[1] The reference here is not to morality ; I expressly mention this, because the expression " pure hands " has been misunderstood. The connection should have made it impossible for a false understanding to arise.

had the fear, or he perceived, that his opponents, including Zwingli, underrated in general the means of grace, that they preached the "spirit," without discerning the importance of the Word. The temptation was very great to teach the presence of the bodily Christ in the Eucharist, because it appeared that thereby the certainty of the inter-connection of Spirit (saving benefit) and means was most conclusively demonstrated. To this temptation Luther yielded, though his yielding was always corrected again by him by means of his original ideas. Secondly, the letter of Scripture seemed to him to admit of no other interpretation, and by this letter he felt himself bound. Accordingly even before the year 1524 he had formed the conviction, that in the Sacrament of the altar forgiveness of sins is so contained that it is conveyed through the outward presentation of the real body and blood of Christ (to be eaten and drunk). The perception of this was first made use of against Carlstadt,[1] whom he sought to counter-work by means of letters. From the year 1525 he turned indirectly, from the year 1526 directly, against Zwingli also, whom he suspected, not quite without ground, of making common cause with the enthusiasts. Zwingli certainly removed the ground of that charge and even by that time held substantially to the doctrine of salvation by justification—not the least cause of this being Luther's writings;—but in order to understand Luther's attitude towards Zwingli, we must keep this suspicion before us. In the correspondence that now began between the two Reformers Luther expounded his view, and when pressed by Zwingli, became ever more deeply involved in Scholasticism.[2] First of all he let himself be

---

[1] Carlstadt had taught that by means of the τοῦτο Christ had pointed to his actual body in which He sat before His disciples.

[2] The earliest writings of Luther on the Eucharist are "Sermon von dem hochwürdigen Sacrament des hl. wahren Leichnams Christi," 1519, "Erkl. Dr. L.'s etlicher Artikel in seinem Sermon v. d. hl. Sacr.," 1520, "Sermon von dem N.T. d. i. v. d. hl. Messe," 1520 (Erlang. Ed., XXVII). "Vom Missbrauch der Messe," 1522, "Von beiderlei Gestalt des Sacraments zu nehmen," 1522, "Vom Anbeten des Sacraments des hl. Leichnams Christi," 1523 (XXVIII.). "Wider die himmlischen Propheten v. d. Bildern u. Sacrament," 1524-5, "Sermon v. d. Sacrament des Leibes u. Blutes Christi, wider die Schwarmgeister," 1526 (XXIX). "Dass diese Worte noch feststehen," 1527, "Bekenntniss vom Abendmahl Christi," 1528 (XXX.). "Kurzes Bekenntniss Dr. M. L.'s vom hl. Sacrament," 1545 (XXXII).

persuaded that the true body must be the body of the exalted Christ; for the historical body ceased of course to have an existence owing to the death on the cross. If it was objected, however, that it was impossible for the glorified body of the Exalted One to be in the bread and wine, his reply was *that he extended to the Exalted One the idea of the inseparable unity of deity and humanity in the historical Christ,* and in order to make this conceivable, called in the aid of Occam's Scholasticism. " The Sophists" (his old enemies!)—so he declares now—"*speak rightly on this matter* when they say:—There are three ways of being in a place, locally or circumscriptively, definitively, repletively (localiter, circumscriptive, definitive, repletive), and, that this may the more easily be understood, I will explain it thus in German."[1]   There then follows a long discussion, in-

Also various letters, more especially the one addressed to the Strassburgers of date Dec., 1524 (see also his opinions about the "Bohemians") with the famous sentence: " I confess that if Carlstadt or any one else had corrected me five years ago by showing that in the Sacrament there is nothing but bread and wine he would have done me a great service. . . . But I am taken captive and cannot escape; the text is too powerful, and no words can drive it from my mind." What first brought Zwingli into the Eucharist controversy was his letter to Alber (Nov., 1524).   Then followed his "Commentarius," his "Klare Underrichtung ' (1526), his "Amica exegesis" (1527), the " Fründlich Verglimpfung" (friendly persuading to believe) "that these words shall have eternally the old sense " (1527).   Letters and writings of the theologians in south-west Germany played an important part in the controversy. The greatest weight attaches to the treatise of Œcolampadius " de genuina verborum domini, etc., expositione liber."   Zwingli regarded the "est" in the words of institution as being = "it signifies," took John VI. as a commentary on the words of institution, allowed therefore only a symbolical explanation of the body and blood of Christ in the sacrament, displayed no assurance and decision in conceiving of the sacrament as a peculiar mode of giving form to the "Word," thought of the observance substantially as sacrificial (nota ecclesiæ, recollection) and yet allowed himself to be led by Luther into the Scholastic-Christological region, where he not only won no laurels by his doctrinaire conception of the two-nature doctrine and his separation of the natures in a way approaching Nestorianism, but betrayed a remarkable lack of religious insight into the problem, together with a wonderful reliance on the significance of sophistic-scholastic formulæ.   The theologians of south-west Germany, so far as they did not, with Brenz, adhere to Luther, spoke in favour of a mystical conception of the Eucharist, which united the defects of the Lutheran with the defects of the Zwinglian conception, and was afterwards embraced by Calvin and Melanchthon. But Œcolampadius did excellent service with his account of the Patristic doctrine.

[1] Bek. v. Abendmahl (XXX., p. 207 ff.). How differently he still expresses himself in the treatise of the year 1519 (XXVII., p. 38): " There are some who exercise their skill and ingenuity in trying to see where the bread remains when it is changed

tended to give further proof of the possibility and certainty of the
presence of Christ's body in the Eucharist. So this Scholasticism
is requisite in order to establish the Christian faith![1] In
following this course he became more and more involved in the
Catholic view, that the Eucharist must be conceived of as the
parallel to and guarantee for the Incarnation.[2] This comes out
most distinctly in the last of his writings, where it is at the
same time apparent how, as the consequence of holding his
doctrine of the Eucharist, the evangelical saving faith became
for Luther resolved into "parts," although he made efforts to
avoid this result.[3]

into Christ's flesh, and the wine into his blood. Also how the whole Christ can be
included under so small a portion of bread and wine. It is of no consequence if thou
dost not seek to understand that ; it is enough for thee to know that it is a divine
sign that Christ's flesh and blood are truly present ; let the how and the where be
left to Him."

[1] From this point the Lutheran doctrine of the communicatio idiomatum then took
its issue.

[2] Undoubtedly Zwingli with his Nestorianism led him on this track.

[3] Kurzes Bekenntniss, p. 413 : "Oh dear man ! if any one will not believe the
article on the Eucharist, how will he ever believe the article on the humanity and
deity of Christ in one person? And if it stumbles thee that thou shouldst receive
with thy mouth the body of Christ when thou eatest the bread from the altar . . .
it must surely stumble thee much more (especially when the hour comes) that the
infinite and incomprehensible deity, who in His essence is and must be everywhere,
should be shut up and enclosed in humanity and in the Virgin's body. . . . And
how is it possible for thee to believe how the Son alone should have become man, not
the Father nor the Holy Ghost, since the three Persons are nothing but the one God
in the supremely one being and nature of the one Godhead. . . . Oh, how they
shall most of all grow excited and reel and make their voices heard, when they
come to this ! Here they will find something to explain, as indeed I hear that they
already march about confidently and courageously with their Eutychianism and
Nestorianism. For that was my thought, and I have stated it too, that this is what
they must come to ; the devil cannot go on holiday when he has made one heresy, he
must make more, and no error remains alone. When the ring is severed at one place
it is no more a ring, it no longer holds together, but goes on breaking. And although
they make a great ado about their believing this article on Christ's person and have
many words about it, believe them not, they are assuredly liars in all that they say of
it. . . . The Turk glories in the name of God, but when they die they find who their
God is. For it is certain of every one who does not rightly believe an article, or will
not believe it, that he believes no article seriously. . . . Hence the word must be, a
belief of all, pure and complete, whole and entire, or a belief of nothing. The Holy
Ghost does not allow himself to be severed or divided, *so that he should let one part
be taught and believed truly and another falsely.*"

It was·not enough that it should be merely asserted that the
true body is in the Eucharist, if this proposition was to describe
a miraculous, external fact, that holds good even apart from
faith.   It was necessary to show *how* the corporeal Christ is
present and is partaken of in the Eucharist.   Here also Luther
adopted hypothetical speculations of the Nominalists.[1]   The
whole Christ is in the elements ; but the elements are not transubstantiated ; neither is there a mingling of the elements with
Christ ; nor again are the two merely side by side, unconnected
and apart ; both remain what they are, but are as perfectly
blended in their properties (idiomata) as Godhead and humanity
are blended in the incarnation.   Accordingly when Melanchthon went to Cassel to hold conferences with Butzer (1534)
Luther could give him the following instruction : " That in and
with the bread the body of Christ is truly partaken of, that
accordingly all that takes place actively and passively in the
bread takes place actively and passively in the body of Christ,
that the latter is distributed, eaten and masticated with the
teeth."[2]   The most objectionable thing here was, that while,
according to Luther, the body and blood of Christ were present
in the Eucharist only for *enjoyment*,[3] the unbeliever and the
heathen were also to receive them.   Thereby there was again
introduced the Catholic doctrine of the Sacrament, with its distinction between the "*objective*" significance of the Sacrament,
and the *saving influence* in the Sacrament.   But at the same time
there was in point of fact a restoration through this separation
of faith in the efficacy of the Sacrament ex opere operato.   It
is not to be wondered at that thereafter, in later Lutheranism,
this faith took the form of a reliance on the objective Sacrament.

[1] See above, Vol., VI., p. 238. In a treatise as early as the de captivitate babyl.,
Luther indicates that Occam's doctrine of consubstantiation was known to him, and
that he was inclined to favour it, without however attaching weight as yet to the
question of the modus of the presence.

[2] As early as in the " Bekenntniss " (1528) he vindicated the opponents of Berengar
(XXX.. p. 297) : " Therefore the enthusiasts are wrong, as is also the gloss in the
ecclesiastical law, when they blame Pope Nicolas for forcing upon Berengar a confession that he enclosed and masticated with his teeth the real body of Christ.
Would to God that all Popes had acted in all matters in as Christian a way ! "

[3] Hence no adoration of the Sacrament ; see the Treatise of the year 1523.

On the other hand there was a reintroducing in this way of the
"awful mystery" (mysterium tremendum) for faith. Whether
the effect was indifference or awe of mystery, in both cases the
original thought connected with the sacred observance, and the
Evangelical view of it, became obscured.

Only with regard to *one* point Luther himself stood firm, or
at least only touched on a view that was foreign to him, and
that was the certainty that what is contemplated in the whole
observance is only *the forgiveness of sins*.[1] Yet what he touched
on, others, though not quite at the beginning, emphasised more
strongly. That is not to be wondered at. If it is to be of
fundamental importance for this observance that Christ is
present here, not for faith merely, but corporeally, then a
presence of such a kind—the receiving of the bodily Christ—
must have also a *specific* effect. But in what else can this effect
be found than in the incorruptibleness of the body of Christ, the
enjoyment of which makes our bodies in a mysterious way incorruptible, or in a mystical union with Christ, which is something still higher than the forgiveness of sins and adoption?

Owing to the way in which Luther conceived of the doctrine of
the Eucharist he involved himself in responsibility for the fact,
that in its Christology, in its doctrine of the sacraments, in its
doctrinairism and in the falseness of the standard by which it
judged of divergent doctrines and pronounced them heresies, the
later Lutheran Church threatened to become a miserable
doublette of the Catholic Church. That this was an impending
danger for this Church, and that even yet it has not been
altogether averted, no one of insight can fail to see. If we look
at the Christianity of Luther and compare it with Catholic
Christianity, we observe that what separates them is real; the
link that binds them together consists only in words. But if we
look at Lutheranism in the form in which it developed itself—
not without Luther's influence—from the second half of the sixteenth century, it must be said that in many important particulars it is only by words that it is separated from Catholicism,
while what unites them is reality; for Catholicism is not the

---

[1] The rudiments of another view have been pointed out by Köstlin and others;
Loofs (l.c., 2nd ed., p. 253) refers to Erlang. Ed. XXX., p. 93 f., 116 ff., 125, 141.

Pope, neither is it the worship of saints or the mass, but it is the slavish dependence on tradition and the false doctrines of Sacrament, of repentance and of faith.

In the theology of Melanchthon, who stands beside Luther the evangelist as the teacher of Ethics, we find the attempts to correct Luther's theology, and Melanchthon, moreover, was guided at every point by the endeavour, first, to secure the freedom, responsibility and seriousness of moral effort that were threatened by the religious quietism that could arise, and, as is well known, did arise from Luther's doctrine; secondly, to strengthen in accordance with this the bond uniting religion and morality; thirdly, to prevent the rise of the sacramentarianism that is akin to religious quietism. These honest and salutary aims, which brought him closer to Calvin, and in themselves contained a tendency to bind together all evangelicals in a powerful practical sympathy, were not asserted with energy by Melanchthon in points of decisive importance ; he was no prophet,—he rather felt himself hampered by the demand made upon him to be the guardian of Lutheranism, and the Lutherans are not to be reproached if in the first instance they were more disposed to go astray with the heroic Luther than to be kept in the leading strings of the faint-hearted Melanchthon. Besides this, the humanistic impulses by which, in addition to those of a religious kind, Melanchthon allowed himself to be influenced, were instinctively felt ,to be something foreign, requiring to be excluded. So at first Lutheranism repelled " Philippism," the founder of which was never popular. It had to pay dearly for this renunciation, and thereafter to learn Melanchthonian truths by a long and bitter discipline. Yet it may be made a question whether that renunciation in the sixteenth century was a misfortune. Would Luther's notion of faith have continued to be maintained in a Lutheran-Philippistic Church? and was the powerful practical exercise of faith in the Germany of that day placed under restriction merely from following a one-sided development of doctrine? was it not above all held in check by the wretched ecclesiasticism and the general political situation ? is there a substantial difference, then, between the Philippistic National Churches of Germany and the Lutheran, and was the development, always becoming more one-sided, of evangelical religion into quietistic doctrine and sacrament-faith, not itself an effect of the restrictive elements in the situation ? These questions must certainly be answered in the affirmative ; but nevertheless the Lutheran Church had to pay dearly for turning away from " legal righteousness," " sacrifice," and " satisfactions." Through having the resolute wish to go back to *religion* and to it alone, it neglected far too much the moral problem, the " Be ye holy, for I am holy."

5. *Concluding Observations.*

In the four preceding sections (p. 168 ff.)—an attempt has been made to state as clearly as possible Luther's attitude towards the Catholic tradition and the old dogma. Our task has not been to describe Luther's theology in the whole breadth of its development. The more difficult problem had to be solved of bringing out the significance of Luther—and thereby of the Reformation—within the *history of dogma*.[1] It has been shown, I hope, that Luther (the Reformation) represents an issue of the history of dogma as much as, in other ways, Post-Tridentine Catholicism and Socinianism. We cannot be made uncertain about this judgment by what has been brought to view in the fourth section ; for it has been shown *that the new view of the gospel taken by Luther forms a complete whole, and that the elements of the old which he retained are not in accord with this whole, nay, that at all points at which he allowed what was Catholic to remain, he at the same time himself indicated the main features of a new structure.*

This complete whole, however, which he outlined with a firm hand, rises superior, not merely to this or that particular dogma, *but to dogmatic Christianity in its entirety :* Christianity is

[1] Compare Berger, Die Kulturaufgaben der Reformation, Einleitung in eine Lutherbiographie, 1895.

something else than a sum of traditional doctrines. Christianity
is not Biblical Theology, nor is it the doctrine of the Councils ;
but it is the *spirit* which the Father of Jesus Christ awakens in
hearts through the Gospel. All authorities which support
dogma are abolished ; how then can dogma maintain itself as
infallible *doctrine ;* but what, again, is a dogma without infallibility ? Christian doctrine establishes its rights only for
faith ; what share, then, can philosophy still have in it ? but
what, again, are dogma and dogmatic Christianity without
philosophy ? Of course one can appeal here to Luther against
Luther, yet only in the same way in which one can raise up
Augustine to reply to Augustine, and in the same way in which
every genius can easily be made away with when a rope to
despatch him has been twisted out of his imperfections and out
of what he shared with his age. The history of dogma comes
to a close with Luther. Any one who lets Luther be Luther,
and regards his main positions as *the valuable possession* of the
evangelical church—who does not merely tolerate them, that is
to say, under stress of circumstances (per angustias temporum)
—has the lofty title and the strict obligation. to conclude the
history of dogma with him.[1] How can there be a history of

[1] In the treatment of the history of dogma from a universal historical point of view
Zwingli may be left out of account.   Anything good that was said by him as the
Reformer, in the way of criticising the hierarchy and with regard to the fundamental
nature of the new piety, is to be found in him as it is to be found in Luther, and his
arriving at greater clearness regarding it he owed to Luther.   The points in which he
diverged from Luther belong to the history of Protestant theology.   There were many
particulars which he understood how to express more lucidly than Luther, and many
negations of the traditional were more definitely shaped by him.   But he was not
less doctrinaire than Luther ; he had that quality rather in a higher degree ;
and he did not always make a beneficial use, for the system of faith,
of his fine Humanistic perceptions.   Calvin, again, is, as a theologian, an
Epigone of Luther.—These sentences of the 1st edition—into which at *one* point
a little more precision is introduced—have been objected to by several critics ;
Dilthey in particular has espoused the cause of Zwingli and Calvin in his articles
referred to above (Archiv. f. Gesch. d. Philos., Vol. V., p. 367 ff. : Ueber Zwingli's
religiös-universellen Theismus, p. 374 ff. : Zwingli's Ergänzung der ausschliesslich
religiösen Moral des Urchristenthums durch sittlich-politische Bethätigung und
Bedeutung dieser That für die Umgestaltung Europas, Vol VI., p. 119 ff. : Zwingli's
Schrift de providentia und der Einfluss der Stoa auf seine Lehre, die sich als Panen-
theismus, Determinismus und die Schranken der positiven Religion übersteigenden
religiösen Universalismus darstellt, Vol. VI., p. 523 ff. : Ueber die Bedeutung der

dogma in Protestantism after Luther's Prefaces to the New
Testament, and after his great Reformation writings? A
history there has been of work carried on with a view to a right
understanding of the Gospel, and for about 150 years this work
was prosecuted within the lines and forms of the old dogma.
But how do 150 years count for the Church! The Roman
Church needed more than 300 years to advance from the
Tridentine to the Vatican Decrees, and how little apparently was
required even about 1550 to bring the Vatican formula within
reach! But Protestantism—some one objects—had a creed-
constructing period; during that period it gave expression to its

Schrift Zwingli's de vera et falsa religione, Vol. VI., p. 528 ff. : Fundamentale und
epochemachende Bedeutung von Calvin's Institutio als synthetische Entwicklung des
ganzen religiösen Stoffs aus dem Wirken Gottes auf den Menschen nach dem in
seinem Rathschluss enthaltenen Zusammenhang seiner Functionem).   Yet after some
hesitation I feel that I must adhere to my position and place the two Reformers outside the boundary lines which I regard as serviceable for the history of dogma.
About these lines there is room for discussion; but if they are correctly drawn, Calvin
at any rate must be left out of view, for there can be no dispute about his being an
Epigone.   But he is to be described as such, not merely when the chief dogma of
justification is placed at the basis of his teaching—as Dilthey asserts—but as regards
the whole sum of what presents itself to view in the new and higher kind of personal
religion, of which Luther had the experience, and to which Luther had given expression, before Calvin (including all important points of theological doctrine).   That he
possessed the incomparable faculty of creating out of this a system, and a principle that
entered powerfully into the institutions of life and revolutionised them, will be denied
by no one, and so in the history of the Church, and in the general history of the
sixteenth and seventeenth centuries, he stands in some respects on a level with Luther
and in some respects above him; but in the history of dogma he stands beside
Melanchthon, though certainly in the power to shape doctrine he far excelled him.
But as regards Zwingli, Dilthey has taught me anew that the conceptions in respect
of which he distinctly and throughout differs from Luther characterise him, not as
the Reformer, but as the thinker and theologian, while at the same time these conceptions are not specially original and did little in determining the nature and course
of Reformation *work* in the period following.   Of course in this question a value-
judgment is partly at work : what worth are we to attach to the determinism, or, say,
the Panentheism of Zwingli and, again, to his Humanistic religious universalism?
My opinion is that we may regard history as teaching us here that these did not
become decisive factors in the great ecclesiastical course of development.   So far, on
the other hand, as they unquestionably contain elements that must be taken account
of if a tenable Christian *theory of the world* is to be framed—for such a theory cannot
be obtained merely from the isolated individual experience of faith that is in accord
with Pauline-Lutheran principles—the problems for solving which they furnish the
guiding lines belong to the Philosophy of Religion.   The elements in Zwingli which
Dilthey brings to view show that he stands on the line, partly of Sebastian Franck,

faith as *dogma;* this period accordingly must also be included within the history of dogma. To this the reply must be: (1) all Lutheran Symbols, with the exception of the Form of Concord, were not thought of at all originally as being symbols in the sense of being regulative doctrinal forms, but were only raised to the position of symbols at a later period, and that position, moreover, was always given to them only by a section of Lutheran Protestants,[1] (2) it was not the *Lutheran* Church that turned them into symbols, but the Empire (1555) and the Princes, the latter having it specially in view to check the quarrelsomeness of theologians, (3) it is as little the case that there have ever been Lutheran Symbols by which all Lutherans have been bound, as that there have ever been Reformed Symbols by which all the Reformed have been united into one, (4), the breach with belief-according-to-symbol within Protestantism which has taken place in the 18th and 19th centuries, can be described by no one as a breach with the Reformation, and *as a matter of fact* even the modern orthodoxy of our days judges the breach very mildly, knowing as it does

partly of Melanchthon (inasmuch as he also was a Ciceronian), partly of mediæval reformers like Wyclif. Nothing is less contemplated in this criticism than a disparagement of the Zürich Reformer ; it will always continue, rather, to be the most noteworthy providential arrangement in the history of the Reformation, that the new knowledge of God made its appearance simultaneously, and in an essentially independent way, in Luther and in the brave Swiss. It is evident that as regards being free and unprejudiced, Zwingli in many respects surpassed Luther (his divergencies from Luther were by no means *merely* due to mediæval motives, they are rather to be traced as much to the ideas of an advancing age), and that he had also a greater faculty for direct organising action, though this last is not to be regarded simply as a product of his religious force. Who will be disposed to estimate in the history of Protestantism what he owes to Luther and what to Zwingli and Calvin? Without the two latter Protestantism might perhaps have ceased altogether to exist ! Or what an unspeakably poor form it might have assumed ! On Zwingli cf. the Histories of Dogma by Loofs and Thomasius-Seeberg. A. Baur, Zwingli's Theol., 2 vols., 1885 ff. Zeller, Das theol. System Z.'s, 1853. Sigwart, u. Zwingli, der Character s. Theol. u. s. w., 1855. Usteri, Zwingli u. Erasmus, 1889. R. Stähelin, Huldr. Zwingli, Leben u. Wirken, 1st vol., 1895.

[1] In what a dim light the Augsburg Confession appears when it is contemplated as the symbol of Lutheranism ; but what an excellent historic record it is, when the estimate formed of it corresponds with what alone it intends itself to be—a statement, in view of opponents, indicating how much harmony with them still exists in spite of the new elements.

that it has itself drifted too far away from the symbols.[1] If these statements are correct,[2] then the "creed-constructing period" during which the "Lutheran Church" declared its "definitive will" is a fable convenue. "This Lutheran Church has never existed at all as an outward whole, and the spokesmen of the strictest 'Lutheran party' have been precisely the worst enemies of such a unification. . . But those who have crowded around the Book of Concord have always been merely a section, though a strong one, of the Lutheran Church, and even among them it has been regarded as a doctrinal law only for particular national churches." But even though this plain historical fact did not admit of being established, yet the opinion would remain true, that the period of the Epigones was not the period of the classic formulation of the evangelical faith, but a noteworthy episode.[3] If one should wish to hold another opinion, he would

[1] This does not prevent it placing before its opponents in an entirely arbitrary way this or that portion of the Creeds, which it regards itself as still adhering to, as outwardly authoritative, while silence, however, is regularly maintained as to its having no wish whatever to deal similarly with other portions.

[2] A very lucid account of things has been given by K. Müller in the Preuss. Jahrbb., Vol. 63, Part 2 : "Die Symbole des Lutherthums." Observe in particular the very excellent concluding words, p. 146 ff. Ritschl's dissertation on the Rise of the Lutheran Church (Ztschr. für K.-Gesch., I., p. 51 ff., II., p. 366 ff.) is of fundamental importance, yet in my opinion the variance of view between Luther and Melanchthon is overdrawn here.

[3] Müller, l.c. : "According to the testimony of its own Fathers, the Church of the Reformation wishes to be regarded as in the first instance a religious, not a legal, magnitude. As religious, however, it cannot find its unity guaranteed by external arrangements of a legal character, but only by the distinctive religious possession which was the basis of its origination and once for all indicated to it its course. But that can never hold good of particular writings, however high they may stand in the estimation of believers. On the soil of the Reformation that holds good simply of the view of Christianity witnessed to by these and numerous other writings, i.e., of the gospel. But through the influence mainly of Melanchthon the gospel lost its original practical-religious character, and, by means derived from a religious age that had been transcended, it was made the subject of theologico-philosophic knowledge, and was rent into parts and in some measure perverted. The period of the Epigones, again, rapidly brought this stage to completion (Melanchthon himself not being without blame for this), and in a course of development which constantly repeats itself in the history of Christianity imposed the products of that theological activity on the Church of the Reformation as a law of faith." But this Church distinguishes itself from the Catholic Church in this, that it possesses the capacity and the means—I should like to continue always without doubt of this—to cast off again the law that has been imposed on it.

require, not only to think of the 18th and 19th centuries as the
period of the Church's apostasy from the Reformation, but also
to blot out Luther's Christianity; for that Christianity cannot
be forced into the scholastic theology of the symbols.   Hence
there are only the two things possible, either to conclude the
history of dogma with Luther's Reformation, or to attach to it,
as a second part, the history of Protestant theology *down to the
present day*.   But this enormous supplement would be something quite different from history of dogma, because while what
would be dealt with in it at the beginning would certainly seem
extremely like the old dogma, it would appear as we proceeded
that the question was rather about understanding the gospel *in
opposition to dogma*.   It would come to view that even Pietism
and Rationalism had a requisite share in the development of
this understanding, that the understanding was materially
developed at important points by Zinzendorf and Wesley, that
it was most powerfully promoted by Schleiermacher, and that
it grew in many respects even within the Pietistic-Confessional
reaction of the 19th century.   It would appear, finally, that
in his description of the gospel, the most disdainfully treated
theologian of the age—Ritschl—has given expression in a
powerful way—though within the limitations that belong to
every individual—to the outcome of two hundred years' work on
the part of evangelical theology in endeavouring to understand
the Reformation, and to the products of criticism of doctrinaire
Lutheranism.

———

The Gospel entered into the world, not as a doctrine, but as a
joyful message and as a power of the Spirit of God, originally
in the forms of Judaism.   It stripped off these forms with
amazing rapidity, and united and amalgamated itself with Greek
science, the Roman Empire and ancient culture, developing, as
a counterpoise to this, renunciation of the world and the striving
after supernatural life, after deification.   All this was summed
up in the old dogma and in dogmatic Christianity.   Augustine
reduced the value of this dogmatic structure, made it subservient

to a purer and more living conception of religion, but yet finally left it standing so far as its foundations and aim were concerned. Under his direction there began in the Middle Ages, from the 11th century, an astonishing course of labour; the retrograde steps are to a large extent only apparent, or are at least counter-balanced by great steps of progress. But no satisfying goal is reached; side by side with dogma, and partly in opposition to it, exists a practical piety and religious self-criticism, which points at the same time forwards and backwards—to the Gospel, but ever the more threatens to vanish amid unrest and languor. An appallingly powerful ecclesiasticism is taking shape, which has already long held in its possession the stolid and indifferent, and takes control of the means whereby the restless may be soothed and the weary gathered in. Dogma assumes a rigid aspect; it is elastic only in the hands of political priests; and it is seen to have degenerated into sophistry; faith takes its flight from it, and leaves the old structure to the guardians of the Church. Then appeared Luther, to restore the "doctrine," on which no one any longer had an inward reliance. But the doctrine which he restored was the Gospel as a glad message and *as a power of God*. That this was what it was, he also pronounced to be the chief, nay the only, principle of theology. What the Gospel is must be ascertained from Holy Scripture; the power of God cannot be construed by thought, it must be experienced; the *faith* in God as the Father of Jesus Christ, which answers to this power, cannot be enticed forth by reason or authority; it must become a part of one's life; all that is not born of faith is alien to the Christian religion and therefore also to Christian theology—all philosophy, as well as all asceticism. Matthew XI. 27 is the basis of faith and of theology. In giving effect to these thoughts, Luther, the most conservative of men, shattered the ancient church and set a goal to the history of dogma. That history has found its goal in a return to the gospel. He did not in this way hand over something complete and finished to Christendom, but set before it a problem, to be developed out of many encumbering surroundings, to be continuously dealt with in connection with the entire life of the spirit and with the social condition of mankind, but to be solved only in faith itself. Christendom must constantly go on to learn, that even in religion the simplest thing is the most difficult, and that everything that is a burden upon religion quenches its seriousness ("a Christian man's business is not to talk grandly about dogmas, but to be always doing arduous and great things in fellowship with God "[1] Zwingli). Therefore the goal of all Christian work, even of all theological work, can only be this—to discern ever more distinctly the simplicity and the seriousness of the gospel, in order to become ever purer and stronger in *spirit*, and ever more loving and brotherly in *action*.

[1] " Christiani hominis est non de dogmatis magnifica loqui, sed cum deo ardua semper et magna facere."

FINIS.

GENERAL INDEX FOR VOLS. I.-VII.[1]

[1] This index was prepared for the *second* edition of the original work.

Antioch, Synods of, III., 94, 216, 222, 230; IV., 2, 5, 55 f., 62, 64 ff., 69, 76, 85, 90, 118, 158; V., 188.

Antiquity, Notion of Ecclesiastical, III., 219.

Antitheses, I., 270, 285.

Antitrinitarians of the Reformation Period, VII., 13, 118-137, 137 ff., 178.

Antonius Melissa, VI., 223.

Antonius, Monk, III., 126, 141; IV., 313; V., 263.

Apelles, I., 255 f., 257 f., 259, 261, 266 ff.; II., 90, 251.

Aphraates, I., 157; II., 17, 37 f.; III., 50, 104; IV., 58.

Aphthartodocetism, I., 260; IV., 178, 237 f., 244, 251, 286, 299.

Apocalypse of John, I., 83, 87 f., 104, 166, 177, 193, 295; II., 50, 95, 107, 294 ff., 299; III., 16, 78, 105, 112, 187, 196 f., 198; V., 152 f.; VII., 24.

Apocalypse of Peter, I., 101, 167.

Apocalypses, I., 100 f., 104 f., 115, 155, 160, 168 f., 173 f., 179, 240; II., 40, 55 f., 65, 297, 300, 317; III., 197; IV., 107.

Apocalyptic hopes, I., 78, 100 f., 167 ff., 223 ff.; VI., 112, v. also Chiliasm and Prophets.

Apocryphal Acts of the Apostles, I., 163, 193, 240, 253, 308, 312 ff.; II., 48, 82.

Apocryphal Gospels, I., 161, 193, 203.

Apocrypha, III., 198; IV., 304; VII., 41.

Apokatastasis, II., 275; III., 186, 189, 298; VII., 128, 131.

Apollinaris of Hierapolis, II., 52; III., 219.

Apollinaris of Laodicea, III., 34, 138, 146, 151, 165, 182, 187, 202, 219, 301, 306; IV., 37, 59, 84, 88, 91, 119, 123 f., 145, 147, 149-163, and in Chap. III. frequently, 264, 266, 286, 335, 340, 351; V., 96.

Apollinarists, III., 185, 221; IV., 150, 157 f., 174, 179, 242; V., 128.

Apollonius of Tyana, I., 120.

Apologists, I., 126, 136, 170, 176, 180, 186, 188; II., 6 ff., 10, 14, 32, 123, 169-229, 230 ff., 243 f., 263, 266, 272, 288; III., 7, 132, 144, 172, 206, 212, 267, 296; IV., 29, 45, 121.

Apostles, I., 98, 143, 147, 158-165, 184, 212 f., 253 f., 278 f., 283; II., 18 f., 25-38, 39-66 ff., 78 ff., 85 ff., 98 f., 103, 107, 141, 348; III., 6, 192.

Apostles, Acts of, I., 56, 162, 295 f., 315; II., 43, 312 ff.; III., 6.

Apostles, Legends of, III., 211 f.; IV., 306.

Apostles' Chairs, III., 219, 221 ff.

Apostolic Brethren, VI., 8.

Apostolic Word, I., 160; II., 51, 65.

Apostol. Constit., I., 186, 293; II., 19, 37, 38, 57, 71, 129 f., 137, 139, 153 f., 304; III., 128, 211 f., 215, 237, 248, 264, 267; IV., 89, 109, 280, 292.

Cerdo, I., 247 f., 250, 266 ff.
Ceremonies (v. Law) I., 173 ff., 291 f., 293 f. ; II., 171 f.
Ceremonial Purity, II., 130.
Cerinthus, I., 167, 246 f., 303 f.; III., 14 ff.
Chalcedonian Formula, I., 28 f., Synod and Symbol, III., 152 f., 209 f., 217, 223-225 ; IV., 178, 195, 196 f., 209 f., 213-226, 226-252, 253, 258, 260 f., 262, 346, 351 ; VII., 244.
Chaldæism, III., 316.
Character indelibilis, V., 157 f.; VI., 211 f., 271 ; VII., 45.
Charisius, IV., 118.
Charisma (v. Prophets) and I., Chap. II., §§ 3, 5, pp. 147, 213; II., 107 f., 232 ; III., 18, 87.
Charlemagne, IV., 133, 135, 320 ; V., 277 ff., 287 f., 302 ff., 327 ; VI., 3, 7, 20, 31.
Charles the Bald, IV., 136 ; V., 27, 300.
Charles of Provence, V., 300.
Charles V., Emperor, VII., 11.
Chateaubriand, VII., 78.
Chemnitz, Martin, VI., 15; VII., 82.
Cherubim, IV., 306.
Chiersey, V., 296, 299 f., 328 ; VI., 55.
Chiliasm, I., 167 ff., 292 ; II., 24, 106 f., 294 ff.; III., 9, 37, 78, 95, 112, 187 f.; IV., 155, 336, 340 ; V., 238.
Chrisma, v. Confirmation.
Christ, I., 184 f. See Jesus.
Christendom, Two Geographical Halves of, II., 149.
Christians outside the Community, I., 151.
Christianity, I., 70 ff., 148, 360;

II., 325 ff., 336, 368 ; III., 100, 107, 330 f., et alibi.
Christianity of second rank, III., 125, 130 f. ; IV., 304 ff.
Christina of Sweden, VII., 169.
Christologies (Beginnings of), I., 76 ff., 80 ff., 92 f., 99 ff., 129 f., 133, 156 f., 183-203, 246, 252 f., 258 ff., 271 f., 275 f., 306, 309 ; II., 98, 180 ff., 218 ff., 235, 373 ; III., 32-50, 69, 76 f., 85, v. Jesus.
Christologies, Philosophical, III., 1-8 ff., 81-118, v. Jesus.
Chronicles, Books of, III., 193.
Chrysantius, I., 355.
Chrysaphius IV., 199.
Chrysostom, I., 165 ; III., 129, 152, 168, 180, 196, 200 f., 205, 213, 215, 222, 226, 235 f., 283, 302, 309 ; IV., 166, 181, 203, 280, 297 ff., 342 f., 344 f., 350 ; V., 190.
Church, I., 43 f., 78 ff., 88 f., 133, 141 ff., 150 ff., 165, 193, 212 ff., 260 f., 324 ; II., 4 f., 43, 46, 61 ff., 67 ff., 71-93, 94-127, 135, 143, 146 f., 287, 293, 295, 303 f., 336, 338 f., 357 f.; III., 3, 25 ff., 79, 108, 110 f., 113 f., 207 ff., 214 ff., 228, 233 ff.; IV., 278 ff., 289, 292 ; V., 10 f., 39 ff., 43 ff., 58, 66, 77, 78 ff., 83, 137, 140-168 ; VI., 118-149, 152 ff., 174 f., 195, 200, 232, 315 ; VII., 9, 161 ff., 187 f., 220, 225, 233, 239 f.
Church as civitas, II., 82 ; V., 137, 151-155.
Church as Mother, II., 76 ; V., 150.
Church and Christ, I., 152 ff. ;

f., IV., 277, 293 ; VI., 201, 211, 230 f. ; VII., 46.

Confutatio, I., 7 ; VII., 10, 226.

Congregations (*v.* also Church), I., 150 ff., 204, 209 ff., 212 ff., 186 f., 252, 324 ; II., 15, 17, 31 ff., 67 ff., 73, 76 f., 86 ff., 137 ; III., 114 f.

Congregatio de auxiliis, VII., 90.

Conservatism of Theologians, III., 137 f.

Consilia, *v.* Twofold Morality.

Constance, Council of, V., 17, 127, 140, 147, 241, 269, 306.

Constans I., IV., 67 f., 243.

Constans II., IV., 256 ff.

Constantia, IV., 62.

Constantine the Great, II., 125, 130 ; III., 126 f., 131, 136, 148, 186, 196, 215, 218, 225 ; IV., 8, 9 f., 43 f., 50 f., 52 ff., 58-63, 93, 221, 333 ; VI., 172.

Constantine II., IV., 67.

Constantine Copronymus, IV., 314, 320, 324 f.

Constantine Pogonatus, IV., 260.

Constantinople, II., 122 ; III., 223 f., 227 f. ; IV., 95, 190 ff., 201, 214, 225, 251, 254 ff., 262, 342 ; V., 241, 247, 302 ; VI., 28 ff.

Constantinople, Synod of, 336, IV., 63, 65.

Constantinople, Synod of, 360, IV., 79.

Constantinople, Synod of, 381, III., 151, 216, 223 ; IV., 94 ff., 118, 158, 219.

Constantinople, Synod of, 382, III., 237 ; IV., 98, 102 f. 118.

Constantinople, Synod of, 383, IV., 104.

Constantinople, Synods of, 448 and 450, IV., 200, 204, 213, 218.

Constantinople, Religious Conference of, 531, IV., 242.

Constantinople, Synod of, 536, IV., 243.

Constantinople, Synod of, 680, III., 157 ; IV., 260 ff., 310.

Constantinople, Synod of, 692, IV., 262, 284.

Constantinople, Synod of, 754, IV., 316, 324 f. ; V., 306, 309.

Constantinople, Synod of, 842, IV. 328.

Constantinople, Synod of, 869, V., 307.

Constantinople, Synod of, 1156, VI., 77.

Constantinopolitan Symbol, III., 209 f. ; IV., 95 ff., 114, 118, 127, 133, 136 ; V., 302 f. ; VII., 40, 84, 134.

Constantius II., IV., 63 ff., 67 ff., 71 ff., 79 f., 91, 94, 222.

Constitution, I., 212 ff., 256, 291 f. ; II., 5 ; III., 126, 211 f., 214 ff., 236, Vols. V.-VII. *passim.*

Consubstantiation, VI., 52, 235 f.

Contarini, VI., 307.

Conventicles, I., 151, 250.

Coornhert, VII., 123, 160.

Copts, IV., 192.

Coptic Monks, see Monks and III., 690 f.

Copula carnalis, VI., 273 f.

Copyists, Errors of, III., 237.

Cordova, V., 283.

Lateran Council of 1179, VI.,
17 f., 188, 203.
Lateran Council of 1215, III.,
224 ; VI., 17, 53 f., 120, 176,
182 f., 203, 232 f., 245, 253.
Lateran Council of 1515, VI.,
127.
Law, Mosaic, I., 43 f., 67, 76 f.,
107 f., 176, 289 ff., 295 f., 302
ff., 314 ; II., 301-311, 348.
Law, New, I., 59, 91, 146, 171,
294 f. ; II., 16, 32, 74, 101 ff.,
121, 139, 214 f., 227 ; III.,
172 f., and Chap. V. ; V., 15,
26, 201 f., 219, 264 f. ; VI.,
131 ff., 137 f., 174 f. ; VII.,
150, 204 f.
Law and Dogma, III., 185 f.,
257 f., 266 ff.
Law, Question of, in the Apostolic Age, I., 86 ff.
Laxism, v. Probabilism.
Lazarus, Gallican Bishop, VI.,
179.
Legal Conceptions in Dog-
matic, II., 135 f., 235 f., 257,
280, 282 ; III., 310 f. ; IV.,
122 f., 136 f., 144 f. ; V., 5
ff., 15 f., 29, 52, 262 ff., 271 ;
VI., 16-23, 118 ff. ; VII., 9,
14, 101 ff., 109.
Leibniz, II., 344 ; V., 3, 74.
Leidrad of Lyons, V., 288, 292.
Leo I., II., 168, 235, 276, 281 ;
III., 94, 148, 153, 157, 217,
224, 226, 307, 312, 314, 336 ;
IV., 131 f., 145, 184, 192 ff.,
197, 199, 200-226, (Ep. ad
Flav., 202, 205), 226 ff., 235
f., 253, 299, 343 ; V., 241,
250, 263.
Leo III., Pope, IV., 133 ; V.,
304.

Leo IX., Pope, VI., 16, 18.
Leo X., Pope, VI., 127 ; VII.,
6, 73.
Leo I., Emperor, IV., 227.
Leo the Armenian, IV., 328.
Leo the Isaurian, IV., 320 f.
Leo, Russian Patriarch, III.,
165.
Leontius of Antioch, IV., 3.
Leontius of Byzantium, III.,
50, 154; IV., 125, 232 ff., 236,
240 ff., 253, 262 ff., 299, 346
ff., 350 ; V., 289 ; VII., 15.
Leontius in Gaul, V., 253.
Leporius, IV., 185.
Lerinum, V., 247, 256.
Lessing, I., 29.
Lessius, VII., 81, 89.
Letter of Holy Scripture, III.,
199 f., 325 f. ; IV., 306.
Leucius, v. Acts of John and
IV., 303.
Leucippus, V., 191.
Libanius, IV., 88 f.
Liberius, IV., 73, 77, 91 ; V.,
59.
Library, Theological, II., 322.
Licinius, IV., 9 f.
Lie, V., 222 f.
Life, Ascetic, v. Monachism.
Life, Eternal, and Resurrection,
I., 84, 118, 145 f., 169 ff., 211
f. ; II., 126, 140, 345 ; III.,
Chaps. II., V., (Part II.) ;
V., 202, v. also Deification,
VI., 40 f., 293 f. ; VII., 142
ff., 153.
Life, Active, VI., 107 ff. ; VII.,
190.
Light and Darkness, III., 324.
Light-God, III., 323 f.
Liguori, Alphonso, VII., 108
f.

Nature, Christian View of, I., 176, 179 ff.; V., 114 f.; VI., 23.

Nazarenes, I., 301, 304.

Neander, I., 32 f.; III., 53; VII., 26.

Nectarius of Constantinople, IV., 95, 103.

Nemesius, IV., 150.

Neocæsarea, Synod of, II., 122.

Neoplatonism, I., 122 f., 231, 233, 336-364; II., 11, 14, 176, 327 f., 344; III., 2, 25, 55 f., 79, 91, 96, 117, 134, 155, 158, 189, 199, 240, 242 f., 248 f., 253 f., 258, 269, 316, 335; IV., 16, 39, 88, 132, 145, 271, 274, 282, 294, 307, 328, 333, 337 f., 346, 349; V., 33 ff., 52, 56, 84, 101 f., 110 ff., 126 f., 131 f., 274, 298; VI., 11, 29, 33 ff., 101, 104, 184.

Neopythagoreans, I., 123, 345.

Nepos, Bishop, II., 299.

Nero, the returning, II., 297; III., 189.

Nestorians and Nestorius, I., 292; III., 32, 40, 171, 193, 201, 212, 238; IV., 124 ff., 180-189, and *passim* in Chap. III., 205, 299, 316, 324, 344; V., 171, 188, 255, 279 ff., 287; VI., 40, 187, 198; VII., 262.

New Testament, I., 48 f., 106, 135, 159, 162, 253 ff., 299; II., 1 ff., 15, 19, 35 f., 38 to 66 (39 critical principles), 87, 93, 103, 106, 112, 121, 151, 230 ff., 289, 301 ff., 348; III., 6, 12 f.; see Holy Scripture.

Nicaea, 1st Council and Canons of, II., 147, 154, 166; III., 75, 100, 117, 139, 151, 216, 223, 225, 229; IV., 12, 26, 50 ff., 65, 72, 83, 219; V., 31, 47.

Nicaea, Synod of 787; III., 218, 252; IV., 303, 304, 311, 314, 316, 326 ff.; V., 306 f., 310; VII., 54.

Niceno-Constantinopolitan Symbol, III., 209 f., 216 f., 217; IV., 51 ff., 64 f., 67 f., 95 ff., 106, 132, 134, 186, 201, 209, 214, 221, 227.

Nice, Synod of, III., 230; IV., 77 f.

Nicephorus, III., 83.

Nicetas of Romatiana, V., 244.

Nicolas of Cusa, VI., 141, 171, 310; VII., 123.

Nicolas of Methone, VI., 51.

Nicolas I., Pope, VI., 7, 16, 18

Nicolas II., Pope, VI., 50.

Nicole, VII., 105.

Nihilianism, VI., 188.

Nilus, IV., 300.

Nisibis, School, III., 193, 205.

Nitrian Monks, IV., 342.

Nitzsch, I., 37; III., 36, 84; VI., 27.

Noailles, VII., 96.

Noëtus and School, I., 196; III., 51, 52 ff., 57 ff., 62 ff., 66, 80, 84.

Nominalism, III., 55; VI., 24, 34 f., 49, 107, 132, 162 ff., 175, 178 ff., 205, 209, 221 f., 225 f., 229, 233, 237 ff., 301-317; VII., 7, 13 f., 16, 58 ff., 92, 120 f., 126 ff., 132, 236, 262, 264; compare Socinianism.

CATALOGUE OF DOVER BOOKS

Books Explaining Science and Mathematics

WHAT IS SCIENCE?, N. Campbell. The role of experiment and measurement, the function of mathematics, the nature of scientific laws, the difference between laws and theories, the limitations of science, and many similarly provocative topics are treated clearly and without technicalities by an eminent scientist. "Still an excellent introduction to scientific philosophy," H. Margenau in PHYSICS TODAY. "A first-rate primer . . . deserves a wide audience," SCIENTIFIC AMERICAN. 192pp. 5⅜ x 8. S43 Paperbound **$1.25**

THE NATURE OF PHYSICAL THEORY, P. W. Bridgman. A Nobel Laureate's clear, non-technical lectures on difficulties and paradoxes connected with frontier research on the physical sciences. Concerned with such central concepts as thought, logic, mathematics, relativity, probability, wave mechanics, etc. he analyzes the contributions of such men as Newton, Einstein, Bohr, Heisenberg, and many others. "Lucid and entertaining . . . recommended to anyone who wants to get some insight into current philosophies of science," THE NEW PHILOSOPHY. Index. xi + 138pp. 5⅜ x 8. S33 Paperbound **$1.25**

EXPERIMENT AND THEORY IN PHYSICS, Max Born. A Nobel Laureate examines the nature of experiment and theory in theoretical physics and analyzes the advances made by the great physicists of our day: Heisenberg, Einstein, Bohr, Planck, Dirac, and others. The actual process of creation is detailed step-by-step by one who participated. A fine examination of the scientific method at work. 44pp. 5⅜ x 8. S308 Paperbound **75¢**

THE PSYCHOLOGY OF INVENTION IN THE MATHEMATICAL FIELD, J. Hadamard. The reports of such men as Descartes, Pascal, Einstein, Poincaré, and others are considered in this investigation of the method of idea-creation in mathematics and other sciences and the thinking process in general. How do ideas originate? What is the role of the unconscious? What is Poincaré's forgetting hypothesis? are some of the fascinating questions treated. A penetrating analysis of Einstein's thought processes concludes the book. xiii + 145pp. 5⅜ x 8. T107 Paperbound **$1.25**

THE NATURE OF LIGHT AND COLOUR IN THE OPEN AIR, M. Minnaert. Why are shadows sometimes blue, sometimes green, or other colors depending on the light and surroundings? What causes mirages? Why do multiple suns and moons appear in the sky? Professor Minnaert explains these unusual phenomena and hundreds of others in simple, easy-to-understand terms based on optical laws and the properties of light and color. No mathematics is required but artists, scientists, students, and everyone fascinated by these "tricks" of nature will find thousands of useful and amazing pieces of information. Hundreds of observational experiments are suggested which require no special equipment. 200 illustrations; 42 photos. xvi + 362pp. 5⅜ x 8. T196 Paperbound **$2.00**

THE UNIVERSE OF LIGHT, W. Bragg. Sir William Bragg, Nobel Laureate and great modern physicist, is also well known for his powers of clear exposition. Here he analyzes all aspects of light for the layman: lenses, reflection, refraction, the optics of vision, x-rays, the photoelectric effect, etc. He tells you what causes the color of spectra, rainbows, and soap bubbles, how magic mirrors work, and much more. Dozens of simple experiments are described. Preface. Index. 199 line drawings and photographs, including 2 full-page color plates. x + 283pp. 5⅜ x 8. T538 Paperbound **$1.85**

SOAP-BUBBLES: THEIR COLOURS AND THE FORCES THAT MOULD THEM, C. V. Boys. For continuing popularity and validity as scientific primer, few books can match this volume of easily-followed experiments, explanations. Lucid exposition of complexities of liquid films, surface tension and related phenomena, bubbles' reaction to heat, motion, music, magnetic fields. Experiments with capillary attraction, soap bubbles on frames, composite bubbles, liquid cylinders and jets, bubbles other than soap, etc. Wonderful introduction to scientific method, natural laws that have many ramifications in areas of modern physics. Only complete edition in print. New Introduction by S. Z. Lewin, New York University. 83 illustrations; 1 full-page color plate. xii + 190pp. 5⅜ x 8½. T542 Paperbound **95¢**

THE STORY OF X-RAYS FROM RONTGEN TO ISOTOPES, A. R. Bleich, M.D. This book, by a member of the American College of Radiology, gives the scientific explanation of x-rays, their applications in medicine, industry and art, and their danger (and that of atmospheric radiation) to the individual and the species. You learn how radiation therapy is applied against cancer, how x-rays diagnose heart disease and other ailments, how they are used to examine mummies for information on diseases of early societies, and industrial materials for hidden weaknesses. 54 illustrations show x-rays of flowers, bones, stomach, gears with flaws, etc. 1st publication. Index. xix + 186pp. 5⅜ x 8.   T622 Paperbound **$1.35**

SPINNING TOPS AND GYROSCOPIC MOTION, John Perry. A classic elementary text of the dynamics of rotation — the behavior and use of rotating bodies such as gyroscopes and tops. In simple, everyday English you are shown how quasi-rigidity is induced in discs of paper, smoke rings, chains, etc., by rapid motions; why a gyrostat falls and why a top rises; precession; how the earth's motion affects climate; and many other phenomena. Appendix on practical use of gyroscopes. 62 figures. 128pp. 5⅜ x 8.   T416 Paperbound **$1.00**

SNOW CRYSTALS, W. A. Bentley, M. J. Humphreys. For almost 50 years W. A. Bentley photographed snow flakes in his laboratory in Jericho, Vermont; in 1931 the American Meteorological Society gathered together the best of his work, some 2400 photographs of snow flakes, plus a few ice flowers, windowpane frosts, dew, frozen rain, and other ice formations. Pictures were selected for beauty and scientific value. A very valuable work to anyone in meteorology, cryology; most interesting to layman; extremely useful for artist who wants beautiful, crystalline designs. All copyright free. Unabridged reprint of 1931 edition. 2453 illustrations. 227pp. 8 x 10½.   T287 Paperbound **$3.00**

A DOVER SCIENCE SAMPLER, edited by George Barkin. A collection of brief, non-technical passages from 44 Dover Books Explaining Science for the enjoyment of the science-minded browser. Includes work of Bertrand Russell, Poincaré, Laplace, Max Born, Galileo, Newton; material on physics, mathematics, metallurgy, anatomy, astronomy, chemistry, etc. You will be fascinated by Martin Gardner's analysis of the sincere pseudo-scientist, Moritz's account of Newton's absentmindedness, Bernard's examples of human vivisection, etc. Illustrations from the Diderot Pictorial Encyclopedia and De Re Metallica. 64 pages.   **FREE**

THE STORY OF ATOMIC THEORY AND ATOMIC ENERGY, J. G. Feinberg. A broader approach to subject of nuclear energy and its cultural implications than any other similar source. Very readable, informal, completely non-technical text. Begins with first atomic theory, 600 B.C. and carries you through the work of Mendelejeff, Röntgen, Madame Curie, to Einstein's equation and the A-bomb. New chapter goes through thermonuclear fission, binding energy, other events up to 1959. Radioactive decay and radiation hazards, future benefits, work of Bohr, moderns, hundreds more topics. "Deserves special mention . . . not only authoritative but thoroughly popular in the best sense of the word," Saturday Review. Formerly, "The Atom Story." Expanded with new chapter. Three appendixes. Index. 34 illustrations. vii + 243pp. 5⅜ x 8.   T625 Paperbound **$1.60**

THE STRANGE STORY OF THE QUANTUM, AN ACCOUNT FOR THE GENERAL READER OF THE GROWTH OF IDEAS UNDERLYING OUR PRESENT ATOMIC KNOWLEDGE, B. Hoffmann. Presents lucidly and expertly, with barest amount of mathematics, the problems and theories which led to modern quantum physics. Dr. Hoffmann begins with the closing years of the 19th century, when certain trifling discrepancies were noticed, and with illuminating analogies and examples takes you through the brilliant concepts of Planck, Einstein, Pauli, Broglie, Bohr, Schroedinger, Heisenberg, Dirac, Sommerfeld, Feynman, etc. This edition includes a new, long postscript carrying the story through 1958. "Of the books attempting an account of the history and contents of our modern atomic physics which have come to my attention, this is the best," H. Margenau, Yale University, in "American Journal of Physics." 32 tables and line illustrations. Index. 275pp. 5⅜ x 8.   T518 Paperbound **$1.50**

SPACE AND TIME, E. Borel. Written by a versatile mathematician of world renown with his customary lucidity and precision, this introduction to relativity for the layman presents scores of examples, analogies, and illustrations that open up new ways of thinking about space and time. It covers abstract geometry and geographical maps, continuity and topology, the propagation of light, the special theory of relativity, the general theory of relativity, theoretical researches, and much more. Mathematical notes. 2 Indexes. 4 Appendices. 15 figures. xvi + 243pp. 5⅜ x 8.   T592 Paperbound **$1.45**

FROM EUCLID TO EDDINGTON: A STUDY OF THE CONCEPTIONS OF THE EXTERNAL WORLD, Sir Edmund Whittaker. A foremost British scientist traces the development of theories of natural philosophy from the western rediscovery of Euclid to Eddington, Einstein, Dirac, etc. The inadequacy of classical physics is contrasted with present day attempts to understand the physical world through relativity, non-Euclidean geometry, space curvature, wave mechanics, etc. 5 major divisions of examination: Space; Time and Movement; the Concepts of Classical Physics; the Concepts of Quantum Mechanics; the Eddington Universe. 212pp. 5⅜ x 8.   T491 Paperbound **$1.35**

Nature, Biology

NATURE RECREATION: Group Guidance for the Out-of-doors, William Gould Vinal. Intended for both the uninitiated nature instructor and the education student on the college level, this complete "how-to" program surveys the entire area of nature education for the young. Philosophy of nature recreation; requirements, responsibilities, important information for group leaders; nature games; suggested group projects; conducting meetings and getting discussions started; etc. Scores of immediately applicable teaching aids, plus completely updated sources of information, pamphlets, field guides, recordings, etc. Bibliography. 74 photographs. + 310pp. 5⅜ x 8½.   T1015 Paperbound **$1.75**

HOW TO KNOW THE WILD FLOWERS, Mrs. William Starr Dana. Classic nature book that has introduced thousands to wonders of American wild flowers. Color-season principle of organization is easy to use, even by those with no botanical training, and the genial, refreshing discussions of history, folklore, uses of over 1,000 native and escape flowers, foliage plants are informative as well as fun to read. Over 170 full-page plates, collected from several editions, may be colored in to make permanent records of finds. Revised to conform with 1950 edition of Gray's Manual of Botany. xlii + 438pp. 5⅜ x 8½.   T332 Paperbound **$2.00**

HOW TO KNOW THE FERNS, F. T. Parsons. Ferns, among our most lovely native plants, are all too little known. This classic of nature lore will enable the layman to identify almost any American fern he may come across. After an introduction on the structure and life of ferns, the 57 most important ferns are fully pictured and described (arranged upon a simple identification key). Index of Latin and English names. 61 illustrations and 42 full-page plates. xiv + 215pp. 5⅜ x 8.   T740 Paperbound **$1.35**

MANUAL OF THE TREES OF NORTH AMERICA, Charles Sprague Sargent. Still unsurpassed as most comprehensive, reliable study of North American tree characteristics, precise locations and distribution. By dean of American dendrologists. Every tree native to U.S., Canada, Alaska, 185 genera, 717 species, described in detail—leaves, flowers, fruit, winterbuds, bark, wood, growth habits etc. plus discussion of varieties and local variants, immaturity variations. Over 100 keys, including unusual 11-page analytical key to genera, aid in identification. 783 clear illustrations of flowers, fruit, leaves. An unmatched permanent reference work for all nature lovers. Second enlarged (1926) edition. Synopsis of families. Analytical key to genera. Glossary of technical terms. Index. 783 illustrations, 1 map. Two volumes. Total of 982pp. 5⅜ x 8.   T277 Vol. I Paperbound **$2.25**
                                                     T278 Vol. II Paperbound **$2.25**
                                                                      The set **$4.50**

TREES OF THE EASTERN AND CENTRAL UNITED STATES AND CANADA, W. M. Harlow. A revised edition of a standard middle-level guide to native trees and important escapes. More than 140 trees are described in detail, and illustrated with more than 600 drawings and photographs. Supplementary keys will enable the careful reader to identify almost any tree he might encounter. xiii + 288pp. 5⅜ x 8.   T395 Paperbound **$1.35**

GUIDE TO SOUTHERN TREES, Ellwood S. Harrar and J. George Harrar. All the essential information about trees indigenous to the South, in an extremely handy format. Introductory essay on methods of tree classification and study, nomenclature, chief divisions of Southern trees, etc. Approximately 100 keys and synopses allow for swift, accurate identification of trees. Numerous excellent illustrations, non-technical text make this a useful book for teachers of biology or natural science, nature lovers, amateur naturalists. Revised 1962 edition. Index. Bibliography. Glossary of technical terms. 920 illustrations; 201 full-page plates. ix + 709pp. 4⅝ x 6⅜.   T945 Paperbound **$2.35**

FRUIT KEY AND TWIG KEY TO TREES AND SHRUBS, W. M. Harlow. Bound together in one volume for the first time, these handy and accurate keys to fruit and twig identification are the only guides of their sort with photographs (up to 3 times natural size). "Fruit Key": Key to over 120 different deciduous and evergreen fruits. 139 photographs and 11 line drawings. Synoptic summary of fruit types. Bibliography. 2 Indexes (common and scientific names). "Twig Key": Key to over 160 different twigs and buds. 173 photographs. Glossary of technical terms. Bibliography. 2 Indexes (common and scientific names). Two volumes bound as one. Total of xvii + 126pp. 5⅝ x 8⅜.   T511 Paperbound **$1.25**

INSECT LIFE AND INSECT NATURAL HISTORY, S. W. Frost. A work emphasizing habits, social life, and ecological relations of insects, rather than more academic aspects of classification and morphology. Prof. Frost's enthusiasm and knowledge are everywhere evident as he discusses insect associations and specialized habits like leaf-rolling, leaf-mining, and case-making, the gall insects, the boring insects, aquatic insects, etc. He examines all sorts of matters not usually covered in general works, such as: insects as human food, insect music and musicians, insect response to electric and radio waves, use of insects in art and literature. The admirably executed purpose of this book, which covers the middle ground between elementary treatment and scholarly monographs, is to excite the reader to observe for himself. Over 700 illustrations. Extensive bibliography. x + 524pp. 5⅜ x 8.   T517 Paperbound **$2.45**

COMMON SPIDERS OF THE UNITED STATES, J. H. Emerton. Here is a nature hobby you can pursue right in your own cellar! Only non-technical, but thorough, reliable guide to spiders for the layman. Over 200 spiders from all parts of the country, arranged by scientific classification, are identified by shape and color, number of eyes, habitat and range, habits, etc. Full text, 501 line drawings and photographs, and valuable introduction explain webs, poisons, threads, capturing and preserving spiders, etc. Index. New synoptic key by S. W. Frost. xxiv + 225pp. 5⅜ x 8.   T223 Paperbound $1.45

THE LIFE STORY OF THE FISH: HIS MANNERS AND MORALS, Brian Curtis. A comprehensive, non-technical survey of just about everything worth knowing about fish. Written for the aquarist, the angler, and the layman with an inquisitive mind, the text covers such topics as evolution, external covering and protective coloration, physics and physiology of vision, maintenance of equilibrium, function of the lateral line canal for auditory and temperature senses, nervous system, function of the air bladder, reproductive system and methods—courtship, mating, spawning, care of young—and many more. Also sections on game fish, the problems of conservation and a fascinating chapter on fish curiosities. "Clear, simple language . . . excellent judgment in choice of subjects . . . delightful sense of humor," New York Times. Revised (1949) edition. Index. Bibliography of 72 items. 6 full-page photographic plates. xii + 284pp. 5⅜ x 8.   T929 Paperbound $1.65

BATS, Glover Morrill Allen. The most comprehensive study of bats as a life-form by the world's foremost authority. A thorough summary of just-about everything known about this fascinating and mysterious flying mammal, including its unique location sense, hibernation and cycles, its habitats and distribution, its wing structure and flying habits, and its relationship to man in the long history of folklore and superstition. Written on a middle-level, the book can be profitably studied by a trained zoologist and thoroughly enjoyed by the layman. "An absorbing text with excellent illustrations. Bats should have more friends and fewer thoughtless detractors as a result of the publication of this volume," William Beebe, Books. Extensive bibliography. 57 photographs and illustrations. x + 368pp. 5⅜ x 8½.
                                              T984 Paperbound $2.00

BIRDS AND THEIR ATTRIBUTES, Glover Morrill Allen. A fine general introduction to birds as living organisms, especially valuable because of emphasis on structure, physiology, habits, behavior. Discusses relationship of bird to man, early attempts at scientific ornithology, feathers and coloration, skeletal structure including bills, legs and feet, wings. Also food habits, evolution and present distribution, feeding and nest-building, still unsolved questions of migrations and location sense, many more similar topics. Final chapter on classification, nomenclature. A good popular-level summary for the biologist; a first-rate introduction for the layman. Reprint of 1925 edition. References and index. 51 illustrations. viii + 338pp. 5⅜ x 8½.   T957 Paperbound $1.85

LIFE HISTORIES OF NORTH AMERICAN BIRDS, Arthur Cleveland Bent. Bent's monumental series of books on North American birds, prepared and published under auspices of Smithsonian Institute, is the definitive coverage of the subject, the most-used single source of information. Now the entire set is to be made available by Dover in inexpensive editions. This encyclopedic collection of detailed, specific observations utilizes reports of hundreds of contemporary observers, writings of such naturalists as Audubon, Burroughs, William Brewster, as well as author's own extensive investigations. Contains literally everything known about life history of each bird considered: nesting, eggs, plumage, distribution and migration, voice, enemies, courtship, etc. These not over-technical works are musts for ornithologists, conservationists, amateur naturalists, anyone seriously interested in American birds.

BIRDS OF PREY. More than 100 subspecies of hawks, falcons, eagles, buzzards, condors and owls, from the common barn owl to the extinct caracara of Guadaloupe Island. 400 photographs. Two volume set. Index for each volume. Bibliographies of 403, 520 items. 197 full-page plates. Total of 907pp. 5⅜ x 8½.   Vol. I T931 Paperbound $2.50
                                              Vol. II T932 Paperbound $2.50

WILD FOWL. Ducks, geese, swans, and tree ducks—73 different subspecies. Two volume set. Index for each volume. Bibliographies of 124, 144 items. 106 full-page plates. Total of 685pp. 5⅜ x 8½.   Vol. I T285 Paperbound $2.50
                                              Vol. II T286 Paperbound $2.50

SHORE BIRDS. 81 varieties (sandpipers, woodcocks, plovers, snipes, phalaropes, curlews, oyster catchers, etc.). More than 200 photographs of eggs, nesting sites, adult and young of important species. Two volume set. Index for each volume. Bibliographies of 261, 188 items. 121 full-page plates. Total of 860pp. 5⅜ x 8½.   Vol. I T933 Paperbound $2.35
                                              Vol. II T934 Paperbound $2.35

THE LIFE OF PASTEUR, R. Vallery-Radot. 13th edition of this definitive biography, cited in Encyclopaedia Britannica. Authoritative, scholarly, well-documented with contemporary quotes, observations; gives complete picture of Pasteur's personal life; especially thorough presentation of scientific activities with silkworms, fermentation, hydrophobia, inoculation, etc. Introduction by Sir William Osler. Index. 505pp. 5⅜ x 8.   T632 Paperbound $2.00

Puzzles, Mathematical Recreations

SYMBOLIC LOGIC and THE GAME OF LOGIC, Lewis Carroll. "Symbolic Logic" is not concerned with modern symbolic logic, but is instead a collection of over 380 problems posed with charm and imagination, using the syllogism, and a fascinating diagrammatic method of drawing conclusions. In "The Game of Logic" Carroll's whimsical imagination devises a logical game played with 2 diagrams and counters (included) to manipulate hundreds of tricky syllogisms. The final section, "Hit or Miss" is a lagniappe of 101 additional puzzles in the delightful Carroll manner. Until this reprint edition, both of these books were rarities costing up to $15 each. Symbolic Logic: Index. xxxi + 199pp. The Game of Logic: 96pp. 2 vols. bound as one. 5⅜ x 8.　　　　　　　　　　　　　　　　　**T492 Paperbound $1.50**

PILLOW PROBLEMS and A TANGLED TALE, Lewis Carroll. One of the rarest of all Carroll's works, "Pillow Problems" contains 72 original math puzzles, all typically ingenious. Particularly fascinating are Carroll's answers which remain exactly as he thought them out, reflecting his actual mental process. The problems in "A Tangled Tale" are in story form, originally appearing as a monthly magazine serial. Carroll not only gives the solutions, but uses answers sent in by readers to discuss wrong approaches and misleading paths, and grades them for insight. Both of these books were rarities until this edition, "Pillow Problems" costing up to $25, and "A Tangled Tale" $15. Pillow Problems: Preface and Introduction by Lewis Carroll. xx + 109pp. A Tangled Tale: 6 illustrations. 152pp. Two vols. bound as one. 5⅜ x 8.　　　　　　　　　　　　　　　　　**T493 Paperbound $1.50**

AMUSEMENTS IN MATHEMATICS, Henry Ernest Dudeney. The foremost British originator of mathematical puzzles is always intriguing, witty, and paradoxical in this classic, one of the largest collections of mathematical amusements. More than 430 puzzles, problems, and paradoxes. Mazes and games, problems on number manipulation, unicursal and other route problems, puzzles on measuring, weighing, packing, age, kinship, chessboards, joiners', crossing river, plane figure dissection, and many others. Solutions. More than 450 illustrations. vii + 258pp. 5⅜ x 8.　　　　　　　　　　　　　　　　　**T473 Paperbound $1.25**

THE CANTERBURY PUZZLES, Henry Dudeney. Chaucer's pilgrims set one another problems in story form. Also Adventures of the Puzzle Club, the Strange Escape of the King's Jester, the Monks of Riddlewell, the Squire's Christmas Puzzle Party, and others. All puzzles are original, based on dissecting plane figures, arithmetic, algebra, elementary calculus and other branches of mathematics, and purely logical ingenuity. "The limit of ingenuity and intricacy," The Observer. Over 110 puzzles. Full Solutions. 150 illustrations. vii + 225pp. 5⅜ x 8.　　　　　　　　　　　　　　　　　**T474 Paperbound $1.25**

MATHEMATICAL EXCURSIONS, H. A. Merrill. Even if you hardly remember your high school math, you'll enjoy the 90 stimulating problems contained in this book and you will come to understand a great many mathematical principles with surprisingly little effort. Many useful shortcuts and diversions not generally known are included: division by inspection, Russian peasant multiplication, memory systems for pi, building odd and even magic squares, square roots by geometry, dyadic systems, and many more. Solutions to difficult problems. 50 illustrations. 145pp. 5⅜ x 8.　　　　　　　　　　　　　　　　　**T350 Paperbound $1.00**

MAGIC SQUARES AND CUBES, W. S. Andrews. Only book-length treatment in English, a thorough non-technical description and analysis. Here are nasik, overlapping, pandiagonal, serrated squares; magic circles, cubes, spheres, rhombuses. Try your hand at 4-dimensional magical figures! Much unusual folklore and tradition included. High school algebra is sufficient. 754 diagrams and illustrations. viii + 419pp. 5⅜ x 8.　　　　　　　　　　　　　　**T658 Paperbound $1.85**

CALIBAN'S PROBLEM BOOK: MATHEMATICAL, INFERENTIAL AND CRYPTOGRAPHIC PUZZLES, H. Phillips (Caliban), S. T. Shovelton, G. S. Marshall. 105 ingenious problems by the greatest living creator of puzzles based on logic and inference. Rigorous, modern, piquant; reflecting their author's unusual personality, these intermediate and advanced puzzles all involve the ability to reason clearly through complex situations; some call for mathematical knowledge, ranging from algebra to number theory. Solutions. xi + 180pp. 5⅜ x 8.
　　　　　　　　　　　　　　　　　　　　　　　　　　　　T736 Paperbound $1.25

MATHEMATICAL PUZZLES FOR BEGINNERS AND ENTHUSIASTS, G. Mott-Smith. 188 mathematical puzzles based on algebra, dissection of plane figures, permutations, and probability, that will test and improve your powers of inference and interpretation. The Odic Force, The Spider's Cousin, Ellipse Drawing, theory and strategy of card and board games like tit-tat-toe, go moku, salvo, and many others. 100 pages of detailed mathematical explanations. Appendix of primes, square roots, etc. 135 illustrations. 2nd revised edition. 248pp. 5⅜ x 8.
　　　　　　　　　　　　　　　　　　　　　　　　　　　　T198 Paperbound $1.00

MATHEMAGIC, MAGIC PUZZLES, AND GAMES WITH NUMBERS, R. V. Heath. More than 60 new puzzles and stunts based on the properties of numbers. Easy techniques for multiplying large numbers mentally, revealing hidden numbers magically, finding the date of any day in any year, and dozens more. Over 30 pages devoted to magic squares, triangles, cubes, circles, etc. Edited by J. S. Meyer. 76 illustrations. 128pp. 5⅜ x 8.　　　　　　**T110 Paperbound $1.00**

CATALOGUE OF DOVER BOOKS

THE BOOK OF MODERN PUZZLES, G. L. Kaufman. A completely new series of puzzles as fascinating as crossword and deduction puzzles but based upon different principles and techniques. Simple 2-minute teasers, word labyrinths, design and pattern puzzles, logic and observation puzzles — over 150 braincrackers. Answers to all problems. 116 illustrations. 192pp. 5⅜ x 8.
T143 Paperbound **$1.00**

NEW WORD PUZZLES, G. L. Kaufman. 100 ENTIRELY NEW puzzles based on words and their combinations that will delight crossword puzzle, Scrabble and Jotto fans. Chess words, based on the moves of the chess king; design-onyms, symmetrical designs made of synonyms; rhymed double-crostics; syllable sentences; addle letter anagrams; alphagrams; linkograms; and many others all brand new. Full solutions. Space to work problems. 196 figures. vi + 122pp. 5⅜ x 8.
T344 Paperbound **$1.00**

MAZES AND LABYRINTHS: A BOOK OF PUZZLES, W. Shepherd. Mazes, formerly associated with mystery and ritual, are still among the most intriguing of intellectual puzzles. This is a novel and different collection of 50 amusements that embody the principle of the maze: mazes in the classical tradition; 3-dimensional, ribbon, and Möbius-strip mazes; hidden messages; spatial arrangements; etc.—almost all built on amusing story situations. 84 illustrations. Essay on maze psychology. Solutions. xv + 122pp. 5⅜ x 8.
T731 Paperbound **$1.00**

MAGIC TRICKS & CARD TRICKS, W. Jonson. Two books bound as one. 52 tricks with cards, 37 tricks with coins, bills, eggs, smoke, ribbons, slates, etc. Details on presentation, misdirection, and routining will help you master such famous tricks as the Changing Card, Card in the Pocket, Four Aces, Coin Through the Hand, Bill in the Egg, Afghan Bands, and over 75 others. If you follow the lucid exposition and key diagrams carefully, you will finish these two books with an astonishing mastery of magic. 106 figures. 224pp. 5⅜ x 8. T909 Paperbound **$1.00**

PANORAMA OF MAGIC, Milbourne Christopher. A profusely illustrated history of stage magic, a unique selection of prints and engravings from the author's private collection of magic memorabilia, the largest of its kind. Apparatus, stage settings and costumes; ingenious ads distributed by the performers and satiric broadsides passed around in the streets ridiculing pompous showmen; programs; decorative souvenirs. The lively text, by one of America's foremost professional magicians, is full of anecdotes about almost legendary wizards: Dede, the Egyptian; Philadelphia, the wonder-worker; Robert-Houdin, "the father of modern magic;" Harry Houdini; scores more. Altogether a pleasure package for anyone interested in magic, stage setting and design, ethnology, psychology, or simply in unusual people. A Dover original. 295 illustrations; 8 in full color. Index. viii + 216pp. 8⅜ x 11¼.
T774 Paperbound **$2.25**

HOUDINI ON MAGIC, Harry Houdini. One of the greatest magicians of modern times explains his most prized secrets. How locks are picked, with illustrated picks and skeleton keys; how a girl is sawed into twins; how to walk through a brick wall — Houdini's explanations of 44 stage tricks with many diagrams. Also included is a fascinating discussion of great magicians of the past and the story of his fight against fraudulent mediums and spiritualists. Edited by W.B. Gibson and M.N. Young. Bibliography. 155 figures, photos. xv + 280pp. 5⅜ x 8.
T384 Paperbound **$1.35**

MATHEMATICS, MAGIC AND MYSTERY, Martin Gardner. Why do card tricks work? How do magicians perform astonishing mathematical feats? How is stage mind-reading possible? This is the first book length study explaining the application of probability, set theory, theory of numbers, topology, etc., to achieve many startling tricks. Non-technical, accurate, detailed! 115 sections discuss tricks with cards, dice, coins, knots, geometrical vanishing illusions, how a Curry square "demonstrates" that the sum of the parts may be greater than the whole, and dozens of others. No sleight of hand necessary! 135 illustrations. xii + 174pp. 5⅜ x 8.
T335 Paperbound **$1.00**

EASY-TO-DO ENTERTAINMENTS AND DIVERSIONS WITH COINS, CARDS, STRING, PAPER AND MATCHES, R. M. Abraham. Over 300 tricks, games and puzzles will provide young readers with absorbing fun. Sections on card games; paper-folding; tricks with coins, matches and pieces of string; games for the agile; toy-making from common household objects; mathematical recreations; and 50 miscellaneous pastimes. Anyone in charge of groups of youngsters, including hard-pressed parents, and in need of suggestions on how to keep children sensibly amused and quietly content will find this book indispensable. Clear, simple text, copious number of delightful line drawings and illustrative diagrams. Originally titled "Winter Nights Entertainments." Introduction by Lord Baden Powell. 329 illustrations. v + 186pp. 5⅜ x 8½.
T921 Paperbound **$1.00**

STRING FIGURES AND HOW TO MAKE THEM, Caroline Furness Jayne. 107 string figures plus variations selected from the best primitive and modern examples developed by Navajo, Apache, pygmies of Africa, Eskimo, in Europe, Australia, China, etc. The most readily understandable, easy-to-follow book in English on perennially popular recreation. Crystal-clear exposition; step-by-step diagrams. Everyone from kindergarten children to adults looking for unusual diversion will be endlessly amused. Index. Bibliography. Introduction by A. C. Haddon. 17 full-page plates. 960 illustrations. xxiii + 401pp. 5⅜ x 8½.
T152 Paperbound **$2.00**

Entertainments, Humor

ODDITIES AND CURIOSITIES OF WORDS AND LITERATURE, C. Bombaugh, edited by M. Gardner. The largest collection of idiosyncratic prose and poetry techniques in English, a legendary work in the curious and amusing bypaths of literary recreations and the play technique in literature—so important in modern works. Contains alphabetic poetry, acrostics, palindromes, scissors verse, centos, emblematic poetry, famous literary puns, hoaxes, notorious slips of the press, hilarious mistranslations, and much more. Revised and enlarged with modern material by Martin Gardner. 368pp. 5⅜ x 8. **T759 Paperbound $1.50**

A NONSENSE ANTHOLOGY, collected by Carolyn Wells. 245 of the best nonsense verses ever written, including nonsense puns, absurd arguments, mock epics and sagas, nonsense ballads, odes, "sick" verses, dog-Latin verses, French nonsense verses, songs. By Edward Lear, Lewis Carroll, Gelett Burgess, W. S. Gilbert, Hilaire Belloc, Peter Newell, Oliver Herford, etc., 83 writers in all plus over four score anonymous nonsense verses. A special section of limericks, plus famous nonsense such as Carroll's "Jabberwocky" and Lear's "The Jumblies" and much excellent verse virtually impossible to locate elsewhere. For 50 years considered the best anthology available. Index of first lines specially prepared for this edition. Introduction by Carolyn Wells. 3 indexes: Title, Author, First lines. xxxiii + 279pp. **T499 Paperbound $1.35**

THE BAD CHILD'S BOOK OF BEASTS, MORE BEASTS FOR WORSE CHILDREN, and A MORAL ALPHABET, H. Belloc. Hardly an anthology of humorous verse has appeared in the last 50 years without at least a couple of these famous nonsense verses. But one must see the entire volumes—with all the delightful original illustrations by Sir Basil Blackwood—to appreciate fully Belloc's charming and witty verses that play so subacidly on the platitudes of life and morals that beset his day—and ours. A great humor classic. Three books in one. Total of 157pp. 5⅜ x 8. **T749 Paperbound $1.00**

THE DEVIL'S DICTIONARY, Ambrose Bierce. Sardonic and irreverent barbs puncturing the pomposities and absurdities of American politics, business, religion, literature, and arts, by the country's greatest satirist in the classic tradition. Epigrammatic as Shaw, piercing as Swift, American as Mark Twain, Will Rogers, and Fred Allen, Bierce will always remain the favorite of a small coterie of enthusiasts, and of writers and speakers whom he supplies with "some of the most gorgeous witticisms of the English language" (H. L. Mencken). Over 1000 entries in alphabetical order. 144pp. 5⅜ x 8. **T487 Paperbound $1.00**

THE PURPLE COW AND OTHER NONSENSE, Gelett Burgess. The best of Burgess's early nonsense, selected from the first edition of the "Burgess Nonsense Book." Contains many of his most unusual and truly awe-inspiring pieces: 36 nonsense quatrains, the Poems of Patagonia, Alphabet of Famous Goops, and the other hilarious (and rare) adult nonsense that place him in the forefront of American humorists. All pieces are accompanied by the original Burgess illustrations. 123 illustrations. xiii + 113pp. 5⅜ x 8. **T772 Paperbound $1.00**

MY PIOUS FRIENDS AND DRUNKEN COMPANIONS and MORE PIOUS FRIENDS AND DRUNKEN COMPANIONS, Frank Shay. Folksingers, amateur and professional, and everyone who loves singing: here, available for the first time in 30 years, is this valued collection of 132 ballads, blues, vaudeville numbers, drinking songs, sea chanties, comedy songs. Songs of pre-Beatnik Bohemia; songs from all over America, England, France, Australia; the great songs of the Naughty Nineties and early twentieth-century America. Over a third with music. Woodcuts by John Held, Jr. convey perfectly the brash insouciance of an era of rollicking unabashed song. 12 illustrations by John Held, Jr. Two indexes (Titles and First lines and Choruses). Introductions by the author. Two volumes bound as one. Total of xvi + 235pp. 5⅜ x 8½. **T946 Paperbound $1.25**

HOW TO TELL THE BIRDS FROM THE FLOWERS, R. W. Wood. How not to confuse a carrot with a parrot, a grape with an ape, a puffin with nuffin. Delightful drawings, clever puns, absurd little poems point out far-fetched resemblances in nature. The author was a leading physicist. Introduction by Margaret Wood White. 106 illus. 60pp. 5⅜ x 8. **T523 Paperbound 75¢**

PECK'S BAD BOY AND HIS PA, George W. Peck. The complete edition, containing both volumes, of one of the most widely read American humor books. The endless ingenious pranks played by bad boy "Hennery" on his pa and the grocery man, the outraged pomposity of Pa, the perpetual ridiculing of middle class institutions, are as entertaining today as they were in 1883. No pale sophistications or subtleties, but rather humor vigorous, raw, earthy, imaginative, and, as folk humor often is, sadistic. This peculiarly fascinating book is also valuable to historians and students of American culture as a portrait of an age. 100 original illustrations by True Williams. Introduction by E. F. Bleiler. 347pp. 5⅜ x 8. **T497 Paperbound $1.35**

CATALOGUE OF DOVER BOOKS

THE HUMOROUS VERSE OF LEWIS CARROLL. Almost every poem Carroll ever wrote, the largest collection ever published, including much never published elsewhere: 150 parodies, burlesques, riddles, ballads, acrostics, etc., with 130 original illustrations by Tenniel, Carroll, and others. "Addicts will be grateful . . . there is nothing for the faithful to do but sit down and fall to the banquet," N. Y. Times. Index to first lines. xiv + 446pp. 5⅜ x 8.
T654 Paperbound $2.00

DIVERSIONS AND DIGRESSIONS OF LEWIS CARROLL. A major new treasure for Carroll fans! Rare privately published humor, fantasy, puzzles, and games by Carroll at his whimsical best, with a new vein of frank satire. Includes many new mathematical amusements and recreations, among them the fragmentary Part III of "Curiosa Mathematica." Contains "The Rectory Umbrella," "The New Belfry," "The Vision of the Three T's," and much more. New 32-page supplement of rare photographs taken by Carroll. x + 375pp. 5⅜ x 8.
T732 Paperbound $1.65

THE COMPLETE NONSENSE OF EDWARD LEAR. This is the only complete edition of this master of gentle madness available at a popular price. A BOOK OF NONSENSE, NONSENSE SONGS, MORE NONSENSE SONGS AND STORIES in their entirety with all the old favorites that have delighted children and adults for years. The Dong With A Luminous Nose, The Jumblies, The Owl and the Pussycat, and hundreds of other bits of wonderful nonsense. 214 limericks, 3 sets of Nonsense Botany, 5 Nonsense Alphabets, 546 drawings by Lear himself, and much more. 320pp. 5⅜ x 8.
T167 Paperbound $1.00

THE MELANCHOLY LUTE, The Humorous Verse of Franklin P. Adams ("FPA"). The author's own selection of light verse, drawn from thirty years of FPA's column, "The Conning Tower," syndicated all over the English-speaking world. Witty, perceptive, literate, these ninety-six poems range from parodies of other poets, Millay, Longfellow, Edgar Guest, Kipling, Masefield, etc., and free and hilarious translations of Horace and other Latin poets, to satiric comments on fabled American institutions—the New York Subways, preposterous ads, suburbanites, sensational journalism, etc. They reveal with vigor and clarity the humor, integrity and restraint of a wise and gentle American satirist. Introduction by Robert Hutchinson. vi + 122pp. 5⅜ x 8½.
T108 Paperbound $1.00

SINGULAR TRAVELS, CAMPAIGNS, AND ADVENTURES OF BARON MUNCHAUSEN, R. E. Raspe, with 90 illustrations by Gustave Doré. The first edition in over 150 years to reestablish the deeds of the Prince of Liars exactly as Raspe first recorded them in 1785—the genuine Baron Munchausen, one of the most popular personalities in English literature. Included also are the best of the many sequels, written by other hands. Introduction on Raspe by J. Carswell. Bibliography of early editions. xliv + 192pp. 5⅜ x 8.
T698 Paperbound $1.00

THE WIT AND HUMOR OF OSCAR WILDE, ed. by Alvin Redman. Wilde at his most brilliant, in 1000 epigrams exposing weaknesses and hypocrisies of "civilized" society. Divided into 49 categories—sin, wealth, women, America, etc.—to aid writers, speakers. Includes excerpts from his trials, books, plays, criticism. Formerly "The Epigrams of Oscar Wilde." Introduction by Vyvyan Holland, Wilde's only living son. Introductory essay by editor. 260pp. 5⅜ x 8.
T602 Paperbound $1.00

MAX AND MORITZ, Wilhelm Busch. Busch is one of the great humorists of all time, as well as the father of the modern comic strip. This volume, translated by H. A. Klein and other hands, contains the perennial favorite "Max and Moritz" (translated by C. T. Brooks), Plisch and Plum, Das Rabennest, Eispeter, and seven other whimsical, sardonic, jovial, diabolical cartoon and verse stories. Lively English translations parallel the original German. This work has delighted millions, since it first appeared in the 19th century, and is guaranteed to please almost anyone. Edited by H. A. Klein, with an afterword. x + 205pp. 5⅝ x 8½.
T181 Paperbound $1.15

HYPOCRITICAL HELENA, Wilhelm Busch. A companion volume to "Max and Moritz," with the title piece (Die Fromme Helena) and 10 other highly amusing cartoon and verse stories, all newly translated by H. A. Klein and M. C. Klein: Adventure on New Year's Eve (Abenteuer in der Neujahrsnacht), Hangover on the Morning after New Year's Eve (Der Katzenjammer am Neujahrsmorgen), etc. English and German in parallel columns. Hours of pleasure, also a fine language aid. x + 205pp. 5⅝ x 8½.
T184 Paperbound $1.00

THE BEAR THAT WASN'T, Frank Tashlin. What does it mean? Is it simply delightful wry humor, or a charming story of a bear who wakes up in the midst of a factory, or a satire on Big Business, or an existential cartoon-story of the human condition, or a symbolization of the struggle between conformity and the individual? New York Herald Tribune said of the first edition: ". . . a fable for grownups that will be fun for children. Sit down with the book and get your own bearings." Long an underground favorite with readers of all ages and opinions. v + 51pp. Illustrated. 5⅜ x 8½.
T939 Paperbound 75¢

RUTHLESS RHYMES FOR HEARTLESS HOMES and MORE RUTHLESS RHYMES FOR HEARTLESS HOMES, Harry Graham ("Col. D. Streamer"). Two volumes of Little Willy and 48 other poetic disasters. A bright, new reprint of oft-quoted, never forgotten, devastating humor by a precursor of today's "sick" joke school. For connoisseurs of wicked, wacky humor and all who delight in the comedy of manners. Original drawings are a perfect complement. 61 illustrations. Index. vi + 69pp. Two vols. bound as one. 5⅜ x 8½.
T930 Paperbound 75¢

Say It language phrase books

These handy phrase books (128 to 196 pages each) make grammatical drills unnecessary for an elementary knowledge of a spoken foreign language. Covering most matters of travel and everyday life each volume contains:

Over 1000 phrases and sentences in immediately useful forms — foreign language plus English.

Modern usage designed for Americans. Specific phrases like, "Give me small change," and "Please call a taxi."

Simplified phonetic transcription you will be able to read at sight.

The only completely indexed phrase books on the market.

Covers scores of important situations: — Greetings, restaurants, sightseeing, useful expressions, etc.

These books are prepared by native linguists who are professors at Columbia, N.Y.U., Fordham and other great universities. Use them independently or with any other book or record course. They provide a supplementary living element that most other courses lack. Individual volumes in:

Russian 75¢	Italian 75¢	Spanish 75¢	German 75¢
Hebrew 75¢	Danish 75¢	Japanese 75¢	Swedish 75¢
Dutch 75¢	Esperanto 75¢	Modern Greek 75¢	Portuguese 75¢
Norwegian 75¢	Polish 75¢	French 75¢	Yiddish 75¢
Turkish 75¢			
English for Italian-speaking people 75¢		English for German-speaking people 75¢	
		English for Spanish-speaking people 75¢	

Large clear type. 128-196 pages each. 3½ x 5¼. Sturdy paper binding.

Listen and Learn language records

LISTEN & LEARN is the only language record course designed especially to meet your travel and everyday needs. It is available in separate sets for FRENCH, SPANISH, GERMAN, JAPANESE, RUSSIAN, MODERN GREEK, PORTUGUESE, ITALIAN and HEBREW, and each set contains three 33⅓ rpm long-playing records—1½ hours of recorded speech by eminent native speakers who are professors at Columbia, New York University, Queens College.

Check the following special features found only in LISTEN & LEARN:

- **Dual-language recording.** 812 **selected phrases and sentences, over 3200 words,** spoken first in English, then in their foreign language equivalents. A suitable pause follows each foreign phrase, allowing you time to repeat the expression. You learn by unconscious assimilation.

- **128 to 206-page manual** contains everything on the records, plus a simple phonetic pronunciation guide.

- **Indexed for convenience. The only set on the market** that is completely indexed. No more puzzling over where to find the phrase you need. Just look in the rear of the manual.

- **Practical.** No time wasted on material you can find in any grammar. LISTEN & LEARN covers central core material with phrase approach. Ideal for the person with limited learning time.

- **Living, modern expressions,** not found in other courses. Hygienic products, modern equipment, shopping—expressions used every day, like "nylon" and "air-conditioned."

- **Limited objective.** Everything you learn, no matter where you stop, is immediately useful. You have to finish other courses, wade through grammar and vocabulary drill, before they help you.

- **High-fidelity recording.** LISTEN & LEARN records equal in clarity and surface-silence any record on the market costing up to $6.

"Excellent . . . the spoken records . . . impress me as being among the very best on the market," **Prof. Mario Pei,** Dept. of Romance Languages, Columbia University. "Inexpensive and well-done . . . it would make an ideal present," CHICAGO SUNDAY TRIBUNE. "More genuinely helpful than anything of its kind which I have previously encountered," **Sidney Clark,** well-known author of "ALL THE BEST" travel books.

UNCONDITIONAL GUARANTEE. Try LISTEN & LEARN, then return it within 10 days for full refund if you are not satisfied.

Each set contains three twelve-inch 33⅓ records, manual, and album.

SPANISH	the set $5.95	GERMAN	the set $5.95
FRENCH	the set $5.95	ITALIAN	the set $5.95
RUSSIAN	the set $5.95	JAPANESE	the set $5.95
PORTUGUESE	the set $5.95	MODERN GREEK	the set $5.95
MODERN HEBREW	the set $5.95		

Americana

THE EYES OF DISCOVERY, J. Bakeless. A vivid reconstruction of how unspoiled America appeared to the first white men. Authentic and enlightening accounts of Hudson's landing in New York, Coronado's trek through the Southwest; scores of explorers, settlers, trappers, soldiers. America's pristine flora, fauna, and Indians in every region and state in fresh and unusual new aspects. "A fascinating view of what the land was like before the first highway went through," Time. 68 contemporary illustrations, 39 newly added in this edition. Index. Bibliography. x + 500pp. 5⅜ x 8.   T761 Paperbound **$2.00**

AUDUBON AND HIS JOURNALS, J. J. Audubon. A collection of fascinating accounts of Europe and America in the early 1800's through Audubon's own eyes. Includes the Missouri River Journals —an eventful trip through America's untouched heartland, the Labrador Journals, the European Journals, the famous "Episodes", and other rare Audubon material, including the descriptive chapters from the original letterpress edition of the "Ornithological Studies", omitted in all later editions. Indispensable for ornithologists, naturalists, and all lovers of Americana and adventure. 70-page biography by Audubon's granddaughter. 38 illustrations. Index. Total of 1106pp. 5⅜ x 8.   T675 Vol I Paperbound **$2.25**
                                                         T676 Vol II Paperbound **$2.25**
                                                         The set **$4.50**

TRAVELS OF WILLIAM BARTRAM, edited by Mark Van Doren. The first inexpensive illustrated edition of one of the 18th century's most delightful books is an excellent source of first-hand material on American geography, anthropology, and natural history. Many descriptions of early Indian tribes are our only source of information on them prior to the infiltration of the white man. "The mind of a scientist with the soul of a poet," John Livingston Lowes. 13 original illustrations and maps. Edited with an introduction by Mark Van Doren. 448pp. 5⅜ x 8.
                                                         T13 Paperbound **$2.00**

GARRETS AND PRETENDERS: A HISTORY OF BOHEMIANISM IN AMERICA, A. Parry. The colorful and fantastic history of American Bohemianism from Poe to Kerouac. This is the only complete record of hoboes, cranks, starving poets, and suicides. Here are Pfaff, Whitman, Crane, Bierce, Pound, and many others. New chapters by the author and by H. T. Moore bring this thorough and well-documented history down to the Beatniks. "An excellent account," N. Y. Times. Scores of cartoons, drawings, and caricatures. Bibliography. Index. xxviii + 421pp. 5⅝ x 8⅜.   T708 Paperbound **$1.95**

THE EXPLORATION OF THE COLORADO RIVER AND ITS CANYONS, J. W. Powell. The thrilling first-hand account of the expedition that filled in the last white space on the map of the United States. Rapids, famine, hostile Indians, and mutiny are among the perils encountered as the unknown Colorado Valley reveals its secrets. This is the only uncut version of Major Powell's classic of exploration that has been printed in the last 60 years. Includes later reflections and subsequent expedition. 250 illustrations, new map. 400pp. 5⅝ x 8⅜.
                                                         T94 Paperbound **$2.25**

THE JOURNAL OF HENRY D. THOREAU, Edited by Bradford Torrey and Francis H. Allen. Henry Thoreau is not only one of the most important figures in American literature and social thought; his voluminous journals (from which his books emerged as selections and crystallizations) constitute both the longest, most sensitive record of personal internal development and a most penetrating description of a historical moment in American culture. This present set, which was first issued in fourteen volumes, contains Thoreau's entire journals from 1837 to 1862, with the exception of the lost years which were found only recently. We are reissuing it, complete and unabridged, with a new introduction by Walter Harding, Secretary of the Thoreau Society. Fourteen volumes reissued in two volumes. Foreword by Henry Seidel Canby. Total of 1888pp. 8⅜ x 12¼.   T312-3 Two volume set, Clothbound **$20.00**

GAMES AND SONGS OF AMERICAN CHILDREN, collected by William Wells Newell. A remarkable collection of 190 games with songs that accompany many of them; cross references to show similarities, differences among them; variations; musical notation for 38 songs. Textual discussions show relations with folk-drama and other aspects of folk tradition. Grouped into categories for ready comparative study: Love-games, histories, playing at work, human life, bird and beast, mythology, guessing-games, etc. New introduction covers relations of songs and dances to timeless heritage of folklore, biographical sketch of Newell, other pertinent data. A good source of inspiration for those in charge of groups of children and a valuable reference for anthropologists, sociologists, psychiatrists. Introduction by Carl Withers. New indexes of first lines, games. 5⅜ x 8½. xii + 242pp.   T354 Paperbound **$1.75**

Art, History of Art, Antiques, Graphic Arts, Handcrafts

ART STUDENTS' ANATOMY, E. J. Farris. Outstanding art anatomy that uses chiefly living objects for its illustrations. 71 photos of undraped men, women, children are accompanied by carefully labeled matching sketches to illustrate the skeletal system, articulations and movements, bony landmarks, the muscular system, skin, fasciae, fat, etc. 9 x-ray photos show movement of joints. Undraped models are shown in such actions as serving in tennis, drawing a bow in archery, playing football, dancing, preparing to spring and to dive. Also discussed and illustrated are proportions, age and sex differences, the anatomy of the smile, etc. 8 plates by the great early 18th century anatomic illustrator Siegfried Albinus are also included. Glossary. 158 figures, 7 in color. x + 159pp. 5⅝ x 8⅜.   **T744 Paperbound $1.50**

AN ATLAS OF ANATOMY FOR ARTISTS, F Schider. A new 3rd edition of this standard text enlarged by 52 new illustrations of hands, anatomical studies by Cloquet, and expressive life studies of the body by Barcsay. 189 clear, detailed plates offer you precise information of impeccable accuracy. 29 plates show all aspects of the skeleton, with closeups of special areas, while 54 full-page plates, mostly in two colors, give human musculature as seen from four different points of view, with cutaways for important portions of the body. 14 full-page plates provide photographs of hand forms, eyelids, female breasts, and indicate the location of muscles upon models. 59 additional plates show how great artists of the past utilized human anatomy. They reproduce sketches and finished work by such artists as Michelangelo, Leonardo da Vinci, Goya, and 15 others. This is a lifetime reference work which will be one of the most important books in any artist's library. "The standard reference tool," AMERICAN LIBRARY ASSOCIATION. "Excellent," AMERICAN ARTIST. Third enlarged edition. 189 plates, 647 illustrations. xxvi + 192pp. 7⅞ x 10⅝.   **T241 Clothbound $6.00**

AN ATLAS OF ANIMAL ANATOMY FOR ARTISTS, W. Ellenberger, H. Baum, H. Dittrich. The largest, richest animal anatomy for artists available in English. 99 detailed anatomical plates of such animals as the horse, dog, cat, lion, deer, seal, kangaroo, flying squirrel, cow, bull, goat, monkey, hare, and bat. Surface features are clearly indicated, while progressive beneath-the-skin pictures show musculature, tendons, and bone structure. Rest and action are exhibited in terms of musculature and skeletal structure and detailed cross-sections are given for heads and important features. The animals chosen are representative of specific families so that a study of these anatomies will provide knowledge of hundreds of related species. "Highly recommended as one of the very few books on the subject worthy of being used as an authoritative guide," DESIGN. "Gives a fundamental knowledge," AMERICAN ARTIST. Second revised, enlarged edition with new plates from Cuvier, Stubbs, etc. 288 illustrations. 153pp. 11⅜ x 9.   **T82 Clothbound $6.00**

THE HUMAN FIGURE IN MOTION, Eadweard Muybridge. The largest selection in print of Muybridge's famous high-speed action photos of the human figure in motion. 4789 photographs illustrate 162 different actions: men, women, children—mostly undraped—are shown walking, running, carrying various objects, sitting, lying down, climbing, throwing, arising, and performing over 150 other actions. Some actions are shown in as many as 150 photographs each. All in all there are more than 500 action strips in this enormous volume, series shots taken at shutter speeds of as high as 1/6000th of a second! These are not posed shots, but true stopped motion. They show bone and muscle in situations that the human eye is not fast enough to have brought. Earlier, smaller editions of these prints have brought $40 and more on the out-of-print market. "A must for artists," ART IN FOCUS. "An unparalleled dictionary of action for all artists," AMERICAN ARTIST. 390 full-page plates, with 4789 photographs. Printed on heavy glossy stock. Reinforced binding with headbands. xxi + 390pp. 7⅞ x 10⅝.
                    T204 Clothbound $10.00

ANIMALS IN MOTION, Eadweard Muybridge. This is the largest collection of animal action photos in print. 34 different animals (horses, mules, oxen, goats, camels, pigs, cats, guanacos, lions, gnus, deer, monkeys, eagles—and 21 others) in 132 characteristic actions. The horse alone is shown in more than 40 different actions. All 3919 photographs are taken in series at speeds up to 1/6000th of a second. The secrets of leg motion, spinal patterns, head movements, strains and contortions shown nowhere else are captured. You will see exactly how a lion sets his foot down; how an elephant's knees are like a human's—and how they differ; the position of a kangaroo's legs in mid-leap; how an ostrich's head bobs; details of the flight of birds—and thousands of facets of motion only the fastest cameras can catch. Photographed from domestic animals and animals in the Philadelphia zoo, it contains neither semiposed artificial shots nor distorted telephoto shots taken under adverse conditions. Artists, biologists, decorators, cartoonists, will find this book indispensable for understanding animals in motion. "A really marvelous series of plates," NATURE (London). "The dry plate's most spectacular early use was by Eadweard Muybridge," LIFE. 3919 photographs; 380 full pages of plates. 440pp. Printed on heavy glossy paper. Deluxe binding with headbands. 7⅞ x 10⅝.   **T203 Clothbound $10.00**

CATALOGUE OF DOVER BOOKS

THE AUTOBIOGRAPHY OF AN IDEA, Louis Sullivan. The pioneer architect whom Frank Lloyd Wright called "the master" reveals an acute sensitivity to social forces and values in this passionately honest account. He records the crystallization of his opinions and theories, the growth of his organic theory of architecture that still influences American designers and architects, contemporary ideas, etc. This volume contains the first appearance of 34 full-page plates of his finest architecture. Unabridged reissue of 1924 edition. New introduction by R. M. Line. Index. xiv + 335pp. 5⅜ x 8.   T281 Paperbound **$2.00**

THE DRAWINGS OF HEINRICH KLEY. The first uncut republication of both of Kley's devastating sketchbooks, which first appeared in pre-World War I Germany. One of the greatest cartoonists and social satirists of modern times, his exuberant and iconoclastic fantasy and his extraordinary technique place him in the great tradition of Bosch, Breughel, and Goya, while his subject matter has all the immediacy and tension of our century. 200 drawings. viii + 128pp. 7¾ x 10¾.   T24 Paperbound **$1.85**

MORE DRAWINGS BY HEINRICH KLEY. All the sketches from Leut' Und Viecher (1912) and Sammel-Album (1923) not included in the previous Dover edition of Drawings. More of the bizarre, mercilessly iconoclastic sketches that shocked and amused on their original publication. Nothing was too sacred, no one too eminent for satirization by this imaginative, individual and accomplished master cartoonist. A total of 158 illustrations. Iv + 104pp. 7¾ x 10¾.   T41 Paperbound **$1.85**

PINE FURNITURE OF EARLY NEW ENGLAND, R. H. Kettell. A rich understanding of one of America's most original folk arts that collectors of antiques, interior decorators, craftsmen, woodworkers, and everyone interested in American history and art will find fascinating and immensely useful. 413 illustrations of more than 300 chairs, benches, racks, beds, cupboards, mirrors, shelves, tables, and other furniture will show all the simple beauty and character of early New England furniture. 55 detailed drawings carefully analyze outstanding pieces. "With its rich store of illustrations, this book emphasizes the individuality and varied design of early American pine furniture. It should be welcomed," ANTIQUES. 413 illustrations and 55 working drawings. 475. 8 x 10¾.   T145 Clothbound **$10.00**

THE HUMAN FIGURE, J. H. Vanderpoel. Every important artistic element of the human figure is pointed out in minutely detailed word descriptions in this classic text and illustrated as well in 430 pencil and charcoal drawings. Thus the text of this book directs your attention to all the characteristic features and subtle differences of the male and female (adults, children, and aged persons), as though a master artist were telling you what to look for at each stage. 2nd edition, revised and enlarged by George Bridgman. Foreword. 430 illustrations. 143pp. 6⅛ x 9¼.   T432 Paperbound **$1.50**

LETTERING AND ALPHABETS, J. A. Cavanagh. This unabridged reissue of LETTERING offers a full discussion, analysis, illustration of 89 basic hand lettering styles — styles derived from Caslons, Bodonis, Garamonds, Gothic, Black Letter, Oriental, and many others. Upper and lower cases, numerals and common signs pictured. Hundreds of technical hints on make-up, construction, artistic validity, strokes, pens, brushes, white areas, etc. May be reproduced without permission! 89 complete alphabets; 72 lettered specimens. 121pp. 9¾ x 8.   T53 Paperbound **$1.35**

STICKS AND STONES, Lewis Mumford. A survey of the forces that have conditioned American architecture and altered its forms. The author discusses the medieval tradition in early New England villages; the Renaissance influence which developed with the rise of the merchant class; the classical influence of Jefferson's time; the "Mechanicsvilles" of Poe's generation; the Brown Decades; the philosophy of the Imperial facade; and finally the modern machine age. "A truly remarkable book," SAT. REV. OF LITERATURE. 2nd revised edition. 21 illustrations. xvii + 228pp. 5⅜ x 8.   T202 Paperbound **$1.65**

THE STANDARD BOOK OF QUILT MAKING AND COLLECTING, Marguerite Ickis. A complete easy-to-follow guide with all the information you need to make beautiful, useful quilts. How to plan, design, cut, sew, appliqué, avoid sewing problems, use rag bag, make borders, tuft, every other aspect. Over 100 traditional quilts shown, including over 40 full-size patterns. At-home hobby for fun, profit. Index. 483 illus. 1 color plate. 287pp. 6¾ x 9½.   T582 Paperbound **$2.00**

THE BOOK OF SIGNS, Rudolf Koch. Formerly $20 to $25 on the out-of-print market, now only $1.00 in this unabridged new edition! 493 symbols from ancient manuscripts, medieval cathedrals, coins, catacombs, pottery, etc. Crosses, monograms of Roman emperors, astrological, chemical, botanical, runes, housemarks, and 7 other categories. Invaluable for handicraft workers, illustrators, scholars, etc., this material may be reproduced without permission. 493 illustrations by Fritz Kredel. 104pp. 6½ x 9¼.   T162 Paperbound **$1.00**

PRIMITIVE ART, Franz Boas. This authoritative and exhaustive work by a great American anthropologist covers the entire gamut of primitive art. Pottery, leatherwork, metal work, stone work, wood, basketry, are treated in detail. Theories of primitive art, historical depth in art history, technical virtuosity, unconscious levels of patterning, symbolism, styles, literature, music, dance, etc. A must book for the interested layman, the anthropologist, artist, handicrafter (hundreds of unusual motifs), and the historian. Over 900 illustrations (50 ceramic vessels, 12 totem poles, etc.). 376pp. 5⅜ x 8.   T25 Paperbound **$2.00**

Fiction

THE LAND THAT TIME FORGOT and THE MOON MAID, Edgar Rice Burroughs. In the opinion of many, Burroughs' best work. The first concerns a strange island where evolution is individual rather than phylogenetic. Speechless anthropoids develop into intelligent human beings within a single generation. The second projects the reader far into the future and describes the first voyage to the Moon (in the year 2025), the conquest of the Earth by the Moon, and years of violence and adventure as the enslaved Earthmen try to regain possession of their planet. "An imaginative tour de force that keeps the reader keyed up and expectant," NEW YORK TIMES. Complete, unabridged text of the original two novels (three parts in each). 5 illustrations by J. Allen St. John. vi + 552pp. 5⅜ x 8½.
T1020 Clothbound **$3.75**
T358 Paperbound **$2.00**

AT THE EARTH'S CORE, PELLUCIDAR, TANAR OF PELLUCIDAR: THREE SCIENCE FICTION NOVELS BY EDGAR RICE BURROUGHS. Complete, unabridged texts of the first three Pellucidar novels. Tales of derring-do by the famous master of science fiction. The locale for these three related stories is the inner surface of the hollow Earth where we discover the world of Pellucidar, complete with all types of bizarre, menacing creatures, strange peoples, and alluring maidens—guaranteed to delight all Burroughs fans and a wide circle of adventure lovers. Illustrated by J. Allen St. John and P. F. Berdanier. vi + 433pp. 5⅜ x 8½.
T1051 Paperbound **$2.00**

THREE MARTIAN NOVELS, Edgar Rice Burroughs. Contains: Thuvia, Maid of Mars; The Chessmen of Mars; and The Master Mind of Mars. High adventure set in an imaginative and intricate conception of the Red Planet. Mars is peopled with an intelligent, heroic human race which lives in densely populated cities and with fierce barbarians who inhabit dead sea bottoms. Other exciting creatures abound amidst an inventive framework of Martian history and geography. Complete unabridged reprintings of the first edition. 16 illustrations by J. Allen St. John. vi + 499pp. 5⅜ x 8½.
T39 Paperbound **$1.85**

TO THE SUN? and OFF ON A COMET!, Jules Verne. Complete texts of two of the most imaginative flights into fancy in world literature display the high adventure that have kept Verne's novels read for nearly a century. Only unabridged edition of the best translation, by Edward Roth. Large, easily readable type. 50 illustrations selected from first editions. 462pp. 5⅜ x 8.
T634 Paperbound **$1.75**

FROM THE EARTH TO THE MOON and ALL AROUND THE MOON, Jules Verne. Complete editions of two of Verne's most successful novels, in finest Edward Roth translations, now available after many years out of print. Verne's visions of submarines, airplanes, television, rockets, interplanetary travel; of scientific and not-so-scientific beliefs; of peculiarities of Americans; all delight and engross us today as much as when they first appeared. Large, easily readable type. 42 illus. from first French edition. 476pp. 5⅜ x 8.
T633 Paperbound **$1.75**

THREE PROPHETIC NOVELS BY H. G. WELLS, edited by E. F. Bleiler. Complete texts of "When the Sleeper Wakes" (1st book printing in 50 years), "A Story of the Days to Come," "The Time Machine" (1st complete printing in book form). Exciting adventures in the future are as enjoyable today as 50 years ago when first printed. Predict TV, movies, intercontinental airplanes, prefabricated houses, air-conditioned cities, etc. First important author to foresee problems of mind control, technological dictatorships. "Absolute best of imaginative fiction," N. Y. Times. Introduction. 335pp. 5⅜ x 8.
T605 Paperbound **$1.50**

SEVEN SCIENCE FICTION NOVELS, H. G. Wells. Full unabridged texts of 7 science-fiction novels of the master. Ranging from biology, physics, chemistry, astronomy to sociology and other studies, Mr. Wells extrapolates whole worlds of strange and intriguing character. "One will have to go far to match this for entertainment, excitement, and sheer pleasure . . . ," NEW YORK TIMES. Contents: The Time Machine, The Island of Dr. Moreau, First Men in the Moon, The Invisible Man, The War of the Worlds, The Food of the Gods, In the Days of the Comet. 1015pp. 5⅜ x 8.
T264 Clothbound **$4.50**

28 SCIENCE FICTION STORIES OF H. G. WELLS. Two full unabridged novels, MEN LIKE GODS and STAR BEGOTTEN, plus 26 short stories by the master science-fiction writer of all time. Stories of space, time, invention, exploration, future adventure—an indispensable part of the library of everyone interested in science and adventure. PARTIAL CONTENTS: Men Like Gods, The Country of the Blind, In the Abyss, The Crystal Egg, The Man Who Could Work Miracles, A Story of the Days to Come, The Valley of Spiders, and 21 more! 928pp. 5⅜ x 8.
T265 Clothbound **$4.50**

THE WAR IN THE AIR, IN THE DAYS OF THE COMET, THE FOOD OF THE GODS: THREE SCIENCE FICTION NOVELS BY H. G. WELLS. Three exciting Wells offerings bearing on vital social and philosophical issues of his and our own day. Here are tales of air power, strategic bombing, East vs. West, the potential miracles of science, the potential disasters from outer space, the relationship between scientific advancement and moral progress, etc. First reprinting of "War in the Air" in almost 50 years. An excellent sampling of Wells at his storytelling best. Complete, unabridged reprintings. 16 illustrations. 645pp. 5⅜ x 8½.
T1135 Paperbound **$2.00**

Music

A GENERAL HISTORY OF MUSIC, Charles Burney. A detailed coverage of music from the Greeks up to 1789, with full information on all types of music: sacred and secular, vocal and instrumental, operatic and symphonic. Theory, notation, forms, instruments, innovators, composers, performers, typical and important works, and much more in an easy, entertaining style. Burney covered much of Europe and spoke with hundreds of authorities and composers so that this work is more than a compilation of records . . . it is a living work of careful and first-hand scholarship. Its account of thoroughbass (18th century) Italian music is probably still the best introduction on the subject. A recent NEW YORK TIMES review said, "Surprisingly few of Burney's statements have been invalidated by modern research . . . still of great value." Edited and corrected by Frank Mercer. 35 figures. Indices. 1915pp. 5⅜ x 8. 2 volumes.   T36 The Set, Clothbound **$12.50**

A DICTIONARY OF HYMNOLOGY, John Julian. This exhaustive and scholarly work has become known as an invaluable source of hundreds of thousands of important and often difficult to obtain facts on the history and use of hymns in the western world. Everyone interested in hymns will be fascinated by the accounts of famous hymns and hymn writers and amazed by the amount of practical information he will find. More than 30,000 entries on individual hymns, giving authorship, date and circumstances of composition, publication, textual variations, translations, denominational and ritual usage, etc. Biographies of more than 9,000 hymn writers, and essays on important topics such as Christmas carols and children's hymns, and much other unusual and valuable information. A 200 page double-columned index of first lines — the largest in print. Total of 1786 pages in two reinforced clothbound volumes. 6¼ x 9¼. The set, T333 Clothbound **$17.50**

MUSIC IN MEDIEVAL BRITAIN, F. Ll. Harrison. The most thorough, up-to-date, and accurate treatment of the subject ever published, beautifully illustrated. Complete account of institutions and choirs; carols, masses, and motets; liturgy and plainsong; and polyphonic music from the Norman Conquest to the Reformation. Discusses the various schools of music and their reciprocal influences; the origin and development of new ritual forms; development and use of instruments; and new evidence on many problems of the period. Reproductions of scores, over 200 excerpts from medieval melodies. Rules of harmony and dissonance; influence of Continental styles; great composers (Dunstable, Cornysh, Fairfax, etc.); and much more. Register and index of more than 400 musicians. Index of titles. General Index. 225-item bibliography. 6 Appendices. xix + 491pp. 5⅝ x 8¾.   T705 Clothbound **$10.00**

THE MUSIC OF SPAIN, Gilbert Chase. Only book in English to give concise, comprehensive account of Iberian music; new Chapter covers music since 1941. Victoria, Albéniz, Cabezón, Pedrell, Turina, hundreds of other composers; popular and folk music; the Gypsies; the guitar; dance, theatre, opera, with only extensive discussion in English of the Zarzuela; virtuosi such as Casals; much more. "Distinguished . . . readable," Saturday Review. 400-item bibliography. Index. 27 photos. 383pp. 5⅜ x 8.   T549 Paperbound **$2.00**

ON STUDYING SINGING, Sergius Kagen. An intelligent method of voice-training, which leads you around pitfalls that waste your time, money, and effort. Exposes rigid, mechanical systems, baseless theories, deleterious exercises. "Logical, clear, convincing . . . dead right," Virgil Thomson, N.Y. Herald Tribune. "I recommend this volume highly," Maggie Teyte, Saturday Review. 119pp. 5⅜ x 8.   T622 Paperbound **$1.25**

Prices subject to change without notice.

Dover publishes books on art, music, philosophy, literature, languages, history, social sciences, psychology, handcrafts, orientalia, puzzles and entertainments, chess, pets and gardens, books explaining science, intermediate and higher mathematics, mathematical physics, engineering, biological sciences, earth sciences, classics of science, etc. Write to:

Dept. catrr.
Dover Publications, Inc.
180 Varick Street, N.Y. 14, N.Y.